30

~~GRADY BRATTIELD~~
~~GA. TECH BOX 35671~~
~~233-1859~~
John A Pehler
Ga. Tech Box 36537
288-2085
Sam Anderson

Cases in Capital Budgeting

Cases in

CAPITAL BUDGETING

By

ROBERT F. VANDELL, D.B.A.

Associate Professor of Business Administration

AND

RICHARD F. VANCIL, D.B.A.

Assistant Professor of Business Administration

BOTH OF THE GRADUATE SCHOOL OF BUSINESS ADMINISTRATION
HARVARD UNIVERSITY

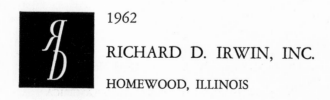

1962

RICHARD D. IRWIN, INC.

HOMEWOOD, ILLINOIS

First Printing, May, 1962
Second Printing, December, 1966

Library of Congress Catalogue Card No. 62–14249

PRINTED IN THE UNITED STATES OF AMERICA

PREFACE

Businessmen are continuously confronted with an array of opportunities for spending available capital resources: Should a new plant be constructed to expand capacity? Should a machine tool be replaced? Should the advertising budget be increased? Should dividends be paid to stockholders? Should bonds be refunded? Should stock be paid to acquire the assets of a competing firm? And so forth. Although the nature and amount of expenditure opportunities change over time, often in unpredictable ways, the essential question remains the same: How much, if any, of our precious capital resources should be spent on each new opportunity?

These decisions cannot be made in a vacuum. Today's opportunity is, in reality, competing for funds against the more vaguely shaped or even unknown opportunities of tomorrow. And the current and prospective availability of capital is an equally important consideration. If current liquid asset balances or prospective cash flow appear inadequate, should new capital be raised through sale of debentures? Should new equity capital be sold? Should a comparatively unprofitable division be liquidated? Should expenses be cut back? Any one of these methods could tend to increase the available capital resources, at least temporarily.

These questions illustrate the range of problems involved in effective acquisition and utilization of capital resources. Capital budgeting, the subject of this book, focuses upon the process by which these decisions are reached. The critical questions raised by the capital budgeting decisional process are: (1) How much capital should be spent and on what opportunities should it be spent? and (2) How much capital should be raised or conserved, and by what means shall it be obtained? Clearly these questions are all highly interrelated.

As we see it, the fundamental, but not exclusive, objective of capital budgeting is for the management of a firm to blend the utilization

v

of available internal and external capital resources in such a manner as to tend to maximize the expected present value of its common stockholders' future receipts from his stock up to some appropriate planning horizon. Since stockholders typically receive income in only two ways —through cash dividends paid by the company, and through appreciation in market value at the time of sale—our analysis focuses on the interrelated effects of capital budgeting policy changes on dividend and appreciation potentials. In this definition we have not included mention of a very important subject, risk, simply because we believe that any changes in risk will affect the future price of a company's common stock, and hence appreciation potential. Like all such broad objectives, it probably should be refined further and qualified more, but we suspect this definition is enough of a mouthful for students to swallow at this juncture.

Objectives are laudable, but unless they can be translated into practical guides for decision-making purposes, they are empty shells. Capital budgeting can often be addressed more directly if some of the policy questions it poses for management are focused upon. For example, at what rate should the firm attempt to grow? How diversified should it be? How much capital should it attempt to borrow? When phrased this way, it is apparent that capital budgeting policies strike at the core of a number of critical business policy decisions.

The systematic study of capital budgeting is a relatively new branch of the theory-of-the-firm school of economics. Both businessmen and economists alike have shown increased interest in addressing more rigorously the problems raised by the capital budgeting process. Consequently, new and highly useful theories and practices are emerging. At the moment, many of the theories have arisen after some small part of the total process—a class of similar problems—has been broken out and studied microscopically. As the quality of these studies has improved, the pressure to integrate the several resulting theories into a uniform, comprehensive conceptual scheme has increased. Valuable contributions toward this end are already available in the literature. However, much remains to be achieved. Because, in our opinion, a satisfactorily comprehensive conceptual scheme is not yet available, we have chosen to illustrate in the balance of this preface some of the most critical elements of the capital budgeting process by word descriptions rather than by mathematical models.

Before proceeding with this description, we wish to comment briefly on the purpose of this book. It consists of a series of case studies;

that is, actual business problems confronting live executives in real companies. These studies have been chosen to illustrate a wide range of capital budgeting decisions. They have been organized to facilitate a step-by-step introduction into the subject's total complexity. In each, the student is asked to put himself squarely in the shoes of an executive, to become involved in the responsibilities associated with the job, to undertake whatever analyses seem appropriate, and to draw these together into a decision and, where appropriate, a formal plan of action. In short, we are asking the student to learn by exposing himself to experience-generating opportunities.

Quite quickly the student should see the advantages of availing himself of knowledge contained in existing theories in the subject area of capital budgeting. These theories provide useful approaches to analyzing certain problems. On the other hand, the student should also see that a wide gap exists between the point where the best of existing theories leave off, and where practice begins. This gap can be bridged only by using the creative resources bestowed upon, but not often enough used by, students in developing their abilities. Many students find this process highly frustrating at first, but we at least have not observed any permanent damage to grey cells as a result.

ALLOCATING FUNDS

In its simplest dimensions, the process of allocating funds involves generating opportunities, evaluating return prospects, screening proposals competitively, and, finally, committing funds to selected opportunities. The commitment generally authorizes the expenditure which formally completes the investment process. Frequently, post audits are conducted to appraise the wisdom of judgments made in the allocation process against the backdrop of actual developments.

In total, these decisions constitute an important determinant of a firm's future. They greatly influence its rate of growth or decline. They determine the extent to which diversification will provide useful protection against risks important to shareholders. The resulting levels of cash flow and their related patterns of variability affect financing opportunities and hence the return on investment realized by shareholders. In short, the cumulative effect of fund allocation on stockholders' long-term welfare is much more significant than it ever appears to be in reaching a single commitment decision.

Appraising expenditure opportunities cannot be undertaken effectively outside the context of the unique cricumstances of a firm. What may be a wonderful expenditure opportunity for one firm may at the same time be an unproductive headache for another, simply because of differing abilities to muster the necessary human and capital resources necessary to make the project a success. More often than not, the difference in people, not in capital resources, will be the vital factor affecting the comparative success of major new expansion or diversification programs.

Context is important in other ways. Each firm faces unique problems that influence the wisdom of choices. Technological and marketing evolutions are continuously interrupting the status quo. So, also, competitors act and react in unpredictable ways. Factors of these kinds shape and change effective capital allocation strategies and tactics, and the policies that must serve as guideposts for managers in allocating funds wisely.

Viva la difference! It is these situational differences between firms that make capital allocation such a challenging and creative set of decisional problems for managements and students alike. However, these differences also limit the degree to which allocating problems can be successfully abstracted and made routine. In the case problems that follow, we have endeavored to preserve the situational flavor that complicates the decisional process, that elevates the analytical process above a pedestrian or theoretical optimum procedure, and that adds practical value to the knowledge gained without sacrifice to comprehensive theoretical understanding.

The most vital factor influencing the success of any given firm's set of allocation decisions relates to the quantity and quality of the opportunities available for expenditures. The most rigorously effective system for appraising opportunities has limited value if most of the opportunities are poor to begin with. How much better it is to be managing the firm that has such a wealth of opportunities that it can afford to make appraisal mistakes in choosing from among the best! It is one thing, however, to recognize the need for creativity in searching for new opportunities; it is another thing to acquire the people with the potential for creativity and to develop an atmosphere that will encourage the emergence of whatever creativity exists latently. It is in the environment that stars can cross. We have seen managements evolve elaborate appraisal systems for improving capital allocation procedures only to find the new system stifling creativity. Solving the wrong problem effectively is a prevalent managerial failing, and one that students have also been known to succumb to when they become immersed in the details relating to a pressing decision.

The capital allocation system is not the only factor affecting corporate atmosphere nor is stimulating creativity the only problem. Capital budgeting is embraced by and influences the entire administrative operation of a company. In large firms this interrelationship works at all tiers of managerial responsibility. The attitude of a firing-line engineer or foreman can influence whether an idea is submitted for consideration and, if submitted, whether it will be considered favorably or not. The attitudes of individuals at the source valves of creativity can be shaped by a number of factors; for example, will the project enhance or detract from prospects for promotion? In many respects these attitudes are shaped more by common law practices evolving from a number of seemingly innocuous precedents than by formal corporate policies. We call these the "rules of the game." In one company we have studied, management attempted to improve the accuracy of rate of return estimates by holding individuals responsible for the variance of actual results from estimates as determined through post audits. Shortly thereafter, the ranks were submitting only expenditure opportunities that could be estimated relatively accurately. By more than happenstance, these projects were among the poorer ones available at the idea level of the organization. For any student who still doubts the importance of "rules of the game," we ask how much of his time is devoted to learning for the sake of learning as compared with "psyching" the teacher, channelling learning accordingly, etc., all for the purpose of receiving a good course grade. It is our belief that the administrative aspects of capital allocation are more important than procedures, and we encourage students to look for these factors in the case situations that follow.

APPRAISING RETURN ON INVESTMENT POTENTIAL

Intuition is an important aspect of capital budgeting decisions in practice. A fuse blows in a factory, shutting off power on an important production line. Should the fuse be replaced? No one stops to consider the return on investment potential of this capital outlay. Instead, people jump to get the fuse replaced and production back on stream as quickly as possible. Why? The benefits from action appear too high to merit delays caused by introducing the sort of thorough-going analysis that could convincingly demonstrate the wisdom of the action. Now, we are not saying that there will never be circumstances when failure to replace the fuse would represent the best course of action; only that, on the average, this is not the appropriate time for such an analysis. This illustrates a simple but vital point: businessmen are action oriented. The purpose of analysis is to make action more effective. When analysis delays action, it carries an implicit cost, and this cost is worthwhile only if it leads to savings derived through improved abilities to make sounder decisions. The obvious best course of action may be justified by, but rarely improved through, analysis.

Unfortunately, an intuitive hunch does not assure that the best course of action will in fact prove to be best for the firm, unless the hunch is coupled with considerable judgment wisdom. This kind of wisdom comes only through understanding and experience. The wise decision maker must understand what the relevant considerations are, and know how they interrelate, as well as be able to supply meaningful data from experience to fit the needs of the circumstances. The first part of this equation—understanding—relates to fundamental rights and wrongs; that is, to principles and to theories. Understanding the theoretically correct procedure for evaluating return potential and knowing the relevant kinds of data pertaining to an analysis are important prerequisites to effective analysis, whether this analysis is formalized or entirely intuitive. The return on investment section of this book affords considerable opportunity for students to develop this theoretical understanding of proper return on investment measurement techniques.

Theoretical understanding, however, can be hypnotic to the extent it creates a false aura of mastery. In practice, theoretically optimum procedures can be mastered readily by clerical personnel. This does not qualify the clerks as wise decision makers. A substantial amount of judgment is still required in selecting the data to be processed by the specified procedures and in determining actions given the formal results of an analysis. These judgment skills can most readily be developed through application in practical settings. Hence, the case studies which follow require more than systematic cranking of formulas before the appropriate course of action is apparent.

There is, at the moment, a single, generally accepted, theoretically correct method of evaluating the return potential of investment opportunities. The students, therefore, may wonder why they are asked to study some of the incorrect procedures for evaluation developed in this section of the book. We believe it is quite important to understand the limitations of some of the less satisfactory methods of analysis for two reasons: Most firms do not now follow the most sophisticated procedures, and even zealous crusaders, as some of you may choose to become, do not often change the course of history overnight. More important, we do not believe it will ever be practical to convert the entire appraisal apparatus over to the most sophisticated techniques available. Indeed, we suspect that the large majority of business decisions can be made more expeditiously and just as soundly by cruder methods once the limitations of a short-cut method are fully understood. In short, practice demands analytical efficiency as well as accuracy.

The first step in any formal appraisal of an investment opportunity involves the identification of relevant alternatives. One set is usually obvious: invest or do not invest. But there are usually more. For example, in appraising a machine replacement opportunity, there frequently are several machines that will perform the desired tasks satisfactorily. Here the question becomes which, if any, new machine is best. Often the existing machine need not be replaced this year. This opens up the time dimension. When should the machine optimally be replaced? This year, next year, or . . . ? The finite possibilities are enormous. Almost all proposals involve alternatives in kind as well as in time. The best decision can hardly be reached unless it begins with the best alternatives. Unfortunately, screening all the feasible alternatives is often impractical.

Appraisal of alternatives requires the determination of the relevant costs and revenues, the time patterns to these cash flows, the earning life of the investment, the size of the initial investment, and similar factors that will affect future cash inflows and outflows. The principle underlying the choice of relevant cash flows is easy to state: they are the cash flows that will change as a consequence of a decision to invest. What is, in fact, an incremental cash flow in a specific situation is less clearly defined. For example, in a decision to replace an outmoded production line, is the liquidation value of the building that houses the line a relevant consideration?

A more difficult set of problems arises in measuring costs or benefits that are relevant. What, for example, is the value of a cafeteria that will serve food at a loss (cost to the firm) to employees? Or what is the value of entering a market with a new product that promises only to provide experience benefits for developing and capitalizing upon possible subsequent products? Measuring relevant costs and revenues, the life of the project and so forth, are often challenging endeavors, and it is here that experience pays off. The cases in this volume should introduce students to some of the problems and pitfalls of measuring these cash flows meaningfully.

EVALUATING RISKS

We would like to distinguish between two types of risks: those relating to a specific project, and those affecting the corporation as a whole. Project risk relates to the uncertainties surrounding the estimating of relevant future cash flows for the specific investment opportunity under study. A shareholder, however, does not experience the effects of project risk in isolation; rather it is the overall risk of the corporation that affects his welfare. As we shall see later, the nature of risks from the stockholder's point of view differs in character from project risks and requires different kinds of analysis. To understand such an analysis effectively requires estimating the impact of the unique riskiness of a project on overall corporate circumstances.

A substantial body of theory has developed toward the end of measuring project risk accurately. The underlying procedure for achieving this objective is mathematical, and involves expected value computations. Essentially, an expected value calculation endeavors to measure what a project will return *on the average,* given probability estimates of the likelihood of a variety of future events and estimates of the profit that would be earned if each possible event occurred.

Students will not be very far along in the measurement of expected profits before they recognize that the procedure requires fairly elaborate calculations even for simple problems. For this reason, most expositions of this theory directed at practitioners have sought to develop rougher approximations of the theoretically correct procedure. Unfortunately, some of these "solutions" have started from the theory and worked toward practice. To us, practice makes a more useful starting place. For example, if we start with the assumption that a businessman needs only to know whether the project proposal is desirable, undesirable, or perhaps marginal but worthy of more careful study, different and much simpler procedures suggest themselves.

Even given a suitable framework for analyzing risk, many problems remain, mostly relating to the value of the data cranked into the equation. These data come from two kinds of sources: objective evidence and subjective opinion. When evaluating objective evidence to determine its predictive value, careful consideration must be given to the data's relevancy and its adequacy. More often than not the data will have to be interpreted and modified from its original form before it is useful for predictive purposes. Subjective opinions also involve questions of relevancy and adequacy—questions that are very difficult to get at without some efforts at formalized analysis. At a minimum (assuming the stakes are high enough, and the issue in doubt), identification of the significant elements of risk seems useful before opinions are formed. However, the degree to which such formalization is desirable appears to us to be a function of the importance and decisional difficulty of the problem under consideration.

THE INVESTMENT DECISION

An idea for a capital expenditure is subjected to a long series of screening appraisals before it ever reaches the point where the decision to invest is made. At any number of points along this road the idea could be killed, set back, or otherwise delayed. Alternatively, it might acquire an aggressive sponsor whose push will assure its approval with utmost speed. In a large organization many people participate in this decisional process. While few hold the ultimate power of final approval, strong positive or negative screening powers are disseminated widely in many hands throughout the organization—indeed, to the very well-springs of the idea itself.

Many more ideas fail along the way than ever are approved. Some of these decisions are made on the basis of very limited information about the potential of the project and sometimes with only the vaguest impression about the overall importance of the project to the affairs of the company. Many of these decisions no doubt would appear wise if subjected to more intensive inquiry. There nevertheless remains an important enough residue to lead us to believe that, in the aggregate, the decision not to invest, made as it is by so many individuals, is as important to the welfare of the firm as decisions to invest. To add some perspective, we think that more firms fail in the relative sense because they spend too little on capital expenditure opportunities than because they spend too much. If the time dimension is added, more firms probably fail because they do not invest funds soon enough than because the investment is made too quickly. Finally, spending funds too cautiously seems often to involve more risks than spending funds too liberally. These factors add important dimensions to the allocation policies affecting the individual investment decision.

On the other hand, any firm that enjoys a modest degree of success in generating new expenditure ideas will not have time to give each of its ideas serious consideration. Many decisions will have to be made quickly and crudely by people far below the policy levels of the firm. Making optimum decisions in each and every instance is an impractical objective. Minimizing the likelihood of serious screening errors seems to be a more worthwhile target.

Whatever the objective, there must be a method of appraisal and standards for screening available to the decision makers. Management faces a major communication problem in any firm where decision powers rests in many hands. The methods and standards must be understandable to those who will use them. They must also seem practical at the operating levels, given whatever limited time is typically available for decisional purposes.

Having an appropriate set of methods and standards is no guarantee of consistency. Estimates of potential demand depend upon too many judgmental factors to hope that a variety of individuals will see different opportunities from the same general perspective. Divergent attitudes toward risk, for example, are hard to eliminate by proclamation, yet these attitudes can have a very significant biasing effect. Even objectivity is a relative term. Illustratively, it often seems to us easier to predict which college will be the NCAA basketball champion two years hence than it is to predict, with good accuracy, demand for a new product. These data limitations must be kept in mind throughout the process of reaching investment decisions, especially when the final decisional power is far removed from the source of the fundamental judgments.

Who should make the required investment decisions? Perhaps this is the most critical question in this subject area. So far, businessmen have groped their way toward a solution. Most agree that many improvements are possible.

Returning to the subject of standards, a minimum satisfactory rate of return (hurdle rate) is generally regarded as the most significant. As we shall discuss shortly, a firm's cost of capital is one important factor influencing the determination of this rate. Essentially, cost of capital describes the minimum rate of return on investment necessary to satisfy a stockholder's investment objectives.

Whenever a firm has more opportunities than it can afford to finance, than are feasible to undertake simultaneously, or than are practical to capitalize upon for other reasons, it is said to be in a state of capital rationing. Under circumstances of capital rationing, the relevant minimum hurdle rate is called the "investment opportunity rate." The investment opportunity rate is the lowest rate of return received from the projects which the company can afford to undertake. Although most firms ration capital in practice, methods for deriving an appropriate (affordable) opportunity rate are not as yet very rigorously thought through.

Once a minimum hurdle rate has been set, many questions remain concerning how it should be applied. For example, should the same rate apply to all divisions of a large firm even though many of these divisions are quite different in character? If there are to be different hurdle rates, how should appropriate differentials be determined? Answers to these perplexing questions are just beginning to be formulated in the literature.

At the heart of these questions are issues of overall corporate strategy. For example, how should the corporation ideally diversify its capital to minimize risk from the shareholder's point of view? We do not believe that the subject of strategic diversification can be addressed rigorously without exploring the relevant risks, as the shareholders may experience them. Nor can they be abstracted from related considerations about appropriate means of financing. These critical subjects are not well understood yet. At the moment, management must rely on its common sense and its experience in its efforts to try to take into account adequately all the wide variety of variables bearing upon these important decisions. In any case, the foregoing suggests that balancing the composition of new capital expenditures requires a top-level perspective, and a long-range point of view—one that is difficult to communicate effectively to lower echelons with more parochial interests—if the many strategic factors not evaluated in return on investment computations are to be considered.

In many senses, the foregoing description of some problems associated with the investment decisions barely scratches the surface of real world complexity. Nevertheless, we hope that the sampling is sufficient for the reader to catch some of the flavor and the challenge of the allocation process as a business problem. We further hope it will help students to see latent problems lying in the background of even the simpler-looking decisional cases which follow.

THE BALANCING POINT

Any firm has a variety of opportunities for investment with differing return potentials, and it has a variety of financing opportunities, each with different cost implications. How should opportunities to spend be brought into balance with opportunities to finance? How low a return on investment is satisfactory? How much is too much for management to pay for its capital? These are complex questions which defy simple, meaningful solutions.

Elementary economics points to a fundamental approach to these issues. In problems involving costs and revenues, profits for a period can be improved by increasing costs up until the point where marginal costs equal marginal revenues. Turning this over, we could say capital should be invested in projects until the marginal returns from the last-most project equal the marginal costs of the capital necessary to finance it, assuming in both instances that the most favorable opportunities are taken first. The comparative inflexibility of capital commitments suggests that a fairly distant planning horizon is necessary to encompass the relevant period for measuring these factors.

We have already indicated that there are methods, admittedly imperfect, for estimating the marginal (or incremental) return potential for capital expenditure opportunities. It follows that, if we can find comparable methods of measuring marginal capital costs, we can at least get to a crude approximation of the point of balance and, from this, establish appropriate minimum return on investment standards—hence, the importance of cost of capital as an integral part of the capital budgeting process.

THE COST OF CAPITAL

The literature presents many ways of measuring the cost of capital. We shall not attempt to review these methods individually here. We can, however, say with confidence that the ultimate answer has not yet been found, and this without minimizing the value of the contributions of several colleagues who disagree with our conclusion. We are also afraid that many of the existing methods of measurement proposed produce badly misleading results in many cases.

At the first level of complexity, capital costs for specific forms of capital are not what they appear to be at first glance. In a very narrow sense, interest rates are a measure of the cost of debt capital. However, debt cannot be added to the capital structure of a firm indiscriminately without affecting risks, from the stockholder's point of view. All other factors being equal, an addition to financial risk would tend to lower the value placed upon earnings in the market place, and, therefore, reduce appreciation opportunities—one of the two sources of stockholder income. In short, there may be opportunity losses associated with the use of debt capital that increase costs above stated interest rates.

The interrelated facets of the cost of one form of capital with another pose questions that are difficult to evaluate. To measure the cost of debt, we must know the impact of the marginal use of debt on market values for the common stock. At the moment, we do not have this knowledge conclusively mastered, although efforts to this end have been and continue to be made.

Certain principles of fundamental importance can be set forth. We should be endeavoring to measure capital costs from the point of view of the common shareholder, not for the corporation as an entity. Whenever capital is raised, the stockholder's long-run position is impaired (relative to no financing) until the capital is put to work. This impairment of earning power takes direct (e.g., interest costs) and indirect forms (e.g., additional financial risks). The indirect cost factors are very difficult to measure. Nevertheless, the focus should remain upon determining the impairment of earning power.

An alternative measurement tack can be developed from the fact that the cost of capital is related to the return on the new capital that is necessary to reestablish long-term earning power on the stock investment at the old status quo. However, this is not a simple problem of relating direct returns to direct costs. For example, stockholders may gain low-cost borrowing capacity when equity is sold, or they may be willing to exchange increased "financial risks" for "increased growth potential" or "increased asset diversification," factors that are not currently measured *satisfactorily* in either cost of capital or return on investment calculations.

The literature employs a device called the "weighed average cost of capital" to overcome some of the foregoing deficiencies. Various of these proposed methods have their unique limitations, but overall the principal deficiency rests with the need for assumptions about optimum dividend and debt policies. Making arbitrary assumptions wishes away the most vital part of the measurement task. Yet there is, in our opinion, too little known as yet to formulate meaningful assumptions.

When measuring capital costs, in short, we believe that it is important to bear in mind the interrelated aspects of the financing and investment decisions. A change in capital allocation objectives flowing from a cost of capital measurement will probably transform the firm's growth characteristics, its composite riskiness, and other factors influencing the stock market's appraisal of the value of the common stock. This feedback mechanism destroys the initial comparability of marginal cost and revenue data. Capital budgeting is a dynamic process and will require dynamic models before theory approaches reality.

The cases we have chosen for the cost-of-capital section of this book are designed to build an inventory of awareness about the problems involved in achieving useful measurements of capital costs. Under such circumstances, it is certainly discomforting to know that decisions are still required, and that the problems are of pressing importance. But then business never promises to be wholly scientific.

RAISING CAPITAL

A book this short cannot begin to deal meaningfully with a subject as complex as financing decisions. We have, however, selected a sampling of cases that illustrate the range of considerations bearing upon financing strategies and tactics and facilitate penetrating probes into the most critical elements of these problems in order to gain a better understanding of the fundamentals.

Our material is broken into two parts: that relating to capital structure policy formulation—the strategy of financing—and that relating to tactical choices among specific financing alternatives under concrete circumstances. It should be clear that the subjects are not unrelated. The amount of debt a firm can afford to carry over time is, in part, a function of the kinds of debt the firm chooses to use.

CAPITAL STRUCTURE POLICIES

Four capital structure policies are especially critical to sound financial management. These are: (1) debt capacity policies, (2) flexibility (or liquidity) policies, (3) dividend policies, and (4) equity policies. Their nature can be best illustrated by posing fundamental questions: (1) How much debt can a firm afford to carry without compromising stockholder objectives? (2) How much capital should management reserve for future needs to protect against the possibility that future adverse conditions in the money market will affect the firm's ability to raise capital on favorable terms? (3) What is the optimum balance between the payment of earnings to stockholders in the form of cash dividends and the retention of earnings within the firm for reinvestment purposes? (4) How frequently, if at all, should management endeavor to raise new capital through sale of equity securities?

We will limit our comments here to the debt capacity policy question. Use of debt involves a classic choice between income and risk. Shall the stockholder eat well or sleep well? When the question is posed in this manner, there are clearly as many answers to the appropriate method of resolving income and risk conflicts as there are shareholders with differing digestive tracts.

Despite this difficulty, answers are necessary and can be improved by means of sophisticated analytical techniques. As with return-on-investment evaluations, analysis of alternative debt policies begins with identifying the relevant dimensions. Existing concepts about "financial leverage," "trading on the equity," and other risk and income factors will be helpful. Nevertheless, the student will have to trace laboriously through the specific effects of proposed policy changes on the likely income and risk circumstances of stockholders if he is to gain the analytical understanding necessary for decisional purposes. From such efforts, clearer understanding of the nature of required judgments and of the methods of balancing conflicting interests should emerge. If so, the student will have made several major strides forward in his ability to make practical decisions concerning debt policy. Our approach to other critical financial policy issues follows along similar lines.

FINANCING TACTICS

Given a set of financing policy objectives, a number of important tactical decisions remain. To illustrate: Should we use debt or equity to finance current capital requirements? If debt, what kind of debt instrument is most appropriate? If equity, should the funds be raised now or later?

Essentially, these problems pose the same kind of analytical demands as return on investment problems—identifying alternatives, determining relevant cost information, appraising risks, and the like. The basic frameworks for analysis are also comparable. We believe it is sufficient at this juncture for the student to be aware that these problems exist and that he will eventually have to deal with them.

This section of the book does require one point of perspective before the specific problems can be viewed properly. Favorable financing opportunities do not automatically flower in the desert. They must be cultivated. They must also be harvested with an eye to the future. In short, financing decisions tend to be more interdependent over time than investment decisions, and this affects the framework in which they should be evaluated.

SUMMARY PERSPECTIVE

We have endeavored to sketch out the full range of problems that will arise in the totality of capital budgeting so that each part may be seen in relation to the whole. We have also attempted to alert students to the kinds of analysis that are necessary to deal with these problems. The result is a skeleton. The cases which follow provide the flesh— a depth and richness to the subject that provides the decision-making challenge. Their purpose is not descriptive, however. The case material provides opportunities for students to build understanding, both through discriminating use of theory and through independent thinking. More important, the student is afforded the chance to develop many of the skills required of successful decision makers in the business world. Over the long run, improved skill in decision making will prove more valuable to the student than any of the substantive knowledge acquired. We hope the student will therefore keep his eye on his personal return on the time he invests as he pursues the educational experience afforded.

ACKNOWLEDGMENTS

To an even greater extent than most casebooks, this volume represents the efforts of many people. We have attempted to compile a set of cases suitable for an integrated course in Capital Budgeting, and have drawn our materials from the interrelated fields of Finance and Managerial Economics. Although we are solely responsible for the selection and organization of the cases, we would like to express our appreciation to the teaching groups in both these areas at the Harvard Business School.

In the Finance teaching group, significant contributions in the development of useful concepts and effective case materials were made by Professors Pearson Hunt, Charles M. Williams, Frank L. Tucker, Lawrence E. Thompson, James T. S. Porterfield (now at Stanford University), James E. Walter, Victor L. Andrews, Alan B. Coleman, and Erich A. Helfert. Several of the cases in this volume will appear simultaneously in the Fourth Edition of *Case Problems in Finance* that is being published this spring.

The Control teaching group has, over the last several years, developed a series of cases for exploring alternative analytical techniques for evaluating capital expenditures. Most of this work has been done by Professors Robert A. Anthony, Charles A. Bliss, Robert O. Schlaifer, Ross G. Walker, Neil E. Harlan, Charles J. Christenson, John R. Yeager, and Robert K. Jaedicke (now at Stanford University), and many of the cases we have included in this area will also appear this spring in *Managerial Economics: Text and Cases.*

In addition to these substantial debts, we wish to express our appreciation to Professors Thomas C. Raymond of Harvard Business School, Harold Bierman, Jr. of Cornell University, Clyde N. Randall of the University of Utah, and J. C. Taylor of the University of Western Ontario for permitting us to use cases they prepared.

We wish to acknowledge the valuable assistance of several research assistants at the Harvard Business School who have prepared many of these cases under our supervision: John H. McArthur, Joseph L. Fromm, Stephen B. Swensrud, and Jerome Bracken. We are also grateful to Miss Sandra Lewis for her cheerful help in preparing various sections of the manuscript for publication.

Finally, we are grateful to a large group of businessmen who have selflessly given their time to cooperate in the preparation of these cases. Without their aid it would have been impossible to approach this subject at the practical level of reality that we have tried to achieve.

The authors accept full responsibility for the contents of this volume.

RFV
RFV

March 1, 1962

TABLE OF CONTENTS

Section I

MEASURING RETURN
ON INVESTMENT

CONSOLIDATED ELECTRICAL PRODUCTS, INC. (A)

In March of 1957, Mr. Holman, treasurer of Consolidated Electrical Products, Inc., faced the task of reviewing the company's capital budgeting policies and practices, and of recommending advantageous changes to the company's executive committee. The present capital budgeting policies and procedures had not been revised significantly for nearly ten years. Recently, a number of company executives had become increasingly critical of the capital budgeting process. This led the company's president to recommend that a thorough-going appraisal of the system be undertaken by the treasurer. Specifically, Mr. Holman was charged with developing (1) minimum return standards for appraising projects, (2) uniform methods for estimating return rates for specific projects, and (3) standardized procedures for allocating funds among the various proposals submitted by the company's operating divisions.

BACKGROUND

Consolidated Electrical Products, Inc. (CONELP), manufactured a broad line of electrical appliances and industrial equipment. The company was organized into five operating divisions, each of which was one of the leading producers in its special field. The major appliance division produced a relatively complete line of consumer products including television sets, refrigerators, ranges, washers, and similar items. The small appliance division also manufactured a range of consumer products such as toasters, radios, electric blankets, mixers, razors, and frying pans. The electrical components division made tubes, transistors, capacitators, and other small electrical parts. The control apparatus divisions designed and manufactured intricate servo-mechanical control devices, computers, and more recently data processing equipment.

Finally, the heavy industrial division manufactured turbines, generators, and similar equipment for power plants. All divisions engaged in some government work, although, in 1956, government contracts constituted less than 20% of the company's sales volume.

CONELP had grown rapidly during and subsequent to World War II. Sales and profits, for example, had more than doubled in the nine years since 1947. During this period, CONELP had undertaken a major expansion program. More than $130 million had been invested in new plant and equipment, while a similar sum was required for related working capital requirements. This expansion program had been financed through retained earnings (management traditionally paid out in dividends roughly 60% to 65% of current earnings) of $95 million, depreciation of $70 million, and two private placements of debentures, totaling $100 million.

At the end of 1956, outstanding debt of $120 million represented 31.9% of CONELP's total capitalization.[1] This factor disturbed several CONELP executives inasmuch as a firm corporate policy limited debt to one-third of total capitalization. These men noted that more than one-half of the new capital required for the postwar expansion program had come from debt sources. Since future expansion was, if anything, expected to accelerate, the need for outside capital would tend to increase. The prospective need to raise equity capital had alarmed these CONELP executives. They considered equity capital comparatively high in cost relative to the company's historic sources of funds—depreciation, retained earnings, and debt. As a result, these officers had urged a thorough review of capital budgeting procedures to ascertain whether limiting expenditures to levels supported by historic fund resources might be more advantageous than expanding more rapidly at the expense of raising equity capital. Some urgency was attached to this review since excess[2] cash balances would largely be depleted by the end of 1957.

A complete set of books was maintained for each division as if it were an independent enterprise. The division managers were held responsible for the rate of return earned on capital invested by CONELP

---

[1] Total capitalization here means the sum total of debt and equity capitalizations as stated on the balance sheet.

[2] For various reasons, the company held continuously cash balances equal to 5% of annual sales volume plus marketable securities equal to outstanding tax liabilities. Liquid asset balances above these levels were considered excess and were generally available for expenditure.

in each division, and for maintaining or improving its share of the market for each of its products. These rates of return on investment for individual divisions were calculated as follows. For each year, profits after depreciation and an allocation for taxes (proportionally distributed by divisions on the basis of profit before tax levels) was divided by a measurement of corporate investment in each division. This investment measure, referred to as gross investment, equaled gross assets (i.e., total assets *before* deducting depreciation) less current liabilities. The unweighted average of opening and closing gross investments for a year actually served as the investment denominator in the rate of return criteria. Sample calculations are shown in Exhibit 1.

In recent years, all but one of the divisions had shown satisfactory increases in sales volume and had improved their market shares. The exception, the major appliance division, although maintaining its market share, had encountered vigorous competition since 1953, and its sales and profit margins had suffered severely. Several observers believed that the major appliance industry would become more like the automobile industry in a few years with only a handful of large manufacturers surviving. CONELP management believed that appliance competition would in any event remain unusually intense for several more years but were confident that the public acceptance of CONELP appliance brand names would make the present transition period less difficult for their company than for most other competitors. Management also expected that the profit levels and sales growth, typical of the major appliance division during the period 1947–1953, would eventually be restored.

Rates of return in the various divisions varied widely as shown in detail in Exhibit 2. Moreover, trends in these rates among divisions also differed. Rates of return in the major appliance division had trended downward sharply, whereas in the heavy industrial equipment division they were declining moderately.[3] The small appliance and electrical components divisions' rates of return were remaining relatively constant, although the latter division had less stability. The control apparatus division, however, had improved its rate of return somewhat in recent years. Over-all, the company's rate of return was falling off. This condition had also led several executives to question the usefulness of present budgeting procedures.

---

[3] Management had discounted this division's higher earning rate experienced in 1956 as attributable to unusually favorable business conditions.

The present capital budgeting policies, when established in 1946, were predicated first on the basic objective that all corporate policies and operating practices should be designed to produce the greatest possible return on investment for the stockholders over the long run. The board of directors and top management were still agreed that a new capital budgeting policy should facilitate achieving this objective.

When implementing this basic objective in 1947, top management had decided that no division should be allowed to go downhill as the result of making new investments that would return less than the division's historic rate of return on gross assets. The historic rate of return here referred to a five-year, unweighted average of rates of return on investments for the division or for the corporation as a whole. (These rate of return calculations have already been described in detail on page 5.) Whenever divisions had historic rates of return less than that for the corporation as a whole, the latter calculation was substituted. This modification was justified in terms of upgrading rates of returns in substandard divisions to the general corporate level.

The five-year average return on investment calculations described above were very important figures in CONELP's capital budgeting policy. Projects were rarely accepted unless they promised rates of return more favorable than the relevant historic rate. Historic rate of return, in short, was employed as cutoff points (i.e., minimum acceptable rate of return criteria) in screening capital expenditure proposals. The current minimum return standards for divisions are shown below:

Division	Five-Year Average Rate of Return	Minimum Return Standards
Major appliance	8.1%	8.1%
Small appliance	13.0	13.0
Electrical components	10.3	10.3
Control apparatus	20.3	20.3
Heavy industrial equipment	6.1	7.0
Total company	7.0	n.a.

n.a. Not available.

Each division was responsible for preparing its own capital budget which itemized and gave relevant details on proposed projects. These budgets were submitted annually in November to the central treasurer's office for preparatory screening.

A divisional capital budget was separated into two parts. Part I consisted of projects to be financed from depreciation resources available within the division. Each divisional manager had the right to commit funds (except for projects involving expenditures on fixed assets in excess of $50,000) up to the forecast level for depreciation (calculated on a straight-line basis—the accounting procedure used in all corporate record keeping). Relatively little information was given for individual projects of this class other than a brief description of the project, the amount of fixed asset investments involved, and a general indication of the purpose of and justification for the expenditure. As a practical matter, projects in this portion of the capital budget were seldom reviewed by top management on an item-by-item basis. The first section of the budget was designed to keep top management and the board of directors informed about how each division was spending its funds.

Part II of the capital budget included projects to be financed from general corporate resources. Each item in this section of the budget required separate approval by top management. The projects covered in the second part of the budget were presented first in summary form, as in the first section, and then, in addition, each project was supported in considerable detail on separate sheets. Each division's project preferences were indicated by the numerical sequence of proposals (i.e., best first) in the summary list.

Each project in Part II of the budget reported the projected return on the proposed investment. Returns here were projected at probable average levels (after depreciation and taxes) over the expected economic life of the investment. These returns were divided by the gross incremental investments in fixed assets and working capital[4] to determine the return rate. Proposals were also supported by cost, market, and such other forms of analysis as appeared useful in giving top management as clear an appreciation of the advantages and limitations of the projects as possible.

Projects in Part II of the budget were categorized into several subgroups to aid top management in its appraisal. Proposed investments in excess of $100,000 were first noted since these projects had to be approved individually by the board of directors. These projects, along with other requests in excess of $50,000, were usually given more intensive study by top management. Next, projects were subdivided into

---

[4] Although working capital estimates were included in the denominator of the return on investment equation, only fixed asset expenditures were formally approved in the budget. Each divisional manager, subject only to broad policy restrictions and general control procedures imposed by top management, was free to commit funds to working capital investments at his discretion. The treasurer held an adequate supply of funds available to cover these working capital requirements as they developed.

four broad categories, generally indicative of the nature of the project request. These categories included: cost reduction or replacement, plant expansion, major processing innovations or new products, and, finally, necessary projects, justified at least partially in terms of intangible benefits not readily reducible to a profit analysis. The last category included such proposals as research facilities, investments to maintain competitive position (i.e., tool and die changes associated with remodeling a product), auxiliary facilities (e.g., power plants), and equipment generally beneficial to the community or employees (e.g., prevention of water pollution, building of cafeterias, etc.). These breakdowns were highly important to top management. While not set forth specifically in policy objectives, top management tended to demand return premiums of at least 5% above minimum levels (i.e., minimum level percentage *plus* 5%) for expansion proposals and of 10% for new products. No specific reasons were given for these return distinctions except that they seemed helpful in equating differences in risks between various types of proposals. Necessary projects were reviewed in terms of the degree of urgency and of the over-all strategic benefits to the company.

Projects were also rated within the context of the various expenditure subgroups, in terms of relative riskiness. Three risk measurements were used—normal, moderate, and high. These ratings reflected the degree of confidence division managers placed in the relative certainty (and/or stability) of return projections. Top management typically reviewed moderate and high-risk proposals more carefully, and oftentimes demanded higher return rates from these projects before approval was granted. There were, however, no established rules of thumb governing the return premiums demanded. Management preferred instead to make *ad hoc* judgments based on the merits of each case.

While divisional managers were aware that top management applied greater selectivity than minimum return standards alone suggested, they were not familiar with specific screening criteria. In anticipation of this selectivity, division managers, themselves, applied screening techniques in keeping with their own concepts of appropriate procedures prior to preparation of the capital budget. Roughly one-quarter of total project proposals, meeting the division's minimum return criteria, was rejected at the divisional level. This proportion, however, varied widely from division to division. Top management normally approved about one-third of the dollar size of Part II—capital budget requests, submitted by the divisions—although this proportion varied among the divisions. Data relevant to project requests and approvals for 1956, a fairly typical year, are shown in Exhibit 3.

Division managers had adopted different standards in selecting the projects that would be presented as Part I expenditures in their capital budget. The small appliance division generally used its depreciation allowance to finance any proposed expenditure involving an investment of less than $10,000. This procedure reduced the amount of executive time spent in preparing and reviewing budgetary fund requests. A simple cash payback approach (i.e., investment divided by profits before taxes and depreciation) was used to justify these expenditures, and only projects with two-year paybacks or less were usually approved. Product managers were delegated the authority to make these commitments, and the division manager rarely reviewed the proposals.

In the heavy industrial equipment division, older equipment caused heavy replacement requirements, and depreciation funds were used to finance these replacements. The divisional manager believed this approach was in keeping with the purpose of depreciation inflows. Simple cash payback calculations, adjusted for taxes (i.e., investment divided by profits after taxes plus depreciation), were used to justify expenditures. Only projects with less than four-year paybacks were approved.

The manager of the electrical components division applied his depreciation resources first to finance "intangible" or "necessary" expenditures. These projects were justified in terms of intangible benefits, and return or payback calculations were rarely prepared. Divisional management had adopted this procedure because it believed it was in the best position to appraise intangible benefits. Remaining funds were used to finance replacement and cost-reduction projects. These projects were also justified in terms of simple paybacks. However, an interest charge, equal to the division's earnings rate as described above, was levied as a cost in the profit calculation. Four-year paybacks or better were required before projects received approval.

The control apparatus division spent its depreciation allocations on projects promising the highest returns after considering relative risks. This procedure, according to the divisional manager, appeared most consistent with the profit maximization objective of the corporation. Returns for Part I commitments were computed on the same basis as Part II proposals. Typically, new products comprised the bulk of these commitments.

In the major appliance division, retooling for model change-overs and new products required sizable fund investments that had to be submitted in Part II of the investment budget. Depreciation resources more than covered remaining investment opportunities. Returns were calculated on the same basis as Part II proposals, and this division used its historic earnings rate as the basic minimum return criterion.

Once divisional budgets were received in the treasurer's office, an economic analysis section screened each Part II request individually, and recommended whether the project should be approved or disapproved. In practice, requests for less than $50,000 were given only cursory review and, unless the project appeared to conflict with a generalized set of standards, were tentatively approved. Larger requests were studied in greater detail. The economic analysis section frequently requested clarification or additional supporting data from the divisions, and occasionally undertook separate investigations (often in conjunction with other staff agencies in the central office) of market potentials, the economic outlook, or other factors of importance to the decision. Whenever a proposal did not appear sufficiently promising, a negative report was prepared. Mr. Holman, the treasurer, personally passed on each negative report before it was appended to the initial request.

In mid-December the over-all budget was submitted to the finance committee which included the president, the executive vice-president, and the vice-presidents for marketing, manufacturing, and finance. The treasurer and the division managers concerned also attended these meetings but did not vote. Each division's budget (Part II) was gone over item by item during the committee meetings. At any point in the review, the division manager had an opportunity to add support to a proposal before it was disapproved. The treasurer's negative recommendations were generally followed unless the division manager could further justify the project, or unless the proposal seemed overridingly strategic to various committee members. Occasionally, the treasurer's positive recommendations were overruled when risks seemed unduly large or when the proposal lacked strategic appeal. When completed, the revised budgets were submitted to the board of directors for formal approval. The board rarely discussed proposed investments with outlays less than $100,000, and almost never overruled the finance committee's decisions on specific projects.

Mr. Holman had discussed possible methods of improving the company's capital budgeting procedures with key members of the board of directors, all top executives concerned, as well as with the divisional managers and their staffs. From these discussions, Mr. Holman had learned there was clearly no unanimity of opinion and, indeed, nearly every officer had some unique approach to present. In order to help in the early stages of his analysis, he had collected and organized (in note form) the various viewpoints expressed under several subheadings:

1. Methods of calculating return on investment for specific projects.
2. Methods of determining appropriate minimum return on investment criteria.
3. Methods of allocating funds among divisions.
4. Methods of allocating funds among projects.

These notes are set forth in the cases that follow.

Exhibit 1

CONSOLIDATED ELECTRICAL PRODUCTS, INC. (A)

DIVISIONAL RATES OF RETURN ON INVESTMENT, 1956

(Dollar figures in thousands)

	Major Appliances	Small Appliances	Electrical Components	Control Apparatus Data Processing	Heavy Industrial Equipment	General Investments	Total
ASSETS							
Cash and marketable securities	$ 9,102	$ 5,309	$ 6,836	$ 3,938	$ 8,450	$37,246	$ 70,881
Accounts receivable	24,446	5,933	17,918	10,252	37,711	....	96,260
Inventories	37,288	22,063	28,566	11,742	52,204	764	152,627
Total current assets	$ 70,836	$ 33,305	$ 53,320	$25,932	$ 98,365	$38,010	$319,768
Gross plant	27,595	26,845	44,480	30,953	59,697	22,710	212,280
Depreciation	7,718	8,893	25,758	4,372	21,582	12,237	80,560
Net plant	$ 19,877	$ 17,952	$ 18,722	$26,581	$ 38,115	$10,473	$131,720
Tools and dies	3,001						3,001
Other assets	1,365	1,575	1,560	974	2,267	1,137	8,878
Goodwill	10,000						10,000
Total assets	$105,079	$ 52,832	$ 73,602	$53,487	$138,747	$49,620	$473,367
LIABILITIES							
Accounts payable	$ 12,433	$ 2,662	$ 3,610	$ 1,976	$ 13,361	$ 1,764	$ 35,806
Accrued expenses	2,439	2,167	6,610	1,981	7,069	1,053	21,319
Tax liabilities						32,300	32,300
Customer advances					10,248		10,248
Current liabilities	$ 14,872	$ 4,829	$ 10,220	$ 3,957	$ 30,678	$35,117	$ 99,673

Net assets	90,207	48,003	63,382	49,530	108,069	14,503	373,694
Gross assets net of current liabilities	97,925	56,896	89,140	53,902	129,651	26,740	454,254
Previous years' gross assets net of current liabilities	92,764	56,107	89,100	49,030	118,204	24,231	429,436
Average gross assets	95,344	56,501	89,120	51,466	123,927	25,485	441,845
Sales	182,046	107,192	136,712	78,764	169,015	......	673,729
Cost of goods sold*	158,819	68,213	111,705	51,894	140,659	......	531,290
	$ 23,227	$ 38,979	$ 25,007	$26,870	$ 28,356	$......	$142,439
Selling and administrative	19,180	24,782	8,401	6,309	11,077	10,640†	80,389
Profit before taxes	$ 4,047	$ 14,197	$ 16,606	$20,561	$ 17,279	$(10,640)	$ 62,050
Taxes	1,790	6,310	7,380	9,140	7,680	......	32,300
Profit after taxes	$ 2,257	$ 7,887	$ 9,226	$11,421	$ 9,599	$(10,640)	$ 29,750
Profit after taxes/average gross assets net of current liabilities	2.4%	13.9%	10.4%	22.1%	7.7%	n.a.	6.7%
	$ 4,016	$ 1,383	$ 3,766	$ 1,287	$ 3,764	$ 1,132	$ 15,348

* Depreciation included in cost of goods sold............
† Includes interest expense of $4,500 less interest income of $781.
n.a. Not available.

Exhibit 2

CONSOLIDATED ELECTRICAL PRODUCTS, INC. (A)

DIVISIONAL RATES OF RETURN ON INVESTMENT, 1947–1956

(Dollar figures in millions)

Major Appliances

Year	Sales	Profit after Tax	Gross Assets Adjusted	Profit after Tax to Gross Assets
1956	$182.0	$2.26	$95.4	2.4%
1955	202.4	4.21	90.2	4.7
1954	219.6	8.22	88.2	9.4
1953	250.9	9.64	88.1	10.9
1952	190.7	8.41	65.5	12.9
1951	185.9	7.88	46.4	17.0
1950	230.4	15.80	45.0	35.1
1949	179.6	7.18	42.6	16.8
1948	159.5	6.38	41.5	15.4
1947	113.2	4.64	37.1	12.5

Small Appliances

Year	Sales	Profit after Tax	Gross Assets Adjusted	Profit after Tax to Gross Assets
1956	$107.2	$7.89	$56.5	13.9%
1955	90.1	7.20	55.9	12.9
1954	84.6	7.02	55.6	12.6
1953	79.9	7.14	54.1	13.2
1952	66.4	5.91	47.3	12.5
1951	61.5	5.90	43.3	13.6
1950	67.4	7.20	40.0	18.0
1949	52.2	5.01	39.2	12.8
1948	54.1	5.42	37.1	14.6
1947	49.0	4.81	35.6	13.5

Electrical Components

Year	Sales	Profit after Tax	Gross Assets Adjusted	Profit after Tax to Gross Asset
1956	$136.7	$9.23	$89.2	10.4%
1955	127.8	9.05	89.0	10.2
1954	109.2	7.17	87.2	8.2
1953	130.6	9.26	81.6	11.3
1952	106.8	8.46	73.1	11.6
1951	90.8	8.30	65.2	12.7
1950	78.4	6.15	60.0	10.2
1949	49.2	4.02	58.7	6.8
1948	47.2	4.31	56.2	7.7
1947	45.3	4.29	51.0	8.4

Control Apparatus—Data Processing

Year	Sales	Profit after Tax	Gross Assets Adjusted	Profit after Tax to Gross Assets
1956	$78.8	$11.42	$51.5	22.1%
1955	72.2	9.96	46.0	21.6
1954	57.5	7.01	38.3	18.3
1953	54.9	6.91	34.1	20.2
1952	46.3	5.78	29.8	19.5
1951	42.3	5.46	27.3	20.0
1950	38.2	5.89	23.8	24.7
1949	28.7	3.50	22.0	15.9
1948	27.0	2.91	17.1	17.0
1947	23.3	2.09	14.0	14.9

Heavy Industrial Equipment

Year	Sales	Profit after Tax	Gross Assets Adjusted	Profit after Tax to Gross Assets
1956	$169.0	$9.60	$123.9	7.7%
1955	135.8	5.63	113.1	5.0
1954	150.5	6.37	108.4	5.9
1953	170.7	6.64	108.4	6.1
1952	137.8	6.04	105.8	5.7
1951	113.9	6.01	86.2	7.0
1950	103.2	7.80	77.6	10.0
1949	95.8	4.75	64.9	7.3
1948	98.0	5.27	57.1	9.2
1947	71.3	3.14	49.7	6.3

Total Company

Year	Sales	Profit after Tax	Gross Assets Adjusted	Profit after Tax to Gross Assets
1956	$673.7	$29.75	$441.8	6.7%
1955	628.2	26.05	420.2	6.2
1954	621.4	26.39	397.7	6.6
1953	687.0	30.79	386.3	8.0
1952	548.0	26.40	341.5	7.7
1951	494.4	25.95	288.4	9.0
1950	517.6	35.84	256.4	14.0
1949	405.5	18.06	247.4	7.3
1948	385.8	18.47	229.0	8.1
1947	302.1	13.77	207.4	6.7

Exhibit 3

CONSOLIDATED ELECTRICAL PRODUCTS, INC. (A)

SUMMARY OF CAPITAL EXPENDITURES APPROVED (DOLLAR VALUES) AT VARIOUS ORGANIZATIONAL LEVELS, 1956

(Dollar figures in thousands)

	Estimate of Projects Requests Prepared at Division Level	At Division Level			At Finance Committee Level		Total Projects Approved	Total Projects Rejected
		Projects Rejected	Projects Approved (Part I)	Projects Requests Submitted (Part II)	Projects Rejected	Projects Approved		
Major appliance division:								
Cost reduction	$ 3,715	$ 175	$ 3,540	......	......	......	$ 3,540	$ 175
Expansion	69	12	57	......	......	......	57	12
New products	1,007	964	43	......	......	......	43	964
Intangibles	3,752	863	125	$ 2,764	$ 1,460	$ 1,304	1,429	2,323
Total	$ 8,543	$ 2,014	$ 3,765	$ 2,764	$ 1,460	$ 1,304	$ 5,069	$ 3,474
Small appliance division:								
Cost reduction	$ 2,788	$ 976	$ 978	$ 834	$ 710	$ 124	$ 1,102	$ 1,686
Expansion	2,156	421	......	1,735	1,392	343	343	1,813
New products	2,416	795	......	1,621	1,621	......	......	2,416
Intangibles	1,544	405	405	734	708	26	431	1,113
Total	$ 8,904	$ 2,597	$ 1,383	$ 4,924	$ 4,431	$ 493	$ 1,876	$ 7,028
Electrical components division:								
Cost reduction	$ 4,892	$ 1,002	$ 525	$ 3,365	$ 2,309	$ 1,056	$ 1,581	$ 3,311
Expansion	2,317	57	......	2,260	2,107	153	153	2,164
New products	1,676	941	......	735	735	......	......	1,676
Intangibles	3,945	704	3,241	......	......	......	3,241	704
Total	$12,830	$ 2,704	$ 3,766	$ 6,360	$ 5,151	$ 1,209	$ 4,975	$ 7,855

Exhibit 3—Continued

	Estimate of Projects Requests Prepared at Division Level	At Division Level		Projects Requests Submitted (Part II)	At Finance Committee Level		Total Projects Approved	Total Projects Rejected
		Projects Rejected	Projects Approved (Part I)		Projects Rejected	Projects Approved		
Control apparatus division:								
Cost reduction	$ 1,604	$ 946	$ 158	$ 500	$ 30	$ 470	$ 628	$ 976
Expansion	3,187	1,234	310	1,643	668	975	1,285	1,902
New products	6,667	2,075	807	3,785	2,256	1,529	2,336	4,331
Intangibles	792	732	12	48	......	48	60	732
Total	$12,250	$ 4,987	$ 1,287	$ 5,976	$ 2,954	$ 3,022	$ 4,309	$ 7,941
Heavy industrial equipment:								
Cost reduction	$ 6,661	$ 642	$ 3,764	$ 2,255	$ 528	$ 1,727	$ 5,491	$ 1,170
Expansion	2,184	208	......	1,976	1,631	345	345	1,839
New products	305	......	......	305	305	......	......	305
Intangibles	3,022	258	......	2,764	2,092	672	672	2,350
Total	$12,172	$ 1,108	$ 3,764	$ 7,300	$ 4,556	$ 2,744	$ 6,508	$ 5,664
Total company:								
Cost reduction	$19,660	$ 3,741	$ 8,965	$ 6,954	$ 3,577	$ 3,377	$12,342	$ 7,318
Expansion	9,913	1,932	367	7,614	5,798	1,816	2,183	7,730
New products	12,071	4,775	850	6,446	4,917	1,529	2,379	9,692
Intangibles	13,055	2,962	3,783	6,310	4,260	2,050	5,833	7,222
Total	$54,699	$13,410	$13,965	$27,324	$18,552	$ 8,772	$22,737	$31,962

CONSOLIDATED ELECTRICAL PRODUCTS, INC. (B)

One of Mr. Holman's first tasks in re-evaluating CONELP's capital budgeting policies was to determine the most useful method of calculating rates of return promised from new investment opportunities. This rate calculation would be one of the primary factors considered in deciding whether new project proposals were sufficiently promising to merit undertaking the necessary investment.

In discussing this task with other members of the CONELP organization, Mr. Holman uncovered a number of widely different viewpoints concerning return calculations, as well as several problem areas that needed clarification. As a result, Mr. Holman had organized his notes, summarizing the various alternatives possible, under three main topics: (1) basic frameworks for computing returns, (2) accounting problems in selecting data for the return equation, and (3) methods for estimating future returns on a comparable basis. This last-most topic developed as an outgrowth of the fact that some individuals within the organization tended to evaluate new projects with an optimistic bias, whereas others were highly conservative in stating return opportunities. Underlying each of these topics was a basic question: Should there be one single procedure, applied throughout the organization, for evaluating the return potential of new projects, or should each division be permitted to use the procedure that seemed most appropriate to its needs?[1] Mr. Holman's notes are set forth below:

I. *Basic Frameworks for Calculating Rate of Return on Investment*

Methods of presenting return on investments computations essentially all relate some measure of funds generated from the new investment to some

---

[1] Because this question was closely related to a larger problem involving the amount of decisional authority delegated to the divisional level, Mr. Holman decided to defer consideration of this problem until a later date. See the CONELP (D) case.

measure of the investment itself. Quite a large number of alternative methods of making this comparison exist, and each produces a unique set of data. In order to explore the implications of these alternatives, each will be used to measure the return potential of the following four hypothetical investment alternates:

(1) An investment of $100,000—$80,000 for plant and $20,000 for working capital—will produce profits after taxes (of 50%) of $10,000 per annum. The expected life of this project is five years, and annual depreciation charges would thus equal $16,000 per annum.

(2) An investment of $100,000—$20,000 for plant and $80,000 for working capital—will produce the same profits after taxes as (1) above. This project also has an expected life of five years with depreciation charges amounting to $4,000 per annum.

(3) The same investment opportunity with the same profit after tax expectations as alternative (1) above. However, the expected life of the project is 40 years. Depreciation charges would, therefore, equal $2,000 per annum.

(4) The same investment opportunity with the same profit after tax expectations as alternative (2) above. This project, however, has an expected life of 40 years. Depreciation charges are $500 per annum.

All the above opportunities are assumed to have no plant salvage value at the end of their expected life, but to have working capital investments that are fully recoverable.

A. *Payback*

In all payback calculations, estimates of annual amounts of return on investment are divided into estimates of the new investment. These formulae all produce an estimate of the number of years necessary to recover capital. If this basic method of evaluation of the return potential of new projects was used, we would have to set some standard based on a minimum number of years to recover capital in evaluating each new project.

Various frameworks for calculating payback are described below. For each, the basic equation is set forth, and, then, this equation is applied to the four investment alternatives outlined above.

1. *Simple Payback*

   a) Basic equation: $\dfrac{\text{Gross Investment}}{\text{Profits before Taxes and Depreciation}}$

   b) Return calculations for sample alternatives (numbers corresponded to investment alternatives):

   (1) $\dfrac{\$100,000}{\$36,000} = 2.8$ Years

   (2) $\dfrac{\$100,000}{\$24,000} = 4.2$ Years

   (3) $\dfrac{\$100,000}{\$22,000} = 4.6$ Years

   (4) $\dfrac{\$100,000}{\$20,500} = 4.9$ Years

2. *After-Tax Payback*

a) Basic equation: $\dfrac{\text{Gross Investment}}{\text{Profits after Taxes Plus Depreciation}}$

b) Return calculations for sample alternatives:

(1) $\dfrac{\$100,000}{\$26,000} = 3.8$ Years

(2) $\dfrac{\$100,000}{\$14,000} = 7.1$ Years

(3) $\dfrac{\$100,000}{\$12,000} = 8.3$ Years

(4) $\dfrac{\$100,000}{\$10,500} = 9.5$ Years

3. *Profit Payback on Average Investment*

a) Basic equation: $\dfrac{\text{Average Investment}}{\text{Profit after Taxes}}$

b) Return calculations for sample alternatives:

(1) $\dfrac{\$60,000}{\$10,000} = 6$ Years

(2) $\dfrac{\$90,000}{\$10,000} = 9$ Years

(3) $\dfrac{\$60,000}{\$10,000} = 6$ Years

(4) $\dfrac{\$90,000}{\$10,000} = 9$ Years

4. *Simple Payback after Capital Costs*

a) Basic equation: $\dfrac{\text{Gross Investment}}{\text{Profits before Depreciation and Taxes—C}}$

where C = an allocation for capital costs, usually stated as a percentage of gross investment (arbitrarily assumed to be 8% of gross investment in the calculations below—in practice this capital cost would equal the minimum return standard), or occasionally average investment (in this case, profits after taxes are used in denominator in lieu of profits before taxes and depreciation).

b) Return calculations for sample alternatives:

Gross Investment	Average Investment
(1) $\dfrac{\$100,000}{\$28,000} = 3.6$ Years	$\dfrac{\$60,000}{\$5,200} = 11.5$ Years
(2) $\dfrac{\$100,000}{\$16,000} = 6.3$ Years	$\dfrac{\$90,000}{\$3,800} = 32.1$ Years
(3) $\dfrac{\$100,000}{\$14,000} = 7.1$ Years	$\dfrac{\$60,000}{\$5,200} = 11.5$ Years
(4) $\dfrac{\$100,000}{\$12,500} = 8.0$ Years	$\dfrac{\$90,000}{\$2,800} = 32.1$ Years

5. *Times Capital Recovered*

 a) Basic equation: This calculation is not strictly a payback figure. It attempts to measure the amount of funds received from an investment (both profits and capital recoveries over the expected life of the investment) in relationship to the total investment. The basic formula is:

$$\frac{\text{Total Profits after Taxes Plus Total Depreciation}}{\text{Gross Investment}}$$

 b) Return calculations for sample alternatives:

(1) $\dfrac{\$50,000 + \$80,000}{\$100,000} = 1.3x$

(2) $\dfrac{\$50,000 + \$20,000}{\$100,000} = 0.7x$

(3) $\dfrac{\$400,000 + \$80,000}{\$100,000} = 4.8x$

(4) $\dfrac{\$400,000 + \$20,000}{\$100,000} = 4.2x$

6. *Other Payback Alternatives*

 a) Variants on the payback alternatives can be developed, using, for example, profits after depreciation but before taxes as the denominator, or using some new combination of the numerators and denominators described above.

B. *Return on Investment*

This framework uses measures of return as the numerator and measures of the investment as the denominator. Minimum return standards would be stated as a percentage of the investment under this proposal.

 1. *Profit Return on Gross Investment* (This is the calculation currently used in our capital budgeting process.)

 a) Basic equation: $\dfrac{\text{Profit after Taxes}}{\text{Gross Investment}}$

 b) Return calculations for sample alternatives:

(1) $\dfrac{\$10,000}{\$100,000} = 10\%$

(2) $\dfrac{\$10,000}{\$100,000} = 10\%$

(3) $\dfrac{\$10,000}{\$100,000} = 10\%$

(4) $\dfrac{\$10,000}{\$100,000} = 10\%$

 2. *Cash Flow Return after Taxes on Gross Investment*

 a) Basic equation: $\dfrac{\text{Profits after Taxes Plus Depreciation}}{\text{Gross Investment}}$

b) Return calculations for sample alternatives:

(1) $\dfrac{\$26,000}{\$100,000} = 26\%$

(2) $\dfrac{\$14,000}{\$100,000} = 14\%$

(3) $\dfrac{\$12,000}{\$100,000} = 12\%$

(4) $\dfrac{\$10,500}{\$100,000} = 10.5\%$

3. *Cash Flow Return before Taxes on Gross Investment*

a) Basic equation: $\dfrac{\text{Profits before Taxes and Depreciation}}{\text{Gross Investment}}$

b) Return calculations for sample alternatives:

(1) $\dfrac{\$36,000}{\$100,000} = 36\%$

(2) $\dfrac{\$24,000}{\$100,000} = 24\%$

(3) $\dfrac{\$22,000}{\$100,000} = 22\%$

(4) $\dfrac{\$20,500}{\$100,000} = 20.5\%$

4. *Profit Return on Average Investment*

a) Basic equation: $\dfrac{\text{Profit after Taxes}}{\text{Average Investment}}$

b) Return calculations on sample alternatives:

(1) $\dfrac{\$10,000}{\$60,000} = 16.7\%$

(2) $\dfrac{\$10,000}{\$90,000} = 11.1\%$

(3) $\dfrac{\$10,000}{\$60,000} = 16.7\%$

(4) $\dfrac{\$10,000}{\$90,000} = 11.1\%$

5. *Similar Frameworks*

a) Other variants to these basic return on investment frameworks exist.

C. *Present Value or the Financial Method*[2]

One of the implicit difficulties with this financial method is the problem involved in explaining it to individuals who must see the tool for evaluating new projects. The measurement procedures, while more complex, can however, be reduced to routines that can be readily handled by clerical personnel.

---

[2] See Appendix, p. 397.

Several alternative approaches to the present value calculation are possible:

1. *Discounted Cash Flow*

   a) Basic equation: Determine the interest rate that will discount future depreciation, profit after taxes, terminal values, and other cash inflows or outflows back to a present value equal to the initial investment.

   b) Return calculations for sample alternatives:

   (1) 13–14%, based on:

   0–4 years...........................$26,000
   5th year........................... 46,000

   (2) 10–11%, based on:

   1–4 years...........................$14,000
   5th year........................... 94,000

   (3) 11–12%, based on:

   1–39 years..........................$12,000
   40th year.......................... 32,000

   (4) 10–11%, based on:

   1–39 years..........................$10,500
   40th year.......................... 90,500

   c) Other considerations: This procedure has an advantage over previous calculations in that it can handle investment opportunities with changing profitability characteristics over time, or with changing investment requirements over time. Consider the following investment alternatives:

   (i) Invest $20,000 in a project with a ten-year life with depreciation recovered at the rate of $2,000 per year (no terminal values) and with the following profits:

Years	*Profits after Tax*
1–3...	$1,000
4–6...	2,000
7–9...	3,000
10...	4,000

   (ii) Invest $20,000 in a project with a ten-year life with depreciation recovered at a rate of $2,000 per year (no terminal values) and with the following profits:

Years	*Profits after Tax*
1...	$4,000
2–4...	3,000
5–7...	2,000
8–10...	1,000

   (iii) Invest $12,000 in a project with a ten-year life but a project which will require a further investment of $8,000 in the fifth year. Depreciation will equal $1,200 per year for the first five years and $2,800 in years six–ten. Profit flows are as follows:

Years	Profits after Taxes
1–5...	.$2,000
6–10...	4,000

The return for each of these projects is shown for various sample frameworks in the table below:

		Project	
Framework	(i)	(ii)	(iii)
Discounted cash flow............................14–15%		19–20%	22–23%
Simple payback.................................3.1 years		3.1 years	2.5 years
After-tax payback..............................2.4 years		2.4 years	4.0 years
Profit payback after capital costs................4.2 years		4.2 years	2.7 years
Profit return in gross investment.................11%		11%	15%
Cash flow return on gross investment.............16%		16%	25%
Profit return on average investment..............21%		21%	37%

2. *Present Value Profitability Ratio*

   a) Basic equation: Discount cash flows (as described in C-1 above) at a specified interest rate (presumably the minimum satisfactory return on investment criterion—arbitrarily assumed to be 8% in the example below) back to their present value. Divide the present value calculation by the actual initial investment to determine the present value index.

   b) Return calculations on sample alternatives:

   (1) $\dfrac{\$115,428}{\$100,000} = 1.154$

   (2) $\dfrac{\$110,372}{\$100,000} = 1.103$

   (3) $\dfrac{\$144,020}{\$100,000} = 1.440$

   (4) $\dfrac{\$127,892}{\$100,000} = 1.279$

3. *Discounted Profits to Net Capital Employed (after Considering Opportunity Costs)*

   a) Basic equation: Discount all capital fund flows (e.g., depreciation terminal values, re-equipment needs, etc.) back to their present value at a specified rate (again, presumably, the minimum acceptable rate of return on investment), and, then, deduct this amount from the initial investment to determine the present value of the net investment (after considering the opportunity costs of employing the capital). Find the present value factor necessary to discount profit after tax flows back to this calculation of the present value of the net investment.

   b) Return calculations for sample alternatives:

   (1) 34–35% ($10,000 discounted to $22,492 over five years)
   (2) 20–21% ($10,000 discounted to $29,548 over five years)
   (3) 13–14% ($10,000 discounted to $75,230 over 40 years)
   (4) 11–12% ($10,000 discounted to $90,768 over 40 years)

4. *Present Value Profitability to Net Capital Index*
   a) Basic equation: This method combines the preceding two methods. First, capital fund flows are discounted back to a present value using the specified rate as described above to produce the present value of the net investment (again, after opportunity costs). Next the present value of profit streams are discounted at the same specified rate. The present value profitability to net capital index measures the ratio of profit present values to capital present values.
   b) Return calculations for sample alternatives:

$$(1) \quad \frac{\$39,930}{\$22,492} = 1.78x$$

$$(2) \quad \frac{\$39,930}{\$29,548} = 1.35x$$

$$(3) \quad \frac{\$119,250}{\$75,230} = 1.59x$$

$$(4) \quad \frac{\$119,250}{\$90,768} = 1.32x$$

5. *Discount Cash Flows before Considering Taxes*
   a) Basic equation: The same as C-1 above except that profits and all similar factors are taken before taxes.
   b) Return calculations for sample alternatives:
      (1) 26–27%
      (2) 20–21%
      (3) 21–22%
      (4) 20–21%

6. *Time Adjusted Rate of Return*
   a) Basic equation: Discount cash flows after taxes back to initial investment, but eliminate consideration of terminal values, if any.
   b) Return calculations for sample alternatives:
      (1) 9–10%
      (2) 0–1%
      (3) 11–12%
      (4) 10–11%

II. *Accounting Problems in Selecting Data for the Return Equation*

The frameworks described in the preceding sections raise questions about how accounting data should be put together, e.g., before or after taxes, on gross or average investment. There are, however, additional and more basic questions about how returns or investments should be measured. These issues are set forth below:

A. *Alternative Measurements of Investment*
   1. *Incremental Investment in Fixed Assets:* Under this alternative, we would use the total amount of new funds to be invested in fixed assets as the measure of investment for a specific project.

2. *Incremental Commitment of Funds:* This differs from alternative one in that incremental working capital requirements, if any, would be added to our fixed asset investments in determining our measure. (Occasionally, a new project may reduce working capital requirements—e.g., a re-equipment opportunity that would reduce work-in-process inventories. In this case, the working capital reduction would be used as an offset to fixed investments.) This alternative raises the question: At what operating level should working capital allowances be made? Capacity requirements might, for example, be substantially higher than average requirements over the course of a business—cycle, etc. The timing of working capital needs may also be significant.

3. *Utilized Capacity:* This alternative builds upon either of the previous two. The utilized capacity approach not only considers incremental investments but certain sunk investments. Illustratively, when we have excess space in one of our plants, and we are considering using this space to produce a new product, the value of the space allocated to the project should be added to the investment base for the project *if and only if* the space might otherwise be used for other productive purposes. Clearly this involves difficult problems in definition. Moreover, it also raises allocation problems in accounting. For example, should we use the historic cost or replacement cost of the space, etc.?

4. *Current Liquidation Value:* Whenever we are faced with a major modernization program, for example, we should not only consider the savings (returns) possible in relation to the new investment required but also what we could realize if we disposed of the existing facilities. Total investments would in this case equal realizable liquidation values plus incremental modernization fund requirements. In effect, this raises the question: Do we want to stay in business?

5. *Current Sunk Investments:* Under this alternative, we would total the book values of related existing facilities and add this to the incremental fund requirements to determine the measure of investment. Using, as an example, a re-equipment proposal, the book loss realized in the disposal of an existing machine would be added to the installed cost of the new machine when estimating the amount of investment.

B. *Alternative Measurements of Profit Flows*

1. *Incremental Profits (or Operating Savings):* This alternative measures incremental profits or operating savings *directly* attributable to the investment. This estimate would be based on incremental revenues less incremental costs or on incremental cost reductions, depending on the nature of the project. This measurement is frequently referred to as "contribution to overhead."

2. *Allocated Indirect Overhead Expenses:* Although new projects may not lead directly to an increase in overhead expenses, they may do

so indirectly. Our research expenditures are, for example, tied fairly closely to the level of sales volume. Any project tending to expand sales volume will indirectly lead to an expansion of research expenditures. Profits from these projects, therefore, it is argued, should be charged with an allocation of indirect overhead items (that tend to be variable over time) before returns are measured realistically. If this approach is used, we will have many problems in determining what overhead cost should be allocated and how they should be allocated.

III. *Comparable Methods for Estimating Future Returns*

In discussing methods of computing return on investment with various officers of CONELP, two special types of problems, relating to differences among individuals who prepare project requests, have come to my attention. These biases, outlined below, can have quite a significant effect on return calculations, and I believe we should attempt to develop a system that will tend to minimize these differences, and to provide top management with return data as comparable as possible. The question is how can this be accomplished?

The first area needing attention is the effect of the personal outlook of individuals responsible for preparing project requests on the return calculations. We have in our organization several individuals who are quite conservative, and who will only consider profit opportunities that are quite certain in their return calculation. Since they omit other return information that will probably be realized, their return calculations tend to understate the true return potentials of their projects. On the other hand, other individuals appear to be perennial optimists and are willing to count as potential returns prospective income that most impartial observers would consider highly improbable. As a result, two individuals can now develop two amazingly different return calculations for the very same project. Since top management and even division management is not usually aware of the bias included in return calculations up for consideration, it is impossible to make either meaningful appraisals or consistent decisions from data in its current form.

The personal outlook of an individual also appears to vary accordingly to the general state of the economy. For example, during a recession, people preparing project requests tend to be more pessimistic about return prospects than they would be under "boom" conditions. In view of the normal lead time of from six months to several years from the date the proposal is first prepared for submission to the date construction is completed and the facility is ready for production, these "economic outlook" biases seem to have limited value over the long run. This is particularly true if, as appears to be the case, division and top management also have similar biases affecting their decisions when they screen the very same proposals.

A. C. CHASE, LTD.[1]

A. C. Chase, Ltd., was a manufacturer of canned goods located near Liverpool, England. It distributed its products to retailers, wholesalers, chain stores, co-operatives, hotels, and restaurants either directly from the factory or from several field warehouses. In recent years, sales had grown so enormously that some of the field warehouses had become too small. One of the warehouses was in Arlington, only 65 miles from the Liverpool plant. In October, 1958, the question arose as to whether the presently rented premises in Arlington should be replaced by a larger, company-owned warehouse, or whether the Arlington area should henceforth be supplied directly from the factory. In order to get a clearer picture of the financial consequences of both alternatives, Mr. Martin, Chase's sales manager, asked his assistant, Mr. Ellington, to gather together some preliminary data which could be used for further discussions.

As a new warehouse could not be completed in any event before 1960, Mr. Ellington based his calculations on the sales estimates for that year, namely: 8,400 tons, or 756,000 cases, of canned goods. He then determined, after considering the size of the present facilities and discussing the proposal with a building contractor, that a new warehouse should contain at least 18,000 square feet of floor space and that building costs would approximate £3[2] per square foot. The additional warehouse equipment required could be purchased for around £2,500. Maintenance costs per annum as estimated by the technical department would be £3,000, excluding depreciation.

The company normally depreciated its buildings of similar con-

---

[1] Copyright 1959, by l'Institute pour l'Etude des Methodes de Direction de l'Enterprise (IMEDE), Lausanne, Switzerland. Reprinted by permission.

[2] The English pound (£) was worth approximately $2.80 in U.S. money. The pound was subdivided into 20 shillings (s.), each worth about $0.14. Shillings were subdivided in 12 pence (d.), each worth slightly more than $0.01. A monetary expression such as 20/6 d. meant 20 shillings and 6 pence.

struction at $2\frac{1}{2}\%$ per annum. While this rate seemed low in comparison with that applied to other fixed assets, Mr. Ellington realized that the proposed warehouse would be what is often called a multi-purpose structure. The equipment, on the other hand, would be amortized over ten years.

Mr. Ellington next turned his attention to the transportation costs between the Liverpool plant and Arlington. Chase did not own a truck fleet of its own, but used the services of Blackpool Truck Company, a Liverpool shipping firm. In 1958, this firm, using 16-ton vehicles for supplying the Arlington warehouse, had charged what was believed to be a favorable rate of 20/6d. per ton for the trip of 65 miles. Blackpool was able to offer this rate only because it got a substantial amount of freight from Arlington to Liverpool. Since Mr. Ellington did not have any idea what the rates would be in 1960, he decided to use those in effect in 1958.

The cost of handling the goods at Arlington, that is, putting them into storage, taking them out, and assembling them for delivery to customers, was estimated at 5s. per ton. Delivery from Arlington was by seven-ton trucks hired from Blackpool. In 1958 the average-size delivery was 29 cases (90 cases = 1 ton), but it was likely that this would decrease as chain stores asked for more and more deliveries to their branches rather than to their central warehouses.

The following list shows the proportion of the goods distributed from Arlington to different kinds of customers. If the trend of the last few years were to continue, about 60% of the "chain stores'" deliveries would be to individual stores within the next five years as against 30% in 1958.

PATTERN OF TRADE DELIVERIES (QUANTITIES—FOR FOUR
MONTHS TO AUGUST, 1958)

Retail	29.0%
Wholesale	29.4
Chain stores	29.9
Co-operatives	7.4
Hotel and restaurant	4.3
	100.0%

The somewhat more than 2,000 customers that might be serviced from Arlington were located at distances from 47 to 110 miles (on the average 80 miles) from Liverpool. From Arlington the average distance was only 25 miles and the delivery cost per 25 miles was

$5\frac{1}{4}d.$ per case, or $39/4d.$ per ton. The total distribution cost per ton was therefore:

	s.	d.
Liverpool plant to Arlington	20	6
Warehouse handling	5	0
Arlington to customers	39	4
Total	64	10

If the new Arlington warehouse were not built, the customers would have to be supplied directly from the factory because it would not be feasible to continue to use the present facilities (which were rented from a railroad on the promise that it would handle a large amount of the in-freight from the Liverpool plant) for part of the volume and to ship the remainder directly from the Liverpool plant. If seven-ton trucks were used, Mr. Ellington estimated that the average delivery cost would be $11\frac{1}{2}d.$ per case, or $86/3d.$ per ton. This rate was determined from the mileage and time consumption involved as well as costs obtained in connection with the first alternative. Instead of seven-ton trucks, Mr. Ellington thought of using 16-ton trucks for the second alternative until he noticed that the time per trip (it would take three days to distribute 16 tons) made this possibility completely unattractive. He therefore compared the distribution cost of alternative one with alternative two assuming the use of seven-ton trucks and arrived at a difference of $21/5d.$ ($86/3d.$ $64/10d.$) per ton, or a total savings of £8,995 for 8,400 tons.

If all shipments were to be made from the Liverpool plant, however, additional storage facilities of about 12,000 square feet would have to be provided, at a cost of about £2 per square foot. The extra equipment necessary would cost £1,000. Mr. Ellington estimated that the handling charges would be $4s.$ per ton at the Liverpool plant and the additional maintenance charges would total £1,500 per year excluding depreciation.

After collecting the foregoing data, Mr. Ellington wondered about how he should present it to Mr. Martin. He realized that he had made a number of assumptions and that many of the figures were approximations only. Both alternatives called for capital expenditures, and therefore the savings of each would have to be measured in some way against the necessary outlay. Intangible factors such as the future of the senior employees at Arlington, the potential growth in the market area, and the likelihood of the demand for more direct shipments to individual stores would all have to be discussed. Mr. Ellington therefore wished to present his findings in such a way that these problems, as well as his assumptions, would be presented clearly.

Question

As Mr. Ellington, prepare what you believe would be an adequate report to Mr. Martin. In your calculations, you may assume that Chase used the straight-line method of depreciation and that the income tax rate was 50%.

CONOVER COUPLING COMPANY

The Conover Coupling Company specialized in the manufacture of pipe couplings for use in industrial and residential construction. The company was a subsidiary of the Houston Housing Supply, Inc., manufacturer of a large line of construction supplies; this line included sewer and house connection pipes which employed Conover couplings.

In the Conover Coupling plant, three-inch to eight-inch diameter sewer and housing connection couplings were machined on two converted metal lathes. These lathes had been purchased in used condition six years previously, and the remaining net book value of each was $4,000 (40% of the initial cost). The lathes were being depreciated on the "straight-line" method. Larger sewer couplings, of 10-inch to 16-inch diameters, were machined on a small boring mill which was fully depreciated. All three pieces of equipment (the two converted lathes and the boring mill) were badly worn, and considerable difficulty had been encountered in machining couplings to meet production specifications. In the opinion of the industrial engineering supervisor, it was necessary either to overhaul or replace the machines. All three machines were considered to have zero salvage value.

One possibility was to replace the present lathes and boring mill with two new 3-inch to 16-inch diameter automatic lathes. The estimated cost of these lathes was $25,000 each; this figure included a 10% allowance to cover installation and delivery costs. The engineering supervisor estimated that the new machines would have a physical life of 12 years each and that they would have 25% greater productivity than the old machines (i.e., that they would permit a 25% increase in physical output with the same labor hours). The new lathes would be depreciated on the "double-declining balance" method over 12 years. The engineer also believed that their installa-

31

tion in place of the old machines would free approximately 300 square feet of floor space; rent, heat, light, and other overhead costs allocated on a space basis were charged at an annual rate of $2 per square foot.

An overhaul of the old lathes, on the other hand, involved the installation of new bedways, headstocks, carriages, and tool feeds—at an estimated cost of $7,700 in direct labor and parts for each lathe. Repairs needed to put the boring mill in satisfactory condition were estimated to cost an additional $1,100 in direct labor and parts. The engineering supervisor thought that these repairs would prolong the life of the lathes and boring mill approximately 12 years, although for income tax purposes the "cost" of the rebuilt machines (present book value plus the cost of overhaul) would be amortized on a straight-line basis over eight years.

Direct labor costs with the present lathes and boring mill had been approximately $24,000 per year, but with the two new lathes, it was estimated that these costs would be cut to about $18,000 per year (by eliminating the "graveyard" shift) for the same volume of production. "Normal" maintenance costs for the two present lathes together were approximately $1,700 higher than estimated mainte-nance costs for the new lathes. The engineering supervisor believed that "normal" maintenance costs would remain roughly unchanged if the present lathes were repaired; an additional $500 per year maintenance outlay was considered necessary, however, to reduce the rejection rate on both of the repaired lathes to that of the new lathes. Current maintenance for the boring mill was $700 annually.

In thinking about the alternatives, the supervisor considered a third possibility—the purchase of one new lathe to take the place of one old lathe. Shipping requirements for couplings were currently being met by operating the lathes and the boring mill six days a week, three eight-hour shifts per day. The same shipping require-ments could be met by operating the new and old lathes and the boring mill on the average of two and one-half shifts per day; in other words, the "graveyard" shift would be eliminated on alternate nights. In the event of an increase in production requirements, additional part-time labor would be available to operate the machines on over-time.

With only one new lathe, breakdowns of a week or less would delay shipments, but breakdowns of a longer duration would un-doubtedly result in increased handling charges and machining costs.

The engineering supervisor estimated that it would cost $1,400 per annum to overcome this risk by maintaining the old discarded lathe as standby equipment. It was thought that it would serve this standby purpose without overhaul.

Looking ahead, company officials were confident that sales would equal, if not exceed, their current volume for the next seven years. Sufficient funds were available and would be allotted for repairs or new equipment when plans were approved by the treasurer of the Houston Housing Supply, Inc., the parent company. The company's corporate income tax rate currently was 50%.

Question

What action, if any, should the company take?

CITY TRANSIT COMPANY

The City Transit Company had been founded in 1910 to provide public transportation to the growing town of Hampton, Ohio. The initial service was an electrified street-railway system. As the town of Hampton grew from a population of 10,000 in 1910 to 50,000 in the 1930's, the operating revenues of City Transit expanded rapidly. Beginning in the late 1920's, however, the company began to feel the competition of increasing private ownership of automobiles. Revenue increases continued during the 1930's, due in part to the effect of the depression on the buying of automobiles, but the company noticed that its revenue per capita was declining. After World War II, City Transit converted its operations to electric buses. The population of Hampton continued to increase during the postwar period and reached a total of 100,000 in 1957. During the years 1950–1957, operating revenues of City Transit were relatively stable, reflecting a continued decrease in revenue per capita, offset by the increasing population of the city.

Annual usage of electricity during this period was approximately 9,300,000 kilowatt-hours. This power was generated in the company's own plant at an annual cost of $154,000, broken into the cost categories shown below:

Coal	$ 67,000
Direct operating cost other than fuel, taxes, supervision, and depreciation	65,000
Real estate tax	5,000
Supervisor's salary	7,000
Depreciation	10,000
	$154,000

In October, 1958, the Hampton Power Company had offered to enter into a contract to supply the power requirements of the City Transit Company. The output of the Hampton Company was twice that of City Transit, and as the Hampton engineers pointed out, their equipment was newer, considerably more efficient, and extremely reliable. The City Transit load would increase Hampton's output by 50% and would

34

lower the unit cost of production for Hampton. The terms of the contract provided for a 20-year period but contained a cancellation clause which could be exercised at the end of ten years by either party.

It was estimated that if City Transit accepted the contract and closed its own power plant, the old plant could be sold for $60,000. The book value of this plant was $100,000; the annual depreciation and taxes were given earlier. The average life of City Transit's generators had been about 20 years. The engineering department felt that the facility now in use would give satisfactory service for at least ten more years, at the end of which time City Transit would need to invest in a major overhaul which would cost $150,000 but which would extend the old facility's service life for an additional ten years.

Under the proposed contract, City Transit's power requirement would be transmitted from Hampton's plant to a new substation which City Transit would have to build. This new substation would cost $400,-000 to build and would have a service life of 20 years with no salvage value at the end of that time. The purpose of this substation was to convert the electric power from alternating to direct current.

The price quoted by the Hampton Company was $\frac{1}{2}$ cent per kilowatt-hour. Hampton would require City Transit to buy at least 8,000,-000 kilowatt-hours annually, and they agreed to furnish a maximum production of 10,000,000 kilowatt-hours annually. Hampton's engineers also pointed out that the estimated operating costs, including real estate taxes but excluding depreciation, for the substation would be about $10,000 per year (which City Transit would have to pay); City Transit's engineers agreed with this estimate.

City Transit estimated that if the present facility were sold, the supervisor could be transferred to another service department within the company where an additional supervisor would soon be needed. If this additional supervisor had to be hired from outside the company, he would have to be paid about $5,000 per year. Because of the present supervisor's tenure with the company, he would be transferred at his present salary, if City Transit decided to do away with the present power facility. The other laborers (cost included under direct operating costs given earlier) would be discharged.

The president of City Transit indicated that the opportunity rate of return which had been used in past investment decisions was 14% after taxes (income taxes were about 50%).

Question

What action should City Transit Company take?

PACIFIC CABLE CORPORATION

In July of 1957, the management of the Pacific Cable Corporation was considering the advisability of constructing facilities for annealing a certain type of copper tape used in the fabrication of submarine cable. Pacific Cable Corporation had been organized in 1953 as a subsidiary of Western Wire Company to engage in the production of underwater transmission cable. The plant was located at Pittsburgh, California. While adapted primarily to the fabrication of submarine cable, the facilities were such that they could readily be converted to the manufacture of other wire and cable products. The plant employed approximately 600 persons when operating at normal capacity, which included three shifts of eight hours each, five days per week. Pittsburgh had been selected as a site because of its water transportation facilities and proximity to the large potential Pacific market for underwater cable. The only other producers of such cable were located on the Atlantic Coast and the European Continent.

The use of submarine cable for transmission of telephone messages was a relatively new market. Experimentation had proven successful, and a long-distance cable from Florida to Cuba had been in operation since as early as 1921. In 1955 a one-way cable was laid across the Atlantic to London, permitting one-way conversation. In 1956 a second cable was laid which made possible two-way conversation. The operation of this cable, based on a very short experience, appeared to be successful. A single cable could carry approximately 37 separate messages at a time.

The use of underwater cable for transmission of telegraph messages had been proven successful by many years of operation since 1866. The useful life of such cables, while somewhat unknown, in the North Atlantic appeared to be 60 to 70 years.

In addition to the future market for submarine cable for transmission of telephone messages, television also appeared to offer a possible

36

outlet. The connection of all the countries of the world in a single television network by underwater cable was a possibility.

The chief alternate facility to underwater cable for transmission of telephone messages, and used almost exclusively from 1927 until recently, was by radio. This means had not proven entirely successful in the North Atlantic area. Weather and atmospheric conditions made the possibility of any contact uncertain. When contact could be made it was often not clear. The possibility of intercepting and "jamming" such telephone messages was considerable. With underwater cable, the messages were almost interceptionproof except on either end or through extensive diving operations.

Conditions in the Pacific area appeared to be different. The contacts and clearness of the messages by radiotelephone were generally successful. On the other hand, no cable had as yet been developed which was immune to the marine life in the South Pacific. The underwater cable seemed to deteriorate faster in this area.

Prior to 1953, the parent company had manufactured some underwater cable, but the market had been small and irregular. Since 1953 the subsidiary, Pacific Cable Corporation, had operated at near capacity. In July of 1957 operations had declined.

An order for submarine cable when received by Pacific was normally for a large quantity and required several months' operation of the plant to complete.

Customer specifications for submarine cable were very rigid. All materials used in the fabrication had to meet exact requirements. In the manufacture of the cable, a very thin copper tape ½-inch wide and weighing eight pounds per one thousand feet was used for wrapping the center structure. The quality of tape required for this purpose was much greater than that needed for ordinary commercial purposes. The needs of copper tape by Pacific, other than for submarine cable production, were very limited.

Pacific had for a number of years purchased the fabricated copper tape from four suppliers at prices shown in Exhibit 1. No one supplier had been willing or able to meet Pacific's needs. Supplies were at times uncertain, but no shutdown of cable production had been necessary because of shortage of tape.

No supplier was willing to invest capital in annealing equipment sufficient to meet Pacific's total demand, nor was any supplier willing to try any new method of annealing copper tape. Often when a shipment arrived, only a part of the expected amount was received. It was suspected that the shortage was caused by spoilage during the annealing process. Pacific's management thought that keeping a two weeks' supply of tape on hand was desirable, but they had found it difficult to maintain more than a few days' supply.

None of Pacific's four suppliers of copper tape were engaged in the production of wire or cable products fabricated by Pacific or its parent company.

The price of copper tape was based on two elements: the price of wire bar electrolytic copper plus freight and a loading charge for processing to various stages. This loading charge fluctuated with the cost of labor and overhead used in processing, and with the profit ratio of the firm from which purchased.

To produce unannealed copper tape of the ordinary commercial variety, three processes were required to reduce the bar copper to tape. A rolling mill converted the bar to a rod $\frac{5}{16}$ inches in diameter. The rod then passed through a drawing machine which reduced it to wire. The wire was fed through a rolling machine and cold-rolled to flat tape. In 1957, these three processes added about 25 cents per pound to the price of the tape. Pacific's management had decided that they did not wish to engage in this fabrication. The further annealing process required by Pacific accounted for approximately 20 cents per pound of the loading charge.

To be useful in the fabrication of long-distance submarine cable, the copper tape had to conform to certain specifications not generally required by the trade. If the tape was not properly kept free from impurities, it tended to become discolored in the process of annealing. There was no positive proof that the discoloring affected the transmission qualities of the product, but Pacific refrained from using discolored tape due to appearances and a policy of rigidly meeting specifications.

During the first nine months of 1956, Pacific ordered 280,352 pounds of copper tape, and 77,165 pounds (about 27%) were rejected upon delivery. In many cases it was not possible to determine whether a package of tape was discolored until it was opened for use at the time needed in the production line. Five per cent of the total quantity accepted by Pacific was subsequently rejected during production. The company had attempted to determine defective qualities in the tape prior to the time of its use, but due to the nature of rolling and packing requirements for storage, no such procedure had been devised.

Each time a roll of tape was rejected at the time of use, a delay of five or six minutes was caused in the cable production line. During

1956 and 1957 these delays had occurred on an average of four or five times per day. The production line at full capacity was operated at a weekly cost of approximately $30,000 for direct and indirect costs, not including direct materials. In addition, a shutdown of the line for a few minutes occasionally resulted in a loss of some materials in process due to excess heating.

Some suppliers had adopted a policy of taking back tape rejected on the production line, while others refused to permit any returns if the tape was accepted at the time of delivery. Those suppliers permitting such returns absorbed the extra cost by increasing their price. The prices given in Exhibit 1 are based on a policy of no returns after original acceptance. When no returns were permitted, Pacific was forced to sell the defective tape at a price averaging 6 cents per pound below the price of wire bar electrolytic copper.

All of Pacific's tape suppliers used the "bell-batch" method of annealing copper tape. The rolls of tape were placed in a steel dome. Atmospheric impurities were removed, and the dome was heated to 500 degrees Fahrenheit for six to eight hours, depending on the size of the batch. The copper was left to cool gradually, with occasional application of water. This method of annealing was generally satisfactory for commercial grade tape, but the removal of atmospheric impurities from the steel dome prior to heating was not positive enough to prevent occasional discoloration of an entire batch. There was no loss of weight in the copper during the annealing process.

Pacific had had considerable experience annealing round copper wire by the "continuous flow" process. Under this method the round wire was heated electrically by short circuit and then cooled as it passed through the processing assembly.

As far as Pacific's management knew, the "continuous flow" process had not been adapted to flat copper tape on a commercial basis. Some laboratory tests of 300- to 400-pound quantities conducted by Pacific had indicated that it could be applied successfully to flat copper tape and that the likelihood of discoloration was not great.

The research department of Pacific Cable Corporation stated that it was not likely that a substitute for flat copper tape used in the fabrication of underwater cable would be found in the near future. The most commonly considered possible substitute was aluminum, which was not considered sufficiently flexible.

Pacific's management was considering the installation of a new unit for the annealing of flat copper tape. None of its present facilities would be usable except building space. The new equipment would require about one thousand square feet of floor space, and that amount would be available.

The new annealing unit would consist of two standard unit processing stands at a cost of $10,000 each and one commercial type heating unit costing $30,000. The cost of adapting the heating unit to the flat tape annealing process was estimated at $10,000. The estimated physical life of the entire unit was 15 years. The functional life of the installation was uncertain due to the fact that specifications for products manufactured by the company changed rather frequently.

The project engineer estimated the theoretical capacity of the unit at $6\frac{1}{2}$ pounds of copper, or about 800 feet of tape, per minute, and he thought that the unit could be operated at about 80 per cent efficiency. Excess capacity would have no use under present production schedules. The unit had to be operated continuously or not at all, could not be constructed to operate efficiently at a lower rate of output, and, in the engineer's opinion, could not be operated practically for periods shorter than one week.

The storage of tape was no problem from a standpoint of space. While no experience was available, some of the production people believed the quality of the tape deteriorated with time. If the new unit was installed, it was anticipated an inventory of 20,000 pounds of annealed tape would be carried. A similar inventory of unannealed tape would be necessary.

It was estimated the operation of the proposed annealing unit would require the services of two men at $2 per hour each for every hour operated. Overhead was estimated at 250% of direct labor costs. Burden allocation included building costs, heat, power, supervision, maintenance, fringe benefits, etc., but did not include depreciation of equipment. In 1955 the company had adopted the "double-declining balance" method of depreciation for both income tax calculations and financial reporting.

The acquisition and installation of the unit would require about four months. From a production standpoint, a slack period with no backlog of orders would be the most advantageous time to complete the installation.

A capital expenditure of the size required for the annealing unit would have to be approved by the board of directors of Western Wire Company, Pacific's parent (see balance sheet, Exhibit 2). Pacific's management knew that the project would be evaluated against Western's investment standards of a two-year "payback period" within which to recover the investment.

Question

Should the management of Pacific Cable Corporation recommend the purchase of the new annealing unit?

Exhibit 1

PACIFIC CABLE CORPORATION

PRICE OF ANNEALED COPPER TAPE

(Per pound)

Period	Base Price of Wire Bar Copper*	Loading Charge for Processing	Total Price
August, 1953	30.00¢	25.66¢	55.66¢
October, 1953	30.00	34.35	64.35
November, 1954	30.00	34.79	64.79
December, 1954	30.00	40.44	70.44
January, 1955	30.00	40.00	70.00
February, 1955	33.00	40.25	73.25
April, 1955	36.00	40.00	76.00
August, 1955	38.00	40.00	78.00
September, 1955	43.00	40.00	83.00
February, 1956	46.00	41.40	87.40
March, 1956	46.00	45.40	91.40
July, 1956	40.00	45.40	85.40
October, 1956	36.00	45.40	81.40
February, 1957	34.00	45.40	79.40
February, 1957	32.00	45.40	77.40
July 3, 1957	29.25	45.40	74.65

* Prices shown are F.O.B. Pacific's plant. The freight cost of returning rejected tape was borne by the supplier.

Exhibit 2

WESTERN WIRE COMPANY

COMPARATIVE BALANCE SHEETS AS OF DECEMBER 31

ASSETS	1955	1956
Government securities	$ 173,093	$ 173,093
Receivables	6,328,916	4,504,307
Inventories	7,222,765	7,156,132
Cash	1,257,291	3,233,592
Total current assets	$14,982,065	$15,067,124
Property and equipment	7,035,726	7,315,353
Prepaid insurance	396,810	157,959
Other investments	110,000	78,000
Total assets	$22,425,601	$22,618,436

LIABILITIES		
Current liabilities	$ 5,575,754	$ 5,036,468
Noncurrent liabilities	2,000,000	. . . .
Capital stock, 120,000 shares—no-par	2,400,000	2,400,000
Surplus	12,448,847	15,181,968
Total liabilities and capital	$22,424,601	$22,618,436
Net current assets	$ 9,406,311	$10,030,656

MONITOR TEXTILE COMPANY (A)

In January, 1961, Mr. Norman Dixon, superintendent of the Monitor Textile Company, was considering replacement of one of the two industrial forklift trucks operating in its plant at Hickory, North Carolina. The two trucks in the plant were gasoline operated and were three and four years old, respectively. The maintenance expenses of the older truck had been rising steadily, and currently they amounted to about $20 per month in addition to normal servicing, gasoline, and oil. This truck was not dependable and was frequently out of service while awaiting repairs. These trucks were both 1,000-pound capacity Columbia trucks and could be used interchangeably.

Exhibit 1 shows the routes traveled by the two fork trucks. One truck was used on the highway truck dock for loading and unloading packages of mohair wool and cloth from highway trucks. This "dock" truck was used only during the day shift because that was the only time when the company's two highway trucks were in operation. On the truck loading dock it was necessary to use a ramp so that the fork truck could be driven into the highway trucks.

The "inside" truck was used to move goods from machines to storage, from dyeing to finishing, and occasionally to take goods to the repair room, as well as to carry drums of chemicals. When used to take a pallet of goods from the machine that stacked pallets, it was promptly returned to this machine to pick up the next loaded pallet. If the truck was delayed during this operation, the machine had to be shut down. For the most part, the inside truck operated on an intermittent schedule, not following any fixed pattern. During the day shift, there was one driver with the inside truck at all times. During the other two shifts, the inside truck was in use about half the time, that is, a total of about eight hours on the second and third shifts.

The Monitor company processed mohair wool into fabrics for upholstery material. In January, 1961, the company was working nearly at capacity and operating on a three-shift basis, six days a week. A large part of the company's capacity was devoted to the manufacture of a special mohair fabric used in arctic clothing for the Army.

Mr. Dixon was undecided whether the company should buy electric or gasoline operated fork trucks. The Stevens Industrial Truck Company, distributors of Columbia fork trucks, was servicing the two Columbia trucks in the Monitor plant. If a new fork truck were bought, it would be bought through the Stevens company. This company offered a service agreement to users of its trucks which provided for a monthly visit by an experienced serviceman who would lubricate and adjust both gas and electric trucks. The rate was $15 per month for the first gas truck and $10 for each additional truck. A flat fee of $10 per month was charged for each electric truck. The difference between the charge for a gas and electric truck represented the cost of an oil filter cartridge that had to be replaced on gas trucks. If additional repairs for either type of truck were required, the cost of parts and the serviceman's time at the rate of $6 per hour for each hour in excess of the average servicing time were charged to the users of the truck.

The power supply for an electric truck of the type being considered by Mr. Dixon was an 18-cell, lead acid, 6.68 kilowatt-hour capacity battery. The cost of this battery was about $1,000. Mr. Suiter, the sales representative for the Stevens company, stated that this battery would provide sufficient power for the truck to travel continuously for eight hours over a level surface and have sufficient power for the operation of the lifting mechanism. This power supply would be adequate for the operation of the inside truck for the day shift. A second battery would be required if the truck were to be used much in excess of one eight-hour shift. On this basis, Mr. Dixon anticipated that two batteries, each charged once a day, would provide sufficient power for the operation of the inside truck on all shifts.

It was difficult to estimate how much of a power drain the ramp would cause for an electric truck. Although Mr. Suiter was confident that the regular charge was adequate for the inside truck, which operated without going up or down any inclines, he was uncertain whether this normal charge would be adequate for ramp operation. The use of the ramp would result in a very heavy drain on the battery. A power failure on the ramp would be very inconvenient, for time would be lost in getting the battery charged to put the truck back into operation.

The life expectancy of a battery was largely dependent on the number of times it was charged and discharged. A battery which was charged once a day could be expected to last approximately five years. When the capacity of a battery became less than 80% of its initial capacity, it was discarded, and Mr. Suiter stated that the Monitor company could count on at least $50 salvage value.

If an electric truck were to be used inside, it would be necessary to change the battery in the truck twice a day. To facilitate this operation, a heavy metal stand with rollers on its top at the same level as the battery roll-out compartment would have to be constructed. This would require $170 worth of materials.

The installation of battery charging equipment was another cost incurred with the electric trucks. The cost of a charger capable of charging one battery at a time was $550. Mr. Suiter recommended the purchase of independent chargers so that in the rare event of a breakdown of a charger, all batteries would not be disabled. A charger was expected to last as long as an electric truck. The installation of a charger necessitated bringing a 550-volt power line from another section of the plant, requiring materials costing $50. The cost of the electricity required to charge the battery for eight hours of operation was about 10 cents. Mr. Dixon understood that this charge would require about three hours.

The two gasoline operated trucks had been using a total of about five gallons of gasoline per day, at a cost of $0.248 per gallon. Mr. Suiter stated that this rate of gasoline consumption was normal for these trucks. They were equipped with two-gallon gasoline tanks as standard equipment, which the manufacturer considered adequate for eight hours of operation.

The initial cost of a gas truck was $3,600. The cost of an electric truck without a battery was $4,700. It was expected that an electric truck would operate efficiently for at least ten years when operated on a one-shift basis, that is, eight hours a day. The life of a gas truck was expected to be six to eight years on the same basis, assuming a major ($200) engine overhaul sometime after the third year. If operated 16 hours a day, as was the case with the inside truck, the expected life of either an electric or a gas truck would be cut in half, and the overhaul of the gas engine would probably be required at the end of two years.

The company paid an income tax of 52% and used the sum-of-digits method of depreciation. Mr. Dixon said he would plan to depreciate either gas or electric trucks on a five-year basis, the same rate at which the present trucks were being depreciated, and would estimate scrap value as 10% of the original cost of the equipment.

Mr. Suiter explained the longer life of the electric trucks by stating that there were a great many more moving parts in a gas truck than in an electric truck. The gas trucks could be "pushed" to get a job done faster at the expense of increasing wear on the moving parts. Because of the power limitations of the electric trucks, excessive wear was largely eliminated.

Mr. Suiter estimated that for about $1,000 the service department of his company could overhaul the older gas truck. Because of the condition of this truck, however, the Stevens service manager recommended a "factory overhaul" that would include installation of a new engine and replacement of practically all moving parts in the truck. This would cost roughly 75% of the cost of a new gas truck. About a week would be required for either type of overhaul, and the Stevens company would lend the Monitor company a truck for that period. Mr. Hunt, the sales manager, had offered the Monitor company a trade-in allowance of $750 for the four-year-old gas truck and $1,000 for the newer truck. The book value of the trucks, which had cost $3,300 each new, was approximately $525 and $725, respectively, at the end of 1960.

Mr. Hunt stated that the Monitor company could expect shipment of a gas truck late in February, or an electric truck in March. The Monitor company enjoyed a strong working capital position, and funds were available for any expenditure for fork trucks that Mr. Dixon might recommend. Based on recent experience, the company expected that funds committed to new investments should earn at least a 10% rate of return after taxes.

Question

What action do you recommend?

Exhibit 1

MONITOR TEXTILE COMPANY (A)

ROUTE TRAVELED BY FORKLIFT TRUCKS

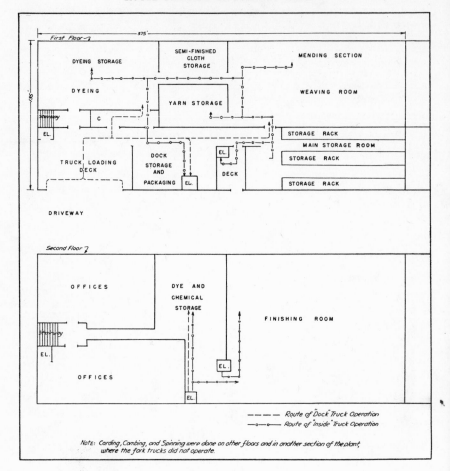

Note: Carding, Combing, and Spinning were done on other floors and in another section of the plant, where the fork trucks did not operate.

FALL RIVER LUMBER COMPANY

The financial analysis department of the Fall River Lumber Company in considering the purchase of equipment for debarking logs prepared the following report:

PROPOSED DEBARKING INSTALLATION FOR FLAKEBOARD PLANT

Introduction

The flakeboard plant is using peeled aspen so that our finished board will contain a light-colored appearance. This lighter appearance is felt to be necessary by the sales department if we wish to continue to point our product toward a higher-quality market.

Moreover, as the plant's operating efficiency is a direct function of the life of its flaker knives, the peeled wood will contribute somewhat to increasing this life by eliminating the abrasive action caused by the sand and dirt that is often found within the bark.

However, the primary consideration in maintaining an adequate knife life is that the moisture content in the aspen be sufficient (above 35% air dry) to act as a cooling agent on the flaker knives.

If the aspen supplied to the plant is too dry, the flaker knives heat up, thereby becoming dull, and the plant's operations are impaired. Past experience has demonstrated to us that the difference in flaker-knife life is almost insignificant between using *freshly peeled aspen* and *freshly unpeeled aspen*, but quite significant between using *dry peeled aspen* and *freshly peeled aspen*.

In the initial stages of operations, the plant used fresh "hand peeled" aspen direct from the wood dealers. However, since the hand peeling (commonly known as sap peeling) season lasts only during the trees' annual growth period (a six-week period from spring to early summer), it is only during this time that a sufficient volume (two cords

47

per man per day) can be maintained. Out of season this type of production drops to one-half cord per man per day, thus becoming uneconomical. While a sufficient year's supply of aspen could possibly be bought during the six-week sap peeling season, the wood would dry out in storage and the problem of flaker-knife life again becomes the critical factor.

Chemical debarking must be ruled out as a possibility since the wood becomes too dry in the one-year period that is required for the tree to die and the bark to fall off.

Thus, the use of some kind of mechanical debarking equipment that would insure a year-round supply of peeled wood with the correct moisture characteristics becomes necessary if we wish to continue producing our lighter-colored flakeboard.

Alternative Solutions

The following proposals exist as possible means of supplying peeled aspen to the flakeboard plant:

1. Installing permanent debarking facilities at Fall River employing King or Elmo equipment.
2. Utilizing portable debarkers at Fall River, such as the Leswork.

Recommendations

This study recommends installing a King debarker out in the woodyard. In addition, it recommends the use of mechanical feeding accessories and a bark burner. The estimated savings would be $40,000 per year compared to our present portable Leswork installation. The total estimated investment would be $70,000. The return on this investment would be at the rate of 57%, or payback in $1\frac{3}{4}$ years.

Discussion of Alternative Solutions

1. *Portable Debarkers at Fall River*

It is possible to utilize *a series* of Leswork portable debarkers for the flakeboard plant's wood requirements. At the present time we are barking approximately 45 rough cords per day ($2\frac{1}{4}$ rough cords per hour $\times$ 20 hours per day). This appears to be maximum capacity for these debarkers. Assuming a 15% bark loss and a 2% wood loss, this results in a production of 37 finished cords per day (45 $\times$ 83%). This is enough capacity for 750,000 square feet of board per month (assuming 1.5 finished cords per 1,000 square feet). Basing our wood requirements at a minimum of 1,000,000 square feet per month, we would need a production of around 50 finished cords per day, which would mean about 60 rough cords per day through these debarkers (only 59 rough cords are required on the Elmo and King equipment due to no wood loss). Thus it would be necessary to invest in a minimum of two more debarkers (one for reserve) to fulfill our minimum production requirements. This would be an investment of $12,000. However, the operating life of a Leswork debarker is only 2,000 hours, and the equipment would have to operate 24 hours per day (60 rough cords divided by $2\frac{1}{2}$ cords per hour) to meet requirements. Even though two machines would be used on a 12 hours per day basis, one machine would have to be replaced every 2.76 months $\left(\dfrac{2,000}{24} = 83 \text{ days}\right)$. Thus a $4,-000 debarker will be purchased, on the average, 4.3 times each year $\left(\dfrac{12 \text{ months}}{2.76 \text{ months}}\right)$, meaning that to the initial investment of $12,000 must be added a continuing *annual* investment of $17,200.

2. Permanent Debarking Facilities

In considering permanent debarking facilities for the Fall River flakeboard operations, the first question that must be answered is what type of bark-removable operation is feasible. Some principal methods of bark removal apart from manual labor with a spud or draw knife are:

a) By means of friction by tumbling or rotating action such as the rotating cylindrical drum at Williamsburg.
b) By hydraulic pressure.
c) By shear principle.
d) By the rosser head, or cutter head, principle such as the present Leswork debarker.

An attempt to debark some aspen in the Williamsburg drum was not successful as the wood was not dry enough to experience sufficient friction for effective bark removal. Since the flakeboard operations demand this higher moisture content in the wood, this generally recognized quick, cheap bark removal system cannot be utilized.

A hydraulic pressure debarker is ruled out chiefly on the grounds of the water pollution problem it would create.

The basic feature of a King-type debarker consists of a blunt edge pressed elastically against the log, which then penetrates the bark down into the cell-forming "cambium" layer between the bark and wood. Tangential pressure against the bark produces shear stresses between bark and wood sufficient to overcome the strength of the cambium layer. The principal feature of such a machine is the removal of bark at a substantially low wood loss. The trade names of debarkers of this type are the King and the Elmo. Both of these debarkers could be used for our flakeboard operations.

The rosser, or "cutter head," principle is employed on the Leswork machine we now are using. While these machines remove the bark sufficiently, the wood loss appears to be higher than with the King type. In addition, as these machines are portable, production is not as great as on the King machines. As an example, the Leswork debarks between 2 to $2\frac{1}{2}$ rough cords per hour as compared to 5 to 10 rough cords per hour on the King. Nevertheless, the Leswork is a proven debarker that could be utilized in our operations.

Both the King and the Elmo have been utilized in flakeboard operations. It is generally felt that the King does an excellent job in debarking, but the maintenance requirements are high. Moreover, there seems to be more of a problem debarking wood with varying diameters with the King than with the Elmo. (Our operations use wood ranging from 4 inches to 15 inches in diameter.)

Since the Elmo has been designed for more rugged operations, its weight is approximately $2\frac{1}{2}$ times the King (22,000 pounds versus 9,000 pounds). Simultaneously, its cost is $20,000 more ($44,000 versus $24,000).

The rating of a barker is dependent on the number of sticks per cord, the per cent of bark removal required, and the infeed system to the debarker. In addition, under wintertime conditions it is necessary to slow down the barker in order to maintain the same per cent of bark removal. For this study, the average rated capacity of the King and Elmo barkers was based on automatic conveying accessories. It should be kept in mind that manual feeding to either of these debarkers would tend to reduce their rated capacity.

Summary of Findings

The problem as outlined in the introduction of this study of determining the most economical and engineering sound method of debarking aspen for the flakeboard plant is complicated.

Basically, it boils down to balancing our rate of production required to supply the flakeboard operations against a capital investment and estimated debarking cost per cord.

Certain assumptions were made. The main ones, subject to the most variability, are:

1. The estimated useful life of the debarkers,
2. The estimated repair and maintenance costs, and
3. The machine production per hour.

The alternative of *buying peeled wood* is not recommended, and such rejection is based mainly on the following considerations:

1. The wide diversity in the location of the aspen stands, creating a difficult peeling setup in the field.
2. The uncertain supply in the winter season.
3. The higher operating costs for the wood dealer necessitated by his increased handling and depreciation expenses.
4. The possible legal problems arising from buying and renting debarkers to the wood dealers.
5. The reluctance of the wood dealers to debark in the field.
6. The uncertainty of getting clean wood.

Rejection of *portable debarkers at Fall River* is primarily based on a pure cost consideration. In order to maintain our estimated production requirements of 1,000,000 square feet per month in the flakeboard plant, it would necessitate reinvesting in portable debarkers at a rate that would more than offset the initial low investment cost. The low production inherent in these debarkers means running them at their capacity practically around the clock and thereby quickly reaching their estimated life of 5,000 cords.

The choice lies between buying a King debarker, either new or used, or an Elmo. A used King is rejected since its return on investment is less than that of a new King. Both the Elmo and King are substantially the same machine as far as the efficiency in debarking the wood goes. However, the rugged design of the Elmo has kept its repair and maintenance charges well under that of the King. While there are over 100 King installations in operation, certain companies, such as the United States Paper Company of Flint, Michigan, are replacing their Kings with Elmos as the latter seemed to hold up better. Nevertheless, the economic advantage as evidenced by the higher rate of return of the new King as compared to the Elmo, 57% versus 49% (see Exhibit 4), takes into consideration this more rugged design of the Elmo, yet this report still concludes that the King investment is the more advantageous for our requirements.

It is well to mention that the inherent savings of using an Elmo or a King debarker lie not only with the increased production (both over twice the hourly capacity of a Leswork), which lowers the total unit cost per cord of wood debarked, but also with the longer estimated life of the machines. The savings are not a result of an over-all reduction in manpower.

While the debarkers themselves do not require operating labor, the machine's higher productive capacities require that such men be utilized as spotters on the infeed and outfeed conveying equipment.

The economics of the study are summarized in the following exhibits. Exhibits 1 through 3 compares the operating costs and investments of a King, an Elmo, and a Leswork debarking installation. Exhibit 4 summarizes the return on investment data of the King and Elmo installations as compared to our present Leswork operations.

Questions

1. Evaluate the return on investment calculations shown in Exhibit 4.
2. Assuming that the "investment opportunity rate" for Fall River is 10% after taxes, which machine should the company buy?

Exhibit 1

FALL RIVER LUMBER COMPANY

COST ESTIMATES FOR FLAKEBOARD PLANT DEBARKERS

	King*	King†	Elmo	Leswork‡
Rated capacity (rough cords per hour)...........	7	6	9	$2\frac{1}{2}$
Debarker cost (with power).....................	$23,200	$16,000	$ 44,000	$4,000
Accessories (conveyors and deck, etc.; see Exhibit 2)......................................	37,425	27,700	52,000	.....
Installation.....................................	9,650	14,600	9,800	300
Total investment..........................	$70,275	$58,300	$105,800	$4,300
Fixed costs per cord...........................	$ 0.82	$ 1.08	$ 0.74	$ 0.95
Variable costs per cord........................	1.16	1.32	0.72	2.87
Total estimated cost per cord...............	$ 1.98	$ 2.40	$ 1.46	$ 3.82

* New King.
† Used King.
‡ Present Fall River operations (estimated three Lesworks required to meet production demands).

Exhibit 2

FALL RIVER LUMBER COMPANY

ANALYSIS OF TOTAL INVESTMENT ESTIMATE FOR FLAKEBOARD PLANT DEBARKERS

	King (New)	King (Used)	Elmo	Leswork
Debarker (with power)	$23,200	$16,000*	$ 44,000	$4,000
Infeed and outfeed conveyors	$ 9,000	$ 6,000	(No exact breakdown given, similar to new King equipment)	
Cross chain conveyor	10,000	10,000		
Bark conveyor	5,000	3,500		
Starting equipment	1,425	1,200		
Bark burner	10,000	3,000		
Special roll conveyor and flipper		2,000		
Spare parts	2,000	2,000		
Total accessories	$37,425	$27,700	$ 52,000	
Dismantling old King equipment and accessories		$ 5,000		
Freight-in	$ 250	200	$ 400	$ 50
Power line to woodyard:		6,400	6,400	
2,100 feet wire at $2 per foot	$4,200			
22 poles on 100 feet intervals at $100 per pole	2,200			
Labor and materials to install equipment (3 men, 3 days)	3,000	3,000	3,000	250
Total installation	$ 9,650	$14,600	$ 9,800	$ 300
Total investment	$70,275	$58,300	$105,800	$ 4,300

* Estimated.

Note: Depreciation for income tax purposes (using our double-declining balance method) would be based on a life of 15 years for the power lines and ten years for the conveyors and other equipment. These lives approximate the estimated physical life of the equipment. The useful life of the debarker is closely related to the number of cords put through the equipment. Depreciation of the debarker (including installation costs) will probably be based on the estimated physical life.

Exhibit 3

FALL RIVER LUMBER COMPANY

ANALYSIS OF COST ESTIMATES PER CORD FOR FALL RIVER FLAKEBOARD PLANT DEBARKERS

	Elmo	King (New)	King (Used)	Leswork (Fall River)
Estimated life (number of hours of operation)	20,000 hrs.	14,000 hrs.	10,000 hrs.	2,000 hrs.
Rated capacity—rough cords per hour	9	7	6	2½

COST ESTIMATE PER CORD

	Elmo	King (New)	King (Used)	Leswork (Fall River)
Fixed costs per cord:				
Depreciation charges: $\dfrac{\text{total equipment cost}}{\text{tot. est. life} \times \text{rated cap.}}$; i.e., $\dfrac{\$106{,}000}{20{,}000 \text{ hrs.} \times 9 \text{ cords/hr.}}$	$0.59	$0.71	$0.96	$0.90
Interest, taxes, insurance: avg. annual invest. × 10%; i.e., $\dfrac{\$106{,}000 \times 0.1}{2 \times 4{,}000 \text{ hr./yr.} \times 9 \text{ cd./hr.}}$	0.15	0.11	0.12	0.05
Total fixed costs	$0.74	$0.82	$1.08	$0.95
Variable costs per cord:				
Repairs and upkeep: 0.125¢/hr.	$0.05*	$0.32*	$0.37*	$0.05
Maintenance (routine lubrication and adjustment; ½ hr./8-hr. shift): $\dfrac{0.125\text{¢/hr.}}{\text{rated capacity}}$	0.01	0.02	0.02	0.05
Operating labor: $\dfrac{2 \text{ men} \times \text{hourly wage} \times 113\%\dagger}{\text{rated capacity}}$; i.e., $\dfrac{2 \text{ men} \times \$2.00/\text{hr.} \times 113\%}{9 \text{ cords/hr.}}$	0.50	0.65	0.75	1.67
Operating supplies and power: 50¢ per hr./rated cap.	0.06	0.07	0.08	0.10
Bark hauling: $\dfrac{\$4/\text{truck/hr.} \times 1 \text{ hr./load}}{4 \text{ cords/truck load}}$				1.00
Bark burning	0.10	0.10	0.10	.....
Total variable costs	$0.72	$1.16	$1.32	$2.87
Total estimated cost per rough cord	$1.46	$1.98	$2.40	$3.82

* Estimated from actual operations at Great Falls Paper Company (Elmo) and Paper Products (King installation).

† 13% increased for social security, workmen's compensation, retirement benefits.

Exhibit 4

FALL RIVER LUMBER COMPANY

ESTIMATED RETURN ON INVESTMENT COMPARING PROPOSED
DEBARKERS WITH PRESENT LESWORK DEBARKER

	Elmo	*King (New)*	*King (Used)*
Estimated savings per rough cord	$ 2.63	$ 1.84	$ 1.42
Estimated required rough cords per year* (59 cords per day × 360 days)	22,000	22,000	22,000
Estimated total savings per year	$ 52,000	$40,000	$31,000
Estimated total investment	$106,000	$70,000	$58,000
Estimated return on investment	49%	57%	54%
Payback period	2 yrs.	1¾ yrs.	1⅘ yrs.

* Based on production requirements of 50 finished cords per day, which provides for 1,000,000 square feet board per month and 15% bark loss.

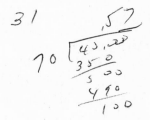

TIME MAGAZINE

In September, 1958, Mr. James A. Linen, publisher of *TIME* magazine, announced that the circulation base rate for advertisers in the domestic edition would be raised from 2,250,000 copies weekly to 2,350,000 copies effective with the March 2, 1959, issue. Immediately, Mr. Bernard M. Auer, circulation director, began thinking about how to incorporate this 100,000-copy increase into his circulation budget (or plan) for 1959. The circulation base rate was an important determinant of the prices at which advertising space was sold by the magazine, and as circulation director, Mr. Auer had primary responsibility for ensuring that the publisher's circulation guarantee was delivered. The long-run pattern of consistently increasing circulation enjoyed by *TIME* was, Mr. Auer thought, attributable to the attractive editorial content of the magazine. In the short run, however, he felt that securing a 100,000 increase in circulation within the next six months was essentially a sales promotion job. He viewed his task as that of securing the required additional circulation in such a manner that it would yield the highest possible net circulation revenue (subscription price less the cost of securing the subscription), consistent with the magazine's policy of conducting its sales promotion in a dignified manner in order to preserve its status in the minds of the public as a high-class magazine.

Mr. Auer recognized that two variables were important in determining the effectiveness with which the sales promotion activities of his department achieved the circulation goal described above. These variables were (1) the type of promotional material used, and (2) the methods of promotion employed. (Several methods used by the magazine industry and commonly called "sources" of circulation are described in Appendix A, p. 66.) Historically, *TIME* magazine made greatest use of direct-mail promotion as its most important source of circulation, and devoted a great deal of effort to the construction of distinctive direct-mail letters and other promotional materials. Although

56

the direct-mail source had been most effective in the past, Mr. Auer felt that securing additional circulation by this method would be increasingly expensive, particularly as postal rates went up, and in deciding how to obtain the new subscriptions required, he felt that he should re-examine several alternative sources, including field-selling organizations.

TIME magazine was published by Time, Inc., publishers of *Life, Fortune, Sports Illustrated, Architectural Forum,* and *House and Home.* In 1958, Time, Inc., was the largest magazine publisher in the United States, was the publisher of international editions of *TIME* and *Life* (having, in themselves, a combined circulation of nearly 1,000,000) and was also engaged in several related activities including book publishing, radio and television broadcasting, and the manufacture of pulp, paperboard, and coated paper. A balance sheet for Time, Inc., as of December 31, 1957, appears in Exhibit 1. Income statements for the years 1956 and 1957 appear in Exhibit 2.

History of Time Magazine

The first issue of *TIME* was published on March 3, 1923. The magazine was launched as a journalistic experiment in the "newsmagazine" concept developed by its founders, Henry Luce and Briton Hadden. These men conceived the idea in 1922 and, after raising $86,000 of original capital, incorporated their venture in 1923. Their contention was that no existing national medium was adapted to provide busy men with clear, complete news of the significant happenings of the week, and their goal was not to see how much news *TIME* could print but "how much it could get off its pages into the minds of its readers."

Circulation of 12,000 for the first issue rose to average 18,500 for the first year of publication. In 1927, average net paid circulation passed 100,000, and in 1935, it exceeded 500,000. Circulation guarantees since 1940 are shown in Exhibit 3.

Advertising revenue also grew rapidly from only $14,635 in 1923 to $501,268 in 1927, when the company showed its first profit. In 1935, pages of advertising exceeded 2,500 for the first time and advertising revenue was $5,116,698. Advertising data for years since 1940 are also shown in Exhibit 3.

Mr. Auer described magazine publishing as being analogous to a three-legged stool, each leg representing one of the three major functions of editorial, advertising, and circulation. Each of the functions was closely related to the other two, and if one of the "legs" were removed the stool would topple over. Because of the close interrelationship of the major functions, long-range and year-by-year goals for each function were determined by top management as a part of the general strategy for the magazine. For example, given a promotion budget of sufficient size, TIME could probably have increased its circulation at an even faster rate than it had achieved. Such a policy, however, might have required a change in the editorial policies of the magazine to broaden its appeal, and this in turn might have required a change in the methods of selling advertising since TIME would then be competing with other "mass magazines" instead of offering a selective audience to its advertisers.

Speaking of the magazine's editorial and circulation policies in 1958, Mr. Auer said, "TIME is a selective mass magazine, that is, its editorial content is aimed at a broader audience than the intellectual magazines such as The Reporter, Atlantic, and Harper's, and yet is not designed for the true mass market catered to by the more popular magazines such as Life, Saturday Evening Post, and Look. Within the framework of this editorial policy, our circulation goal is to achieve consistent growth and an increasing saturation of our market through imaginative promotion which is aggressive but also smart and civilized."

Sources of Subscriptions

A wide variety of methods of obtaining subscriptions was used by the magazine publishing industry. In order to prevent extravagant and unsubstantiated claims, the publishing industry had formed the Audit Bureau of Circulation (ABC) for the purpose of verifying each member publication's circulation data. Publishers participating in ABC (all major publishers were participants) issued a semiannual "Publishers' Statement" reporting various data on circulation and subscription sources, terms, and prices. These statements were audited by ABC, and both unaudited "Publishers' Statements" and ABC Audit Reports (based on examination of the publishers' records) were distributed by ABC at nominal cost to advertisers and other interested parties. Circulation statistics for 1957 for selected magazines are shown in Exhibit 4. Brief ABC definitions of each of the sources of subscriptions are quoted in Appendix A, page 66.

The magazine steering committee of the Association of National Advertisers (ANA) made frequent analyses of the circulation data distributed by ABC. Excerpts from a 1958 ANA publication entitled *Magazine Circulation and Rate Trends, 1940–1957* are given below, reflecting that committee's evaluations of the quality of circulation sources from the advertisers' point of view:

A.B.C. supplies quantitative facts on circulation, not qualitative measures of the relative merits of circulation methods. However, A.B.C. figures may be used to form opinions concerning values of various channels of distribution and also as a basis of questions to publishers regarding changing emphasis on circulation methods employed.

As with other products, magazines can be oversold to the extent that the purchaser sooner or later feels he has not received full value. This situation can occur with any of the presently used circulation methods, though some methods lend themselves more readily to such abuse than others. In other words, channels of distribution are not inherently good or bad, but the methods of using such channels may be good or bad to the purchaser (and consequently to the advertiser) depending on the intent, purpose and use by the publisher.

Even though one method of circulation distribution cannot be considered essentially more "honest" or "dishonest" than another method, the amount of sales pressure which can be exercised, the degree of direct control by the publisher, and the cost of obtaining circulation, varies widely with each method.

Because a subscription is expensive to secure does not necessarily indicate that it is "poor" circulation for the advertiser; in fact, it may be the very best that can be obtained. The following may be helpful in understanding the use of various channels of distribution, the ways sales pressure may be applied, and the control or lack of control a publisher can exercise in using the various methods.

Subscription Sales (Paragraph 6)

(a) *Ordered by mail.* Normally, the most important and profitable method of obtaining renewal subscriptions and frequently the largest source for new subscriptions. A high degree of control can be exercised over subscriptions mailed direct to publisher or through other publishers and department stores.

While no direct sales pressure can be applied by this method of subscription production, since all sales are by mail, considerable attractiveness can be offered in the form of short-term subscriptions at a special price, long-term subscriptions at substantial savings, attractive combination offers, premium, or payments during service.

(b) Ordered through salesmen.

. . . . .

(2) *Publisher's own and other publisher's salesmen,* and (3) *Independent agencies salesmen.* Field selling staffs may be directly controlled by a publisher or they may be independently owned and operated. Furthermore, they may be sponsored by a local civic or charitable organization (not school, church or fraternal organizations, which are reported separately under A.B.C. Paragraph 6 (b) 5) or may be unsponsored.

With all of these four variations of field selling staffs, a publisher has very little control over the activities of the agents or the amount or type of sales pressure used. While he can set up the rules under which he wants the agents to operate (for example, no sympathy appeals, full payment on first call, part payments with balance mailed to agency, installment payments, premiums, combinations, etc.) he doesn't know how closely the rules are observed unless he verifies orders by mail or field supervision.

· · · · ·

The 1959 Circulation Promotion Budget

The circulation promotion budget Mr. Auer was preparing in September, 1958, was a plan for the operations of the circulation department during 1959, showing in detail the sources for securing new subscriptions that were to be employed during that year. Of the subscriptions in effect in 1958, Mr. Auer knew how many would expire during 1959 and could estimate with reasonable accuracy the number of expiring subscriptions that would be renewed. The difference between total expirations and renewals was 600,000 subscriptions, and Mr. Auer knew that this many new subscriptions would have to be sold in 1959 in order to maintain circulation at the 1958 level. In addition, 100,000 new subscriptions would be required before March, 1959, in order to provide the increase in circulation over 1958 that had been guaranteed to advertisers after that date. Since TIME's newsstand sales had been relatively constant for several years, Mr. Auer felt that the quantity of circulation sold through retail outlets probably would not change significantly during 1959. Therefore, he determined that his 1959 promotion budget should plan to produce a total of 700,000 new subscriptions.

Of the 700,000 new subscriptions required, Mr. Auer estimated that approximately 400,000 would come in as the result of continuing promotional programs: order cards inserted in newsstand copies; the activities of independent magazine agents (catalogue agencies and independent agents); direct-mail pieces to residents of top suburban areas, book and record club members, college students, educators, clergy, etc.; the standard Christmas-gift promotion; and over-the-counter orders in department stores, etc. All of these continuing programs were in the "ordered by mail" source category except orders from the independent magazine agents.

The remaining 300,000 new subscriptions could be secured through a variety of sources. The continuing programs provided specific coverage to those segments of the population which TIME regarded as its natural market (educators, businessmen, college students, etc.). Therefore, the primary criteria for choosing the sources to be employed for the final 300,000 subscriptions were the relative costs of the alternative methods and the effect of each method on the public's "image" of the magazine.

Participating in a panel discussion on the subject "Forecasting and Budgeting Circulation . . . Cost Control" conducted by the Magazine Publishers Association, Inc., in March, 1957, Mr. Rhett Austell, the assistant circulation director of *TIME* made the following statement concerning the approach used by *TIME* magazine in choosing among promotion alternatives:

We look at any group of new subscriptions as you might look at a paid-up annuity. We put a certain amount of money down . . . our promotion costs . . . in the expectation of securing future income payments. These payments do not stop coming in when that particular group of new subs expires. Some of these subs renew and in so doing provide additional income. In turn, some of these renewals renew and so on. In fact, it takes about 20 years for the last of these original subscribers to drop off the books. Renewals, then, . . . or, if you will . . . future income payments . . . are the heart of the problem. Our primary cost control technique is, therefore, to set up a "chain of circulation" through which we test the renewability of all our various sources of new business.

Now, obviously, if we expect renewals to be high, we can afford to pay a lot for the first group of new subs. The trick is to know precisely what sources of "annuity" you are buying when you shop around for different sources of business, to know precisely what sort of income payment (or renewal business) you are going to receive in the future. Some sources offer a terrific first-cost bargain. Payment on the initial term alone may, and probably will, put you ahead of the game. But that payment may be the last you will ever get. If it exceeds the initial cost, of course, you could continue to buy this type of annuity and always show some profit. But we have found that we can often substitute for or supplement this type of annuity with sources which cost more to start with but which will pay us income for a longer period. Whatever sources you are using, it is vital to know what you are getting for your money. We have found that costs in this business are not often what they seem to be.

So now I come to the first step in our system of cost control, . . . which is to rate every source of business on the basis of its initial cost and the income which it is expected to provide through its renewals over the course of years. We then arrange these sources in descending order from the most profitable to the least profitable indicating in each case the volume of circulation which each source is able to maintain. We are always adding to the list because new promotion ideas and projects are always coming up. And we are constantly revising the ratings as the latest renewal data become available (for what was a good source relatively speaking a year ago may not be today).

Once we have prepared and updated this list of ratings, we face the practical decision-making involved in setting up a sales campaign. As Marge Dyer [another panelist] pointed out, our budgets show us the number of new subs needed at any one time to offset expires and to reach the new growth goals which management has set down. With this information as to requirments in hand, we dig down into our barrel of sources only so far as we need to meet these requirements. And, of course, our constant challenge is to develop a less expensive way of selling the lowest batch of subs in the barrel.

This system of cost control has one added advantage in TIME's case and that is the cost ratings seem to bear an inverse relationship to quality. In other words, our new subscriber surveys and our renewal percentages indicate that those sources of business which provide the largest annuity payments are also the best in terms of subscriber quality. This makes sense, we think, because renewals play such a large part in this system of cost accounting, and we believe that TIME, as an editorial product, appeals to a certain group of people whose education and income are above the average.

Field-Selling Organizations

In deciding how the remaining 300,000 new subscriptions required during 1959 should be obtained, Mr. Auer felt he should re-examine the use of field sales agencies to obtain part or all of the required amount. Early in 1955, TIME had begun the small-scale use of field sales agencies on an experimental basis in order to obtain some experience with this source. Based on the 1956 and 1957 results, Mr. Auer decided that the cost of field selling did not compare favorably with the use of direct mail for certain mailing lists which could be used to produce an estimated 200,000 new subscriptions during 1959. Therefore, his decision concerning the use of field sales agents involved only the final segment of 100,000 new subscriptions for which he had the alternative of using a direct-mail list with higher estimated costs of securing the initial subscriptions.

Field-selling organizations were used by many publishers as an important subscription source. Two of the largest publishers had their own field-selling organizations, and there were also several independent field agencies. Both types of organization operated in a similar fashion, employing door-to-door salesmen to sell a "package" of magazines on an installment plan. Sales were made by professional solicitors or, in some cases, high school or college students who were working part time. The salesmen were only permitted to sell in certain designated sections of a city; they were not allowed to sell in low-income areas where the collection of installments was difficult. They might sell a group of, say, four publications, from a list of 25 or 30 magazines. The usual offer was for a three-year subscription with monthly payments of $1 or $1.50 covering the cost of the entire package. These subscriptions were referred to by the magazine industry as PDS (Paid during Service).

If *TIME* were to use PDS during 1959 it would sign a contract with an agency to accept 100,000 subscriptions for a three-year term at a subscription price of $14. The agency's commission per subscription would be $10, which included the agency's fees for both selling the subscription and collecting the installments. The contract would stipulate that the entire block of subscriptions would be delivered between January 1 and March 1, 1959. Mr. Auer's experience with field sales agencies convinced him that the agent could deliver the subscriptions within the stated time. In order to minimize accounting problems, the agreement would state that the agency would pay *TIME* $4 (the net between the subscription price and the agency commission) at the time the subscription was delivered. All future installment payments collected by the company would then belong exclusively to the agency.

Mr. Auer estimated, based on his and other publishers' experience, that approximately 10% of the PDS subscriptions would renew at the end of the initial term in response to a direct-mail solicitation. Although a variety of renewal alternatives were offered to the holder of an expiring subscription, the average renewal was for a two-year term at a price of $11. The cost of obtaining a renewal was 50 cents. After the first renewal, Mr. Auer knew that approximately 75% of the subscriptions expiring would be renewed. Thus of the 100,000 initial PDS subscriptions, 10,000 could be expected to make one renewal, 7,500 a second renewal, and 75% of the decreasing number would renew over and over.

Direct Mail

If the field-selling agency was not used in 1959, Mr. Auer would plan to increase his direct-mail campaign. In addition to the mailing lists already tentatively included in his 1959 program, he had a list of 12,500,000 names of homeowners in selected metropolitan and suburban areas throughout the nation. From his experience with such lists in the past, Mr. Auer expected he might get an 0.8% (0.008) response, thus providing 100,000 new subscriptions. The offer to be made would be for a one-year subscription at the introductory price of $5. Mr. Auer expected that 52% of the initial subscribers from a list such as this one might renew at the end of the first year, and thereafter the 75% renewal ratio was expected. Renewal prices, costs, and terms would be the same as that estimated for renewals of PDS subscriptions.

At the request of Mr. Auer, Mr. Austell prepared an estimate of the cost of the direct-mail promotion as follows:

Printing the sales literature, enclosure cards, etc., 12,500,000
    at $17.55 per thousand.....................................$219,000
Renting mailing list and addressing envelopes 12,500,000 at $18
    per thousand... 225,000
Postage, 12,500,000 at $20 per thousand..................... 250,000
    Total promotion costs...............................$694,000

Cost per subscription, assuming 0.8% response
    $694,000 ÷ 100,000......................................$ 6.94
Cost of postage on airmail reply card........................   0.06
    Total cost per new subscription.......................$ 7.00

Upon presenting the above cost estimate to Mr. Auer, Mr. Austell commented that, while he was fairly confident of the reliability of the estimates of the cost of putting out the mailing, the final figure of $7 as a cost per new subscription was heavily dependent on the number of reply cards received. Although careful records were maintained of the results of previous mailings with other lists, Mr. Austell felt that the response to this mailing might easily vary as much as 10% either way from the estimated 0.8%. And there was always the possibility that the department's copywriters might score another creative breakthrough as they had many times in the past when new approaches in art and copy had pulled 50% to 100% more orders than expected.

If this direct-mail campaign were undertaken, it would be accomplished during the months of January and February, 1959. Although the magazine offered a "bill-you-later" plan, for all practical purposes Mr. Austell expected that the bulk of the subscriptions would be collected by the end of February.

Income Tax Regulations concerning Circulation Income and Expense

In 1958, after several years of litigation by the magazine publishing industry, the determination of taxable net circulation income (the difference between circulation revenue and promotion expenses) was the subject of several Treasury Department rulings. The effect of these rulings was to give the publisher permission to handle subscription promotion costs and revenue as follows: promotion costs could be deducted in the year in which they were incurred or paid, while subscription revenue could be apportioned as income over the number of years in the life of the subscription; only a pro rata share of the subscription price had to be treated as income for each year in which deliveries against the subscription were made.

This method of treating circulation net income, which was used by Time, Inc., and most major publishers, was particularly advantageous for subscriptions having a high promotion cost and a long term. Under the PDS contract described above, for example, Time, Inc., could deduct the $10 agency commission as an expense in the first year, and recognize one-third of the $14 subscription price as income in each of the three years during which the subscription was in effect.

For purposes of recognizing the impact of income taxes in comparing alternative circulation sources, Mr. Auer used a 50% tax rate and treated tax payments as being made in one amount at the end of each calendar year; he believed that this procedure gave a rough approximation of the actual tax rate and schedule of payments.

Limitation on the 1959 Promotion Budget

In trying to decide between PDS and direct mail for securing the necessary 100,000 subscriptions in 1959, Mr. Auer was troubled by the fact that there was a significant difference between net dollar income or outgo during 1959 between the two methods. To find out if he should consider any over-all limitation on the dollar amount of his 1959 budget, he decided to discuss the problem with Mr. John Harvey, controller of Time, Inc. Mr. Harvey stated that there was no rigid dollar limitation, but that if Mr. Auer decided to use direct mail which would have a net cash loss in 1959, instead of PDS which would show an immediate cash profit, he should be able to justify his decision. Such a justification would probably need to show that the greater profits in later years using direct mail would more than offset the first-year loss, even considering that the corporation had been able to earn 14% to 22% on capital invested in the business during recent years (Exhibit 1). Mr. Harvey felt that 15% might be a reasonable estimate of the company's earnings rate in the future.

Question

Which method of selling 100,000 new subscriptions should be used by *TIME* magazine in 1958?

APPENDIX A

Excerpts from Audit Bureau of Circulation Bylaws and Rules, *Edition Z*
—August, 1957
Published by Audit Bureau of Circulations
123 North Wacker Drive, Chicago 6, Illinois

Chapter B
Article I, Section 1. Paid Circulation Defined

Paid circulation is hereby defined to be copies of publications which have been paid for by the purchasers, not for resale, under the following conditions, viz.:

(a) If the sale be a single copy sale, it shall be paid for at not less than 50 per cent of the basic single copy price.

(b) On term order for a year the subscription must be paid for at not less than 50 per cent of the basic annual price. In case of a subscription for more than one year the subscription must be paid for at not less than 50 per cent of a pro rata of the basic annual price for the period covered by the order. If the subscription is for a period of less than one year, it must be paid for at not less than 50 per cent of the basic price for the period offered. If there is no basic price for the period offered, it must be paid for at not less than 50 per cent of a pro rata of the basic price for the next shorter period. If there is no basic price for the term offered nor for a shorter term, it must be paid for at not less than 50 per cent of a pro rata of the basic price for the next longer term.

A price for a period of less than one year that is less than a pro rata of the basic annual price shall not be considered a basic price.

(c) Subscriptions for one year or more, or for less than one year if sold at not less than 50 per cent of basic annual price, may be served for no longer than three consecutive months immediately following the expiration date, and such arrears may be included in paid circulation.

Chapter F
Article IX, Section 1.   Channels of Subscription Sales

Subscription production shall be classified by channels in Paragraph 6 of Bureau reports designed for magazines in accordance with the following definitions and instructions:

(a) Ordered by mail:

Subscriptions produced by a publisher, individually or in behalf of other publishers; department stores; or other media may be classified as "Ordered by Mail" if the subscription order is received through the mail as the result of a voluntary effort by the subscriber.

Subscriptions sent in by mail as the result of solicitation by a field salesman shall be classified as "Ordered through Salesmen."

(b) Ordered through salesmen:

(1) Catalog agencies and individual agents:

A catalog agency is a concern which publishes in substantial volume a wholesale price list and/or a retail price list, commonly known as a "catalog." Catalog agencies generally accept subscriptions for many and often for all publications. The retail price catalogs are mailed direct to prospective subscribers by catalog agencies. The wholesale catalogs are distributed to subagents, such as individual agents, department stores, bookstores, newsdealers, postmasters, or others dealing directly with prospective subscribers. Subagents employ various forms of solicitation, such as direct mail, telephone, newspaper and periodical advertising and door-to-door canvass. Retail catalogs are usually furnished subagents by catalog agencies for mailing. The subagents or agencies send the subscriptions which they originate to the wholesale catalog agency which in turn clears them to respective publishers. The term "individual agents" is intended to apply to subscription salesmen who are not attached to the staff of a field selling organization, such as referred to in (b) (2) below. It also applies to agencies which do not publish a wholesale trade price list and/or a retail price list. Such agents are either part or full time workers who are compensated by either cash commission or merchandise reward. They include individuals and concerns variously described as "pin-money salesmen," "personal effort solicitors," individual salesmen, newsdealers, bookstores, postmasters, etc.

(2) Publisher's own and other publishers' salesmen:
   Subscriptions produced by the publisher through:
   (a) Full time field selling employees.
   (b) Appointed independent field selling contractors who report directly to the publisher.
   (c) A field selling subscription agency jointly owned by two or more publishers.

shall be shown in Bureau reports as having been ordered through "publisher's own and other publishers' salesmen."

(3) Independent agencies' salesmen:
   Subscriptions produced by outside field selling organizations which are totally unaffiliated with publisher except as subscription producers shall be shown in Bureau reports as having been ordered through "independent agencies' salesmen."

Note: the distinguishing characteristics of field selling staffs listed in (b) (2) and (b) (3) above are:

That the personal solicitation involved is conducted by professional salesmen who have chosen subscription selling as their principal means of livelihood.

These salesmen are usually, although not necessarily, associated with others in crews.

These salesmen usually take subscriptions for publications in accordance with authority specifically granted by the publishers.

(4) Newspaper agencies:

A newspaper agency operates under three main methods:

Method (a) Subscriptions ordered by direct mail.

Method (b) Subscriptions ordered through an advertisement in the sponsoring newspaper which carries an order form to be mailed to the publisher.

Method (c) Subscriptions ordered under a plan whereby the newspaper carrier solicits subscriptions to periodicals and in which said carrier collects for the periodical or periodicals when making collections for the newspaper.

The major part of the orders produced by these methods covers subscriptions to one or more magazines and farm publications and the sponsoring newspaper.

Subscriptions produced by organizations such as above described shall be included in the subdivision "Newspaper agencies."

(5) Members of schools, churches, fraternal and similar organizations:

Subscriptions in which sponsorship is involved shall be included in the subdivision "Members of schools, churches, fraternal and similar organizations" unless specifically provided for elsewhere.

This provision shall apply even though the production of the sponsoring organization is cleared through a catalog agency or any other channel whatsoever.

The Bureau shall prepare lists of field selling staffs as defined by this rule and distribute some to publisher members with appropriate instructions as a guide in properly classifying their production.

(c) Association membership:

Subscriptions received as the result of membership in an association shall be included in the subdivision "Association memberships."

Exhibit 1

TIME MAGAZINE

CONDENSED CONSOLIDATED BALANCE SHEET,
DECEMBER 31, 1957, FOR TIME, INC.

Current assets	$101,345,001
Investments	15,318,457
Property and equipment (net)	73,155,781
Intangible assets	15,669,442
Other assets and deferred charges	2,571,662
Total assets	$208,060,343
Current liabilities	$ 28,541,116
Long-term indebtedness	44,778,945
Deferred income—unearned portion of paid subscriptions	42,301,242
Minority interests, reserves, other deferred income	4,873,429
Total liabilities	$120,494,732
Capital stock	1,961,114
Surplus	85,604,497
Total liabilities and capital	$208,060,343

Return on investment:	1957	1956	1955	1954	1953
			(000 Omitted)		
Net income before special items	$12,024	$13,850	$ 9,196	$ 8,057	$ 8,144
Stockholders' equity	$87,566	$64,821	$44,456	$40,563	$37,111
Per cent	13.7%	21.4%	20.7%	19.9%	21.9%

Source: Corporate annual reports.

Exhibit 2

TIME MAGAZINE

CONSOLIDATED STATEMENT OF INCOME YEARS ENDED
DECEMBER 31, 1956, AND 1957 FOR TIME, INC.

	1957	1956
Revenues: From sales of magazines, advertising, and books; radio and television broadcasting; pulp and paperboard; paperboard containers; timber, poles, and piling; printing plates and scanned negatives; and miscellaneous products and services—less discounts, commissions, allowances, returns, etc.	$254,095,798	$229,373,627
Costs and expenses: Production, distribution, selling, editorial, and general	232,679,098	204,340,283
Operating income	$ 21,416,700	$ 25,033,344
Other income	3,751,117	2,913,475
	$ 25,167,817	$ 27,946,819
Other deductions	2,022,516	1,319,595
Income before taxes on income	$ 23,145,301	$ 26,627,224
Federal and foreign taxes on income	11,121,754	12,777,087
Net income before special items	$ 12,023,547	$ 13,850,137
Special items: Extraordinary capital gains (losses) after effect of capital gains taxes:		
From sales of 350,000 shares of St. Regis Paper Company common stock	7,709,290	
From sales of preferred stocks	(2,004,885)	
From liquidation of investment in Houston Oil Company of Texas		15,113,733
Net income	$ 17,727,952	$ 28,963,870

Source: Corporate annual reports.

Exhibit 3

TIME MAGAZINE

ADVERTISING STATISTICS

(Domestic edition only)

Year	Effective Date of Guarantee	Guaranteed Circulation	Pages of Advertising	Gross Advertising Revenue
1941	Sept., 1941	770,000	2,817	$ 8,648,519
1942	Sept., 1942	880,000	2,924	9,718,180
1943	Sept., 1943	1,000,000	3,313	12,267,564
1944			3,433	13,743,612
1945			3,509	13,910,407
1946	Mar., 1946	1,300,000	3,693	18,537,057
1947	Mar., 1947	1,500,000	3,676	23,204,329
1948			3,580	25,005,083
1949			3,316	23,771,732
1950			3,333	23,793,870
1951	Feb., 1951	1,600,000	3,809	29,950,738
1952			3,562	32,664,222
1953	Jan., 1953	1,700,000	3,561	35,391,178
1954	Jan. 4, 1954	1,800,000	3,268	35,143,779
1955	Jan. 3, 1955	1,900,000	3,302	37,891,943
1956	Jan. 2, 1956	2,000,000	3,450	42,598,778
1957	Jan. 1, 1957	2,100,000	3,361	45,112,621
1958	Jan. 6, 1958	2,250,000		
1959	Mar., 1959	2,350,000		

Source: Company records.

Exhibit 4

TIME MAGAZINE

CIRCULATION ANALYSIS AND SUBSCRIPTION SOURCES OF SELECTED LEADING MAGAZINES IN 1957

I. Circulation Analysis

	Total	Average Net Paid Circulation			
		Subscription	% to Total	Single Copy	% to Total
Life	5,906,161	5,073,878	85.9	832,283	14.1
Saturday Evening Post	5,301,042	3,827,438	72.2	1,473,604	27.8
Look	5,192,406	4,329,714	83.4	862,692	16.6
Time	2,171,476	1,935,326	89.1	236,150	10.9
Newsweek	1,136,568	1,000,430	88.0	136,138	12.0
U.S. News & World Report	949,013	819,542	86.4	129,471	13.6
Holiday	918,272	752,488	81.9	165,784	18.1
Esquire	827,016	552,009	66.7	275,007	33.3
New Yorker	420,026	300,709	71.6	119,317	28.4

II. Sources of Subscriptions Sold

	Total Subscriptions Sold	Subscriptions Ordered by Mail		Catalog Agencies and Independent Agents		Subscriptions Ordered through Salesmen										All Other Sources	
						Publishers' Salesmen		Independent Agencies Salesmen		Newspaper Agencies		Schools, Civic Organizations					
		Number	%	Number	%	Number	%	Number	%	Number	%	Number	%			Number	%
Life	4,192,071	2,730,328	65.1	686,088	16.4	551,236	13.1	8,875	0.2	14,728	0.4	200,677	4.8			139	...
Saturday Evening Post	2,857,849	1,040,658	36.4	276,300	9.7	822,334	28.8	286,717	10.0	76,306	2.7	339,140	11.9			16,394	0.5
Look	2,743,999	1,041,392	38.0	96,446	3.5	881,725	32.1	406,725	14.8	198,569	7.2	108,736	4.0			10,406	0.4
Time	1,795,412	1,303,183	72.6	334,432	18.6	65,519	3.6	13,609	0.8	4	...	78,605	4.4			56	...
Newsweek	821,428	563,641	68.6	96,105	11.7	28,554	3.5	84,442	10.3	......	...	48,686	5.9			......	...
U.S. News & World Report	721,818	621,530	86.1	100,288	13.9	......	...										
Holiday	644,308	314,126	48.8	85,169	13.2	138,790	21.5	31,575	4.9	18,082	2.8	50,107	7.8			......	...
Esquire	300,086	101,479	33.9	42,447	14.1	60,531	20.2	42,927	14.3	40,630	13.5	12,072	4.0			6,459	1.0
New Yorker	270,539	185,767	68.7	84,772	31.3	......	...										

Source: Publishers' statements submitted to the Audit Bureau of Circulation.

Section II

EVALUATING RISKINESS

CONSOLIDATED ELECTRICAL
PRODUCTS, INC. (E)

METHODS OF ALLOCATING FUNDS AMONG VARIOUS TYPES OF PROJECTS

Once Mr. Holman had settled on minimum return standards for each of the five operating divisions, he planned to investigate what types of criteria should be used in deciding how to allocate funds among the various projects submitted by division management. Historically, CONELP used two classification systems to differentiate among various types of capital budgeting proposals. Projects were first classified into four groups in accordance with the purpose of the individual funds request. These classifications were: cost reduction or replacement, new products or processes, expansion, and "necessary" projects. Each request for funds was further classified by the degree of risk inherent in the proposal. These risk categories were: normal, moderate, and high. As one of his tasks, Mr. Holman was attempting to develop new classification procedures to aid either division or top management in the screening process.

These historic classifications had proven to be quite important in evaluating new requests for funds. Cost reduction or replacement projects frequently were approved if the proposals promised returns greater than the relevant division's minimum-return standard. Top management, however, usually demanded a return rate equal to the minimum standard plus 5% for expansion proposals, and the minimum standard plus 10% for new product or process proposals. These differentials seemed appropriate to top management in view of differences in the basic risk characteristics among these types of proposals. Necessary projects were not justified in terms of return potentials but rather in terms of their strategic advantages.

75

Top management also made use of the risk classifications in reaching its allocation decisions. While no firm guide lines had been established, the finance committee usually reviewed more carefully and tended to demand higher returns from projects classified as moderate risks. Only a few of the most promising high-risk projects typically were ever approved.

Mr. Holman was personally quite disturbed by present procedures for classifying projects by degree of risk. Top management had never attempted to define the meaning of these risk categories. As a result, division personnel, responsible for preparing appropriation requests, had each developed his own interpretation of the terms normal, moderate, and high risk. Mr. Holman knew from experience that these interpretations differed widely from individual to individual; yet it was difficult to detect the bias expressed in the rating given on any specific proposal. Since the treasurer's office and the finance committee were under severe time pressure during the screening process, considerable reliance had to be placed on the stated risk rating. This was particularly problematical for projects rated "normal" risks since these proposals were often given only cursory review. Mr. Holman believed that the finance committee's decisions were probably unwittingly inconsistent as a consequence.

Nevertheless, the task of defining differing degrees of risk seemed prodigious to Mr. Holman. The forms of exposure to risk were both numerous and difficult to measure precisely. New product proposals, for example, typically involved estimates of current and potential demand for the basic product, of consumer acceptance of CONELP's product, of the current and prospective competitive situation for the product, of vulnerability to technological risks, and of other marketing considerations. These estimates, in turn, had to be converted into appraisals of the size of product demand, pricing opportunities, costs necessary to preserve the future market share, and the expected life of the product. Technological risks were also important. These proposals had to appraise the ability to solve complex engineering and manufacturing problems, to determine cost levels, to gauge exposure to adverse cost trends such as inflation, and so forth. Any one of these estimates could be in serious error and suggest a high level of risk. These elements of exposure to risk were so unique to a particular project that Mr. Holman found it difficult to define differences in degree of risk in a concrete yet generally applicable manner.

Defining differences in risk was but a part of the problem confronting Mr. Holman. He also had to decide how much of a premium, if any, should be demanded from projects considered more risky in order to compensate for CONELP's greater exposure. Existing return premiums demanded from new products proposals, for example, had been set arbitrarily. Mr. Holman found that CONELP's officers were about equally divided among believing this differential was either too high, or too low, or just about right. Significantly, these opinions seemed largely based on "gut feel" rather than substantive evidence. The task of developing useful differentials in the demanded rate of return from proposals with more severe risk characteristics consequently appeared formidable.

Mr. Holman had actively solicited the opinions of various interested members of the CONELP organization on ways of resolving these issues. His notes—never fully organized—are abstracted below:

Nothing will ever replace the value of human judgment in deciding the appropriate amount of incremental return to demand from a risky project. We consequently ought to leave these judgments to the people most capable of making them—those closest to the situation. Each new expenditure proposal regardless of its purpose should be compared with competing investment opportunities at the plant level, and a priority list should be prepared there, ranking the projects from best to worst in accordance with their over-all income and risk characteristics. At the division level, each plant's priority list should then be integrated into a composite priority list—perhaps discarding a few unworthy proposals from the bottom of each plant list. At this stage of the screening process, division management should not be allowed to alter significantly the plant's priority schedule but rather should focus on dovetailing the various plant schedules into a composite schedule on the basis of the over-all competitive attractiveness of the proposals. The treasurer's office would perform a similar integrating function by developing a master priority schedule once division priority lists are received. Next, the master list would be divided into three parts: clearly acceptable projects, clearly unacceptable projects, and (hopefully a small portion of the total) marginal projects. The treasurer's office and the finance committee both could then focus their attention on comprehensive analysis of marginal projects and have as a guide the foregoing priority judgments. In order to avoid the risk of having mid-management "slip an undesirable project up towards the top of their priority list to assure acceptance," we would, of course, have to follow up on the comparative success of accepted projects and hold relevant personnel accountable for their judgments.

. . . . .

Top management is the only authority in a position to determine an appropriate balance between income and risk considerations in keeping with basic desires of CONELP's stockholders. Since the mix of income and risk for any proposal is unique, it is next to impossible to develop standards for decision making at lower echelons. The only way to make consistent evaluations is to have a single body—namely the finance committee—responsible for the decisions (except perhaps for projects requiring investments so small in amount as to be unworthy of their attention). In contrast, delegation of authority would only lead to a hodgepodge of judgments. Perhaps present difficulties can be traced to the fact that capital budgeting is now undertaken on a crash basis, once a year. If, instead, we were to adopt a procedure allowing for submission of project requests throughout the year, work loads would be spread out sufficiently to allow careful consideration of each and every proposal.

. . . . .

The risk characteristics of each division differ substantially, and basic return differentials should consequently be tailored to meet the specific risk circumstances at the division level. Historically, our policies have provided highly artificial distinctions as shown in the table below:

Division	Current Minimum-Return Standard	Current Minimum-Return Standard for New Products	Return Premium Demanded for New Products, Stated as a Percentage of Minimum Standards
Major appliance	8.1%	18.1%	122%
Small appliance	13.0	23.0	77
Electrical components	10.3	20.3	97
Control apparatus	20.3	30.3	49
Heavy industrial equipment	7.0	17.0	143

Two years ago we permitted the major appliance division to invest funds in equipping for "hi-fi" production, a project promising a 20% return on investment and rated "normal" risk. In contrast, cost reduction proposals promising the same return (but offering greater certainty) are currently rejected if they are submitted by the control apparatus division. These decisions seem inconsistent, largely because they have not taken basic risk differences among the divisions adequately into account.

. . . . .

When we talk of risk, we are really most concerned about the size of our losses in the event the venture proves unsuccessful and about the probability of such an event occurring. What we need, then, is an index which will measure exposure to losses of this nature. We could develop just such an index by the following means. We sink certain sums of money into a project, only part of which could be realized in the event of failure either through sale of the useless assets or through putting the assets to alternative worthwhile employment. The net difference between the sums invested and the potential amounts recovered represents the maximum exposure to loss. If we multiply this maximum loss by the probability of failure, we would have an estimate of the expected size of losses. Restating this product as a percentage of the initial investment would produce the desired index. The lower the index value is, the safer will be the investment. Through experience, we could gradually develop appropriate return differentials to demand from new proposals, given the index. This index suggests, for example, that we should prefer working capital investments to plant investments, multipurpose plant investments to special-purpose equipment investments, etc., whenever promised returns are identical.

.   .   .   .   .

Although there are many varieties of risks, they are all essentially of two kinds: ability to realize marketing expectations and ability to realize technological expectations. We can devise a useful procedure for equating risks if we focus on these two risk areas. I propose evaluating every project, irrespective of its purpose on the same basis. This would involve grading the project in terms of relative riskiness in each of these areas on a scale running from, say, 0.80 (very risky) to 1.00 (negligible risks). I would then use these two risk factors (the above grades) to modify return calculations in accordance with the following formula:

$$A = M \times T \times R$$

Where:

A = Rate of return on investment, adjusted for risk
M = Marketability risk factor
T = Technological risk factor
R = Initial return on investment before adjusting for risk

For instance, a project initially promising a rate of return of 30%, but with a marketability risk factor of 0.85 and a technological risk factor of 0.90, would have a risk-adjusted rate of return 22.05%. This figure for the risk-adjusted rate of return on a specific project would then be compared with the minimum-return standard in deciding whether or not the project should be accepted. This proposal has the primary advantage of developing precedents, which will tend to assure consistency over time. Division managers, when submitting an appropriation request, will have to justify not only the validity of their return on investment calculation but also the appropriateness of the two risk factors used. Top management could then confine itself to a judiciary review of the validity of these judgments—striving, in the process, for consistency.

.   .   .   .   .

Should we use present value as a method of computing returns on investment, we have the flexibility to consider risk in our basic calculations. Illustratively, returns during the first few years of an investment may be highly certain and could, therefore, be discounted at a low rate (about the level of the minimum-return standard). If more distant returns for the same project were more uncertain, we could, then, use a higher discount rate (to reflect the higher risk) in bringing these returns back to their present value. Similarly, depreciation estimates might be regarded as more certain than profit estimates and could be discounted at a lower rate. In short, we could examine each element of the return calculation to determine its relative certainty, and, then, select an appropriate discount factor to calculate the present value of the element. Once the present values for each element of the computation had been determined, these present value amounts would be summed. The resulting figure (already adjusted for risk) could then be compared with the amount of the investment to determine the advisability of the investment. Whenever the present value computation exceeds the amount of the investment, we presumably would wish to approve the appropriation request.

· · · · ·

There are two—or possibly three—aspects of risk that are of major concern in evaluating capital budgeting proposals. We are uncertain about our estimates of the amount of returns from the investment, of the length of life of the project, and possibly of the amount of the investment. These elements of risk can be subjected to statistical analysis, and the results used to adjust returns for differences in risk.[1] For instance, we could assign probabilities in keeping with our expectations, to various possible estimates of the amount of return and, through statistical analysis, derive expected return levels that were certainty equivalents. Similarly, we could derive through probability analysis an expected life for the project. These two figures[2] could, then, be used in present value calculations to determine the expected rate of return on the investment.[3] This expected return value would, then, serve as a basis for subsequent risk adjustments. In the process of obtaining expected values for returns or for project-life, we will have developed data that could be used to determine the standard deviation (a statistical term indicating the relative uncertainty of a mean estimate) of possible returns from their expected value (or mean), etc. The larger such a standard deviation estimate is, the greater will be the riskiness of the project. We can then use standard deviation calculations to develop criteria for adjusting basic return computations downward to reflect differences in risk. It will, of course, take time to develop an adequate experience base to know what are appropriate adjustments for specific standard deviation figures; however, once this experience base is acquired, we will have a consistent basis for appraising the relative importance of income and risk for any given proposal.

· · · · ·

---

[1] Although Mr. Holman was intrigued by this suggestion, he wondered whether it could ever be sold to either top or division managers. Historically, these men had resisted what they regarded as oversophisticated or academic approaches to problems.

[2] One individual objected to discounting the expected value of returns, given an expected life figure, back to its present value. He believed that it was statistically more correct to estimate the probability of each possible return level, year by year, and, then, to discount independently the product of each probability and return estimate back to its present value. Estimates of life expectancy implicitly were built into the assignment of probabilities in any given year. This procedure, also, skips calculating expected values of returns for any year, developing instead an expected over-all rate of return.

[3] Whenever the size of the investment is uncertain, it, too, could be estimated by means of a probability analysis.

In considering the implications of risk on investment decisions, we should first consider what risk means to our stockholders. Stockholders never see the results of any given project, and, indeed, they are interested only in the composite results of our investment decisions. If we overestimate the returns on any given investment, we may well underestimate the returns on another. To the extent these misestimates cancel out, stockholders never suffer from the risks we consider in evaluating individual projects. Since we invest in a large number of projects each year, the opportunities for misestimates canceling out are sizable. This is, in effect, the old law of averages at work. Whereas we may not realize the estimated return on a given project, we will tend to realize the estimated return on all investments. Consequently, we should not bother with attempting to adjust return calculations for differences in risk; instead, we should treat each return estimate as if it were certain, and make our decisions on this basis alone.

Our stockholders are, however, concerned by two other kinds of risk excluding those inherent in our financing policies. They might suffer, for example, if we make all our investments in projects that were tied to the same form of risk; e.g., the same market, such as is true in our major appliance division. It seems clear that the major appliance division would be considered a more risky stock investment than CONELP is if it were a separate company. We, therefore, should strive for a balance in our future investments to assure our stockholders of adequate diversification of investment risks. In effect, this suggests we should concern ourselves more with the strategic diversity of total investment risks rather than with the relative riskiness of a single project.

Stockholders are also concerned by the over-all volatility of corporate earnings. The more stable our growth pattern is, the more favorably will our stock be received on the market. We, therefore, should prefer to invest in projects with relatively stable returns over the course of a business cycle. On the other hand, we should demand higher returns from projects, which will tend to magnify the present cyclical characteristics of earnings. Since the cyclicality of earnings is a risk that affects the value of our stockholders' holdings, we should give it more weight in our analysis of the suitability of investment opportunities.

. . . . .

The greatest fault with our present capital budgeting system is that too much money is allocated to projects justified solely on the basis of necessity. For instance, the major appliance division invests sizable sums each year in model change-overs, justified entirely on the basis of necessity. Although we must consider the importance of maintaining the major appliance division's competitive position, it is impossible to gauge whether adequate value is received from the specific change-over investment recommended without having estimates of the return values (or loss savings) associated with distinct subunits of the model change-over proposal. In contrast, the control apparatus division must make investments in new products to stay competitive. However, these projects are reviewed with strict minimum-return criteria in mind (currently 30%) and have greater difficulty receiving approval. The fairest capital budgeting policy would consequently require that all projects be justified by their return characteristics first and their strategic values second—as opposed to current practice. Although there may be many problems involved in assigning quantitative values to certain intangible considerations, management would nevertheless have a more objective basis for evaluating the projects and appraising the assumptions if all returns were expressed quantitatively. This would further assure that the allocation of funds among projects would be conducted on a more competitive basis.

WACO WILDCAT COMPANY

In September, 1958, Mr. Arthur Bennett, exploration vice-president of Waco Wildcat Company, was trying to decide what action to take regarding the company's lease No. 4783. The lease, which gave the company exclusive rights to explore for oil and gas on 40 acres of west Texas land owned by Mr. W. T. Hatcher, had been purchased by Waco in July, 1954, for a bonus payment of $5,000. Annual rentals, payable in advance each year until drilling operations began, of $400 had been paid—a total of $2,000. The lease provided that in the event that oil or gas were found, Mr. Hatcher was to receive one-eighth of the gross production from the well, with the other seven-eighths to go to Waco. All costs of drilling and completing any well and bringing the oil or gas to the surface were to be paid by Waco.

The lease contained an automatic cancellation provision if drilling was not started within five years from the date of the lease. During the four years since the lease had been signed, Waco had not been in a position to begin drilling on the property because the company had all its funds employed in investment opportunities which it considered more attractive. The company was a medium-sized oil producer with sales in 1957 of approximately $20,000,000 and profits after taxes of about $3,000,000. In a normal year the company invested between five and six million dollars in oil exploration ventures.

Mr. Bennett knew that he must reach a decision on lease No. 4783 within a month or so if he wished to consider the alternative of "selling" (assigning Waco's rights to another party) the lease to another oil company. He believed that because the oil field in which the lease was located had proved out so well during the last four years, Waco should be able to sell the lease for approximately $15,000. In order to give the purchaser time to act on the lease, Mr. Bennett thought that it should be put on the market by the first of November, 1958.

Mr. Bennett was more interested in the possibility of having Waco

drill for oil on the site of lease No. 4783. The lease was located in the
Sandusky oil field, an area of roughly 35 square miles containing an
unknown number of large oil and natural gas pools. The productiveness
of any particular well was determined by the subsurface geological formations underneath the well. The topography in the Sandusky field was
relatively uniform, but the subsurface formations varied; therefore, the
results of any particular exploratory well were difficult to predict. Since
exploration of the field began, 70 wildcat wells had been completed by
the 23 operators active in the field. Referring to data collected by an oil
industry trade association, Mr. Bennett was able to determine that 21 of
these were dry holes (nonproductive), 28 were gas wells, 14 were
combination oil and gas wells, and seven were oil wells. In addition, 18
wildcat dry holes had been drilled on the fringes of the field during the
process of determining what the apparent boundaries of the productive
zone were. Within the productive zone thus defined, the location of
productive wildcats followed no particular pattern. Therefore, Mr. Bennett had no specific guide as to whether a well drilled on lease No.
4783 would be productive, but he did know that the land was clearly
situated within the productive zone of the field.

From the trade association data, Mr. Bennett was also able to determine the average amount of oil and gas reserves that were recoverable
from a productive well in the Sandusky field. He computed the net
profit that Waco could expect each year over the ten-year life of a typical well, and found that the total, discounted to its present value, was
approximately $150,000 for a gas well, $200,000 for a combination
well, and $300,000 for an oil well. These amounts were the discounted
total profits from the well, after deducting royalty payments and operating expenses but before deducting the estimated $100,000 cost of
drilling the well.

Several of the major oil companies had been active in the exploration of the Sandusky field and had employed an exploration technique
with which Waco had had no experience. These companies conducted a
"seismic test" to determine in advance of drilling the type of subsurface
formations that were beneath the proposed drilling site. The seismic
test required a highly trained crew to bury and detonate an explosive
charge, and expensive equipment to record the shock waves produced
by the explosion. The resulting seismograph was then interpreted by a
geologist who could predict the subsurface formations with great accuracy. In the Sandusky field, three main types of formations were commonly found. Of the 30 seismic tests that had been "shot," type A for-

mation was indicated 12 times; time B, 15 times; and type C, 3 times.

In each case in which the tested site had then been drilled, the formation predicted by the seismic test had been actually encountered. Only four of the "A" formations had been drilled, as this was generally thought to be an unproductive type of formation. Of these four, three were dry and the fourth was a gas producing well. The B type formation was known to be a formation likely to contain gas pools. Of the 15 wells drilled on tested "B" sites, nine were gas producers and the other six were combination oil and gas wells. The "C" formation almost always yielded an oil well, and on the three "C" sites located by seismic tests, an oil well had been brought in.

Reviewing this information, Mr. Bennett was uncertain as to what action to take. Upon inquiry, however, he found that the cost of a seismic test on lease No. 4783 would be $30,000, and he suspected that the cost of the test would be impossible to justify in economic terms. He also knew that having a seismic test made would, if it yielded negative results, kill the market for the lease since no competitor would want to speculate on it if Waco had tested it and then decided not to drill on it.

Question

What course of action should Mr. Bennett take? It is suggested that you ignore the effect of income taxes in your analysis of this case.

ALLEN DISTRIBUTION COMPANY

On June 16, 1954, Mr. William McConnell of the mid-Atlantic office of the Allen Distribution Company was considering whether his company should extend a credit limit of $1,000 to the Morse Photo Company of Harrisburg, Pennsylvania. Mr. McConnell had recently transferred from his job as credit representative in one of the company's western branch offices to become credit manager of the mid-Atlantic branch office where he assumed full responsibility for initiating and supervising the branch's credit policies. When he assumed this position, Mr. McConnell had asked the five credit representatives who had been handling the branch's accounts on their own to submit to him for review a few borderline credit accounts pending the establishment of a credit limit. Mr. McConnell believed that his decision and method of analysis might prove helpful in "setting the tone" of future operations in the credit department. Therefore, he planned to write out his analysis and decision so that it could be circulated.

The Allen Distribution Company, a subsidiary of the Allen Electric Company, one of the nation's largest manufacturers of electrical appliances and lighting equipment, was a national wholesale distributor of the parent company's products. Merchandise sold by the Allen Distribution Company ranged from refrigerators and television sets to electric light bulbs. Its competition included other nationally known wholesalers and small regional wholesalers of the Allen line as well as wholesalers of a number of competing product lines.

The parent company sold goods to the Allen Distribution Company on the same terms that it sold to independent wholesalers. Allen Distribution in turn usually sold its merchandise at the wholesale prices and on the terms suggested by the parent company, as did most other wholesalers of the Allen line; however, Allen Distribution maintained the right to set its own prices, and occasionally, when price competition developed in local areas, prices were reduced for short periods.

86

Since wholesale prices for competing products tended to be uniform, the intense competition for retail outlets and intermediary wholesale houses handling the Allen line caused the company to give major attention to the services offered these customers including co-operative advertising, store displays, inventory control, and credit arrangements. However, the slight differences in the quality of services rendered by the large wholesalers of Allen's products were not fully appreciated by customers, and sales often depended more on the personal relationships developed between the customer and company salesmen. For this reason, Allen Distribution's salesmen tended to concentrate on maintaining current accounts and on expanding sales by securing outlets carrying competing product lines where brand differentials could be emphasized.

These salesmen were paid a straight commission of 1% for net sales in their territory. An additional 1% commission was given salesmen on net sales to new accounts during the first year. Salesmen were not held responsible for bad debt losses resulting from their sales efforts, although they sometimes helped in collecting overdue receivables.

Sales during the first four months of 1954 for the entire company, as well as the mid-Atlantic branch, had decreased 2% in comparison with the similar period in 1953 even though the number of customers serviced remained relatively unchanged. In late May, 1954, the president of Allen Distribution had called together the branch managers and announced an intensified sales campaign for new outlets to offset the sales decline. Sales quotas by branch and by salesmen were established, and a prize system was devised to reward sales personnel for successful efforts. Mr. McConnell knew that the mid-Atlantic branch manager was actively supporting the program and that he wanted the branch to make a good showing.

The mid-Atlantic branch office of Allen Distribution had net sales of $78 million in 1953. A percentage analysis of the branch's 1953 income statement is shown below:

Net sales	100.0%	
Cost of merchandise	92.0	(All costs variable)
Gross profit	8.0%	
Operating and other expenses:		
Warehouse	4.1	(Variable portion: 1.2% of sales)
Selling	1.4	(Variable portion: 1.1% of sales)
Administrative	1.1	(Variable portion: 0.1% of sales)
Bad debt loss	0.13	
Interest expense	0.27	
Total	7.0%	
Net profit before taxes	1.0%	

Mr. McConnell found that throughout 1953 the branch's outstanding receivables had averaged $5.6 million, of which approximately $150,000 represented overdue amounts. The active accounts, numbering 15,000, were turning over approximately every 25 days. Twelve people were employed in the credit department, and its operating expenses (included in the administrative expenses above) were $100,000 per year. This did not include bad debt losses, which were 0.13% of sales in 1953 and had averaged 0.14% of sales in recent years. These bad debt losses derived principally from the marginal accounts and they were, therefore, approximately 1.4% of sales to the marginal accounts.

In Mr. McConnell's belief, a credit department should have little difficulty in approving good accounts and rejecting the bad ones. The real core of the credit department's operation rested in the evaluation of marginal accounts. Although Mr. McConnell had not made a study of the branch's operation, it was his opinion that the good accounts covered Allen Distribution's total operating and overhead costs, whereas the selection and handling of marginal accounts made the difference between profit and loss. Furthermore, Mr. McConnell believed that the purpose of a credit department was not to minimize credit losses but rather to maximize profits. He thought it was significant to recognize that an increase in sales volume for Allen Distribution usually meant increased sales for the parent company.

In evaluating a marginal account, Mr. McConnell considered: the cost of handling the account, the current and potential profitability of the account, and the inherent risks. Although Mr. McConnell did not know how much more it cost a credit department to maintain a marginal account, he knew the credit department spent at least twice as much time maintaining credit files and collecting overdue amounts on marginal accounts than on good accounts. He estimated that 20% of the branch's accounts, accounting for nearly 10% of sales, were marginal firms. Nevertheless, collections from these companies tended to be on the average only five to ten days slower than good accounts. Mr. McConnell had not determined an appropriate basis for distributing these costs to marginal firms, but he thought they should bear a substantial portion of the credit department's operating expenses. He also believed that the 3% interest charge on bank loans, which roughly paralleled the size of the account receivable balance, was a cost factor chargeable to his department. Although Mr. McConnell was not certain how it might apply, he knew that management of the parent company expected new investments to promise returns of 20% or more (before taxes) before the investment was considered acceptable.

Although Mr. McConnell hesitated to define a good account in specific terms, he generally considered that companies with a two-to-one current ratio and with an equity investment greater than outstanding debt fitted into this category. He also examined, when appropriate, acid test ratios, net working capital, inventory turnover, and other balance sheet and income statement relationships, but found it difficult to establish rules to cover every situation. Unsatisfactory credit requests were also difficult to define in terms of specific ratios. With experience, a good credit analyst was able to handle good and bad accounts in a routine manner. Real judgment, however, was required to select from the marginal applications those worthy of credit. In evaluating a marginal account, Mr. McConnell thought the principal's character, although difficult to ascertain, was as important as the company's financial status. In an analysis of a credit application, two factors were considered important: (1) the risk of losing all or part of the outstanding receivable balance through bankruptcy; and (2) the cost of having to carry the amount due beyond the net period. Since the credit department screened almost 1,000 new requests for credit annually, Mr. McConnell knew that the evaluative procedures would have to be "streamlined."

Mr. McConnell thought that the most difficult aspect of his new job would be translating any changes in credit policy into appropriate action by the credit representatives. Consequently, he planned to analyze a few selected marginal accounts so he might set forth the reasons for accepting or rejecting the accounts as a step toward establishing new credit standards. The Morse Photo Company was the first situation he had decided to review.

A credit file on the Morse Photo Company had been established on the basis of the following memo dated May 16, 1954, from the company's Harrisburg salesman:

Have sold Mr. Anthony V. Morse, president of Morse Photo Company, 280 Carlisle Avenue, Harrisburg, Pennsylvania, on the idea of switching from Oliver Electric Company's flash bulbs to ours. Sales would be $5,000 a year on current volume, and the Morse company is a real grower. Tony Morse is a terrific salesman and should sell a whale of a lot of bulbs for us. He wants $1,000 worth of bulbs as a starter.

Photographic flash bulbs were not a major product item and for statistical purposes were grouped with electric lighting equipment which accounted for 25% of Allen Distribution's sales volume. These electrical lighting supplies normally carried gross margins of 7% to 10% for Allen Distribution, but photo bulbs, one of the highest profit items sold by the company, had a gross margin of 17% after cash discounts. In addition, the parent company earned a profit margin of 20% (before taxes) on its sales of photo bulbs.

The Morse Photo Company was similar to a number of Allen's customers. Almost half of Allen's 15,000 credit accounts purchased only lighting supplies from them. Many of these accounts were small wholesale houses or regional chain stores whose annual purchases were in the $5,000 to $20,000 range.

Largely in order to control the retail price, photo bulbs were sold only on a consignment basis, but the practice had possible financial significance. Although a supply of bulbs was delivered to a customer, Allen remained the owner until the bulbs were sold by the consignee. Hence, Allen was entitled to recover its bulbs at any time from the consignee's stock. To insure recovery, segregation of inventory was agreed to by the customer. This meant that his stock of Allen bulbs should be plainly marked and physically separated from the remainder of his inventory.

After a sale of bulbs by the consignee, the latter was supposed to keep the resulting receivables or cash separate from its other accounts or funds until payment was made to Allen. Therefore, if the prescribed procedures were followed, it was possible to identify, as Allen's, the total value of a consignment, either in inventory, receivables, or cash. Thus, in the event of liquidation, no other creditor could make claim against these items.

Owing to the inconvenience of keeping separate stocks, accounts, and funds, the safeguards associated with Allen's consignment shipments were not often observed in practice. Allen made little effort to verify whether a separate inventory was actually maintained by its photo bulb customers. Nevertheless, it was believed that the company might have some protection in recovering consigned merchandise in the event of a customer's bankruptcy, since the bulbs carried Allen's brand name. More significantly, Allen made no effort to enforce segregation of funds after bulb sales were made by the customer. In consequence, Allen stood in the same general position as other creditors from the time the bulbs were sold by the consignee until remittance was made. Mr. McConnell, therefore, concluded that the consignment method afforded little financial protection in practice and appraised these accounts in the same way as open accounts.

At each month's end, the consignee inventoried the bulb supply and made payment in the amount of actual sales, less its 25% trade discount. Credit terms were 5% ten E. O. M. All photo bulb consignees were on a one-year contract basis, whereby the customer agreed to sell Allen's bulbs exclusively, and Allen agreed to supply the customer's needs up to a predetermined limit ($1,000 in the case of Morse Photo Company), provided payments were made within terms.

In the Morse Photo Company's credit file, Mr. McConnell found a credit report (Exhibit 1), four letters in reply to credit inquiries sent out by a branch credit representative (Exhibit 2), and balance sheet and income statements obtained from the Morse Photo Company by the Harrisburg salesman (Exhibits 3 and 4).

Exhibit 1

ASSOCIATED CREDIT AGENCY REPORT, MAY 27, 1954

Company: Morse Photo Company, 280 Carlisle Avenue, Harrisburg, Pennsylvania.

Rating: Limited (unchanged frem previous report).

Business: Commercial developing and photographic finishing. Also does a small volume of wholesaling films and camera supplies. Its distribution includes about 300 drug and periodical stores within a 130 mile radius of Harrisburg.

Management: Anthony W. Morse, president and principal stockholder.

History: Business started as proprietorship in May, 1948, with limited capital. On November 12, 1949, present owner purchased the assets but did not assume the liabilities for a reported $11,000; $2,000 was derived from savings and the balance was financed through a bank loan under the G. I. bill of rights. On April 30, 1952, the proprietorship was succeeded by the present corporation, which corporation took over assets and assumed liabilities of the predecessor business.

Sales terms: 2% ten days, net 30.

Employees: Twelve individuals of which three are salesmen.

Exhibit 1—Continued

BALANCE SHEETS FOR THE PERIOD ENDED APRIL 30, 1953, AND 1954

(Figured in even dollars)

ASSETS	April 30, 1954	April 30, 1953
Cash	$ 439	$ 320
Accounts receivable, net	16,201	11,503
Inventory at cost	12,681	12,712
Total current assets	$ 29,321	$ 24,535
Fixed assets, net	72,082	45,758
Other assets	9,641	2,839
Total assets	$111,044	$ 73,132

LIABILITIES		
Accounts payable	$ 22,311	$ 9,953
Note payable—bank	9,360	5,136
Notes payable—other	15,158	9,127
Other payables	4,529	3,321
Total current liabilities	$ 51,358	$ 27,537
Long-term notes payable	3,458	3,412
6% bonds	14,000	....
8% preferred stock	10,000	10,000
Common stock	32,100	32,100
Earned surplus	128	83
Total liabilities and net worth	$111,044	$ 72,132

INCOME STATEMENT FOR FISCAL YEARS 1953 AND 1954

	April 30, 1954	April 30, 1953
Net sales	$269,461	$162,898
Cost of goods sold	197,391	121,257
Gross profit	$ 72,070	$ 41,641
Selling and administrative expense	71,252	41,360
Profits before taxes	$ 818	$ 281
Tax	373	198
Earnings	$ 445	$ 83
Dividends	400	nil
Earnings transferred to surplus	$ 45	$ 83

Analysis of Financial Statements:

This seven-year old concern has expanded rapidly since its founding. This has been accomplished by expanding from a local territory to a radius of 130 miles and by giving 24-hour service to its customers. In order to accomplish this, there has been a substantial increase in fixed assets and approximately a 60% increase during the last year under review. This has been made possible in part by acquiring the Meade Photo Company in September, 1953. While the net earnings transferred to surplus have been small, there has been an increase in capital. During 1952, an 8% preferred stock issue of $10,000 was made, and in 1954 bonds were issued for $14,000. In connection with the acquisition of the Meade Photo Company for $24,000, $7,000 was borrowed from the Harrisburg Fidelity and Trust Company and the seller was given a chattel mortgage for $17,000, payable $180 a week. In addition Meade receives a payment of 10% of the net sales which is transacted from their former customers for a period of five years. During the year more equipment was purchased with money obtained in the form of notes from the bank. The amount due the bank is made up of five installment notes, secured by various pieces of equipment. Other notes payable consist of $5,500 payable to a large film manufacturer; $8,500 payable to Meade Photo; and the balance to others. Notes payable after one year are due to Meade Photo. Mr. Morse, the president, estimates that sales during the fiscal year, 1955, will be $320,000.

Exhibit 1—*Continued*

CREDIT RECORD, MAY 15, 1954

High Credit	Owes Currently	Past Due	Terms	Payments
3,000	0	0	Net 30	Prompt
2,693	0	0	2% 10 E.O.M.	Prompt
2,740	245	127	Net 30	Slow 8 months
582	0	0	2% 10	Prompt to slow 60 days
108	108	108	Net 10	Slow
2,518	2,518	0	Net 30	Prompt
582	61	0	2% 10	Prompt
9,308	8,854	4,601	2% 10, net 30	Slow 30 to 60 days
5,000	4,800	4,800	2% 10 E.O.M.	Slow 90 to 120 days
4,492	3,452	3,452	2% 10 E.O.M.	Slow 90 to 120 days
167	0	0	· Net 30	Slow 60 days
118	118	118	Net 15	Slow 60 to 90 days

Exhibit 2

ALLEN DISTRIBUTION COMPANY

LETTER FROM THE HARRISBURG FIDELITY AND TRUST COMPANY

Allen Distribution Company June 6, 1954
Philadelphia, Pennsylvania

Attention: Credit Manager

GENTLEMEN:

Morse Photo Company has maintained a satisfactory account with us for a number of years and such accommodation as we have extended them is cared for as agreed. It is our feeling that they are entitled to their reasonable trade requirements.

Yours very truly,

(*Signed*) GEORGE GRUBB
Assistant Vice-President
Harrisburg Fidelity and Trust Company

LETTER FROM A LARGE FILM MANUFACTURER

Allen Distribution Company June 4, 1954
Philadelphia, Pennsylvania

Attention: Credit Manager

GENTLEMEN:

Re: Morse Photo Company

With reference to your inquiry regarding the above account, we wish to advise that we have been doing business with them since 1948.

Recently we have had a fair amount of trouble with them because of overexpansion in relation to their net worth. In the past, customer's promises for payment could not be depended upon, although there has been a decided improvement in the last six months. Around the first of the year we had to take notes totaling $7,500 for the past-due accounts. At the present time $2,500 is still outstanding, but the notes are not in default. In April, we extended them $2,700 worth of credit, $2,600 of which was under the term ⅓ payable every ten days. The last payment was not received until June 1, whereas it was

Exhibit 2—Continued

due May 22. At the present time the concern owes us outside of the notes $115 of which $76.70 represents the April charge which is past due in our books.

To sum the whole thing up we are willing to extend credit up to $5,000 but must watch the account carefully.

Yours very truly,

(*Signed*) ALFRED WHITTIER
Credit Manager

LETTER FROM A LARGE CHEMICAL COMPANY

Allen Distribution Company   June 7, 1954
Philadelphia, Pennsylvania

Attention: Credit Manager

GENTLEMEN:

The following summary is the information you requested with respect to Morse Photo Company:

How Long Sold—May, 1952
Last Sale—June, 1954
Highest Credit—$700
Amount Owing—$700
Past Due—0
Terms—2% ten days
Amount Secured—None
Manner of Payment—Previous sales C.O.D.

This is a trial order on restricted credit terms. Future policy will be determined by payment record.

Yours very truly,

(*Signed*) ARNOLD HEAD
Credit Manager

LETTER FROM OLIVER ELECTRIC COMPANY

Allen Distribution Company   June 9, 1954
Philadelphia, Pennsylvania

Attention: Credit Manager

GENTLEMEN:

Re: Morse Photo Company
How Long Sold—July, 1949
Date of Last Sale—April, 1954
High Credit—$1,600
Amount Owing—$630
Past Due—$630
Terms—2% Ten End of the Month

Other comments:

We would suggest watching this account carefully. It has been up to nine months slow with us.

Yours very truly,

(*Signed*) J. E. STEWART
Credit Manager

Exhibit 3

ALLEN DISTRIBUTION COMPANY
MORSE PHOTO COMPANY
BALANCE SHEETS, APRIL 30, 1953, AND 1954
(Figured in even dollars)

ASSETS	April 30, 1954	April 30, 1953
Cash	$ 439	$ 320
Accounts receivable, net	16,201	11,503
Inventory at cost	12,681	12,712
Total current assets	$ 29,321	$24,535
Fixed assets:		
Cost	93,574	58,331
Depreciation	21,492	12,573
Net	$ 72,082	$45,758
Other assets	9,641	2,839
Total assets	$111,044	$73,132

LIABILITIES		
Accounts payable	$ 22,311	$ 9,953
Note payable—bank	9,360	5,136
Notes payable—other	15,158	9,127
Income tax	373	198
Other tax	2,546	3,123
Interest payable	96	. . . .
Payroll payable	1,514	. . . .
Total current liabilities	$ 51,358	$27,537
Other liabilities:		
Notes payable—officers	2,648	2,648
Notes payable—bank	. . . .	764
Notes payable—other	810	. . . .
Bond payable	14,000	. . . .
Total liabilities	$ 68,816	$30,949
Net worth:		
Preferred stock	10,000	10,000
Common stock	32,100	32,100
Earned surplus	128	83
Total net worth	$ 42,228	$42,183
Total liabilities and net worth	$111,044	$72,132

Exhibit 4

ALLEN DISTRIBUTION COMPANY

Morse Photo Company

Income Statements for Fiscal Years Ending April 30, 1953, and 1954

(Figured in even dollars)

	April 30, 1954	April 30, 1953
Net sales	$269,461	$162,898
Less cost of goods sold:		
Material	88,079	58,453
Wages	65,263	33,963
Other	44,049	28,841
Total cost of goods sold	$197,391	$121,257
Gross profit	72,070	41,641
Administrative and selling expense:		
Officers' salaries	22,000	12,000
Office salaries	10,000	5,733
Sales commissions	3,568	....
Depreciation	10,071	7,848
Other	25,613	15,779
Total administration and selling expense	$ 71,252	$ 41,360
Net earnings before tax	818	281
Income tax	373	198
Earnings	$ 445	$ 83
Dividends	400	nil
Earnings transferred to surplus	$ 45	$ 83

CONSOLIDATED MINING AND MANUFACTURING CORPORATION[1]

||

In the middle of 1949 the Consolidated Mining and Manufacturing Corporation was considering the storage of a reserve supply of the mineral impervium[1] in order to avoid a repetition of the severe losses which the company had incurred in 1948 after a stoppage of the supply of this mineral had forced the company to shut down the larger part of its manufacturing activities. The Consolidated Mining and Manufacturing Corporation comprised two divisions. Division A extracted ore containing the mineral impervium from a single mine in Mexico and separated the mineral from the ore at a mill located near the mine. Consolidated's production constituted about a half of the total North American production of impervium, the rest being divided among a number of smaller firms. A part of the impervium produced by Division A was sold by Consolidated to a number of outside concerns, but the larger part—about two-thirds of the total—was transferred to Consolidated's Division B. This division manufactured a wide variety of products for both industrial and domestic use. Some of these products contained impervium as an essential constituent, while others used none of the mineral.

In 1947 and 1948 Consolidated had had serious labor difficulties at its mine, culminating in a four-month strike.[2] These difficulties had had no repercussions among the labor force in the manufacturing plant of Division B, which was located in the United States about 800 miles from the mine in Mexico, but the loss of the company's impervium supply had ultimately forced the manufacturing plant to cease production of all products containing the mineral. The losses incurred by Division B as a result of this partial shutdown were so severe, and the labor situa-

---

[1] Fictitious name.

[2] Other impervium producers were not affected by this strike.

tion at the mine continued so unstable, that the president of the company, Mr. Adams, decided to study the possibility of storing a reserve supply of impervium large enough to permit continuous operation of the manufacturing plant in spite of any strike that might occur at the mine in the future.

Mr. Adams realized, however, that the creation and maintenance of such a reserve would involve a considerable investment, and feared that serious operating costs might be involved in addition. He decided, therefore, to have a systematic study made of both the costs involved in the storage scheme and the losses which might be incurred in the absence of such a scheme. The task of collecting and analyzing the necessary data he assigned to Mr. Fox, a young assistant whom he had just hired for this very purpose of making analyses of special problems outside of the ordinary routine of the business. Wishing to profit by as fresh a look as possible at the problem, Mr. Adams outlined the problem to his assistant very briefly. The only specific instructions and information which he gave Mr. Fox were the following:

1. The losses actually occurred as a result of the stoppage in 1948 were not to be considered a reliable basis for estimating losses in case of a future stoppage, since the sellers' market which had prevailed in 1947–1948 had made it possible to shift productive facilities from one product to another in a way which would not be possible under normal conditions. During a strike, Mr. Adams opined, a number of Consolidated's normal customers could be expected to defer shipment on their orders until the end of the strike, so that only about one-half of the normal sales volume for the strike period would be irretrievably lost. Moreover, in view of Consolidated's predominant position in the market, virtually all of the company's customers who had had their requirements temporarily filled by another supplier would return to Consolidated after the strike.

2. It was not a part of Mr. Fox's assignment to predict the exact frequency or duration of future strikes, since this was a decision for which Mr. Adams believed that he himself would have to take the responsibility. The labor situation was in such a state that he had not even reached a tentative decision as yet, although he was convinced that no strike was likely to last more than six months and told Mr. Fox that he need not consider the possibility of a longer strike.

3. Mr. Adams had already definitely decided that if storage facilities were built at all, they should be built in the United States. (Impervium entered the United States duty-free.) The most suitable location was on a 20-acre piece of property which had already been offered for sale to the company in whole or in part at a price of $500 an acre. This property was located a few miles from the plant of Division B and was on the railroad which connected the mine with the plant.

4. In considering the advisability of new capital expenditures, the company had usually been guided by a rule of thumb according to which the least acceptable return was 10% after taxes. (You may assume a tax rate of 50%.)

Mr. Adams told his assistant that he was free to request figures and other information from any department of the company. The first line of inquiry which Mr. Fox decided to pursue was determination of the magnitude of the losses which would be incurred by Division B in case of another stoppage of impervium supplies. For figures on the total amount of sales which would be lost in such a case, Mr. Fox applied to the sales department for information. This department had recently made an extensive study of the probable future annual sales of each of the company's products. The study consisted essentially of the projection on the basis of prewar sales of a "normal trend" for each of the company's products; sales were expected to fluctuate cyclically about this "normal trend." In computing this trend all values had been converted to 1949 prices by use of an "internal" price index, and the projection was on the same basis. A trend was computed separately for each of the company's products, and the total sales trend was simply the sum of the trends for the individual products. This "normal trend" of total sales by Division B showed a value of $70,000,000 for 1950, the first year in which the president expected a more or less normal market. The trend line had a slope of 3.27% per annum. To determine the effect of a stoppage of impervium supplies on the division's sales under normal conditions, Mr. Fox also obtained from the sales department a subtotal trend consisting simply of the total of the trends for all the products containing no impervium. This trend showed a value of $30,-000,000 for 1950, and had a slope of 2.98% per annum. The chart supplied by the sales department is shown in Exhibit 1.

In order to determine the net income which would be lost if the annual rate of sales fell from $70 to $30 million as a result of an impervium stoppage, Mr. Fox first turned to Mr. Walsh, the company's chief cost accountant. Mr. Walsh stated that the problem was very easy to solve, and that he could supply not only the cost figures corresponding to the total predicted sales of $70 million but also a breakdown of these costs into those chargeable to the products containing impervium and those with none of the mineral. This was possible, he said, because standards of hours and materials per unit of product had been carefully set up before the war, and actual performance had been found to be very close to these standards over a long period of time, the only notable exceptions being due to abnormal wartime conditions which had already virtually disappeared. At Mr. Fox's request, Mr. Walsh prepared such a prediction and breakdown on the basis of the volume of sales forecast for 1950, using the current prices for labor and materials. In accordance with the standard policy of the company, established by top management, the cost of the impervium transferred from Division A to Division B was taken at the price F.O.B. mine at which the company sold to outsiders, plus freight from the mine to the plant of Division B. Indirect expenses were allocated to products in the same ratio as their sale value bore to the total sales of the division. Mr. Walsh's figures are shown in Exhibit 2.

Despite Mr. Walsh's confidence in the accuracy of his figures, Mr. Fox was hesitant to accept them, especially as an indication of what the costs would be if only those products were produced which contained no impervium, since he knew that allocation of costs to specific products was generally considered to be difficult and at best somewhat imprecise. As a check on Mr. Walsh's figures, he decided to get the historical costs of operation at a time when total sales amounted to approximately the same sum as the sales department predicted for impervium-free products alone in 1950. Looking at the chart supplied by the sales department, he observed that the year with total sales closest to $30,000,000 was 1920, and he asked the accounting department to supply him with the operating statement for that year. As a double check he asked the accounting department itself to check through all the operating statements and send him the one with total sales closest to $30,000,000. In response to these requests, the accounting department sent him the operating statements for 1920 and 1928, shown in Exhibit 3.

Mr. Fox was considerably puzzled by the inconsistencies among the statements of costs which he had thus obtained, and after studying them for some went in person to the accounting department to see if he could obtain any additional information on the probable behavior of costs if sales should be reduced to about $30 million. Here he was referred to the section in charge of the annual budget, which he was told was the only possible source of information in addition to that which he had already been given. In the budget section he learned that preparation of the budget for 1950 was only beginning, but he was given the following data on the Division B cost budget for 1949:

Direct labor and materials: Expected to vary directly with sales, since the company sold at a uniform markup, and since the company had always followed a policy of immediately releasing workers for whom no work was available.

Factory burden: $1,200,000 fixed expense per month plus $1.057 per dollar of direct labor.

Selling expense: $250,000 fixed expense per month plus $0.05 per dollar of sales.

Administrative and general expense: $135,000 per month plus $0.0125 per dollar of sales.

Further inquiry around the company's offices failed to produce any additional information on the variation of costs with volume, and Mr. Fox turned to the problem of the calculation of the cost of storing a reserve supply of impervium. His first step was to inquire into the existing storage facilities of Division B, and he was told that the very limited space at the manufacturing plant held about ten days' supply at the current rate of consumption. Supplies arrived almost continuously, and since about five days were required in transit from the mine to the plant, this meant that about five days' supply was in transit at any time.

For figures on the cost of the stored impervium, Mr. Fox first got in touch directly with Mr. Spear, the general manager of Division A. Mr. Spear stated that provided that he was not obliged to increase his current rate of production by more than 4,000 tons a month, the "out-of-pocket" cost of the additional production would be $17.35 per ton at the mine. The only other information which Mr. Fox could find on the current cost of producing the mineral was in the company's operating statement for the first six months of 1949, which had just been prepared for internal use. This statement showed a profit for Division A of $319,000 before taxes on a total production of 61,500 tons, all of which had been either sold to outsiders or transferred to Division B at a price of $37.50 per ton F.O.B. mine.

For figures on the cost of building and operating a storage warehouse, Mr. Adams had told his assistant to employ the firm of consulting engineers which the company had used for a number of years on all of its construction projects and whose estimates had always proved very reliable. This firm supplied estimates of costs and of useful lives for warehouses of three different capacities as specified by Mr. Fox; these estimates are shown in Exhibit 4.

Questions

1. Should Consolidated Mining and Manufacturing Corporation build a warehouse to store impervium?

2. Assuming that a strike of three-month duration will occur randomly one year out of four, how big a warehouse should be built?

3. Recognizing Mr. Adams' uncertainty about the frequency and duration of future strikes, how would you recommend he proceed to reach a decision on this problem?

Exhibit 1

CONSOLIDATED MINING AND MANUFACTURING CORPORATION

SALES RECORDS AND PROJECTIONS

(All values in 1949 dollars)

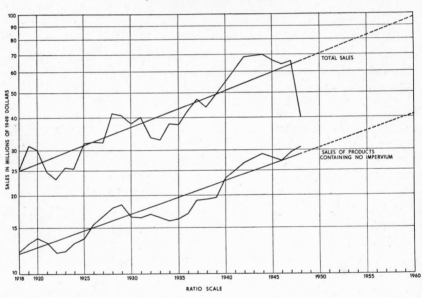

Exhibit 2

CONSOLIDATED MINING AND MANUFACTURING CORPORATION

DIVISION B, PROJECTED COSTS OF OPERATION, 1950

(Based on sales department's forecast of sales)

(All amounts in thousands)

	Products Containing Impervium		Products Containing No Impervium		Total	
	Amount	%	Amount	%	Amount	%
Sales	$40,000	100.0	$30,000	100.0	$70,000	100.0
Manufacturing costs:						
Direct labor	$ 6,150	15.4	$ 4,350	14.5	$10,500	15.0
Direct materials	7,350*	18.4	3,650	12.2	11,000	15.7
Factory burden	15,100	37.7	10,400	34.7	25,500	36.5
Division B expenses:						
Salesmen, sales office, and promotion costs	3,700	9.2	2,800	9.3	6,500	9.3
Administrative and general	1,450	3.6	1,050	3.5	2,500	3.6
Real and property taxes	550	1.4	450	1.5	1,000	1.4
General Corporation expenses allocated to Division B	2,550	6.4	1,950	6.5	4,500	6.4
Total cost and expense	$36,850	92.1	$24,650	82.2	$61,500	87.9
Estimated profit before taxes	$ 3,150	7.9	$ 5,350	17.8	$ 8,500	12.1

* Including $3 million for 80,000 tons of impervium transferred from Division A at $37.50 per ton. The freight charges on these shipments of $973,600 is a part of the remaining $4,350,000 of direct materials.

Exhibit 3

CONSOLIDATED MINING AND MANUFACTURING CORPORATION

DIVISION B, OPERATING STATEMENTS, 1920 AND 1928

(Not adjusted to 1949 dollars)

	1920		1928	
	Amount	%	Amount	%
Sales	$13,598	100.0	$30,239	100.0
Manufacturing costs:				
Direct labor	$ 1,619	11.9	$ 3,998	13.2
Direct materials	1,895*	13.9	4,169†	13.8
Factory burden	3,932	28.9	8,144	26.9
Division B expenses:				
Salesmen, sales office, and promotion	1,827	13.4	4,018	13.3
Administrative and general	748	5.5	1,087	3.6
Real and property taxes	54	0.4	73	0.2
General Corporation expense allocation	1,122	8.3	2,281	7.6
Total cost and expenses	$11,197	82.3	$23,770	78.6
Profit before taxes	$ 2,401	17.7	$ 6,469	21.4

* Including $931,500 (before freight) for impervium transferred from Division A.
† Including $2,398,500 (before freight) for impervium transferred from Division A.

Exhibit 4

CONSOLIDATED MINING AND MANUFACTURING CORPORATION

COSTS OF WAREHOUSING IMPERVIUM

CAPITAL INVESTMENT

	Life* (Years)	Cost of Facilities for Storing		
		10,000 Tons	20,000 Tons	40,000 Tons
Land..	....	$ 1,000	$ 2,000	$ 4,000
Land improvements:				
Railways, grading sewers, etc......................	25	8,500	10,000	12,500
Water supply, electrical connections................	20	10,000	10,000	10,000
Driveways.......................................	15	3,500	4,500	7,000
Buildings...	40	123,500	217,000	394,000
Equipment..	10	9,500	9,500	9,500
		$156,000	$253,000	$437,000

EXPENSES

Operating costs.....................................	$ 1,500	$ 1,750	$ 2,000
Real and property taxes............................	13,000	24,000	45,500
Insurance..	1,000	2,000	3,500

MEMORANDUM APPENDED TO THE ENGINEERS' REPORT

"Up to the present no method of shipment and storage has been found practical for impervium other than in cloth bags. Unless these bags are replaced every five years, there is serious danger that they will rot and that the mineral they contain will be lost or spoiled. It would be difficult to transfer the stored mineral from old bags into new ones, and would probably be cheaper to renew the stored mineral on a rotation basis. We estimate that the cost of removing mineral from the warehouse and trucking it to the factory, plus the cost of unloading fresh supplies from the freight cars and placing it in the warehouse, will amount to $3.667 per ton exchanged, this figure being in addition to the cost of operating the warehouse given in our estimate above."

* This estimate of the physical life of the facilities would also be used for income tax determination (straight-line depreciation).

CHESTER GOLD CORPORATION

Shortly after 10:20 A.M. on October 27, 1960, Mr. E. G. Byers, purchasing manager for the Chester Gold Corporation of Philadelphia, Pennsylvania, received his usual morning telephone call detailing the opening of the New York Cocoa Exchange. As he jotted down figures quoted by the broker who had called, Mr. Byers noted that the market had risen slightly from the previous day's close, contrary to the pattern of softness and lack of buyer interest which had prevailed for several weeks. According to the broker, the rise was due to a cable received by the exchange that morning from Dr. Felio Tosta, director of the Brazilian Cocoa Trade Commission. The message expressed doubt that the current year's cocoa harvest in Brazil would live up to earlier expectations, and indicated that quite possibly no additional shipping contracts of Bahia cocoa would be made for the 1960–1961 season. To Mr. Byers, this news served to point up the need for finalizing the Gold company's cocoa purchasing strategy for the current season.

The present upswing in the market, Mr. Byers realized, was probably more a reflection of various "short" interests attempting to cover positions they had taken believing that the Bahia yield would be higher than an indication of what the cocoa market would do generally. But at the same time he believed that in view of the Gold company's present cocoa position, and because of the company's unusual financial situation, Gold would do well to formulate a general policy concerning cocoa purchases which would encompass the many relevant factors and provide a framework within which his activities, as purchasing manager, could be performed. He therefore decided to organize and consolidate his own thinking on the matter, and to present his views as soon as possible to various other company executives.

The Chester Gold Corporation, which operated as an independent company although it had been purchased by one of the nation's larger food-processing firms in 1958, was a long-established manufacturer of high-quality candies. The Gold company's product lines included more than 200 varieties of candy, packaged in approximately 700 combinations. These products ranged from 5-cent candy bars to $5 boxes of fancy candy, and all were nationally marketed. In 1959, roughly 60% of Gold's nearly $23 million in sales stemmed from the fancy, or boxed, candy lines; bulk candy, hard and bar candy, and miscellaneous or speciality items accounted for the remainder. The 60% figure represented a sizable gain over preceding years and reflected improved marketing of fancy candy products.

Sales of candy were characterized by large seasonal swings, particularly for boxed products. Typically the periods of greatest consumer demand fell between Halloween and Mother's day, with Christmas or Valentine's day marking the high point. To the manufacturer, these seasonal sales characteristics meant that deliveries began to pick up in August or September, peaked in December or January, and then tapered off rapidly to midsummer lows. Monthly sales in the latter period were often less than 15% of those during the peak winter months. Virtually all sales were made to franchised distributors who were able to service the numerous local outlets serving the consumer market.

Gold's manufacturing process was "intermittent." Beans were processed into chocolate in batches, and each of the six chocolates used were then stored in vats. Similarly, fillings were produced in batches. In the coating process, the "factory" made long runs of single pieces of candy for economic reasons. These were stored for subsequent packing. The chocolate vats typically contained one-half week's supply of material stored pending production, and there normally was at least another half-week's supply of finished pieces in storage at any one time. Even in the periods of lowest finished goods inventories, production could usually be scheduled in advance to suit the convenience of the factory without fear of substantial interruption because of rush orders.

The Chester Gold Corporation's sales volume had been expanding significantly since the mid 1950's, following several years of relatively stable performance (Exhibit 1). New top management, strongly oriented toward an aggressive marketing policy, succeeded in raising sales from slightly more than $16 million in 1955 to $22,699,000 in 1959; and for 1960, recently revised forecasts indicated that sales revenues would exceed $27 million. Despite expanding volume, however, the effect of increased sales on corporate finances had not proven severe until the spring of 1960. Gold's plant and facilities were quite modern, and substantial excess capacity had (and still) existed so that modest repair and improvement expenditures had been easily financed from depreciation resources. Retained earnings, plus cash funds available at the low point in seasonal funds needs, had until recently been adequate to meet permanent working capital requirements; temporary capital required to cover seasonal peaks had been met through borrowings from local banks. Although the company had always attempted to produce as levelly as possible, the fact that the production department has underestimated sales by significant margins in each of the past several years had reduced inventories of finished goods below expectations in the late winter and early spring months, and facilitated cleaning up the short-term loans at that time. A contraction in the size of raw material inventories had also been helpful in this regard since 1958.

In the spring of 1960, however, Gold for the first time had been unable to liquidate its seasonal loans from internal sources. This fact was especially troublesome because a term loan negotiated by the firm which now owned Gold carried a proviso whereby consolidated borrowings of the two firms were to be cleaned up annually, and to meet this requirement Gold was forced to borrow $900,000 directly from the parent organization. (Exhibit 2 includes a monthly summary of the Gold company's borrowing during the past 24 months.) Such intracompany loans did not appear on the consolidated statements and thus did not violate the loan agreement; but since the parent company was also expanding rapidly and had increasing needs for funds itself, there was some doubt as to whether it would have sufficient excess funds to make a similar arrangement in the future. Moreover, since the seasonal lows of the two firms coincided, considerable pressure was on Gold to clean up its own loans in the spring. The principal alternative, raising long-term debt capital to finance Gold's permanent fund needs, also posed parent-subsidiary financial complications which Gold's management preferred not to face until there was reliable evidence that such action would bring about substantial benefits; but if additional capital were required, Gold's needs would have to be justified in terms of promising returns of better than 10% after taxes. In view of the foregoing, the liquidation of seasonal loans in the spring of 1961 was an important factor in all phases of the Gold company's current planning activities.

Despite the marked improvement in sales outlook, profits for the Gold company were not expected to improve in 1960 over the preceding year. Increased production, especially since some of it had not been forecasted, had led to disproportionately higher processing costs in the spring and summer of 1960, pending adjustment of the production process to higher rates. Labor costs, also, had increased during the year, and costs of some raw materials (primarily "box" goods) had gone up. These factors, combined with the fact that retail prices for candy goods were quite inflexible, resulted in a cost-price squeeze. Consumers resisted price increases relative to other "gift" opportunities (and fancy candies were normally sold for gift purposes), with the result that retail price increases almost invariably resulted in greatly reduced demand. Although many manufacturers reacted to cost increases by maintaining their prices but using less expensive, lower-quality ingredients, or by reducing the size of their products, Gold's management had always adhered rigorously to the high-quality features of the company's products. Company officials were convinced that "quality tells over time" and that consumer differentiation was sufficiently acute so that a lessening of quality would do permanent harm to the company's excellent reputation. Even for cost-cutting firms, profit margins remained slim, with 2% after-tax profit on sales reflecting average industry experience in 1959; and as a consequence of the margin squeeze, management did not expect retained earnings in 1960 to exceed $400,000 (after payment of a $100,000 dividend to the parent company), with depreciation less planned capital expenditures providing an additional $300,000 in funds for working capital over the same period.

One of the critical areas in which the cost-price squeeze created pressures pertained to the purchasing and processing of raw materials for candy. Gold was one of the few fancy candy producers which had remained vertically integrated. The company produced both fillings and coatings for its products, as opposed to other producers who merely combined commercially manufactured materials into finished products. By so doing, Gold was able to realize certain production economies and to control quality standards more closely than otherwise would have been possible; but at the same time, the company was forced into the position of having to deal in commodities with highly volatile price patterns. By far the most significant of these were cocoa beans, the raw material from which chocolate was manufactured.

The timing of cocoa purchases to take advantage of favorable prices was of considerable importance to Gold. In 1959, for example, the cost of cocoa used in the manufacturing process was equivalent to almost 7% of company sales revenues, and comprised approximately 14% of the value of all raw materials included in cost of goods sold. The average price of this cocoa was nearly 37 cents per pound (much of it having been contracted for in the fall of 1958), so that a difference of only 1 cent per pound on all cocoa purchased would have altered the company's pretax profits by about $37,000. Actually, as may be seen from Exhibits 5 and 7, the price of cocoa fluctuated by far more than 1 cent per pound during the year.

The price of cocoa had been in fairly steady decline for the past two years. In July, 1958, "spot" Accra in New York (which, in the industry, was usually taken to be the representative price) had sold at 48.9 cents per pound; by September, 1960, the comparable price was less than 28 cents. The decline was largely the result of successively more bountiful harvests in the 1958–1959 and 1959–1960 seasons, and of prospects for an even better year in 1960–1961. Harvest prospects were one of the two major influences on cocoa prices, the other being economic or political conditions in the cocoa producing countries.

The 1960–1961 harvest outlook was generally bright around the world for two reasons: first, physical factors in the growing countries were favorable. Climatic conditions through the summer of 1960 had been ideal; damage from cocoa tree diseases such as "swollen shoot" or sahlbergella, or from insect pests such as the cocoa moth, was expected to be unusually light; and early indications of yield, based on the number of bean pods evident on cocoa trees during the early stages of ripening, led many authorities to predict that 1960–1961 would produce the best harvest ever. Harvest time was still from one to six months away, depending on geographic location of the various growing areas, and these conditions could alter radically before the crop was in; but the market, in October, 1960, did not appear particularly concerned with this possibility.

The second reason for optimism about the 1960–1961 harvest stemmed from an expected increase during the year in the productive cocoa tree population. Several years earlier (in 1953–1954), cocoa had been in very short supply, and during this period many new trees were planted. These trees were only now coming to maturity and beginning to bear fruit. Their presence would probably augment

1960–1961 production by 5–10%, and in succeeding years by even more.

The influence of economic and political conditions in cocoa producing countries on cocoa prices was more difficult to interpret than the influence of harvest prospects, although potentially these factors could have a tremendous impact. One such consideration in October, 1960, pertained to efforts by cocoa growers in some areas to stabilize the price they were paid for their production. Under their plan, the growers would receive a set price for all beans harvested, in good years and in bad. If such guaranteed prices were established, their presence would stabilize the bottom side of the market at prices which most authorities conceded would be at least 5 cents or more per pound above the current level. Interest in the plan was particularly prevalent in Brazil, but the idea had also gained popularity in various African states, particularly those which had but recently gained independence. While attempts to institute the plan did not appear likely to succeed in 1960–1961, it was possible that the market effect of an extremely high harvest would add enough momentum to the idea so that price guarantees would be enforced in the 1961–1963 or 1962–1963 seasons.

Another possibility which could have a similar effect on the cocoa market was that the United States government, particularly under a new administration, might endeavor to support higher prices for commodities produced in "less developed" countries. Although such support could take several forms, the result for the cocoa bean user would almost surely be higher material costs. As in the case of price stabilization by the growers, the likelihood of this measure being taken in the current year was extremely remote. Nevertheless, there was widespread belief among persons active in the cocoa market that the presence of these two possibilities would effectively prohibit the price of cocoa (in terms of spot Accra) from falling much below 22 cents per pound, with the absolute bottom at 20 cents per pound.

Influences of a more short-range nature than the above were constantly operating in the cocoa market, affecting the day-to-day prices. The cable from Dr. Tosta was an example. By modifying previous estimates of the important Brazilian cocoa production, Dr. Tosta changed the basis on which cocoa transactions had been taking place. Were Bahia cocoa to be in short supply during 1960–1961, chocolate manufacturers who used Bahia beans would either have to pay more to fulfill their needs or they would be forced to use other, comparable beans in their processes. Their efforts to purchase substitute beans would increase the demand, and the price, for those items. Because of this obvious price effect, however, many purchasers were inclined to discount pronouncements from the marketing agencies of producing countries, at least until further substantiation of reduced prospects was available. In Mr. Byers opinion, the Tosta telegram would not produce a significant change in the market for several weeks because of this fact, although if additional pessimistic indications were received the market response could be sizable, amounting to perhaps 5 cents per pound for many beans.

In addition to general market considerations, Gold's cocoa purchasing problems were complicated by the fact that nine and sometimes ten distinctly different beans were required to produce the company's six basic coatings (Exhibits 3 and 4 present detailed information on the various beans used by the company). Quality standards severely limited the degree to which one bean could be substituted for another. Of Gold's requirements, only Bahia beans could be replaced without seriously altering the characteristics of the coatings in which they were used. Either Accra beans or Lagos beans (from Nigeria) could be used in place of Bahia, although the reverse was not true and Bahia could not be substituted for Accra. There was, however, some freedom to change the mix of coatings used in various fancy candy assortments, and thereby make small adjustments to the amount of specific beans required in any given year (Exhibit 3 gives the composition of each major coating). In the past the production department had been able to make such changes when, for one reason or another, certain beans were out of stock and impossible to procure.

The cocoa beans used by Gold were grown in different parts of the world, principally Africa and South America. Since the characteristics of the beans differed from area to area, the company was dependent on the success of several different crops for its supplies. In addition, since other manufacturers were often willing to make substitutions on the basis of price differentials, Gold's profit margin and competitive position were affected by the success of other crops for which the company itself had no need.

Harvest times for cocoa varied with both geographical area and climatic conditions. Bahia cocoa, for example, usually matured between December and March, while Accra (from Ghana) was normally ready for shipment two or three months earlier. So-called

"Seasons Arriba" cocoa, from Equador, matured in two crops: the first coming between September and December; the second between December and April.[1] Inasmuch as the harvest peaks changed from year to year, prices of the various cocoas were often affected by whether the crop came in early or late during the season. In 1960, indications were for an early crop in Africa and a normal crop in South America.

Two basic types of purchase contracts could be negotiated. Under a "delivery" agreement (which Gold used almost exclusively), the broker agreed to deliver a specified quantity of a particular type and grade of bean sometime during a specified month within the shipping period. Typically such a contract involved a premium of $\frac{1}{2}$ cent per pound over the more widely used "shipment contract," wherein the seller agreed only to ship the desired beans from the port of origin at sometime during a specified three-month period. Although most frequently shipping dates fell in the middle month of this period, shipment could and did occur at either extreme, depending largely upon the availability of dockside stocks and appropriate carrier vessels. Shipping times varied depending upon the area of the world in which the originating port was located, but this factor was fairly predictable. From African ports, shipment ordinarily took 30–40 days; and from South America (Brazil), shipping time was approximately 20–30 days.

Although Gold was not an important factor in the market for any specific type of cocoa (the company's purchases did not exceed 1% of the supply for any type), certain "flavor beans" such as "Trinidad," "Agua Clara," or "Seasons Arriba" usually had to be purchased prior to the harvest season to insure an adequate supply. The market for these beans was relatively small, and speculators (brokers or warehousers who were willing to buy beans on shipment and store them, hoping for more favorable prices later) were reluctant to take a position in them. Consequently, once the shipping season was over, few or none of these beans were available from warehouse stocks. As a result, Mr. Byers' principal decisional discretion for these beans related to the timing of purchase contracts. In the past two years, prices had tended to decline in these beans by 4 to 6 cents per pound

---

[1] The above dates refer to the "main" and largest crop; additional crops, the "mid" or intermediate harvest, matured during the May–August period in certain growing areas. This mid-crop, however, was small by comparison with the main crop, and for Gold it was unsuitable for the production of coatings.

between the earliest contract date and the harvest time. If supply or demand factors changed materially as the harvest came near, however, prices could rise sharply. In 1957, for example, the failure of roughly 10% of the expected Trinidad crop to materialize forced prices for that bean to soar by 30% at the beginning of the harvest season.

For more widely used beans, such as Accra, Sanchez, or Bahia, secondary sources existed from which Gold could usually supplement its supplies after the growing season was concluded. Brokers offered contracts specifying delivery several months after the shipping period, which they would cover with purchases of their own before the season had ended. Typically, such contracts involved a premium of three-fourths of a cent per pound per month above the market price at the time of negotiation, for each month following the season. The premium covered the broker's storage costs and provided him with a small profit. There was also a significant speculative (spot) market in primary beans where prices were relatively more volatile, as evidenced by the spot Accra prices shown in Exhibit 5. Over the past two years those who had purchased on the spot market had generally fared quite well, to the detriment of the speculators. This was due to declining prices over the period which had meant that prices for future deliveries were almost invariably higher than spot prices at the time of delivery.

The Gold Company did not have an effective means of "hedging" its price exposure in cocoa beans, and was per force involved in cocoa speculation. Hedging was usually accomplished by selling a "futures" contract at the time a purchase was made. By this device the purchaser could protect himself against the possibility of price change over the period he held the purchased cocoa in inventory. If the price was to decline, he could buy back his contract at a lower price, making up his inventory loss on the profit from his short sale. If the price rose, his inventory would presumably be more valuable by an equal amount. For Gold, however, the latter was not the case, since price increases could not easily be passed on to the public through higher retail prices and an upgraded inventory value merely reduced profits. Moreover, futures contracts were always made in terms of the cheapest bean on the market, and the price of these beans did not necessarily fluctuate in the same way as the price for some of the more specialized beans used at Gold.

In order to assure that the manufacture of chocolate coatings proceeded smoothly, Gold's management had elected to follow a protective cocoa inventory policy. Sufficient cocoa to cover "anticipated" production requirements for the forthcoming three months was maintained as a minimum stock at all times. Cocoa purchases, therefore, had to be scheduled in relation to anticipated production at least three months hence. During periods when cocoa was not being harvested, greater supplies had to be held on hand or on firm order to provide the desired level of protection. This protective policy, however, had not been the subject of critical review for several years, during which both the nature of Gold's demand and the price structure of the cocoa market had changed materially.

As of October 27, 1960, Gold held in stock sufficient cocoa of most types to meet forecasted production rates for the next four months (see Exhibit 4). These stocks had been acquired at an average cost of 30.62 cents per pound. In addition, purchase commitments due for delivery during the next three months could cover production needs for two additional months. The beans on order were priced at an average of 27.41 cents per pound. The discrepancy between these average prices and the apparent existing market was due to the fact that the largest portion of the beans on order, as well as on hand, was composed of lower-grade items such as Sanchez beans. Over a period of time, Gold's average price on all beans typically would be approximately 4–6 cents per pound above the price of Accra.

The recent surge in sales had placed pressures on both the production scheduling and the purchasing departments. For example, the original sales estimate for 1960 appeared by the middle of October to be nearly $2.4 million short of what actual performance would be. Moreover, the production department had regarded the original 1960 sales forecast as overoptimistic and had initially scheduled production at a more conservative rate. The production rate had been increased throughout 1960 and particularly sharply in July to avoid depletion of finished goods stocks during the peak selling season. This action, in turn, had forced Mr. Byers to step up cocoa purchases in the off-season. Fortunately, prices had fallen so that no adverse cost consequences materialized from these spot purchases.

The outlook for 1961 was again somewhat confused. Sales personnel were confidently predicting sales of $33.5 million, and in fact thought $35 million a more likely level, with $37.5 million a distinct possibility. On the other hand, production personnel were reluctant to plan on producing for a higher level than $32 million in sales, at

least initially, for fear of accumulating excess finished goods inventories. As sales (seasonally adjusted) began exceeding production schedules, production rates would be adjusted upward. Thus, as
Mr. Byers began planning his purchase schedules for the balance of
1960 and the remainder of the cocoa crop season, he was highly
uncertain whether bean requirements would be 6.0 million or 7.1
million pounds, corresponding with requirements for sales of $32 or
$37.5 million. Moreover, he was uncertain whether production rates in
the final six months of 1961 would be at a $32 million level or at a $40
million level.

Mr. Byers' problem was further complicated by the fact that there
was still uncertainty as to what the sales breakdown by specific
products would be in 1961. He had heard opinions expressed that
the national economy would undergo a mild recession in 1961, and
from experience he knew that in relatively unprosperous years consumers were more interested in bar candy than in fancy assortments.
Whereas in 1960 sales of fancy candies had far outstripped those of
bar candy (bar candy accounted for about 25% of total sales), in
1961 bar candy might be a more popular item. Such a situation, as
evidenced in Exhibit 3, would significantly alter the company's needs
for specific beans.

Among the many cocoa brokers with whom Mr. Byers regularly
talked, he had found little agreement as to what direction the market
would take in the future. Several brokers ventured the opinion that
prices would hold at low levels at least through the current season
(until May, 1961) and possibly for the next year; but others declared
that three outstanding years of cocoa production in a row was highly
unusual, and to expect a fourth was foolhardy. They reasoned that
prices might start moving upward as early as March, 1961, if there
were early indications at that time of a less successful harvest in the
1961–1962 season. Mr. Byers felt that a good concensus of opinion
had been expressed by the broker who recently had written: "This
is a topsy-turvy world we live in, especially at this time. Therefore,
we believe it would be prudent to at least buy on the declines or, in
any event, build up a good substantial inventory of supply."

This last suggestion, Mr. Byers knew, was one Gold could afford
to follow at the moment if cocoa storage were the only consideration.
The company maintained warehouse space on its premises adequate
to hold as much as 15 million pounds of cocoa. Since most costs
associated with the facility were fixed, the incremental expense

(excluding financial costs) of storing additional beans would amount to only 1 cent per pound per year.

Mr. Byers also knew, however, that Gold was especially cramped for adequate finished goods storage space; existing facilities were capable of holding finished inventories with values up to roughly $5.5 million. In recent months, the company had paid out $30,000 (a figure that was likely to increase substantially in future years if production volume rose) to rent public space to house excess finished goods inventories. At the moment, the company's comptroller was studying a proposal to spend $100,000 for converting the raw material storage facilities, in part, into space suitable for warehousing finished candy. If this proposal were adopted, there would be room to store only 2.0 million pounds of raw beans. Any excess beans would then have to be stored in local public warehouses (specifically suited for the purpose) at a cost of $0.01 per pound per month. Mr. Byers knew he would have to comment on this proposal shortly.

As the final background consideration for his analysis, Mr. Byers knew that Gold's top management had become quite "cost conscious." Recent profits had proven somewhat disappointing, and various executives from the parent company had exerted pressure to increase profits as well as sales in 1961.

Exhibit 1

CHESTER GOLD CORPORATION

INCOME STATEMENTS, 1958 AND 1959, NINE MONTHS 1959 AND 1960

(Dollar amounts in thousands)

	Year				Nine Months			
	1959	%	1958	%	1960	%	1959	%
Net sales	$22,600	100.0	$20,090	100.0	$15,610	100.0	$12,870	100.0
Cost of goods sold	17,290	76.5	15,900	79.1	11,670	74.8	9,410	73.1
Gross profit	$ 5,310	23.5	$ 4,190	20.9	$ 3,940	25.2	$ 3,460	26.9
Operating expenses	3,730	16.5	3,150	15.7	3,530	22.6	2,831	22.0
Operating profit	$ 1,580	7.0	$ 1,040	5.2	$ 410	2.6	$ 629	4.9
Other income†	112		118		137		90	
Total income	$ 1,692		$ 1,158		$ 547		$ 719	
Other expenses‡	854		705		494		525	
Profit before taxes	$ 838		$ 453		$ 53		$ 194	
Federal income taxes	436		227		27		107	
Profit after taxes	$ 402		$ 226		$ 26		$ 87	

*Sales and profits in prior years were as follows (in thousands of dollars):

Year	Sales	Profit after tax
1955	$16,320	$353
1956	17,230	217
1957	18,760	81

† Includes discounts earned.
‡ Includes discounts given and contribution to profit sharing trust.

Exhibit 2

CHESTER GOLD CORPORATION

SELECTED INCOME STATEMENT AND BALANCE SHEET ACCOUNTS—OCTOBER, 1957–SEPTEMBER, 1960

(Dollar amounts in thousands)

| | Income Accounts | | | Balance Sheet Accounts (E.O.M.) | | | | | | |
	Sales	Production	Raw Material to Production	Accounts Receivable	Total Inventory	Finished Goods	Total Raw Material	Cocoa Beans	Notes Payable	Total Assets
1958:										
October	n.a.	n.a.	$ 941	$1,077	$ 7,490	$4,741	$1,024	$ 270	$1,900	$14,578
November	n.a.	n.a.	846	1,904	6,670	3,877	1,135	283	1,900	15,021
December	n.a.	n.a.	886	2,315	5,716	2,821	2,313	333	500	13,990
1959:										
January	$2,551	$1,516	936	2,028	5,239	2,173	1,412	599	-0-	13,467
February	1,689	1,277	721	1,428	5,361	2,127	1,555	789	-0-	13,402
March	1,282	1,189	645	1,127	5,752	2,295	1,784	816	-0-	13,505
April	911	1,462	813	903	6,391	2,975	1,665	827	-0-	13,555
May	667	1,238	684	699	7,256	3,739	1,811	853	950	14,357
June	583	1,210	698	765	8,073	4,530	1,826	839	1,900	14,903
July*	463	988	610	791	8,632	4,982	1,771	808	3,100	15,765
August	1,148	1,492	940	1,239	9,574	5,597	2,169	1,013	3,800	16,708
September	3,046	2,286	1,501	2,650	9,293	5,543	2,002	824	4,300	17,934
October	2,718	1,801	1,131	2,504	8,447	5,163	1,490	610	3,700	17,146
November	3,707	1,803	1,170	3,771	7,370	4,075	1,443	552	3,700	17,551
December	3,853	2,016	1,303	3,156	6,406	3,130	1,399	461	1,800	15,842
1960:										
January	2,745	1,731	1,075	3,214	5,837	2,658	1,321	492	2,200	16,004
February	2,242	1,428	830	2,215	5,766	2,361	1,557	693	900†	14,781
March	1,732	1,883	1,088	1,538	6,623	2,944	1,857	791	600†	14,752
April	1,365	1,463	851	1,337	6,947	3,327	1,892	777	1,400	14,791
May	918	1,648	957	950	7,968	4,255	1,935	716	1,900	15,411
June	790	1,980	1,165	1,013	9,334	5,470	1,957	633	3,600	17,086
July*	670	1,056	679	933	9,701	5,802	1,753	438	4,300	17,606
August	1,508	2,407	1,623	1,717	10,716	6,743	1,605	454	6,400	19,734
September	3,640	1,729	1,085	3,109	9,635	5,575	1,517	491	6,400	20,123

* In July the company closed down for approximately 14 days for employee vacations and equipment maintenance.
† Borrowed from parent company to liquidate bank notes.
n.a. Not available.

Exhibit 3

CHESTER GOLD CORPORATION

COMPOSITION AND RELATIVE USAGE OF VARIOUS COATINGS

	Composition		*% of Total Coatings Produced†*			
Coating Name	*Type of Cocoa*	*% of Total Cocoa Used*	*9 mos. 1960*	*1959*	*1958*	*1957*
Ordinary No. 100 (milk chocolate)*..	Accra	66.6	38	35	34	39
	Trinidad	33.4				
Ordinary No. 200 (bittersweet)*......	Sanchez	63.8	22	20	20	24
	S. Arriba	36.2				
Fancy coating No. 300 (special)......	Agua Clara	31.0				
	S. Arriba	24.9	15	17	12	12
	Cameroon	12.7				
	Panamara	12.7				
	Trinidad	18.7				
Fancy coating No. 400 (bitter).......	Accra	12.5				
	Agua Clara	30.0	14	15	17	13
	S. Arriba	20.8				
	Bahia	12.5				
	Sanchez	18.5				
	Trinidad	5.7				
Fancy coating No. 500 (dark)........	Accra	11.9				
	Agua Clara	10.7	8	9	13	10
	S. Arriba	20.6				
	Bahia	11.9				
	Sanchez	18.7				
	San Thomé	26.2				
Fancy coating No. 600 (especial).....	Accra	14.3	3	4	4	2
	S. Arriba	28.6				
	Bahia	14.3				
	Trinidad	42.8				

* Approximately 10% of these coatings were used for fancy candies, 80% for candy bars, and 10% for miscellaneous items.

† Coating usage was somewhat seasonal and less predictable on a month-to-month basis.

Exhibit 4

Holdings and Commitments for Cocoa as of October 27, 1960 (in Thousands of Pounds)

Information About Various Beans

Type of Bean	Amount on Hand	Total on Order	Amount Each Contract	Contract Delivery Month	Contract Cost per Pound	Type of Bean	Country Where Grown	Appropriate Harvest Season	1960-1961 Prospects	"Normal" Price Relation to Spot Accra	Current Price Spot	Current Price Nov.-Dec.	Current Price Jan.-Mar.
Accra	155.7	200.0	100.0	Dec.	28.00¢	Base Grade	Ghana	Sept.–Jan.	Excellent	...	26.50¢	26.63¢	26.88¢
			100.0	Jan.	27.63								
Agua Clara	297.6	75.0	75.0	Jan.	27.88	Flavor	Venezuala	Nov.–Feb.	Good	+5.0¢	30.25	30.00	30.25
Bahia	142.1	....				Base grade	Brazil	Sept.–Dec.	Fair	–1.5	26.50	26.38	26.75
Cameroon	25.0	....				Base grade	Cameroons	Sept.–Nov.	Excellent	±0	None	26.63	26.75
Panamara	87.1	60.0	60.0	Nov.	25.63	Base grade	Panama	All year	Good	–1.5	26.25	25.88	26.25
Seasons Arriba	341.0	75.0	75.0	Jan.	27.38	Flavor	Equador	Aug.–Dec.	Excellent	+3.5	27.13	27.25	27.50
Sanchez	449.0	541.0	16.0	Nov.	26.88	Bulk	Dominican Republic	Dec.–April	Good	–2.0	25.63	25.88	26.25
			75.0	Nov.	26.88			Sept.–May					
			75.0	Dec.	25.95								
			75.0	Dec.	25.75								
			75.0	Dec.	26.00								
			75.0	Dec.	26.13								
			75.0	Jan.	25.75								
			75.0	Jan.	26.25								
San Thomé	75.4	....				Flavor	San Thomé	Sept.–Nov.	Good	+2.5	28.13	28.38	28.50
Trinidad	132.0	116.0	16.0	Nov.	37.50	Flavor	Trinidad	Nov.–Feb.	Good	+9.0	38.00	32.50	32.50
			50.0	Feb.	32.00								
			50.0	Mar.	32.00								
Total	1,704.9	1,067.0		Weighted average....27.01									

Exhibit 5

CHESTER GOLD CORPORATION

SPOT ACCRA BEAN PRICES—MONTHLY AVERAGE

(Cents per pound)

Month	1957	1958	1959	1960
January	23.1	41.5	36.8	30.3
February	23.4	44.3	35.8	28.7
March	22.3	43.7	37.8	27.4
April	25.5	42.9	36.8	27.5
May	25.3	46.0	37.8	29.6
June	30.5	48.3	38.1	28.3
July	30.5	48.9	35.8	29.8
August	32.1	46.3	37.0	28.5
September	34.6	42.7	38.3	28.0
October	35.4	37.4	35.8	29.5
November	42.7	43.8	33.0	
December	39.9	41.0	30.9	
Average*	30.5	43.9	36.2	

* Average prices in other years were:

1952	35.4	1955	37.4
1953	37.1	1956	27.2
1954	57.7		

Exhibit 6

CHESTER GOLD CORPORATION

WORLD COCOA PRODUCTION

(Millions of pounds)

Country	1956–1957	1957–1958	1958–1959	1959–1960
Brazil	367.9	380.0	383.0	410.0
Colombia	30.0	25.8	29.0	31.0
Dominican Republic	78.7	78.0	67.9	77.2
Equador	68.0	68.0	64.0	70.0
Cameroons	129.2	147.7	134.0	145.5
Ghana	589.9	474.3	575.0	660.0
Ivory Coast	170.0	99.2	120.0	145.0
Nigeria	303.0	180.0	314.0	310.0
San Thomé	20.0	20.0	19.0	20.0
Trinidad	17.0	19.0	18.5	21.0
Venezuela	39.6	35.0	30.0	33.0
Other	76.2	83.0	84.6	90.3
World total	2,017.7	1,736.3	1,976.2	2,160.6

Exhibit 7

CHESTER GOLD CORPORATION

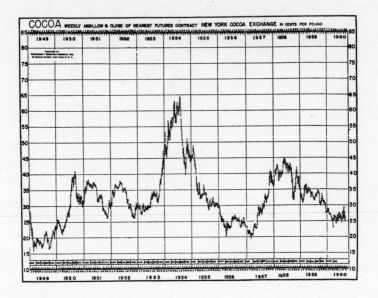

WHITE EAGLE OIL COMPANY (D)

In December, 1957, Mr. Walter H. Helmerich, III, executive vice-president of White Eagle Oil Company, called a meeting of the exploration committee of the company. The White Eagle Oil Company was an independent oil producing and contract drilling company located in Tulsa, Oklahoma.

Regular members of the exploration committee, in addition to the executive vice-president, were as follows: Mr. V. H. Zoller, vice-president—exploration; Mr. Harry Saye, vice-president—production; Mr. R. W. Haigh, financial vice-president; Mr. D. R. Toll, assistant to the president; Mr. E. H. Leede, landman in the exploration department; and Mr. F. O. Bennett, geologist in the exploration department. Other members of the exploration department occasionally attended these meetings when they happened to be in town, or if they had a special interest in the project being discussed.

The purpose of the meeting on December 6, among other things, was to consider the request from the exploration department for approval to begin exploratory drilling in the Central Kansas area. When the committee addressed itself to this topic, the following discussion ensued:

VICE-PRESIDENT—EXPLORATION: For the last several months we have been working to develop a group of exploration prospects in the Central Kansas area. Our recommended drilling program in this area is designed to maintain current oil production while the search for large reserves goes on elsewhere. That is, reserve potential is not high, perhaps 300,000 to 450,000 barrels per six-well pool, but it could be developed cheaply and produced quickly. To date, we have screened over a hundred prospects and have purchased acreage on about 50 of these. Each prospect contains an average of one-half to a full section (320–640 acres), which has been purchased at an average lease bonus of $5 per acre.

We are now in the process of having seismic work done on each of the prospects. The average cost of the seismic work is about $1,000 per prospect.

123

Of the 30 that have been "shot" to date, we have picked ten which we would like to use for the initial exploratory drilling program. These will be shallow wells, and we estimate that it will cost about $18,000 to drill each wildcat. Completion costs on successful wells will run about $22,000 each. Thus, in terms of the exploration department budget, we are asking for an appropriation of $180,000 for drilling these ten wildcats. The completion costs of any successful well, and the cost of drilling any further development wells, would, of course, be handled by the production department. This $180,000 represents about one-third of the total exploration department budget for drilling activities in fiscal year 1958.

We think the prospects we have put together in this package are particularly good ones, certainly far better than the average. We feel sure that this drilling program will be a profitable experience.

FINANCIAL VICE-PRESIDENT: You say the reserve potential is not high. In terms of barrels of reserves per well, what sort of experience would you expect in this area?

GEOLOGIST: Well, of course, reserves per well are the function of the size of the pool and the number of wells that you drill into it. In Kansas we are allowed [by state regulatory authorities] to drill development wells on 20-acre spacing, but the "hickeys" [the geological structure in which the oil is trapped] are small. The usual experience in this area has been that each successful well will bring in 50,000 to 100,000 barrels of oil. Occasionally reserves run as low as 30,000 barrels per well, and sometimes up as high as 150,000. The most likely estimate is about 50,000 barrels per well.

FINANCIAL VICE-PRESIDENT: What's been the usual experience on the size of the pool? That is, how many development wells is it usually feasible to drill around a successful wildcat?

GEOLOGIST: Well, we know that these prospects are not likely to discover any big pools, but we think it is quite likely that each one will lead to two or three development wells.

FINANCIAL VICE-PRESIDENT: If you drilled these ten wildcats, how many of them do you think will hit oil?

VICE-PRESIDENT—EXPLORATION: We can't answer that question, of course. We think it is very unlikely that we will miss on all ten, and expect that most likely we will hit on two or three of them. If we hit on three wildcats and each one permits three additional development wells, that will give us 12 productive wells each with 50,000 barrels of reserves or a total of 600,000 barrels of oil. It looks pretty good, don't you think?

FINANCIAL VICE-PRESIDENT: Well, I don't know. We will have quite an expense for dry holes, and it will cost us $40,000 to drill and equip each productive well. Then, too, if this area is going to justify continuing investments in the future, we should expect to recover all of our land acquisition costs, lease rentals, the overhead of the exploration department, administrative costs, and a reasonable profit. . . . I just don't know. I wonder how this whole prospect stacks up in terms of return on investment.

VICE-PRESIDENT—EXPLORATION: Well, we haven't figured any involved economics, but it looks like a good deal to us. A success ration of two to three out of ten on exploratory wells is just about as good an average as anyone can be expected to achieve in this business.

FINANCIAL VICE-PRESIDENT: That's true, but there are so many factors, such as success ratios, investment costs, reserves per well, number of development wells per prospect, production costs, that I just can't tell whether or not the whole deal represents a good investment for the company without making detailed projections and working up a return on investment. Let me play around with this thing for a week or so, and I will report back to you at the next meeting as to what the rate of return looks like.

EXECUTIVE VICE-PRESIDENT: Well, it's not particularly important for us to resolve this problem today. Bob, why don't you work up some figures for our next meeting as to what the rate of return looks like. We will consider the Central Kansas program further at that time.

The meeting then turned to discussion of other topics.

Immediately after the meeting Mr. Haigh summoned his staff and began work on an analysis of the Central Kansas exploration project.

The Overhead Loading Factor

One of the first problems to be resolved in the analysis was how to allow for overhead expenses. Mr. Haigh knew that the land acquisition costs, as well as the salaries and other expenses of the exploration department, were "sunk costs," and that they should not influence the decision as to whether or not to drill the Central Kansas prospects already on hand. Mr. Haigh was, however, very much interested in determining whether or not Central Kansas was, over a longer period of time, a good place for White Eagle Oil Company to be exploring for and developing oil reserves. Mr. Haigh knew that land acquisition costs and exploratory overhead costs were material in amount. In some recent years, for example, land and exploration overhead costs had exceeded expenditures for exploratory drilling. Thus, he felt these costs could not be overlooked in sizing up the exploration prospects of a particular area.

Mr. Haigh was also actively interested in improving White Eagle's over-all rate of return on investment. Based upon published information about comparable oil companies (Exhibit 1), he had set 15% after taxes as a company-wide target for rate of return. He decided that this goal would be more readily understood by the other executives if he applied the same standard for new investments (15% return) to all departments of the company. As Mr. Haigh saw the problem, if overhead costs were not included in evaluating exploration prospects, this would mean that a higher "target rate of return" should be used in judging exploration projects than if the overhead costs were included as part of the investment of these projects.

Moreover, Mr. Haigh had encouraged all department heads to take a conservative approach in evaluating capital expenditure projects, and inclusion of overhead costs was in line with this objective. Finally, Mr. Haigh believed that it was easy to forget overhead and land costs in looking at the return on oil finding activities, and he felt that inclusion of these costs would help to develop long-run exploration policies and decisions that were more realistic for the company. For these reasons, therefore, he decided to determine an overhead loading factor to be added to the exploratory drilling investment for projects in the exploration department.

For fiscal year 1958, the budget of the exploration department provided for $600,000 of exploratory drilling investments, $450,000 for lease investments, and $390,000 of other overhead costs in the department. The last item was for the relatively fixed costs, such as salaries, annual rentals on leases, expenses of regional land offices, and so forth. Lease investments were actually capital expenditures, but were made in such small individual amounts that specific approval of expenditures for this item was not required. Many leases which were purchased were never drilled on, and those that were had to be approved when the drilling project was put before the exploration committee. Mr. Haigh computed that lease investments amounted to 75% of drilling costs and that other overhead amounted to 65%, and he decided to use these factors in computing the investment on exploratory drilling projects.

In order to simplify exploration analyses, Mr. Haigh felt it would be satisfactory to use the same land and overhead factors in different areas, such as Central Kansas and West Texas, even though the factors actually varied from area to area. The factors also varied from year to year in any one area, depending upon the amount of exploratory drilling done, changes in overhead staffing, the amounts of lease purchases, and so on. Mr. Haigh recognized these factors, but he felt that a simple method accomplished his purposes without significantly distorting the conclusions that might be reached on any one exploration area or prospect.

Central Kansas Exploratory Study

Exhibits 2 through 8 comprise the "Central Kansas Exploratory Study" prepared by Mr. Haigh's department. Exhibit 3 computes the per-barrel costs of finding and developing oil for 40 possible combinations of the number of successful wildcats and the number of development wells per successful wildcat. For example, if only one of the ten wildcats were successful, and there were no successful development wells, the exploration and development costs were expected to be $304,000. In Exhibit 2, these costs are detailed for three sample situations. In a separate computation (on a form called the evaluation work sheet), Mr. Haigh's staff estimated the amount of oil that would be recovered each year and figured the cash flow after taxes that would be received from the sale of this oil. These results are shown in the column labeled "Net Cash Returned" in Exhibit 4.

The handling of tax deductions was especially complicated due to the nature of certain tax provisions affecting the oil industry. As shown in Exhibit 2, the drilling costs of dry holes and exploration overhead costs (other than lease investments) were immediately deductible because these expenses were not successful in producing an income stream against which the costs could be amortized. The drilling costs of successful wells were likewise deductible for tax purposes in the year incurred. Tax credits derived from the drilling costs of successful wells were taken into account in calculating the net cash returns after taxes shown in Exhibit 4.[1] Lease investment costs and geophysical costs on successful prospects were capitalized, and they were recoverable for tax purposes through depletion allowances. The depletion deduction could be based on actual costs, or the statutory "percentage depletion" deduction could be used, at the option of the taxpayer. For most productive wells, percentage depletion was more advantageous. In addition to a depletion deduction, depreciation of the actual cost of productive equipment was also allowable over the life of the well. The annual tax deductions for depletion and depreciation were taken into account in determining the "Net Cash Return" after taxes in Exhibit 4.

By stating the finding costs in Exhibit 3 and the total revenue in Exhibit 4 on a per-barrel basis, Mr. Haigh was able to prepare Exhibit 5 which indicated the "time-adjusted" rate of return for any combination of successes, given the assumption of 50,000 gross barrels of reserves per well. Exhibits 6, 7, and 8 provide the same computations for the assumption of 104,000 gross barrels of reserves per well.

[1] See Exhibit 12 as an illustration of the evaluation work sheets on which the net cash returns of Exhibit 4 were computed.

As an additional part of his preparation for the next meeting of the exploration committee, Mr. Haigh prepared the information shown in Exhibits 9, 10, and 11. Exhibit 9 presents success ratios for all exploratory wells drilled in the United States for the period 1944 through 1957. Exhibit 10 is a rough measure of the efficiency of various techniques for finding oil. Geophysics, which was the most sophisticated technique, included seismic tests and other instrumented analyses. Exhibit 11 indicates drilling experience in the state of Kansas in 1954.

The Meeting on December 13, 1957

On December 13, 1957, the exploration committee reconvened and the following discussion took place on the subject of the Central Kansas exploration project:

VICE-PRESIDENT—EXPLORATION: This is a very interesting study, Bob. Let me make sure I understand it. If all our wells had 50,000 gross barrels of reserves, and if we hit on three out of the ten wildcats, and if we also can drill four development wells on each successful wildcat, then we will earn a 15% rate of return. Is that right?

FINANCIAL VICE-PRESIDENT: That's right. But remember, this study is meant to be a tool for evaluating the oil finding and development prospects of the Central Kansas area. Since the study includes costs already incurred, the study does not measure the incremental return on investment that we would derive from drilling the specific prospects we now have on hand. The study is rough in many respects, but we are all feeling our way in this general area of exploration investment analysis.

VICE-PRESIDENT—EXPLORATION: Looking at these figures, I am not sure now whether or not we should go ahead with this program. Frankly, I expected somewhat better results. Perhaps we had better put our $180,000 in some other area.

GEOLOGIST: Well, I don't know either. After giving Mr. Haigh my estimates at the last meeting, I took another look at this group of prospects. The chances are real small, maybe one out of ten, that we won't hit on any of these wildcats. I'd say the chances are 50–50 that we would hit on three or more of them, although the chances of hitting on four are probably only one out of ten. The number of development wells are not as good as I had originally thought, however. Probably three times out of ten the substructure, even if we hit, will be so poor that it wouldn't pay to drill any development wells. And I'll bet the chances of having four development wells is only one out of ten. So my best guess is a toss-up between one, two, or three development wells. This would mean, from looking at Exhibit 5, that we would have a return between 2% and 11%, probably about 7%. There is always the chance, however —maybe as good as three out of ten—that we might hit the larger reserves, in which case, our return would go to 20%. Since this is unlikely, however, my best guess is that our rate of return will be less than 10%.

VICE-PRESIDENT—PRODUCTION: I think we ought to take this program. We've got to take some risks in order to have some development wells to drill. Besides, we're gamblers—that's why we are in the oil business.

LANDMAN: We shouldn't forget that we have an awful lot invested in this program already. In addition to about $100,000 in lease investment, this project has occupied one of my assistants for nearly a full year, not to mention the time spent by the geological department and the cost of all the seismic tests. I'm particularly concerned about the amount of time we have spent developing these prospects. There are plenty of other exploratory oil deals being offered on a partnership basis by other oil companies, so it isn't a problem of finding a place to invest our money. It's that we don't have time to investigate all of the deals offered to us, and the really good deals don't get put on the market anyway. So, we have to develop some prospects on our own, and when we do then we probably should drill them.

VICE-PRESIDENT—EXPLORATION: Well, these prospects are good ones; there's no doubt about that. I am sure we could recover something on our investment by farming these prospects out to other operators on one basis or another while retaining an interest for White Eagle. The real question is whether or not we should invest $180,000 of our own money in drilling these prospects. (*Pause.*) You know, I'm beginning to have doubts about the method of analysis we are using here. I wonder if any oil prospect could show us a satisfactory rate of return, after we loaded all these things into it. What we need is to see some other prospects figured on the same basis.

FINANCIAL VICE-PRESIDENT: You're absolutely right. Rate of return, as figured here, is just a ranking device, and what we need to know now is how this program ranks against some of the other drilling prospects that we have available. Let's table this item once more, and for the next meeting I'll work up some comparable figures on that Oklahoma deal we have been thinking about.

The R. A. Hoff "A" Prospect

After the December 13 meeting, Mr. Haigh instructed his staff to prepare a comparable set of figures for the Hoff prospect in Oklahoma. The Hoff prospect was a somewhat deeper, more expensive wildcat which was expected to yield larger reserves if it was successful. Exploratory drilling costs for this well were $45,000, and completion costs an additional $40,000. The geologist's estimate of the "most likely" reserves was 114,000 gross barrels. As a result of the Central Kansas exploratory study, Mr. Haigh and his staff developed a method of analyzing exploratory oil drilling prospects. The work sheet presented in Exhibit 12 indicates the computations necessary to arrive at the "Net Cash Return" column on Exhibit 4. Column 30 of

Exhibit 12 is the net cash return for the Hoff prospect. Most of the columns in Exhibit 12 are self-explanatory. Column 6, totaling $36,000, represented the depreciation of the completion (equipment) costs less salvage value shown in Columns 24 and 25. The company used the statutory percentage depletion allowance instead of using cost depletion, so that for the first year there was no depletion allowance because the heavy expenses of the intangible drilling costs (Column 4) produced an operating loss for the first year. In Column 32, the discounted present value of the amounts in Column 30 were found to total approximately $85,000, an amount equal to the estimated investment in a well. This indicated that if the well were successful, and the reserves were 114,000 barrels, the rate of return would be 28% (ignoring overhead costs). Exhibits 13 and 14 are similar to Exhibits 2 and 4 for the Central Kansas study, computing the per-barrel cost of finding oil and the per-barrel discounted revenue from the oil. Exhibit 15 is the "Recommendation to Drill" form developed by Mr. Haigh for presenting the results of his analyses. Based on information from the company geologist, Mr. Haigh had figured the most likely estimate on the assumption of a one-in-four success ratio, with 14 successful development wells drilled on the prospect and one dry development well. These assumptions yielded a 20% rate of return on investment. The results of other assumptions, above and below the "most likely expectations," were also computed and entered on the form.

After Exhibit 15 was completed, Mr. Haigh felt that the Hoff prospect was stated in terms reasonably comparable with those of the Central Kansas study. Based upon previous discussions, however, he anticipated that some problems might develop at the forthcoming meeting in comparing the rates of return for the two investments. With ten prospects in the Central Kansas program, a success ratio had a meaning, but there was only one exploratory drilling site on the Hoff prospect, and it would either be successful or dry. Thus, some men would undoubtedly argue that the Hoff prospect was considerably more risky than the Central Kansas venture. Moreover, some men would undoubtedly be interested in comparing the risks of a single wildcat well from among the Kansas prospects with the single Hoff well. Since the dry hole cost of the Hoff well ($45,000) was 2.5 times as large as a single Kansas dry hole, the Hoff well would require a much greater commitment from the exploration budget than a single Kansas well. In a real sense, therefore, it might

Exhibit 1

WHITE EAGLE OIL COMPANY (D)

RETURN ON BORROWED AND INVESTED CAPITAL EARNED BY
OIL PRODUCING* COMPANIES, 1920–1952

Year	Number in Group	Median	Interquartile Average	Arithmetic Average
1920	9	12.9%	14.2%	15.2%
1921	16	3.8	4.5	3.8
1922	18	5.9	5.7	7.9
1923	19	3.3	3.0	5.1
1924	24	5.1	5.1	7.8
1925	24	7.1	7.9	13.3
1926	23	11.5	11.9	16.2
1927	26	4.1	4.7	7.5
1928	24	3.8	3.2	5.0
1929	27	9.4	8.6	13.2
1930	28	5.1	5.8	9.3
1931	27	(0.1)	(0.7)	0.1
1932	30	1.9	2.7	6.5
1933	28	1.9	1.8	4.3
1934	26	6.3	7.0	9.7
1935	24	5.6	6.3	9.3
1936	30	9.1	9.1	13.0
1937	30	9.6	11.2	14.9
1938	31	9.2	9.6	11.9
1939	32	6.9	6.8	8.6
1940	32	6.1	6.0	7.0
1941	32	9.7	9.1	10.3
1942	32	9.4	9.1	10.2
1943	31	9.8	10.5	11.6
1944	31	10.7	11.5	11.8
1945	31	9.6	10.0	10.4
1946	31	9.5	10.0	11.3
1947	31	16.8	17.4	20.9
1948	28	24.6	24.9	24.9
1949	28	18.0	15.9	17.0
1950	27	11.8	13.4	13.9
1951	26	14.9	13.8	13.4
1952	23	11.2	12.5	11.9

Note: Net income was taken after taxes but before interest charges and income applicable to minority interests. Borrowed and invested capital included
common stock, surplus, preferred stock, long-term debt, and the equity of minority
stockholders in consolidated subsidiaries.

* The data tabulated in this exhibit is for nonintegrated oil producing companies, i.e., those companies with no significant participation in the refining or
marketing activities of the oil industry. Comparable data for other classifications
of oil companies will be found in the source cited.

Source: John G. McLean and Robert Wm. Haigh, *The Growth of Integrated
Oil Companies* (Boston: Division of Research, Harvard Business School, 1954),
p. 680.

be argued that the Hoff well was riskier than individual Kansas
wells. Mr. Haigh wanted to resolve these problems prior to the
meeting. If the risks were greater on the Hoff well, he felt he should
be prepared to state how these greater risks might be evaluated in
the light of the higher rate of return forecast for the Hoff well.

Questions

1. What action, if any, should the exploration committee approve regarding the Central Kansas and Hoff drilling prospects?

2. What is your evaluation of the method of analysis developed by Mr. Haigh? Should the exploration department overhead be included as a part of the investment in evaluating exploratory drilling prospects?

3. Comment on the use of probability estimates in preparing these analyses. Has this tool been properly used? Could it be used more effectively?

Exhibit 2

WHITE EAGLE OIL COMPANY (D)

CENTRAL KANSAS EXPLORATORY STUDY
PER-BARREL FINDING AND DEVELOPMENT COSTS

(50,000 gross barrels of reserves per well)

	Total	Per Barrel
One-in-ten success ratio—no development wells:		
Drilling costs—10 wells @ $18,000	$180,000	
Completion cost—1 well @ $22,000	22,000	
Other exploratory costs—140% of $180,000	252,000	
Total costs .... ~~← 75% + 65%~~	$454,000	
Less: Tax credits not taken on evaluation work sheet:		
Drilling costs of dry holes: 9 wildcats @ $18,000 ....$162,000		
Expensible "other costs"—65% of $180,000 117,000		
Total deductions at 54%* $279,000	150,000	
Net costs—after credits	$304,000	
Net reserves: 50,000 ×(0.875 net interest) = 43,770 barrels		$6.95
Two-in-ten success ratio—no development wells:		
Net costs—as computed above for one success	$304,000	
Add completion cost for second successful well	22,000	
Add back tax credit for drilling successful well (drilling and completion costs of productive wells are deducted on the evaluation work sheet)	10,000	
Net costs—after credits	$336,000	
Net reserves: 50,000 × 0.875 × 2 wells = 87,500 barrels		3.84
One-in-ten success ratio—one development well:		
Net costs as computed above for 1-in-10 success ratio	$304,000	
Add drilling and completion costs for one well (tax credit taken on the evaluation work sheet)	40,000	
Net costs—after credits	$344,000	
Net reserves: 50,000 × 0.875 × 2 wells = 87,500 barrels		3.94

* 54% is the federal income tax rate for corporations with subsidiaries reported on a consolidated basis.

working
interest (7/8)
Net Prod.

Exhibit 3

WHITE EAGLE OIL COMPANY (D)

CENTRAL KANSAS EXPLORATORY STUDY
PER-BARREL FINDING AND DEVELOPMENT COSTS

(50,000 gross barrels of reserves per well)

development wells per wildcat (successful)

successful wildcats/lease

Number of Wells per Lease	*Success Ratio* One in Ten	*Two in Ten*	*Three in Ten*	*Four in Ten*	*Five in Ten*
1	$304,000 43,770 bbls. $6.95	$336,000 87,540 bbls. $3.84	$ 368,000 131,310 bbls. $2.80	$ 400,000 175,080 bbls. $2.28	$ 432,000 218,850 bbls. $1.97
2	$344,000 87,540 bbls. $3.94	$416,000 175,080 bbls. $2.38	$ 488,000 262,620 bbls. $1.86	$ 560,000 350,160 bbls. $1.60	$ 632,000 437,700 bbls. $1.44
3	$384,000 131,310 bbls. $2.92	$496,000 262,620 bbls. $1.89	$ 608,000 393,930 bbls. $1.54	$ 720,000 525,240 bbls. $1.37	$ 832,000 656,550 bbls. $1.27
4	$424,000 175,080 bbls. $2.42	$576,000 350,160 bbls. $1.64	$ 728,000 525,240 bbls. $1.39	$ 880,000 700,320 bbls. $1.26	$1,032,000 875,400 bbls. $1.18
5	$464,000 218,850 bbls. $2.12	$656,000 437,700 bbls. $1.50	$ 848,000 656,550 bbls. $1.29	$1,040,000 875,400 bbls. $1.19	$1,232,000 1,094,250 bbls. $1.13
6	$504,000 262,620 bbls. $1.92	$736,000 525,240 bbls. $1.40	$ 968,000 787,860 bbls. $1.23	$1,200,000 1,050,480 bbls. $1.14	$1,432,000 1,313,100 bbls. $1.09
7	$544,000 306,390 bbls. $1.78	$816,000 612,780 bbls. $1.33	$1,088,000 919,170 bbls. $1.18	$1,360,000 1,225,560 bbls. $1.11	$1,632,000 1,531,950 bbls. $1.07
8	$584,000 350,160 bbls. $1.67	$896,000 700,320 bbls. $1.28	$1,208,000 1,050,480 bbls. $1.15	$1,520,000 1,400,640 bbls. $1.09	$1,832,000 1,750,000 bbls. $1.05

Exhibit 4

WHITE EAGLE OIL COMPANY (D)

CENTRAL KANSAS EXPLORATORY STUDY
CASH FLOW, AFTER TAXES, FROM 50,000 BARRELS OF GROSS RESERVES

Year	Net Cash Return	Present Value of Net Cash Return						
		2%	6%	10%	15%	20%	30%	40%
1...............	$19,240	$18,860	$18,140	$17,490	$16,740	$16,030	$14,800	$13,740
2...............	15,420	14,820	13,720	12,740	11,660	10,700	9,130	7,860
3...............	15,420	14,530	12,960	11,580	10,150	8,930	7,020	5,610
4...............	11,920	11,010	9,440	8,140	6,820	5,750	4,170	3,100
5...............	8,290	7,510	6,190	5,150	4,120	3,330	2,230	1,540
6...............	6,080	5,400	4,290	3,430	2,630	2,040	1,260	810
7...............	4,010	3,490	2,670	2,060	1,510	1,120	640	380
8...............	2,610	2,230	1,640	1,220	850	610	320	180
9...............	1,380	1,160	820	590	390	270	130	70
10...............	1,870	1,530	1,040	720	460	300	140	70
Total...........	$86,240	$80,540	$70,910	$63,120	$55,330	$49,080	$39,840	$33,360
Per barrel*.......	$1.97	$1.84	$1.62	$1.44	$1.26	$1.12	$0.91	$0.76

* 43,770 barrels of net reserves.

Exhibit 5

WHITE EAGLE OIL COMPANY (D)

CENTRAL KANSAS EXPLORATORY STUDY
PER CENT RETURN ON EXPLORATORY AND DEVELOPMENT INVESTMENT
(50,000 gross barrels of reserves per well)

Number of Wells per Lease	One in Ten	Two in Ten	Three in Ten	Four in Ten	Five in Ten
1............0%	0%	0%	0%	0%	
2............0	0	2	6	10	
3............0	2	7	12	15	
4............0	5	11	15	18	
5............0	8	15	18	19	
6............1	11	17	19	21	
7............3	13	18	20	22	
8............5	15	19	21	23	

Exhibit 6

WHITE EAGLE OIL COMPANY (D)

CENTRAL KANSAS EXPLORATORY STUDY
PER-BARREL FINDING AND DEVELOPMENT COSTS
(104,000 gross barrels of reserves per well)

Number of Wells per Lease	Success Ratio				
	One in Ten	*Two in Ten*	*Three in Ten*	*Four in Ten*	*Five in Ten*
1	$304,000 90,920 bbls. $3.34	$ 336,000 181,840 bbls. $1.85	$ 368,000 272,760 bbls. $1.35	$ 400,000 363,680 bbls. $1.10	$ 432,000 454,600 bbls. $0.95
2	$344,000 181,840 bbls. $1.89	$ 416,000 363,680 bbls. $1.14	$ 488,000 545,520 bbls. $0.89	$ 560,000 727,360 bbls. $0.77	$ 632,000 909,200 bbls. $0.70
3	$384,000 272,760 bbls. $1.41	$ 496,000 545,520 bbls. $0.91	$ 608,000 818,280 bbls. $0.74	$ 720,000 1,091,040 bbls. $0.66	$ 832,000 1,363,800 bbls. $0.61
4	$424,000 363,680 bbls. $1.17	$ 576,000 727,360 bbls. $0.79	$ 728,000 1,091,040 bbls. $0.67	$ 880,000 1,454,720 bbls. $0.60	$1,032,000 1,818,400 bbls. $0.57
5	$464,000 454,600 bbls. $1.02	$ 656,000 909,200 bbls. $0.72	$ 848,000 1,363,800 bbls. $0.62	$1,040,000 1,818,400 bbls. $0.57	$1,232,000 2,273,000 bbls. $0.54
6	$504,000 545,520 bbls. $0.92	$ 736,000 1,091,040 bbls. $0.67	$ 968,000 1,636,560 bbls. $0.59	$1,200,000 2,182,080 bbls. $0.55	$1,432,000 2,727,600 bbls. $0.53
7	$544,000 636,440 bbls. $0.85	$ 816,000 1,272,880 bbls. $0.64	$1,088,000 1,909,320 bbls. $0.57	$1,360,000 2,545,760 bbls. $0.53	$1,632,000 3,182,200 bbls. $0.51
8	$584,000 727,360 bbls. $0.80	$ 896,000 1,454,720 bbls. $0.62	$1,208,000 2,182,080 bbls. $0.55	$1,520,000 2,909,440 bbls. $0.52	$1,832,000 3,636,800 bbls. $0.50

Exhibit 7

WHITE EAGLE OIL COMPANY (D)

CENTRAL KANSAS EXPLORATORY STUDY
CASH FLOW, AFTER TAXES, FROM 104,000 BARRELS OF GROSS RESERVES

Year	Net Cash Return	Present Value of Net Cash Return						
		2%	*6%*	*10%*	*15%*	*20%*	*30%*	*40%*
1	$ 19,240	$ 18,860	$ 18,140	$ 17,490	$16,740	$16,030	$14,800	$13,740
2–9	123,360	110,746	90,346	74,787	60,169	49,313	34,695	25,674
10–16	36,160	28,709	18,393	12,018	7,249	4,496	1,840	818
Total	$178,760	$158,315	$126,879	$104,295	$84,158	$69,839	$51,335	$40,232
Per barrel*	$1.96	$1.74	$1.40	$1.15	$0.93	$0.77	$0.56	$0.44

* 90,920 barrels of net reserves.

Exhibit 8

WHITE EAGLE OIL COMPANY (D)

CENTRAL KANSAS EXPLORATORY STUDY

PER CENT RETURN ON EXPLORATORY AND DEVELOPMENT INVESTMENT

(104,000 gross barrels of reserves per well)

Number of Wells per Lease	Success Ratio				
	One in Ten	*Two in Ten*	*Three in Ten*	*Four in Ten*	*Five in Ten*
1............	0%	1%	7%	11%	14%
2............	1	10	16	20	23
3............	6	15	20	24	27
4............	9	19	23	27	29
5............	12	22	26	29	31
6............	15	23	28	30	32
7............	17	25	29	32	33
8............	18	26	30	33	34

Exhibit 9

WHITE EAGLE OIL COMPANY (D)

EXPLORATORY WELLS DRILLED IN UNITED STATES

	All Exploratory Wells			New Field (Strict Wildcat) Exploratory Wells		
Year	*No. Drilled*	*No. Dry*	*% Dry*	*No. Drilled*	*No. Dry*	*% Dry*
1944.............	4,796	3,852	80.3	3,094	2,752	88.9
1945.............	5,613	4,399	78.4	3,037	2,685	88.4
1946.............	5,759	4,622	80.3	3,133	2,800	89.4
1947.............	6,775	5,397	79.7	3,480	3,086	88.7
1948.............	8,013	6,550	81.7	4,296	3,795	88.3
1949.............	9,058	7,228	79.8	4,449	3,943	88.6
1950.............	10,306	8,292	80.5	5,290	4,698	88.8
1951.............	11,756	9,539	81.1	6,189	5,505	88.9
1952.............	12,425	10,090	81.2	6,698	5,957	88.9
1953.............	13,313	10,633	79.9	6,925	6,151	88.8
1954.............	13,097	10,389	79.3	7,380	6,478	87.8
1955.............	14,937	11,832	79.2	8,104	7,186	88.7
1956.............	16,137	13,077	80.9	8,709	7,841	90.0
1957.............	14,707	11,897	80.9	8,014	7,142	89.1

Source: *Bulletin of the American Association of Petroleum Geologists.*

Exhibit 10

WHITE EAGLE OIL COMPANY (D)

BASIS FOR LOCATING NEW FIELD WILDCATS—1957

(For all states reported in the United States)

	No. Drilled	*Producers*	*Dry*	*% Dry*
Geology	4,825	445	4,380	90.8
Geophysics	611	114	497	81.3
Geology and geophysics	1,140	176	964	84.6
Total technical	6,576	735	5,841	88.8
Nontechnical	550	26	524	95.3
Unknown	888	111	777	87.5
Total	8,014	872	7,142	89.1

Source: B. W. Blanpied, "Exploratory Drilling in 1957," *Bulletin of American Association of Petroleum Geologists,* June, 1958, p. 1125ff.

Exhibit 11

WHITE EAGLE OIL COMPANY (D)

WELLS DRILLED IN KANSAS, BY TYPES, IN 1954

	Total	*Producers*	*Dry*	*% Dry*
1. Total number of wells drilled	4,581	3,071	1,510	33.0
2. Exploratory wells drilled:				
a) Outposts (drilling for long extension of a partly developed pool)	497	195	302	60.8
b) New pool wildcats (drilling for a new pool on a structure or in a geological environment already productive, typically, drilling outside the limits of the proved area of the pool or drilling within the proved area for a new pool above or below the known pool)	647	130	517	79.9
c) New field wildcats (drilling for a new field on a structure or in an environment never before productive)	285	30	255	89.5
d) Total exploratory wells	1,429	355	1,074	75.2
3. Development wells drilled	3,152	2,716	436	13.8

Sources:
1. Bureau of the Census: 1954 Census of Mineral Industries, *Oil and Gas Field Contraci Services.*
2. Frederic H. Lahee, *Bulletin of the American Association of Petroleum Geologists.*
3. By deduction: 1 − 2*d*.

Exhibit 12

WHITE EAGLE OIL COMPANY (D)

Purchase Price - Or Book Value as of

Lease Cost (Development)	45,000.00
Producing Equipment	40,000.00
Total	85,000.00

White Eagle Net Revenue Barrels 0.875

EVALUATION WORK SHEET
OIL AND/OR GAS PRODUCING PROPERTY

EVALUATION AS OF _____

COMPUTATION OF NET INCOME FOR DETERMINING PERCENTAGE DEPLETION LIMITATION — WORKING INTEREST BEING — BASIS OF DETERMINING ALLOWABLE DEPLETION

Figures are in Thousands

Year	Gross Production Bbls Oil	Gross Production Mcf Gas	(a) Gross Income After Royalty, OR's & OP (1)	Prod. Expense @200/Well Month or /Net Bbl (2)	Prod. Tax 5% of Gross Income (3)	Development Cost Chargeable to Intangible Drlg. or Production Expense (4)	Total Col. 2+3+4 (5)	Depreciation .36 Per Net Bbl or MCF / Per $ Gross Revenue (6)	Administrative Overhead 20% of Cols. 2 & 4 (7)	Total Expense For Determining % Depletion Limit (Col. 5+6+7) (8)	Net Income For Determining Percentage Depletion Limit (Col. 1-8) (9)	Cost Depletion Per Net Bbl or MCF / Per $ Gross Revenue (10)	27 1/2% of Gross Income (.275 x Col. 1) (11)	50% of Column 9 (12)	Applicable Allowance (13)
1	16,000	14,000	42,000	2,400	2,100	45,000	49,500	5,050	9,480	64,030	(22,030)	–	11,550	(1,015)	–
2	16,000	14,000	42,000	2,400	2,100	–	4,500	5,050	480	10,030	31,970	–	11,550	15,985	11,550
3	16,000	14,000	42,000	2,400	2,100	–	4,500	5,050	480	10,030	31,970	–	11,550	15,985	11,550
4	13,000	11,350	34,050	2,400	1,700	–	4,100	4,100	480	8,680	25,370	–	9,364	12,685	9,364
5	10,700	9,300	27,900	2,400	1,400	–	3,800	3,350	480	7,630	20,270	–	7,672	10,135	7,672
6	8,700	7,600	22,800	2,400	1,150	–	3,550	2,750	480	6,780	16,020	–	6,270	8,010	6,270
7	7,200	6,300	18,900	2,400	950	–	3,350	2,275	480	6,105	12,795	–	5,198	6,398	5,198
8	6,000	5,200	15,600	2,400	780	–	3,180	1,875	480	5,535	10,065	–	4,290	5,032	4,290
9	4,900	4,300	12,900	2,400	650	–	3,050	1,550	480	5,080	7,820	–	3,548	3,910	3,548

Oil and Gas — Production, Revenue and Expense Worksheet

12	2,700	2,400	6,000	2,400	300	–	2,700	725	480	3,905	2,095	–	1,650	1,555
13	2,200	2,000	4,800	2,400	300	–	2,640	575	480	3,695	1,105	–	1,320	552
14	1,800	1,600	3,900	2,400	240	–	2,595	475	480	3,550	350	–	1,072	175
15	1,500	1,300		2,400	195	–			480					175
Total	114,000	99,750	299,250	36,000	15,000	45,000	96,000	36,000	16,200	148,200	151,050	–		67,820

(a) Price of Oil or Gas: 3.00

(b) Basis for Determining Deduction for Depreciation and Cost Depletion

$$\text{Depreciation (Column 6)} = \frac{\text{Book Value of Equipment Less } 10\% \text{ Salvage}}{\text{Net Reserves – Bbl or Mcf or Gross Revenue}} = \frac{36,000}{99,750 \text{ bbls.}} = .361 \text{¢ Per Net Bbl or Mcf or \$ Gross Revenue}$$

$$\text{Depletion (Column 10)} = \frac{\text{Book Value of Lease Cost}}{\text{Net Reserves – Bbl or Mcf or Gross Revenue}} = \$\_\_\_\_ \text{ ¢ Per Net Bbl or Mcf or \$ Gross Revenue}$$

(c) The lesser of Column 11 or 12, but not less than column 10 provided cost has not been fully returned through percentage depletion

(d) Income Tax Rate: 52%

(e) Taxable gain on equipment recovery – if any – is handled in column 19.

8

Exhibit 12—Continued

Properties Owned By: **White Eagle Oil Company**
Description: **NW SW NW Sec. 24-26S-21E**
Oklahoma
R. A. Hoff "A" No. 1

CONSIDERED

	Direct Expense (Column 5)	Interest @ % on Unrecovered Outlay at Beginning of Year	Administrative Overhead	Sub-Total (Col. 14 + 15 + 16)	Depletion Allowance (Column 13)	Depreciation (Column 9)	Total Deductions (Col. 17 + 18 + 19)	Taxable Income (Col. 1 - 20)	Federal and State (d)	Total Expense (Col. 17 + 22)	Development Cost Chargeable to Producing Equipment Investment	Net Salvage (Credit) For Equipment to Be Recovered (e)	Total Annual Cash Outlay (Col. 23 + 24 - 25)	Net Cash Return (Column 1 - 26)	Payout Status at End of Year	Net Cash Return (Col. 27) Discounted @ % for Present Worth	Before Disc.	30%	28%	%
Col.	14	15	16	17	18	19	20	21	22	23	24	25	26	27	28	29	30	31	32	33
	49,500	-	-	49,500	-	5,050	54,550	(12,550	(6,777	42,723	40,000	-	82,723	(40,723)	(40,723)	-	44,277	34,049	34,580	
	4,500	-	-	4,500	11,550	5,050	21,100	20,900	11,286	15,786	-	-	15,786	26,214	(14,509)	-	26,214	15,519	15,991	
	4,500	-	-	4,500	11,550	5,050	21,100	20,900	11,286	15,786	-	-	15,786	26,214	11,705	-	26,214	11,927	12,504	
	4,100	-	-	4,100	9,364	4,100	17,564	16,486	8,902	13,002	-	-	13,002	21,048	32,753	-	21,048	7,367	7,851	
	3,800	-	-	3,800	7,672	3,350	14,822	13,078	7,062	10,862	-	-	10,862	17,038	49,791	-	17,038	4,583	4,958	
	3,550	-	-	3,550	6,270	2,750	12,570	10,230	5,524	9,074	-	-	9,074	13,726	63,517	-	13,726	2,841	3,116	
	3,350	-	-	3,350	5,198	2,275	10,823	8,077	4,362	7,712	-	-	7,712	11,188	74,705	-	11,188	1,779	1,991	
	3,180	-	-	3,180	4,290	1,875	9,345	6,255	3,378	6,558	-	-	6,558	9,042	83,747	-	9,042	1,112	1,257	
	3,050	-	-	3,050	3,548	1,550	8,148	4,752	3,566	5,616	-	-	5,616	7,284	91,031	-	7,284	685	787	

														1/4
2,700	-	1,048	4,473	1,527	825	3,525	-	3,525	2,475	107,004	-	2,475	82	99
2,640	-	552	3,767	1,033	558	3,198	-	3,198	1,602	108,606	-	1,602	40	51
2,595	-	175	3,245	655	354	2,949	4,000	(1,051)	4,951	113,557	-	4,951	99	124
96,000		67,820	99,820	99,430	53,693	149,693	4,000	185,693	113,557		-	198,557	80,894	84,262

Payout Time __2.5__ Years

Barrels required to payout __36,000__

Barrels remaining after payout __63,750__

Rate of Return __28__ % On __$85,000__

Exhibit 13

WHITE EAGLE OIL COMPANY (D)

R. A. HOFF "A" No. 1

PER-BARREL FINDING AND DEVELOPMENT COSTS

(114,000 gross barrels of reserves per well)

	Investment	Tax Credits — Deducted from Investment	Tax Credits — Deducted on Evaluation Work Sheet
Exploratory costs (1-in-4 success ratio):			
Drilling costs: 1 productive wildcat..................	$ 45,000		Column 4
3 dry wildcats @ $45,000................$135,000			
Less: Dry hole contributions @ $12,200...........36,600	98,400	$ 98,400	
Lease investment: 75% of exploratory drilling costs			Column 13 (actual costs not deductible if percentage depletion used)
4 × $45,000 × 75%............................	135,000		
Other overhead costs: 65% of exploratory drilling costs			
4 × $45,000 × 65%............................	117,000	117,000	
Development costs (14 successful development wells in 15):			
Drilling costs: 14 productive development wells @ $45,000.....	630,000		Column 4
1 dry development well........................	45,000	45,000	
Completion (equipment) costs: 15 productive wildcat and development wells @ $40,000.........................	600,000		Column 6 (net of Columns 24 and 25)
Totals.......................	$1,670,000	$260,400	
Less: Tax credit: 54% of $260,400................	140,616		
Net investment after some tax credits..........	$1,529,384		
Net reserves: 114,000 × 0.875 net interest × 15 productive wells = ...	1,496,250 bbls.		
Finding and development costs per barrel............	$ 1.022		

Exhibit 14

WHITE EAGLE OIL COMPANY (D)

R. A. HOFF "A" NO. 1

CASH FLOW, AFTER TAXES, FROM 114,000 BARRELS OF
GROSS RESERVES FROM "EVALUATION WORK SHEET"

Year	Net Cash Return	Present Value of Net Cash Return	
		18%	20%
1	$ 44,277	$ 37,503	$ 36,883
2	26,214	18,822	18,193
3	26,214	15,964	15,178
4	21,048	10,861	10,145
5	17,038	7,446	6,849
6	13,726	5,079	4,598
7	11,188	3,513	3,121
8	9,042	2,405	2,107
9	7,284	1,639	1,413
10	5,733	1,095	929
11	4,424	717	597
12	3,341	458	374
13	2,475	287	230
14	1,602	159	125
15	4,951	416	322
Total	$198,557	$106,364	$101,064
Per barrel*	$1.991	$1.0663	$1.013

* 99.750 barrels of net reserves.

Exhibit 15

WHITE EAGLE OIL COMPANY (D)

WHITE EAGLE OIL COMPANY
RECOMMENDATION TO DRILL EXPLORATORY TEST   DATE   January 6, 1958

General Information:

Quarter Fiscal Year	Second	Must Commence	February 1, 1958
Operator	White Eagle Oil Co.	Must Complete	
Lease Acres in Block	1,280	Lease Name	R. A. Hoff "A"
Spacing	80	Lease No.	010182
Proposed Depth	5500	Well Name	Hoff "A" #1
Probable Horizons	Mississippian	Field	Wildcat
White Eagle Working Interest	100%	Location	NWSWNW Sec. 24–26S–21E
Net Revenue Interest	87.5%	County	
Other Working Interest	None	State	Oklahoma

Cost and Price Data:

Drilling Cost—Gross per Well	$45,000.00	Crude Price	
Drilling Cost—Net per Well	$45,000.00	(per Barrel)	$3.00
Completion Cost—Gross per Well	$40,000.00	Allowable (per	
Completion Cost—Net per Well	$40,000.00	Calendar Day)	43-BOPD
Direct Operating Cost per Well		Income Tax Rate	54%
per Month	$200.00	Severance Taxes	5% of Gross
Other Exploratory Costs per		Number of Years	
Dollar of Exploratory Drilling		at Allowable	3
Costs	$1.40	Total Life of Well	15
Dry Hole Contribution	$12,200.00	Trucking Cost	(not used in
White Eagle Net Reserves		(per Barrel)	$0.77 evaluation)
(Most Likely per Well)	99,750		

Principal Evaluation Data:	*Below Expectations*	*Most Likely*	*Above Expectations*
Probability of Success	1 in 8	1 in 4	1 in 2
Number of Successful Development Wells per Prospect	10	14	19
Reserves per Well (Gross)	80,000 bbls.	114,000 bbls.	154,000 bbls.
Number of Dry Development Wells per Prospect	2	1	0
Return on Investment	Less than 2 %	20 %	34 %

Reason for Recommendation: Located 6 miles west of the Trestle Pool on a well-defined structure similar to that on which the latter Pool was drilled.

Geological Recommendations: Drill stem test any favorable shows above the top of the Mississippian. Core the Mississippian to a sufficient depth to test a zone.

Engineer Recommendations:

Data on Area and Nearby Wells: Nearest Mississippian test is White Eagle's R. A. Hoff No. 6 producing from X Zone, R Zone not perforated.

WHITE EAGLE OIL COMPANY (E)

In January, 1958, the members of the exploration committee of the White Eagle Oil Company were trying to decide what action the company should take with regard to a group of oil drilling prospects in the Central Kansas area. Background information about the Central Kansas prospects was presented in the (D) case of this series. A report entitled the "Central Kansas Exploratory Study" (Exhibits 2 through 8 in the D case) had been prepared by the financial vice-president, and indicated that the potential profitability of the program varied widely depending upon the number of wildcat wells that were successful and the number of development wells per successful wildcat.

At a meeting of the exploration committee on December 20, 1957, Mr. W. H. Helmerich, III, executive vice-president, suggested that the drilling of the Central Kansas prospects be deferred by White Eagle until the alternative of taking in partners in high income tax brackets was fully explored. Mr. Helmerich pointed out that the effective income tax rate greatly influenced the degree of risk taken and the rates of return earned on oil exploration activities. He noted that individual investors having high personal federal income tax rates would gain maximum utilization of the tax deductions permitted for percentage depletion and the expenses of drilling unsuccessful wildcats. Therefore, he felt it might be possible to devise a partnership proposal for the Central Kansas prospects with individuals in high income tax brackets that would be attractive to the potential investors, and, at the same time, would either (1) increase White Eagle's rate of return in the program, or (2) reduce the risk of loss to be borne by White Eagle.

Mr. Helmerich asked Mr. Daniel R. Toll, assistant to the president, to prepare a descriptive brochure that might be useful in explaining a possible partnership venture to outside investors. At the same time, he asked Mr. Toll and Mr. Haigh, the financial vice-president, to analyze several possible partnership deals from the standpoint of an outside investor and from the standpoint of White Eagle Oil Company.

A partnership arrangement in an oil exploration venture required a clear agreement as to (1) the amount and nature of the investment to be made by each partner, and (2) the method to be used in computing each partner's share of the proceeds of any successful wells. The program finally devised by Mr. Toll and other members of the exploration committee specified that the entire investment for exploratory and development drilling would be made by the "tax partner." The partner would be entitled to receive all the oil flowing from successful wells until such time as he had recovered his initial investment. After "pay-out," White Eagle and the partner would share equally in the net profits from the wells. In order to maximize the partner's tax credits, White Eagle's share of the profits would be in the form of "oil payments"; that is, White Eagle would receive title to a sufficient number of barrels of oil each year to yield proceeds equal to White Eagle's 50% share of the net profits. The partner would thus own a greater proportion of the annual oil production after pay-out, but would be responsible for paying all operating costs of the well. This arrangement would give the partner a larger gross income basis on which to compute his percentage depletion. In addition to its share of future profits, White Eagle would also be entitled to a 5% fee on all investment and operating costs in return for providing managerial and engineering services.

After the idea for the partnership proposal had been worked out, Mr. Toll prepared the material shown in Exhibits 1 through 5. This was the material that Mr. Toll would propose to give to potential investors, and was intended to illustrate the attractiveness of the investment from the partner's point of view. Exhibit 1 specified the details of the partnership arrangement. It was planned to offer 15 drilling prospects, from which the investor would pick ten for actual exploratory drilling. Exhibit 5 provided a detailed analysis of the investor's cash flows, assuming one successful wildcat out of ten, three successful development wells out of four, and a 90% tax bracket for the investor. The results of similar calculations for other combinations of success ratios and tax brackets was shown in Exhibit 4. As graphed in Exhibit 3, the proposal offered the investor a high rate of return on an after-tax basis. Mr. Toll felt that this proposal would be sufficiently attractive to make it relatively easy to obtain a partner in the deal.

Mr. Toll next turned to an analysis of the partnership proposal from White Eagle's point of view. He noted that the original Central Kansas exploratory study had indicated that White Eagle's rate of return for one successful wildcat and three development wells was estimated at 11% (see Exhibit 5 in the D case). Mr. Toll, working with Mr. Haigh's staff, prepared Exhibit 6 to substantiate this calculation, and to state it on a basis comparable with his further calculations described below. They next computed the cash flows that White Eagle would receive under the partnership agreement. This is shown in Exhibit 7. In addition to White Eagle's oil payments as shown in Exhibit 5, the company would also receive $27,080 of income in the form of management fees to be charged to the partner (Column 15). White Eagle would also be entitled to a depletion allowance, and Mr. Toll computed it on a "cost" basis, using the estimated cost of the lease investment as provided in the original study (Column 10). Using these assumptions, Mr. Toll estimated that White Eagle's net cash return would be $138,966, for a one-in-ten success ratio. In Exhibit 8, Mr. Toll converted his calculations from Exhibit 7 to reflect a three-in-ten success ratio, and computed the discounted rate of return on the investment. Since no additional investment would actually be required by White Eagle, he used as his investment for this calculation the amounts included as "overhead loading" in the original study. An 8% rate of return was indicated by this calculation.

Finally, in Exhibit 9, Mr. Toll computed the return that White Eagle would earn on its incremental investment if it were to carry out the Central Kansas program alone rather than through the use of a partner. This was done by subtracting the net cash return and net investment in Exhibit 8 from the comparable figures of Exhibit 6. This computation resulted in an indicated rate of return of 14% on the incremental investment. It should be noted that this 14% return was the return on incremental investment available to the company above and beyond that available through use of a tax partner.

After completing his computations, Mr. Toll decided to discuss the results with Mr. Haigh before preparing his recommendation for the exploration committee. Reviewing the figures, the two men were able to list several questions which needed to be resolved before a recommendation could be made:

1. How should the "sunk costs" representing lease investments and exploratory overhead be treated? As a result of having incurred these expenses, White Eagle had created a position which had a definite cash value. For ex-

ample, in the Central Kansas area, the value of White Eagle's position in absolute dollars was $262,818, as estimated in Exhibit 8. By taking in a partner, White Eagle could, in effect, "cash in" on its overhead expenditure without making any additional investment. But, if overhead costs were to be ignored in computing the rate of return on a project being evaluated, would it also be logical to ignore that portion of the cash flows from the project that could be related to its "trading value"?

2. How should rates of return be computed on exploratory projects in the future? To use the method of Exhibit 9 would require a determination of the best possible results to be obtained from "trading out" the position, in order to determine what White Eagle's incremental cash flows would be. These incremental cash flows would then be related to the additional investment required. This procedure seemed quite long and complicated.

3. If White Eagle's incremental return on the Central Kansas venture were 14% rather than 11% as indicated in the original study, should the company undertake the venture on its own, or should it seek a partner on the terms described above?

4. What would be the implications, in terms of company policy, if White Eagle were to take in a partner on the Central Kansas deal? One of the expansion goals of the company was to increase its oil production, and taking in a partner seemed inconsistent with this goal.

Exhibit 1

WHITE EAGLE OIL COMPANY (E)

GENTLEMEN:

This Brochure contains fifteen drilling prospects situated on the Barton Arch Trend in Central Kansas. These drilling blocks were purchased on subsurface geology by White Eagle Oil Company in the maintenance of an acreage inventory for its exploratory program and were later evaluated by seismograph work. White Eagle intends to sell a drilling program consisting of ten of these prospects to be selected by the investor from among the fifteen included herein.

The drilling program is offered on the following terms and conditions:
1. All costs of securing and evaluating the ten selected prospects will be absorbed by White Eagle.
2. The participating partner will drill the ten wells required at its sole cost and expense and take all tax write-offs involved.
3. White Eagle will operate the properties under the terms of the industry accepted Model Form 1956 Operating Agreement plus a management fee of 5 per cent of the total monies expended under such operating agreement.
4. The participating partner will own all production of oil and gas from each prospect until pay-out. Pay-out on each prospect is defined as: "The end of the first month in which the participating partner has received, through sales of oil and gas or other revenues and credits, an amount sufficient to recover all of the tangible, intangible, and operating costs which the participating partner has incurred on the prospect, including the cost of dry holes and the 5 per cent management fee."
5. At pay-out on each prospect White Eagle Oil Company will acquire an undivided one-half interest of the net profit from each prospect in the form of an oil payment and will continue to operate the prospect for the joint account of White Eagle and the participating partner.
6. Within 90 days after pay-out on each prospect the participating partner has the option to sell (and White Eagle Oil Company is obligated to purchase) the partici-

Exhibit 1—*Continued*

pating partner's one-half interest in the remaining reserves in each prospect at a price which will, in the opinion of a qualified petroleum engineer, permit White Eagle to earn a 10 per cent return on its investment after taxes by producing this one-half interest in such remaining reserves.

Yours very truly,
WHITE EAGLE OIL COMPANY

By_____

Exhibit 2

WHITE EAGLE OIL COMPANY (E)

FINANCIAL ANALYSIS OF THE BARTON ARCH DRILLING PROGRAM

The financial results for the investor in this program are shown in the following exhibits. As an example, the graph on the next page [Exhibit 3] shows the results of the program for a 70% tax bracket investor. The following statistical table [Exhibit 4] summarizes the results for 70%, 80%, and 90% tax positions. Also included is the detailed evaluation work sheet which White Eagle uses to analyze its drilling prospects. This work sheet has been completed for one of the nine sets of conditions shown in Exhibit 4 in order to show the precise method of analysis employed.

The key variables incorporated in the analysis are these:
1. Out of ten prospects tested by wildcat wells, results are shown for one, two, and three discoveries. Higher results are certainly possible, but just these assumptions will demonstrate the value of the program.
2. The effect of the tax structure is shown for 70%, 80%, and 90% brackets.

The key assumptions are these:
1. Oil reserves for each successful well are 50,000 barrels.
2. Each discovery well will lead to three successful development wells and one dry development well, for a total of four successful wells on each successful prospect.
3. Oil reserves are produced at allowable level (25 barrels per day) for four years, and thereafter decline in a straight line to economic limit over the remaining four years of normal life.
4. All exploratory and development drilling is completed within the first year after the program's inception. On each successful prospect the wells produce for only three months in the first year, leading to a nine-month carry-over of production into a ninth year of the program's life.

Exhibit 3

WHITE EAGLE OIL COMPANY (E)

BARTON ARCH DRILLING PROGRAM

SAMPLE ILLUSTRATION OF INVESTMENT, CASH RETURN, AND
PER CENT GAIN FOR 70% TAX BRACKET

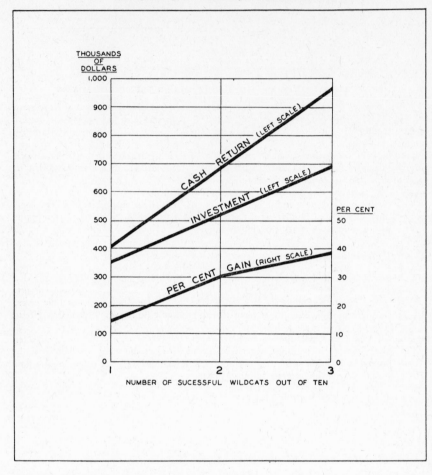

Exhibit 4

WHITE EAGLE OIL COMPANY (E)

FINANCIAL ANALYSIS OF THE BARTON ARCH DRILLING PROGRAM

	One Out of Ten Success (Tax Bracket)			Two Out of Ten Success (Tax Bracket)			Three Out of Ten Success (Tax Bracket)		
	70%	80%	90%	70%	80%	90%	70%	80%	90%
I. CASH GAIN									
A. Successful Prospects									
Gross income	428.4			856.8			1,285.2		
Less: Direct expense	208.6			417.2			625.8		
Administrative expense	9.6			19.2			28.8		
Depreciation	88.0			176.0			264.0		
Depletion	94.6			189.2			283.8		
Total	400.8			801.6			1,202.4		
Taxable income	27.6	27.6	27.6	55.2	55.2	55.2	82.8	82.8	82.8
Tax	19.3	22.1	24.8	38.6	44.2	49.6	57.9	66.3	74.4
Net income	8.3	5.5	2.8	16.6	11.0	5.6	24.9	16.5	8.4
Add back: Depletion	94.6	94.6	94.6	189.2	189.2	189.2	283.8	283.8	283.8
Cash gain	102.9	100.1	97.4	205.8	200.2	194.8	308.7	300.3	292.2
B. Unsuccessful Wildcats									
Gross cost	170.1	170.1	170.1	151.2	151.2	151.2	132.3	132.3	132.3
Less: Tax credit	119.1	136.1	153.1	105.8	121.0	136.1	92.6	105.8	119.1
Net cost	51.0	34.0	17.0	45.4	30.2	15.1	39.7	26.5	13.2
C. Total Program									
Cash gain from successful prospects (A)	102.9	100.1	97.4	205.8	200.2	194.8	308.7	300.3	292.2
Less: Net cost of unsuccessful wildcats (B)	51.0	34.0	17.0	45.4	30.2	15.1	39.7	26.5	13.2
Cash gain from total program	51.9	66.1	80.4	160.4	170.0	179.7	269.0	273.8	279.0
II. INVESTMENT									
Successful prospects	186.9			373.8			560.7		
Unsuccessful wildcats	170.1			151.2			132.3		
Total	357.0	357.0	357.0	525.0	525.0	525.0	693.0	693.0	693.0
III. RETURN ON INVESTMENT	14.5%	18.5%	22.5%	30.5%	32.4%	34.3%	38.8%	39.4%	40.1%

Exhibit 5

WHITE EAGLE OIL COMPANY (E)
BARTON ARCH DRILLING PROGRAM
ONE OUT OF TEN SUCCESS
90% TAX
(All figures in thousands)

EVALUATION WORK SHEET

OIL AND/OR GAS PRODUCING PROPERTY

EVALUATION AS OF _____

Purchase Price - Or Book Value as of _____
Lease Cost (Oil & Gas Reserves) _____
Producing Equipment _____
Total _____

Year	Full Interest of Properties Involved — Gross Production Bbls Oil	Mcf Gas	Working Interest (7/8) Net Production Bbls Oil	$	Less White Eagle Interest* Bbls Oil	$	Net Production after White Eagle Interest Bbls Oil	$	(a) Gross Income After Royalty, OR's & OP (1)	Prod. Expense $.210@/well Month /Net Bbl Mcf (2)	Prod. Tax .0525% of Gross Income (3)	Development Cost Chargeable to Intangible Drlg. or Production Expense (4)	Total Col. 2+3+4 (5)	Depreciation* (b) Per Net Bbl or MCF or Per $ Gross Revenue (6)	Administrative Overhead Per Net Bbl or MCF or Per $ Gross Revenue (7)	Total Expense For Determining % Depletion Limit Col. 5+6+7 (8)	Net Income For Determining Percentage Depletion Limit (Col. 1-8) (9)	Cost Depletion (a) Per Net Bbl or MCF or Per $ Gross Revenue (10)	27 1/2% of Gross Income (.275 x Col. 1) (11)	50% of Column 9 (12)	Applicable Allowance (c) (13)
			87-1/2%																		
1	9.1		8.0	25.0			8.0		25.0	2.5	1.3	98.9	102.7	5.2	0.3	108.2	(83.2)	--	6.9	--	--
2	36.6		32.0	101.0			32.0		101.0	10.1	5.3		15.4	20.7	1.2	37.3	63.7	27.8	27.8	31.8	27.8
3	36.5		32.0	101.0	0.5	1.6	31.5		99.4	10.1	5.3		15.4	20.4	1.2	37.0	62.4	27.3	27.3	31.2	27.3
4	36.6		32.0	101.0	13.4	42.3	18.6		58.7	10.1	5.3		15.4	12.0	1.2	28.6	30.1	16.1	16.1	15.0	15.0

Form — Oil & Gas Production Revenue and Expense Worksheet (rotated)

7	14.1	12.3	38.7	4.0	12.7	8.3	26.0	10.1	2.0	12.1	5.3	1.2	18.6	7.4	7.2	3.7	3.7
8	7.7	6.7	21.3	1.4	4.5	5.3	16.8	10.1	1.1	11.2	3.4	1.2	15.8	1.0	4.6	0.5	0.5
9	5.1	4.5	14.2	0.8	2.5	3.7	11.7	7.6	0.7	8.3	2.4	0.9	11.6	0.1	3.2	--	--
T	200.0	175.0	551.4	39.0	123.0	136.0	428.4	80.8	28.9	208.9 / 98.9	88.0	9.6	306.2	122.2	117.8	102.5	94.6

Total

(Left margin: All Production Revenue and Expense)

(a) Price of Oil or Gas: **$3.15/bbl.**

(b) Basis for Determining Deduction for Depreciation and Cost Depletion

Depreciation (Column 6) = $\dfrac{\text{Book Value of Equipment Less \% Salvage}}{\text{Net Reserves - Bbl or Mcf or Gross Revenue}}$ = $\dfrac{\$88}{136}$ = **64.7** ¢ Per Net Bbl or Mcf or $ Gross Revenue

Depletion (Column 10) = $\dfrac{\text{Book Value of Lease Cost}}{\text{Net Reserves - Bbl or Mcf or Gross Revenue}}$ = $\$\underline{\hspace{1cm}}$ = $\underline{\hspace{1cm}}$ ¢ Per Net Bbl or Mcf or $ Gross Revenue

(c) The lesser of Column 11 or 12, but not less than column 10 provided cost has not been fully returned through percentage depletion

(d) Income Tax Rate: **90%**

(e) Taxable gain on equipment recovery - if any - is handled in column 19.

Exhibit 5—Continued

Properties Owned By __White Eagle Oil Company__

Description:

CONSIDERED

	DEDUCTIONS FROM GROSS INCOME FOR COMPUTING INCOME TAX							INCOME TAX									Prospect Return	Tax Cr. Total on Dry Return Wildcat Disc.		
Direct Expense (Column 5)	Interest % on Unrecovered Outlay at Beginning of Year	Administrative Overhead	Sub-Total (Col. 14 + 15 + 16)	Depletion Allowance (Column 13)	Depreciation (Column 9)	Total Deductions (Col. 17 + 18 + 19)	Taxable Income (Col. 1 - 20)	Federal and State (d)	Total Expense (Col. 17 + 22)	Development Cost Chargeable to Producing Equipment Investment	Net Salvage (Credit) For Equipment to Be Recovered (e)	Total Annual Cash Outlay (Col. 23 + 24 - 25)	Net Cash Return (Column 1 - 26)	Payout Status at End of Year	Net Cash Return (Col. 27) Discounted @ % for Present Worth	Before Disc.	Discounted for Present Worth ###	Total	14%
14	15	16	17	18	19	20	21	22	23	24	25	26	27	28	29	30	31	32	33
102.7	--	0.3	103.0	--	5.2	108.2	(83.2)	(74.9)	28.1	88.0	--	116.1	(91.1)	(91.1)		95.8	153.1	248.9	232.0
15.4		1.2	16.6	27.8	20.7	65.1	35.9	32.3	48.9			48.9	52.1	(39.0)		52.1		52.1	42.6
15.4		1.2	16.6	27.3	20.4	64.3	35.1	31.6	48.2			48.2	51.2	12.2		51.2		51.2	36.8
15.4		1.2	16.6	15.0	12.0	43.6	15.1	13.6	30.2			30.2	28.5	40.7		28.5		28.5	17.9
14.9		.2	16.1	13.1	11.1	40.3	13.2	11.9	28.0			28.0	25.5	66.2		25.5		25.5	14.1

12.1	1.2	13.3	3.7	22.3	5.3	3.7	3.3	16.6		16.6	9.4	91.0	9.4		9.4	4.0
11.2	1.2	12.4	0.5	16.3	3.4	0.5	0.4	12.8		12.8	4.0	95.0	4.0		4.0	1.5
8.3	0.9	9.2	--	11.6	2.4	0.1	0.1	9.3		9.3	2.4	97.4	2.4		2.4	0.8
															--	--
208.6	--	9.6 218.2	94.6	400.8	88.0	27.6	24.8 243.0	88.0		331.0 97.4			284.3 153.1		437.4	357.1

Investment 186.9   357.0

Cash Gain 97.4   80.4

Discounted

*   1/2 of net profit after payout = column 9

** $26.25 per well per month

*** 90% x $170,100 (9 wells x $18,000 ÷ 5%)

Payout Time __3-1/8__ Years

Barrels required to payout __73.8__

Barrels remaining after payout __62.2__

Rate of Return __14__ % on __Total Investment ($357.0)__

Exhibit 7

WHITE EAGLE OIL COMPANY (E)

BARTON ARCH DRILLING PROGRAM

ASSUMING ONE OUT OF TEN SUCCESSFUL WILDCATS AND THREE OUT OF FOUR PRODUCTIVE DEVELOPMENT WELLS

EVALUATION WORK SHEET

OIL AND/OR GAS PRODUCING PROPERTY

EVALUATION AS OF January 6, 1958

Purchase Price - Or Book Value as of ___

Lease Cost (Oil & Gas Reserves) ___

Producing Equipment ___

Total ___

Full Interest of Properties Involved

$s are in Thousands

Year	Gross Production Bbls Oil	Gross Production Mcf Gas	Working Interest (7/8) Net Production Bbls Oil	Amount	White Eagle Oil Payments (Equal to 50% of Profits after Payout) Bbls Oil	Amount	1 — Gross Income After Royalty, OR'S & OP	2 — Prod. Expense @ ___ /Well Month /Net Bbl or Mcf	3 — Estd. Tax 5.25 % of Gross Income	4 — Development Cost Chargeable to Intangible Drlg. or Production Expense	5 — Total Col. 2 + 3 + 4	6 — Depreciation Per Net Bbl or MCF or Per $ Gross Revenue	7 — Administrative Overhead Per Net Bbl or MCF or Per $ Gross Revenue	8 — Total Expense For Determining % Depletion Limit (Col. 5 + 6 + 7)	9 — Net Income For Determining Percentage Depletion Limit (Col. 1 - 8)	10 — Cost Depletion 3.46 Per Net Bbl or MCF or Per $ Gross Revenue	11 — 27 1/2% of Gross Income (.275 x Col. 1)	12 — 50% of Column 9	13 — Applicable Allowance
1	9.1		8.0	25.0			1,600	-	-	-	-	-	-	-	84	-	-	-	-
2	36.6		32.0	101.0				-	-	-	-	-	-	-	-	-	-	-	-
3	36.6		32.0	101.0	.5	1.6		-	84	84	84	-	-	84	1,516	1,730	440	758	1,730
4	36.6		32.0	101.0	13.4	42.3	42,300	-	2,221	2,221	2,221	-	-	2,221	40,079	46,364	411,633	20,040	46,364

7	14.1	12.3	38.7	4.0	12.7	12,700	667	667	667	-	12,033	13,840	3,493	6,017	13,840
8	7.7	6.7	21.3	1.4	4.5	4,500	236	236	236	-	4,264	4,844	1,238	2,132	4,844
9	5.1	4.5	14.2	.8	2.5	2,500	131	131	131	-	2,369	2,828	688	1,185	2,828
total	200.0	175.0	551.4	39.0	123.0	123,000	6,458	6,458	6,458	-	116,542	135,000	33,828	52,273	135,000

All Production Revenue and Expens[e]

(a) Price of Oil or Gas: **$3.15/bbl.**

(b) Basis for Determining Deduction for Depreciation and Cost Depletion { Depreciation (Column 6) = $\frac{\text{Book Value of Equipment Less \% Salvage}}{\text{Net Reserves - Bbl or Mcf or Gross Revenue}}$ = \$ _____ = \$ _____ ¢Per Net Bbl or Mcf or \$ Gross Revenue

Depletion (Column 10) = $\frac{\text{Book Value of Lease Cost}}{\text{Net Reserves - Bbl or Mcf or Gross Revenue}}$ = $\frac{\$ \underline{135,000}}{39,000 \text{ bbls}}$ = **$3.46** ¢Per Net Bbl

(c) The lesser of Column 11 or 12, but not less than column 10 provided cost has not been fully returned through percentage depletion

(d) Income Tax Rate:

(e) Taxable gain on equipment recovery - if any - is handled in column 19.

Total

Exhibit 7—Continued

Properties Owned By __White Eagle Oil Company__

Description: _____

	CONSIDERED																			Return Available for Retirement of Purchase Price and Development Cost, or Profit (Col. 27 ÷ Col. 4 and 24)				
	DEDUCTIONS FROM GROSS INCOME FOR COMPUTING INCOME TAX							INCOME TAX (d)												Discounted for Present Worth @		
Direct Expense (Column 5)	Mgmt. Fee (Income)	Administrative Overhead	Sub-Total (Col. 14 + 15 + 16)	Depletion Allowance (Column 13)	Depreciation (Column 6)	Total Deductions (Col. 17 + 18 + 19)	Taxable Income (Col. 1 - 20)	Federal and State	Total Expense (Col. 17 + 22)	Development Cost Chargeable to Producing Equipment Investment	Net Salvage (Credit) For Equipment to Be Recovered (e)	Total Annual Cash Outlay (Col. 23 + 24 - 25)	Net Cash Return (Column 1 - 26)	Payout Status at End of Year	Net Cash Return (Col. 27) Discounted @ ___% for Present Worth	Before Disc.	___%	___%	___%
14	15	16	17	18	19	20	21	22	23	24	25	26	27	28	29	30	31	32	33
-	(17,315)	-	(17,315)	-	-	(17,315)	17,315	9,350	(7,965)	-	-	(7,965)	7,965						
-	(1,260)	-	(1,260)	-	-	(1,260)	1,260	680	(580)	-	-	(580)	580						
84	(1,260)	-	(1,176)	1,730	-	554	1,046	565	(611)	-	-	(611)	2,211						
2,221	(1,260)	-	961	46,364	-	47,325	(5,025)	(2,714)	(1,753)	-	-	(1,753)	44,053						
1,969	(1,260)	-	709	41,174	-	41,883	28,242	2,671	(6,589)	-	-	(1,658)	39,158						

MILLER PRTG. CO. TULSA

	(1,200)	-	(593)	13,840	-	13,240	(547)	(295)	(888)	-	(888)	15,588
236	(1,260)	-	(1,024)	4,844	-	3,820	680	367	(657)	-	(657)	5,157
131	(945)	-	(814)	2,828	-	2,014	486	263	(551)	-	(551)	3,051
6,458	(27,080)	-	(20,622)	135,000	-	114,378	8,622	4,656	15,966	-	(15,966)	138,966

Payout Time _____ Years

Barrels required to payout _____

Barrels remaining after payout _____

Rate of Return _____ % On _____

Exhibit 6

WHITE EAGLE OIL COMPANY (E)

RATE OF RETURN EARNED BY WHITE EAGLE ON CENTRAL KANSAS PROGRAM
COMPANY DRILLS AND EQUIPS WELLS

Year	Net Cash Return from One 50,000- Barrel Well	Net Cash Return from 12 Wells	Present Value of Net Cash Return	
			10%	12%
1	$19,240	$ 230,880	$209,870	$206,176
2	15,420	185,040	152,843	147,477
3	15,420	185,040	138,965	131,748
4	11,920	143,040	97,696	90,973
5	8,290	99,480	61,777	56,405
6	6,080	72,960	41,149	36,991
7	4,010	48,120	24,686	21,750
8	2,610	31,320	14,626	12,653
9	1,380	16,560	7,021	5,978
10	1,870	22,440	8,662	7,226
Total	$86,240	$1,034,880	$757,295	$717,377

Net investment (Exhibit 3 in Case [D]): $728,000.
Indicated rate of return: 11% + (per Exhibit 5 in Case [D]).

Exhibit 8

WHITE EAGLE OIL COMPANY (E)

RATE OF RETURN EARNED BY WHITE EAGLE UNDER PARTNERSHIP PROPOSAL

Year	(1) Net Cash Return One Success in Ten (Exhibit 7)	(2) Less Tax Shield of Cost Depletion (54% of $135,000)	(3) Partial Cash (No Depletion Shield) (Col. 1 − 2)	(4) Partial Cash on Three Successes (Col. 3 × 3)	Net Cash Return on Three Successes (Col. 4 + 2)	Present Value of Net Cash Return 8%	Present Value of Net Cash Return 10%
1	$ 7,965	.....	$ 7,965	$ 15,615*	$ 15,615	$ 14,459	$ 14,194
2	580	.....	580	1,740	1,740	1,491	1,437
3	2,211	$ 934	1,277	3,831	4,765	3,783	3,579
4	44,053	25,037	19,016	57,048	82,085	60,332	56,064
5	39,158	22,233	16,925	50,775	73,008	49,718	45,338
6	23,203	13,079	10,124	30,372	43,451	27,374	24,506
7	13,588	7,474	6,114	18,342	25,816	15,051	13,244
8	5,157	2,616	2,541	7,623	10,239	5,529	4,782
9	3,051	1,527	1,524	4,572	6,099	3,050	2,586
Total	$138,966	$72,900	$66,066	$189,918*	$262,818	$180,787	$155,730

Net investment (stated on basis comparable to the original Central Kansas study):

Other exploratory costs—140% of $180,000. .... $252,000

Less: Tax shield on expensible costs:

65% of $180,000 = $117,000 × 54% tax. 63,180

Net investment. $188,820

Indicated rate of return: 8%.

* First-year management fee for three out of ten successes computed as follows:

Investment by partner: Drill 10 wildcats and 12 development wells @ $18,000. ... $396,000

Complete 12 successful wells @ $22,000. 264,000

Subtotal. $660,000

5% management fee. 33,000

Partner's investment (per Exhibit 4). $693,000

Management fee: $33,000 plus $315 first-year operating fee on each of 3 sites. $33,945

Less: Tax on fees @ 54%. 18,330

Net first-year management fee. $15,615

Exhibit 9

WHITE EAGLE OIL COMPANY (E)

RATE OF RETURN EARNED BY WHITE EAGLE ON THE INCREMENTAL
INVESTMENT REQUIRED TO RETAIN FULL WORKING INTEREST RATHER
THAN USING A TAX PARTNER

Year	(1) Net Cash Return 100% White Eagle (Ex. 6)	(2) Net Cash Return with Tax Partner (Ex. 8)	(3) Incremental Cash Return (Col. 1 − 2)	Present Value of Net Cash Return 14%	15%
1	$ 230,880	$ 15,615	$215,265	$188,787	$187,281
2	185,040	1,740	183,300	140,958	138,575
3	185,040	4,765	180,275	121,686	118,621
4	143,040	82,085	60,955	36,085	34,866
5	99,480	73,008	26,472	13,739	13,157
6	72,960	43,451	29,509	13,456	12,748
7	48,120	25,816	22,304	8,922	8,386
8	31,320	10,239	21,081	7,399	6,893
9	16,560	6,099	10,461	3,222	2,971
10	22,440	....	22,440	6,059	5,543
Total	$1,034,880	$262,818	$772,062	$540,313	$529,041

Incremental investment:
100% White Eagle program........$728,000
Program with tax partner.......... 188,820
Incremental investment............$539,180

Indicated rate of return: 14%

QUANDROW BEARINGS COMPANY

In early 1960, Mr. Rudolf Carnap, a recent graduate of the Harvard Business School and capital expenditure project analyst at Quandrow Bearings Company (QB), was studying two related capital investment proposals designed to facilitate a rapid expansion of the company's railroad freight car antifriction bearing sales.[1] The projects involving sizable investments had been under active study for about two years by several staff and functional groups in the areas of product development, manufacturing, sales, accounting, and economic analysis. Mr. Carnap's job was to study the work of these groups and to help them prepare a final analysis and proposal for presentation to top management.

The antifriction bearing analysis was one of Mr. Carnap's first major assignments at QB. As a consequence, he was particularly mindful of the fact that the amount of the proposed investments was quite sizable for QB, and that the profits involved were very significant relative to existing levels. Also, he remembered that Mr. John Dewey, the financial vice-president, had been seeking a man who, among other things, could apply "new techniques of systematic analysis, creatively and usefully" for the job he now held.

Quandrow Bearings Company was a large manufacturer of antifriction bearings and metal products. During 1959, QB's sales and net income had reached $160 million and $17 million, respectively; and at the year's end the firm's net worth was approximately $105 million. Over a period of years, however, the sales and profits of the company were subject to relatively frequent and sizable fluctuation, as may be seen from Exhibits 1 and 2.

---

[1] Although the product has been disguised to protect the identity of the firm on which this case is based, every effort has been made to keep product information as realistic as possible.

163

Capital Budgeting Policies

In screening new capital expenditure proposals such as those under consideration, QB management used the firm's cost of capital as a cutoff rate, and all projects justified on economic grounds alone had to meet this standard. The cost-of-capital measurement was based upon the product of a "typical" earnings per share/market price ratio and an adjustment factor, anticipating the effects of ten years' annual compound rate of growth on earnings per share. This cost measurement, which at present equaled 13.6% after taxes, constituted QB's cost of capital.

QB's growth had been entirely financed by retained earnings (approximately 50% of earnings were ordinarily paid as dividends). Like its principal competitors, the firm had not had to borrow funds in the postwar period, and there were no immediate plans to raise debt. Although QB's financial vice-president, Mr. Dewey, believed that the company could borrow a modest proportion, perhaps 20%, of its total capital (limited by the cyclical character of its industry), he did not think that the use of debt would affect the cost-of-capital calculations since any borrowing would eventually have to be repaid through retained earnings. The same logic applied to lease financing.

Two formal risk appraisals were made for each capital expenditure proposal submitted. The first estimated the operating level at which the project would barely return 13.6% on investment, and the relationship between this minimum level and the actual expected operating level. The second estimated the potential amount of capital which would be lost through shrinkage of assets in the event the project proved to be a dud. These two figures provided top management with a framework for evaluating the specific risks envisioned for a project. In the case of antifriction bearings, the risk of capital loss seemed smaller than usual, since most of the equipment could probably be utilized, after some delay, in other production departments.

Antifriction Bearings

QB's antifriction bearings were the sole product of an operating subdivision which competed in the market with several other well-established firms. The subdivision's total sales for 1959 of $10.5 million represented approximately 12% to 15% of total bearing sales to the railroad industry, and roughly 65% of total antifriction bearing sales.

The antifriction bearing was a relatively new development for use on railroad cars. Historically, freight car wheels had been equipped with sleeve-type friction bearings; but with the introduction of diesel locomotives, automated signal equipment, and similar innovations, train speeds increased and equipment was used more fully. These developments placed increasing strain on friction bearings, making them susceptible to more rapid failure. Since the failure of a friction bearing could, at worst, cause train derailment, frequent inspection (usually undertaken while cars were standing still) of journal boxes in which bearings were housed became a necessary, although very costly and problematical, safety measure. Maintenance of friction bearings, with its associated loss of equipment use, also proved costly. As a result, railroad men were anxious to lick the so-called "hotbox" problem which characterized bearing failure. Early efforts toward this end were concerned with improved lubricants, but these experiments did not prove particularly encouraging. As a result, the railroads gave increasing attention to the possibilities of using newly developed "antifriction" bearings.

In 1946, QB developed and began to promote an antifriction-type bearing for use on car wheels. After extensive testing on sample railroad cars, a special committee of railroad men, appointed to study the hotbox problem, reported that this bearing appeared to have a life[2] of about 500,000 car-miles. This compared with only 150,000 car-miles for the friction-type bearing and was equal to the historic average life for a freight car. Newer freight cars, however, were expected to have an average useful life of 600,000 car-miles. Although the roller-type bearings cost approximately twice as much as the friction bearings, potential savings afforded railroads from the installation of new antifriction bearings appeared sufficiently significant to insure swift adoption of the product.

In 1949, engineers at the Hercules Company, a principal competitor, developed a different type of friction roller bearing, which appeared to have superior life characteristics to the sleeve-type and other roller-type car wheel bearings. The Hercules product was still under use test, and after an average of approximately 170,000 test

---

[2] "Life" here refers to the car mileage point where only 90% of equipment is still operative.

miles per car, no Hercules bearing had yet failed in service. QB would not know for several years' time whether the life of the Hercules product would prove in actual service to be as good as the QB bearing or whether it might eventually prove substantially better. QB engineers had, however, estimated that the life of the Hercules product would be at least 500,000 car-miles, and more probably 650,000, thereby giving Hercules at least equivalent selling points. The Hercules product was also somewhat easier to inspect and service, if and when necessary. Both products sold for the same price, $120 per unit, and appeared to involve equal production costs. Hercules was already experiencing significant demand for its product and had recently begun to construct new, highly automated plant facilities that would increase its roller-bearing capacity from 32,000 units to 88,000 units annually; this capacity would be sufficient to supply 20% to 30% of the estimated antifriction bearing market for freight cars in 1961. Moreover, Hercules' facilities appeared adequate to permit expansion of capacity to 150,000 units fairly quickly, if this ever proved desirable.

The QB's initial production line was currently operating at its capacity of 80,000 units per year, and orders were booked several months in advance. Sales were being turned away, and although no systematic records had been kept, the sales manager believed orders at the rate of at least 4,000 units per year were currently being lost due to unacceptable delivery availability, perhaps with adverse long-term competitive consequences.

Two other bearing companies (having a combined annual capacity of 15,000–20,000 antifriction units in 1960) had begun testing antifriction-type bearings similar in character to the "approved" QB product. These tests, still in their early stages, had not yet shown the capabilities of these products, although QB engineers did not think it likely that the "new" roller bearings would prove much, if at all, superior to the QB product. This left Hercules as a lone wolf backing the new type freight car bearings and could, depending on the results of the use test, prove a competitive advantage or disadvantage.

QB's present freight car bearing production facilities were housed and spaced in one of QB's least efficient plants. There was sufficient free space in this plant to house the equipment necessary to expand production of cylindrical bearings to a maximum of 120,000 units per year. If and when further capacity proved necessary and desirable, a new more efficient plant would have to be constructed and existing bearing production facilities would be moved at that time. Although there were no other immediate plans for using free space in the existing plant, it could probably be put to some constructive use within a year's time.

On the basis of early performance indications and the demand which had materialized for the QB antifriction bearing, studies had been initiated by the firm's management in late 1957 as to the desirability of expanding antifriction bearing production's capacity. The two proposals which had come to Mr. Carnap's attention were outgrowths of these studies. Under the first plan, which called for an investment of slightly more than $780,000, new equipment would be purchased and housed in an existing plant. This equipment would increase QB's capacity to 120,000 antifriction bearing units per year.

According to the second plan, involving a considerably greater financial outlay, a new plant would be constructed and equipped (partly with existing equipment) with an initial capacity of 160,000 units per year and space for 320,000 units per year if deemed necessary in the future.

If the first plan were adopted, from four to six months would be required to install the equipment and produce bearings in volume. Under the second plan, smooth production would not be achieved for 15 to 18 months after the go-ahead was given. This constituted something of a disadvantage since, in view of present and prospective unsatisfied demand for QB's bearings, management was under considerable pressure to formulate its expansion plans quickly. Mr. Carnap was keenly aware of this consideration as he began to develop his method of analyzing the situation.

Analysis of Potential Market

As the first step in his analysis, Mr. Carnap gave his attention to an estimate of future demand for antifriction freight car bearings. Since there appeared little reason to anticipate a replacement market of any proportions in the foreseeable future (the economies of replacing worn "old-type" bearings with antifriction bearings on freight car fleets had not yet gained, nor seemed likely to win, ready acceptance in the railroad industry), he focused on potential demand generated by new railroad car sales.

The demand for new railroad cars was extremely cyclical and very difficult to forecast precisely. Mr. Carnap believed that demand typically followed an approximate cycle of two poor and three good years, as shown in Exhibit 3. Although demand for new cars and replacement orders would be highly cyclical, total demand for railway journal box bearings did not seem likely to grow significantly over the next 15 years. Largely this lack of over-all expected increase stemmed from unusual freight car production patterns during and following World War II.

To estimate expected demand for new freight cars in good and poor years, Mr. Carnap had prepared the charts shown in Exhibit 4 to derive probabilities. These probabilities were used as shown below to estimate expected sales in a poor year:

Demand for New Cars	Incremental Demand	Probabilities of Incremental Demand	Expected Demand
33,200	33,200	1.00	33,200
35,000	1,800	0.89	1,600
37,500	2,500	0.67	1,675
40,000	2,500	0.40	1,000

Expected new car deliveries in poor years 37,975

By similar procedures, Mr. Carnap estimated that new freight car deliveries would run at an expected level of 80,200 units in good years. Average expected demand for new freight cars was then estimated as follows:

Nature of Demand	Expected Demand (in Units)	Probability of Demand	Long-Run Expected Deliveries (in Units)
Good 80,200		0.6	48,120
Poor 37,975		0.4	15,200

Long-run expected delivery in units 63,320

Mr. Carnap then turned to estimating QB's probable share of the total railroad car bearing market which would be represented by antifriction bearings. As an initial step, he plotted (as shown in Exhibit 5) the historic proportion of antifriction bearing sales for freight cars to total industry demand and determined a fit using a logistical curve. This trend line suggested that antifriction bearing sales might constitute as much as 49% of the total market in 1960. When these estimates were shown to the sales department, responsible sales officials considered them conservative. They expressed the opinion that the two most recent years were more nearly indicative of the trend; if a curve were fitted using these data, antifriction bearing sales equaling 64% of the total might be reached in 1960. In either case, it appeared likely that antifriction bearings would capture almost the entire market sometime within the next ten years. Since antifriction bearing sales were estimated at only 38% of the total in 1959, Mr. Carnap decided to work with a conservative figure of 40% in his initial calculations.

To ascertain QB's share of the antifriction market, Mr. Carnap discussed the problem with Mr. Edmund Husserl, marketing manager for antifriction bearings, who said:

We ought to maintain a 50% share of the roller-bearing market as an absolute minimum, since the use tests show a 500,000 car-mile life. If Centro's [Centro was an important competitor that had introduced experimental bearings for testing in 1959] new bearing works out, we probably won't end up with more than 60% of the market because of that company's reciprocity position. Their previous antifriction bearing failed miserably, but the engineers tell me the new one looks about as good as ours. If, as seems unlikely, Centro's bearing fails again, we might even get 75% to 80% of the market; and for the next few years we may benefit from skepticism about the Centro product. If Hercules' bearing should prove to have a life of 650,000 car-miles, and we can't beat 500,000 by much, we'd have a real selling job to make up for their servicing advantages and longer life; but we have the sales staff to do this job. I think we might still end up with 60% to 70% of the market, depending again upon how good Centro's product is.

Most likely we'll get at least 60% even if all the other bearings pass the life test. In fact, this is the goal we're shooting for, with every indication that's where we'll be in a year or two.

Mr. Carnap found it difficult to reduce these statements to a probability distribution reflecting estimated market share. Moreover, he was uncertain whether Mr. Husserl's observations reflected any bias. From what little he knew of Mr. Husserl, Mr. Carnap was inclined to believe that the marketing manager was somewhat optimistic by nature and reluctant to lose sales opportunities for want of production capacity. On the other hand, QB's bonus reward system was such that marketing personnel benefited considerably by underestimating expected performance in budget forecasts. These or similar considerations might have affected Mr. Husserl's objectivity. For the purpose of preliminary investigation, Mr. Carnap decided to assume the conservative market share level of 50%.

Using the 63,320-car estimate of long-run annual demand for new cars, and the assumed 40% and 50% roller-to-friction-bearing and share-of-market estimates, Mr. Carnap estimated that QB's average sales would be 12,700 car sets (or 101,600 roller bearings, assuming eight bearings per car set) per year. Mr. Carnap planned to use these conservative estimates in preparing a preliminary report to use in evaluating whether the minimum equipment necessary to produce 120,000 units should be purchased in the near future so as to minimize expansion delays.

Since under the first expansion proposed the company's capacity would be limited to 120,000 bearings, QB's expected long-range activity level would be less than the 101,600 bearings indicated above. The company would not be able to capitalize fully on sales in the very best years (or, in other words, would be unable to maintain its market share in the years of highest demand). After making allowance for this factor in the demand estimates used above for good years, the following demand projection resulted:

Nature of Demand	Expected Demand for QB Bearings	Probability of Demand	Expected Demand
Good	120,000 (capacity)	0.6	72,000
Bad	60,760	0.4	24,304
			96,304

As it developed, the expected sales of 96,304 bearings represented about 80.3% of the proposed 120,000 bearing capacity. Since the company's experience indicated that average utilization of plant capacity tended to be about 80%, projects were generally recalculated at an 80% operating rate if the rate of return were based on an assumed operating per cent significantly in excess of this 80% figure.

Mr. Carnap had also prepared the estimates shown in Exhibit 6 to illustrate the impact of an incorrect estimate for either the 40% or 50% market share assumptions. These calculations followed procedures already outlined.

The next major factor Mr. Carnap decided to take into account was the immediate economic outlook. Although the current sales conditions were highly favorable, the company's economists predicted that there would be an economic downturn affecting the railroad car industry during the last quarter of 1960 and continuing through 1961. As described above, the demand for railway car bearings for new car deliveries tended to fall in cycles of roughly two bad and three good years. The company economists expected that the downturn they were projecting would follow this typical pattern.

Considerations Relating to Expansion in Current Facilities

After giving careful consideration to all these factors, Mr. Carnap decided to use demand estimates of roughly 101,000 bearings in 1960 and 1961 (allowing for inventory accumulation), and 96,000 units (80% of capacity) thereafter in his preliminary conservative analysis of the desirability of expanding roller-bearing capacity in current facilities. These assumptions were followed in preparing the cash flow forecast shown in Exhibit 7. The cost figures shown in this forecast reflect variable costs of unit production and special fixed costs directly associated with the manufacture of antifriction freight car bearings. Depreciation was scheduled after an item-by-item analysis. These figures promised a present value return on investment of 15.7%.

In view of QB's experience with manufacturing antifriction bearings, Mr. Carnap was quite confident that the cost data was relatively accurate, with the exception of the 1% allowance for sales returns. The historic average for sales returns was 0.89% of sales, but this had varied between 0.5% and 4.0% in recent years. Experience with similar projects showed sales return loss ranging up to 10%, with the following approximate relative frequencies: returns of 0–1%, 60% of total observations; 1–3%, 20%; 3–5%, 12%; 5–10%, 8%. Mr. Carnap had used 1% in his analysis after assurance from the engineering staff that this was the most likely occurrence. As the following figures show, higher losses resulting from sales returns had a significant effect on the return on investment calculation:

Percentage Loss Resulting from Returns	Rate of Return
1%	15.7%
3	13.3
5	11.3
10	6.5

Mr. Carnap's analysis of "return-loss" possibilities showed a return of 14.76%, based on a graphic interpolation of return on investment due to the average loss from returns, as shown below:

Average % Loss Resulting from Returns	Probability	Interpolated Rate of Return	Expected Value
0.5%	0.60	16.2%	9.72%
2.0	0.20	14.4	2.88
4.0	0.12	12.2	1.46
7.5	0.08	8.7	0.70
Expected rate of return			14.76%

One of the problems faced by Mr. Carnap in preparing these estimates was how to determine the time interval over which returns would be estimated. The equipment used in manufacturing antifriction bearings had useful lives ranging from 5 to 40 years, and the product appeared safe from technological obsolescence for at least 20 years. Thus, many life assumptions were possible. Mr. Carnap solved this problem by taking a weighted average of the economic life and dollar value of the equipment. On this basis he established an average life for equipment of 15 years, the estimate used in his return calculations. Allowance was then made in the present value calculations for the cost of replacing equipment with shorter lives than 15 years (see Exhibit 8).

As Exhibit 8 shows, the equipment investment required for a 120,-000 capacity was $3,028,900. Of this amount, $2,250,000 represented an estimate of the liquidation value of equipment already used by the company in the manufacture of freight car bearings. Although QB normally followed an incremental approach in which only "out-of-pocket" expenditures were analyzed, Mr. Carnap believed that a decision to expand was essentially the antithesis of a decision to liquidate—and that therefore the liquidation value of "sunk investments" was a relevant incremental consideration. No allowance had been made, however, for the floor space utilized, even though the replacement cost of this space was $450,000. In addition, finance personnel estimated that working capital requirements to support sales of 96,000 units per year would amount to $4,213,000 (of which $2,597,100 represented funds already invested, and $1,009,000 reflected the need to replenish overly depleted inventories).

Mr. Carnap had also prepared the data shown in Exhibit 9 to trace the effects of changes in assumptions pertaining to operating levels on cash flows.

Considerations Relating to Construction of New Facilities to House Freight Car Bearing Production

The aforementioned investment information pertained only to the alternative of expanding the present plant. The second alternative, involving construction of new facilities, would provide initial capacity for producing 160,000 units per year and sufficient plant space to support eventual production of 320,000 units per year. Data collected by Mr. Carnap to analyze this alternative (assuming construction was started in 1960) are shown in Exhibit 10. Since the costs of new plant and equipment were continuing to rise at about 1.0% to 1.5% per year, any delay in expansion would increase the total investment required.

Construction of new facilities provided several potential advantages. Working capital requirements would be reduced as the result of better production cycling. At a 96,000-unit operating level, for example, working capital requirements would be reduced by $600,000. Variable costs would also be reduced. Illustratively, at an operating level of 96,000 units, variable costs would be reduced by $3.00 per unit before depreciation and taxes, or by a total of $288,000. Finally and most important, the new facilities would permit QB to take advantage of favorable market conditions, if and when they developed.

Mr. Carnap believed that one factor that would complicate his analysis arose because the land and building costs associated with the facilities expansion program would be financed entirely by means of a sale-and-leaseback agreement, as plans stood at the moment. Rental fees would amortize the sales price over 25 years and provide the lessor with compound interest at the rate of 4.6% per annum; thereafter the lease was renewable for 15 years at a gross annual rental of 2.5%.

Having carried his analysis this far, Mr. Carnap believed he was in a position to formulate some preliminary conclusions as to the form and content of the proposal which would ultimately go to top management. He was certain, however, that some additional information would be helpful and that parts of his analysis would bear further scrutiny or, perhaps, revision. At the same time he was aware of the urgency of the situation and the need to make some recommendation within a very short time.

At this point, Mr. Carnap learned that actual levels of total new freight car deliveries and new freight cars equipped with antifriction bearings were 37,819 and 10,526, respectively, in 1959. As both these figures were considerably below previous estimates (see Exhibit 3) due in large part to the steel strike, he wondered how conservative his previous estimates would prove to be.

Exhibit 1

QUANDROW BEARINGS COMPANY

SALES AND INCOME DATA, 1950–1958

(Dollar figures in millions)

Year	Net Sales	Operating Profit	Net Income
1950	$108.9	$24.5	$11.4
1951	141.1	34.8	10.5
1952	134.3	27.1	7.4
1953	133.5	28.8	8.4
1954	101.8	16.5	7.9
1955	147.1	37.0	16.7
1956	161.5	34.2	15.9
1957	154.5	31.7	15.2
1958	124.3	16.5	8.1

Exhibit 2

QUANDROW BEARINGS COMPANY

YEAR-END BALANCE SHEETS, 1955–1958

(Dollar figures in millions)

ASSETS	1955	1956	1957	1958
Cash and securities.................$11.7		$15.6	$ 20.8	$ 16.7
Accounts receivable................. 14.2		14.5	13.9	11.2
Inventory.......................... 30.8		31.8	33.9	35.5
Other assets (net)................. 34.3		34.9	38.0	44.8
Total assets.....................$91.0		$96.8	$106.6	$108.2

LIABILITIES				
Current liabilities...................$12.9		$10.6	$ 12.6	$ 13.8
Net worth........................ 78.1		86.2	94.0	94.4
Total liabilities.................$91.0		$96.8	$106.6	$108.2

Exhibit 3

QUANDROW BEARINGS COMPANY

TOTAL FREIGHT CAR PRODUCTION AND CARS EQUIPPED WITH
ANTIFRICTION ROLLER BEARINGS, 1946–1959

Year	Total New Freight Cars Delivered	Total New Freight Cars Equipped with Anti-friction Bearings
1946....................... 41,955 (P)		6
1947....................... 68,522 (G)		57
1948.......................112,640 (G)		498
1949....................... 92,562 (G)		948
1950....................... 43,991 (P)		344
1951....................... 95,993 (G)		932
1952....................... 77,833 (G)		1,111
1953....................... 81,021 (G)		2,286
1954....................... 35,696 (P)		2,870
1955....................... 37,545 (P)		2,923
1956....................... 67,080 (G)		4,985
1957....................... 99,290 (G)		11,215
1958....................... 42,760 (P)		6,953
1959 estimate............... 41,000 (P)*		15,170

* Adversely affected by prolonged steel strike.
Note: The symbols (G) and (P) reflect the categorization of these deliveries into good and poor years, respectively.
Source: *Car Facts* (American Railway Car Institute), February, 1959. edition.

Exhibit 4

QUANDROW BEARINGS COMPANY

ESTIMATE OF EXPECTED SALES IN GOOD AND POOR YEARS

(Data based on 1946–1958, as shown in Exhibit 3)

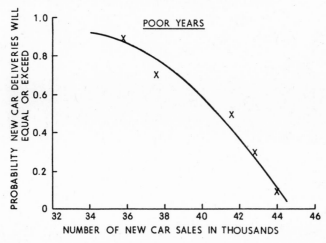

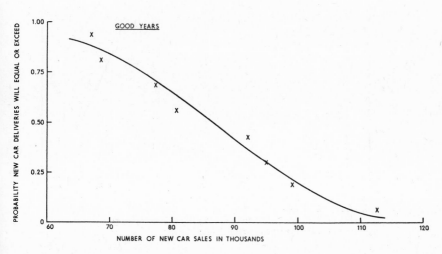

Exhibit 5

QUANDROW BEARINGS COMPANY

CHART SHOWING PER CENT NONROLLER-BEARING CAR DELIVERIES

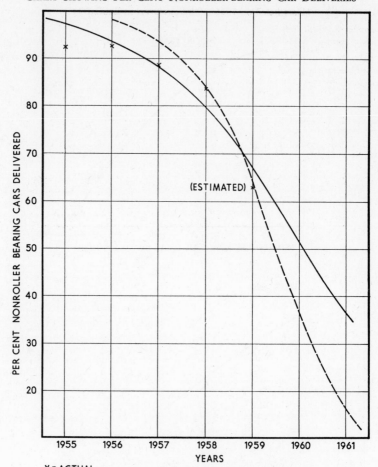

X = ACTUAL
———— FITTED TO FOUR YEARS' DATA (LEAST SQUARES)
— — FITTED TO LAST TWO YEARS' DATA

Exhibit 6

QUANDROW BEARINGS COMPANY

MARKET POTENTIAL UNDER VARIOUS MARKET SHARE ASSUMPTIONS

Quandrow Bearings Company's Share of Antifriction Market		*Antifriction Bearings' Share of Total Market*				
		40%	*50%*	*60%*	*70%*	*100%*
Capacity Limited to 120,000 Bearings per Year	50%	96,304	102,380	108,456	114,532	120,000
	60%	100,564	108,456	115,747	120,000	120,000
	70%	106,025	114,532	120,000	120,000	120,000
Unlimited Capacity	50%	101,296	126,620	151,944	177,268	253,240
	60%	121,555	151,944	182,332	212,720	303,888
	70%	141,814	177,268	212,720	248,175	354,536

Exhibit 7

QUANDROW BEARINGS COMPANY

ESTIMATED RETURNS FROM EXPANSION OF EXISTING FACILITIES, ASSUMING SALES OF 96,000 UNITS PER YEAR

(Dollar figures in thousands)

	1	2	3	4	5	6	7	8	9	10	11–15
Unit sales	101,000*	101,000*	96,000	96,000	96,000	96,000	96,000	96,000	96,000	96,000	480,000
Sales values	$12,120.0	$12,120.0	$11,520.0	$11,520.0	$11,520.0	$11,520.0	$11,520.0	$11,520.0	$11,520.0	$11,520.0	$57,600.0
Cost of sales:											
Manufacturing cost	$ 7,175.6	$ 7,175.6	$ 6,814.5	$ 6,814.5	$ 6,814.5	$ 6,814.5	$ 6,814.5	$ 6,814.5	$ 6,814.5	$ 6,814.5	$34,072.5
Inventory scrap	170.7	170.7	155.4	155.4	155.4	155.4	155.4	155.4	155.4	155.4	810.0
Production reconstruction	72.9	72.9	60.0	60.0	60.0	60.0	60.0	60.0	60.0	60.0	300.0
Loss on returns	121.2	121.2	115.5	115.5	115.5	115.5	115.5	115.5	115.5	115.5	577.5
Storage and shipping	270.8	270.8	236.3	236.3	236.3	236.3	236.3	236.3	36.3	236.3	1,181.5
Depreciation	551.6	418.9	327.0	262.1	217.5	408.3	261.3	207.8	213.0	175.5	1,395.0
Total cost of sales	$ 8,362.8	$ 8,230.1	$ 7,708.7	$ 7,643.8	$ 7,599.2	$ 7,790.0	$ 7,643.0	$ 7,589.5	$ 7,594.7	$ 7,557.2	$38,336.5
Gross margin	$ 3,757.2	$ 3,889.9	$ 3,811.3	$ 3,876.2	$ 3,920.8	$ 3,730.0	$ 3,877.0	$ 3,930.5	$ 3,925.3	$ 3,962.8	$19,263.5
Startup	$ 30.9	....	....	....	....	....	....	....	....	....	....
Social insurance and pensions	$ 644.7	$ 644.7	$ 586.9	$ 586.9	$ 586.9	$ 586.9	$ 586.9	$ 586.9	$ 586.9	$ 586.9	$ 2,934.5
Sales and engineering expenses	656.5	656.5	656.5	656.5	656.5	656.5	656.5	656.5	656.5	656.5	3,282.5
Commercial expenses	619.3	619.3	564.5	564.5	564.5	564.5	564.5	564.5	564.5	564.5	2,822.5
Local taxes	121.7	121.7	115.5	115.5	115.5	115.5	115.5	115.5	115.5	115.5	577.5
Total other expenses	$ 2,073.1	$ 2,042.2	$ 1,923.4	$ 1,923.4	$ 1,923.4	$ 1,923.4	$ 1,923.4	$ 1,923.4	$ 1,923.4	$ 1,923.4	$ 9,617.0
Profit before tax	$ 1,684.1	$ 1,847.7	$ 1,887.9	$ 1,952.8	$ 1,997.4	$ 1,806.6	$ 1,953.6	$ 2,007.1	$ 2,001.9	$ 2,039.4	$ 9,646.5
After 52% tax	$ 808.3	$ 886.9	$ 906.2	$ 937.3	$ 958.7	$ 867.2	$ 937.7	$ 963.4	$ 960.9	$ 978.9	$ 4,630.3
CASH PICKUP											
Depreciation	$ 551.6	$ 418.9	$ 327.0	$ 262.1	$ 217.5	$ 408.3	$ 261.3	$ 207.8	$ 213.0	$ 175.5	$ 1,395.0
Profit after tax	808.3	886.9	906.2	937.3	958.7	867.2	937.7	963.4	960.9	978.9	4,630.3
Total pickup	$ 1,359.9	$ 1,305.8	$ 1,233.2	$ 1,199.4	$ 1,176.5	$ 1,275.5	$ 1,199.0	$ 1,171.2	$ 1,173.9	$ 1,154.4	$ 6,025.3

* Permits desired inventory accumulation of 10,000 units.

Exhibit 8

QUANDROW BEARINGS COMPANY

ESTIMATED INVESTMENT REQUIREMENTS FOR EXPANSION OF EXISTING
FACILITIES AND RELATED RETURN ON INVESTMENT COMPUTATIONS

(Dollar figures in thousands)

Year	Equipment Investment	Working Capital	Installation Cost after Taxes	Cash Pickup (Ex. 7)	Net After-Tax Cash Flow	Present Value at: 15%	16%
−½ to 0	$−3,028.9		$−118.4		$−3,147.3	$−3,268.5	$−3,276.7
1		$−2,477.2		$1,359.9	−1,117.3	−1,037.5	−1,032.5
2		−1,735.8		1,305.8	− 430.0	− 343.9	− 338.9
3				1,233.2	+1,233.2	+ 848.3	+ 827.5
4				1,199.4	+1,199.4	+ 710.2	+ 685.8
5	− 527.5			1,176.5	+ 649.0	+ 330.7	+ 316.2
6				1,275.5	+1,275.5	+ 559.4	+ 529.6
7				1,199.0	+1,199.0	+ 452.6	+ 424.2
8	− 522.0			1,171.2	+ 649.2	+ 211.0	+ 195.7
9				1,173.9	+1,163.9	+ 328.3	+ 301.6
10	− 527.5			1,154.4	+ 626.9	+ 150.9	+ 137.2
11–15	− 983.3			6,025.3	+5,042.0	+ 791.6	+ 700.8
Residual value	+ 561.2	+4,213.0			+4,774.2	+ 503.2	+ 433.0
Present value, Total						+ 236.3	− 96.5

$$15\% + \left(\frac{236.3}{332.8} \times 1\%\right)$$

Present value rate of return = 15.7%

Exhibit 9
QUANDROW BEARINGS COMPANY
RETURN POTENTIALS AT VARIOUS LEVELS OF OPERATION
(Dollar figures in thousands)

Units	70,000	80,000	90,000	100,000	110,000	120,000
Sales value	$ 8,400	$ 9,600	$10,800	$ 12,000	$ 13,200	$ 14,400
Variable cost	$ 6,294.5	$ 7,184.8	$ 8,083.7	$ 8,978.3	$ 9,876.1	$ 10,778.3
Fixed expenses	666.0	666.0	675.0	682.5	682.5	682.5
Depreciation*	337.5	337.5	337.5	337.5	337.5	337.5
Total costs	$ 7,298.0	$ 8,188.3	$ 9,096.2	$ 9,998.3	$ 10,896.1	$ 11,798.3
Profit before tax†	$ 1,102.0	$ 1,411.7	$ 1,703.8	$ 2.001.7	$ 2,303.9	$ 2,601.7
Tax at 52%	573.0	734.1	886.0	1,040.9	1,198.0	1,352.9
Profit after tax	$ 529.0	$ 677.6	$ 817.8	$ 960.8	$ 1,105.9	$ 1,248.8
Depreciation	337.5	337.5	337.5	337.5	337.5	337.5
Cash pickup	$ 866.5	$ 1,015.1	$ 1,155.3	$ 1,298.3	$ 1,443.4	$ 1,586.3

* Represents an increase of $71,400 over estimated levels if no expanison were undertaken.
† Really contribution to overhead.

Exhibit 10
QUANDROW BEARINGS COMPANY
CAPITAL REQUIREMENTS AND RETURN POTENTIALS UNDER
PROPOSED PLANT EXPANSION PROGRAM
(Dollar figures in thousands)

PART I

	1961	1962	1963	1964
Target capacity (units)	160,000	192,000	276,000	320,000
	Total		Incremental	
Building cost	$ 1,450.0			
Land cost	365.0			
Value equipment on hand	2,250.0			
Moving expense (after tax)	376.2*			
Equipment capacity per 120,000	878.9			
Additional new equipment†	4,637.0	$1,997.9	$2,448.3	$1,366.2
Working capital needs (80% activity)	4,795.0	325.3	520.3	260.5
Less: Value of space freed	(450.0)			
Current working capital (96,000 per year)	(4,213.0)			
Total investment	$10,089.1	$2,323.2	$2,968.6	$1,626.7

PART 2

	1961	1962	1963	1964
Expected revenues:				
Sales at 80% capacity	$15,360.0	$18,432.0	$26,496.0	$30,720.0
Expected costs and profits at 80% of capacity:				
Variable cost of goods sold per unit	$ 61.80	$ 61.56	$ 61.32	$ 61.20
Variable cost of goods sold	$ 7,910.0	$ 9,455.6	$13,539.5	$15,667.2
Depreciation‡	913.3	726.0	607.2	532.1
Total other expenses	2,631.0	3,026.2	3,672.5	4,200.8
Total costs	$11,454.7	$13,207.8	$17,819.2	$20,400.1
Before taxes contribution to overhead	$ 3,905.3	$ 5,224.2	$ 8,676.8	$10,319.9
Taxes @ 52%	2,030.8	2,716.6	4,511.9	5,366.3
Profit after tax	$ 1,874.5	$ 2,507.6	$ 4,164.9	$ 4,943.6
Depreciation	913.3	726.0	607.2	532.1
Cash throw-off	$ 2,787.8	$ 3,233.6	$ 4,772.1	$ 5,475.7

* Would be $458.8 if capacity of existing plant expanded first.
† Same depreciation % as before.
‡ Based on proposed investment schedule, assuming plant and land are purchased, not leased, plant depreciation equals approximately 12% of total annual depreciation.

Section III

MEASURING THE COST OF CAPITAL

CONSOLIDATED ELECTRICAL PRODUCTS, INC. (C)

SELECTION OF A MINIMUM STANDARD FOR EVALUATING ACCEPTABLE RETURNS ON PROSPECTIVE INVESTMENTS

The opinions expressed by various members of CONELP management with respect to alternative methods of establishing minimum acceptable return on investment criteria fell into two broad categories. The first related to using some historic measure of return on assets as a cutoff point in evaluating new capital expenditure programs. Alternatively, several officers preferred to follow a measurement approach referred to as the "cost-of-capital" method. Each of these basic measurement alternatives could be calculated by several procedures, all with significantly different results. Moreover, opinions among management differed widely both as to which basic approach and as to which subsidiary procedure would provide the most useful basis for determining the desired cutoff point. In an effort to resolve the resulting conflict, Mr. Holman had summarized the alternatives suggested to him as shown below:

I. *The "Historic Return on Assets" Approach*

Stockholders have invested in CONELP stock largely because they are satisfied with the manner in which we run our affairs. In particular, they are satisfied with the success we have had in employing capital effectively. In formulating capital budgeting policies, we must strive to employ our capital as well in future years as we have done in the past if we are to fulfill our responsibilities to stockholders. This means we cannot afford to let our historic return on assets decline. The surest method of accomplishing this objective is to reject projects whose returns are below the historic rate of return. By these arguments, then, historic rate of return on assets is a useful method of determining minimum return standards.

There have been several procedures suggested for measuring historic return on assets. Each of these procedures is outlined below.

A. *Alternative Basic Return on Investment Calculations*

1. *Net Return on Gross Investment.* This is the procedure currently
employed by CONELP. Essentially, profits after depreciation and taxes
serve as numerator for the equation while total book assets, gross of
depreciation but net of current liabilities, form the denominator. (See
Exhibit 1 in the CONELP (A) case for sample calculations.)

Several executives strongly urge the continuance of this procedure.
They believe, first of all, that over the years CONELP management has
developed considerable experience in applying this criterion and that
any change from it would involve significant readjustments of a super-
sensitive yet vital ingredient, the judgment skills of management. They
also argue that the current procedures would have successfully imple-
mented basic objectives were it not for the unexpected and abnormal
depression of profit levels in the major appliance division. To support this view, they point out that over-all corporate profit levels would
return to earlier postwar levels with only a partial restoration of profit
rates in the major appliance division. Finally, a number of executives
think this procedure is the most realistic and meaningful method of
establishing a minimum return criterion.

2. *Cash Flow to Gross Investment.* One executive believes that the sum
of profits after taxes and of depreciation is a more suitable numerator
for the equation than the profit after-tax figure used currently. Depreciation inflows are, in his mind, as important, if not more important,
than profit flows. Depreciation, he noted, is unrestrictedly available
for investment, whereas profits, in part, are distributed to stockholders.
Depreciation consequently provides a valuable means of sustaining
expansion. Since stockholders are largely interested in growth, they
will not want their cash flows as a percentage of investments to fall
off. The procedure outlined above affords a means of avoiding this
danger.

3. *Net Return on Net Investment.* Under this alternative, total assets, net
of depreciation and current liabilities, would be used as the equation's
denominator. Net investment is simply another method of expressing
total capitalization (i.e., the sum of debt, preferred stock, common
stock, and surplus book values). Several officers believe that we should
attempt to maintain or improve the return on total capitalization, the
justification being expressed in terms of maintaining stockholder
values.

4. *Net Return on Equity Book Values.* Common stock book values, both
capital and surplus accounts, would be used here as the denominator of
the equation. Stockholders have a vested interest in seeing the returns
on their investment hold constant or improve. Several officers believe
that common stock book values consequently constitute the most acceptable means of establishing cutoff points, consistent with stock-

holder objectives. This procedure has one inherent difficulty. Divisional records summarize total capital advanced from the parent company but do not differentiate between debt and equity funds. Hence, some problems may exist in allocating the book values of the common stock to divisions. In particular, one division manager objected to a distribution in proportion to total capitalization because "investments in his division are substantially less risky than some others, and consequently his division should command a higher proportion of debt and a lower proportion of equity than the corporate average." He has not, however, suggested an alternative basis for distribution.

5. *Net Return on Replacement Values.* In this equation, the denominator would be measured by adding the gross replacement value of property and subtracting from it current liabilities. The argument for this alternative starts from the opinion that book values reflect accounting oversimplifications and are not true values in the sense of reflecting current market worth. The argument continues: revaluing assets in terms of their present worth creates a more realistic picture of their true value to stockholders. Illustratively, the inventory values in the electrical components division were understated by at least $10 million because of Lifo accounting procedures. Inventories in other divisions evaluated mostly by Fifo procedures were, in contrast, stated according to their approximate current worth. Gross plant book values in both the electrical component division and the heavy industrial equipment divisions were stated at less than half current replacement costs, whereas in the remaining divisions, gross plant book values were approximately 90% of current replacement values. In particular, these differences would change profit rates within various divisions—in some instances significantly. The officer most in favor of this measurement procedure also believed depreciation was unrealistically stated and should be revised in profit calculations.

6. *Miscellaneous Alternatives.* The aforementioned variations in procedure suggest single substitutions in the measurement equation. Several additional combinations are possible—e.g., cash flow return on net investment. The possibility of advantageously combining some of these alternatives should consequently not be ignored.

B. *Other Variations in Methodology*

1. *Method of Calculating Profits at the Divisional Level.* Under present procedures, expenses of a division are charged to that division. However, expenses of the central office are not. Unless these central expenses, variously referred to as "club dues," are allocated to the divisions, the divisions' profit rates, as used in calculating cutoff points, are not realistic. Although this argument has considerable support, there is no agreement as to whether sales, profits, gross investment, or some other measure might be the most appropriate basis for accomplishing this allocation.

There is also some support for a system that would distribute central corporate assets to divisions before computing their cutoff points. Arguments in favor of this approach are similar.

2. *Methods of Weighing.* We now employ a system of computing five-year unweighted averages to determine the cutoff point. The five-year figure is admittedly arbitrary and has been subjected to sharp criticism. On the one hand, several believe the use of more current figures, attune with the times, would lead to more useful standards. However, others feel strongly that the standard is already too volatile and has shifted downward significantly, yet without just cause merely because of the major appliance division's current adverse earnings. The number of years included in the weighting clearly will need more systematic resolution than arbitrarily selecting five years. There is also the possibility of using weighted averages (e.g., weighting the most recent years more heavily) in this calculation.

II. The "Cost-of-Capital" Approach

Money or capital, the fuel for a capital expenditure program, is a commodity that may be purchased in various forms and at various prices. As long as the return opportunities from projected investments exceed the cost of desirable forms of capital, available to the company for its use, stockholders would benefit by employing the capital and by making the investments. Thus, a desirable cutoff point for appraising marginal investment opportunities is the "cost of capital." These essentially are the arguments put forward in support of the cost-of-capital approach.

Perhaps the biggest difficulty associated with the cost-of-capital approach is the problem of finding agreement as to how costs are to be measured. In this company, there are sharply contrasting opinions as to just how capital costs should be measured. These disagreements arise about both the framework and the procedures for calculating costs. A summary of these disagreements and of other related problems is indicated below:

A. *Frameworks for Computing a Cost of Capital for Minimum Return Purposes.*

1. *The Least Expensive Increment of Capital.* This framework suggests that all projects with returns above the least costly form of capital are desirable, and that the cost of this least expensive source of capital should serve as a minimum return criterion. Illustratively, debt capital, at the moment, costs only $4\frac{3}{4}\%$ and appears generally to be the least expensive source of capital available to us. A project returning profits in excess of this cost (e.g., 5%) would therefore add to stockholders' earnings per share. Since maximizing earnings per share is one of our corporate objectives, this alternative should be accepted.

2. *The Most Expensive Increment of Capital.* The alternative outlined above may have as one of its flaws, the limiting condition that the cutoff rate can't be maintained. A low cutoff point would probably lead to extremely heavy investment—beyond the level supportable by debt

resources. Once debt funds are depleted—the low cost capital resources consumed—management will have to fall back upon more expensive forms of capital. The cutoff point must then be raised to the next most expensive increment, etc., until finally it arrives at the level of the most expensive form of capital. In order to avoid discontinuity, and the financing of projects with lower returns than prove acceptable over time, the use of the cost of the most expensive increment of capital will prove most desirable. In our company, this means setting the cutoff point at the level of the cost of equity capital.

3. *The Weighted-Average Cost of Capital (Present Book Values)*. We are already employing considerable sums of capital. These capital accumulations are worth something on the market. Indeed, we can approximate the cost or worth of our capital by computing the cost we would have to pay if we were to replace these funds in today's markets. At the moment our capital structure is as follows:

	Amount	*% of Total*	*Weight*
Debenture (3.75%)............................	$120 million	32.1%	0.321
Noncallable preferred (6.0% dividend).........	50 million	13.4	0.134
Capital stock (7 million shares)...............	70 million	18.7	0.187
Earned surplus..............................	134 million	35.8	0.358
Total................................	$374 million	100.0%	1.000

By multiplying the weight column above and the cost of each form of capital, and then summing the products, we can ascertain the average cost of capital under today's market conditions. This figure can then serve as the cutoff point.

4. *The Weighted-Average Cost of Capital (Ideal Capital Structure)*. Our present capital structure is not without its flaws. In the future, we anticipate shifting this capital structure towards a more satisfactory balance. This ideal balance envisioned in current policies would have book values as shown below:

	% of Total
Debentures...	33.3%
Preferred stock...	10.0
Common stock and earned surplus.......................	56.7
Total...	100.0%

These percentages can be employed in the weighting and averaging process described above.

5. *The Weighted-Average Cost of Capital (Market Values)*. The capital structure can be described in terms of market values, and a weighting system developed from these values. Illustratively, there are seven million common shares outstanding, each with a market worth of $48 per share (average market price—1956). The common stock's total market value is thus $336 million. The value of outstanding debt can be measured by dividing prevailing interest rates (4.75%) into total in-

terest payments (of $4.5 million). Debt has a market value of $95 million by this calculation. The market value of the preferred may also be calculated by a similar process to be $65 million. From this data, the following weights can be obtained:

	Amount	% of Total
Debt	$ 95	19.1%
Preferred stock	65	13.1
Common stock	336	67.8
Total	$496	100.0

These weightings can then be employed in measuring average cost of capital by the procedures outlined above. Note, however, that the specific market values described above are not the only figures that could be developed for this purpose.

6. *The Weighted-Average Cost of Future Capital.* Forecasts of future fund requirements reveal a totally different picture of capitalization proportions than do measures based on present balance sheet relationships. According to five-year projections, retained earnings for the period have been estimated at $65 million. An additional $150 million must be raised from outside sources to cover fully expansion requirements during this five-year period. Since present debt policy limits the use of debt to one-third of total capitalization, at least $74 million of the funds required must be raised from equity sources. No further use of preferred stock is contemplated in the immediate future. Hence, an approximate weighting system using funds required as a base is shown below:

Source	Estimated Amount of Funds Raised	% of Total
Debt	$ 76 million	35.4%
Equity capital issue	74	34.3
Retained earnings	65	30.3
Total	$215 million	100.0%

Average capital costs may be computed by using these weightings.

7. *The Weighted-Average Cost of Cash Flows.* None of the foregoing systems take into consideration the existence of depreciation resources which tend to support expenditure levels. Illustratively, depreciation resources for the forthcoming five-year period were estimated at $85 million. Hence, the weighted proportions of capital we anticipate employing in the next five years is as shown below:

Source	Estimated Amount of Funds Raised	% of Total
Depreciation	$ 85	28.3%
Debt	76	25.3
Equity capital issues	74	24.7
Retained earnings	65	21.7
Total	$300	100.0%

After computing a cost for depreciation funds, an average cost of capital can be computed by the usual weighting procedures.

8. *The Cost of the Most Expensive Incremental Package of Capital.* The present expansion plans are predicated on the assumption it will be desirable to use all the resources outlined above. This assumption would not be valid if an integral portion of the funds required were financed from a source more expensive in cost than the return opportunities available within the company. Illustratively, the fund resources outlined above can be broken into two meaningful parts: funds available (including added debt resources) as an outgrowth of our internally generated source of funds, and funds available as the result of raising additional equity capital. Each of these capital packages has an independent cost, which may be computed separately. The weightings would be as follows:

PACKAGE 1*

Source	Amount	% of Total
Depreciation	$ 85.0	45.0%
Debt	39.0	20.6
Retained earnings	65.0	34.4
Total	$189.0	100.0%

* This package can presumably be broken into smaller units. However, under this alternative, only the most expensive package has relevance. We are interested in the subpackage that has the highest cost and is incremental in the sense management has the power to raise or to reject the funds.

PACKAGE 2

Source	Amount	% of Total
Debt	$ 37.0	33.3%
Issue of equity capital	74.0	66.7
Total	$111.0	100.0%

Package 2 presumably is the more expensive increment, and consequently should be employed in calculating the cutoff point by the conventional weighted-average process.

B. *Methods of Measuring the Cost of Various Forms of Capital*

Various methods of measuring the cost of the several forms of capital involved in the weighting schemes discussed above have been suggested and are summarized below. (The need for tax adjustments to an after-tax basis is implicitly assumed and not discussed.)

1. *Debt Capital.* Four basic measurement alternatives are available. They are:

a) Stated interest rates: The stated interest coupons on outstanding debt are 3.75%.

b) Present interest rates: Debentures similar in quality to CONELP's (i.e., rated Aa by Moody's Investment Service) currently sell to·

yield approximately 4.75% on the market. New issues of this same rating are being marketed at slightly higher yields—approximately 5%.

  c) *Historic average yield:* In the postwar years, Aa bonds have yielded in the market between 2.8% and 4.8%, with 3.2% being an approximate average for the period.

  d) *Expected level of future yields:* This approach involves projecting probable yields for securities of the quality we normally employ. Here, we would have to project the yield trends for Aa bonds for some relevant period in the future.

2. *Preferred Capital.* The alternatives for measuring the cost of preferred resemble those for debt.

  a) *Stated dividend rates:* The rate is 6%.

  b) *Present yield in market price:* The dividend is $6, and the current market price (the stock is listed on the New York Exchange) is $130. Yield on this market price is 4.6%. The average market price for the preferred during 1956 was $139.

  c) *Historic average yield:* In the postwar years, the 6% preferred has yielded between 3.7% and 5.1% on the market, with 4.2% reflecting a rough approximation of an average yield.

  d) *Expected future yields:* This involves forecasting preferred yields for an appropriate period in the future.

3. *New Issues of Equity Capital.* For the preceding forms of capital, the essential aspects of measurement involve relating a payment (e.g., interest fees) to the amount of capital that could, given a fixture as to point in time, be acquired for that payment. While the same measurement problem exists for equity capital, the complications are more notable.

  a) *Numerator in the cost equation:* A number of individuals consider dividends per share the most appropriate measure of income obligations for the common stock. They argue that the dividend rate represents the only out-of-pocket payment made for capital employed and hence is its cost. Secondly, dividend rates exert a more important influence in determining market prices, and, by this token, can be considered the most appropriate cost measurement. Raw evidence, allegedly supporting this viewpoint is shown in the summary of market data given in Exhibit 1.

  In contrast, others believe that earnings per share are a more meaningful base for measuring equity costs. Stockholders, they argue, place some value on retained earnings as well as on dividends. Retained earnings are reinvested in the firm and build a base for future earnings and dividend per-share growth. Moreover, retained earnings act as a cushion, protecting the safety (or stability) of the dividend during periods of adverse earnings. If we are to preserve the reinvestment and cushion value of retained earnings, earnings per share should be used as the cost of capital measure.

b) *Denominator in the cost equation:* The differences here arise because several individuals believe that the issue price per share is a more appropriate figure for the calculation than the customary market price per share. Because of underwriting discounts and fees, and of other issuing costs, the final issuing price is usually below the market price (e.g., an issue price equal to 95% of market price might serve as a satisfactory rule of thumb). Since the company only gains funds equal to the issue price, it must invest these funds at a cost ratio based on issue price in order to avoid dilution.

c) *Alternative sources of data:* Even after these previous issues have been settled, there still remains the task of selecting specific data to plug into the derived equations. The following differences in point of view as to appropriate sources of data for measuring the cost have arisen:

(1) *Present relationships:* Accept the most recent data only.

(2) *Historical averages:* Take a weighted or unweighted average of calculations for several recent years.

(3) *Projections of relationship at the expected date of issuance:* Use a projection of the most probable relationship at the expected future time of issue.

(4) *Average of future earnings or dividends per share:* Under this alternative, average future earnings (or dividends) per share (estimated by assuming no equity capital is raised) would be related to the current market price.

(5) *The earnings or dividend discount factor:* Illustratively, we would first project earnings (or dividends) per share into the future. The rate necessary to discount the present value of this stream of earnings per share to the current market price would then be taken as the cost measurement.

4. *Retained Earnings.* Several alternative methods of measuring the cost of retained earnings are available. These are:

a) *Zero cost:* The argument in support of the contention that retained earnings have no cost runs as follows: CONELP is already paying out a generous proportion of earnings in cash dividends (approximately 60% pay-out on the average). Stockholders have not complained about this policy and must, therefore, consider the pay-out fair. Stockholders, moreover, expect some earnings retention, and, indeed, dividends might become highly unstable (viz., 1950–1951 in Exhibit 1) if a higher proportion of earnings were actually paid out. In view of the prospects of greater instability, stockholders might actually attach a negative value to any further increase in dividends. These factors all suggest that retained earnings do not have any real cost.

b) *Cost of an equity issue:* Retaining earnings is merely an alternative means of raising equity capital, and therefore its cost is the same (or nearly so) as the cost of an equity issue. See the alternative outlined above.

c) *The personal income tax factor:* Because cash dividend distributions are subject to personal income taxation—often at high rates —it is more advantageous to retain an equitable portion of earnings than pay out all earnings in dividends, and then subsequently raise equity capital. Retained earnings must consequently have a lower cost than equity capital.

    Since CONELP stockholders have a wide variety of tax situations, the specific application of this cost measurement, if any, has yet to be worked out.

5. *Depreciation:* The following suggestions for measuring the cost of depreciation have been made:

a) *Zero cost:* Depreciation is capital already within the company. Since it does not need to be raised, even in the indirect sense of retained earnings, it clearly has no cost.

b) *Historic return on assets:* The main purpose that depreciation serves is to preserve corporate earning power. As assets deteriorate, they must be renovated or replaced if earnings are to be maintained. Depreciation funds provide the wherewithal. On these grounds, one of the historic return on asset criteria discussed above appears to be an appropriate basis for measuring the cost of depreciation.

c) *Cost of capital:* Depreciation is a return of capital previously invested. It is consequently equivalent in cost to the historic composite for capital employed within the company. The cost of depreciation then can be taken as one of the weighted-average costs already discussed.

d) *Erosion cost:* New capital is employed to add new earning power, according to the cost definitions outlined above. However, a number of investments must be made to offset the erosion of earning power taking place within the company. This profit erosion is not only attributed to machine obsolescence and wear and tear but also to product obsolescence, to the adverse effects of advances made by competitors, to creeping cost increases, etc. In short, a number of investments must be made to avoid losing ground on the profit treadmill. Depreciation is the prime source of funds for this purpose. The "total cost of depreciation" is then the dollar decline in earnings that would take place if no further investments were made. This figure can be readily restated in terms of a percentage of depreciation resources.

C. *Other Cost-of-Capital Considerations*

    One of the primary drawbacks to using costs of capital as a measurement standard for minimum returns on investment is that computations below the corporate level are highly problematical. Consequently, there is no real basis for distinguishing between the return cutoff points of independent divisions. A suggestion for avoiding this dilemma is to compare each division with comparable competing companies in industry and determine appropriate cost data and cutoff points by this indirect means. Illustratively, the control apparatus division has shown extraordinary growth in postwar years. Since similar growth companies have high price-earnings ratios in the order of, say, 20, this division's cost of equity capital could be estimated as 5% after taxes. On the other hand, heavy equipment manufacturers with similar earnings records to our industrial division have price-earnings ratios in the neighborhood of eight. This suggests that the cost of equity funds for the industrial division might approximate 12.5% after taxes. Other bases for distinguishing between division's capital costs are apparent. The less risky divisions might be able to carry a higher debt proportion, replacement requirements among divisions differ widely, and other similar important areas of contrast exist. These elements of contrast form the basis for imputing capital costs to each division.

A second disturbing condition is that most all of these cost-of-capital measurements suggest that we should become less selective in undertaking projects than we have been historically. The finance committee, on the other hand, believes intuitively that we are already dipping too far down in the list of available projects. Are these cost-of-capital figures conclusive enough to argue for a change in capital expenditure policies (i.e., lowering the cutoff standard) which would cause a sharp increase in our dependence upon equity capital? That is, do these figures really prove that top managements' judgment is in error?

Exhibit 1

CONSOLIDATED ELECTRICAL PRODUCTS, INC. (C)

EARNINGS, DIVIDEND, AND MARKET PRICE DATA, 1947–1956

	Earnings per Share*	Dividends per Share	Average Market Price	Price-Earnings Ratio	Dividend Yield
1956	$3.82	$2.25	$48	12.6	4.7%
1955	3.29	2.00	45½	13.8	4.4
1954	3.34	2.00	38½	11.5	5.2
1953	3.97	2.00	40¾	10.3	4.9
1952	3.37	2.00	39⅜	11.7	5.1
1951	3.28	2.00	37⅜	11.4	5.4
1950	4.69	1.60	29⅛	6.2	5.5
1949	2.15	1.20	24	11.2	5.0
1948	2.21	1.00	21¼	9.6	4.7
1947	1.55	0.80	18⅛	11.6	4.4
Ten-year average				11.0	4.9%

* After preferred dividends; 7,000,000 common shares outstanding throughout the period after adjusting for stock splits.

VIKING STEEL CORPORATION (A)

In January, 1960, at the conclusion of a long steel strike, the board of directors of the Viking Steel Corporation decided to raise $10 million for expansion and modernization by selling a new issue of common stock in May, 1960. Subsequent to this decision, the market price of Viking's common stock fell from $49 to $38 per share. At the mid-February board meeting, Mr. Togni, one of the outside directors, noted the downward trend in market prices and posed the following question: "At what market price would it be more desirable to issue debt rather than continue with the proposed sale of equity?" After a brief discussion, the question was referred to Mr. O'Hearth, financial vice-president and director, for further study and recommendations. As a first step in this analysis, Mr. O'Hearth planned to investigate the relative desirability of selling stock at an issue price of $35 per share.

The Viking Steel Corporation was founded by a small group of businessmen in 1900. Operations began in 1902 with the completion of four open-hearth furnaces, a blooming mill, a billet mill, and two hot strip mills. Prior to 1930 the company began production of cold-rolled strip steel as well as stainless and other alloy strip steels. In 1930 and the years which followed, the company suffered severe operating losses. Sales in 1932 amounted to only 27% of 1929 sales, and finishing mill operations averaged under 30% of capacity. The company incurred sizable losses during six of the nine years from 1930 to 1938 (the largest loss was $2 million). At the close of the war in 1945, the company resumed its long-run program of development. During the postwar period, negotiations were completed for the acquisition of seven formerly independent concerns. The company also joined with another firm to set up a subsidiary which produced and fabricated titanium, zirconium, hafnium, columbium, and thorium. In 1960, the company and its subsidiaries produced a wide range of products, including: steel bar and plates; carbon, alloy, and stainless hot- and cold-rolled strip;

194

coal, coke, and chemical by-products; strapping; and various specialty metals. Exhibits 1 through 4 show some of the company's recent financial development.

During 1958 the company's board of directors installed a new management to help strengthen Viking's competitive position. The new president, Mr. Rab Dellor, realized the company's production facilities were badly in need of modernization, since Viking was one of the highest cost producers in the industry. The company's sales organization also needed attention if Viking was to capitalize fully on available market opportunities. Mr. Dellor recognized that Viking was still largely a producer of basic steel products and that further vertical integration towards the market was required. Management believed the solution of these problems would enable Viking both to reduce the cyclical character of sales and increase profitability.

Mr. Dellor and his new management team first concentrated on improving the sales organization, and although it was too early in January, 1960, to measure the results of their efforts, they were pleased with the progress made. In particular, it was thought that the company would henceforth operate closer to capacity, due to improved selling, and that it would be somewhat less subject to cyclical sales fluctuations.

Executives of the company had prepared a detailed modernization plan involving the expenditure of $12 million in 1960 and early 1961. This expenditure was expected to increase finishing capacity by 15%, to raise operating income by nearly $4 million at the operating level envisioned for 1960, and to improve efficiency at lower levels of activity. For example, Mr. Dellor anticipated that the modernization program would insure a minimum operating profit (EBIT) of $3.5 million in the future, even under such severely depressed sales conditions as Viking had experienced in 1958.

Although Viking's sales and profits had demonstrated considerable instability during the postwar period, the company had always maintained a strong current position. During the most recent five years, for example, net working capital had ranged between $33.4 and $38.6 million, and total current assets between $51.1 and $54.3 million. To maintain this relatively strong current position, management had adopted a firm policy of maintaining a minimum $4 million reserve in marketable securities to cushion sudden changes in financial requirements.

Mr. Dellor also recommended that the board change Viking's dividend policy. In the past, dividends had been closely related to profits and consequently had undergone frequent change, despite a determined effort on the part of the board to maintain a minimum $2 annual dividend rate. Mr. Dellor believed the frequent changes in dividend payments had hurt the reputation of the Viking Steel Corporation in the financial community. In view of this situation, the board recently had approved an annual dividend rate of $2.40 per share, to be paid, insofar as possible, during both profitable and unprofitable years. This new stable dividend rate was regarded as a minimum by the board, but would be continued until the long-term earnings outlook changed materially. When this new dividend policy was announced publicly in December, 1959, it was favorably received.

In planning the financing aspect of the proposed modernization program, Mr. O'Hearth projected operating profits of $11 million during the first half of 1960, followed by $7 million in the second half of the year. This prediction assumed a relatively strong level of demand throughout the year, with some decline during the last half of the year once customers' inventories were rebuilt from the depleted levels existent following the steel strike in late 1959. Retained earnings (before considering the effect of the proposed financing) had been forecast at $5.8 million in 1960, with depreciation remaining at $3.8 million. These internally generated sources of funds and the proposed sale of $10 million in stock would be used as follows: $12 million modernization program, $3.5 million increase in inventories and receivables, $500,000 sinking fund payment, and $3.6 million added to Viking's cash balance for use in subsequent expansion programs.

In view of the considerable sales and profit uncertainties associated with the future, Mr. O'Hearth did not believe the company could forecast fund flows beyond 1960 with a useful degree of accuracy. Since experience indicated that funds generated through depreciation charges would be required to support the company's normal capital expenditures, future funds requirements for expansion and diversification would have to be financed with retained earnings and new external capital in the forseeable future. Total capital expenditures probably would average about $7.0 million per year after 1960.

In planning the financing of the proposed modernization program, company officials considered a number of alternative debt and common stock proposals. After careful analysis they narrowed the choice to either a privately placed issue of debentures or common stock.

A large pension trust had agreed to buy a debenture issue from Viking. The $5\frac{3}{4}\%$ debentures would mature in 20 years and would involve no sinking fund payments during the first five years. Thereafter there would be a $500,000 annual repayment with a balloon maturity. (The currently outstanding debentures carried a 4½% interest rate and a $500,000 annual sinking fund payment.) The proposed debentures would be subject to the following restrictions: (1) additional long-term debt would be limited to 75% of net working capital; and (2) dividends could not be paid in excess of profits earned subsequent to 1959. Additional covenants appeared normal and in no way restrictive or threatening.

The exact terms on the proposed common stock issue could not be set until just prior to issuance. In January, 1960, when the market price was $49, the company was told by investment bankers that it probably could net $45 per share. Sale of common stock would involve additional expenses of about $70,000.

On the basis of this information, Mr. Dellor had prepared a detailed analysis of these alternatives. Excerpts from this analysis are shown in Exhibit 5. After careful review of all the available information, management had recommended, and the board had approved, the common stock alternative on the following grounds: the sacrifice in earnings per share appeared justified in view of the greater risk associated with the debt alternative; the timing of an equity sale seemed "right" in view of the high market price of the stock, whereas interest rates on debt were at a postwar high; and the stock alternative allowed for greater financial flexibility by keeping Viking's debt to total capitalization ratio within range of the industry's average of 18.7%.

After this decision was reached, stock prices on the New York Stock Exchange broke sharply downward, and by mid-February were a full 10% below January's highs. Viking's market price had also fallen from $49 to $38 per share. Following this experience, leading investment bankers expressed considerable uncertainty regarding the likely movement of the market over the next few months. In view of this uncertainty, Mr. O'Hearth was unable to get any firm estimate about the level of the stock market, or the likely price of Viking's stock, during the period preceding the proposed midyear stock sale.

This situation led Mr. Togni to question whether the decline in the price of the company's stock justified a reappraisal of the alternative methods of financing the modernization program. Mr. Togni pointed out that in view of the basic market uncertainties, the board would quite likely have to examine the same proposition after every major market movement up to the proposed date of issue in mid-May. Mr. Togni suggested, therefore, that the board determine the lowest acceptable issue price for common stock (before the debenture alternative looked more attractive than a new issue of common stock). In this way, he argued, the board would have a firm basis for action until the day preceding the offering date when a final decision would be made. Mr. Dellor admitted that he had never looked at the question in this way, but, because it seemed a useful approach, agreed to have Mr. O'Hearth prepare such an analysis prior to the next scheduled board meeting in early March. As a preliminary step in this investigation, Mr. O'Hearth planned to explore the implications of selling the stock to net $45, $40, $35, and $30 per share (see Exhibit 5). As a basis for comparison, Mr. O'Hearth had collected the data on selected steel companies shown in Exhibit 6.

Exhibit 1

VIKING STEEL CORPORATION (A)

BALANCE SHEET, DECEMBER 31, 1959

(Dollar figures in thousands)

ASSETS		LIABILITIES	
Cash	$ 5,641	Accounts payable	$ 5,544
Market securities	5,121	Accrued wages	3,360
Accounts receivable	13,496	Accrued taxes	3,474
Inventories	30,042	Other current liabilities	3,358
Total current assets	$ 54,300	Total current liabilities	$ 15,736
Investments in affiliates	7,000	4½% debentures of 1970	12,000
		Total debt	$ 27,736
Net fixed assets	43,697		
Other assets	502	Common stock (1.1 million shares outstanding)	$ 33,312
		Earned surplus	44,451
		Total equity	$ 77,763
Total assets	$105,499	Total liabilities	$105,499

Percentage long-term debt to total capitalization:
1. December 31, 1959 .... 13.4%

2. Pro forma (assuming debt alternative) 22.0%

Exhibit 2

VIKING STEEL CORPORATION (A)

INCOME STATEMENTS FOR THE YEARS ENDING DECEMBER 31, 1947, TO 1959

(Dollar figures in thousands)

Years	Sales	Profits before Taxes	Profits after Taxes	Dividends	Depreciation	Capital Expenditures
1947	$ 89,307	$11,147	$6,722	$2,200	$1,471	$ 2,901
1948	118,462	15,609	9,234	3,520	1,965	11,418
1949	89,543	5,065	3,325	2,200	2,247	3,497
1950	135,409	19,611	9,284	3,300	2,469	2,371
1951	168,958	28,041	8,861	4,190	2,603	4,667
1952	131,305	8,045	5,120	4,400	3,024	5,674
1953	167,240	14,309	6,709	4,400	3,617	4,834
1954	98,219	5,084	3,134	2,750	3,973	5,766
1955	171,180	16,187	7,987	3,025	4,714	9,443
1956	178,682	13,378	6,905	3,300	4,070	9,381
1957	150,361	7,652	4,048	3,300	4,038	11,276
1958	99,591	550	220	2,200	3,678	4,053
1959	119,760	4,462	2,409	2,310	3,811	5,942

Exhibit 3

VIKING STEEL CORPORATION (A)

CHART SHOWING AVERAGE ANNUAL EARNINGS AND DIVIDENDS PER SHARE,
MARKET PRICE, YIELD, AND PRICE-EARNINGS RATIOS

Year	EPS	DPS	Average Market Price	Dividend Yield	Price-Earnings Ratio
1947	$ 7.26	$2.00	$22.2	9.0%	3.1x
1948	9.97	3.20	26.1	12.2	2.6x
1949	3.59	2.00	19.2	10.4	5.4x
1950	10.03	3.00	22.2	13.6	2.2x
1951	8.06	3.80	40.7	9.3	5.0x
1952	4.65	4.00	39.6	10.2	8.5x
1953	6.10	4.00	39.2	10.2	6.4x
1954	2.85	2.50	31.0	8.1	10.1x
1955	7.26	2.75	39.3	7.0	5.4x
1956	6.28	3.00	46.7	6.4	7.4x
1957	3.68	3.00	45.4	6.6	12.4x
1958	0.20	2.00	33.4	6.0	167.0x
1959	2.19	2.10	42.8	4.9	19.5x

Exhibit 4

VIKING STEEL CORPORATION (A)

CHART SHOWING QUARTERLY EARNINGS, DIVIDENDS, MARKET PRICES, YIELDS,
AND PRICE-EARNINGS RATIOS

		EPS	Four-Quarter Cumulative EPS	DPS	Four Times Current DPS	Market Price	Dividend Yield	Price-Earnings Ratio
1953	1	$1.69	$5.09	$1.00	$4.00	$40.1	10.0%	7.9x
	2	2.04	7.52	1.00	4.00	41.1	9.7	5.5x
	3	1.53	7.78	1.00	4.00	39.9	10.0	5.1x
	4	0.84	6.10	1.00	4.00	35.6	11.2	5.8x
1954	1	0.06	4.47	1.00	4.00	36.4	11.0	8.1x
	2	0.52	2.95	0.50	2.00	31.3	6.4	10.6x
	3	0.46	1.88	0.50	2.00	27.2	7.3	14.4x
	4	1.81	2.85	0.50	2.00	28.1	7.1	9.9x
1955	1	2.03	4.82	0.50	2.00	31.1	6.4	6.5x
	2	2.05	6.35	0.75	3.00	39.6	7.6	6.2x
	3	1.62	7.51	0.75	3.00	42.4	7.1	5.6x
	4	1.56	7.62	0.75	3.00	44.0	6.8	6.0x
1956	1	2.05	7.28	0.75	3.00	47.2	6.4	6.5x
	2	1.88	7.11	0.75	3.00	45.6	6.7	6.4x
	3	0.27	5.76	0.75	3.00	45.3	6.6	7.9x
	4	2.08	6.28	0.75	3.00	48.7	6.2	7.8x
1957	1	1.45	5.68	0.75	3.00	50.1	6.0	8.8x
	2	1.03	4.83	0.75	3.00	49.6	6.1	10.3x
	3	0.19	4.75	0.75	3.00	47.1	6.4	9.9x
	4	1.01	3.68	0.75	3.00	35.0	8.6	9.5x
1958	1	(0.26)	1.97	0.50	2.00	30.6	6.5	15.5x
	2	(0.67)	0.27	0.50	2.00	31.4	6.4	116.0x
	3	0.06	0.14	0.50	2.00	35.7	5.6	254.0x
	4	1.07	0.20	0.50	2.00	37.0	5.4	185.0x
1959	1	1.54	2.00	0.50	2.00	39.2	5.1	19.6x
	2	2.51	5.18	0.50	2.00	42.3	4.7	8.2x
	3	(1.62)	3.50	0.50	2.00	41.0	4.9	11.7x
	4	(0.24)	2.19	0.60	2.40	48.6	4.9	22.1x

Exhibit 5

VIKING STEEL CORPORATION (A)

EFFECT ON INCOME OF FINANCING ALTERNATIVES AT EBIT LEVELS OF $6 AND $18 MILLION

$6 Million EBIT

	Debt	Common Stock*			
		$45	$40	$35	$30
EBIT	$6,000	$6,000	$6,000	$6,000	$6,000
Interest	1,115	540	540	540	540
PBT	$4,885	$5,460	$5,460	$5,460	$5,460
Taxes (@ 52%)	2,540	2,840	2,840	2,840	2,840
PAT	$2,345	$2,620	$2,620	$2,620	$2,620
Sinking fund	1,000	500	500	500	500
UPAT	$1,345	$2,120	$2,120	$2,120	$2,120
No. of common shares (million)	1.100	1.322	1.350	1.386	1.434
EPS ($ per share)	$2.12	$1.99	$1.94	$1.89	$1.83
UEPS ($ per share)	$1.22	$1.62	$1.57	$1.53	$1.48
Coverage of interest and sinking funds†	1.88x	3.80x	3.80x	3.80x	3.80x

$18 Million EBIT

	Debt	Common Stock*			
		$45	$40	$35	$30
EBIT	$18,000	$18,000	$18,000	$18,000	$18,000
Interest	1,115	540	540	540	540
PBT	$16,885	$17,460	$17,460	$17,460	$17,460
Taxes (@ 52%)	8,780	9,079	9,079	9,079	9,079
PAT	$ 8,105	$ 8,381	$ 8,381	$ 8,381	$ 8,381
Sinking fund	1,000	500	500	500	500
UPAT	$ 7,105	$ 7,881	$ 7,881	$ 7,881	$ 7,881
No. of common shares (million)	1.100	1.322	1.350	1.386	1.434
EPS ($ per share)	$7.37	$6.34	$6.22	$6.06	$5.84
UEPS ($ per share)	$6.46	$5.96	$5.84	$5.69	$5.49
Coverage of interest and sinking funds†	5.64x	11.40x	11.40x	11.40x	11.40x

* Net proceeds per share under various issuing conditions.
† Calculated as follows for debt alternative:

(*Thousands of Dollars*)

Interest	$1,115
Sinking fund (before taxes)	2,080
Total burden	$3,195
EBIT	6,000
Coverage ($6,000/$3,195)	1.88x

Note: If no financing were undertaken in 1960, EPS would be $7.61 at an EBIT level of $18 million.

Exhibit 6

VIKING STEEL CORPORATION (A)

FINANCIAL ANALYSIS OF THE STEEL INDUSTRY

Company	Year	Ingot Capacity Net Tons (Millions)	Ingot Production Net Tons (Millions)	Per Cent of Capacity Operated
U.S. Steel Corporation............	1958	40.2	23.8	59.2
	1957	39.5	33.7	85.2
	1956	39.5	33.4	85.2
	1955	38.8	35.3	90.8
	1954	38.7	28.3	73.2
Bethlehem Steel Corporation..........	1958	23.0	13.3	58.2
	1957	20.5	19.1	93.3
	1956	20.0	18.3	91.6
	1955	19.1	18.8	98.5
	1954	18.5	13.8	74.6
Armco Steel Corporation.............	1958	6.3	4.5	70.5
	1957	5.9	5.4	90.9
	1956	5.1	5.2	101.4
	1955	4.9	5.0	103.0
	1954	4.9	4.4	90.8
Inland Steel Company...............	1958	5.8	4.7	81.3
	1957	5.5	5.5	100.0
	1956	5.2	4.9	94.5
	1955	5.0	5.1	103.8
	1954	4.7	4.5	96.2
Viking Steel Corporation............	1958	1.9	0.7	39.7
	1957	1.8	1.2	63.5
	1956	1.7	1.5	85.6
	1955	1.5	1.5	98.6
	1954	1.5	0.8	54.6
Kaiser Steel Corporation............	1958	1.5	1.4	95.5
	1957	1.5	1.5	103.5
	1956	1.5	1.6	105.3
	1955	1.5	1.4	93.3
	1954	1.5	1.3	90.0
Detroit Steel Corporation...........	1958	1.5	0.4	30.0
	1957	1.5	0.5	37.0
	1956	1.2	1.0	80.0
	1955	1.2	0.8	68.9
	1954	0.6	0.4	67.1

Net Sales (Millions)	Net Income (Millions)	Net Income Per Cent of Sales	Capitalization: Per Cent Long-Term Debt	Per Cent Sales to Total Assets	Per Cent Net Income to Total Assets	Per Cent Net Income to Net Worth
$3,472	$301	8.7	13.5	77.5	6.8	9.7
4,413	419	9.5	6.7	107.4	10.3	14.0
4,228	348	8.2	8.1	109.4	9.1	12.6
4,097	370	9.0	9.9	112.7	10.2	14.3
3,250	195	6.0	12.1	96.8	5.8	8.3
2,024	137	6.8	8.9	109.4	6.3	8.5
2,624	191	7.3	9.7	115.2	12.0	29.2
2,343	161	6.9	17.3	111.3	7.7	12.1
2,114	180	8.5	22.1	104.9	9.1	15.2
1,667	132	8.0	12.4	102.7	8.2	12.3
867	57	6.6	14.4	96.7	6.4	9.0
776	55	7.1	15.8	102.4	7.6	10.8
761	65	8.6	10.7	124.3	10.2	14.6
692	64	9.3	12.9	123.0	11.4	16.6
532	41	7.7	15.9	108.5	8.4	12.1
661	47	7.3	28.3	95.6	7.0	11.5
772	58	7.7	30.2	115.2	8.9	14.5
731	52	7.3	25.9	127.0	7.3	14.4
663	52	8.0	20.2	128.4	10.2	15.8
537	41	7.7	25.2	115.7	8.9	14.4
99	0.2	0.2	13.2	94.6	0.002	0.003
151	4	2.7	14.3	141.2	3.8	5.1
180	6	3.8	5.6	164.2	6.4	8.8
173	7	4.6	6.8	184.9	8.6	11.7
99	3	3.2	9.1	117.2	3.7	5.0
181	5	3.0	60.0	37.6	1.0	3.0
208	21	10.3	61.9	46.4	4.7	14.6
201	23	11.7	48.5	68.7	7.9	18.2
136	5	4.2	52.1	50.6	1.9	4.7
128	7	6.2	55.2	49.0	2.7	6.7
61	1	1.9	26.9	56.3	0.9	1.7
82	3	3.6	28.3	75.6	2.8	4.9
123	8	7.1	29.6	108.0	7.0	13.0
101	6	6.2	32.7	95.2	5.7	10.4
51	1	2.3	46.5	56.9	1.1	2.5

VIKING STEEL CORPORATION (B)

In January, 1960, while Mr. O'Hearth, financial vice-president of Viking Steel Corporation, was considering whether it would be more appropriate to raise $10 million required for expansion purposes by means of debentures or common stock (see Viking Steel Corporation [A]), his attention was drawn to a problem which he believed might be highly interrelated. For several months Mr. O'Hearth had been appraising Viking's capital budgeting procedures with a particular eye toward establishing a minimum acceptable return on investment criterion (opportunity or hurdle rate) against which new capital expenditure opportunities could be appraised. His early investigations had led him to believe that the "cost" of Viking's capital might be an important factor affecting the setting of a useful hurdle rate. Consequently, he wondered whether the proposed financing would influence the hurdle-rate decision, or whether, in contrast, the financing decision should be influenced by what appeared to be a useful minimum return on investment criterion. In either case, he thought it would be appropriate to recommend a new return on investment hurdle-rate criterion as well as to propose financing plans at the next board of directors' meeting.

Prior to 1960, the Viking Steel Corporation evaluated capital expenditure proposals by a simple return on investment formula (profits after taxes divided by total gross investment). Projects with returns in excess of 10% after taxes had usually been approved, assuming that other considerations were favorable.

During the latter part of 1959, Viking began changing from the simple rate of return to a discounted cash flow method of measuring return on investment. At the time of this change, however, Mr. Dellor and Mr. O'Hearth had both been disturbed because the discounted cash flow rates of return ran higher (about five percentage points) than those calculated under the simple return formula. This meant that a greater dollar volume of projects would now qualify than was formerly true, assuming the cutoff rate remained at 10%. As a consequence, Mr. Dellor asked Mr. O'Hearth to report whether it would be more desirable to increase the amount of capital expenditures, as suggested by the new formula, or alternatively, to raise the cutoff point to approximately 15%.

Management was also concerned about the company's historic return on assets. Viking's historic return had averaged 4.5% over the most recent five years, a figure well below the industry average. Management believed a substantially higher cutoff rate than 5% was necessary to assure improved performance in the future.

While he was in the midst of thinking this problem through, Mr. O'Hearth attended a thought-provoking talk on the subject "cost of capital." The speaker recommended that a firm base its cutoff point on its weighted average cost of capital.[1] In Viking's case, Mr. O'Hearth understood this would involve the costing and weighting of debt, equity, and retained earnings.

Mr. O'Hearth was somewhat confused concerning the weights he should use in the calculation of Viking's cost of capital. If Mr. O'Hearth used the firm's existing capital structure, he found he would arrive at one set of weights. However, the capital structure and the weights would change after the financing and would depend upon the method of financing actually used. He, therefore, wondered which, if any, of these weights were appropriate to his firm's circumstances.

When he turned to measuring the costs of the various sources of funds, he found himself confused by the speaker's recommendation concerning the calculation of the cost of equity funds. It was suggested that the cost of equity was simply current earnings per share divided by current market price. Although he was impressed by the logic and simplicity of this argument, Mr. O'Hearth wondered how these concepts would have to be modified, if at all, to be useful in Viking's situation.

As a final guide in attempting to set a minimum return on investment standard, Mr. O'Hearth estimated the dollar amount of capital expenditure opportunities (including those for modernization) that would be approved at different cutoff points in any "normal" year in the future. Although this was admittedly difficult in view of the large element of uncertainty surrounding the outcome of Viking's plans for the future, Mr. O'Hearth and his assistants believed that the following estimates were as useful as any that could be prepared in the time available:

---

[1] Essentially this speaker made the same points as appear in Hunt, Williams, and Donaldson, *Basic Business Finance* (Homewood, Ill.: Richard D. Irwin, Inc., 1961), chap. 21.

Discounted Cash Flow Return on Investment (after Taxes)	"Comparable" Rate of Return on Investment, Old Measurement Method*	Expected "Normal" Year Capital Expenditures Approved at Varying Cutoff Rates (Millions of Dollars)	(Cumulative)
22% and over	15.4% or over	$ 0.9	$ 0.9
19% to 21%	13.0% to 15.3%	1.6	2.5
16% to 18%	10.7% to 12.9%	2.1	4.6
13% to 15%	8.5% to 10.6%	2.6	7.2
10% to 12%	6.3% to 8.4%	3.5	10.7
7% to 9%	4.2% to 6.2%	5.2	15.9

Projects justified on grounds of absolute necessity.............. 1.1

Total available projects................................$17.0

* Assuming ten-year life, straight-line depreciation, etc.

JOHNS-MANVILLE CORPORATION

In early September, 1956, James Thurston learned that Johns-Manville Corporation planned to offer 650,000 shares of common stock to its shareholders. The offering, at the rate of one new share for every ten shares held, was scheduled for October 1; rights to subscribe to the new issue would be issued to stockholders of record September 28 and would expire October 17. Thurston held 180 shares of J-M common and realized that he soon would have to decide either to sell the forthcoming rights or increase his present investment in the company.

Thurston's ownership of Johns-Manville stock dated back to early 1946 when he had invested $4,500 in 30 shares at $150 per share. The stock had attracted him as an investment opportunity at that time because of the company's size and important position in the building materials industry. The large expansion program of the company also had seemed opportunely timed to take advantage of an expected postwar upsurge in construction activity.

In retrospect, Thurston realized that his objectives for common stock investments in 1946 had been more or less evenly divided between the desire for a reasonable dividend return and substantial capital appreciation. Income had been important as a supplement to the $12,000 salary which he was receiving as credit manager of a medium-sized eastern manufacturing company. Capital appreciation, on the other hand, had been regarded as a much less immediate objective. Thurston, then 36 years old, had accumulated $10,000 in liquid assets and a sizable additional sum in the cash surrender value of his insurance. He also had what seemed to be a reasonably secure and promising future with his company and therefore did not anticipate an emergency or early need to liquidate his security holdings.

During his first year as a Johns-Manville shareholder, Thurston received $105 in dividends ($3.50 per share), a 2.3 per cent yield on the purchase price of his stock. Over the next five years the company experienced a steady growth in earnings, and its dividend rate was increased each year. By 1951 Thurston was receiving $382.50, or an 8.5 per cent return on his original investment. The price of the stock, however, had not advanced in line with earnings and dividend increases during this period. In early 1951 the market value of Thurston's shares was approximately equal to what he had paid for them in 1946 (Appendix A, Exhibit 5, p. 215).

After 1951 the market price of J-M common had begun to rise. By early September, 1956, as the result of a three-for-one stock split in 1947 and a two-for-one split in March, 1956, Thurston owned 180 shares with a market value of $55 per share. The total value of his investment, $9,900, represented a capital gain of more than 100 per cent for the ten-year period. Johns-Manville had stabilized its dividend payments after 1951, and consequently Thurston had received $382.50 in dividends annually for the past five years.

The rights issue, which posed a problem for Thurston, was the first new equity offering by Johns-Manville since 1945.[1] It was prompted by management's belief that the company should look forward to a period of further expansion of plants and facilities. The situation was similar in this respect to that which had first attracted Thurston to the company in 1946, and his initial reaction was to subscribe to the new issue. On later reflection he realized, however, that his investment objectives had changed since 1946, and he therefore decided that the offering presented an appropriate occasion for reappraising his investment in Johns-Manville.

Thurston's professional progress had borne out his earlier expectations, and by 1956 he had advanced to the post of treasurer of the same eastern company. With an annual salary of $25,000, he was considerably less interested in current dividend income than he had been ten years previously. Capital appreciation, which would build up the value of his retirement fund and estate, had become increasingly important and was now his dominant investment objective.

Since he was fundamentally interested in the value of his holdings 10 to 15 years in the future, Thurston concentrated his attention on Johns-Manville's capital expansion and financial policies. To his mind, these policies and the standards used in putting them into practice

---

[1] In 1945, J-M had sold $17 million of convertible preferred stock, all of which was subsequently converted into common. In 1947 the company had borrowed $5 million in long-term notes from two insurance companies; this was the company's first use of fixed debt. (See Appendix A, pp. 215–16.)

would have a critical effect on the company's future performance and the ultimate value of his investment. He therefore resolved to find out as much as he could about them.

Several days later, Thurston learned from a Johns-Manville official that the company generally regarded 15 per cent as a minimum acceptable rate of return for new investment projects. This figure had been derived from a study of the average return which the company had earned in the past on capital and retained earnings. Thurston's informant pointed out, however, that this standard was a flexible one and that management had not hesitated to depart from it when circumstances warranted. In recent years, for example, the number of acceptable investment projects had been larger than the company's engineering and administrative staff could handle. Consequently, only the most profitable projects had been undertaken, and the effective standard had thus been raised well above 15 per cent. As a further example of the flexibility of the standard, Thurston was told that timber lands had sometimes been purchased despite estimates of something less than a 10% return. Because of the nature of the company's business, timber reserves were considered "essential" regardless of their formally calculated return.

In order to obtain further insight into the reasoning behind Johns-Manville's financial policies, Thurston studied a financial manual which had been prepared for the use of the company's executives.[2] Selected excerpts from this manual are presented here as Appendix B. A digest of other information which Thurston assembled from financial services and his own file of Johns-Manville annual reports, letters to stockholders, and similar company communications appears as Appendix A.

On September 28, Johns-Manville announced that the offering price of the new issue would be $40 per share, and that stockholders, as previously announced, would receive rights to subscribe to one new share for each ten shares held. On the same day the stock was traded (cum rights) between 49 and 50⅛. Thurston's immediate decision on the new issue therefore involved a choice between investing an additional $720 or realizing a much smaller but still somewhat uncertain sum from the sale of his rights. Beyond this lay the larger question, in dollar terms, of the disposition of his present 180 shares.

---

[2] *Financial Analysis of Johns-Manville Operations* (Revised), by Alvin Brown, vice-president for finance.

APPENDIX A
RECENT FINANCIAL HISTORY
OF THE JOHNS-MANVILLE CORPORATION

Johns-Manville Corporation is the largest producer of asbestos fiber in the world, dating from a business established in 1858. The company mines, manufactures, and sells temperature-control and soundproofing materials, and products for the protection of buildings against fire, weather, and wear. Johns-Manville's more important products include asbestos and asphalt flooring, siding and roofing materials, shingles, rock wool insulation, sound control tile, roof cements, "Transite" asbestos-cement pipe, and marine sheathing. Materials used in building construction and maintenance costitute slightly less than 40 per cent of sales.

The company operates 21 manufacturing plants throughout the United States and Canada, and one plant in Belgium. Asbestos mines are owned in Canada and southern Rhodesia. Sales are handled through offices in 59 cities in the United States and Canada, and the Johns-Manville International Corporation subsidiary.

At the end of World War II, the company initiated an extensive program of expansion. Capital expenditures, which were at a seven-year high of $3.2 million in 1945, increased to $11.9 million in 1946, and averaged over $20 million in each of the next two years. Gross value of properties and plants increased from $62 million in 1945 to $110 million in 1948. The program included the construction of new "Transite" and other asbestos products plants in Louisiana, New Jersey, Ontario, Mississippi, and New Hampshire; major expansions in Quebec, California, and Illinois; and approximately 3,500 other projects of varying size.

Large additions to properties and plants were resumed in 1951, and by the end of 1955 the gross property account had risen to almost $194 million. Capital expenditure in 1955 amounted to $18.3 million, and for the entire decade 1946–1955 averaged $16 million annually (Exhibit 4). Of the total additions of $160 million, slightly under 50 per cent was spent for new plants and acquisitions, about 20 per cent for new and improved products, 15 per cent each for cost reduction projects and replacement, and about 5 per cent for improved working conditions.

Paralleling this capital growth, sales increased regularly from $86 million in 1945 to $285 million in 1955, with the exception of a small setback in 1949. Pretax earnings, however, behaved more erratically. They climbed from $6.6 million in 1945 to an all-time high of $48.7 million in 1951, and then declined steadily to $28.6 million in 1954 despite the continued growth in sales. A rise in earnings was resumed in 1955, up to $42 million, and continued during the first half of 1956 (Exhibit 1).

Management explained the shrinking profit margin in the early 1950's as the result of a temporary decline in world demand for asbestos attributable to stockpiling of inventories, a competitive pressure on prices combined with rising costs, fluctuations in the building construction industry, and accelerated depreciation allowances on the large new capital acquisitions. On this last point, chairman of the board L. M. Cassidy stated at a stockholders' meeting that if the company had employed straight-line depreciation methods instead of the accelerated rate, earnings per share would have been $3.55 rather than $3.10 in 1953, and $3.10 rather than $2.62 in 1954. Mr. Cassidy explained that the annual "cash savings" of over $2 million dollars resulting from accelerated depreciation charges "provides additional means for paying out a higher proportion of stated earnings in dividends and for improving the long-range future position of the company, which could increase substantially the value of the stockholder's equity."

Johns-Manville financed approximately $135 million of the $160 million of postwar capital growth with funds derived from company operations. The company had for many years followed a policy of segregating a part of cash inflow from operations in an account termed "Fund for Deferred Expenditure." This asset account, which appeared in the balance sheet separated from the classifications of current and fixed assets, represented an earmarking of cash resources, and was invested for the most part in U.S. Treasury notes and bonds. According to the company's annual report, the fund was "established to provide cash when needed for contingencies and for additions to plant facilities."

Although in the past the Fund for Deferred Expenditure had varied between $2 and $4 million, it was built up during 1943 and 1944 until it stood at approximately $14 million by the end of the war. At that time, Johns-Manville did not have any funded debt, the capital structure consisting entirely of common stock. In the summer of 1945, the company prepared to meet the anticipated requirements of the postwar years with the modernization and expansion program described above. To augment the resources accumulated in the Fund for Deferred Expenditure, Johns-Manville sold $17 million of 3½ per cent cumulative convertible preferred stock in August, 1945. Thus the company entered the postwar period with total liquid funds of $33 million, apart from cash included in working capital.

In the course of the expansion program, the Fund was gradually drawn down until it stood at $6 million in 1948. In 1949, working capital was decreased by $8 million, and the sum of $10 million in cash was added to the Fund. During the next three years (to 1952) while capital expenditures were continuing at an annual rate of $13 million, the company nevertheless managed to add to its liquid holdings until the Fund totaled almost $34 million in 1952. Thereafter, the Fund was drawn down to $19.6 million at the end of 1955 (Exhibit 2).

The preferred stock issue was called in two installments, in August, 1946, and in February, 1950. At the time of the first call, management stated: "In the interest of financial stability and flexibility it is the general objective of the company to have only common stock outstanding. When the preferred stock was issued, therefore, it was the expectation of the board of directors that stockholders would find it desirable to convert their stock." These two moves to force conversion were successful, and led to an approximate 10% increase in the number of common shares outstanding.

Johns-Manville introduced funded debt into its capital structure for the first time in its history in July, 1947, when it established a $25 million line of credit, available through 1950, with the Metropolitan Life Insurance Company and the Mutual Life Insurance Company of New York. Subsequently, $5 million of this credit was taken down and the remainder of the line was allowed to expire. The notes carried a 2.7% interest charge, and were payable at the rate of $250,000 annually from July 16, 1952, with the balance due July 16, 1967. The company also had an option to prepay additional notes of $250,000 per year beginning in 1952; this option had not been exercised up to mid-1956. The changes which occurred in Johns-Manville capitalization during the period of expansion from 1945 to 1955 are summarized in Exhibit 2.

The external financing described above accounted for approximately 15 per cent of the total capital expansion of $160 million. Most of the program was financed internally, out of the approximately $245 million in after-tax earnings and depreciation representing the cash inflow from operations over the period. A total of $100 million was paid out in cash dividends (preferred and common).

In March, 1956, with the common stock selling in the high 90's, the board of directors proposed a two-for-one stock split. At the stock-holders' meeting, Board Chairman L. M. Cassidy stated: "Aside from the added shares required for the proposed stock split, we have no defi-nite plans for the use of any additional stock. However, this situation could change because I must point out that we are studying a number of interesting expansion projects. . . ." The shareholders almost unani-mously approved the proposed split.

On September 5, 1956, the board of directors announced plans to raise approximately $25.5 million by means of new equity. The com-pany would offer 648,696 shares of new common stock to present shareholders at a price of $40 per share, on the basis of one share for each ten shares held of record September 28, 1956. A standby under-writing agreement was concluded with a syndicate headed by Morgan Stanley & Company.

According to the prospectus, the proceeds of the sale of new equity were to be applied to the cost of a large plant expansion and improve-ment program, and to additional working capital in anticipation of in-creased sales; no part of the proceeds, however, was allocated to any specific purpose. As of October, 1956, the company had under construc-tion new plants and facilities estimated to cost $23.2 million, and plans called for additional capital expenditures of $32.2 million in the near future. Sometime earlier Johns-Manville had announced a budget of $28 million for capital expenditures in 1956. These figures, compared with actual outlays of $18 million in 1955 and $20 million in 1954 (Exhibit 4). Among the chief items in the 1956 construction program were an asbestos fiber mill in Asbestos, Quebec (Canada's largest build-ing in terms of floor space), and new plants in Savannah, Georgia, for the manufacture of asphalt roofing; North Bay, Ontario, for insulating board; and Lompoc, California, for synthetic silicates. Plans were set for entering the gypsum business with extensive explorations in southern Nevada; for beginning manufacture of hardboard at a new factory in Natchez, Mississippi; for a floor tile plant in Marrero, Louisiana; and for two new "Transite" pipe and insulating board plants at Stockton, California, and Klamath Falls, Oregon.

Exhibit 1

JOHNS-MANVILLE CORPORATION

SELECTED INCOME STATEMENT FIGURES, 1945–1956

(Dollar figures in millions)

Year	Net Sales	Earnings before Taxes	Pretax Earnings as Per Cent of Sales	Earnings after Taxes	Common Dividends Paid
1956 (6 mo.).............$147.4		$22.3	15.2%	$12.6	$ 6.4
1955..................... 284.7		41.8	14.7	23.5	13.6
1954..................... 253.2		28.6	11.3	16.7	13.5
1953..................... 252.6		34.7	13.7	19.7	13.5
1952..................... 244.7		39.7	16.2	22.6	13.5
1951..................... 238.0		48.7	20.5	24.5	13.4
1950..................... 203.3		38.5	19.0	22.8	11.0
1949..................... 162.6		22.2	13.7	14.4	7.3
1948..................... 173.5		25.1	14.5	15.4	5.8
1947..................... 133.9		15.3	11.4	9.5	4.0
1946..................... 92.0		5.9	6.4	5.8	3.2
1945..................... 86.0		6.6	7.7	5.1	2.8

Source: Moody's *Industrial Manual.*

Exhibit 2

JOHNS-MANVILLE CORPORATION

SELECTED BALANCE SHEET FIGURES, 1945–1956

(Dollar figures in millions)

Year	Net Working Capital	Fund for Deferred Expenditures	Gross Property and Plant	Book Equity	Capitalization		
					Long-Term Debt (%)	Preferred Stock (%)	Common Stock Equity (%)
1956.....$42.6		$17.9	$202.6	$171.8	2.1	....	97.9
1955..... 37.2		19.6	193.7	166.3	2.2	....	97.8
1954..... 29.4		22.7	177.5	154.6	2.6	....	97.4
1953..... 26.2		30.9	160.9	150.7	2.9	....	97.1
1952..... 28.0		33.8	144.4	144.2	3.2	....	96.8
1951..... 27.9		33.3	131.8	134.9	3.6	....	96.4
1950..... 32.5		22.5	121.2	123.4	4.2	....	95.8
1949..... 27.7		16.3	118.4	102.6	5.1	6.5	88.4
1948..... 35.2		6.3	110.8	95.0	5.5	7.3	87.2
1947..... 26.9		15.3	96.0	85.5	6.2	8.1	85.7
1946..... 24.6		27.8	73.3	77.4	0.8	9.6	89.6
1945..... 25.8		32.0	62.2	63.9	....	23.2	76.8

All figures as of December 31, except those for 1956 which are June 30.
Source: Moody's *Industrial Manual.*

Exhibit 3

JOHNS-MANVILLE CORPORATION

RELATION OF NET INCOME TO ASSETS AND NET WORTH

Year	Net Income as Per Cent of Total Assets	Net Income as Per Cent of Net Worth
1955	10.8%	14.1%
1954	8.4	10.8
1953	10.3	13.0
1952	12.3	15.7
1951	13.9	18.2
1950	14.5	18.5
1949	10.7	14.1
1948	12.1	16.3
1947	8.2	11.1
1946	6.1	7.6
1945	5.7	7.0

Exhibit 4

JOHNS-MANVILLE CORPORATION

CAPITAL EXPENDITURES, 1944–1955

(Thousands)

1955	$18,278
1954	20,208
1953	21,526
1952	15,048
1951	13,104
1950	9,413
1949	9,271
1948	17,323
1947	23,709
1946	11,871
1945	3,156
1944	1,428

Exhibit 5

JOHNS-MANVILLE CORPORATION

SELECTED COMMON STOCK FIGURES, 1945–1956

Year	Number of Shares (Millions)	Market Price Range	Earnings per Share	Dividends per Share	Dividend Pay-out Ratio
1956	6.46*	58¾–41*	$1.73†	$1.00†	58%
1955	3.19	48½–38¾	3.68	2.12½	58
1954	3.18	45¾–30⅞	2.62	2.12½	81
1953	3.17	37¼–28⅞	3.10	2.12½	69
1952	3.17	39⅜–31⅜	3.57	2.12½	60
1951	3.16	35¼–23½	3.88	2.12½	55
1950	3.13	25¾–18¼	3.64	1.75	48
1949	2.91	25⅛–15¼	2.42	1.25	52
1948	2.91	21⅛–16⅝	2.61	1.00	38
1947	2.85	23¼–17⅞	1.61	0.70	42
1946	0.89	28 –19⅛	1.00	0.58	58
1945	0.85	24⅛–16⅞	0.95	0.54	57

All per-share figures have been adjusted for stock splits: two-for-one in 1956: three-for-one in 1947.
* To September 28, 1956.
† Six months to June 30, 1956.
Source: Moody's *Industrial Manual.*

Exhibit 6

JOHNS-MANVILLE CORPORATION

COMPARATIVE COMMON STOCK RECORD, 1945–1956

STOCK PRICE INDEX* (1941–1943 = 10)

Year	Standard & Poor's 425 Industrials	Building Materials Industry†	J-M
1956 (6 mos.)................	49.2	50.8	43.1
1955.........................	42.4	45.0	38.9
1954.........................	30.2	31.8	32.7
1953.........................	24.8	24.3	28.8
1952.........................	24.8	25.9	32.1
1951.........................	22.7	24.3	26.2
1950.........................	18.3	22.0	20.5
1949.........................	15.0	19.1	17.4
1948.........................	15.3	20.7	16.8
1947.........................	14.8	21.0	18.9
1946.........................	16.5	22.4	22.0
1945.........................	14.7	18.2	18.4

PRICE-EARNINGS RATIO*

Year	Standard & Poor's 425 Industrials	Building Materials Industry‡	J-M
1956 (6 mos.)................	13.4	10.7	11.9
1955.........................	12.8	9.6	11.8
1954.........................	11.4	8.8	14.0
1953.........................	9.4	7.9	10.4
1952.........................	10.4	9.5	10.1
1951.........................	8.4	7.4	7.6
1950.........................	6.7	5.5	6.3
1949.........................	6.2	7.6	8.0
1948.........................	7.6	5.3	7.2
1947.........................	9.8	7.0	13.1
1946.........................	19.0	11.7	23.3
1945.........................	17.5	23.2	21.5

YIELD*

Year	Standard & Poor's 425 Industrials	Building Materials Industry‡	J-M
1956 (6 mos.)................	4.0%	4.8%	4.7%
1955.........................	4.0	4.9	4.9
1954.........................	4.9	6.2	5.8
1953.........................	5.9	7.0	6.6
1952.........................	5.9	6.6	5.9
1951.........................	6.2	7.1	7.2
1950.........................	6.7	7.7	7.6
1949.........................	6.6	7.4	6.5
1948.........................	5.5	6.3	5.3
1947.........................	4.9	4.0	3.3
1946.........................	3.8	2.9	2.5
1945.........................	4.1	2.8	2.6

* Based on yearly average of prices. The average price of Johns-Manville stock adjusted for stock splits equals 112 per cent of index figures shown; average price computed from *Value-Line* data.
† Standard and Poor's Index for "Building Materials—Roofing and Wallboard" includes the following stocks: Celotex Corporation, Certain-teed Products, Flintkoke, Johns-Manville, Masonite Corporation (from 1947 on), National Gypsum (from 1947 on), Ruberoid, U.S. Gypsum, Barker Asphalt (to 1947 only), and Paraffine (to 1947 only).
‡ These figures are for the above-mentioned companies, with the following omissions: 1945–1947, Barker Asphalt and Paraffine; 1956, Certain-teed Products.

APPENDIX B

Selected Excerpts[3]

Financial Analysis of Johns-Manville Operations

I. Responsibility to Stockholders

. . . . .

The sole purpose of industrial enterprise is to earn money. For this purpose it employs the funds of its owners, and it completes this purpose by paying dividends to those owners.

. . . . .

Excess funds. If owners entrust money to an enterprise so that it will earn a profit, the converse is implied: they would not do so if it were not to earn a profit. As we have seen, also, cash not needed for operating the enterprise can be regarded no differently than cash contributed by the owners. What the owners would not have done should be undone. That is: *Money in excess of the needs of an enterprise should be paid to the owners.*

Of course, the "needs" of an enterprise requires some definition, and obviously it is to be defined from the viewpoint of the owners, who alone are concerned.

We have already, it will be remembered, found reason for an enterprise to have a safety margin of cash, and, having utility, that safety margin is to be considered a need.

There may also be some occasions when it is in the interest of owners to retain funds against a future need. There may be times when an enterprise foresees the need of money at a time when it cannot be obtained from owners—which is to say, when stock cannot be sold; although this usually refers, not to an impossibility, but to a disadvantage to present owners. In such a case, the alternative of borrowing may be available but undesirable, either because the terms will be unfavorable or because the fixed charges and fixed date of repayment are regarded as too burdensome. When, and to the extent that, such times can be foreseen, money may be said to be needed; but the need should be appraised reasonably and, above all, from the viewpoint of the interest of the owners.

In such appraisal, it should be considered that some inconvenience to most owners always attends a call for contributions of additional

---

[3] These excerpts are not presented in the exact order in which they appear in the manual, *Financial Analysis of Johns-Manville Operations.* Outline headings have been added. Other italicized sentences and phrases are reproduced as they appear in the manual.

funds. In considering whether to pay idle funds to the owners in the face of a prospective need for funds, the owners' advantage of having the money must be weighed against the inconvenience of returning it. Thus, if the funds will be needed within a year, it is unlikely that use by the owners for that period is worth the inconvenience, while the answer seems plainly contrary if the interval is five years.

. . . . .

Present obligation is to present owners. So, in balancing a disposition of idle funds against a future demand upon the owner, the effect upon those owners who will not contribute their share must be considered. This requires comparison of normal market value of stock with probable market value when the demand is made. Normal value, like normal earnings, is to be conceived as the average of a business cycle.

Let us say, for example, that the normal market value of a share of stock in an enterprise is appraised at 100, upon which normal earnings are 15 per cent. If, then, demand for new funds is made by sale of stock at 150, the owners thereafter will have an increased average earnings per share. The owner who does not contribute his proportion will gain an advantage over the owner who does. If, on the other hand, the stock is sold at 50, the average earning per share will be decreased. The owner who does not contribute his proportion will lose as compared to the owner who does. It is the same as saying, of course, to buy low and sell high.

For the owner who is free to make his own choice, the enterprise need have no concern. That is the case when stock is sold at a relatively high price, for then he loses nothing (or gains) by not contributing. But the enterprise should have concern for the owner who may not be free to make his own choice. That is the case when the stock is sold at a relatively low price. Thus, it will be to the disadvantage of owners to pay idle funds to them if later the enterprise must sell stock at an amount significantly below its normal market value.

. . . . .

 II. Capital Budgeting

 A. *General Observations and Concepts*

. . . . .

A standard for operating expenditure has been supplied very simply by the concept that expenditure is desirable if it will procure more than its amount in income. This standard can be applied because the operating expenditure is promptly recouped in the form of income. Industry can, in a manner of speaking, look in its cash drawer at the end of the day and see whether it is ahead.

. . . . .

An expenditure for facilities, on the other hand, is not recouped. It is a permanent expenditure, and the desirability of that kind of expenditure cannot be tested by simple subtraction. Some other device must be found as a basis for ascertaining whether earnings justify such an expenditure.

. . . . .

In each case of contemplated expenditure for a facility, the actual (forecasted) rate of earnings will be computed, and compared with the demanded rate. Subject to whatever scope there may be for exercise of judgment, that comparison will enable the conclusion whether the expenditure should be made or not.

. . . . .

The importance of a correct standard must obviously not be lost sight of. The consequences could be severe. If the standard is too low, earnings run down hill. If it is too high, opportunities are missed. Both are bad, because there is no difference between making a bad expenditure and failing to make a good one. Either is a failure to realize earnings.

. . . . .

Maximum income. It is as much an error (*even if not equal in degree*) *to adopt a course that yields earnings lower than possible, as to adopt a course that yields inadequate earnings.* A demanded rate of earnings is, in other words, only a minimum demand: it should not encourage an enterprise to accept, or to be content with, earnings that are less than can be had. The enterprise should seek, not merely profit, but the most profit.

. . . . .

In general, a profitable and seasoned enterprise can get all the money it needs for expenditures that will increase its earnings without diluting their ratio to investment. On the other hand, experience shows plainly that the opportunities to spend money soundly are not unlimited. The limiting factor, in other words, is the opportunity, not the funds.

There may be one exception to this. In a period of depression, when the sale of stock might dilute the interest of existing stockholders and when borrowing may be undesirable, the limitation of available funds may require a choice among opportunities to spend.

. . . . .

B. *Demanded Rate of Earnings*
   1. *Past Earnings as a Standard*

. . . . .

What we expect from a permanent expenditure is annual earnings, more or less uniform, of unlimited duration. The former cannot be subtracted from the latter, but the latter can be expressed as a ratio to the former. Thus we obtain a rate of earnings.

That still, however, does not provide a standard that will tell us what rate of earnings is an acceptable one and what not. For such a standard, however, we need not look far. In advancing their money, owners must be assumed to have some expectation of earnings. Since the money is being spent in their behalf, it should be spent according to their expectation. The question becomes one of interpreting the owners' expectation.

For this purpose, let us try to penetrate the mental process of the owner. In effect, by buying or holding the stock of the enterprise, he has said this to the enterprise:

> I have observed the record of this enterprise. I observe what it has earned in the past. I count on its earning the same in the future. (I may have a sneaking hope it will earn more, but I do not stipulate that as a condition of my contribution.) Here, then, is my money. Take it and use it as you have used money in the past.

Is not that what the owner must be presumed to think? Can anything else be inferred from his act? If he were satisfied to earn less, would he give his money to the enterprise? No, because rate of earnings measures risk, and if he is willing to accept a lower rate he can presumably find a lower risk. If he would be satisfied only to earn more, would he give his money to the enterprise? No, because he has no assurance that the enterprise will increase its rate of earnings.

Past earnings afford the basis of a standard for expenditures for facilities. The owners have expressed this fact themselves by buying and holding their stock.

. . . . .

It might be asked whether an enterprise should not try to increase its rate of earning, rather than be content with past experience. The answer is, assuredly, provided the attempt does not lead the enterprise to neglect expenditures that measure up to the acceptable experience of the past. The enterprise should make all the expenditures that are desirable by its standards; if the effect is to increase the earnings, so much the better, but that effect should not be the primary object.

. . . . .

2. Cost of Borrowed Funds Fallacy

· · · · ·

The worst invitation to error, however, grows out of funds an enterprise may borrow. An enterprise will borrow for two reasons. (1) Almost always, money can be borrowed at a rate of interest less than the experienced rate of earnings of the enterprise. Thus, when the enterprise borrows, it uses funds from which the owners, with no contribution by themselves, derive a margin of profit. This is the advantage of borrowing. There are also disadvantages: borrowings must be repaid, and money borrowed now may impair the enterprise's borrowing ability at a time when it is needed. The fiscal judgment of an enterprise will weigh these opposing considerations and decide its policy as seems best to it.

An enterprise may also borrow at times for more expedient reasons: because it may be disadvantageous to the owners if they are asked to contribute more capital, or because funds will presently be available from the operations of the enterprise and in the meantime it is more convenient to borrow than to ask the owners for funds that would soon be returned.

When money is being borrowed for either reason, the unthinking man will say, "Money is only costing us three per cent; look there, we are borrowing at three per cent; ergo, anything we can earn more than three per cent gives us a profit."

The fallacy in this reasoning, so plausible, perhaps, on its surface, is that the borrowing is not for any particular use, but for the general purposes of the enterprise. Obviously, the cost of borrowed funds could not be made the test of all expenditures, for how, then, could the experienced rate of earnings be preserved? Only a portion of the enterprise's earnings can come from the use of borrowed funds; in the use of equity capital, the enterprise must stand solidly on the maintenance of the experienced rate. If the cost of borrowing is not a valid test for all expenditures, then how can it be valid for any of them?

The most that could be conceded to this argument is that the demanded rate of earnings might be reduced by the leverage derived from the borrowed money. If the enterprise borrows one-fifth of its capital, its experienced rate being 15 per cent and the interest rate 3 per cent, it could allow its rate of earnings to fall to 12 per cent and still earn 15 per cent on the owners' contribution of funds. But this does not say that some particular expenditure should be made at, perhaps, 6 per cent, merely because that rate is more than the interest rate. It is still necessary to earn an average rate of 12 per cent, and the enterprise could accept one at 6 per cent only because it is assured of others high enough to offset it; not merely because it is better than a rate of interest.

But even this concession is usually too much to make. How shall the enterprise know that the time will not come when it will find reasons to pay off the borrowing? If that happens, then the enterprise will be left with a diluted rate of earnings. Judgment will usually bid the enterprise maintain its demanded rate for the *use* of funds, giving the owners a higher return during the period of borrowing.

. . . . .

No one can accept the principle that the experienced rate of earnings should not be diluted, and at the same time tolerate investment (or continuation of investment) at a low rate on the notion that money costs only interest.

. . . . .

✳ 3. *Problems of Determining a Standard Rate for J-M*

. . . . .

As we saw when discussing the concept, the standard of earnings to be procured by expenditures for facilities—the demanded rate of earnings—should be derived from the experience of the enterprise. And, in view of the basis of the rate, this means experience in two respects: expenditure and earnings.

. . . . .

We have seen that the only way to deal rationally with forecasts of sales and earnings is at their normal amount, as this has been defined: the average of a business cycle. Since this is so, a standard for earnings must speak in the same terms. The experienced earnings must, therefore, be translated to a normal basis.

. . . . .

Here we shall say, then, that the rate is to be computed as the ratio of characteristic earnings to the investment in the enterprise, generally as expressed by the balance sheet. What adjustments this requires in the analyst's thought will be considered presently.

It is, however, necessary to define "investment." Basically, it is, of course, the amount shown in the balance sheet to have been contributed by the owners of the enterprise, plus the amount of earnings that has been retained. To this should be added the amount of borrowing—the amount, that is, of any liabilities that do not arise naturally and involuntarily from the character of operations. To this should be added, also, if the amount is to be accurate, any "write-offs" that did not reflect actual losses or depreciation and depletion; and, of course, any "write-ups" should be deducted.

. . . . .

If we look at the period of 20 years or so from which the Johns-Manville demanded rate of 15 per cent was derived, we shall find that accumulated depreciation varied from 40 per cent to 60 per cent of the cost of wearable facilities. Over the whole period, the approximate mean was about one-half. Wearable facilities were included in investment, that is, at half the amount of expenditure for them.

So far, in other words, as the demanded rate was derived from wearable facilities, it is not 15 per cent of expenditure, but 15 per cent of one-half of expenditure. It is, thus, only $7\frac{1}{2}$ per cent of original expenditure. As applied to wearable facilities, the standard would say, not, get 15 per cent of expenditure, but, get $7\frac{1}{2}$ per cent of expenditure.

. . . . .

The principal conclusion from these investigations [of depreciation of book asset values] is that the demanded rate of earnings, so far as based upon wearable facilities, has been based upon one-half their cost.

. . . . .

A valid rate requires, of course, that investment and earnings be expressed in dollars of the same value. The only counsel that can be given, then, where earnings are inflated and investment is a hodgepodge, is to adjust both to a common value of the dollar.

For the same reasons that apply to earnings, investment must be averaged over the period from which the amount of normal earnings is derived. If, however, there has been a considerable variation in the amount of investment, it may prove more accurate to compute the ratios of normal earnings to investment at various dates, and then to average the rates. Indeed, it would be a reasonable statistical method to do both, and compare them.

. . . . .

It is, of course, impossible to apply a standard of *average* earning to an individual case. The only standard by which an individual case can be judged is one that is a *minimum*. Therefore, the standard must be expressed as the minimum that will cause the rates of earnings from all future expenditures, at and above the minimum, to average the rate of the past. For use as a standard, accordingly, the rate of earnings will be reduced from the experience of the past.

Such a minimum is, plainly, impossible of exact calculation. From time to time, however, the expenditures of a recent period can be reviewed and the weighted-average rate of earnings can be computed. Then, if that average is above or below the experience of the past, the standard employed in that period can be adjusted proportionately. There is, indeed, nothing immutable about a demanded rate of earnings: it should be changed whenever there is reason to do so.

. . . . .

If the minimum rate is actually used as the standard, it may also be called the *demanded* rate. But management in its discretion may set a higher rate as a standard. Various considerations may induce this, such as desire to offer an incentive to concentrate on finding the more profitable opportunities of expenditure, or a period when it is desired to place some limitation on expenditure. Such a rate, fixed by management, becomes the demanded rate as distinguished from the minimum rate.

True, there is another possible means of deciding such an expenditure. That is to seek the highest aggregate rate of earnings within some limit of aggregate expenditure. That is, of course, a sensible proceeding when the funds for expenditure are limited. It is the course one would expect followed by an endowment fund or an insurance company. But the usual industrial enterprise is not so limited: it can obtain all the funds that can be desirably expended. To use a limit of expenditure as a test rather than a demanded rate, then, would infringe the concept that it is an error to fail to make a desirable expenditure.

. . . . .

  ⓒ   4. *Judgment Required in Applying Standard*

. . . . .

As will have been evident from the description of its derivation, the demanded rate of earnings is not a measure of precision. Precision is impossible, even if it were appropriate for the measurement of facts that, because they are mainly forecasts, are not themselves precise. The demanded rate is, on the contrary, a very practical measure, based, as we have seen, upon experience, and asking only that the results of the future conform in reasonable degree to the satisfactory results of the past.

These circumstances should be kept in mind when applying the standard. Because it is expressed as a single figure, the analyst—and the decider of expenditure—will be tempted to regard it as an exact line of demarcation between expenditure and no-expenditure. If, for example, the demanded rate is 15 per cent, the analyst will be tempted to regard an actual return of 15 per cent as justifying an expenditure *per se,* and an actual return of 14.9 per cent as rendering expenditure undesirable. This would be a mistake. It is no such precise measure, and it should not be thus automatically applied.

Remember again its origin. It is, at best, an approximation of the minimum rate of earnings that, with all the greater rates, will yield the average of the past. Remember, also, that it is applied to approximation [sic] of future earnings. These approximations will be variable in their probabilities. The forecasts of some earnings may be highly probable as to accuracy; others will be of only moderate, or even low, probability. These variations invite discretion in the use of the demanded rate. Undoubtedly, with a demanded rate of 15 per cent, some expenditures offering 20 per cent, but with low probability of accuracy, should be rejected. On the other hand, it is not inconceivable that supporting inducements might invite decision to make an expenditure that offered only 13 or 14 per cent.

The demanded rate, in brief, is not a fixed level, but a mean level that may have a high and a low tide.

. . . . .

C. *The Actual (Forecasted) Rate of Return*

. . . . .

For computing the actual rate, then, *ultimate average investment* includes expenditures for wearable facilities at half their amount; for other facilities, at their full amount. If an expenditure is, however, currently deductible for income tax purposes, there is a proportionate tax saving; and the amount to be included in ultimate average investment is the expenditure less the applicable tax.

Earnings will be computed at the amount of income, less related operating expenditures, less provision for depreciation of wearable facilities. No deduction should be made from income of any part of a permanent or nonrecurring expenditure, even though currently deductible for tax purposes.

Moreover, the earnings so computed should be at their normal rate, for so they are in the demanded rate.

. . . . .

Additions to earnings come from three principal sources: (1) reduction in operating expenditure—i.e., cost reduction; (2) increase in volume of sale of existing products; (3) manufacture and sale of new products. Additions of any kind almost always depend, in part, upon expenditures for facilities.

. . . . .

Within the scope of the enterprise, there is no general reason, as we have seen, to decline an expenditure that offers earnings acceptable to the standard. Yet we have recognized circumstances that, for temporary periods, may justify limitation of expenditure. In any such period, then, there should be a criterion of selection of expenditure. The weightiest criterion is, naturally, the extent of expected earnings: such funds as are spent will seek the highest earning. But the value of those earnings depends upon their character as well as upon the bare mathematics of rate.

Let us, then, consider what will influence a choice among varieties of added earnings.

Stability of earnings. Considerable value must be attributed to stability of earnings.

. . . . .

Reduction in cost. A reduction in cost implies the same quantity of physical production and sales at less operating expenditure (together with provision for renewal of facilities).

. . . . .

Usually, the forecasts of earnings from cost reduction can be more accurately evaluated than can earnings added from other sources. More importantly, however, cost reduction is never impaired as sales may be. In proportion to volume, cost reduction is just as productive of earnings in hard times as in good times, whereas added sales have a trick of disappearing.

. . . . .

Increase in volume. As a source of added earnings, an increase in the sale of existing products is to be preferred to the sale of new products.

Forecasts of ability to increase volume are usually more reliable than forecasts of ability to sell new products, and so conclusions are usually more probable. New products usually add more to fixed expense than does an addition to the volume of existing products, and so usually reduce unit cost less. More important, probably, is the greater possibility of latent, unsuspected difficulties in the manufacture and sale of new products.

. . . . .

New products. The comparative worth of added earnings from new products has been appraised by the conclusions about other added earnings . . .

. . . . .

The following table of rates of earnings, while based upon judgment rather than evidence, expresses reasonably well the extent of preference for one kind of earnings over another:

RATE OF EARNING

Rating	Cost Reduction	Increased Volume	Net Products
1	100% and over	150% and over	200% and over
2	65% to 99%	100% to 149%	130% to 199%
3	40 to 64	60 to 99	80 to 129
4	25 to 39	37 to 59	50 to 79
5	15 to 24	22 to 36	30 to 49
6		15 to 21	20 to 29
7			15 to 19

．　．　．　．　．

There are also certain expenditures that cannot be appraised in terms of monetary income, and therefore may not yield the demanded rate. Such are employee benefits, safety measures, improvements of working conditions, and cash retained as a safety margin or for future expenditure. For these, it will be prudent to make some allowance.

TUBER ELECTRONICS CORPORATION

On January 15, 1960, Mr. Conrad Dencer, financial vice-president of the Tuber Electronics Corporation, read an article on "The Cost of Capital" in a leading business publication. The article suggested that minimum standards for evaluating new project proposals should be determined by calculating a weighted-average "cost of capital" based on a firm's present capitalization. Since Tuber's existing minimum standards of a 20% return before taxes had been established on a rather arbitrary basis, Mr. Dencer decided to explore whether the cost-of-capital method might provide a more useful basis for determining a cutoff point or hurdle rate in screening new capital expenditure opportunities. The analysis would be particularly timely, he believed, in view of the fact that recently the 20% rate had been subjected to considerable criticism by several other Tuber executives.

The Tuber Electronics Corporation, a firm engaged in the design, development, and manufacture of control devices for industry (65% of sales volume in 1959) and for the Department of Defense, had grown extremely rapidly since World War II; 1959 sales of $294 million and profits of $20 million were nearly four times the comparable figures for 1947, indicating that the company had expanded at a compound rate of better than 12% per year over the period. (Selected financial information is presented in Exhibits 1 and 2, and a compound rate of growth table is shown in Exhibit 6.)

In order to finance the expansion, Tuber had spent approximately $235 million during the past 14 years. These funds had been generated as follows:

Depreciation	$ 61 million
Retained earnings	74
Debt financing	90
Excess cash on hand, beginning of 1947	10
Total	$235 million

In Mr. Dencer's opinion, the greatest part of Tuber's growth had been financed with funds provided by retained earnings and debt and, to a less important degree, the excess cash available in early 1947. Of these sources, debt accounted for 51.8%, while retained earnings supplied only 42.5%. Depreciation generations over the period had not really contributed to the company's expansion, since these funds had been barely adequate to permit reinvestment necessary to offset the high rate of obsolescence prevalent in the electronics industry.

The availability of debt financing in the past had been an important factor contributing to the ease with which Tuber had been able to grow, and management had relied heavily on this resource. The company had entered the postwar era in a highly liquid position and with no long-term obligations, but since 1947 long-term borrowing had provided capital equal to approximately 122% of retained earnings. By 1959, Tuber's debt position had been brought to almost 40% of total capitalization.

The 40% ratio had been strongly resisted by several members of Tuber's management as being too high, and in Mr. Dencer's judgment it represented the maximum debt level which the firm could hope to maintain in the future. As a result, Mr. Dencer could foresee that the company's future ability to generate funds would be limited to depreciation resources plus retained earnings and whatever new debt capacity these earnings allowed, unless new equity financing were provided. Assuming that the existing debt-to-equity policy remained in effect, each $1.00 of new equity would permit only $0.667 of additional debt in the future, in contrast with the $1.22 of the past.

The prospect of a new common stock issue, in the event that Tuber's minimum-return standards were met by more projects than could be financed from internal funds generations, was the subject of considerable heated controversy among the firm's management. Mr. Dencer himself had objected to previous stock issue proposals on the grounds that they would mean sharing the firm's future earnings with new stockholders, to the detriment of existing owners. The possibility of issuing stock on a privileged subscription basis, which would alleviate this problem to some degree, was out of the question since roughly 30% of the company's outstanding stock was owned by the direct descendants of the founder, H. Erich Tuber, and these individuals were not in a position to increase their investment. Indeed, they seemed primarily interested in the income aspects of stock ownership and both recently and in the past had been adamant in their insistence that Tuber's 50% dividend pay-out policy be maintained, even though several members of management had suggested that a cut in the dividend rate would yield valuable funds for the company's growth.

Several Tuber executives had expressed the opinion that while Tuber's stock was actively traded and listed on a major exchange, a new issue of common would have an adverse effect on the market price of Tuber shares. This affect would be disadvantageous both to present investors and to key executives who held options for the purchase of some 20,000 shares at various prices ranging from $16 to $25 per share.

In light of the resistance to common stock financing evident within the company, Mr. Dencer had become worried during the past year about the utility of Tuber's present 20% minimum standard for accepting capital expenditure proposals. Historically, the ratio of annual retained earnings increments to total capitalization at the beginning of a year had, on the average, held steady at roughly 5.0%. If this relationship were to continue in the future, as seemed likely, then capital expenditures (including net additions to working capital) would have to be restricted to an annual rate of 8.3% of opening total capitalization (based on new retained earnings plus additional borrowing capacity generated). Annual capital expenditures since 1947, however, had averaged nearly 12% of total opening capitalization. Thus, it appeared that if such expenditures were henceforth to be approved at a reduced rate, Tuber would have to be more selective with respect to which proposals were accepted. This possibility would create concern among various divisional vice-presidents in charge of manufacturing operations, Mr. Dencer was aware, for these men had criticized even the present cutoff point as being too high. They believed that Tuber could become a more important force in the industry if its sales were greater and its rate of growth more rapid.

To complicate matters further, research expenditures had increased sharply since 1955, from 5% to 8% of commercial sales (exclusive of research sponsored under government contract). The fruits of the added research had begun to show by late 1959, and the number of acceptable expenditure opportunities for 1960 had increased, proportional to total opening capitalization, to 15% (see data in Exhibit 3). As a result, Tuber was now in the position of having a greater number of expenditure opportunities at just the time when less capital (on a percentage basis) would be available for investment.

From an analysis of the current expenditure opportunities, Mr.

Dencer had estimated that the impact of Tuber's present situation would be to limit project approvals to those with returns of 24% or more before taxes, provided no new common stock equity were issued. He estimated that retained earnings in 1960 would approximate $11.4 million, and these, combined with the additional $7.6 million of borrowing power thus created, would enable Tuber to finance expenditures (other than those funded by depreciation) of only $19 million. In order to gain perspective as to what effect adoption of a 24% cutoff rate would have on future earnings per share, Mr. Dencer had prepared the forecast shown in Exhibit 4. These calculations showed that the firm's earnings per share rate of growth would decline to an average rate of 10.8% over the following ten years, versus the 11.2% average per year since 1947.

Mr. Dencer believed that the projections shown in Exhibit 4 probably understated the profit potential developing from the increased selectivity in accepting new projects. In the past, Tuber had been growing so rapidly that finding trained technical and managerial manpower was a perennial and increasing critical problem. As a consequence, responsibility was often thrust upon young personnel before their experience justified the promotion. Moreover, the very push for expansion created pressures which interfered with effective managerial planning, coordination, and control, probably to the detriment of profits. In particular, Mr. Dencer was concerned about research activities. He believed the sharp step-up in research efforts after 1955 might have led to a significant decrease in the over-all quality of the research. A slower rate of new capital expenditures, perhaps coupled with a cutback in research efforts (to 6% or 7% of commercial sales), might, then, favorably affect profits. For example, a 1 percentage point decrease in research expenditures alone would increase projected profits before taxes for 1960 by $1.91 million.

In an effort to appraise the effects of issuing common stock to allow maintenance of the existing 20% (before taxes) cutoff point on expenditure proposals, Mr. Dencer had also prepared the earnings forecasts shown in Exhibit 5. In this analysis he had reluctantly assumed that stock could be sold at a price of 40 times the previous year's earnings, despite the fact that the stock had sold at this high ratio for less than a year. These figures showed, perhaps optimistically, earnings per share growth over the next ten years averaging 14.9% per year.

While his two earnings projections had proved interesting, Mr. Dencer did not believe they really provided an answer to the question he had posed: What should Tuber's cutoff point be in order best to achieve optimum growth? He wondered if the weighted-average cost-of-capital approach outlined in a magazine article might provide a clue toward solution of this problem.

At the present time Tuber's interest charges on the outstanding $90 million in long-term debt averaged exactly 4%, and hence this figure appeared to represent the effective cost for the debt portion of the company's capitalization. Recent borrowing had cost as much as 5%, and there was little likelihood that borrowing in the near future could be accomplished at less than this rate; but rates on older debt were lower than the 4% average.

In contrast to the relative ease of computing debt costs, there were several possible methods of calculating the cost of equity. Mr. Dencer decided, as a start, to use book value as the basis for his analysis. He assumed that the cost of retained earnings and new equity would be the same, although he had some doubts as to whether this assumption was wholly accurate. The results of his calculation are shown below:

	Capitalization	Percentage of Capitalization	Weight	Cost of Capital	Weight × Cost
Debt	$ 90 million	39.5%	0.395	4.00%	1.580%
Equity	138	60.5	0.605	5.09*	3.079
				Weighted-average	
Total	$228 million	100.0%		cost of capital	4.659%

* Computed as follows:
a) Current rate of E.P.S./Current MP = $1.12/$44 = 2.545% after taxes.
b) Cost after taxes/1 − tax rate = 2.545/0.5 = 5.09%

According to this analysis, Tuber would apparently be correct in accepting any expenditure proposal which promised a return of more than 4.66%. Mr. Dencer had noted that, as recently as October, 1959, the U.S. Treasury had issued bonds carrying an interest rate of 5%, and logically Tuber would have been justified in issuing common stock for the express purpose of purchasing some of these bonds, if his calculation were correct. Mr. Dencer was suspicious of the validity of such reasoning, however, and he began to wonder whether there might be a more useful way of using the cost-of-capital approach as an aid in determining Tuber's ideal cutoff rate.

Exhibit 1

TUBER ELECTRONICS CORPORATION

BALANCE SHEET, DECEMBER 31, 1959*

(Dollar amounts in millions)

ASSETS

Cash..$ 15.0
Accounts receivable.. 45.1
Inventories... 60.3
Prepaid items... 1.5

Total current assets.......................................$121.9
Investments in foreign subsidiaries........................... 20.0
Net plant and equipment.................................... 122.4
Other assets.. 4.9

Total assets...$269.2

LIABILITIES

Accounts payable..$ 20.1
Miscellaneous accruals...................................... 10.7
Federal income tax... 10.4

Total current liabilities....................................$ 41.2
Debentures†... 90.0
Common stock (20,000,000 shares at $1.00 par value)†........... 20.0
Capital surplus†.. 28.0
Earned surplus†... 90.0

Total liabilities and net worth..............................$269.2

* An unaudited, preliminary statement.
† Total capitalization equals $228.0, of which debentures represent 39.5%.

Exhibit 2

TUBER ELECTRONICS CORPORATION

EARNINGS PER SHARE, DIVIDEND AND MARKET PRICE INFORMATION

(Adjusted for stock splits)

Year	Earnings per Share	Dividends per Share	Dividend Pay-out Percentage	Average Market Price	Price-Earnings Ratio	Dividend Yield
1947	$0.26	$0.10	39%	$2.22	8.6x	4.5%
1948	0.28	0.16	57	3.03	10.8	5.3
1949	0.38	0.18	47	3.27	8.6	5.5
1950	0.60	0.20	33	4.61	7.7	4.3
1951	0.40	0.24	60	6.17	15.4	3.9
1952	0.38	0.24	63	6.54	17.2	3.7
1953	0.42	0.24	57	7.61	18.1	3.2
1954	0.61	0.32	52	11.10	18.2	2.9
1955	0.79	0.37	47	15.31	19.4	2.4
1956	0.85	0.44	52	18.98	22.4	2.3
1957	0.79	0.44	56	23.54	29.8	1.9
1958	0.81	0.44	54	23.25	28.7	2.0
1959	1.00	0.50	50	35.00	35.0	1.4

Average 51%

Note: On January 15, 1960, Tuber's common stock was selling at $44 per share, relative to antici-
pated earnings per share in 1960 of $1.12 (P.E. ratio of 39.2) and anticipated dividends per share
of $0.55 (yield of 1.25%).

Exhibit 3

TUBER ELECTRONICS CORPORATION

CAPITAL EXPENDITURE OPPORTUNITIES, 1960*

Discounted Cash Flow, Present Value Rate of Return (before Taxes)	*Amount of Acceptable Expenditure Opportunities*	*Cumulative Expenditure Opportunities*	*Cumulative Expenditure Opportunities as % of Total Capitalization*	*1955 Capital Expenditure Opportunities as % of Total Capitalization*
32% and above.........	†	†	†	‡
30–31.9%..............$	3.6 million	$ 3.6 million	1.6%	‡
28–29.9%..............	4.2	7.8	3.4	1.7%
26–27.9%..............	5.0	12.8	5.6	3.6
24–25.9%..............	6.2	19.0	8.3	5.9
22–23.9%..............	7.0	26.0	11.4	8.7
20–21.9%..............	8.0	34.0	14.9	12.0

OTHER AVAILABLE EXPENDITURE OPPORTUNITIES§

18–19.9%..............$	9.1 million	$43.1 million	18.9%	15.2% §
16–17.9%..............	10.4	53.5	23.5	
14–14.9%..............	12.0	65.5	28.7	
12–13.9%..............	14.0	79.5	34.8	
10–11.9%..............	18.0	97.5	42.7	

* Based on staff estimates.
† Depreciation generations of $19.0 million were expected to finance projects with returns, before taxes, of 32% or more.
‡ Depreciation funds financed these expenditures.
§ Based on estimates prepared by staff in research departments.

Exhibit 4

TUBER ELECTRONICS CORPORATION

PROJECTION OF EARNINGS PER SHARE ASSUMING 24% CUTOFF RATE, NO NEW EQUITY

(Dollar amounts in thousands)

	1960	1961	1962	1963	1964	1965	1966	1967	1968	1969
Profit before interest and taxes, prior year		$48,400	$53,634	$59,324	$65,618	$72,581	$80,284	$88,805	$ 98,243	$108,672
Plus incremental profits @ 27.5% previous year's investment*		5,234	5,690	6,294	6,963	7,703	8,521	9,438	10,429	11,541
Profit before interest and taxes	$48,400	$53,634	$59,324	$65,618	$72,581	$80,284	$88,805	$98,243	$108,672	$120,213
Interest†	3,600	3,980	4,394	4,852	5,358	5,918	6,538	7,224	7,979	8,818
Profit before taxes	$44,800	$49,654	$54,930	$60,766	$67,223	$74,366	$82,367	$91,019	$100,695	$111,395
Taxes at 50%	22,400	24,827	27,465	30,383	33,611	37,183	41,183	45,509	50,347	55,697
Profit after taxes	$22,400	$24,827	$27,465	$30,383	$33,612	$37,183	$41,184	$45,510	$ 50,348	$ 55,698
Dividends, estimated at 50% (except 1960), of P.A.T.	11,000	12,413	13,732	15,191	16,806	18,591	20,592	22,755	25,174	27,849
Retained earnings	$11,400	$12,414	$13,733	$15,192	$16,806	$18,592	$20,592	$22,755	$ 25,174	$ 27,849
Additional borrowing capacity (two-thirds retained earnings)	7,600	8,276	9,155	10,128	11,204	12,394	13,728	15,170	16,783	18,566
Total new capital available	$19,000	$20,690	$22,888	$25,320	$28,010	$30,986	$34,320	$37,925	$ 41,957	$ 46,415
Earnings per share	$1.12	$1.24	$1.37	$1.52	$1.68	$1.86	$2.06	$2.28	$2.52	$2.78
Dividends per share	$0.55	$0.62	$0.69	$0.76	$0.84	$0.93	$1.03	$1.14	$1.26	$1.39

* Calculated as follows, based on data in Exhibit 3:

Amount Invested	Estimated Return	Dollar Return
$ 3,600	31%	$1,116
4,200	29	1,218
5,000	27	1,350
6,200	25	1,550
$19,000		$5,234

$5,234/$19,000 = 27.5% return on investment before taxes.

† Interest at 4% on outstanding $90 million in debt, plus 5% on additional debt..

Exhibit 5

TUBER ELECTRONICS CORPORATION

PROJECTION OF EARNINGS PER SHARE ASSUMING 20% CUTOFF RATE, NEW EQUITY AS REQUIRED

(Dollar amounts in thousands)

	1960	1961	1962	1963	1964	1965	1966	1967	1968	1969
Profit before interest and taxes, prior year......		$ 48,400	$ 56,934	$ 66,733	$ 77,992	$ 90,928	$105,791	$122,869	$142,743	$165,290
Plus incremental profits @ 25.1% of previous year's investments*......		8,514	9,799	11,259	12,936	14,863	17,078	19,874	22,547	25,906
Profit before interest and taxes......	$ 48,400	$ 56,914	$ 66,733	$ 77,992	$ 90,928	$105,791	$122,869	$142,743	$165,290	$191,196
Interest†......	3,600	4,280	5,061	5,958	6,989	8,173	9,534	11,098	12,895	14,959
Profit before taxes......	$ 44,800	$ 52,634	$ 61,672	$ 72,034	$ 83,938	$ 97,618	$113,335	$131,645	$152,395	$176,237
Taxes at 50%......	22,400	26,317	30,836	36,017	41,969	48,809	56,667	65,822	76,197	88,118
Profit after taxes......	$ 22,400	$ 26,317	$ 30,836	$ 36,017	$ 41,969	$ 48,809	$ 56,668	$ 65,823	$ 76,198	$ 88,119
Dividends estimated @ 50% (except 1960) of P.A.T.......	11,000	13,158	15,418	18,008	20,984	24,404	28,334	32,911	38,099	44,059
Retained earnings......	$ 11,400	$ 13,159	$ 15,418	$ 18,009	$ 20,985	$ 24,405	$ 28,334	$ 32,912	$ 38,099	$ 44,050
Additional borrowing capacity (two-thirds retained earnings)......	7,600	8,772	10,279	12,006	13,990	16,270	18,889	21,941	25,399	29,706
Total new capital available......	$ 19,000	$ 21,931	$ 25,697	$ 30,015	$ 34,975	$ 40,675	$ 47,223	$ 54,853	$ 63,498	$ 73,756
Total capitalization, beginning of year......	$228,000	$262,000	$301,038	$345,893	$397,431	$456,648	$524,689	$602,868	$692,695	$795,907
Funds required (14.9% of opening total capitalization)......	$ 34,000	$ 39,038	$ 44,855	$ 51,538	$ 59,217	$ 68,041	$ 78,179	$ 89,827	$103,212	$118,590
Less total new capital available, per above......	19,000	21,931	25,697	30,015	34,975	40,675	47,223	54,853	63,498	73,756
Additional capital required from debt and equity sources......	$ 15,000	$ 17,107	$ 19,158	$ 21,523	$ 24,242	$ 27,366	$ 30,953	$ 34,974	$ 39,714	$ 44,834
Additional capital obtained from debt (40% of above)......	6,000	6,842	7,663	8,609	9,697	10,946	12,382	13,990	15,886	17,934
Balance of capital obtained from equity (60% of above)......	$ 9,000	$ 10,265	$ 11,495	$ 12,914	$ 14,545	$ 16,420	$ 18,574	$ 20,984	$ 23,828	$ 26,900

Market price per share of stock (40 times prior year E.P.S.)	$ 40.00	$ 44.40	$ 51.60	$ 59.60	$ 68.80	$ 79.60	$ 91.60	$ 105.20	$ 121.20	$ 139.20
New shares required to be issued (thousands)	225	231	223	217	211	206	203	199	197	193
Shares outstanding at beginning of year (thousands)	20,000	20,225	20,456	20,679	20,896	21,107	21,313	21,516	21,715	21,912
Total shares outstanding at end of year	20,225	20,456	20,679	20,896	21,107	21,313	21,516	21,715	21,912	22,105
Earning's per share (on total shares outstanding at end of year)	$1.11	$1.29	$1.49	$1.72	$1.99	$2.29	$2.63	$3.03	$3.48	$3.99
Dividends per share (on total shares outstanding at end of year)	0.54	0.64	0.74	0.86	0.99	1.14	1.31	1.51	1.76	1.99

* Calculated as follows, based upon data in Exhibit 3:

Amount Invested	Return	Dollar Return
$ 3,600	31%	$1,116
4,200	29	1,218
5,000	27	1,350
6,200	25	1,550
7,000	23	1,610
8,000	21	1,680
$34,000		$8,524

$\frac{8,524}{34,000}$ = 25.1% return on investment before taxes.

† Interest at 4% on outstanding $90 million in debt, plus 5% on additional debt.

Exhibit 6

TUBER ELECTRONICS CORPORATION

COMPOUND RATE OF GROWTH TABLE*

Compound Rate of Growth— % per Year	\multicolumn{12}{c}{Value of 1 — Year (n)}
		1	2	3	4	5	6	7	8	9	10	15	20
1%.........1.01	1.020	1.030	1.041	1.051	1.062	1.072	1.083	1.094	1.105	1.161	1.220
2..........1.020	1.040	1.061	1.082	1.104	1.126	1.149	1.172	1.195	1.219	1.346	1.373
3..........1.030	1.061	1.093	1.126	1.159	1.194	1.230	1.267	1.305	1.344	1.558	1.806
4..........1.040	1.082	1.125	1.170	1.217	1.265	1.316	1.369	1.423	1.480	1.801	2.191
5..........1.050	1.103	1.158	1.216	1.276	1.340	1.407	1.477	1.551	1.629	2.079	2.653
6..........1.060	1.124	1.191	1.262	1.338	1.419	1.504	1.594	1.689	1.791	2.340	3.207
7..........1.070	1.145	1.225	1.311	1.403	1.501	1.606	1.718	1.838	1.967	2.759	3.870
8..........1.080	1.166	1.260	1.360	1.469	1.587	1.714	1.851	1.999	2.159	3.172	4.661
9..........1.090	1.188	1.295	1.412	1.539	1.677	1.828	1.993	2.172	2.367	3.642	5.604
10..........1.100	1.210	1.331	1.464	1.611	1.772	1.949	2.144	2.358	2.594	4.177	6.727
11..........1.110	1.232	1.368	1.518	1.685	1.870	2.076	2.305	2.558	2.839	4.785	8.062
12..........1.120	1.254	1.405	1.574	1.762	1.974	2.211	2.476	2.773	3.106	5.474	9.646
13..........1.130	1.277	1.443	1.630	1.842	2.082	2.352	2.658	3.004	3.395	6.254	11.523
14..........1.140	1.300	1.482	1.689	1.925	2.195	2.502	2.853	3.252	3.707	7.138	13.743
15..........1.150	1.323	1.521	1.749	2.011	2.313	2.660	3.059	3.518	4.046	8.137	16.366
20..........1.200	1.440	1.728	2.074	2.488	2.986	3.583	4.300	5.160	6.192	15.407	38.334
25..........1.250	1.563	1.953	2.441	3.052	3.815	6.275	5.960	7.451	9.313	51.186	86.736
30..........1.300	1.690	2.197	2.856	3.713	4.827	6.275	8.157	10.604	13.786	51.186	190.049
40..........1.400	1.960	2.744	3.842	5.378	7.530	10.541	14.758	20.661	28.925	155.568	836.681
50..........1.500	2.250	3.375	5.063	7.594	11.391	17.086	25.629	38.443	57.665	437.893	332.524

* Based on compound interest computation according to the formula $s = (1 + i)n$.

Section IV
CAPITAL STRUCTURE PLANNING

MANSFIELD CHEMICAL COMPANY

In early 1957 Mansfield Chemical Company launched a five-year $180 million expansion program, the largest in the company's history. Mansfield planned to finance the expansion program and other requirements of $10 million from internally generated sources totaling $145 million and through the sale of a new $45 million debt issue. During the planning period preparatory to the expansion program, management had reviewed a total of $300 million in capital expenditure project requests, all of which promised attractive returns. However, the limited financial resources necessitated careful screening of all expenditure proposals and elimination of $120 million of projects in order to keep the size of the program within the limits of the funds available.

Following these decisions, several company officers argued that the emphasis on fund conservation had precluded approving projects promising significant return opportunities. They believed that corporate earnings would grow more rapidly through accelerated expansion if only the artificial restrictions imposed by present debt policy objectives could be liberalized to free more funds for expansion. Notwithstanding these purported advantages to be gained from a change in debt policy, other members of top management believed that present debt limitations already reflected a healthy balance between risk considerations and income opportunities. An exploratory discussion of debt policies at the February board of directors meeting had not resolved but instead had heightened the elements of disagreement raised by top management. As a consequence, the board of directors asked Mr. William Gates, financial vice-president, to prepare a thorough review of alternative debt policies, including his personal recommendations, for discussion at the forthcoming March meeting of the board.

Mansfield Chemical Company commenced operations in 1895 producing coal derivatives, such as tar, asphalt, and coke, from the low-grade surface coal deposits found in southwestern Ohio. In the early 1900's, the company actively entered into the production of basic chemicals from various mineral resources. Expansion and diversification continued thereafter at a rapid pace until, by the 1930's, the company was a significant factor in the basic chemicals industry.

After World War II, Mansfield recorded a fairly rapid growth in sales but only a moderate growth in earnings. Many of the capital investments made during the postwar period were for plant modernization and cost reduction projects, projects carrying lower rates of return than was typical for the chemical industry. Furthermore, as other companies entered the basic chemicals industry, competition increased and profit margins were reduced. As a result, Mansfield's earnings failed to grow as rapidly as sales. After considering the diluting effect of two equity issues, earnings per share showed only modest gains over the ten-year postwar period.

Exhibit 1 gives comparative balance sheets as of December 31, 1947, and 1956, as well as a source and application of funds statement for the period. Exhibit 2 summarizes Mansfield's operations for 1947 through 1956 and also shows market prices of the common stock for these years.

In early 1956 a young and aggressive group of officers assumed management of Mansfield Chemical Company. One of the first objectives established by the new management group was greater emphasis on corporate growth. However, before commencing a "helter-skelter" expansion program for the mere sake of expansion, management took careful stock of its situation. Mansfield's competitive status was explored product by product. Simultaneously, market research teams were drawing up careful estimates of long-term market potentials of current and of possible new product lines.

These studies suggested several significant conclusions. Management found that the company was overdiversified to the point where it could not compete effectively in many of its product lines because of limited production. Similarly, much effort was currently being expended in developing product lines that showed comparatively little future promise, whereas areas with outstanding growth prospects were being overlooked. In particular, Mansfield had lagged behind its competitors in upgrading basic chemical output to more profitable intermediate products. Research and development expenditures were low by industry standards and were not directed toward the most rewarding activities. Despite these developments, the company learned it held significant resource advantages in manpower, technology, and materials in a number of promising areas.

The study focused management's attention on the need for a carefully planned expansion program. Research expenditures, for example, were increased sharply, and emphasis was shifted to the most strategic opportunities available. Immediate studies were launched into the possibilities of upgrading basic output to an intermediate level wherever growth potentials seemed highly significant. In short, the company set out to follow a path of intensive but highly selective growth.

In establishing a framework for developing an expansion program to achieve these objectives, management first set a five-year period as the most desirable planning horizon. All capital expenditure proposals would have to meet the standards of Mansfield's capital investment policy for return on investment. The company had based its standard on the historic performance of Mansfield for the last five years, which showed an average after-tax return on invested capital of 5.2%.[1] Since the return on investment for similar chemical companies had averaged somewhat higher than Mansfield's during the same period, management set its own standards above Mansfield's historic rate. In this way, it was hoped to improve the company's performance over time. Generally, the standards were set for minimum risk projects and required a 15% return after taxes for any new product or process, 12% for expansion of present product capacity, 10% for replacement or improvement projects, and 8% for cost reduction projects. Lower rates of return were acceptable for "strategic" investments necessary to maintain competitive position, replace or improve vital facilities, or provide other intangible benefits of importance. However, projects with greater than minimum risk required proportionately higher rates of return. No specific method had evolved for equating these risks, each case being decided by an individual evaluation. The company anticipated that in five years new products, now unknown to Mansfield, would make up 30% of total sales.

As the next step in the planning process, division managers were

---

[1] For instance, after-taxes return in 1956 (from Exhibits 1 and 2) :

$$\frac{\text{Profit after Taxes}}{\text{Total Assets}} \times 100 = \frac{\$10,878}{\$199,002} \times 100 = 5.45\%.$$

allowed several months to prepare and submit their projects for the program. During that time, all available and prospective projects were analyzed and rigorously screened. The division managers finally submitted projects totaling nearly $300 million, all meeting the prescribed investment criteria. For the most part, the projects also offered desirable growth opportunities and fell within the selected areas of concentration. The top-management group, meeting in continuous session for over a week, pared the projects to $180 million, a limit that appeared financially feasible. Of the total program, $145 million was for investment in plant and equipment and the balance of $35 million would be invested in working capital. An additional $10 million was required to meet sinking fund payments on outstanding debt.

While the capital budgeting and selection process was under way, the treasurer's office prepared a forecast of the sources of funds available to finance the expansion program. Sales projections were based on market appraisals of sales prospects for current product lines plus planned additions growing out of the approved expansion program. Earnings projections were forecast on the basis of anticipated larger margins, reduced to some extent by heavy starting-up expenses, research and development charges, and advertising costs. In line with past dividend policy, a pay-out of 60% of earnings after taxes was projected. From these data, including projected depreciation charges, the treasurer forecast internally generated funds at $145 million over the program's five-year planning horizon. Exhibit 3 presents a summary of the final forecast. Capital expenditure levels in this forecast have been revised to reflect in full the proposed expansion program.

On the basis of preliminary forecasts, top management concluded that internally generated funds would not be adequate to cover all desirable expenditure opportunities and that additional funds would have to be raised from some outside source.

The issuance of common stock was eliminated for the following reasons:

1. Mansfield common was currently selling at a comparatively low price to earnings ratio, both for Mansfield historically as well as for the rest of the chemical industry.

2. The issuance of a large number of new common shares would cause an immediate dilution of earnings per share, thereby reducing the relative benefits of the expansion program for the present stockholders.

3. The company dividend policy, which for various reasons the board of

directors did not wish to change, made equity capital relatively expensive. More-over, an equity issue was considered the most expensive method of raising capital.

4. The two postwar issues of Mansfield common stock had diluted earnings per share, and as a result, the Mansfield stockholder had not participated as fully in the postwar growth of the chemical industry as had stockholders in other chemical companies. Management consequently believed stockholders should be allowed the opportunity to see their stock values appreciate significantly without further threats of dilution.

5. More favorable financing opportunities were available.

Similarly, it was decided not to issue preferred stock for three reasons:

1. Preferred dividend rates were near their postwar high.
2. The dividends were paid from after-tax earnings.
3. The pre-emptive rights of the present common stockholders, granted by the company charter, virtually eliminated the possibility of private placement at more favorable rates.

Consequently, management finally decided that long-term debentures were the best method of raising the additional capital needed to supplement funds generated from internal sources.

Mr. Gates, the financial vice-president, next planned to analyze how much debt financing Mansfield could carry safely. In his opinion, the interests of the common stockholder were the most important factor in making such a decision. Historically, the company had been run conservatively, carrying little or no debt, and Mr. Gates believed that the present stockholders had invested in the company's securities largely for this reason. He further believed that the common stockholders' interests would be injured if Mansfield altered its debt policy drastically.

Mr. Gates also had undertaken an analysis of recent debt levels stated as a per cent of total capitalization (long-term debt plus stock plus surplus) for 14 other chemical companies. From this analysis, he determined the industry average debt outstanding was roughly 30% of total capitalization. In view of Mansfield's conservative financial history, he reasoned that a limit of 25% debt to total capitalization (or debt equal to one-third of the equity base) was safely below the industry average. This debt policy, applied to the present capital structure, would allow Mansfield to market a new debenture issue of $45 million, after considering debt obligations of $9.8 million already outstanding.

Mr. Gates next met with investment bankers and discussed the prospects of raising $45 million through a public debenture issue. The bankers told him that they would be able to sell such an issue at close to the lowest prevailing interest rate for long-term debt, 4.75%. Despite the tight money market, an issue with a 25- or 30-year maturity would be salable, and sinking fund payments could be arranged to commence in five or ten years. The debenture would probably carry a Moody's "A" rating. Other restrictions relating to dividend payments, sale or purchase of assets, and maintenance of minimum working capital levels did not appear to limit management's freedom of action significantly. On the basis of his talks with the underwriters, Mr. Gates concluded that the proposed debt limit was reasonably conservative.

In December, 1956, the board of directors concurred with Mr. Gates' findings. The board approved his recommendation to raise $45 million through debt financing, along with formally approving the proposed $180 million capital-expenditure program.

Criticism of Mansfield's debt policy did not arise until early 1957 when the expansion program was already under way. Then several of the division managers expressed concern over the fact that projects with obviously attractive returns on investment had been eliminated from consideration because adequate funds were not available. The division managers suggested that more funds would be available if the present conservative debt limit were abandoned.

When the subject of debt policy was raised at the February, 1957, board meeting, the resulting discussion lasted well over an hour, with all directors expressing definite, although diverse, views. Mr. Gates finally agreed to review the company's debt policy and to prepare recommendations for presentation at the next board meeting in March. Mr. Gates further agreed to analyze and discuss in his report each of the viewpoints raised by the various board members. These viewpoints are summarized in the following paragraphs:

CONTRASTING VIEWPOINTS ON AN APPROPRIATE DEBT POLICY PRESENTED DURING THE FEBRUARY MEETING OF MANSFIELD'S BOARD OF DIRECTORS[2]

Stockholder Preferences

Traditionally, we have been a conservatively run, soundly financed company. Many stockholders have acquired their holdings on the assumption that we will continue to run their company in a manner tending to minimize, as far as feasible, the relative riskiness of their investment. A radical change in our debt structure, bringing with it excessive leverage and lower safety factors, would

---

[2] Comments of individual directors are identified on the following pages by dotted paragraph breaks.

consequently constitute a breach of trust. Excessive leverage would, for example, make earnings per share and market prices more volatile, thereby replacing our characteristic elements of stability with wider speculative fluctuations. This argues for holding our debt position to a prudent level—certainly less than the average for companies in our industry.

. . . . .

We should not tailor our financial policies around the preferences for conservatism attributed, perhaps erroneously, to our present stockholders. Rather, we must take advantage of available opportunities, as fully and aggressively as seems economically justified. We have significant opportunities for growth available to us at this moment. If we earnestly attempt to capitalize fully on these opportunities, we will, through favorable growth trends, attract new (and more desirable) stockholders whose goals are more consistent with our corporate opportunities. Were we to strive for unwarranted stability at the expense of less rapid growth, we would be doing our stockholders a disservice. I see no need to sacrifice significant income opportunities unjustifiably on a prehistoric altar of safety. By this, I am not suggesting that we should abandon prudence and borrow excessively risky amounts of debt. I don't believe, however, that our present debt commitment of $45 million begins to approach this limit. For example, several of our competitors have borrowed in excess of 40% of their total capitalization, yet their stocks are not considered excessively leveraged or speculative. None of these companies (e.g., Dow Chemical, Hooker Electrochemical) appears to be on the verge of bankruptcy either.

Equally important, I believe that the great majority of our present stockholders would prefer us to maximize growth within the limits of prudence rather than maximize safety within the confines of allowing only modest growth. The historic price-earnings ratio of our stock is more nearly similar to ratios for other growth stocks than to stocks exhibiting unusual stability. Here is concrete evidence of our stockholder's preference. More liberal use of debt promises higher earnings per share levels, and perhaps more favorable market reception (i.e., higher price-earnings ratios) for the common stock. Even if I am wrong about stockholder preferences, those stockholders wishing to switch to a stock like American Telephone and Telegraph can undoubtedly do so at a very favorable market price.

. . . . .

Elements of Risk

The safest course of action is to avoid debt entirely. However, the income advantages from financing by debt are so significant we can't afford the safest policy. On the other hand, none of us wants to follow a course of action that might bring us anywhere near the brink of financial disaster. This means to me that we ought to borrow as much as we can as long as the sum borrowed involves no significant measure of risk. The question then becomes how much can we borrow without adding any significant degree of risk. In answer, we should only borrow sums where we know we can safely discharge fixed debt obligations (interest and sinking funds) from profits earned under adverse circumstances. Illustratively, in our worst postwar year (1948) we earned roughly $10.7 million before taxes. Sinking funds typically run about 5% of funds borrowed, or 10% on a tax adjusted basis. At worst, interest charges would be 5%, leading to a total burden of 15% before taxes. Our worst earnings year consequently could only cover about $70 million of debt $\dfrac{(\$10.7 \text{ Million})}{0.15} = \$70$ Million). We currently plan to borrow a total of $54 million. The difference appears to be a minimal allowance for safety. Consequently, any plan to increase the debt level above current proposals seems unwise in view of the added element of risk.

· · · · ·

In considering coverage ratios, let's not forget the rather large noncash depreciation charges which provide funds for meeting fixed obligations. Including these depreciation funds in coverage ratios improves the picture considerably. All this makes larger amounts of debt appear clearly safe.

· · · · ·

Call me a pessimist if you will, but I cannot forget what happened to the company during the depression. In 1932 our sales were less than one-half the 1929 level, and our earnings less than one-fifth. Perhaps we won't see anything like this again but who can say for sure. A really safe debt policy, in any event, should take possibilities like this into account. How will the proposed debt level look if profits before taxes should fall to one-fifth of their current levels? The answer is we could not begin to cover our fixed obligations.

Secondly, the postwar period has been a boom era where the chemical industry has had to run hard to catch up with demand. During this period we haven't seen anything but minor economic tremors in the chemical industry— nothing truly recessionary in nature. Today, notwithstanding the promising long-term outlook, the industry has about caught up with demand. In this framework, periods of temporary oversupply and recessions seem more probable in future years. Moreover, the nature of the industry has changed considerably. In particular, I call your attention to the new relationship between fixed and variable expenses. Skilled operators performing automated functions, research activities, accounting and other staff functions, advertising—all these and other costs are now more difficult to cut back during sales declines without jeopardizing our competitive position. Comparatively moderate sales declines may consequently cause sharper earnings declines than was true historically. This argues for greater emphasis on safety. I have grave doubts about the wisdom of the proposed borrowing level, except as a temporary expedient, and don't find any justification for increasing these risks any further.

· · · · ·

So far we've talked about coverage and safety entirely from the point of view of satisfying bondholder's interests. I like to think that I represent the point of view of the common shareholders. These shareholders have a natural interest in the safety of their income, and I suspect they would like us to consider maintaining the stability of their dividends as an informal obligation in formulating wise debt policies. How do their dividends fare coveragewise under the various debt alternatives proposed? Not so well I fear.

· · · · ·

All this discussion of coverage seems a little academic to me. You don't pay obligations with profits; rather, you use cash. As long as we have an adequate cash supply to meet these demands, we're safe. Let's examine this principle closely. During the depression, when sales declined, inventory and receivable investments were reduced. As a result, cash balances increased. At the end of 1932, for example, liquid asset balances were 20% of sales volume for that year. By today's standards, we were extremely liquid in 1932. I can't see that additional debt poses any real threat for this reason.

· · · · ·

Safety is just one element of risk. A more important element is the protection of our market reputation. Our growth aims suggest we will be requiring capital again in the future, and it would indeed be unfortunate if we jeopardized our future ability to risk these funds by a rash action today. Credit worthiness is a valuable asset for a growth company, and we should act to preserve it. As I see it, this means limiting outside financing to high-grade securities (e.g., debentures rated "A" or better by Moody's). This may prove more restrictive than our safety criterion would suggest; but by assuring access to the various capital markets on favorable cost terms in the future, we should benefit manifold from this added precaution.

· · · · ·

Permanence of Borrowing Ability and Long-Term Debt Policy Considerations
I regard the use of debt capital as a temporary expedient necessary today only to get our current expansion program off the ground. Eventually, I hope we will be able to reduce the amount of debt outstanding to a level more in keeping with historic objectives. Let us examine the implications of this goal. Once we have committed the company to a heavy debt position, we clearly cannot count on borrowing similar sums again without jeopardizing our basic principle of safety. We must consequently face the problem of meeting sinking fund requirements from future internally generated sources. This need to allocate portions of our primary fund resource to debt retirement, tends to reduce our ability to take advantage of future opportunities, perhaps more promising than those we have available today. We must, in short, be aware of the potential opportunity costs associated with sinking fund payments. Excessively heavy borrowing today would only tend to aggravate this situation. We are just beginning a promising long-term expansion program. A little caution at the outset will better insure our ability to continue growing rapidly for many years to come.

· · · · ·

A company the size of Mansfield should be able to count on its ability to carry a certain portion of its capitalization permanently in the form of debt. Hence, if we decide 25% of total capitalization is a prudent level today (after allowing for an adequate margin of safety), it presumably will be prudent in the foreseeable future. In this framework, I cannot regard sinking fund payments as having opportunity costs. Repayment recreates the opportunity to reborrow by restoring unused borrowing capacity. If sinking fund payments threaten opportunity costs in the future by absorbing useful internally generated resources, we have the opportunity to finance repayments by reborrowing,[3] and still live within the confines of our established policy objectives. Sinking fund payments consequently do not constitute a true drain on our resources.

. . . . .

It seems to me we have been rather shortsighted in our policy discussion to date. We have considered our borrowing ability only in terms of our present position without regard to our future position. Let us assume, illustratively, we agree that a debt to total capitalization ratio of 25% is prudent as a long-term policy objective. Over the course of the next five years, our projections show that we will retain earnings of $32 million. This will add $10 million directly to our borrowing capacity. Perhaps this is counting chickens before they hatch, but I can't see why we shouldn't consider these projected debt resources as available for use in financing the immediate expansion program. Secondly, projected profit before tax levels increase sizably over the period. This means better future coverage of interest charges, carrying with it the opportunity to liberalize our debt policy without jeopardizing our safety objectives. Should not this factor be considered today? Finally, our internally generated sources will, according to these projections, increase to twice the size of corresponding 1956 flows. This development and my previous points further add to the arguments against believing sinking fund payments involve opportunity costs.

. . . . .

Flexibility

In forecasting our future fund requirements, we have made practically no allowance for unforeseen contingencies. However, I doubt if any of us believe that the forecast is without sizable elements of uncertainty. Supposing, for example, profits declined sharply in one or two years in this period. If at all possible, we probably would wish to maintain the common dividend. This means we would have to replace the retained earnings, forecasted, with new issues of capital to keep the expansion program going. If we are borrowed to the hilt, where will we get these funds? The equity capital market? No! Then, we must save some unused borrowing capacity to cover possible unforeseen contingencies.

. . . . .

The time to borrow is when things are going well, not when profits are down and the company appears generally more risky. In formulating a debt policy, we must not only consider the amount of debt we can borrow under today's favorable conditions but also consider the amount we can, if necessary, borrow under adverse circumstances. That is, if we want to count on having debt funds available to cover contingencies, we must take precautions to insure our credit worthiness under any and all business conditions. Once we have established this maximum debt limit, we must, then, set aside an appropriate amount as unused capacity to protect ourselves.

At the moment, we hold only sufficient liquid assets to cover probable requirements over one forward year. In contrast, many large chemical companies

---

[3] One director questioned whether it would be practical to borrow small sums of the size involved in sinking fund payments.

hold liquid asset balances in excess of 10% of their sales volumes and, in addition, fund their federal income tax payments. We are without this sort of protection. Consequently, it is not fair to compare our debt position with theirs. Since we have substantially lower liquid asset balances, we must protect ourselves through more conservative use of debt.

. . . . .

We are just getting off the ground on a long-term expansion program. Our research and development expenditures, for example, haven't begun to produce the results we expect from them in a few years. Expansion opportunities in the future should be substantially better than they are today. If we rush headlong into debt today, we will only be depriving ourselves of the ability to finance new and better projects in the future. We ought, instead, to reserve some of our borrowing capacity to use when opportunities become more favorable.

. . . . .

A rapid rate of expansion provides the best basis for sustaining expansion. New capital expenditures will generate new profits, which will provide funds for accelerating the rate of expansion. Moreover, new depreciation funds will be available. Since replacement demands will not increase proportionally for eight or ten years, these funds can also be used to finance continued growth. Finally, growth will strengthen our position in the capital markets. We will have more favorable coverage ratios on debt obligations. Market prices for the common stock will undoubtedly increase more rapidly, leaving us in a favorable position to finance by means of an equity issue. In summary, the faster we grow in the immediate future, the better able we will be to sustain this growth. All this argues for increased use of debt today.

. . . . .

Let's strike while the iron is hot and let the future take care of itself. I hate to hold idle cash—and that's what unused debt capacity amounts to on vague promises of better things to come. We're in an inflationary era. This argues for maximum use of debt by itself. The best way to maximize long-term profits is to start by maximizing them today. So let's use our debt resources fully today.

. . . . .

Cost Considerations

All I can see is that we have debt capital available for use, costing 5% or less before taxes. On the other hand, we have projects available promising earnings returns four times this cost. Why forego unnecessarily these current profit opportunities? The incremental profits alone will cover the incremental interest costs severalfold, thereby assuring safety. What further proof do we need that further borrowing will be highly profitable?

. . . . .

Interest costs are only one part of the cost of debt. As we borrow larger and larger sums, several cost factors besides interest charges become important. The added elements of risk represent potential source of severe opportunity costs in the event unforeseen and highly adverse circumstances develop. Secondly, restrictive clauses in the indenture have more bite, thereby threatening to limit management's freedom to act solely in the best interests of stockholders without regard to creditor's interests. As I have mentioned, sinking fund payments carry potential opportunity costs. Excessive borrowing also limits our flexibility, perhaps leaving us, at some future date, with a Hobson's choice of either foregoing desirable expansion or raising capital at a disadvantageous time. Finally, the leverage added to our stock should adversely affect our stock's price-earnings ratio. All these factors are opportunity costs (admitted intangible and difficult to measure), which add substantially to the cost of any incremental borrowing. It is the total of these costs that is the germane consideration, and I suspect that if we knew how high these costs really ran, we would refrain from any further borrowing.

·   ·   ·   ·   ·

A growth stock that really grows is favored with a high price-earnings ratio. The better the growth is, the higher the price-earnings ratio becomes (I believe). If we grow as rapidly as we can, our stockholders will receive dual rewards—higher earnings per share and higher price-earnings ratios. In view of these advantages, the cost and risk implications of further borrowing appear truly minor.

·   ·   ·   ·   ·

This is a particularly poor time to be raising debt capital. Interest rates are at their highest postwar level. We have talked a great deal about coverage. The higher the interest charges are, the lower will be the coverage for any given amount of debt. If coverage is the limiting factor, we ought to attempt to time debt issues in periods when interest rates are low. For example, debt today costs nearly 5%. If we could wait and raise debt when interest costs were $2\frac{1}{2}\%$, let us say, we could raise twice the amount of debt and still have the same coverage ratio. Consequently, when we borrow at high interest rates, we are giving up the opportunity to borrow larger sums at later dates. We must consider this long-term "cost" disadvantage while examining how much we borrow today.

·   ·   ·   ·   ·

The treasurer, Mr. Gates, began his analysis of the debt policy by having his staff prepare several comparison tables to aid him. The first, Exhibit 4, presented a comparison of selected companies in the chemical industry, ranking them according to size, cash flows, nature of debt financing, and performance of the common stock among other factors. Mr. Gates thought that coverage of interest charges and stability of earnings were important in determining debt policy. It was more difficult to evaluate coverage of sinking fund payments since many companies had deferred payments well into the future or had related the level of sinking fund payments to future earnings.

A chart, Exhibit 5, showed the performance of interest rates in the postwar period. Recent debenture issues of other chemical companies were shown on the chart to indicate the premium rate that a company had to pay to market a new issue.

Mr. Gates also expected to make use of the cash flow projections for Mansfield given in Exhibit 3. No allowance had been made in that table for sinking fund payments, since it was expected that any sinking fund could be deferred until long after 1962. In other respects Mr. Gates realized that this forecast reflected optimistic conditions of sales and earnings growth, and no allowance had been made for unforeseen reversals, such as an economic downturn or accelerated product-obsolescence. However, Mr. Gates believed that the forecast represented the program as realistically as a forecast could.

Mr. Gates had also begun an exploration of the possible effects of an acceleration of the expansion program. An analysis of unapproved, although available, project requests provided the following information:

Dollar Amount of Unapproved Projects	Average Projected Return on Investment before Interest and Taxes*
$15 million	24%
15 million	22
30 million	21
50 million	20

* These returns were adjusted to equate risks to the level of certainty of cost reduction projects.

Mr. Gates anticipated that any additional expenditures approved would be spread evenly throughout the five-year planning period. Plant equipment investments would account for 70% of additional fund requirements, with working capital needs contributing the balance. Depreciation would total $7\frac{1}{2}\%$ of the plant investments and would start the year following the expenditures. Incremental profits, because of start-up time lags, would not begin until the second year following the investment.

Following the suggestion of one of the directors, Mr. Gates had learned that fixed expenses accounted for slightly more than one quarter of operating, selling, research, and administrative expenses. While some of these expenses undoubtedly could be cut somewhat under severe pressures, management clearly preferred to avoid such a situation if at all possible. After considering the possibility of time lags, the remaining expenses appeared generally variable. Mr. Gates expected these cost proportions would remain unchanged as the company grew.

In further discussion with investment bankers, Mr. Gates learned that any borrowing in excess of $45 million would carry a higher interest rate than 4.75%. From these discussions, the following approximate schedule was obtained: Legal and other expenses were estimated at $50,000 plus 0.1% of the total amount of any new issue.

Amount of New Debt	Per Cent of Total Capitalization Including Debt Outstanding	Interest Rate	Probable Moody's Rating*
$ 45 million	25%	4.75%	A
60 million	30	4.80	A
75 million	34	4.90	Baa
90 million	38	5.10	Baa
105 million	41	5.40	Ba

* Moody's Investor's Service rates corporate debenture issues according to their value as long-term investments. Factors evaluated include coverage of interest payments, security of principal, fluctuations of protective elements, relative position in the total capitalization. Ratings range from Aaa on highest grade, "gilt-edged" bonds to C on highly speculative bonds with little or no long-term investment qualities.

A 25- to 30-year maturity was suggested with any sinking fund pay-ments deferred for 15 years, or until 1972. In that year, an annual sinking fund of 5% of the initial borrowing would commence, leaving a balloon maturity coming due in the final year. The issue would be noncallable during the first five years. During the next ten years a call premium starting at 5% and decreasing over the period would be re-quired. After 15 years there would be no call premium.

In addition, the underwriters stated that if debt exceeded 35% of total capitalization, additional restrictions would be necessary: Dividend payments would be limited to undistributed earnings accumulated after January 1, 1957, plus $3 million; net working capital would have to be maintained at over $40 million; the company would have to seek prior permission from the new debenture holders before increasing total long-term debt above 40% of total capitalization. All other covenants appeared conventional.

Mr. Gates believed that if he developed a complete set of recom-mendations, the board would approve his report without alteration. However, he was wondering what weight he should give in his de-cision to the viewpoints of the various directors, and what weight he should place on his analysis of the financial data.

Exhibit 1

MANSFIELD CHEMICAL COMPANY

COMPARATIVE BALANCE SHEETS AND FUNDS FLOW STATEMENT,
DECEMBER 31, 1947–DECEMBER 31, 1956

(Dollar figures in thousands)

ASSETS	1947	Source	Use	1956
Current assets:				
Cash	$ 7,971	$ 42		$ 8,013
U.S. Government securities	3,201		2,664	5,865
Accounts receivable	9,174		16,986	26,160
Inventories	28,500		10,905	39,405
Total current assets	$48,846			$ 79,443
Plant, property, and equipment	99,090		143,244	242,334
Less: Reserve for depreciation, depletion, and amortization	54,795	$ 77,214*		132,009
Net plant, property, and equipment	$44,295			$110,325
Other assets and deferred charges	2,745		6,489	9,234
Total assets	$95,886			$199,002
LIABILITIES				
Current liabilities:				
Notes payable	$ 345	1,395		$ 1,740
Accounts payable	7,101	6,939		14,040
Federal income taxes	4,473	3,288		7,761
Other current liabilities	2,790	1,128		3,918
Total current liabilities	$14,709			$ 27,459
Long-term debt:				
3½% term loan (payable $3 million annually)		9,810		9,810
Capital stock:				
Common stock, no par	43,575	55,068		98,643
Retained earnings	37,602	25,488†		63,090
Total capital	$81,177			$161,733
Total liabilities and capital	$95,886			$199,002
Total sources and uses		$180,330	$180,330	

* Gross change in depreciation account; for yearly charges see Exhibit 2.
† Net of profits after taxes less dividend payments and other charges to surplus. For yearly profits and dividend payments, see Exhibit 2.

Exhibit 2

MANSFIELD CHEMICAL COMPANY

SUMMARY PROFIT AND LOSS AND COMMON STOCK DATA

(Dollar figures in thousands)

	1947	1948	1949	1950	1951	1952	1953	1954	1955	1956
Net sales	$89,916	$ 97,293	$ 99,519	$119,943	$142,665	$172,452	$177,633	$174,372	$203,325	$208,251
Income before taxes	12,306	10,740	13,260	23,868	30,543	18,876	19,182	18,603	21,324	21,684
Income after taxes	7,668	6,852	8,061	12,018	10,626	9,654	9,318	10,173	10,452	10,878
Dividends declared	4,311	3,903	4,596	5,889	5,994	6,150	6,339	6,876	6,876	6,897
Earnings retained	3,357	2,949	3,465	6,129	4,632	3,504	2,979	3,297	3,576	3,981
Depreciation charged	3,531	4,671	5,991	6,261	7,269	10,179	11,724	14,880	16,197	17,538
Total assets	95,886	106,296	116,574	143,184	173,544	190,542	195,021	188,319	196,338	199,002
Per common share:										
Earnings	$4.92	$4.17	$4.95	$5.96	$4.95	$3.89	$3.75	$4.10	$4.20	$4.38*
Dividends	2.70	2.25	2.70	3.40	3.00	2.55	2.55	2.75	2.75	2.75
Average market price	67½	62⅝	58⅛	79⅛	93	85⅜	69⅜	70½	72¾	70⅞

* Shares outstanding: 2,480,000.

Exhibit 3

MANSFIELD CHEMICAL COMPANY
FIVE-YEAR EXPANSION PROGRAM, PROJECTIONS OF FUNDS FLOWS
(Dollar figures in millions)

	1957	1958	1959	1960	1961	1962
Sales	$234.0	$264.0	$294.0	$333.0	$360.0	$405.0
Operating profit	25.8	29.1	35.4	39.9	46.8	52.8
Interest charges	2.5	2.4	2.3	2.1	2.1	2.1
Federal income taxes at 52%	12.1	13.9	17.2	19.7	22.8	26.4
Net earnings	$ 11.2	$ 12.8	$ 15.9	$ 18.1	$ 21.9	$ 24.3
Dividends paid—60% earnings	6.7	7.7	9.5	10.9	13.1	14.6
Earnings retained	$ 4.5	$ 5.1	$ 6.4	$ 7.2	$ 8.8	$ 9.7
Depreciation charges, 7½% of opening gross plant	18.3	20.1	22.5	25.2	27.3	28.8
Internally generated sources of funds	$ 22.8	$ 25.2	$ 28.9	$ 32.4	$ 36.1	$ 38.5
Debt financing	45.0					
Total sources	$ 67.8	$ 25.2	$ 28.9	$ 32.4	$ 36.1	$ 38.5
Investment in plant and equipment	25.5	31.5	37.5	27.0	22.5	Not
Increase in working capital	4.5	6.0	7.5	7.5	10.5	Projected
Sinking fund—3½% term loan	3.0	3.0	3.9			
Total applications	$ 33.0	$ 40.5	$ 48.9	$ 34.5	$ 33.0	
Sources less applications	34.8	(15.3)	(20.0)	(2.1)	3.1	
Cumulative sources less applications	34.8	19.5	(0.5)	(2.6)	0.5	
Earnings per share	$ 4.52	$ 5.16	$ 6.41	$ 7.30	$ 8.85	$ 9.81

Exhibit 4

MANSFIELD CHEMICAL COMPANY

COMPARATIVE FINANCIAL DATA ON LEADING CHEMICAL COMPANIES,
FISCAL YEAR ENDING 1956

	Mansfield	Allied Chemical	American Cyanamid	Commercial Solvents
Total capitalization (000's)	$171,543	$625,643	$462,203	$64,894
Net sales (000's)	208,251	668,937	500,651	58,745
Earnings before interest and taxes (000's)	22,356	86,647	88,739	7,093
Depreciation charged (000's)	17,538	50,392	30,094	3,157
Cash and marketable securities to sales (%)	6.7	8.5	31.5	18.3
Debt financing:				
Amount (000's)	$ 9,810	$200,000	$ 94,750	$25,000
Interest rate (%)	3½	3½	2¾–3¾	3¾
Per cent of total capitalization	5.7	31.97	20.36	37.86
Moody's rating	....	Aa	....	......
Interest payments (000's)	$ 474	$ 7,000	$ 3,492	$ 938
Times charges earned—1956	47.00	12.48	28.60	7.57
1955	45.96	14.22	21.39	7.27
Sinking fund payments (000's), 1956	$ 1,000	$ 7,000	$ 1,250	$ 1,560
Coverage by profit after tax plus depreciation	28.42	13.8	61.5	2.1
Maximum debt, 1950–1956 (%)	6.3	36.75	31.94	40.06
Maximum decline in one year—earnings before interest and taxes, 1950–1956 (%)	38.0	23.5	40.5	73.7
Common stock:				
Earnings per share 1956	$ 4.38	$ 4.74	$ 2.11	$ 1.20
Five-year average	$ 4.08	$ 4.68	$ 1.75	$ 0.98
Ratio: 1955, 1956; 1947, 1948	0.8	1.5	2.4	0.4
Price to earnings ratio, 1956	16.1	22.3	16.8	15.7
Five-year average	18.2	17.9	16.1	17.6
Yield %	3.9	2.7	3.9	5.3
Five-year average	3.7	3.5	4.0	5.0
Dividend pay-out as per cent of earnings	60	62	61	100
Five-year average				

Diamond Alkali	Dow	DuPont	Hooker Electro-chemical	Monsanto	Pennsalt	Union Carbide	Victor Chemical
$115,294	$545,624	$2,220,782	$112,029	$531,799	$72,181	$1,222,092	$40,689
121,261	565,260	1,888,446	109,979	541,883	72,416	1,324,506	50,146
24,320	122,908	643,767	24,518	77,181	7,815	308,198	7,336
9,933	73,857	115,205	7,169	38,449	5,846	113,888	4,548
7.2	12.9	18.5	10.1	7.0	18.8	19.9	18.0
		No debt					
$ 35,805	$139,074		$ 37,660	$172,750	18,850	$ 410,515	$ 8,550
3–3⅜	2.35–3¼		3–3¾	2.65–3¾	3.45	2.70–4.0	3
31.0	29.90		28.46	29.46	26.11	33.59	19.66
A	Aa, A		....	....	A	....	......
$ 1,188	$ 5,863		$ 1,384	$ 5,420	$ 520	$ 14,861	$ 269
21.7	20.48		17.59	13.81	15.03	20.67	27.31
19.5	9.50		22.63	17.18	13.94	19.81	28.98
$ 2,644	$ 3,500		$ 2,000	$ 2,750	$ 580	$ 2,000	$ 450
7.7	38.0		9.3	28.0	16.4	100+	18.2
31.0	43.44		41.94	31.33	26.11	38.37	23.60
43.5	30.5		12.0	25.3	36.4	22.5	22.5
$ 3.83	$ 2.47	$ 8.20	$ 1.75	$ 1.80	$ 2.92	$ 4.86	$ 2.02
$ 2.70	$ 1.68	$ 6.89	$ 1.32	$ 1.62	$ 2.71	$ 3.95	$ 1.66
1.6	2.4	3.0	1.8	1.5	0.9	1.6	1.7
13.4	23.3	25.5	24.2	22.7	19.0	24.2	14.7
13.6	24.6	20.8	21.1	20.8	18.7	21.5	16.2
3.0	1.8	3.1	2.4	2.4	3.4	2.7	4.7
4.2	2.5	3.8	3.0	2.5	3.6	3.3	4.3
42	50	67+	60	52	65	60	68
	+ Stock	GM Divs.					

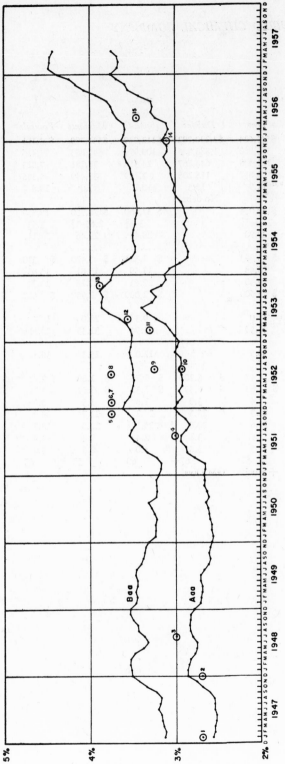

Exhibit 5

MANSFIELD CHEMICAL COMPANY

BOND INTEREST RATES

Showing selected chemical company new issues

Notes to Exhibit 5
CHEMICAL COMPANY ISSUES

Name	Date	Stated Int. Rate	Size (Millions)	Maturity Years	Moody's Rating
1. Dow	Jan. 1, 1947	2.70%	$ 35	25	Term loan
2. Union Carbide	Dec. 3, 1947	2.20	150	20	Term loan
3. Diamond Alkali	July 1, 1948	3.00	10	20	Private Placement
4. Victor Chemical	June 21, 1951	3.00	9	20	Term loan
5. Union Carbide	Nov. 1, 1951	3.75	300	100	Term loan
6. Am. Cyanamid	Jan. 1, 1952	3.75	75	35	Term loan
7. Monsanto*	Jan. 1, 1952	3.75	66	50	Private Placement
8. Hooker	May 1, 1952	3.75	20	25	Term loan
9. Dow	July 1, 1952	3.25	90	25	Term loan
10. Dow†	July 1, 1952	2.925‡	100	30	A
11. Diamond Alkali	Feb. 1, 1953	3.30‡	15	25	A
12. Allied Chemical	Apr. 1, 1953	3.56‡	200	25	Aa
13. Stauffer	Sept. 15, 1953	3.875	15	20	A
14. Diamond Alkali	Dec. 31, 1955	3.125	12	10	Serial notes
15. Pennsalt	Apr. 1, 1956	3.45	15	25	A

* Income debenture.
† Convertible debenture.
‡ Yield to maturity.

SUPPLEMENT TO MANSFIELD CHEMICAL COMPANY

REFORECAST ASSUMING $90 MILLION OF NEW DEBT

	1957	1958	1959	1960	1961	1962
EBIT: Currently projected...........	25.8	29.1	35.4	39.9	46.8	52.8
EBIT: Added expansions.............	...	...	2.0	4.0	6.0	8.0
Total.........................	25.8	29.1	37.4	43.9	52.8	60.8
Less interest: Old...................	0.4	0.3	0.2	...	...	...
New.................	2.1	2.1	3.6	4.4	4.4	4.4
PBT.............................	23.3	26.7	33.6	39.5	48.4	56.4
PAT of 52%......................	11.2	12.8	16.2	19.0	23.4	27.1
Dividends at 60%..................	6.7	7.7	9.7	11.4	14.0	16.3
Retained earnings..................	4.5	5.1	6.5	7.6	9.4	10.8
Depreciation: Currently projected.....	18.3	20.1	22.5	25.2	27.3	28.8
Added expansions......	...	0.5	0.9	1.4	1.9	2.4
Total internal sources...........	22.8	25.7	29.9	34.2	38.6	42.0
Plus added debt....................	45.0	...	30.0	15.0	...	...
Total sources..................	67.8	25.7	59.9	49.2	38.6	42.0
Investment in plant and equipment:						
Currently projected..............	25.5	31.5	37.5	27.0	22.5	Not
Added expansions................	6.3	6.3	6.3	6.3	6.3	Projected
Increase in working capital:						
Currently projected..............	4.5	6.0	7.5	7.5	10.5	''
Added expansions................	0	2.7	2.7	2.7	2.7	2.7
Sinking fund—3½% loan............	3.0	3.0	3.8	...	...	Not
Total applications.............	39.3	49.5	57.8	43.5	42.0	Projected
Sources less applications............	28.5	(23.8)	2.1	5.7	(3.4)	''
Cumulative.......................	28.5	4.7	6.8	12.5	10.1	''
Earnings per share.................	4.52	5.16	6.53	7.66	9.44	10.93
Old debt..........................	6.8	3.8	...	...	...	
New debt.........................	45.0	45.0	75.0	90.0	90.0	
Total debt.....................	51.8	48.8	75.0	90.0	90.0	
Equity base.......................	161.7	166.2	171.3	177.8	185.4	
Plus: RE.........................	4.5	5.1	6.5	7.6	9.4	
New equity base..................	166.2	171.3	177.8	185.4	194.8	
Total capitalization................	218.0	220.1	252.8	275.4	284.8	
Total debt.......................	51.8	48.8	75.0	90.0	90.0	
Less liquid reserves................	28.5	4.7	6.8	12.5	10.1	
Debt required.....................	23.3	44.1	68.2	77.5	79.9	
Debt to total capitalization..........	23.8%	22.2%	29.7%	32.7%	31.6%	
30% debt to total capitalization......	65.4	66.0	75.8	82.6	85.4	

SUPPLEMENT TO MANSFIELD CHEMICAL COMPANY

REFORECAST ASSUMING $120 MILLION OF NEW DEBT

	1957	1958	1959	1960	1961	1962
EBIT: Currently projected	25.8	29.1	35.4	39.9	46.8	52.8
EBIT: Added expansions	...	...	3.3	6.5	9.7	12.9
Total	25.8	29.1	38.7	46.4	56.5	68.7
Less interest: Old	0.4	0.3	0.2	...	...	...
New	2.9	2.9	4.4	5.4	5.9	5.9
PBT	22.5	25.9	34.1	41.0	50.6	62.8
PAT of 52%	10.8	12.4	16.4	19.6	24.3	30.2
Dividends at 60%	6.5	7.4	9.8	11.8	14.5	18.1
Retained earnings	4.3	5.0	6.6	7.8	9.8	12.1
Depreciation: Currently projected	18.3	20.1	22.5	25.2	27.3	28.8
Added expansions	...	0.8	1.6	2.4	3.1	3.9
Total internal sources	22.6	25.9	30.7	35.4	40.2	44.8
Plus added debt	60.0	...	30.0	20.0	10.0	...
Total sources	82.6	25.9	60.7	55.4	50.2	44.8
Investment in plant and equipment:						
Currently projected	25.5	31.5	37.5	27.0	22.5	Not
Added expansions	10.5	10.5	10.5	10.5	10.5	Projected
Increase in working capital:						
Currently projected	4.5	6.0	7.5	7.5	10.5	"
Added expansions	0	4.5	4.5	4.5	4.5	4.5
Sinking fund—3½% loan	3.0	3.0	3.8	...	...	Not
Total applications	43.5	55.5	63.8	49.5	48.0	Projected
Sources less applications	39.1	(29.6)	(3.8)	5.9	2.2	"
Cumulative	39.1	9.5	5.7	11.6	13.8	"
Earnings per share	4.35	5.00	6.61	7.90	9.80	12.18
Old debt	6.8	3.8	...	...	...	
New debt	60.0	60.0	90.0	110.0	120.0	
Total debt	66.8	63.8	90.0	110.0	120.0	
Equity base	161.7	166.0	171.0	177.6	185.4	
Plus: RE	4.3	5.0	6.6	7.8	9.8	
New equity base	166.0	171.0	177.6	185.4	195.2	
Total capitalization	232.8	234.8	267.6	295.4	315.2	
Total debt	66.8	63.8	90.0	110.0	120.0	
Less liquid reserves	39.1	9.5	5.7	11.6	13.8	
Debt required	27.7	54.3	84.3	98.4	106.2	
Debt to total capitalization	28.7%	27.2%	33.6%	37.2%	38.1%	
30% debt to total capitalization	69.8	70.4	80.3	88.6	94.6	

BRUSHWELL PAINT AND
CHEMICAL COMPANY

In early 1958 Mr. Weilman, financial vice-president of the Brush-well Paint and Chemical Company, was considering several alternative strategies for financing a major expansion program, proposed for the forthcoming five-year planning period. Initially, Mr. Weilman had planned to finance the program through combined use of debt and equity capital resources. However, the prospects of heavy dilution, arising as the result of sale of common stock, had caused concern among Brushwell's top management. Two alternatives, both aimed at reducing dependence on external equity capital resources, had subsequently been advanced. The first alternative involved reducing the dollar size of planned capital expenditures by a significant amount. The second alternative suggested a major change in dividend policy, leading to a substantially lower dividend pay-out for stockholders. Mr. Weilman was charged with writing a report for the president and the board of directors resolving these and related policy questions, and with recommenidng a tentative financial program for the five-year period.

The Brushwell Paint and Chemical Company was founded in 1832 by Nicholas Croates to manufacture a new industrial coating product. After several years of struggle and near bankruptcy, the company began to grow steadily. Domestic, as well as new industrial, paints were gradually added to the product line until, in 1958, the company was one of the six largest broad-line paint manufacturers in the country. Following World War I, Brushwell had diversified into the chemical field. Opportunities existing in the chemical field allowed acceleration in the rate of sales growth. By 1958, nearly 60% of total sales volume came from Brushwell's line of basic and intermediate inorganic chemicals.

264

Brushwell's growth following World War II had been particularly rapid. Sales volume and profits had more than doubled during the 11-year period from 1947 to 1957. (Recent balance sheets and income statements are shown in Exhibits 1 and 2.) Management, in early 1958, was convinced the future held opportunities for growth that were every bit as attractive as those that had existed immediately after World War II.

During the postwar period, Brushwell had undertaken a major modernization and expansion program. Over $350 million had been spent on new plant and equipment in the 11 years after 1946. Funds for these investments, as well as for related working capital requirements, had come from three sources: retained earnings of $130 million, depreciation of $163 million, and new debt capital of $160 million. (Exhibit 3 contains a source and application of funds statement for the period 1947 through 1957.)

In recent years, various members of Brushwell's top management had become increasingly concerned by the fact retained earnings provided only a small portion—29%—of total fund requirements during the postwar period. For every $100 of earnings retained in this 11-year period, $123 of debt capital was raised. These proportions clearly could not be maintained indefinitely, and, indeed, by 1955, Brushwell had reached a debt level that appeared to management as high in proportion to total capitalization as seemed prudent. Future fund requirements for expansion consequently would have to be financed from some new capital source—presumably equity capital. The Croates family,[1] who owned 20% of the outstanding shares of Brushwell's common stock, had not welcomed this development.

This situation had been further complicated by three additional factors. The company's research and development program had been accelerated in 1953, and recently there had been a sharp increase in the number and quality of capital expenditure opportunities. Mr. Weilman consequently expected future fund requirements would be substantially larger than was true in the past. Secondly, the trend of annually increasing depreciation charges, which had served as an important source of funds in recent years, was about to be reversed temporarily. Rapid am-

---

[1] No family member was currently active in managing Brushwell. Six of the eleven members of the board of directors were, however, closely associated with the Croates family.

ortization privileges associated with plant investments during the latter years of the Korean conflict were about to expire, and the related decrease in depreciation charges would be only partially offset by new investments. Finally, sinking fund payments on outstanding debentures began taking effect in 1958. All these factors pointed towards greater future capital requirements that would have to be financed from new, as well as current, capital sources.

Nevertheless, Brushwell's top management had laid the groundwork for an expansion program that would more than double sales volume within a ten-year period beginning with 1958. Top management was firmly convinced the company's long-term future was more promising and offered more opportunities for growth than did the preceding 11-year period. Plans had consequently been prepared to capitalize as fully on these opportunities as possible.

In order to gauge future fund requirements, Mr. Weilman had prepared a five-year forecast in November, 1957. The forecast for the first two years had subsequently been revised to give fuller consideration to the business recession in progress during late 1957 and early 1958. The revised forecast is shown in Exhibit 5.

Mr. Weilman believed that, barring the development of a recession of major proportions, sales and earnings projections were conservatively stated in this forecast. Market research personnel had given him repeated assurance that demand for Brushwell's products was holding up well or improving despite the adverse business conditions prevailing generally. Other elements of the forecast represented management's best judgment as to likely future requirements. Each element had been estimated with considerable care, but nevertheless these estimates were subject (particularly more distant estimates) to some measure of uncertainty. These plans made no allowance for capital charges arising from new capital issues.

Mr. Weilman had also begun considering strategy associated with financing this expansion program in the most favorable manner. As background for this analysis, he kept in mind certain established financial policies.

The company's current dividend policy had initially been formulated in 1946 as the fairest and most equitable means of satisfying stockholders' diverse interests in immediate income and in capital appreciation. Management had set as a target the payment of 65% of earnings in dividends. However, in order to avoid dividend cuts, management had decided to pass on only a portion, usually half, of an indicated dividend increase in any given year. Increases usually first took the form of year-end extra payments but were incorporated as a part of regular quarterly payments as soon as seemed desirable. Management normally was cautious in increasing regular quarterly payments. Since stockholders appeared to regard regular dividends as permanent, management wanted to avoid, insofar as possible, a situation where the regular dividend might have to be reduced. Based on these policies, Mr. Weilman submitted a quarterly dividend recommendation to the board of directors for their approval. Approval by the board was virtually automatic. (See Exhibit 4 for historic dividend payment record.)

The company, also, had a firm debt policy which limited long-term borrowing to one-third of total capitalization (long-term debt, preferred and common stocks, and surplus accounts), expressed at book value. While many members of management believed it was possible to borrow larger amounts without excessive risks, this privilege was reserved for genuine emergency conditions. This policy had recently been restudied, and management was firmly convinced the present limitation represented the wisest compromise between income and market-reputation risks. The limiting features of this debt policy on Brushwell's future ability to raise capital through sale of debentures are illustrated in Exhibit 5.

In accordance with capital budgeting policies, each project was evaluated by a present value breakeven analysis. That is, management ascertained the discount rate for projected fund inflows (profits *after* taxes plus depreciation) and outflows that was necessary to equate the present value of these flows with immediate investment outlays.[2] A breakeven discount rate of 10% (after taxes) represented the minimum acceptable standard used for evaluating new projects. Management normally demanded higher returns from projects characterized by larger elements of risks, and these decisions related to predetermined

---

[2] To illustrate the nature of this calculation, consider the following simplified example. A project requires an initial investment of $110,000 in equipment and $30,000 in working capital. The equipment has an estimated life of ten years and a scrap value of $10,000. Working capital will be recoverable at the end of ten years. Depreciation will be charged on a straight-line basis of $10,000 per year, and profits after taxes are estimated at $10,100 per year. The discount rate necessary to equate the present values for the cash inflows (profit after tax plus depreciation) of $20,100 per year for ten years and for the terminal inflow of $40,000 to the initial outlay of $140,000 is, in this example, 10%. This "breakeven" discount rate was then used to compare the relative economic advantages of the various capital expenditure proposals.

return premiums above the minimum-return standard. The minimum-return standard had been adopted on an experimental basis when the present capital budgeting procedures had been installed in 1954. This standard had not subsequently been reviewed critically.

Initially, Mr. Weilman had planned to use debt funds as fully as possible in the expansion program. He knew, of course, that outstanding debt (in accordance with accepted debt policies) could not exceed one-half of the preferred and common stock equity bases, as shown by book values. For various economic reasons, he did not want to raise less than $40 million of debt at any one point of time. Current market conditions suggested an interest rate of $4\frac{1}{2}\%$, and annual sinking funds to amortize the loan in 20 equal installments were necessary to secure market acceptance of new debt issues. Remaining funds would have to be raised from equity sources.

Mr. Weilman had considered the possibility of financing a portion of equity requirements through sale of preferred stock. He had, however, decided it would be undesirable to have more than 10% of total capitalization in the form of preferred issues. This ruled out a preferred issue as an immediate alternative, but this source might be a factor later in the expansion program. The outstanding preferred (noncallable) currently yielded 4.4% on the market, and over the past ten years the yield range was between 3.5% and 4.9%.

Mr. Weilman had also eliminated various types of convertible issues from immediate consideration. He believed that these convertible issues should be counted as a part of outstanding debt or preferred capital, depending upon their nature, until converted, and that present capitalization proportions did not permit additional senior securities of the amount contemplated.

Mr. Weilman had tentatively decided to raise the first $50 million of future fund requirements by means of a sale of common stock in June of 1958. He had not, however, decided whether the issuance should be made by means of rights or through public sale. A public sale, it appeared, could be sold at a price 4% below the then current market price. Further, underwriting fees and associated costs would approximate 2% of the market price. A rights sale would require a minimum underpricing of 10% below the market, but underwriting and related costs would be only $\frac{1}{2}\%$.

Mr. Weilman personally preferred a public sale on the grounds that a higher market price would tend to minimize capital costs. The treasurer, Mr. Krantz, disagreed. He thought that the added underpricing associated with a rights issue was akin to giving stockholders a stock dividend in disguise. As stock dividends or stock splits did not involve capital costs, Mr. Krantz argued rights discounts would not. He also observed that many stockholders would regard the rights issue as a bargain opportunity, or, if they were unable to subscribe, the sale of rights as a windfall dividend. He consequently saw no harm and perhaps some benefit in offering the stockholders a real bargain by underpricing the rights issue by as much as 30%. Finally, he observed that underwriting fees were less under a rights issue. Since the company received more of the funds paid by stockholders for the new shares, capital costs were clearly less under the rights alternative.

Subsequent to these discussions, several factors had developed which changed the perspective and broadened the scope of the initial decision. First of all, the market price of the common stock had declined from a peak of $81 per share in July of 1957 to a level of $69 in January of 1958. Moreover, the full impact of the business recession on the stock market was not known. Mr. Weilman thought that in view of these uncertainties, the time might not be ripe for an issue of equity capital. Moreover, equity capital had become relatively more costly.

Mr. Krantz had again disagreed. He observed that if a rights issue could have been sold at $56, a 30% discount from the peak market price, without adversely affecting capital costs, it could still be sold at $56 without penalizing capital costs. Stockholders would merely receive less of a bargain. He consequently argued that timing was not nearly as important a consideration when rights were used. Finally, he noted that an increase in the quarterly dividend rate from $0.50 to $0.60 was indicated for the March dividend date. He thought this development would have a buoyant effect on the market price of Brushwell's stock— particularly since it underscored management's confidence in a strong earnings record during 1958. Hence, future issuing conditions were more likely to be favorable than was true at the moment.

When Mr. Weilman had first approached Mr. Eastlander, president of Brushwell, with the proposal to issue common stock in June of 1958, the latter had reacted adversely. Mr. Eastlander had never liked the prospect of an equity issue because of its diluting effect on earnings per share. He observed that, whereas in the past the company had striven for maximum sales and earnings, the time may have come for greater emphasis on maximizing earnings per share. He recognized that some equity sales undoubtedly were inevitable, but thought they should be as small and as infrequent as possible. One method of achieving this objective appeared to involve increased selectivity in approving new capital expenditure proposals. He suggested that Mr. Weilman consider the implications of a change in the minimum-return standard, applied to capital expenditure proposals, on equity capital fund requirements. As an initial point for analysis, he recommended testing the effect of an increase in the minimum-return standard to 12% after taxes.

Mr. Weilman had not had time to complete this examination subsequent to his meeting with Mr. Eastlander. However, he had learned that the higher standard would reduce the amount of approved expenditures for plant and equipment by about 10% in 1958 and by about 25% in each of the four years 1959–1962. If this plan were adopted, incremental sales and profits after 1958 would probably be reduced by 20%. Incremental working capital requirements would also be reduced by 20% after 1958. Depreciation charges would fall below forecast levels at the cumulative rate of $1.0 million per year after 1959. In forecasting fund requirements under this proposal, dividend payments would also have to be adjusted to conform with new earnings levels and historic dividend policy. Finally, minimum cash balance requirements were estimated at 5% of annual sales volume.

Mr. Eastlander's openmindedness toward innovation had stirred Mr. Weilman to suggest an alternative that he long had considered attractive. This alternative had at its heart a fundamental change in the company's dividend policy. Mr. Weilman believed that a growth company, such as Brushwell, should pay out a smaller proportion of current earnings in dividends. He argued that stockholders were more interested in appreciation than immediate income. This factor alone suggested more earnings should be retained than paid out. Indeed, the only value of dividend income seemed to be its stabilizing influence on market prices. Mr. Weilman consequently believed a target pay-out objective of 40% was more appropriate than the current policy.

Mr. Weilman did not believe the company could adjust to a 40% pay-out policy without an immediate, unfavorable market reaction. Instead, he proposed that the company maintain its current $0.50 quarterly dividend until the company's earnings per share reached a level of $5. Thereafter, dividends would be increased in accordance with present methods of adjustment, using the 40% pay-out policy as a guide. During the intervening years no extra dividends would be declared. Mr. Weilman did not believe the elimination of the $0.40 extra dividend would have a significant effect on market price of the common stock. The market did not seem to weight extra dividends as highly as regular quarterly dividends. As evidence, Mr. Weilman pointed out the fact that market prices had not fallen following the 1954 cut in extra dividend payments and that market prices had not risen after the 1957 increase in the extra dividend. Mr. Eastlander agreed that this alternative merited further consideration but was not entirely convinced stockholders would welcome such a radical change in dividend policy.

Mr. Weilman had collected certain data which he believed would be helpful in appraising the proposed change in dividend policy. He had prepared a chart of market price ranges for Brushwell common stock by quarters from 1947 through 1957 (see Exhibit 6). Since dividend changes were announced toward the end of each quarter, the market's reaction to "surprises" could often be judged by price movements in the subsequent quarter. He had also collected selective data (see Exhibit 7) on market price relationships for comparable companies in the paint and chemical industries.

While preparing to analyze the various alternative methods of financing the proposed expansion program, Mr. Weilman had taken advantage of the opportunity to discuss the proposals with two key members of the board of directors. Mr. Lane, a lawyer who generally represented the interests of the Croates family, reported that by and large the Croates clan were interested in long-term capital appreciation but that a few members valued their current income highly. In deference to these latter individuals, Mr. Lane suggested that the extra dividend should not be cut. He also noted that only half of the Croates shares would exercise their subscription privileges in the event of a rights issue. Finally, Mr. Lane was opposed to any plan which might seriously impair the family's present position of effective working control of the company.

Mr. Abbey, a director who frequently adopted the viewpoint of nonfamily stockholders, was concerned by the proposed dividend policy change. He stated that many investment analysts were freely predicting Brushwell would increase its quarterly dividend to $0.60 at the March meeting. Failure to pass on the expected dividend increase would, in his opinion, cause nearly as severe a market reaction as a dividend cut. He thought management should avoid any unnecessary action, which might be interpreted adversely in a period when market prices were already severely depressed. While not objecting to the proposed change in dividend policy, he did not want in any case to cut the dividend below last year's level of $2.40. Beyond this, Mr. Abbey stated he would support the proposal which appeared to offer greatest opportunity for appreciation in stockholders' market values over the long term.

Mr. Weilman had recently scanned the list of stockholders. There were, first of all, 16 separate family units of Croates holding a total of two million shares. Approximately one million shares were held by large investment trusts, many of which were growth oriented. The remaining seven million shares were held largely by 28,000 individual accounts. From this group, about 10,000 individuals held less than 100 shares of stock apiece with their total holdings amounting to less than 400,000 shares.

Mr. Eastlander had suggested that Mr. Weilman prepare a report for himself and the board of directors outlining the relative advantages and disadvantages of the various proposals for financing the proposed expansion program as well as recommending a tentative financial program for the five-year period. Considerable urgency was attached to this report inasmuch as related capital expenditure, dividend, and equity financing decisions would have to be made soon to be effective.

In his initial approach to the problem, Mr. Weilman planned to evaluate the relative attractiveness of three basic alternatives. These alternatives were:

1. A public sale of $50 million in common stock during June of 1958 at an approximate issuing price of $64.75 per share (after discounts and underwriting fees), followed by further debt and/or equity financings as necessary during the period 1958–1962.

2. Adoption of a 40% dividend policy, coupled with an immediate reduction in dividends to an annual rate of $2 per share. Additional funds required, if any, would be financed through public issues of debt and/or equity capital.

3. A reduction in capital expenditures as proposed by Mr. Eastlander, plus supplementary financings as necessary during the five-year period.

Upon completion of this analysis, Mr. Weilman planned to appraise how alternative methods (such as use of rights, timing of equity issues, maintenance of the $0.40 extra dividend) of implementing basic objectives might modify his findings on the relative attractiveness of the three basic alternatives.

Exhibit 1

BRUSHWELL PAINT AND CHEMICAL COMPANY

BALANCE SHEET DECEMBER 31, 1957

(Dollar figures in millions)

ASSETS		LIABILITIES	
Cash	$ 15.7	Accounts payable	$ 18.4
Marketable securities	30.0	Accrued liabilities	20.1
Accounts receivable	31.2	Taxes payable	40.6
Inventories	103.6	Less: Tax anticipation notes	40.6
Total current assets	$180.5	Net tax liability	....
		Total current liabilities	$ 38.5
Gross plant	$628.1		
Depreciation	242.0	Long-term debt*	160.0
Net plant	$386.1	5% preferred	50.0
Miscellaneous investments	12.7	Common stock, 10,000,000 shares	100.0
Total assets	$579.3	Earned surplus	230.8
		Total equity capital base	$380.8
		Total capitalization	540.8
		Total liabilities and net worth	579.3

* Debt to total capitalization ratio was 29.6% $\frac{(\$160.0)}{(\$540.8)}$ on December 31, 1957.

Exhibit 2

BRUSHWELL PAINT AND CHEMICAL COMPANY

ANNUAL INCOME STATEMENTS, 1953–1957

(Dollar figures in millions)

	1953	1954	1955	1956	1957
Sales	$235.1	$205.2	$257.9	$270.1	$301.4
Cost of goods sold*	129.2	113.1	136.5	145.7	158.3
Gross profit	$105.9	$ 92.1	$121.4	$124.4	$143.1
Selling and administration*	38.9	38.2	41.4	42.2	47.8
Operating profit	$ 67.0	$ 53.9	$ 80.0	$ 82.2	$ 95.3
Miscellaneous net income	1.0	1.1	1.0	1.0	1.0
Earnings before interest	$ 68.0	$ 55.0	$ 81.0	$ 83.2	$ 96.3
Interest	3.2	3.2	3.2	4.5	7.2
Profit before taxes	$ 64.8	$ 51.8	$ 77.8	$ 78.7	$ 89.1
Taxes	35.7	26.1	39.1	39.7	45.1
Profit after taxes	$ 29.1	$ 25.7	$ 38.7	$ 39.0	$ 44.0
Preferred dividends	2.5	2.5	2.5	2.5	2.5
Income to common stockholders	$ 26.6	$ 23.2	$ 36.2	$ 36.5	$ 41.5
Common dividends	17.0	16.0	20.0	22.0	24.0
Retained earnings	$ 9.6	$ 7.2	$ 16.2	$ 14.5	$ 17.5
* Includes depreciation of	$ 17.1	$ 18.2	$ 20.2	$ 22.6	$ 23.3

Exhibit 3

BRUSHWELL PAINT AND CHEMICAL COMPANY

SUMMARY SOURCE AND APPLICATION OF FUNDS STATEMENT, 1947–1957

(Dollar figures in millions)

Sources:	1947–1955	1956–1957	Total
Profit after taxes	$263.5	$ 83.0	$346.5
Depreciation	116.7	45.9	162.6
Long-term debt	80.0	80.0	160.0
Current liabilities	12.1	4.1	16.2
Total sources	$472.3	$213.0	$685.3
Opening cash and market securities	20.2	15.2	20.2
Total	$492.5	$228.2	$705.5
Applications:			
Accounts receivable	$ 14.6	$ 5.1	$ 19.7
Inventories	39.7	25.2	64.9
Plant and equipment	251.8	100.3	352.1
Preferred dividends	22.5	5.0	27.5
Common dividends	143.0	46.0	189.0
Miscellaneous other	5.7	0.9	6.6
Total applications	$477.3	$182.5	$659.8
Closing cash and market securities	15.2	45.7	45.7
Total	$492.5	$228.2	$705.5

Exhibit 4

BRUSHWELL PAINT AND CHEMICAL COMPANY

EARNINGS DIVIDEND, AND MARKET PRICE DATA, 1947–1957

Year	E.P.S.	D.P.S.	1st Q.	2d Q.	3d Q.	4th Q.	Extra	Ave. MP*	P.E. Ratio	Yield
1947	1.99	1.00	0.20	0.20	0.20	0.20	0.20	23¾	11.9	4.2%
1948	2.66	1.30	0.25	0.25	0.25	0.25	0.30	27	10.1	4.8
1949	2.40	1.40	0.30	0.30	0.30	0.30	0.20	27½	11.5	5.1
1950	3.23	1.70	0.30	0.30	0.30	0.30	0.50	31½	9.8	5.4
1951	2.70	1.70	0.30	0.30	0.30	0.40	0.40	47	17.4	3.6
1952	2.56	1.70	0.40	0.40	0.40	0.40	0.10	43½	17.0	3.9
1953	2.66	1.70	0.40	0.40	0.40	0.40	0.10	46	17.3	3.7
1954	2.32	1.60	0.40	0.40	0.40	0.40	nil	47	20.2	3.4
1955	3.62	2.00	0.40	0.40	0.40	0.40	0.40	55½	15.3	3.5
1956	3.65	2.20	0.50	0.50	0.50	0.50	0.20	68¾	18.8	3.2
1957	4.15	2.40	0.50	0.50	0.50	0.50	0.40	73	17.6	3.3

* Unweighted average of midpoint of monthly market price ranges.

STANDARD AND POOR 425 INDUSTRIALS

Year	Ave. MP	P.E. Ratio	Yield
1947	$14.94	9.8	5.0%
1948	15.44	7.6	5.5
1949	15.13	6.2	6.8
1950	18.64	6.7	7.0
1951	22.72	8.4	6.9
1952	25.41	10.4	5.7
1953	24.45	9.4	5.9
1954	31.84	11.4	4.8
1955	43.87	12.7	3.9
1956	50.14	13.6	4.0
1957	46.71	13.0	4.1

Exhibit 5

BRUSHWELL PAINT AND CHEMICAL COMPANY

FIVE-YEAR FORECAST OF FUND REQUIREMENTS

(Dollar figures in millions)

	1958	1959	1960	1961	1962
Sales	$320.0	$340.0	$375.0	$420.0	$470.0
Cost of goods sold	173.0	180.0	199.0	221.0	254.0
Selling and administrative	50.0	54.0	60.0	67.0	72.0
Miscellaneous net	6.0	6.0	6.0	6.0	6.0
Taxes	46.0	50.0	55.0	63.0	69.0
Profit after taxes	$ 45.0	$ 50.0	$ 55.0	$ 63.0	$ 69.0
Preferred dividends	2.5	2.5	2.5	2.5	2.5
Common dividends	26.0	29.0	32.0	36.0	40.0
Retained earnings	$ 16.5	$ 18.5	$ 20.5	$ 24.5	$ 26.5
Depreciation	23.1	22.9	25.6	28.3	31.1
Total internally generated sources	$ 39.6	$ 41.4	$ 46.1	$ 52.8	$ 57.6
Opening cash and market securities	45.7	16.0	17.0	19.0	21.0
Total resources	$ 85.3	$ 57.4	$ 63.1	$ 71.8	$ 78.6
Projected earnings per share	4.25	4.75	5.25	6.05	6.65
Projected dividends per share	2.60	2.90	3.20	3.60	4.00
Applications:					
Sinking fund payments	5.0	5.0	5.0	5.0	10.0
Plant and equipment	60.8	55.0	65.0	75.0	90.0
Inventories	7.6	6.5	10.9	14.0	14.5
Accounts receivable	2.1	2.1	3.6	4.6	5.0
Total applications	$ 75.5	$ 68.6	$ 84.5	$ 98.6	$119.5
Closing cash requirement	16.0	17.0	19.0	21.0	24.0
Total	$ 91.5	$ 85.6	$103.5	$119.6	$143.5
Sources less applications	(6.2)	(28.2)	(40.4)	(47.8)	(64.9)
Cumulative requirements	(6.2)	(34.4)	(74.8)	(122.6)	(187.5)
Opening equity base	380.8	397.3	415.8	436.3	460.8
Add retained earnings	16.5	18.5	20.5	24.5	26.5
Closing equity base	$397.3	$415.8	$436.3	$460.8	$487.3
Debt capacity end of period (½ equity base):	198.6	207.9	218.1	230.4	243.6
Outstanding debt, end of period	155.0	150.0	145.0	140.0	130.0
Available borrowing capacity	$ 43.6	$ 57.9	$ 73.1	$ 90.4	$113.6

Exhibit 6
BRUSHWELL PAINT & CHEMICAL COMPANY
MARKET PRICE DATA
Brushwell Common and Standard and Poor's 425 Industrial Stocks

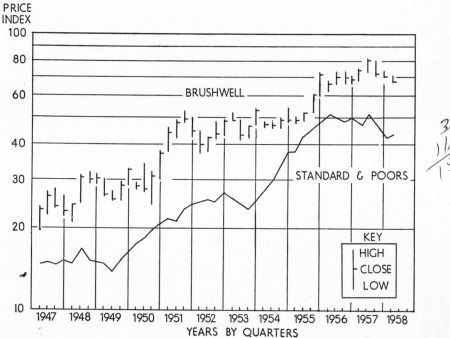

Exhibit 7

BRUSHWELL PAINT AND CHEMICAL COMPANY

SELECTED FINANCIAL DATA FOR COMPANIES
RELATIVELY COMPARABLE TO BRUSHWELL

(See explanatory notes)

Company	Annual Rate of Earnings Growth	Annual Pay-out	Dividend Yield	Price-Earnings Ratio
Company A...................	14.9%	41.0%	1.9%	21.4
Company B...................	13.1	61.3	2.7	22.5
Company C...................	12.2	24.8	1.7	14.2
Company D...................	12.1	60.2	2.9	20.8
Company E*..................	11.9	39.7	2.3	17.0
Company F...................	11.0	42.1	2.7	15.6
Company G...................	10.2	39.0	2.7	14.2
Brushwell...................	10.1	60.4	3.5	17.4
Company H*..................	9.9	59.7	3.5	17.2
Company I...................	8.2	64.9	4.4	14.6
Company J*..................	8.2	65.1	4.5	14.5
Company K...................	8.0	60.7	4.3	14.0

Notes:

1. "Comparable companies" are all of Brushwell's approximate size, manufacture similar products, are actively traded on the New York Stock Exchange, are generally regarded as growth stocks, and have fairly similar capitalization ratios.

2. Annual rate of earnings growth computed on the basis of a weighted average of percentage changes in earnings per share for years 1948–1957. Weights applied on the following basis: 1957, 10; 1956, 9; 1955, 8; . . . ; 1948, 1. Illustratively for Brushwell:

Year	Weight	Percentage Increase or Decrease in E.P.S.	Wt. × Percentage Change
1957...................	10	+13.7%	+137.0
1956...................	9	+ 0.8	+ 7.2
....	.	....	....
1954...................	7	−12.8	− 89.6
....	.	....	....
1948...................	1	+33.7	+ 33.7
Total..................	55		+553.5; Wt. Ave. = 10.1%

3. Annual pay-out data represents total cash dividends per share, 1953–1957, divided by total earnings per share, 1953–1957.

4. Dividend yields and price-earnings ratios are unweighted averages for the period 1953–1957.

5. All data are adjusted for stock splits and dividends.

* Companies E, H, and J alone from the group have financed their expansion programs in part through sale of common stock; none of these three used rights issues.

TEXAS NORTHERN ELECTRIC COMPANY

In early February, 1960, the board of directors of Texas Northern Electric Company (TENECO) met to discuss the following financial plan which was prepared for the board by Stone & Webster Service Corporation. The latter was a consulting firm whose services TENECO customarily employed for advice on their planning.

· · · · ·

To the Director of
Texas Northern Electric Company

At the last directors' meeting you were informed of the rapidly growing demand for service in the territory served by the company. You also were advised of the necessity for raising substantial amounts of new capital to pay for major plant additions if the demands for service are to be satisfied. Since those preliminary discussions took place, in co-operation with company personnel we have made projections of loads and kilowatt-hour requirements and from them have prepared estimates of revenues, expenses, and construction requirements. These have been carefully reviewed and analyzed and represent our best judgment of what reasonably may be expected in the foreseeable future, assuming continuation of favorable economic levels. In accordance with your instructions, the results of our studies and our recommendations are presented herewith for your consideration.

The primary purpose of this report is to anticipate the effect of the expected growth on the company's earnings and to determine the extent of, and the ability to finance, cash requirements for the next few years. The following comments are therefore limited to a discussion of the financial aspects and the details of revenue, expense, and construction estimates and the assumptions and supporting data upon which the estimates are based have been omitted:

Construction Requirements

During the five-year period, cash required for construction is estimated to aggregate $20,536,000. The amounts by years, taken from the cash estimate, are as follows:

1960	$ 5,897,000
1961	4,568,000
1962	5,756,000
1963	2,767,000
1964	1,548,000
	$20,536,000

Construction costs shown include provision for new generating capacity and necessary additions to the transmission and distribution systems to serve the projected loads. The magnitude of this program in relation to the present plant is indicated by the fact that additions for 1960 through 1962 are equivalent to 62%, and for the five-year period are nearly 78%, of gross plant at the end of 1959.

Five-Year Financing Program

In addition to the cash generated within the company through depreciation accruals and retained earnings, it is anticipated that $13,493,000 of cash will be needed from permanent financing and bank loans in the 1960–1964 period. A proposed financing program to raise the required capital is summarized below (dollar figures in thousands):

Date	Security	1960	1961	1962	1963	1964
6/60	50,000 shares common stock at $37 net	$1,850				
10/60	$5\frac{3}{8}$% first-mortgage bonds	3,000				
10/61	15,000 shares $5\frac{3}{4}$% preferred stock		$1,500			
6/62	42,000 shares common stock at $41.50 net			$1,743		
10/62	$5\frac{3}{8}$% first-mortgage bonds			4,000		
4/64	14,000 shares $5\frac{3}{4}$% preferred stock					$1,400
	Bank loans—net change (decrease)		2,000	(1,300)	$1,100	(1,800)
	Total proceeds	$4,850	$3,500	$4,443	$1,100	$ (400)

FIVE-YEAR TOTALS

First-mortgage bonds	$ 7,000
Preferred stock	2,900
Common stock	3,593
Bank loans (net)	0
Total proceeds	$13,493

Recommended Financing for the Year 1960

Projected cash requirements for 1960 construction amount to $5,900,000. It is estimated that approximately $1,100,000 of this will be available from operations, making it necessary to raise the balance of approximately $4,800,000 from outside sources.

During the past few years there has been a gradual improvement in the capital structure from that which existed at the time the company's stock was distributed to the public. Because of the need for additional common equity to balance out the over-all financing, the company should take advantage of present favorable common stock markets. We, therefore, recommend the sale of common stock as soon as possible to raise approximately $1,850,000 as the first step in the program for 1960, to be followed later this year by the sale of first-mortgage bonds.

Since it appears appropriate to sell common stock in the immediate future, every attempt should be made to assure the attractiveness of the common stock from an investment standpoint. While it cannot be said with certainty what factors have the greatest effect on market values of utility common stocks, dividend policy undoubtedly plays a major part. For this reason we feel that consideration should be given now to increasing the quarterly dividend.

The present annual dividend of $1.40 per share established in early 1958 would represent a payment of 60% of estimated 1960 earnings of $2.33 per share on the 449,500 shares to be outstanding after a proposed sale of 50,000 shares in June of this year. On earnings of $2.44 per share based on average shares outstanding during the year a dividend of $1.40 would be equivalent to 57% of earnings. We believe the dividend rate might be increased at this time to $1.70 per share, or 73% of estimated 1960 earnings of $2.33 per share mentioned previously. This rate of payment is in line with the average pay-out ratio of other electric utility companies of its size. Assuming no adverse changes in the general price levels for utility securities, we would expect the proposed increase in dividends, if made effective before the sale of new shares, to improve considerably the price for the new stock. Accordingly, if our recommendation for the sale of common stock is acted upon favorably, we think that the dividend rate should be increased at this meeting to a suggested quarterly rate of $42\frac{1}{2}$ cents per share in order to have the company obtain the maximum benefit from the stock sale.

With respect to the amount of common stock to be sold, from an examination of the estimates of cash requirements for the years 1960, 1961, and 1962 it seems certain that some form of permanent financing will be needed in each of the three years. The estimates provide for part of this to be accomplished through the sales of common stock in 1960 and 1962. There appears to be little question as to the desirability of selling common stock this year, and the principal point for consideration should be the amount of stock to be sold. Utility stocks presently are in good demand, but the market for equity securities can disappear rapidly. For this reason we favor selling now, enough shares of common stock to provide the equity needed for approximately the next two years. At an estimated net price to the company of $37 per share based on current market relationships[1] the sale of 50,000 shares of common stock would realize $1,850,000 in cash and provide sufficient common stock equity to maintain reasonable balance in the program for this year and next. Estimated earnings are sufficient to absorb the dilution caused by the increased number of shares and provide a modest further improvement over 1959 results. In consideration of the various factors, it is our judgment that the sale of common stock in the amounts mentioned should be made, and we so recommend.

With a sufficient amount of bondable property additions available, we believe the sale of $3,000,000 of first-mortgage bonds is the logical step to

---

[1] Calculated as follows:
$1.70 ÷ 0.044 = $38.50 − $1.50 = $37.00 (Dividend ÷ Yield − Underwriter's Commission)

$38.50 ÷ $2.33 = 16.5 P.E. ratio (Market Price ÷ Earnings per Share Expected in 1960)

raise the balance of 1960 capital requirements. We have projected such a sale for October 1. The $5\frac{3}{8}\%$ rate of interest reflects the approximate level of rates for bonds of similar quality sold within the past 30 days.

Projected Financing for 1961 through 1964

The cash estimate shows that $3,500,000 of new money will be needed in 1961 and about $4,400,000 in 1962. At this point we need to sell preferred stock to restore proper balance to the capital structure; consequently, we have scheduled the sale of $1,500,000 preferred stock for October 1, 1961. The rate of $5\frac{3}{4}\%$ which has been used in the estimates is an approximation based on today's situation. While the ratio of common equity temporarily will drop below the 32% level attained by the proposed sale of common stock in 1960, the change should not be sufficiently great to affect the bond rating. Aside from this, we believe it is desirable, where possible, to space common stock sales at less frequent intervals. The balance of 1961 requirements, estimated to be $2,000,000, should be obtainable through short-term bank credit.

In 1962 an additional common stock sale will be necessary if an improved common equity ratio is to be accomplished. Therefore permanent financing projected for that year consists of the sale of an estimated 42,000 shares of common stock on or about June 1, 1962, to net $1,743,000 and the sale on October 1 of $4,000,000 principal amount of first-mortgage bonds. Assuming payment of common dividends in the range of 74% of available earnings, the annual rate could be $1.90 when the common stock is sold in 1962. Based on such a dividend and anticipating about the same yield basis as estimated for the 1960 sale, we have estimated a price of $41.50 per share net to the company.

Completion of the permanent financing program, insofar as it is possible to make recommendations for such future dates, contemplates the sale of an additional 14,000 shares ($1,400,000) of preferred stock on April 1, 1964, to retire bank loans assumed to be issued for temporary financing of 1963 construction and the balance carried over from 1962.

Capital Structure

The condensed table which follows (given in thousands of dollars and in per cent) shows the changes in capitalization ratios and related dollar figures over the period:

	Actual 1959	Estimated 1960	1961	1962	1963	1964
Bonds (net of retirements)	$10,020	$12,960	$12,900	$16,840	$16,780	$16,720
Debentures (net of retirements)	2,825	2,750	2,675	2,600	2,525	2,450
Total long-term debt	$12,845	$15,710	$15,575	$19,440	$19,305	$19,170
Bank loans	.....	.....	2,000	700	1,800	.....
Total debt	$12,845	$15,710	$17,575	$20,140	$21,105	$19,170
Preferred stock (net of retirements)	2,750	2,750	4,168	4,085	3,957	5,229
Common equity	6,589	8,749	9,093	11,187	11,585	12,010
Total capitalization	$22,184	$27,209	$30,836	$35,412	$36,647	$36,409

	Actual	Estimated				
	1959	1960	1961	1962	1963	1964
Bonds	45.2%	47.6%	41.8%	47.5%	45.8%	45.9%
Debentures	12.7	10.1	8.7	7.4	6.9	6.7
Total long-term debt	57.9%	57.7%	50.5%	54.9%	52.7%	52.6%
Bank loans	....	....	6.5	2.0	4.9	....
Total debt	57.9%	57.7%	57.0%	56.9%	57.6%	52.6%
Preferred stock	12.4	10.1	13.5	11.5	10.8	14.4
Common equity	29.7	32.2	29.5	31.6	31.6	33.0
Total capitalization	100.0%	100.0%	100.0%	100.0%	100.0%	100.0%

The principal effect of the proposed financing schedule is a reduction in total long-term debt from 57.9% of the total capitalization at the beginning of the five-year period to 52.6% at the end of 1964. This reduction is brought about by increasing the proportion of preferred stock from 12.4% in 1959 to 14.4% estimated in 1964 and by an improvement in the common equity ratio from 29.7% for 1959 to 33.0% at the end of 1964, together with the operation of debenture sinking funds and the increase in total capitalization.

Earnings and Dividends

The following tabulation summarizes estimated earnings and dividends and the percentages of earnings paid in the form of common dividends:

Year	Average Earnings per Share	Annual Dividend Rate	Total Dividends ÷ Total Earnings
1959, actual	$2.17	$1.40	64.5%
1960, estimated	2.33	1.70	67.0
1961	2.46	1.70	69.0
1962	2.55	1.90	69.6
1963	2.71	1.90	70.1
1964	2.86	2.00	69.8

The earnings per share shown in the above tabulation are based on shares outstanding at the end of the year. Computed on average shares they would be $2.44 and $2.64 in 1960 and 1962, respectively. The annual dividend rate is the rate in effect at the year-end, and in 1960 and 1962 it reflects changes during the respective years. This explains the apparent discrepancies in those two years in the ratios of dividends paid to earnings available for common stock which are computed on aggregate dollar dividends and earnings.

Conclusions and Recommendations

It is our recommendation that the company proceed with the immediate sale of 50,000 shares of common stock. If work on this proposed sale is begun now, it should be possible to close on or about June 1. To improve the marketability of the stock and obtain the most advantageous price, we also recommend increasing the dividend on the common stock from the present basis of $1.40 annually to $1.70 per annum by declaring a quarterly dividend of 42½ cents per share, effective with the next dividend payable on May 1,

1960. Preliminary steps should also be taken looking to the sale of $3,000,000 of first-mortgage bonds not later than the last quarter of this year.

The various financing steps suggested beyond these immediate proposals should be considered as tentative. It is felt that they represent a reasonable program for raising the amounts needed but because of changing market conditions and the possibility of revised operating requirements, they should be subject to review as each successive step is taken. Although changes are inevitable, the basic plan set forth should maintain the company's credit and permit a moderate increase in the earnings for the common shares.

Respectfully submitted,
STONE & WEBSTER SERVICE CORPORATION

. . . . .

The Texas Northern Electric Company began operations in Border-town, Texas, during the early 1900's. The company engaged in the generation, purchase, and sale of electricity in an area of north central Texas approximately 70 miles long and 30 miles wide centered around the city of Bordertown. For many years TENECO exhibited below-average growth, but beginning in the early 1940's had become one of the country's more rapidly growing electric utilities. The population of the area served by the company increased by 20% from 1950 to 1960, until it currently numbered over 200,000 people. This annual rate of increase was about 4%, compared with 1.7% for the country as a whole.

All the company's outstanding common stock was held by three very wealthy individuals (whose marginal tax rate on dividends was 87%) until 1955, when the owners made a secondary stock offering to provide a market value for estate planning purposes and to create wider public interest in TENECO'S affairs. The original stockholders had also wished to increase the diversity of their portfolios and were no longer willing to add further to their investments in TENECO. By 1960, these individuals had reduced their holdings to 40% of outstanding shares, and they contemplated no further sales of their stock. One block of common, constituting 20% of total shares, had been placed directly with a large nontaxable charitable foundation. Otherwise, the stock was owned by 2,700 individuals, most of whom owned 100 shares or less and lived in surrounding areas. In the future, management planned to sell any additional common stock offerings through a New York under-writer in order to attract wider interest in the company's securities, particularly among large eastern investors such as the pension trust funds. Management hoped that wider distribution would enhance the stock's market reputation and facilitate issuing bonds, debentures, and pre-ferred stock on more favorable terms in the future.

Managements in the electric utility industry were usually able to plan their financial requirements with a high degree of accuracy for several years ahead. Previous five-year forecasts prepared by Stone & Webster had proved quite reliable because the stable rate of growth in TENECO'S area provided a ready basis for forecasting kilowatt-hour demand and load requirements. In the past, facility needs beyond three years had occasionally been underestimated, but this did not prove serious as the first few years of the forecast were usually fairly accurate.

In the discussion that developed out of the 1960 Stone & Webster report for TENECO, the board focused its attention on three areas: (1) the recommendation to increase the common stock dividend; (2) a suggested change in debt policy; and (3) the sequence, amounts, and security types proposed by the report.

Prior to 1960, the company followed a policy of paying out approximately 60% of current earnings in dividends, although actual payment varied somewhat from year to year. In contrast, Stone & Webster recommended an increase in pay-out ratio to 70% of earnings in future years. This proposed change would place TENECO more in line with the industry average, which approximated 75% of earnings. In March, 1958, the board had increased the quarterly dividend rate from 30.0 cents to 35.0 cents per share. Stone & Webster proposed an immediate increase in the quarterly rate to 42.5 cents per share. The proposed change in pay-out hopefully would increase the yield, broaden the marketability of the stock, and might drive up the common stock market price to a level where fewer shares would be required to support future capital requirements.

During the early postwar period, when its debt was held privately, TENECO's debt capitalization was heavy compared with that of other comparable companies. Beginning in 1955, management had attempted to bring capitalization ratios more in line with industry averages:

	1952	1955	1958	Present Target Capitalization Ratio as per TENECO Policy
Mortgage bonds	47%	49%	51%	46%
Debentures (general claims)	.19	11	6	12
Preferred stock	4	6	12	12
Common stock and surplus	.30	34	31	30

First-mortgage bond indentures contained a provision limiting total mortgage bonds to 60% of net utility property. This restriction did not affect TENECO's ability to raise debentures or borrow short-term funds.

In its 1960 report, Stone & Webster recommended that TENECO reduce the debt proportion to 52% of capitalization over the next five years. Ideal target capitalization ratios suggested by Stone & Webster were: long-term debt, 50%; preferred stock, 15%; and common stock, 35%. As a matter of long-standing practice, Stone & Webster had advocated these policies to its electric utility clients, and many utilities had debt ratios in line with this recommendation. Moreover, the Securities and Exchange Commission, after passage of the Public Utility Holding Company Act of 1935, had actively encouraged electric and gas companies under its purview to reduce debt to 50% of capitalization.

Moody's Investors Service, widely used by utility analysts, had rated TENECO's public issues of mortgage bonds and debentures A and Baa, respectively. Normally, the debentures[2] of a utility were rated one grade below its mortgage bonds. Although Moody's never divulged its bases for making bond evaluations, TENECO's small size and dependence upon the prosperity of one area made it very unlikely that the company's mortgage debt would be rated above A by Moody's in the foreseeable future. However, TENECO could probably continue to earn A ratings on its mortgage bonds provided total debt did not exceed "prudent" levels, very generally regarded as about 57% of capitalization for companies of its size. The many financial and nonfinancial factors (attitudes of local regulatory authorities, marketability of the securities, etc.) considered by Moody's made a precise upper limit difficult to determine.

Generally speaking, the factors considered most important in Moody's bond ratings, for companies comparable to TENECO, were as follows: earnings coverage of long-term debt charges; over-all coverage; capitalization ratios; size of company (it was unusual for a company with total revenues under $10 million to have more than a Baa rating on its mortgage bonds); proportion of debt to net plant; and the distribution of revenues and customers by kind of service. (See Exhibit 5 for a summary of information relating to some of these factors on 20 companies comparable to TENECO.) Other important factors included: territory served; degree of competition with public power; diversification of industrial customers; and over-all evaluation of management. TENECO appeared favorably situated with regard to this latter group of factors.

In view of the magnitude of TENECO's estimated construction pro-

---

[2] Recently, TENECO had paid approximately ⅜% more for its debentures than its bonds.

gram (and, hence, future capital requirements), Stone & Webster recommended that the company aim at a 52% debt to capitalization policy for three primary reasons: The 52% ratio would be more in line with industry averages and might, as a consequence, have a favorable effect upon capital costs for preferred and common stock as well as debt. Such a ratio would better assure future A ratings on mortgaged debt. (Since Moody's revised ratings whenever circumstances seemed appropriate, a firm treading too near the A–Baa borderline might expose itself unduly to a lower bond rating in the event unforeseen adversity developed.) Finally, the new debt policy would allow greater flexibility in timing future capital issues.

Management was particularly anxious to preserve an A rating on TENECO's mortgage bonds. Once a Baa rating was placed on mortgage bonds, all the firm's securities would become more difficult to market (some institutional investors were restricted by law, others by policy, as to the quality of securities in their portfolios). As shown in Exhibit 4, Baa bonds sold at a higher yield than higher-grade bonds. In addition, it was true that yields varied slightly within the A range, depending on market evaluation of quality. Bond ratings also affected preferred yields in a similar fashion, and lower ratings might adversely affect the market prices of a firm's common stock. Once a rating dropped to Baa, major improvement in corporate affairs was necessary to receive an improved rating; also, any reduction in bond rating was not easy to erase from the minds of potential investors.

Many insurance companies and pension trusts have staffs that appraise independently new bond issues. These ratings do not always agree with Moody's. It was generally believed that the debt restriction in the first-mortgage bond indenture was likely to satisfy these institutional investors' safety requirements, provided TENECO's coverage of interest was not significantly out of line with the industry at the moment. These investors were actively seeking securities with higher yields, and had found lower-quality A or higher-quality Baa bonds particularly attractive. As a result, yield differentials between lowest A and highest B were currently less than $\frac{1}{8}$%, and occasionally Baa's carried lower yields than A's. (Bond marketability was a less important consideration for these investors.) In short, TENECO would not have immediate difficulty placing new debt issues, even those rated Baa, and the only disadvantage of current debt policy arose from the possibility of slightly higher interest and other financial costs.

It was accepted for purposes of analysis that the proposed changes in financial policies would not have any effect on future rate determinations by utility commissions. In short, TENECO management had the same incentives to minimize capital costs as any unregulated company.

SELECTED COMMENTS BY DIRECTORS ON THE DEBT POLICY QUESTION

1. TENECO's president: "I've become convinced A bond ratings are extremely important in this industry, and this factor should be our single most important consideration."

2. Manufacturing company president: "Current debt levels are much too risky for a company owned in part by small stockholders, and should be reduced. I would like to see TENECO move immediately to a 52% debt to total capitalization ratio."

3. Department store owner: "Companies in the department store industry often have comparably high debt to capitalization ratios (after capitalizing leases) despite less inherent profit stability."

4. A second manufacturing company president: "The financial plan requires too heavy dependence on short-term bank loans in view of money market uncertainties."

5. A retired manufacturer: "Reduction in debt proportions will increase new common equity requirements, add undesirable dilution, and unnecessarily limit appreciation opportunities in which our stockholders are most interested."

6. Commercial banker: "Too much emphasis has been placed upon bond ratings. We should instead continue present plans to minimize capital costs."

Although management personally valued the views of each board member, it was recognized that the board's inexperience in utility management occasionally created difficulties in areas where public-utility problems were unique.

Exhibit 1

TEXAS NORTHERN ELECTRIC COMPANY

SUMMARY OF DATA SUPPORTING STONE & WEBSTER REPORT

(Dollar figures in thousands)

	Actual			Estimated		
	1959	*1960*	*1961*	*1962*	*1963*	*1964*
1. Operating revenues	$ 7,030	$ 7,682	$ 8,350	$ 9,530	$ 10,865	$ 11,864
2. Income before interest and taxes	2,249	2,707	2,932	3,414	3,777	4,111
3. Interest on present bonds	312	310	308	306	304	302
4. Interest on new bonds (@ 5⅜%)	....	41	162	216	377	377
5. Interest on debentures	97	95	92	89	87	85
6. Interest on short-term credit	21	37	58	93	58	35
7. Interest charged to construction*	(165)	(118)	(192)	(204)	(111)	(12)
8. Income before federal taxes	$ 1,984	$ 2,342	$ 2,504	$ 2,914	$ 3,062	$ 3,324
9. Federal taxes (@ 50%)	992	1,171	1,252	1,457	1,531	1,662
10. Net income	$ 992	$ 1,171	$ 1,252	$ 1,457	$ 1,531	$ 1,662
11. Preferred dividends on present stock	124	124	120	117	111	105
12. Preferred dividends on new stock (@ 5¾%)	....	....	24	87	88	149
13. Balance for common stock	$ 868	$ 1,047	$ 1,108	$ 1,253	$ 1,332	$ 1,408
14. Dividends on common stock	560	702	764	872	934	983
15. Balance to retained earnings	$ 308	$ 345	$ 344	$ 381	$ 398	$ 425
16. Shares outstanding (end of period)	399,500	449,500	449,500	491,500	491,500	491,500
17. Earnings per share (end of period)	$2.17	$2.33	$2.46	$2.55	$2.71	$2.86
18. Dividends per share (quarter made effective)	1.40	1.70(2)	1.70	1.90(2)	1.90	2.00
19. Fixed charges and preferred dividends times earned†	3.23	3.14	2.93	2.77	2.46	2.35

* State regulatory commissions usually require that interest accrued during construction be capitalized.
† Coverage ratios computed as follows:

	1959	*1960*	*1961*	*1962*	*1963*	*1964*
Income before interest and taxes	$ 2,249	$ 2,707	$ 2,932	$ 3,414	$ 3,777	$ 4,111
Federal taxes (@ 50%)	992	1,171	1,252	1,457	1,531	1,662
Gross income	$ 1,257	$ 1,536	$ 1,680	$ 1,957	$ 2,246	$ 2,449
Interest charges (net of construction credit)	265	365	428	500	715	787
Preferred dividends	124	124	144	204	199	254
Total fixed charges and preferred dividends	$ 389	$ 489	$ 572	$ 704	$ 914	$ 1,041
Coverage ratios (gross income divided by total fixed charges and preferred dividend)	3.23	3.14	2.93	2.77	2.46	2.35

Exhibit 2

TEXAS NORTHERN ELECTRIC COMPANY

CHART SHOWING CUMULATIVE CAPITAL REQUIREMENTS ASSUMING EXISTING FINANCIAL POLICIES

(Dollar figures in millions)

	1960 Existing Policies	%	1961 Existing Policies	%	1962 Existing Policies	%	1964 Existing Policies	%
Target year-end capitalizations:								
Bonds	$12.52	46	$14.18	46	$16.29	46	$16.75	46
Debentures	3.26	12	3.70	12	4.25	12	4.37	12
Preferred stock	3.26	12	3.70	12	4.25	12	4.37	12
Common equity	8.17	30	9.26	30	10.62	30	10.92	30
Total	$27.21	100	$30.84	100	$35.41	100	$36.41	100
Actual capital structure on December 31 (before consideration of new issues):								
Bonds (after sinking fund)	$ 9.96		$ 9.90		$ 9.84		$ 9.72	
Debentures (after sinking fund)	2.75		2.68		2.60		2.45	
Preferred stock	2.75		2.66		2.58		2.33	
Common equity (including additional retained earnings)*	7.01		7.45		7.95		9.05	
Total	$22.47		$22.69		$22.97		$23.55	
Cumulative additional capital requirements to meet target capitalization ratios:								
Bonds	$ 2.56		$ 4.28		$ 6.45		$ 7.03	
Debentures	0.51		1.02		1.65		1.92	
Preferred stock	0.51		1.04		1.67		2.04	
Common stock	1.16		1.81		2.67		1.87	
Total	$ 4.74		$ 8.15		$12.44		$12.86	
Maximum limit to total bonds under first-mortgage bond indenture	$13.52		$15.61		$18.34		$18.98	

* Incremental dividends under 70% pay-out policy are:

1960	$ 74,000
1961	99,000
1962	120,000
1963	134,000
1964	138,000
Total	$565,000

Exhibit 3

TEXAS NORTHERN ELECTRIC COMPANY

MOODY'S COMMON STOCK AVERAGES COVERING TWENTY-FOUR UTILITIES

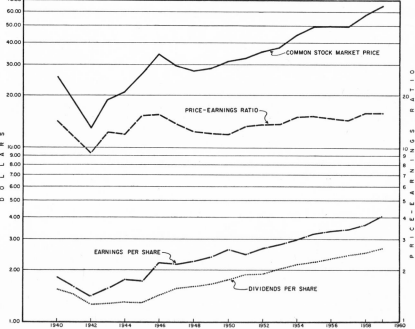

Exhibit 4

TEXAS NORTHERN ELECTRIC COMPANY

MOODY'S PUBLIC UTILITY BOND YIELDS BY RATINGS*

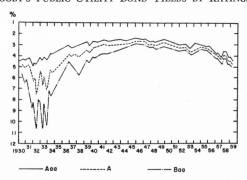

* These are average yields and do not necessarily represent yields on new issues.

Exhibit 5

TEXAS NORTHERN ELECTRIC COMPANY*

SELECTED INDUSTRY STATISTICS FOR COMPANIES WITH REVENUES
LESS THAN $25 MILLION*

(Based on most recent data)

	P.E. Ratio (1)	Dividend Yield (2)	Growth Rate (3)	Pay-out Ratio (4)
1. Public Service, New Mexico	23.3	2.8%	14.0%	66%
2. Central Louisiana Electric	21.5	4.0	3.6	86
3. Colorado Central Power	21.1	3.4	6.6	72
4. El Paso Electric	20.6	3.3	8.3	69
5. California Oregon Power	17.9	4.8	−3.4	85
6. Southwestern Electric	17.1	4.2	5.4	72
7. Upper Peninsular Power	16.6	5.6	−5.1	92
8. Missouri Utilities	16.6	4.9	−1.7	81
9. Southern Nevada Power	16.2	3.8	11.1	61
10. Arkansas-Missouri	16.1	4.6	4.2	75
11. Sierra Pacific Power	16.0	4.2	9.4	67
12. Southern Colorado Power	15.8	5.0	1.4	78
13. Green Mountain Power	15.3	5.7	2.6	88
14. Fitchburg Gas & Electric	15.2	5.4	0.4	82
15. Iowa Southern Utilities	14.1	4.8	5.7	67
16. Northwestern Public Service	13.9	5.2	1.3	72
17. Edison Sault Electric	13.4	4.7	5.1	63
18. Black Hills Power & Light	12.9	4.5†	4.5	59
19. Newport Electric	12.9	5.2	4.5	67
20. Bangor Hydro Electric	12.6	5.1	4.2	64
Average of 20 companies	16.5	4.6	4.1	73
21. Teneco	17.7	3.7	7.3	64

(1) Ratio market price 1/29/60 to most recent published earnings per share.
(2) Existing dividend rate divided by market price 1/29/60.
(3) The rate which will discount average 1958–1959 earnings per share to equal the average 1955–1956 earnings per share.
(4) Current dividend rate divided by most recent reported earnings per share.
(5) Earnings after taxes but before fixed charges divided by fixed charges.

Debt Ratio	Common Equity Ratio	1958 Times Interest Covered after Taxes (5)	1959 Times Fixed Charges + Pfd. Dividends Covered	(Actual) or Estimated Moody's Bond Rating	Operating Revenue (Millions of Dollars)
53.4%	33.5%	4.16	3.53	A	17.1
57.1	31.2	3.12	2.73	(Baa)	19.2
49.8	45.1	3.25	2.87	Baa	6.5
49.7	35.6	6.07	3.80	(Aa)	17.1
57.2	33.4	2.84	2.15	(A)	23.7
57.6	27.4	4.52	2.43	Baa	3.6
59.9	29.1	2.59	2.09	(Baa)	6.3
56.0	34.3	2.70	2.20	Baa	7.9
54.8	39.5	2.31	2.19	(Baa)	9.1
58.2	30.2	2.86	2.29	Baa	12.3
58.0	30.4	3.29	2.55	(Baa)	12.0
48.5	33.8	5.67	3.83	Baa	7.9
57.9	35.6	3.18	2.68	Baa	6.7
43.9	48.2	4.02	3.16	Baa	5.4
57.3	38.1	2.81	2.55	(Baa)	16.5
56.0	30.3	2.91	2.22	(Baa)	11.5
57.9	31.9	2.93	2.48	Baa	2.7
54.6	36.3	3.24	2.43	Baa	6.8
54.0	34.0	2.57	2.12	Baa	2.8
51.5	33.3	3.42	2.22	A	8.0
54.7‡	34.5	3.42	2.63		
57.9	29.7	4.74	3.23	A	7.0

* Common stock of all these companies was traded over the counter.
† Plus stock dividend.
‡ Average of 125 companies: 51.7% debt.
Sources:
1. Bear, Stearns & Company, *Monthly Comparison of Electric Utility Common Stocks.*
2. *Moody's Public Utility Manual.*

294 CASES IN CAPITAL BUDGETING

Exhibit 6

TEXAS NORTHERN ELECTRIC COMPANY

GRAPH SHOWING RELATIONSHIP BETWEEN PRICE-EARNINGS RATIO, DIVIDEND
PAY-OUT RATE, AND RATE OF EARNINGS GROWTH PER SHARE

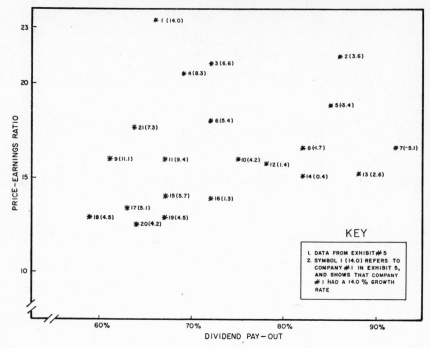

Section V

CHOICE AMONG FINANCING ALTERNATIVES

THE RIZZO MANUFACTURING COMPANY

On December 10, 1954, Mr. George Rizzo, president of The Rizzo Manufacturing Company, was considering whether to finance the purchase of a $120,000 profile molding machine required for competitive reasons by means of a three-year conditional sales contract with the manufacturer, W. P. Swanson & Company, or a ten-year purchase mortgage note with the Manufacturers Credit Corporation. Since the size and timing of payments and the financing costs varied significantly, Mr. Rizzo planned to analyze the alternatives carefully prior to reaching a decision.

In August, 1951, Mr. Rizzo had founded the Rizzo Manufacturing so he might gain financially from his intimate knowledge of the aircraft industry's mold and die requirements. He had noted a growing reliance by airframe manufacturers on machine tool subcontractors to supply specialized molds and dies required on short notice. Since there was a general shortage of mold and die capacity in Glendale, California, late deliveries often caused costly production delays for the aircraft manufacturers located nearby. Mr. Rizzo further believed that a number of the aircraft industry's mold and die requirements could be handled, in all but slack production periods, more efficiently and rapidly by independent job order machine shops. Consequently, he had decided to invest his life savings of $192,000 in what he thought would be a profitable venture. In addition, two friends had contributed $50,000 each to the initial common stock capitalization.

The company's initial capital investment of $292,000 was soon consumed by the purchase of a few multipurpose machine tools and a plant to house the production facilities. Although the company was able to accept a sufficient volume of orders to insure a profitable level of operations from the start, a large number of orders had to be

297

turned down because the equipment had limited capabilities. Since this meant inefficient use of several machines as well as loss of potential profits, Mr. Rizzo had undertaken a rapid expansion of fixed assets to balance machine utilization, increase total capacity, and enlarge the variety of mold and die orders that could be accepted. During 1952, 1953, and 1954, $250,000 was spent on enlarging plant facilities and purchasing new machine tools. In addition, $321,000 in equipment had been leased[1] from manufacturers by 1954.

Sales and profits had shown a pronounced upward trend from the beginning, and all profits had been retained in the business. Nevertheless, the heavy fixed asset expansion had drained the company's working capital position, and twice Mr. Rizzo was forced to resort to outside sources to meet commitments. In January, 1953, $100,000 was borrowed from a local investor. Although this loan required no periodic interest payments, it was repayable in five years at $150,000. In October, 1954, the company also borrowed $100,000 at 5% interest from a large Los Angeles bank on 90-day unsecured demand notes. When the loan was arranged, the loan officer indicated that $100,000 represented the maximum commitment the bank was willing to make at that time. However, the loan officer stated that the loan agreement's renewal every 90 days would be fairly automatic unless unfavorable circumstances developed. (Balance sheet and income statement information for 1953 and 1954 is shown in Exhibits 1 and 2.)

Although the company's working capital position had always been tight, it had never been critical. Mr. Rizzo believed this was due largely to the favorable terms on which credit was extended to the company and to the rapid turnover of inventories and receivables. Materials accounted for 50% of cost of goods sold, and all purchases were made on net 60-day terms. Mr. Rizzo had endeavored to pay creditors promptly but had found them willing to carry delinquencies for short periods when his cash position was low. A two-month supply of raw materials, required to meet all production specifications from stock without delay, formed the bulk of inventories. Completed job orders were shipped immediately and processing generally required less than one week's time after being scheduled into the plant. Although Rizzo's sales terms were net 15 days, collections generally required about 30 days.

---

[1] The manufacturers' lease agreements included options to purchase the machinery at specified prices after a designated period of rental. The options, if exercised, would require $25,000 in 1957, $60,000 in 1958, and $25,000 in 1959.

In December, 1954, the immediate outlook for sales looked promising to Mr. Rizzo. Since August of that year, sales volume had averaged $200,000 a month, and Mr. Rizzo believed that this could be increased to $250,000 per month in 1955 when a profile molding machine was purchased. Mr. Rizzo realized that over the long run, capacity operations would depend on continued national defense expenditures, since 80% of the company's business was government aircraft subcontracts. He thought, however, that an annual sales volume of $1,000,000 could be maintained even under the worst industry conditions.

By December, 1954, Mr. Rizzo had completed the major portion of the fixed asset expansion program he considered necessary to operate profitably under the prevailing conditions of a shortage in machine tool capacity. He realized, however, that over the long run the company's competitive position would depend on its ability to manufacture all of the aircraft industry's wide variety of mold and die requirements. The company still needed four specialized machine tools costing a total of $400,000 to accomplish this objective. Mr. Rizzo thus planned to purchase a $120,000 profile molding machine in early 1955 and the remaining machinery in late 1955 or early 1956. Mr. Rizzo believed the addition of other new equipment would be highly desirable from a profit standpoint. For example, one machine costing $100,000 promised to return profits averaging $20,000 per year after depreciation and taxes over a ten-year life.

In November, 1954, Mr. Rizzo had discussed the time payment terms with Mr. Kahn, sales representative of W. P. Swanson & Company, manufacturer of the profile molding machine he wished to purchase. Swanson financed most of its time sales by means of three-year conditional sales contracts[2] but arranged purchase mortgage notes[3] when longer terms were required. Mr. Kahn had explained the terms of the conditional sales contract as summarized in Exhibit 3.

---

[2] As a result of a conditional sales contract, the purchaser acquires use of the machinery, but title remains with the seller or his assigned agent until the full purchase price is paid.

[3] On a purchase mortgage note, title is held by the purchaser and the lender is secured by a chattel mortgage lien on the machinery purchased. Since these notes are frequently endorsed by the vendor, the lender may have recourse to the vendor in the event of default of installment payments by the purchaser. W. P. Swanson & Company endorsed all purchase mortgage notes sold to finance companies. These notes were endorsed at face value, and no service charge was levied against Swanson. However, 5% of the notes' face value was withheld as a reserve by the finance company until repayment of the note was completed.

Although Mr. Kahn had agreed to endorse any purchase mortgage note that Mr. Rizzo found would meet the company's needs, he urged full consideration of the favorable interest rate on the conditional sales contract before accepting an "expensive" purchase mortgage. Subsequently, Mr. Rizzo had examined several purchase mortgage agreements but did not find the terms sufficiently better than the conditional sales contract to merit further consideration. For example, the most favorable purchase mortgage agreement available required a 25% down payment, amortization of the principal in equal monthly installments over five years, and interest at the rate of 6% per annum on the original amount of the principal. Mr. Rizzo was preparing to accept the conditional sales contract when he read a newspaper advertisement of the Manufacturers' Credit Corporation, a nationally known finance company specializing in industrial chattel mortgage loans. Three aspects of MCC's loan terms as described in the advertisement seemed particularly attractive to Mr. Rizzo: (1) the interest rate was only 4.25%; (2) repayment terms as long as ten years were arranged; and (3) repayments were tied to depreciation rates so, in effect, the major portion of the purchase price would be written off as an expense. Shortly thereafter, Mr. Thelma, regional sales representative of MCC, called at Mr. Rizzo's request and discussed the terms of its purchase mortgage note. The repayment schedule was limited to the depreciable life of the equipment of ten years, whichever was shorter. Since the molding machine had an estimated life of 15 years, repayments could be made over a ten-year period. These repayments were related to the sum-of-the-digits depreciation schedule,[4] approved for federal income tax determination in the Revenue Act of 1954. The additional terms of MCC's note are summarized in Exhibit 3. Mr. Rizzo had also prepared the data in Exhibit 4 to compare the repayment schedules of the two financing alternatives.

---

[4] The sum-of-the-digits depreciation is a recognized method of accelerating depreciation deductions. Its mechanics are best explained by illustration. Assume a $60,000 machine with a three-year depreciable life is purchased. The integers 1, 2, and 3, representing the three-year life of the machine are added to reach the total (referred to as the sum-of-the-digits), 6. Depreciation in any one year is calculated by dividing the number of years of undepreciated life remaining by the sum of the digits, and then multiplying the resultant and the original depreciable value of the property. In the case of the $60,000 machine, depreciation in the first year equals 3 (years of undepreciated life remaining) /6 (sum-of-the-digits) of $60,000 (original depreciable value) or $30,000; in the second year 2/6 of $60,000, or $20,000; and in the third year 1/6 of $60,000, or $10,000. Application of this principle to the $120,000 molding machine is shown in Exhibit 5 of the case.

Mr. Rizzo believed one factor that might have an important bearing on his decision would be the rate at which he wished to depreciate the new machinery. Depreciation on present plant and equipment totaled $64 thousand per year and was calculated on a straight-line basis, thus writing off initial costs evenly over the estimated life of the facilities. A new federal tax law revision, however, permitted the calculation of depreciation rates on newly acquired equipment by several alternative ways, one of which was the sum-of-the-digits method. To contrast the effects of the sum-of-the-digits and straight-line depreciation schedules on the proposed equipment purchases, Mr. Rizzo had prepared the table shown in Exhibit 5. He had also prepared the table shown in Exhibit 6 to compare the total annual deductions from income for federal income tax purposes under the three alternatives. Mr. Rizzo was particularly interested in the managerial implications of a change in the depreciation methods of write-off, and planned to explore the alternatives thoroughly.

Since the company's working capital position was still tight in December, 1954, Mr. Rizzo thought that the size and timing of payments would be as important considerations in reaching a decision as the cost of financing. Consequently, he began analyzing the prospective sources and applications of funds. Mr. Rizzo first prepared pro forma income statements (shown in Exhibit 7) for capacity operations in 1955 and 1956, ultimate capacity when expansion was completed, and a minimum sales level of $1,000,000, which he believed could be maintained even under the most adverse circumstances. These calculations did not include provisions for the cost of financing nor depreciation expenses on the new molding machine.

Mr. Rizzo believed that future funds would be limited to internally generated sources. He thus planned to modify his pro forma calculations to determine retained earnings. In addition to the deductible expenses on the new equipment purchase and federal income taxes at 50%, Mr. Rizzo also had to consider dividend payments. To satisfy his two friends, who had invested $100,000 when the company was started, Mr. Rizzo had agreed to begin paying out 50% of future earnings after taxes in cash dividends. Mr. Rizzo had also summarized prospective cash drains as shown in Exhibit 8. Finally, he believed that a minimum cash position of $50,000 was required to meet all future payments when they came due.

Exhibit 1

THE RIZZO MANUFACTURING COMPANY

AUDITED BALANCE SHEETS AUGUST 31, 1953, AND 1954, AND ESTIMATED
NOVEMBER 30, 1954

(Dollar figures in thousands)

	Aug. 31, 1953	Aug. 31, 1954	Nov. 30, 1954*
Cash	$173.1	$ 95.5	$ 102.3
Accounts receivable	108.9	128.7	187.8
Inventory	153.3	131.4	180.0
Total current assets	$435.3	$355.6	$ 470.1
Land and buildings (gross)	$180.0	$232.6	$ 284.6
Machinery and equipment (gross)	300.5	390.6	390.6
Less: Reserve for depreciation	39.5	91.8	107.7
Net property	$441.0	$530.4	$ 567.5
Prepaid items	10.7	9.8	10.7
Total assets	$887.0	$897.0	$1,048.3
Bank loan			$ 100.0
Accounts payable	$226.5	$149.8	158.1
Accrued payables	180.2	185.4	194.3
Taxes payable	29.5	40.5	52.5
Total current liabilities	$436.2	$375.7	$ 504.9
Debentures	100.0	100.0	100.0
Common stock	292.0	292.0	292.0
Earned surplus	58.8	129.3	151.4
	$887.0	$897.0	$1,048.3

* Estimated.

Exhibit 2

THE RIZZO MANUFACTURING COMPANY

INCOME STATEMENTS FISCAL YEARS 1953 AND 1954, AND
FIRST QUARTER 1955

(Dollar figures in thousands)

	Year Ending Aug. 31, 1953	Year Ending Aug. 31, 1954	Three Months* Sept.–Nov., 1954
Net sales	$1,353.1	$1,595.9	$601.2
Cost of goods sold	1,093.3	1,162.2	451.1
Gross profit	$ 259.8	$ 433.7	$150.1
Selling and administrative expense	126.1	197.2	50.1
Lease rentals	18.4	78.3	20.0
Depreciation	31.0	52.3	15.9
Net profit before taxes	$ 84.3	$ 106.0	$ 64.1
Federal income tax	29.5	40.5	32.0
Net profit	$ 54.8	$ 65.5†	$ 32.1

* Estimated.
† This profit constituted a return of 7.3% on average net assets for fiscal 1954. Mr. Rizzo knew
that this return was slightly below the industry average of 8%.

Exhibit 3

THE RIZZO MANUFACTURING COMPANY

SUMMARY OF ALTERNATIVE PURCHASE TERMS ON $120,000
MOLDING MACHINE

	Three-Year Conditional Sales Contract	Ten-Year Purchase Mortgage Note
Down payment made by Rizzo.	$20,000	$30,000
Time payment principal.......	100,000	90,000
Interest rate.................	5% interest per annum on the original time payment principal	4¼% interest per annum on the original time payment principal
Method of payment...........	Principal repaid in 36 equal monthly installments of $2,777.78 plus monthly interest payments of $416.67	120 monthly installments based on diminishing annual payments (see Exhibit 4)
Total interest charges........	$100,000 × 5% × 3 yrs. = $15,000	$90,000 × 4¼% × 10 yrs. = $38,250
Total payments, including down payment...................	$135,000	$158,250

Exhibit 4

THE RIZZO MANUFACTURING COMPANY

Comparison of Alternative Payment Schedules for Purchase of $120,000 Molding Machine

	Conditional Sales Contract				Ten-Year Purchase Mortgage Note			
Year	Principal Payments	Interest Payments	Total Payments	Cumulative Payments	Principal Payments	Interest Payments	Total Payments	Cumulative Payments
1955	$ 33,334	$ 5,000	$ 38,334	$ 38,334	$16,205	$ 6,880	$ 23,085	$ 23,085
1956	33,333	5,000	38,333	76,667	15,106	6,440	21,546	44,631
1957	33,333	5,000	38,333	115,000	12,968	5,500	18,468	63,099
1958					11,879	5,050	16,929	80,028
1959					10,810	4,580	15,390	95,418
1960					8,642	3,670	12,312	107,730
1961					5,395	2,300	7,695	115,425
1962					4,316	1,840	6,156	121,581
1963					3,237	1,380	4,617	126,198
1964					1,442	610	2,052	128,250
Total	$100,000	$15,000	$115,000		$90,000	$38,250	$128,250	

Payment Differentials*

Year	Principal Payments	Interest Payments	Interest Payments after Taxes	Principal Payments Plus Interest Payments after Taxes
1955	$ 17,129	$ (1,880)	$ (940)	$ 16,189
1956	18,227	(1,440)	(720)	17,507
1957	20,365	(500)	(250)	20,115
1958	(11,879)	(5,050)	(2,525)	(14,404)
1959	(10,810)	(4,580)	(2,290)	(13,100)
1960	(8,642)	(3,670)	(1,835)	(10,477)
1961	(5,395)	(2,300)	(1,150)	(6,545)
1962	(4,316)	(1,840)	(920)	(5,236)
1963	(3,237)	(1,380)	(690)	(3,927)
1964	(1,442)	(610)	(305)	(1,747)
Total	$(10,000)	$(23,250)	$(11,625)	$ (1,625)

* Conditional sales contract payments minus ten-year purchase mortgage payments.

Exhibit 5

THE RIZZO MANUFACTURING COMPANY

DEPRECIATION TABLE, STRAIGHT LINE AND SUM-OF-DIGITS FOR $120,000
MOLDING MACHINE

Year	Rate	Sum of Digits		Straight Line		Difference	
		Annual	Cumulative	Annual	Cumulative	Annual	Cumulative
1955	15/120	$ 15,000	$ 15,000	$ 8,000	$ 8,000	$7,000	$ 7,000
1956	14/120	14,000	29,000	8,000	16,000	6,000	13,000
1957	13/120	13,000	42,000	8,000	24,000	5,000	18,000
1958	12/120	12,000	54,000	8,000	32,000	4,000	22,000
1959	11/120	11,000	65,000	8,000	40,000	3,000	25,000
1960	10/120	10,000	75,000	8,000	48,000	2,000	27,000
1961	9/120	9,000	84,000	8,000	56,000	1,000	28,000
1962	8/120	8,000	92,000	8,000	64,000	-0-	28,000
1963	7/120	7,000	99,000	8,000	72,000	(1,000)	27,000
1964	6/120	6,000	105,000	8,000	80,000	(2,000)	25,000
1965	5/120	5,000	110,000	8,000	88,000	(3,000)	22,000
1966	4/120	4,000	114,000	8,000	96,000	(4,000)	18,000
1967	3/120	3,000	117,000	8,000	104,000	(5,000)	13,000
1968	2/120	2,000	119,000	8,000	112,000	(6,000)	7,000
1969	1/120	1,000	120,000	8,000	120,000	(7,000)	-0-
Total	120/120	$120,000		$120,000		$ -0-	

Exhibit 6

THE RIZZO MANUFACTURING COMPANY

SUMMARY OF INCOME TAX DEDUCTIONS (DEPRECIATION AND INTEREST)
UNDER ALTERNATIVE PURCHASING ARRANGEMENTS FOR $120,000
MOLDING MACHINE

Year	Condition Sales Contract		Purchase Mortgage,
	Straight-Line Depreciation	Sum-of-Digits Depreciation	Sum-of-Digits Depreciation
1955	$13,000	$20,000	$21,880
1956	13,000	19,000	20,440
1957	13,000	18,000	18,500
1958	8,000	12,000	17,050
1959	8,000	11,000	15,580
1960	8,000	10,000	13,670
1961	8,000	9,000	11,300
1962	8,000	8,000	9,840
1963	8,000	7,000	8,380
1964	8,000	6,000	6,610
1965	8,000	5,000	5,000
1966	8,000	4,000	4,000
1967	8,000	3,000	3,000
1968	8,000	2,000	2,000
1969	8,000	1,000	1,000

Exhibit 7

THE RIZZO MANUFACTURING COMPANY

PRO FORMA INCOME STATEMENTS FOR 1955, 1956, ULTIMATE PLANNED
CAPACITY AND ESTIMATED MINIMUM OPERATING LEVELS

(Dollar figures in thousands)

	Year Ending Aug. 31, 1955	Year Ending Aug. 31, 1956	Ultimate Capacity	Minimum Operating Level
Sales	$2,700	$3,000	$4,000	$1,000
Variable cost of goods sold (60% of sales)	1,620	1,800	2,400	600
Fixed cost of goods sold	400	400	450	200
Total cost of goods sold	$2,020	$2,200	$2,850	$ 800
Gross profit	$ 680	$ 800	$1,150	$ 200
Selling and administrative expense	250	250	300	200
Operating profit	$ 430	$ 550	$ 700	$ 0
Other expenses:				
Interest on bank loan	$ 5	$ 5	$ 5	$ 5
Depreciation	64	64	64	64
Lease rentals	80	80	*	*
Finance costs and depreciation on molding machine	†	†	†	†
Total other expenses				
Profit before taxes				
Less taxes at 50%				
Profit after taxes				
Less dividends				
Retained earnings				
Plus total depreciation				
Internal source of funds				

* Rental payments declined after 1956 to $55,000 in 1957; $15,000 in 1958; and $0.00 in 1959 assuming, as Mr. Rizzo planned, purchase options were exercised when they became available. Exercising purchase options would cost $25,000 in 1957, $60,000 in 1958, and $25,000 in 1959.

† Mr. Rizzo planned to complete these calculations by using the figures he had developed in Exhibit 6 as appropriate.

Exhibit 8

THE RIZZO MANUFACTURING COMPANY

ESTIMATED CASH DRAINS BY YEAR ENDING AUGUST 31, 1955–1961

(Dollar figures in thousands)

	1955	1956	1957	1958	1959	1960	1961
Working capital increase	$50	....	$ 50	....	...	...	...
Repayment of debentures		....	....	$150	...	...	...
Purchase of leased equipment		....	25	60	$25	...	...
Replacement of fixed assets	10	$ 10	10	10	10	$75	$75
Purchase of additional machine tools†		140	70	70	...	...	...
Down payment—molding machine	30	....	....	...	...	...	...
Total	$90	$150	$155	$290	$35	$75	$75
Payment schedule—molding machine	*	*	*	*	*	*	*
Total cash drain							

* Information from Exhibit 4, as appropriate.

† In 1956, Mr. Rizzo hoped to purchase three additional machine tools with an aggregate cost of $280,000. For guidance he had included a 25% down payment on this equipment in 1956, and three equal payments of 25% in 1956, 1957, and 1958.

MONITOR TEXTILE COMPANY (B)

In January, 1961, the Monitor Textile Company was considering replacement of one of its industrial forklift trucks. Operating data about gasoline and electric trucks, and price quotations from the Stevens Industrial Truck Company for the new trucks, were given in the Monitor Textile Company (A) case.

The Stevens company also offered to lease a truck to Monitor under four different leasing plans. Regardless of the plan chosen, Stevens would maintain the equipment and guarantee to keep it in serviceable condition at all times. In the event of a major breakdown, Stevens would provide a replacement truck, at its expense, within four hours. The cost of the lease plans, summarized below, varied depending on the minimum term of the contract signed by the lessee:

Plan	Term of Contract	Gas Truck	Electric Truck
1	No minimum term	$25 per day or $75 per week	$30 per day or $100 per week
2	Four months minimum, 30-day cancellation thereafter	$207 per month	$267 per month
3	Three years minimum, 30-day cancellation thereafter	$145 per month	$179 per month
4	Five years minimum, 30-day cancellation thereafter	$132 per month	$159 per month

Questions

1. Why are the monthly payments less on longer-term leases?
2. Which lease is most advantageous for Monitor?
3. Should Monitor buy a truck or lease one?

ANSCOTT CORPORATION

In October, 1960, Mr. L. Paul Manley, controller of Anscott Corporation, was trying to decide whether his company should lease its new data processing equipment from the manufacturer or from a third-party lessor. The decision concerning the type of equipment to acquire had been made in June, and during the intervening months the company had been preparing to convert its punched-card system to a combination card-and-magnetic-tape system involving an electronic computer. At the time that the equipment decisions were made, Anscott had deferred a final decision as to whether the equipment would be leased from the manufacturer or acquired in some other manner, the decision which now faced Mr. Manley.

Anscott Corporation was one of the country's largest manufacturers of diversified industrial products. Net assets of the company amounted to over $300 million, and the company's common stock was publicly traded and held by more than 7,000 stockholders. The company had had an excellent growth record since 1946, earnings per share having increased 9% per year, on the average. The common stock was currently selling at a price-earnings rate of 18, was providing a dividend yield of 3%, and was highly regarded in financial circles as a "blue-chip" investment.

Anscott's management prided itself on its conservative financial practices; the company had no preferred stock outstanding, and limited the amount of long-term debt to only 20% of the company's total capitalization. A large proportion of the funds for expansion were provided by retained earnings. In 1954 and 1958, the company had sold rather sizable issues of debentures, which had the effect of increasing the debt portion of its capital structure to 20%. Seasonal bank loans, when occasionally used by the company, were readily available at the rate offered to prime borrowers. Anscott's management was agressive in seeking out new investment opportunities, and the company tried to avoid investment projects which did not hold out the promise of a 10% rate of return after taxes.

Anscott's operations were sufficiently diversified and decentralized that management had not found it necessary to be an innovator in the use of electronic computers for data processing. The company had used IBM punched-card equipment for many years and had watched the development of computers carefully. In 1959, an intensive study of the potential benefits of electronic equipment was undertaken under Mr. Manley's direction. As a result of this study, Mr. Manley recommended that the company modernize its data processing operations by acquiring a medium-sized computer, the IBM 1401. This recommendation was justified by an analysis which indicated that annual costs with the new equipment (primarily costs for equipment rental and clerical personnel) would be approximately the same as the costs with existing equipment, so that the additional benefits of faster processing time and greater machine capacity would be obtained for practically no additional cost. After Mr. Manley's recommendation was approved, he began taking the necessary steps to convert to the new system. A new air-conditioning system and an extensive modification and rewiring of the existing facilities were required. In addition, Mr. Manley established a programming group within his department to be responsible for the operation of the new equipment. Mr. Manley estimated that the total costs of installation and initial programming for the new system would require an expenditure of approximately $100,000 before the equipment was delivered.

In his initial analysis of computer systems, Mr. Manley had assumed that Anscott would lease any new equipment from IBM in the same manner that it had leased its punched-card equipment in the past. The standard IBM lease contract provided an initial lease period of one year, after which time the lease was automatically renewed. After the first year the contract could be canceled at will by the lessee upon giving 90 days' notice of intention to cancel. Under the lease, IBM also assumed all responsibility for maintenance of the equipment, and for paying the costs of insurance and property taxes.

In June, 1960, Mr. Manley received a letter from Bankers Leasing Corporation which made him wonder if he should consider another method of acquisition. The letter, reproduced in Exhibit 1, implied that it would be much cheaper to lease from Bankers than from IBM, and Mr. Manley decided to investigate the possibility.

In response to Mr. Manley's letter of inquiry, Mr. Alvin Zises, president of Bankers Leasing Corporation, requested that Mr. Manley provide the following additional information:

1. A list of the equipment to be acquired indicating both the purchase price and the annual rental charged by IBM.
2. The annual cost of the maintenance contract for each item of equipment which IBM offered to purchasers of the equipment, and
3. Mr. Manley's estimate of the "economic life" of the equipment.

Mr. Manley had no trouble obtaining the first two pieces of information from the IBM representative. He had somewhat more trouble, however, estimating the utilization period. The entire system that he planned for Anscott would be a collection of several items of equipment, some of it new (such as the computer), some of it which the company had been leasing for only a few months, and some of it (primarily key punch equipment) which the company had been leasing from IBM for several years. Mr. Manley summarized Anscott's equipment requitements into categories by age, as shown on Exhibit 2, and sent a copy of that schedule to Mr. Zises.

In his covering letter, Mr. Manley said that it was his best guess that IBM equipment would have an average life of about nine years. Therefore, he stated, the new equipment ought to last for nine years from the date of installation, the one-year-old equipment ought to be good for eight years, and the older equipment might have an average remaining life of about four years. In part, Mr. Manley based his nine-year estimate on the fact that the IBM trade-in schedule for used equipment (the amount which IBM indicated it would allow the owner of used equipment against the purchase price of new equipment) showed that the equipment would have no value after seven years. Based on his own experience, Mr. Manley thought seven years might be too conservative because the property would have some resale value at the end of seven years, and that a nine-year life was more realistic. The trade-in schedule is shown below:

IBM TRADE-IN SCHEDULE

Age of Equipment (in Months)	Trade-in Value as Per Cent of Original Cost
12	60%
24	48
36	36
48	24
60	15
72	7½
84	1½
Over 84	0

A couple of weeks after sending off the data, Mr. Manley received a letter from Bankers Leasing Corporation forwarding the schedule reproduced in Exhibit 3. In his letter, Mr. Zises made the following points:

1. Great savings would accrue to Anscott if it leased from Bankers. Assuming that all of the equipment were leased for nine years, and taking advantage of the favorable renewal options, total savings would amount to nearly half a million dollars. Even if the equipment were only leased for four, eight, or nine years, according to age, the savings would amount to over $333,000.

2. Because of Anscott's excellent credit standing, Bankers had been able to offer a lease under which the interest cost was only $6\frac{1}{4}\%$ per year. While this rate was substantially higher than the $4\frac{1}{2}\%$ prime rate at the time, Mr. Zises pointed out that compensating balances raised the effective rate, that the money was being provided over a long term, and that Anscott would probably have to pay at least 5% for a loan of similar duration. In addition, by leasing, Anscott avoided all the extra "hidden costs" of debt such as legal fees, investment bankers' fees, and the like.

3. The leasing proposal offered two tax advantages: (1) In effect, Anscott would be amortizing the cost of the equipment over its economic life, and this amortization would be tax deductible. Thus, for the new equipment, Anscott would amortize the full cost over nine years which would be more advantageous than depreciation under which Anscott would probably have to use a ten-year life and provide a 10% scrap value. (2) The monthly lease payments were composed of level amortization of the cost of the equipment plus interest at $6\frac{1}{4}\%$ of the unamortized balance. This meant that lease payments in the early years were higher than the payments in the later years, thus providing larger tax deductions in the early years than would be possible if a "level payment" lease were used. The monthly payments would be due at the beginning of each month.

4. The renewal provisions of the lease were quite favorable to Anscott. After the initial, noncancellable term, Anscott could continue to lease the equipment for an annual cost of one-half of 1 per cent of the cost of the equipment, payable at the rate of one-twenty-fourth of 1 per cent per month.

5. The lease contract would provide desirable flexibility for Anscott by permitting the lessee to dispose of any piece of equipment at any time by requesting Bankers to sell the equipment. In such an event, Anscott would be responsible for making sure that Bankers recovered the unamortized cost of the equipment, but if any excess over the unamortized cost were realized, Bankers would refund the excess to Anscott as an "adjustment of rent."

6. Anscott would receive the full benefit of any residual value of the equipment after the initial term of the lease. Any proceeds from the disposal of the equipment after it was fully amortized would be paid to Anscott as an "adjustment of rent."

Mr. Zises stated that the terms of this offer were firm, but were subject to adjustment in the event that the purchase price of the equipment were to change before execution of the agreement, in which event the terms of the lease would be adjusted pro rata. He also pointed out that the lease would be a "net lease," under which Anscott would be responsible for the payment of property taxes and insurance.

In examining the proposal from Bankers Leasing Corporation, Mr. Manley could think of only three adjustments that needed to be made to the cost comparison. The cost of property taxes and insurance on the equipment, while minor, would probably amount to about 3% of the unamortized cost of the equipment, assuming a straight-line amortization over ten years rather than the sum-of-digits depreciation which the company ordinarily used for income tax purposes. The maintenance costs included in the comparison were only the cost of the IBM service contract, and Mr. Manley knew that, in addition, the owner of a piece of equipment might have to bear the cost of certain replacement parts which would be replaced free if the equipment were leased from IBM. Finally, the cost comparison had ignored the federal excise tax on the equipment. This tax amounted to 10% of the purchase price of the equipment, or 10% of each year's lease payment when the equipment was leased from the manufacturer.[2] The tax applied only to machines and not to "systems" which meant that all of the equipment with model numbers in the 1400 series would not be subject to the tax.

Mr. Manley knew that all of these minor considerations would have little impact on the calculations shown in Exhibit 3, and he was favorably impressed by the potential savings offered by the leasing company. Considering the heavy initial costs of installing the new system, Mr. Manley thought that it was quite likely that Anscott would continue to use the equipment for many years, and he wondered if it would be wise for the company to pay a heavy "insurance premium" to IBM in order to protect itself against obsolescence of the equipment.

Question

What action should Mr. Manley take?

[2] If the equipment were leased from Bankers Leasing Company, the excise tax would be paid by Bankers when the equipment was purchased from IBM. The terms quoted by Bankers in Exhibit 3 would be proportionately higher to permit the recovery of this additional cost.

Exhibit 1

ANSCOTT CORPORATION

LETTER FROM BANKERS LEASING CORPORATION

June 22, 1960

Mr. L. Paul Manley
Controller
Anscott Corporation
43 Broad Street
Baltimore, Maryland

DEAR MR. MANLEY:

We are pleased to inform you that we have just executed leasing agreements on an electronic computer installation with Public Service Electric and Gas Company, New Jersey.

This is one of a number of such data processing and computer installations, manufactured by companies with outstanding reputations, which we, with the sponsorship of The First National Bank of Boston, lease to industry.

You may be interested to know why our leasees made the determination to lease from us rather than from the equipment manufacturer. In one ten-year comparison of our rentals with those of a well-known manufacturer (after reduction of the manufacturer's rentals by the amount charged for maintenance and service), the total difference in rents on an installation having a cost of $1,000,000 was $570,000 in favor of our program.

When a manufacturer of computers charges rent, the components within his rental charges generally include:

1. Amortization of the cost of the equipment over as short a period as possible for quick recovery of the cost by the manufacturer. This period may be as short as 50 months for equipment with a possible life of eight to ten years.
2. A reserve or "insurance premium" for obsolescence. In the ordinary rental program offered by some manufacturers, the reserve for obsolescence is sometimes sufficiently high to more than doubly recover any possible obsolescence charges. As prudent businessmen, some manufacturers strive to achieve a "loss ratio" on obsolescence of less than 50% of the reserve.
3. A reserve for physical maintenance and service.
4. A cost-of-capital charge which, depending upon the manufacturer, may run from over 15% to over 30% per annum (pretax) to enable the manufacturer's shareholders to receive an acceptable return on their investment in ownership of the equipment.
5. After fully recovering the cost of the asset the manufacturer usually may continue the rent at or near the same level.
6. Additional rents are charged for extra-shift operations.

In the leasing program which we offer to lessees of excellent credit, rent has the following components:

1. A lower monthly amortization charge because the asset is amortized over a period which closely corresponds to the economic life. For purposes of computing rent the amortization period may be eight or even ten years.
2. After full amortization, the monthly rent drops to an insignificant amount.
3. A cost of capital which is based not on the manufacturer's pretax equity requirements but on the excellent credit of your company. The cost-of-capital component compares not unfavorably with your total cost of debt financing.

Our lessees, after careful consideration, have determined that the high cost of programming effectively "locks" them into a computer installation for a period of time which may approximate the amortization period of our lease. Some manufacturers concur that programming costs of major installations make it economically unfeasible to change an installation before eight or even ten years. Consequently, our lessees pay no reserve for obsolescence which, in fact, may not occur.

Nevertheless, our lessees are accorded needed flexibility during much of the lease term. If our lessees desire to replace a unit of equipment with a new leased asset, the

Exhibit 1—Continued

lessee incurs only the actual obsolescence cost which may, under some circumstances, be nothing. Upon retirement of a leased asset by our lessee he receives an adjustment in rent. If the asset is retired at a figure less than the net unamortized balance, the lessee pays the deficiency. If the asset is retired during or after the amortization period at a figure more than the net unamortized balance, the lessee receives the excess.

This technique enables our lessee to pay only for the obsolescence cost, if any, actually incurred.

Physical maintenance and service is obtained by our lessees through direct contractual relationship with the manufacturer at published rates. Our lessees inform us that no service problems have occurred as a result of leasing through our program. We pay the manufacturer in full upon acceptance by, and approval of, our lessee. Through the service contract the manufacturer maintains a continuing relationship with his customer.

Upon request we will be pleased to submit a specific proposal which you may compare with your present or planned computer rental costs.

Sincerely,
BANKERS LEASING CORPORATION
ALVIN ZISES
President

AZ:nb

Exhibit 2

ANSCOTT CORPORATION

SUMMARY OF IBM EQUIPMENT COSTS

Number of Units	Type of Machine	Model Number	Purchase Price	Annual Rental	Annual Maintenance Contract if Purchased		
					Years 1–3	Years 4–6	Years 7–9
1	Computer	1401-E4	$144,100.00	$ 38,520	$ 1,536	$ 1,617	$ 1,740
1	Card reader	1402	24,800.00	6,600	588	783	1,065
1	Printer	1403	30,800.00	9,300	2,244	2,496	2,784
1	Extra storage unit	1406	20,100.00	6,900	162	165	195
3	Magnetic tape units	7330	57,000.00	16,200	1,881	2,097	2,313
	Subtotal for system		$276,800.00	$ 77,520	$ 6,411	$ 7,158	$ 8,097
1	High-speed card sorter	084	10,000.00	3,330	396	459	522
1	Card interpreter	548	5,300.00	1,320	195	270	312
	Total new equipment		$292,100.00	$ 82,170	$ 7,002	$ 7,887	$ 8,931
1	High-speed collator	088	$ 15,401.25	4,884	$ 714	$ 1,020	$ 1,320
1	Alphabetic accounting machine	403	23,015.16	7,854	1,154	1,314	1,470
1	Gang punch and summary punch	523	3,066.68	1,095	138	198	255
	Total one-year-old equipment		$ 41,483.09	$ 13,833	$ 2,006	$ 2,532	$ 3,045
1	Portable key punch	010	$ 380.00	$ 132	$ 9	$ 15	$ 18
3	Key punch machines	024	2,713.76	1,488	678	738	798
2	Verifying machines	056	1,200.00	1,200	660	660	660
1	Reproducing machines	514	6,346.07	2,676	744	744	843
	Total older equipment		$ 10,639.83	$ 5,496	$ 2,091	$ 2,157	$ 2,313
	Grand totals		$344,222.92	$101,499	$11,099	$12,576	$14,289

Exhibit 3

ANSCOTT CORPORATION

SUMMARY COMPARISON PREPARED FOR ANSCOTT CORPORATION

COST OF LEASING

IBM VERSUS BANKERS LEASING CORPORATION

SCHEDULE A

Bankers Leasing Corporation	Purchase Price	1	2	3	4	5
9-year rent.....	$292,100.00	$ 49,782.08	$ 47,753.62	$ 45,725.16	$ 43,696.68	$ 41,668.20
9-year maintenance......		7,002.00	7,002.00	7,002.00	7,887.00	7,887.00
8-year rent.....	41,483.09	7,629.59	7,305.51	6,981.42	6,657.31	6,333.23
8-year maintenance......		2,006.00	2,006.00	2,006.00	2,532.00	2,532.00
4-year rent.....	10,639.83	3,248.84	3,082.58	2,916.33	2,749.74	
4-year maintenance......		2,091.00	2,091.00	2,091.00	2,157.00	
Total per year.....	$344,222.92	$ 71,759.51	$ 69,240.71	$ 66,721.91	$ 65,679.73	$ 58,420.43
IBM..........		101,499.00	101,499.00	101,499.00	101,499.00	96,003.00
Net savings....		$ 29,739.49	$ 32,258.29	$ 34,777.09	$ 35,819.27	$ 37,582.57

SCHEDULE B

Bankers Leasing Corporation					
9-year rent.....	$ 49,782.08	$ 47,753.62	$ 45,725.16	$ 43,696.68	$ 41,668.20
8-year rent.....	7,629.59	7,305.51	6,981.42	6,657.31	6,333.23
4-year rent.....	3,248.84	3,082.58	2,916.33	2,749.74	53.20
Maintenance...	11,099.00	11,099.00	11,099.00	12,576.00	12,576.00
Total......	$ 71,759.51	$ 69,240.71	$ 66,721.91	$ 65,679.73	$ 60,630.63
IBM..........	101,499.00	101,499.00	101,499.00	101,499.00	101,499.00
Net savings....	$ 29,739.49	$ 32,258.29	$ 34,777.09	$ 35,819.27	$ 40,868.37

6	7	8	9	10	Total
			Year		
$ 39,639.72	$ 37,611.26	$ 35,582.80	$ 33,554.28		
7,887.00	8,931.00	8,931.00	8,931.00		
6,009.15	5,685.06	5,360.52			
2,532.00	3,045.00	3,045.00			
$ 56,067.87	$ 55,272.32	$ 52,919.32	$ 42,485.28		$ 538,567.08
96,003.00	96,003.00	96,003.00	92,170.00		872,178.00
$ 39,935.13	$ 40,730.68	$ 43,083.68	$ 49,684.72		$ 333,610.92
$ 39,639.72	$ 37,611.26	$ 35,582.80	$ 33,554.28	$ 1,460.50	
6,009.15	5,685.06	5,360.52	207.42	207.42	
53.20	53.20	53.20	53.20	53.20	
12,576.00	14,289.00	14,289.00	14,289.00	14,289.00	
$ 58,278.07	$ 57,638.52	$ 55,285.52	$ 48,103.90	$ 16,010.12	$ 569,348.62
101,499.00	101,499.00	101,499.00	101,499.00	101,499.00	1,014,990.00
$ 43,220.93	$ 43,860.48	$ 46,213.48	$ 53,395.10	$ 85,488.88	$ 445,641.38

SPLASH SOAP CORPORATION

Mr. William Cavanaugh, treasurer of Splash Soap Corporation, was considering how the company should finance the expansion of facilities located in Chicago, Illinois. The vice-president in charge of production had introduced two different proposals for expanding capacity in Chicago at the last monthly meeting of management in December, 1958. However, no decision had been reached until Mr. Cavanaugh could analyze the financial aspects and present his recommendations at the next meeting to be held in January, 1959.

The two proposals introduced by Mr. Badin Farley, production vice-president, called for the construction of a new plant to be completed late in 1960 or for a two-stage expansion program for the present plant. After contacting several financing sources, Mr. Cavanaugh had obtained an offer of a term loan from Morrissey Life Insurance Company for the two-stage expansion to the present plant. He had also obtained an offer from Dillon National Bank for a sale-and-leaseback arrangement in connection with the construction of a new plant. Splash Soap Corporation had used both methods of financing in the past.

Splash Soap Corporation was a medium-sized company engaged in the manufacture and sale of powdered and liquid detergents and cleaning agents for commercial dishwashing and household use. In 1958 sales of commercial dishwashing and household products accounted for about 55% and 35% of total sales, respectively. The remaining 10% of sales came from different types of automatic dispensers of dry and liquid detergents. These dispensers were sold to customers for installation on dishwashing equipment to improve the efficiency of the company's detergents.

In 1958, Splash Soap Corporation conducted manufacturing operations in three plants. The main plant and office building, located in Syracuse, New York, were leased from Morrissey Life Insurance Company under a sale-and-leaseback arrangement. Plants located in Chicago

318

and Los Angeles were owned outright by the company. In addition, the company leased sales offices and space in public warehouses in various cities throughout the United States and Canada.

Mr. Cavanaugh had become acquainted with sale-and-leasebacks in December, 1952, when the company had sold its main plant and office building to Morrissey Life Insurance Company for $275,000 and leased it back for a period of 20 years with options to renew for an additional 15 years. Splash Soap Corporation had sold the facilities in Syracuse at a loss of $25,000 and had used the loss as an offset against excess profits taxes. In addition the company had been able to obtain rent deductions that were more favorable than depreciation allowances. For example, the Syracuse facilities had been constructed in the fall of 1947 at a cost of $280,000 for the building and $55,000 for land. The buildings were being depreciated over 40 years, at $7,000 per year. Under the terms of the sale-and-leaseback, rental payments for the first 20 years were $22,000 per annum.

Other terms of the sale-and-leaseback agreement had included the following:

1. Lease renewable for three periods of five years each at the following rental rates:
    a) $8,250 per year during the first five-year period.
    b) $6,875 per year during the next five-year period.
    c) $5,500 per year during the last five-year period.
2. Tenant shall pay all taxes and assessments.
3. Tenant shall maintain the improvements and every part thereof.
4. Tenant may construct and reconstruct accessory buildings.
5. Tenant to provide fire and extended coverage in amounts for not less than 80% of full insurable value.

In June, 1957, the management of Splash Soap Corporation had decided to open a plant on the West Coast. Mr. Cavanaugh had requested a sale-and-leaseback from Morrissey Life for a new plant scheduled for construction in Los Angeles. He had considered negotiating a temporary construction loan from Dillon National Bank to handle construction costs until the completed plant could be sold to Morrissey Life.

However, Mr. Harvey Zahm, vice-president of Morrissey Life, had expressed a lack of interest in a sale-and-leaseback proposition at that time. He stated that the insurance company had been out of the market for this investment medium since mid-1956. Because of factors peculiar to sale-and-leasebacks, the insurance company insisted on a yield at least one-half of 1 per cent greater than other forms of investment media.

This incremental interest rate had been required by the insurance company to compensate for the risk assumed in making what was essentially a 100% loan on fixed assets. By assuming legal ownership, Morrissey Life would not have the position of a general creditor which would be the case in a term loan. The general counsel of the insurance company had advised Mr. Zahm that in previous court cases, claims amounting only to the equivalent of one year's rental had been allowed in the case of straight bankruptcy, and three years in the case of reorganization.

A second reason for requiring a higher yield was the "nuisance" involved. In past sale-and-leaseback transactions, the insurance company had been asked to provide funds for improvements and renewal in the terms of the lease. As property owners, Morrissey Life felt a moral obligation to assist its tenants whenever possible. This had often involved the cost and nuisance of reconsidering and rewriting long leases and of committing additional funds at times when other investments seemed preferable.

In conjunction with this nuisance factor, Mr. Zahm had pointed out that the insurance company also viewed these periodic renewals and rewritings as postponements of their equity claims on the residual value of the leases. Morrissey Life considered real estate investment as one of two ways by which an insurance company could hedge against inflation; the other being common stocks. Since investments in common stocks were severely limited, insurers often hedged against rising prices by means of real estate ownership. As a result, the insurance company wanted to obtain residual value as soon as possible so that it could realize any capital appreciation that may have taken place.

Mr. Zahm had shown a chart to Mr. Cavanaugh that the insurance company used to compare yields from mortgage loans and yields from new issues of electric power utility bonds with "A" Moody ratings (Exhibit 10). He explained that the company considered a sale-and-leaseback to be comparable to a mortgage loan. Until August, 1956, mortgage loans had sold at a premium ranging between one-half of 1 per cent and 1 per cent above new issues of "A" utility bonds. However, after August the yields had narrowed, and in June, 1957, "A" utility bonds and mortgage loans were both yielding about 5%. Mr. Zahm stated that the insurance company would not consider sale-and-leaseback at that time unless it could obtain a yield of $5\frac{1}{2}\%$ to 6%.

Mr. Cavanaugh considered the interest rate requested by Morrissey Life Insurance Company for a sale-and-leaseback too high. He subsequently had negotiated a 20-year term loan of $300,000 at 5% with

Dillon National Bank for the construction of the Los Angeles plant. The provisions of the loan agreement had been as follows:

1. *Noncallable* prior to July 1, 1962.
2. *Indebtedness:* Up to $200,000 additional term debt permitted if pro forma term debt would not exceed 33% of total capitalization.
3. *Consolidation and merger:* Not permitted without consent.
4. *Sales of assets:* Sale of all or substantially all assets prohibited.
5. *Minimum working capital:*
    a) Initially $800,000 to increase to $1,250,000 as of the date of issue of the additional debt.
    b) Current ratio not to be less than 2:1.
6. *Dividends and stock retirements:* Total amount of all dividends not to exceed $200,000 plus 75% of net income subsequent to June 30, 1957.
7. *Investments:* None permitted except:
    a) Direct obligations to the United States government.
    b) Securities acquired to satisfy debts incurred in the ordinary course of business.

The present Chicago plant, a multistory building, had been built in 1946 at a cost of $140,000. Between 1946 and 1958 the number of products produced in the Chicago plant had increased from 2 to 18. Similarly, tonnage output had increased from 4 million tons to 11 million tons per year. Production operations had changed requiring more complex formulas and methods of mixing and packaging. Moreover, the loading and unloading facilities had become insufficient to handle the present volume of the plant.

Mr. Farley believed that the capacity of present mixing equipment, mixing pit, materials handling system, and packaging equipment would be reached during 1959. The practical tonnage capacity of the plant for optimum operation was 10 million tons. However, Mr. Farley thought that he could turn out close to 12 million tons if hard pressed but cautioned that operations for incremental production above 11 million tons would be less efficient. The marketing department estimated that sales in 1968 would be able to absorb somewhere between 17 and 20 million tons from the Chicago plant.

When the need for expanded capacity in the Chicago plant became evident, Mr. Farley drew up two plans for expansion: Plan A, the construction of a new plant; and Plan B, a two-stage expansion to the present plant (Exhibit 4).

Under Plan A, Mr. Farley proposed abandoning the present plant and constructing a completely new plant with capacity for annual production of 20 million tons. The new plant would be located on a railroad siding and thus would decrease delivery expenses. It would be a one-story structure with air-conditioned offices. The new plant would permit a more straightforward layout and improved operating efficiencies. Mr. Farley considered the cost savings as nebulous and difficult to put on a monetary basis. He guessed that these savings would probably average $30,000 per year before taxes, at an 11-million-ton operating level.

Because of the delays involved in purchasing the land, drawing up final blueprints, and obtaining bids from contractors, construction of the plant could not be started until August, 1959. Mr. Farley did not think the plant could be completed and equipped before December, 1960.

Mr. Farley estimated that the new plant would have about 28,000 square feet of floor space and would involve a total net investment of $450,000. He estimated the land would cost $50,000; buildings, $400,-000; and new equipment, $100,000. Mr. Farley then estimated that $150,000 net after capital gains taxes might be realized from the sale of the present plant. The new plant would be depreciated over 40 years on the basis of the declining balance method if it were owned outright, and the equipment would be depreciated over ten years using the sum-of-years-digits method.

Under Plan B, Mr. Farley had proposed that the expansion of the present plant be undertaken in two steps. The first step would provide an additional 6,000 square feet, an increase of 60%. The additional area would be used for storage space and would free production area currently used for storage. Plant capacity would be increased from 12 million to 15 million tons. Mr. Farley thought the first step could be started by May, 1959, and completed in about eight months. He estimated a cost of $80,000 for the plant expansion and an additional $5,000 for repairing and reinstalling machinery that had been stored on vacant land adjacent to the plant.

The second step, according to Mr. Farley's proposal, would not begin until additional capacity was required. He suggested beginning the second step of expansion in mid-1961 for completion early in 1962. This phase of the program would involve the construction of an additional 10,000 square feet of floor space for processing and packaging. The tonnage capacity would be increased to 18 million tons. Mr. Farley estimated $150,000 for construction and then added $15,000 for increases in construction costs. He also included $100,000 for new equipment, the same equipment that would be purchased for the new building. The total cost of Plan B would approximate $350,000.

Mr. Cavanaugh consulted a tax authority to learn how the depreciation on the plant additions should be handled. The present building was being depreciated on a straight-line basis over a useful life of 40 years. He knew that the 1954 Internal Revenue Code permitted the use of declining balance depreciation for new facilities constructed after January 1, 1954, but he was uncertain as to whether additions to existing facilities would qualify. The tax counsel had ascertained that declining balance depreciation could be applied only to the expenditures for plant improvement or expansion. He did not think that the useful life of the original plant would be extended because of the plant expansion. Therefore, the new plant expenditures of $80,000 and $165,000 could be amortized over the remaining life of the existing plant, or 26 years and 24 years, respectively. The existing structure would have to continue to be depreciated on a straight-line basis. The machinery and equipment currently in use in the Chicago plant were fully depreciated.

After the preliminary discussion in the December, 1958, meeting of management, the president of Splash Soap Corporation had requested Mr. Cavanaugh to prepare his recommendation for financing the expansion and to present it at the January meeting. Mr. Cavanaugh contacted Mr. Zahm at Morrissey Life to see if the insurance company had renewed its interest in sale-and-leasebacks. Mr. Zahm stated that Morrissey Life was not entering into sale-and-leaseback transactions at the time because of uncertainties in the outlook for federal income taxes on life insurance companies. Mr. Zahm stated that Congress was in the process of revising life insurance tax laws and the 1958 tax rate had not been determined yet. Morrissey Life was not considering any sale-and-leasebacks until new legislation had been enacted.

In lieu of a sale-and-leaseback, Mr. Zahm offered Splash Soap Corporation a term loan of $350,000 at $4\frac{1}{2}\%$ with a takedown of $100,-000 in July, 1959, and $250,000 in July, 1961. Splash Soap Corporation would begin annual payments of $32,600 in 1962 that would amortize the loan over 15 years.

Mr. Cavanaugh also called on Dillon National Bank to inquire about a sale-and-leaseback arrangement with a pension fund administered by the bank. Income received by these funds was not subject to federal income tax. Mr. Lyons, a trust officer of Dillon National Bank, expressed interest in the new building. He proposed a lease of 25 years with annual rental payments of $31,930 beginning in 1961. These payments would amortize the $450,000 net investment over the 25-year period at 5%. He also implied that the bank would be willing to include an option whereby Splash Soap Corporation could repurchase the land and building at the end of 25 years. However, no specific repurchase price could be stated in the agreement because of rulings by the Bureau of Internal Revenue. The repurchase price would have to depend upon arm's-length market prices in 1985. A similar leaseback on the existing plant could also be arranged on equivalent terms for a sum not to exceed $200,000.

After reviewing these financing alternatives, Mr. Cavanaugh decided to compute the discounted cash flows under each alternative (assuming the new plant would be leased as compared with term loan financing of expansion of existing facilities) from 1959 through 1985 when the lease on the new building would be terminated and the existing building would be fully depreciated (Exhibit 5). He assumed a tax rate of 52% in all of his calculations. Mr. Cavanaugh computed that the sale-and-leaseback was more expensive up to a discount rate of 50% if he did not include the repurchase cost of the land and building under the sale-and-leaseback or the cost savings of the new plant.

Mr. Cavanaugh wondered whether the sale-and-leaseback might be less expensive if the estimated cost savings were included. However, he had not yet made this appraisal. Mr. Cavanaugh was also uncertain about what cost to use for repurchasing the new plant in his calculations. He decided to use the book value of $107,544 for the plant in 1958 after declining balance depreciation and the current value of the land of $50,000. However, he had become concerned about inflation and wondered if these estimates were valid.

Before making a decision on the two financing alternatives, Mr. Cavanaugh discussed his computations with the controller, Mr. Patrick Stephanowsky. The latter did not agree with the use of book value of the new plant under declining balance method of depreciation. He argued that this method of depreciation was merely a "gimmick" for tax purposes and was not related to the actual depreciation of the plant. Mr. Stephanowsky also believed that the cost of replacing the existing plant should be considered a cost under the term loan if the cost of repurchasing the new plant were included as a cost under the sale-and-leaseback. By 1985 the existing plant will be fully depreciated and probably obsolete.

Secondly, Mr. Stephanowsky questioned whether some imputed cost should be charged to the loan alternative for carrying charges of the land. If the company continued to own the present land and buildings, funds would be tied up. Part of these funds were recouped through depreciation charges on the building but not on the land. On the other hand, through the sale-and-leaseback, the land would be amortized through the tax deductible rental payments. In order to make the two financing alternatives comparable, Mr. Stephanowsky argued that an imputed carrying charge for land should be included under the cost of owning the plant and property.

Finally, Mr. Stephanowsky questioned whether the two alternatives could be compared against each other at all since the sale-and-leaseback involved $100,000 more in net investment. He raised the point that perhaps Mr. Cavanaugh should adjust the cost of the sale-and-leaseback for the additional $100,000.

Mr. Cavanaugh decided to reanalyze his computations before deciding between the two financing alternatives.

Exhibit 1

SPLASH SOAP CORPORATION

COMPARATIVE BALANCE SHEETS AS OF DECEMBER 31, 1957, AND 1958

(Dollar figures in thousands)

ASSETS	1957		1958	
Current assets:				
Cash..............................$307		$342		
Accounts receivable................ 708		791		
Inventories........................ 799		766		
Prepaid expenses................... 48		57		
Total current assets..............		$1,862		$1,956
Property, plant, and equipment:				
Land..............................	$ 66		$ 66	
Building.........................$345		$540		
Less: Allowance for depreciation... 39	306		62	478
Machinery and equipment..........$465		$465		
Less: Allowance for depreciation... 255		323		
	210		142	
		582		686
Investments and other assets..........		66		66
Intangibles.........................		99		92
Total assets...................		$2,609		$2,800

LIABILITIES	1957		1958	
Current liabilities:				
Accounts payable.................$326		$315		
Dividends payable................. 27		29		
Federal and state taxes on income.... 232		214		
Current maturities for long-term debt. 57		31		
Total current liabilities...........	$ 642		$ 589	
Long-term debt......................	216		344	
Preferred stock......................	109		106	
Common and surplus:				
Common.........................$400		$400		
Paid-in surplus.................... 516		516		
Retained earnings................. 726		845		
	1,642		1,761	
Total liabilities.................		$2,609		$2,800

Exhibit 2

SPLASH SOAP CORPORATION

STATEMENT OF INCOME

(Dollar figures in thousands)

	1957		1958	
Net sales..........................		$6,068		$6,545
Cost and expenses:*				
Cost of sales......................	$2,622		$2,797	
Selling and advertising.............	2,334		2,607	
General and administrative.........	561		581	
Employees' retirement..............	47		47	
Other...........................	35		39	
		5,599		6,071
Net income before taxes.............		$ 469		$ 474
Federal taxes on income.............		247		250
Net earnings......................		$ 222		$ 224

* Including provisions for depreciation and amortization of $91,286—1958; $76,265—1957.

Exhibit 3

SPLASH SOAP CORPORATION

SUMMARY DATA

(Dollar figures in thousands)

Year	Net Sales	Earnings before Income Taxes	Federal Income Taxes	Net Earnings	Earnings Reinvested in the Business	Current Assets	Current Liabilities	Working Capital
1949	$1,844	$ 76	$ 32	$ 44	$ 22	$ 338	$164	$ 174
1950	2,203	160	66	94	71	416	224	192
1951	2,697	158	72	86	61	572	320	252
1952	3,100	164	84	80	52	756	386	370
1953	3,490	150	65	85	58	817	441	376
1954	3,887	219	117	102	68	883	412	471
1955	4,527	351	189	162	119	1,320	604	716
1956	5,291	397	207	190	140	1,438	715	723
1957	6,068	469	247	222	142	1,862	642	1,220
1958	6,545	474	250	224	119	1,956	589	1,367

Exhibit 4

SPLASH SOAP CORPORATION

EXPANSION PROPOSALS SUBMITTED BY VICE-PRESIDENT OF PRODUCTION

(Dollar figures in thousands)

	Plan A (New Plant)	Plan B (Expansion of Present Plant) Step No. 1	Plan B (Expansion of Present Plant) Step No. 2
Begin program	August, 1959	May, 1959	May, 1961
Finish program	December, 1960	December, 1959	January, 1962
Land	$ 50		
Building	400*	$80†	$150‡
Equipment: Repairs		5	
New§	100	...	100
Expected cost	$550	$85	$250
Plus 10% for increases in construction costs between 1959–1961	....	...	15
	$550	$85	$265
Less: Sale of present plant‖	150		
	$400		$350

* Interest charges for a construction loan were estimated at $5,000 in 1959 and $15,000 in 1960.
† To be depreciated over 26 years on the declining balance method (Exhibit 8).
‡ To be depreciated over 24 years on the declining balance method (Exhibit 8).
§ To be depreciated over ten years on the sum-of-years-digits method (Exhibit 9).
‖ Net after capital gains taxes.

Exhibit 5

SPLASH SOAP CORPORATION

NET CASH FLOW COMPARISON BETWEEN SALE-AND-LEASEBACK
AND TERM LOAN

(For results of discounted cash flow, see Exhibit 6)

Year	Sale-and-Leaseback (Note A)	Term Loan (Note B)	Difference
1959	$ 2,400	$ 3,480	$ (1,080)
1960	7,200	(1,039)	8,239
1961	5,872	87	5,785
1962	6,817	3,262	3,555
1963	7,763	5,407	2,356
1964	8,708	7,504	1,204
1965	9,654	9,559	95
1966	10,599	11,578	(979)
1967	11,544	13,566	(2,022)
1968	12,495	15,529	(3,034)
1969	13,436	17,471	(4,035)
1970	14,381	19,396	(5,015)
1971	15,326	21,310	(5,984)
1972	15,326	23,216	(7,890)
1973	15,326	24,171	(8,845)
1974	15,326	25,039	(9,713)
1975	15,326	25,707	(10,381)
1976	15,326	26,295	(10,969)
1977	15,326	(5,469)	20,795
1978	15,326	(5,469)	20,795
1979–1985*	15,326	(5,469)	20,795
Total for 27 years	$340,759	$202,317	$138,442

* Each year.

Note A: Includes interest payments of $5,000 in 1959 and $15,000 in 1960; lease payments of $31,930 per year between 1961–1985; and machinery depreciation (Exhibit 9) between 1961–1970.

Note B: Includes machinery repairs of $5,000 in 1959; interest payments (Exhibit 7); loan repayments of $32,600 per year between 1962–1976; building depreciation (Exhibit 8); and machinery depreciation (Exhibit 9) between 1962–1971.

Exhibit 6

SPLASH SOAP CORPORATION

RESULTS OF DISCOUNTING NET CASH FLOWS SHOWN IN
EXHIBIT 5

Per Cent	Sale-and-Leaseback	Term Loan	Difference
2	$249,663	$164,450	$85,213
4	189,086	133,957	55,129
6	146,019	109,405	36,614
8	115,314	89,824	25,490
10	92,972	74,220	18,752
12	76,408	61,696	14,712
15	59,158	47,366	11,792
20	40,617	31,577	9,040
25	30,058	21,979	8,079
30	23,424	15,961	7,463
50	11,678	6,229	5,449

Exhibit 7

SPLASH SOAP CORPORATION

AMORTIZATION SCHEDULE FOR 4½% TERM LOAN FROM MORRISSEY
LIFE INSURANCE COMPANY

(Repayable in equal annual installments of $32,600 between
1962–1976)

Year	Principal at End of Year	Annual Payments Principal	Interest
1959	$100,000	. . . .	$ 2,250
1960	100,000	. . . .	4,500
1961	350,000	. . . .	10,125
1962	333,150	$16,850	15,750
1963	315,542	17,608	14,992
1964	297,141	18,401	14,199
1965	277,912	19,229	13,371
1966	257,818	20,094	12,506
1967	236,820	20,998	11,602
1968	214,877	21,943	10,657
1969	191,946	22,931	9,669
1970	167,984	23,962	8,638
1971	142,943	25,041	7,559
1972	116,775	26,168	6,432
1973	89,430	27,345	5,255
1974	60,854	28,576	4,024
1975	30,992	29,862	2,738
1976	. . . .	30,992	1,608

Exhibit 8

SPLASH SOAP CORPORATION

INCREMENTAL DEPRECIATION SCHEDULE FOR PLANT FACILITIES

Year	Present Building	Existing Facilities Expansion Step No. 1*	Existing Facilities Expansion Step No. 2†	Total	New Facilities
1960	‡	$6,152	....	$ 6,152	$20,000
1961	$3,500	5,679	....	9,179	19,000
1962	3,500	5,242	$13,745	22,487	18,050
1963	3,500	4,839	12,600	20,939	17,148
1964	3,500	4,467	11,550	19,517	16,290
1965	3,500	4,123	10,588	18,211	15,476
1966	3,500	3,806	9,706	17,012	14,702
1967	3,500	3,514	8,897	15,911	13,967
1968	3,500	3,243	8,156	14,899	13,268
1969	3,500	2,994	7,477	13,971	12,605
1970	3,500	2,764	6,854	13,118	11,975
1971	3,500	2,551	6,283	12,334	11,376
1972	3,500	2,355	5,760	11,615	10,807
1973	3,500	2,175§	5,280	10,955	10,267
1974	3,500	2,175	4,842§	10,517	9,753
1975–1985‖	3,500	2,175	4,842	10,517	**

* Declining balance with a useful life of 26 years on a cost of $80,000.
† Declining balance with a useful life of 24 years on a cost of $165,000.
‡ No depreciation charge in 1960 because the present building would be owned under both expansion plans.
§ The company expected to charge to straight-line depreciation when charges under the declining balance method fell below the straight-line charge. For example, in Step No. 1, the straight-line charge in 1973 would be $2,175 (book value of $28,271 at the end of 1972 divided by remaining life of 13 years), which is greater than the $2,174 ($28,271 × declining balance rate of 7.69%).
‖ Each year.
** 1975 .... $9,266
　　1976 8,802
　　1977 8,362
　　1978 7,944
　　1979 7,547
　　1980 fwd 7,170

Exhibit 9

SPLASH SOAP CORPORATION

DEPRECIATION SCHEDULE FOR EQUIPMENT

(Sum-of-years'-digits with useful life of ten years
on cost of $100,000)

Year	Depreciation
1	$18,182
2	16,364
3	14,545
4	12,727
5	10,909
6	9,091
7	7,273
8	5,455
9	3,636
10	1,818

Exhibit 10

SPLASH SOAP CORPORATION

COMPARATIVE YIELDS, 1953–1957

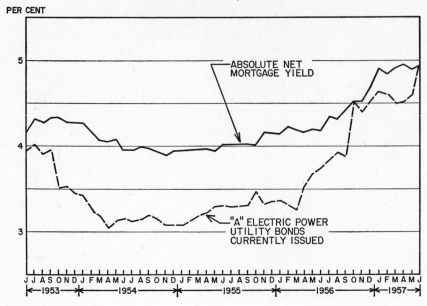

FISCHER PHARMACEUTICAL
COMPANY

In January, 1955, Mr. Patrick O'Conner, treasurer of the Fischer Pharmaceutical Company, decided to issue $30 million in common stock to provide funds for meeting a term-loan balloon maturity payable in June, 1955, and for expanding the company's product line. When Mr. O'Conner discussed the proposed issue with an underwriting firm, the underwriter pointed out that successful issuance of common stock depended on future stock market developments. The underwriter argued that the stock market was in a state of flux and might be subject to radical downward pressures. In view of this Mr. O'Conner decided to consider a privately placed issue of debentures as an alternative method of raising the required funds. Fischer's December 31, 1954, balance sheet and selected income statement information for the years 1948–1954 are shown in Exhibits 1 and 2.

Fischer Pharmaceutical Company was one of the largest companies engaged in the development, manufacture, and distribution of quality chemicals, which it sold chiefly for medicinal, nutritional, industrial, and laboratory purposes. Approximately 25% of the company's sales were made directly to pharmaceutical houses, food processors, and other industrial users. The remainder of its sales, including prescription chemicals and ethical drugs for medicinal and household use, were made directly to wholesale and retail distributors. The ethical drug industry was a highly competitive and constantly changing field in sales of existing products as well as research for new and improved products.

The discovery of new wonder drugs beginning in the late 1930's, together with the large requirement for drugs resulting from World War II and later the Korean conflict, encouraged a rapid expansion of production facilities in the ethical drug industry. In late 1950 and 1951, distributors, fearing a wartime drug shortage, had heavily stocked their inventories. Unaware of this false layer of demand, the industry continued expanding its productive capacity. Suddenly, in late 1951, a condition of general oversupply became evident, and ethical drug manufacturers undertook drastic competitive action. Prices on all major products were cut substantially, some as much as 40%, and profit margins were reduced to postwar lows. After three years of depressed earnings there were some indications in early 1955 that profit margins were stronger and that demand was increasing.

Fischer's dollar sales volume had increased fivefold from 1941 to 1950. This rapid expansion had been financed primarily through equity sources. During this period, $20 million or nearly 50% of earnings after taxes was retained in the business, and three stock issues were successfully floated: an $8 million common stock issue in 1942; a $9 million issue of $3.50 cumulative preferred stock in 1944; and a $10 million issue of $4 cumulative convertible preferred stock in early 1947. Nine months after the issuance of the convertible preferred stock, the market price of the common had risen to a level where the company was able to call the issue and successfully force conversion.

In June, 1950, Fischer negotiated a five-year $20 million term loan with the Broad Street National Bank of New York. The loan, carrying a 3% interest rate, was repayable in semiannual installments of $1 million with a balloon maturity of $11 million due in June, 1955. Under the provisions of the term loan, the company, without the prior written consent of the bank, could not declare or pay any dividend on its outstanding stock or purchase or redeem any shares of its outstanding stock if these expenditures amounted in the aggregate to more than net additions to earned surplus accruing from net earnings after December 31, 1949, plus $3 million.

In October, 1951, Fischer successfully sold a 200,000 share issue of $4 cumulative convertible preferred stock at $100 per share. It was convertible into common stock in the ratio of four shares of common for each share of preferred and was callable at $106 per share. At the time of the offering, Mr. O'Conner believed the market value of the common stock would appreciate sufficiently within a two-year period to enable the company to force conversion. However, with adverse developments affecting the ethical drug industry's profits, the market price of Fischer's common fell below the point where conversion could be forced. (Market prices from 1948–1954 for Fischer convertible preferred and common stock are shown in Exhibit 3.)

The company's inability to force the convertible stock conversion was a matter of serious concern to Mr. O'Conner. He believed that sophisticated investors would regard the issue as unsuccessful and would be less receptive to future stock offerings made by the company. This, in turn, put pressure on the company to make certain that its next public offering would be favorably accepted. The "frozen" convertible preferred stock issue, in Mr. O'Conner's opinion, eliminated a preferred issue as an alternative method of financing new capital requirements because the company's proportion of preferred capital was substantially larger than other companies in its industry, as shown below:

Capital Structure	Fischer December 31, 1954	Average of Nine Other Leading Drug Companies December 31, 1953
Debt	11%	2%
Preferred stock	28	10
Common stock and earned surplus	61	88
	100%	100%

Because the company had no intention of ever passing a preferred dividend payment, Mr. O'Conner regarded preferred stock as a form of subordinated debt. From this standpoint, he considered the company's debt ratio too high and hoped it would be reduced as the term loan was repaid. He believed that the "top should be kept open" for emergency use, and that the company's financial position could not bear more debt without a substantial increase in equity.

Thus, Mr. O'Conner had made strenuous efforts to "keep the bottom open" for favorable issuance of common stock. Despite the fact that earnings had fallen off sharply after 1951, the dividend rate was maintained at $0.60 per share in order to lend maximum support to the common stock's market price. However, depreciation and the small amount of retained earnings did not cover the necessary capital replacement costs and the maturities of the term loan. As a result, the company's cash balance was reduced to a minimum level of $10 million by December 31, 1954.

In looking to the future, Mr. O'Conner foresaw the need for additional cash by June, 1955. With lifesaving drugs pouring out of laboratories in bewildering numbers, old "new wonder drugs" rapidly became obsolete. In order to hedge against possible declines in demand for any of its major specialty drug products, Fischer had decided to begin a $19 million expansion program in the summer of 1955 aimed at widening the company's product line of consumer drugs. The final maturity of the term loan, $11 million, was also to be repaid in June, thus bringing the company's total fund requirements to $30 million.

In Fischer's laboratories, several promising new antibiotics were nearing the final stage of development. Although it was not expected that commercial production could be begun until early 1956, an additional $15 million would be required to purchase processing equipment. When these products were developed, it would be necessary to move rapidly in order to establish a market before competitors could develop substitutes. Consequently, Mr. O'Conner was expected to have outside sources of capital readily available for this purpose. Mr. O'Conner had not projected capital requirements beyond early 1956 but was certain that additional external financings would be required for future expansion programs.

Mr. O'Conner believed a new common stock issue would be the most desirable method of raising the required $30 million but, as previously indicated, he decided in January, 1955, to investigate other possible alternatives. After discussing Fischer's fund requirements with several banks and insurance companies, Mr. O'Conner concluded that only a privately placed debenture issue merited further consideration. The Municipal Life Insurance Company expressed a willingness to accept a $30 million, 15-year debenture issue at 4% interest. The debentures would carry an annual sinking fund provision of $2 million. The first sinking fund payment would not be scheduled until two years after the loan agreement was completed thus leaving a $4 million balloon maturity at the end of 15 years. Approximately one month's time would be required to complete negotiations. Although restrictions were not discussed in detail, Mr. O'Conner gathered the impression that the insurance company would insist on a provision limiting dividend payments and stock retirements to future net earnings after providing for sinking fund requirements. He had also discussed the possibility of a smaller 15-year loan but found that the insurance company would require the same general sinking fund repayment schedules and restrictions. Mr. O'Conner had rejected this alternative because he believed the sinking fund requirement would prove burdensome during a period of expansion.

In February, 1955, when he discussed a $30 million common stock issue with a large underwriting firm in New York, Mr. O'Conner learned that an issue of this size would require a substantial discount from market price in order to insure acceptance. Although Fischer's common stock was selling at $19 a share at the time, the underwriter doubted if the company would net more than $15 per share after all expenses even though the company's stock was widely held and well known. On this basis, approximately 2 million shares would have to be issued. The underwriters indicated that the arrangements for issuing common stock, including registering with the SEC, etc., would take about three months. During this period, the final issuing price would be subject to modifications necessitated by changes in stock market conditions affecting the market price of Fischer's stock. The underwriter pointed out that after a strong advance in November and December, 1954, the stock market had taken an erratic course. Opinion of market experts was sharply divided between those who anticipated a sharp downward readjustment and those who expected a continued upward trend after a short period of instability. In any event, Fischer common appeared to be relatively vulnerable to a decline, if it came, since the stock was "priced high in relation to its current earnings." (Weekly Standard and Poor's Industrial Averages from November 1, 1954, to March 18, 1955, are shown in Exhibit 4.)

Although the market price of Fischer's common had been relatively stable since early February, 1955, trading in a range between $18\frac{1}{2}$–$19\frac{1}{2}$, Mr. O'Conner believed there was a substantial degree of uncertainty involved in issuing stock. Consequently he decided, on March 18, 1955, to review other considerations relative to a new common stock issue. Since he expected to maintain the common stock dividend at $0.60 per share, an additional cash drain of $1.2 million would be imposed on the company. This represented a 4% cost after taxes on the money received or approximately 8% before taxes based on a 50% tax rate. Since the new funds were not being used to expand the company's earning power, the new stock issue would be a pure dilution of stockholder's earnings per share, and this in turn might adversely affect future opportunities for common stock marketings. A further complication was the existence of the unconverted preferred stock. This stock contained the provision that in the event of a new issue of stock the conversion ratio had to be adjusted upward so as not to dilute the preferred stockholders' rights to acquire common. Mr. O'Conner felt that the possibility of conversion might adversely affect the market price of the common during the period of the offering. Finally, Mr. O'Conner believed that Fischer's current market price was temporarily depressed by the recent unfavorable developments in the pharmaceutical industry. If earnings recovered as expected, it might be possible to issue common stock at some future date on more favorable terms.

On the basis of this analysis, Mr. O'Conner thought it would be desirable to continue active consideration of a private issue of debentures to the Municipal Life Insurance Company. If he decided to issue common stock, he thought it would be important to make the decision within a week's time, so the issue could be marketed before the end of June, 1955. He planned to defer consideration of other factors of a common stock issuance, including whether rights would be used, until a later stage of the arrangements.

Mr. O'Conner estimated that profits before taxes would approximate $15 million in 1955 and expected this to increase an average of $1 million per year in the future. Future taxes were estimated at 50% of profits. Depreciation would contribute about $4 million to available cash, but necessary capital replacements would absorb about $2.5 million of these funds. Preferred dividend requirements were $1,115,000 per year, and there were no sinking funds on the outstanding preferred issues. Mr. O'Conner had projected a statement of source and application of funds (see Exhibit 5) through June, 1957, based on the assumption that 2 million shares of common stock would be sold in June, 1955. After modifying this projection to reflect the $300,000 quarterly interest payments on the debentures, and the $2 million annual sinking fund, payable beginning June, 1957, Mr. O'Conner planned to compare the effects of the two alternative methods of financing the required $30 million on future financial needs.

Exhibit 1

FISCHER PHARMACEUTICAL COMPANY

BALANCE SHEET, DECEMBER 31, 1954

(Dollar figures in millions)

ASSETS		LIABILITIES	
Cash	$ 10.7	Accounts payable	$ 5.2
Accounts receivable	10.3	Accruals	2.0
Inventory	32.9	Taxes payable	9.3
Total current assets	$ 53.9	Total current liabilities	$ 16.5
Fixed assets, net	59.0	Term loan (due June, 1955)	11.0
Investment in subsidiaries	4.6	$3.50 cumulative preferred ($100 par)	9.0
Deferred charges	1.5	$4.00 convertible preferred ($100 par)	20.0
Total assets	$119.0	Common stock ($5 par)	36.5
		Earned surplus	26.0
		Total liabilities and net worth	$119.0

Exhibit 2

FISCHER PHARMACEUTICAL COMPANY

SELECTED INCOME STATEMENT INFORMATION, 1948–1954

(Dollar figures in thousands)

Year	Net Sales	Gross Operating Profits	Interest	Net Profit before Tax	Provision for Tax	Net Income
1948	$51,390	$19,590	nil	$ 9,904	$ 3,749	$6,155
1949	51,886	18,674	nil	8,452	3,319	5,133
1950	71,177	28,174	$300	17,226	8,735*	8,491
1951	90,519	41,588	540	28,189	18,768*	9,421
1952	78,898	30,343	480	14,386	8,015*	6,371
1953	82,515	31,219	420	12,624	6,983	5,641
1954	71,551	29,570	360	13,792	7,202	6,590

Year	Preferred Dividends	Income Applicable to Common Stock	Common Shares Outstanding	Earnings per Share	Dividends per Share
1948	$ 315	$5,840	7,300,000	$0.80	$0.40
1949	315	4,818	7,300,000	0.66	0.40
1950	315	8,176	7,300,000	1.12	0.40
1951	515	8,906	7,300,000	1.22	0.60
1952	1,115	5,256	7,300,000	0.72	0.60
1953	1,115	4,526	7,300,000	0.62	0.60
1954	1,115	5,475	7,300,000	0.75	0.60

* Includes excess profits tax.

Exhibit 3

FISCHER PHARMACEUTICAL COMPANY

COMPARATIVE NEW YORK STOCK EXCHANGE MARKET PRICES, 1948–MARCH 18, 1955

Year	Fischer Common Stock		Yield on Common Stock: Range	Price-Earnings Ratio: Range	Fischer $4 Convertible Preferred	
	High	*Low*			*High*	*Low*
1948	$ 7⅞	$ 5⅝	5.2%–7.2%	9.8– 7.0		
1949	10⅞	6¾	3.7 –5.9	16.5–10.2		
1950	16½	10⅛	2.4 –4.0	14.7– 9.0		
1951	29⅛	15	2.0 –4.0	24.5–12.3	122½–113	
1952	26¼	16⅞	2.3 –3.6	36.5–23.4	121 –104	
1953	19⅞	13½	3.0 –4.4	32.1–21.8	104½–101	
1954	17¼	12½	3.5 –4.8	23.0–16.7	109 –102¾	
Through March 18, 1955	19¾	16½			109 –105¾	
Closing price March 18, 1955	19⅜				108½	

Exhibit 4

FISCHER PHARMACEUTICAL COMPANY

STANDARD AND POOR'S INDUSTRIAL AVERAGES (50 STOCKS) BY WEEKS,
NOVEMBER 1, 1954–MARCH 18, 1955

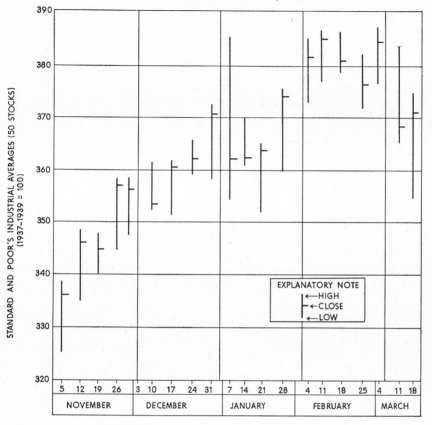

WEEK ENDING...

Source: Standard and Poor's Statistical Survey.

Exhibit 5

FISCHER PHARMACEUTICAL COMPANY

PROJECTED SOURCE AND APPLICATION OF FUNDS, BY SIX-MONTH PERIODS
JANUARY, 1955–JUNE, 1957

(Dollar figures in thousands)

	January–June *1955*	*July–December* *1955*	*January–June* *1956*	*July–December* *1956*	*January–June* *1957*
Projected profits before taxes...	$ 7,500	$ 7,500	$ 8,000	$ 8,000	$ 8,500
Estimated taxes..............	3,750	3,750	4,000	4,000	4,250
Sources:					
Profit after taxes...........	$ 3,750	$ 3,750	$ 4,000	$ 4,000	$ 4,250
Depreciation, amortization, etc.................	2,000	2,000	2,000	2,000	2,000
Outside financing...........	30,000	......	15,000	......	......
Total sources..........	$35,750	$ 5,750	$21,000	$ 6,000	$ 6,250
Applications:					
Preferred dividends.........	$ 557	$ 558	$ 557	$ 558	$ 557
Common dividends.........	2,190	2,790	2,790	2,790	2,790
Maturity term loan.........	11,000	......	......	......	......
Capital expansion program...	......	19,000	15,000	*	*
Capital replacements........	1,250	1,250	1,250	1,250	1,250
Total applications......	$14,997	$23,598	$19,597	$ 4,598	$ 4,597
Opening cash balance.........	$10,700	$31,453	$13,605	$15,008	$16,410
Plus sources.................	35,750	5,750	21,000	6,000	6,250
	$46,450	$37,203	$34,605	$21,008	$22,660
Less applications.............	14,997	23,598	19,597	4,598	4,597
Closing cash balance..........	$31,453	$13,605	$15,008	$16,410	$18,063

* Not projected after June, 1956.

Section VI

CAPITAL RATIONING

MCCARTHY'S BOWL INN

In August, 1955, Mr. Justin McCarthy was trying to decide whether or not he should make an additional investment in his new bowling alley venture, McCarthy's Bowl Inn. Mr. McCarthy was a partner in a law firm located in Boston, Massachusetts. Having some personal funds available for investment, Mr. McCarthy had decided to open a new business and to operate it in his spare time. After some investigation, he decided that an amusement business, which could take advantage of the increased amount of leisure time being enjoyed by the population, would find a ready market. He finally selected ten-pin bowling as a suitable amusement. Ten-pin bowling was more popular in the Midwest and western parts of the United States, but Mr. McCarthy felt that it was likely to spread into New England, and that a ten-pin bowling alley in the right location in the Boston area would be successful.

During 1954, Mr. McCarthy had spent a considerable amount of his leisure time searching for a suitable location for his first bowling alley. He ultimately selected and purchased two sites, one located on Route 9, west of Boston, and the other on Route 1 near the junction of Route 128. In each case, the lot that he purchased was in a rapidly developing commercial area and had some frontage on the busy highway. The Route 9 location cost $30,000; the Route 1 location cost $25,000.

Mr. McCarthy decided to exploit the Route 9 location first because he thought it offered a better potential for immediate success. In July, 1955, Mr. McCarthy completed a complicated financial transaction with Mr. Anderson, a real estate developer and general construction contractor. Mr. Anderson purchased the Route 9 location from Mr. McCarthy for $30,000 and agreed to erect on the site a building suitable for a 16-lane bowling alley. Mr. McCarthy obtained a 15-year lease on the building at a monthly rental of $1,400, with an option to renew for an additional ten years at a reduced rental. Mr. Anderson was

345

responsible for paying all taxes, insurance, and maintaining the building. The lease provided that the building was to be air-conditioned, with the initial equipment and the maintenance of it to be the responsibility of Mr. Anderson. Mr. McCarthy knew that bowling was a seasonal sport, being more popular in the winter, but he hoped that providing an air-conditioned facility would reduce the seasonality of his business.

Mr. McCarthy had had no previous experience in the bowling alley business, but he had attempted to estimate what his operating expenses would be. He planned to hire a full-time manager because he would be able to devote only general supervision to the operation of the business. He estimated the manager's salary at about $6,000 per year. He also knew that he would need to hire two additional persons: a cashier-clerk at $4,000 per year and a janitor and utility man for about $3,600 a year. He estimated his heating and electricity bill at approximately $4,000 a year, to cover the costs of lights, operation of the air-conditioning equipment, and heating of the building during the winter. Supplies and maintenance were difficult costs to estimate, particularly the latter because when the alleys were new they would require a minimum amount of maintenance, but as they aged, maintenance costs would no doubt rise. He estimated an average annual expenditure of $8,000 for these expenses. Payroll taxes and workmen's compensation insurance would amount to approximately 5% of his labor costs. Income taxes would be about 40% of net profits.

In late July, 1955, Mr. McCarthy contracted with a firm in Chicago, Illinois, for the installation of 16 bowling alleys. The cost of these alleys and accessory equipment was just under $4,000 each, a total of $60,000. The Chicago firm told Mr. McCarthy he could expect a life from the hardwood alleys of about 15 years. Mr. McCarthy made a down payment of $30,000, and the supplier permitted him to pay off the balance over five years with equal payments (interest and principal) of $625 each month.

Mr. McCarthy planned to permit an outside operator to establish and run the concessions in his first Bowl Inn. These concessions, which would rent bowling shoes and lockers as well as offering a full line of refreshments, were expected to provide Mr. McCarthy with a net income of $10,000 per year.

Thus, by August, 1955, Mr. McCarthy's plans for the Route 9 Bowl Inn were complete except for the decision as to the method to be used to reset pins. Mr. McCarthy was trying to decide whether to use pinboys or whether he should buy or lease pinsetting machines.

Pinboys

Mr. McCarthy knew that the initial cost would be low if the decision were made to use pinboys. He was afraid, however, that there was a chance that the presence of pinboys might have an adverse effect on the type of customers he hoped to attract. He expected that a large part of his business would come from children, families, and mixed bowling leagues. He had noticed that pinboys working at other alleys sometimes behaved in a manner which might not make the best impression on this type of customer. In any case, he knew that careful supervision would be necessary.

The only additional investment required if pinboys were employed would be about $25 per alley for pinsetting guides. The going rate in the area for setting pins was 12 cents a string; payroll taxes and other fringe benefits would add about 8%. Five boys were usually needed to operate four alleys; a total of 20 would be required for the proposed 16 alleys. These employees would have to be drawn from the 16- to 18-year age group since the minimum legal age was 16 and boys over 18 could normally find higher paying jobs.

Pinsetting Machines

Two makes of pinsetting machines were available: "Speedy" pinsetters, made by the Griswold Machine Corporation of Everett, Massachusetts; and "Reliable" pinsetters, made by Old Reliable Machine Tool Corporation of Akron, Ohio. Both machines could be either bought or leased.

Both machines had a list price of $3,600 per machine, and 16 machines would be required. Freight and installation charges on the Reliable machines were paid by the manufacturer, but the customer paid for these charges on the Speedy machines. Griswold Corporation charged $125 per machine for installation and estimated that the freight cost to Mr. McCarthy would be $10 per alley. The parts of Reliable machines were guaranteed for one year; Speedy's warranty covered only 90 days. If the machines were purchased for cash upon completion of installation, both manufacturers offered a 20% discount off the list price; the net cash price was $2,880.

Financing could be arranged by both companies. Reliable agreed to finance 75% of the net cash price over 48 months, and Speedy would finance 80% over 36 months. Both firms charged interest of 6% per year on the total original amount of the loan, based on net cash price. Thus, if 16 machines were purchased from Speedy, the total

cash price would be $46,080. If the purchase was financed, Mr.
McCarthy would make a down payment of $9,216, and in each of the
three following years he would pay $12,288 on the principal (one-
third of 46,080 — $9,216) plus $2,212 in interest (6% of $36,864).
The installment payments of $1,208.33 would be paid each month for
36 months.

Speedy and Reliable machines could be leased under the following
conditions: The rent on the Speedy machine was $720 a year for four
years, and would probably be $420 thereafter. An initial lease of four
years would be required, followed by four-year leases at the option of
the lessee. The uncertainty of the rental fee after the initial lease period was due to the fact that very few machines had been in operation
for four years, and fees for subsequent lease periods would be subject
to negotiation. Freight and installation costs on the Speedy machine
would be paid by the lessee; insurance on the machine would be paid
by the manufacturer.

The rental fee on Reliable machines was 10 cents a string, with a
minimum fee of $40 a month on an initial lease for four years. Sub-
sequent four-year leases could probably be negotiated at 5 cents a
string and $40 a month minimum. The manufacturer of the Reliable
machines paid the freight, installation, and insurance costs. The manufacturers of both Speedy and Reliable pinsetters employed servicemen
to do major repair work on the machines; most alleys, however, did
their own minor repair work and maintenance. If the machines were
purchased, Mr. McCarthy expected that, after the initial warranty period, maintenance services purchased from the manufacturer might
cost an average of $50 per year per machine. These services would be
provided at no cost by the manufacturer if the machines were leased.

The lease arrangements for the Speedy machines gave the lessee
an option to buy the machine at three different points during the four-
year lease. When the machine was six months old, it could be purchased with 80% of the total past rental payments applied to the
original list price. At 24 months, 60% of the past rents could be applied to the purchase price; at 48 months, 40% of the past rents could
be applied.

There was also included in the Speedy lease an option to substitute
a seven-year lease at $540 a year. This option could be exercised only
after 16 months of the original lease, and would thereby extend the
total lease period to eight years, four months. If this option were
elected, the purchase option would no longer apply unless the $15 a

month difference were paid for all the months in which the reduced rent had been paid. If the machines were purchased, they could be depreciated for tax purposes over an eight-year life, and Mr. McCarthy planned to use the double-declining balance method. Lease payments were deductible for tax purposes in the year in which paid.

Volume of Business

One of the important considerations, in Mr. McCarthy's opinion, in deciding between pinboys and pinsetting machines, concerned the expected volume of business that the new Bowl Inn might achieve. In his initial planning, Mr. McCarthy had tried to estimate the volume of business under the assumption that he would use pinboys. He planned that the alleys would be open daily from 2 P.M. to 11 P.M., although he knew that the evening hours were much more popular for bowling. Initially he had expected to charge 25 cents a string before 5 P.M., and 35 cents from 5 P.M. until 11 P.M. Mr. McCarthy thought that with an alley in constant use, a pinboy would set an average of six strings an hour. He expected to obtain 100% utilization during the hours of 7 to 10 P.M.; about 60% utilization during the hours of 5 to 7 P.M., and 10 to 11 P.M.; and perhaps a 40% utilization during the afternoon hours. The Bowl Inn would be open every day of the year.

The capacity of pinsetting machines was about eight strings per hour, and was one of the primary advantages of the machines over the pinboys. If he acquired the machines, Mr. McCarthy was uncertain as to how he should exploit this advantage. He knew that most bowlers, and in particular, league bowlers, like the greater speed of bowling with the machines and might be expected to pay a premium for this advantage. Thus, he felt that if he offered machines, he might be able to charge a price of a nickel a string more than if he used pinboys, without suffering a decline in his expected volume. On the other hand, if he kept his prices at 25 and 35 cents, which were the going rates in the area for manually set pins, Mr. McCarthy felt that he might achieve a greater volume with the machines, particularly in the evening hours, because of the greater capacity of the alleys. He was dubious that afternoon bowlers would pay any premium for the use of machines.

Some Additional Factors

There were some additional factors which Mr. McCarthy had to consider. Each machine would require electrical power extensions costing about $150 per alley. If he bought the machines, his annual property insurance costs would rise $14 per alley. He would have to hire a maintenance man for around $75 a week whether he bought or rented the machines.

Electrical power costs were expected to be relatively insignificant. Each machine had six fractional horsepower motors: a one-third and one-sixth horsepower motor ran continuously; the other four, which amounted to one horsepower (about 1,000 watts), ran 11 seconds during each cycle; about 12 cycles were required, on the average, to process a string. The electrical power would cost $0.01 per kilowatt-hour.

Mr. McCarthy examined both makes of machines in operation and came to the conclusion that there was little difference in their reliability or speed. The Speedy machine was perhaps slightly less noisy, but on the whole each did the job satisfactorily. In addition, there seemed to be no reason why one machine would last longer than another, although just how long they would last was difficult to determine. They would surely last for five years, and probably for ten. All machines could be easily modified as a part of normal maintenance activities, the manufacturers said, to keep abreast of design improvements. If this were done, the machines would almost certainly last for ten years. There had been almost no major improvements over the past three years, and none of the companies appeared to be working on any radical improvements for the near future.

Mr. McCarthy was quite optimistic about the potential success of his Route 9 Bowl Inn. He felt that his judgment in launching the venture had been substantiated because he had recently been approached by Mr. Carl Peterson, the operator of a nearby amusement park, who had offered to buy him out (that is, take over the lease and make the remaining payments on the alleys which were being installed) for $40,000. Mr. McCarthy felt that this prospective $10,000 immediate profit was partly in compensation for his efforts in locating the site and getting the business underway, but also reflected the potential high profitability of the enterprise. Mr. McCarthy declined to sell because he did not need the money and was hoping to use the Route 9 Bowl Inn as the first of a chain of such ventures.

Mr. McCarthy still had approximately $15,000 available for investment in his bowling alley venture. He thought that about $5,000 would be needed for working capital and a "safety margin" at the Route 9 location, and the remaining $10,000 could be used to make the down payment on the pinsetting machines if he decided to purchase them. As an alternative, however, he was also toying with the idea of proceeding immediately with the exploitation of his Route 1 site. Assuming that the land could be sold and leased back as he had done on Route 9, the $25,000 proceeds plus his available $10,000 would be sufficient to make the down payment on the alleys and provide working capital at Route 1.

Mr. McCarthy was less confident of the immediate profitability of the Route 1 location because he knew that his operating expenses would be about the same as on Route 9, while his best estimate of the volume was that it would range between 15% and 30% lower to begin with. On the other hand, he was convinced of the ultimate profitability of the Route 1 location, and felt that establishing it as soon as possible might discourage any potential competitors from building in that area.

Question

What course of action would you recommend to Mr. McCarthy?

FRONTIER RUBBER COMPANY

At the December, 1958, meeting of the finance committee of Frontier Rubber Company, four capital expenditure proposals were brought up for review. The finance committee met quarterly to consider requests for the appropriation of funds for projects to be started within the next year. The committee previously had approved expenditures totaling $70 million for 1959, a figure that represented the highest appropriations since World War II. The committee had reviewed the projects currently under consideration earlier in the year but, at that time, had decided to allocate the available funds to projects promising a higher rate of return, considered to be more urgent, or appearing to be less risky. However, management expected 1959 profits to run higher than originally estimated, thereby providing an additional source of approximately $5 million. Therefore, the finance committee decided to rescreen requests that previously had been rejected to see whether any of these projects were sufficiently promising to merit approval.

COMPANY BACKGROUND

Frontier Rubber Company was one of the major producers of rubber tires in the country. The company also produced a wide line of other rubber and nonrubber products. Rubber products included radiator hoses, floor mats, molded and extruded mechanical rubber goods, fan belts, latex thread, and cushion material for mattresses. During World War II the company had entered the chemicals and plastics field with the manufacture of vinyl, styrene, and other types of plastic resins; agricultural chemicals such as fungicides and nitricides; acids; textile resins and organic chemicals for use in petroleum, rubber, plastics, and other industries.

The company had been organized in 1911 as the result of a merger between two medium-sized rubber companies. In the period prior to

World War II, growth had resulted from a series of acquisitions of many smaller companies. During World War II, Frontier Rubber had been a major supplier of military products for the government. After the war, sales had increased from $443 million in 1946 to $907 million in 1957. Net income had also increased from a low in 1949 of $26 million to $60 million in 1957.

Capital expenditures for plant expansion and improvement since the end of World War II had been substantial. The company had undertaken two major programs prior to the current one. The first expansion program had been undertaken in the immediate postwar period as the company resumed production for civilian consumption. In 1949 the company had increased expenditures for the addition of facilities to handle new products in the plastics and chemicals fields and for improvements to existing plants. The current program had been started in 1955. The company had financed these expansion programs by the public sale of debentures and by retained earnings. On December 31, 1957, it had outstanding $151 million of long-term debt which represented 28% of total capitalization (long-term debt plus common stock and surplus). Recent balance sheets are shown in Exhibit 1.

CAPITAL EXPENDITURE PROGRAM

In 1947 the directors of Frontier Rubber had established long-range expansion goals with the hope of furnishing a basis for the budgeting of time, money, materials, and manpower in a purposeful manner. In conjunction with these long-range goals, the directors had approved a rolling five-year capital expenditure program. This program had been adopted to provide management with budgets beyond the yearly budget normally drawn up by the treasurer.

The objective of the capital expenditure programs was to increase earnings per share. The directors also wished, in the implementation of the programs, to stay within certain established financial policies. These involved maintaining a dividend pay-out ratio of approximately 65% and a long-term debt ratio of less than 35% of total capitalization.

In establishing capital expenditure policies, management set up minimum expected rates of return on investments, which had to be met before project proposals could be approved. These return criteria were disseminated throughout the organization to be used as a guide by division managers and their staffs. Division managers sponsored nearly all project proposals and, in turn, were held accountable for their forecasts and projections. Despite these minimum standards, more proposals were submitted than could be met by the funds available. As a result, all sizable proposals were given a critical appraisal throughout the review process. Typically, about one-third of all projects submitted by the division managers were rejected during the screening process.

The minimum-return standards were based on the historical return on net assets of the company modified by comparisons with other companies in the rubber industry. For instance, during the five-year period, 1942–1946, Frontier Rubber's average rate of return (net income after taxes divided by net assets) was 5.68%. Other large rubber companies, on the other hand, earned between 6.26% and 7.42% on net assets in that period. After reviewing this evidence, officers of Frontier Rubber had established the minimum acceptable rate of return for projects at 12% after taxes. Management hoped that a high cutoff rate of return would help to improve its earnings position more rapidly and raise its return on investment to levels comparable with competitors.

This minimum-return criterion was not applied uniformly to all projects because of the uncertainties involved in forecasting. The 12% rate was used for projects for improvement or replacement of existing facilities where expected earnings and expenditures could be forecast with reasonable accuracy over relatively long periods of time. Projects of this type generally involved laborsaving devices and other equipment purchases. Because of experience gained from equipment already in use, management had confidence in the estimates of division managers concerning these projects.

However, management expected higher rates of return from projects that appeared to be more uncertain. For instance, ventures into new products were expected to return at least 20% because of the greater risks that typically existed. New products could easily result in failure because demand did not match expectations or because of hidden costs that may not have been anticipated. Moreover, projects of this nature generally involved the expenditure of greater sums of money.

In another instance, management expected a minimum rate of return of 17% on projects for expansion of existing facilities. Although the company did not have to establish new markets, these projects were regarded as relatively risky because of the uncertainties involved in forecasting demands and costs.

In contrast to the emphasis placed upon the rates of return for the above projects, the officers of Frontier Rubber considered return criterion less important for projects designed wholly to reduce costs. They believed that any savings in cost were beneficial to the company regardless of the rate of return. However, with a limited supply of funds for capital investment, management decided to restrict expenditures by some means. It therefore used the minimum acceptable rate of return of 12% for projects of cost reduction.

The method chosen for computing rates of return was based upon the incremental investment required for the project and the ten-year average of expected earnings. Gross plant expenditures and funds required for working capital comprised the incremental investment. Expected earnings under "normal" future business conditions were computed after taxes and normal straight-line depreciation.[1] Division managers used detailed engineering and market surveys in their computations of expected earnings. Management did not require projections beyond ten years, because it did not think that accurate forecasts could be made beyond that period. Moreover, ten years was a typical obsolescence period for many products in the rubber industry.

Frontier Rubber made an exception to its method of computing rates of return in the case of expenditures for replacement or improvement of facilities. In this instance, management believed that expected earnings should take into consideration the income that would be lost if the existing facility under consideration were to cease operations. Moreover, it was believed that investment should include the net book value of the existing facility plus the new capital being requested. This procedure had been adopted to avoid sinking additional money into projects already yielding a low rate of return on existing book value.

PROCESSING CAPITAL EXPENDITURE REQUESTS

The first step in the system of processing capital expenditure requests was separation of the proposed projects into three basic categories:

Class A—Projects amounting to $15,000 or more which covered new products, new plants, or new processes; or any project costing $100,-000 or more.

Class B—Projects above $5,000 which did not fall into the Class A category.

Class C—Projects below $5,000.

In establishing these categories, management felt that closer surveillance should be given to all projects requiring large expenditures, and

---

[1] The company used the declining balance method of depreciation for accounting purposes.

to new projects because of the inherent risks. As a result, Class A proposals went through a thorough system of review before they were approved. In Class B projects, the proposals did not go through so rigorous a review, but nevertheless, they were considered carefully before final approval was given. (See Exhibit 6 for a schematic diagram of the appropriations procedure for Class A and B projects.)

Class C projects, which included mainly maintenance expenditures, did not fall within the appropriations procedure but were allowed for and approved in total in the annual budget review. Division managers grouped requests for projects of less than $5,000 together and submitted them in a lump sum for budget approval. Officers of the company seldom questioned these requests but approved them on the basis of need. However, management felt that the system had a built-in control because each division manager was aware that he would decrease his chance for approval of Class A or B projects if he requested excessive amounts for Class C projects. Officers believed that, in practice, division managers limited Class C expenditure to essential projects.

When the capital expenditure program had been established, the directors had appointed two committees, the budget committee and the finance committee, to review project proposals before they were submitted to the president and to the board of directors.

In the first step of the approval procedure, division managers submitted all proposed projects to the budget committee for inclusion in the five-year capital expenditure program. The committee was assigned the task of looking ahead, anticipating desirable expenditures opportunities, and testing the company's capacity to finance them. Each year at the May meeting, the committee revised the program and subsequently submitted it to the board of directors for approval. Unanticipated yet urgent requests were submitted to the directors as they were received. The budget committee included the president, the six division managers, the treasurer, the director of research and development, the personnel manager, and the assistant to the president. It reviewed projects as initially conceived—sometimes while still in advanced stages of research and often several years before they were ready for construction. Market information, process know-how, details on products, and estimated operating costs were used as a rough estimate to support each project proposal insofar as possible. Projects were evaluated on the basis of available resources, needs of the company, and expected rates of return on investment.

If the directors approved the projects in the five-year budget, the new projects were sent to the finance committee for more detailed analysis when the project was ready for construction. The division manager sponsoring the project prepared a detailed request for funds called an "appropriation request." This request embodied more detailed estimates of costs and earnings than the budget committee required. The time lag between approval by the budget committee and the appropriation of funds by the finance committee had varied from five months to five years. The finance committee consisted of the president, executive vice-president, treasurer, director of research and development, the division manager sponsoring the project, and another division manager who was not concerned with the project.

The four projects currently under consideration were presently at the finance committee awaiting the appropriation of funds. The projects were: (1) renovation of the molding process for rubber goods; (2) expansion of an existing acid plant; (3) construction of a laboratory for research into the commercial applications of atomic energy; (4) and construction of a new plastics plant on the West Coast. These projects had been approved by the budget committee at previous meetings and subsequently had been made a part of the company's five-year investment program. The appropriation requests had been submitted to the finance committee earlier in the year but had not been approved because funds had been limited and because other projects were expected to yield a higher rate of return, were less risky, or were more urgent. All of the projects that had been granted funds for 1959 were expected to yield at least 15% on the investment, or the equivalent.

RENOVATION OF MOLDING PROCESS FOR RUBBER GOODS

In December, 1958, the factor of urgency became more imminent for one of the four projects listed above, renovation of the molding process for rubber goods at the Buffalo, New York, plant. Recurring mechanical failures had continued to plague the compression molding presses at Buffalo, one of the three plants of the company producing molded rubber goods. Mr. Jordan, the division manager for rubber goods, believed that the Buffalo plant would have to be shut down if renovation were not started within a few months.

Sales of molded rubber goods had declined during 1957 and 1958 because of the general economic recession. However, Mr. Jordan expressed his confidence that sales of nontire rubber products would continue to expand with the economy (i.e., about 4% per year) as it usually had in the past. Moreover, he pointed out the plant had been earning between 14% in good years and 10% in poor years on net assets. In 1959, he expected the plant to earn about $230,000 after taxes and depreciation, provided repairs were undertaken immediately. On the basis of the December, 1958, net book value of the plant of $1.9 million, operations yielded a higher rate of return on net assets than the over-all average for the company. In December, 1958, the appraised value of these assets was approximately $2.9 million, a sum that could possibly be realized in the event of liquidation of this facility. Mr. Jordan expected direct, nonrecurring costs of closing the plant to approximate $200,000, after taxes.

In the compression molding process, uncured compounded rubber was prepared to the correct weight, placed into the press cavity, and forced into the contour of the cavity by the pressure of the mold closing in the press. Cavities in the mold ran from one to hundreds, depending upon the size of the product being made. The plant had expanded gradually throughout the years so that many of the presses were small and inefficient. For example, rubber had to be inserted by hand into each of the cavities.

A minimum expenditure of $290,000 was now absolutely necessary to keep the presses in operation. Otherwise the plant would gradually have to be shut down. The repairs would be only a stop-gap measure, but Mr. Jordan estimated that probably no additional repairs would be required for another three years. The expenditure would be charged against current operations. The existing plant was being depreciated at a rate of $100,000 per year. The present molding presses were fully depreciated and had only nominal salvage value.

Mr. Jordan pointed out that the existing presses would eventually require a complete mechanical overhaul. If they were overhauled in conjunction with the repairs, the total cost (including repairs) would approximate $650,000. He estimated that $45,000 after taxes and straight-line depreciation could be saved each year after mechanical overhaul through the elimination of inefficiencies. The machines, when overhauled, would have a new life for depreciation purposes of seven years. Mr. Jordan indicated that the cost for overhauling the presses would still approximate $650,000 at current market prices if the overhauling were done after the repairs had been made.

As a third possibility the company could replace the existing presses with new injection molding machines. These new presses utilized a power-driven plunger to force the unvulcanized rubber into a tightly closed mold. Forcing the rubber through small passages under high pressure increased the temperature of the injected compound sufficiently to reduce the curing time considerably. The machines would be automatic except for the removal of the product from the cavity. The new machines would cost a total of $2.4 million at current market prices but were not necessary to keep the plant in operation. They would have a life of 12 years for depreciation purposes.

As part of the request for appropriations, Mr. Jordan estimated that installation of the new equipment would result in average cost savings of about $230,000 per year, after taxes and straight-line depreciation. About 75% of these reduced operating costs would result from a reduction in the labor force since the new equipment would be almost fully automatic. The remaining cost savings would be realized from the use of less fuel. In his estimates Mr. Jordan included only those cost savings that he could definitely expect during the ten-year forecast. However, he believed that these savings would continue beyond the ten years of the forecast. He expected the new machines to last for at least 20 years with only nominal interim repairs.

In addition to the above labor and fuel savings, Mr. Jordan thought that approximately $500,000 after taxes could be saved by a reduction of indirect expenses during the first ten years of their use. Since the new equipment would be more compact, he thought the machines, when installed, would free 20% of existing floor space for further expansion when this became desirable. Moreover, preventive maintenance and proper handling of the new equipment would cut repair bills, particularly in later years. This would also reduce time lost and would benefit the company by improving customer relations. With the repeated mechanical failures of the existing presses, the shipment of several orders had been held up. One of the company's more important customers had threatened to seek a new supplier if his orders were not delivered on schedule.

However, Mr. Jordan did not include these indirect savings in his return on investment computation because he could not be absolutely sure that they would be realized. He knew that he would be held accountable for the project when completed and would be expected to achieve the rate of return as forecasted. Until he had gained more experience with the new equipment, he did not want to assume the responsibility for the cost savings that were possible but either uncertain or intangible.

ACID PLANT EXPANSION

The expansion of the sulfuric acid plant in Newark, New Jersey, was planned as part of the original engineering work when the plant had been built in 1949. Demand at the time had not warranted building the entire plant, but it had been designed to allow an increase in capacity at a later date. Since the plant had been opened in 1949, the production of sulfuric acid in the United States had increased more than 50%, from 10.9 million short tons in 1947 to 16.5 million short tons in 1956. In December, 1957, Mr. Branner, the chemical division manager, had requested $2,250,000 for expansion of the plant. This request had included $1,200,000 for the plant, $800,000 for machinery and equipment, and $225,000 for working capital. However, funds had not been allocated because members of the finance committee had not been convinced that general business activity in 1958 would warrant expansion at that time.

Frontier Rubber had begun the production of industrial acids in 1949 as part of the company's diversification program. During 1957 Mr. Branner had felt that space limitations had placed pressure upon his plant personnel to fulfill the demands of his current customers. At one period, orders from new customers had been turned down. The economic recession in 1958 had left the plant operating at 80% of capacity. Mr. Branner had already noted an increase in the demand for acids by December, 1958, and expected them to be in short supply by mid-1959. The expansion program would double existing capacity.

With the recovery from the 1957–1958 recession well under way by December, 1958, Mr. Branner was convinced that the industrial market soon would be able to absorb the output of the expanded plant within a few years' time. He therefore resubmitted his proposal. He further estimated that construction, machinery, and equipment costs would increase by approximately 5% and therefore requested an additional $100,000 for a total request of $2,325,000. Mr. Branner expected that earnings after taxes and straight-line depreciation would be approximately $200,000 a year for the first two years when the plant would be operating at less than peak capacity. Thereafter, earnings would increase gradually to $600,000 per year in the fifth year as demand increased (Exhibit 4). The plant would be depreciated over 40 years, while the machinery and equipment would be depreciated over ten years.

Mr. Branner decided to resubmit his proposal in conjunction with the company's policy of upgrading its acid products. Initially, the company had produced only heavy acids such as sulfuric, nitric, and hydrochloric acids. Recently, it had established a policy of converting the basic chemical products into higher grades of fine acids which generally yielded higher profit margins, had stabler markets, and offered better returns on investment. For instance, the company now produced sulfuric acid to make ammonium sulphate for mixing into fertilizer. The company was also considering the manufacture of sulphonates for detergents. Expansion of the acid plant would be necessary if the company expected to continue its policy of upgrading its acid products yet wished to preserve the current basic acids market. Mr. Branner anticipated a strong growth pattern in the demand for end products such as detergents which, in turn, would increase the demand for fine acids. Consequently, additional heavy acids would be required for the manufacture of fine acids. His projections indicated that the present capacity would be entirely captive by 1965 (in contrast with being only 20% captive in 1958), suggesting further expansion would be necessary within a few years.

In discussing his proposal with the finance committee, Mr. Branner commented that product obsolescence was not a great problem. Sulfuric acid was used so widely that a decrease in one use was often offset by an increase in another. For instance, new and increased uses in rayon and film manufacture, and increased manufacture of sodium alkylsulfates as detergents, had offset the obsolescence of the salt-sulfuric acid process for manufacturing hydrochloric acid, petroleum refining by hydrogenation, and partial replacement in the fertilizer industry by nitric and phosphoric acids.

Mr. Branner felt confident that the expanded plant would be producing in the year 2000 with only moderate, interim equipment replacement. However, he pointed out the danger of the competition from other companies. In the past, a number of companies had been attracted to the chemical industry because of the high rate of return on investment and growth prospects. Because heavy acid plants required modest investment, an increasing number of companies were entering the field. Moreover, large users of sulfuric acid, such as fertilizer and explosive manufacturers, were acquiring smaller companies because they found it cheaper to make acid than to buy it. Consequently, occasional periods of overcapacity and cyclical fluctuations in plant usages had occurred. However, Mr. Branner pointed out that technical know-how was an important factor which tended to minimize the ease of entry into the sulfuric acid field.

An additional reason for resubmitting the proposal for expansion of the plant was Mr. Branner's argument that Frontier Rubber would be able to improve the return on investment of the entire sulfuric acid plant. The original plant costing $3.5 million (and returning profits of $400,000 on net assets of $3.0 million) had been built with excess floor space. Part of the basic structure had been designed to provide for further expansion. In addition some service facilities such as a power plant would not be required. Therefore, the plant expansion would provide a greater increase in capacity in proportion to the nominal investment expense and the rate of return for the entire plant would be improved.

CONSTRUCTION OF AN ATOMIC ENERGY LABORATORY

The third project before the finance committee was a proposal by Mr. Wilbur, the director of research and development, for the construction of a new laboratory for research into atomic energy. He pointed out that the major rubber companies, as well as many companies in construction, mining, petroleum, chemicals, plastics, machine tools, electrical instruments, metals, and aircraft, were involved in some research of nuclear technology and its commercial counterparts. The function of the laboratory would be to explore the effects of radiation on chemical structures pertaining to the rubber industry and related products of Frontier Rubber.

Because of the hazards of radiation, a specially designed building would have to be constructed for the new research laboratory. After visiting other nuclear research laboratories and talking to architects and engineers, Mr. Wilbur had drawn up plans for a building, machinery, and equipment that would cost approximately $2.2 million. This amount included $200,000 for an air-conditioning system with an expected life of ten years. He estimated that an additional $500,000 would be needed each year for manpower and other operating costs of the laboratory.

Mr. Wilbur recognized that the investment would have to be made with a look toward the long run. He admitted that he would be surprised if tangible benefits would result during the first five years because of immediate emphasis on basic research. He pointed out, however, that this form of basic research might eventually lead to extremely significant findings such as revolutionary new products or processes of major importance. Consequently, Mr. Wilbur believed the laboratory should be given high priority. He had become alarmed over the apathy for the project that had been shown by several officers of the company. These people, he felt, failed to recognize that all of the major competitors of Frontier Rubber were now actively engaged or about to begin research in atomic energy. The laboratory, he concluded, was necessary to keep up with competition and if postponed for another year would put the company behind its competitors. He thought research leadership was particularly important if the company were going to establish itself as a dynamic and aggressive organization.

CONSTRUCTION OF A PLASTICS PLANT

The fourth proposed project was the construction of a plastics plant, which represented a completely new venture for Frontier Rubber. Recently the company had been offered an option to acquire the process rights to produce vinyl sheeting of a thinner gauge than currently on the market. This new sheeting would have the strength and quality of current plastics. The new finishing process would permit the production of more sheeting per pound of vinyl resin. The new process, combined with a nearby resin plant, would give Frontier a 15%–20% cost advantage over competing sheeting. Several companies were tooling up to produce this thinner gauge plastic in the East and Midwest but, at the moment, a market potential existed for entry into the West Coast area. In 1957, a number of relatively small vinyl chloride polymer plants had been built in various parts of the country, but the West Coast was still relatively free from competition in producing this material.

Rubber companies had played an important role in the plastics industry since the immediate post–World War II period when Goodrich began producing vinyl resin and film. By the time that Frontier Rubber had entered the vinyl resin industry, Firestone and Goodyear were producing both resin and film. Frontier had sold all of its resin to independent film and sheeting producers and manufacturers of end products such as vinyl garden hose, vinyl flooring, and vinyl-coated fabrics.

The vinyl industry had been highly competitive since 1952, and prices had been unstable. For instance, prices per pound of vinyl resin dropped from 38 cents to 31 cents in 1955 and to 27 cents in 1956. Imports of lower-priced foreign resin and pressure from vinyl film producers were largely responsible for the price cuts. On the other hand, vinyl film and sheeting manufacturers were able to maintain relatively stable price margins. Many vinyl resin producers began to produce their own vinyl film or sheeting in order to have a stable market for their vinyl resin without getting into the competitive pricing pressures from outside customers.

When the company policy of upgrading as many of the basic products as possible was formulated, management of Frontier began to look for an opportunity to manufacture its own vinyl film or sheeting. Several advantages of the new plastics plant had been pointed out by the division manager, Mr. Sterling. One important aspect would be the technical know-how gained with this product. If, at a later date, the company decided to upgrade its plastic products even further into production of consumer goods, this technical know-how would be an important factor. Secondly, the new plastic process would enable the company to begin building the sales force needed for further penetration into the plastic fields and consumer goods.

A final important consideration with respect to the new process was the opportunity that it would give to the company to establish a captive market for its adjacent vinyl resin plant thereby avoiding the competitive price struggle. Purchases of vinyl resin from the adjacent plant would probably absorb about 35% of the capacity of the plant. Moreover, the adjacent plant would realize a stable profit of $175,000. These profits were not included in the calculations on the rate of return by Mr. Sterling.

The project proposal for the manufacture of sheeting called for a special-purpose plant costing approximately $1.5 million and machinery and equipment of $800,000. Land adjacent to the existing plastics plant had been offered to the company for $200,000. (This land could also be used for construction of additional facilities in future years.) An additional $300,000 had been requested for working capital. Although the plant would have limited value if the project did not work out as expected, it would have to be depreciated over 40 years. The machinery and equipment could be depreciated over ten years. Management could foresee nothing that might replace vinyl products for the next three to four years. In fact trade publications estimated that production of vinyl resin for the entire industry would increase from 845 million pounds in 1957 to 1,200 million pounds by 1961. However, product obsolescence growing out of technical obsolescence in the plastic industry was quite high, with a typical product life expectancy of eight to ten years.

Mr. Sterling estimated earnings after taxes and straight-line deductions at $500,000, during the shakedown period of the first two years, $800,000 in years three through five, and $1 million thereafter. Some members of the finance committee had questioned these estimates when the project had been introduced earlier in the year. Mr. Sterling had based his projection on the expanding uses for vinyl sheeting such as vinyl-line irrigation ditches and farm ponds, vinyl-covered greenhouses and home swimming pools. He had assumed that a market already existed for these products and would result in production close to the capacity of the plant. Those who had disagreed felt that the projection should be based upon current production figures for the industry, which had shown a leveling off in the demand for vinyl sheeting. They had been doubtful that current demand would assure operations of more than 75% of operating capacity, or profits of $400,000 per year at this level.

Other members of the finance committee had believed that the sales potential was between full capacity and 75% of capacity. One committee member had suggested returning the proposal to Mr. Sterling for further study at the division level. With a nominal cost of approximately $25,000 for architectural and engineering fees, the capacity of the plant could be scaled down. He had estimated roughly that profit from the investment would be about 75% of Mr. Sterling's original estimate. He also had estimated that the cost of constructing the smaller plant would be about 90% of anticipated expenditures. After thorough discussion when the proposal had been introduced the first time, the members of the committee had agreed that all of the points of view concerning potential demand and earnings had some merit. Since they were generally agreed that the company would not know what the operating level would be until the plant was put on stream, Mr. Sterling had resubmitted his initial estimates.

In addition to questioning the potential market size for the vinyl sheeting, one committee member had questioned the availability of marketing personnel. The company had salesmen who were experienced in selling vinyl resin but did not have anyone skilled in selling film or sheeting. The two products, resin and sheeting, would be sold to different end-product markets. For instance, vinyl sheeting would be sold primarily to the upholstery field. Other uses would be for handbags, wallets, belts, and carrying cases. Vinyl resin, on the other hand, was sold to manufacturers of vinyl film and sheeting. Different selling techniques would have to be used for the two vinyl products because of the different end uses. The committee member who had raised the point questioned, first of all, whether the company could recruit enough good salesmen for the job and, secondly, whether the present vinyl resin salesmen would be able to train the new salesmen for the vinyl sheeting.

After reviewing the proposed projects the finance committee had to decide whether any or all of the projects should be allocated funds for construction in 1959.

Exhibit 1

FRONTIER RUBBER COMPANY

BALANCE SHEET, DECEMBER 31, 1956, AND 1957

(Dollar figures in millions)

ASSETS	1956		1957	
Current assets:				
Cash...................................$ 27.0			$ 23.6	
Marketable securities..................... 63.6			32.3	
Accounts receivable..................... 151.8			147.1	
Inventories............................ 181.6			208.2	
Total current assets....................		$424.0		$411.2
Investments.............................		26.9		32.7
Gross plant, machinery, and equipment......$286.6			$320.8	
Less: Reserve for depreciation............ 99.6			115.7	
Net fixed assets.......................		187.0		205.1
Deferred charges.........................		2.7		2.3
Total assets.........................		$640.6		$651.3
LIABILITIES				
Current liabilities:				
Bank loan..............................$ 1.5			$ 5.3	
Accounts payable....................... 39.4			35.7	
Accrued taxes.......................... 40.5			45.9	
Other accruals......................... 22.7			23.3	
Total current liabilities................		$104.1		$110.2
Long-term debt..........................		159.7		151.3
Common and surplus......................		376.8		389.8
Total liabilities.....................		$640.6		$651.3

Exhibit 2

FRONTIER RUBBER COMPANY

SUMMARY OF SALES AND EARNINGS

(Dollar figures in millions)

	Sales	Income before Taxes	Income Tax	Net Income
1944	$517	$ 32.7	$18.0	$14.7
1945	449	31.8	16.5	15.3
1946	443	65.3	33.7	31.6
1947	507	59.9	31.0	28.9
1948	523	60.7	31.6	29.1
1949	489	53.7	28.0	25.7
1950	680	90.2	46.4	43.8
1951	797	92.4	48.6	43.8
1952	780	85.7	45.3	40.4
1953	835	87.3	44.7	42.6
1954	781	100.2	51.9	48.3
1955	902	119.1	62.4	56.7
1956	891	112.6	58.5	54.1
1957	907	122.3	62.7	59.6

Exhibit 3

FRONTIER RUBBER COMPANY

SUMMARY OF EXPECTED RATES OF RETURN ON INVESTMENT AS CALCULATED BY THE COMPANY FOR RENOVATION OF THE MOLDING PROCESS FOR RUBBER GOODS

(All earnings figures are after taxes and straight-line depreciation)

Basic data:

Expected net earnings in 1958 ....$ 230,000
Net book value of plant (December, 1958)........................ 1,900,000
Current return on book value.................................... 12.1%

I. Temporary repairs:
   Net investment—$290,000
   Return on investment—

$$\frac{\text{Income That Would Be Lost If Closed Down}}{\text{Net Book Value} + \text{Net Investment}} = 10.5\%$$

II. Overhaul:
   Net investment—$650,000
   Expected cost savings—$45,000
   Return on investment—

$$\frac{\text{Income That Would Be Lost If Closed Down} + \text{Expected Cost Savings}}{\text{Net Book Value} + \text{Net Investment}} = 10.8\%$$

III. Replacement with new machinery:
   Net investment—$2,400,000
   Expected cost savings—$230,000
   Return on investment—

$$\frac{\text{Income That Would Be Lost If Closed Down} + \text{Expected Cost Savings}}{\text{Net Book Value} + \text{Net Investment}} = 10.7\%$$

Exhibit 4

FRONTIER RUBBER COMPANY

SUMMARY OF EXPECTED RATE OF RETURN ON INVESTMENT
AS CALCULATED BY THE COMPANY FOR EXPANSION
OF THE ACID PLANT

(All earnings figures are after taxes and straight-line depreciation)

Net investment:

Plant	$1,260,000
Machinery and equipment	840,000
Working capital	225,000
	$2,325,000

Expected earnings:

Year	Earnings
1	$ 200,000
2	200,000
3	330,000
4	460,000
5	600,000
6	600,000
7	600,000
8	600,000
9	600,000
10	600,000
	$4,790,000

Return on investment: $\dfrac{\text{Average Expected Earnings}}{\text{Net Investment}} = 20.6\%$

Exhibit 5

FRONTIER RUBBER COMPANY

SUMMARY OF EXPECTED RATES OF RETURN ON INVESTMENT AS CALCULATED
BY THE COMPANY FOR CONSTRUCTION OF A PLASTICS PLANT

(All earnings figures are after taxes and straight-line depreciation)

Net investment:

Plant	$1,500,000
Machinery and equipment	800,000
Land	200,000
Working capital	300,000
	$2,800,000

Expected earnings:

Year	Per Year
1–2	$ 500,000
3–5	800,000
6–10	1,000,000
Total expected earnings	$8,400,000

Return on investment: $\dfrac{\text{Average Expected Earnings}}{\text{Net Investment}} = 30.0\%$

Exhibit 6

FRONTIER RUBBER COMPANY

SUMMARY OF APPROPRIATION REQUEST PROCEDURE REVIEW
AND APPROVAL REQUIREMENTS

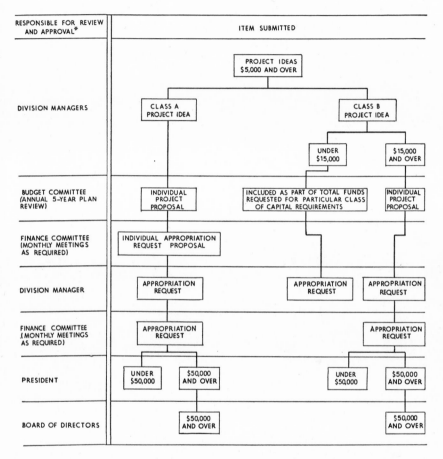

* Formal approval to spend funds comes only after approval is received from last authority noted on this diagram.

Section VII

THE STRATEGY OF
CAPITAL BUDGETING

CONSOLIDATED ELECTRICAL
PRODUCTS, INC. (D)

ALLOCATING FUNDS AMONG DIVISIONS

Each of CONELP's divisions competes for a share of the relatively limited amount of capital available to the company. Even after the questions associated with selecting a procedure for calculating minimum acceptable return on investment criterion have been satisfactorily resolved, suitable procedures for applying this standard to the problems of allocating the available supply of funds among divisions has to be determined. The most critical allocation question was whether a single standard applied uniformly to all divisions would be a more appropriate screening criterion than multiple standards each of which could be tailored more specifically to the needs and special problems of a single division. Also to be decided was the issue of how much authority division managers should have in making capital budgeting commitments. Mr. Holman, CONELP's treasurer, had yet to resolve these questions.

Mr. Holman's notes, which summarized various opinions relevant to these questions, are shown below.

A. *Single or Multiple Minimum-Return Standards*

Many individuals believe that we should move to a single minimum-return standard. This standard would be applied to all projects irrespective of the divisions from which they originated. In support of this position, advocates cite the fact that projects with returns of 20% from one division are currently being rejected, while at the same time projects from other divisions with returns of 8% or less are accepted. This discrimination does not make sense and, clearly, is to the disadvantage of stockholders. A single return standard also appears to fulfill more satisfactorily the basic policy objective upon which the capital budgeting procedures were initially established. This policy objective

373

states that management ought to attempt to maximize stockholders' earnings over the long term.

There are also a number of executives who support the use of multiple cut-off points. These men argue that each division is competing in a virtually separate industry and that each industry has its own unique return characteristics. One would hardly expect to find that such contrasting companies as International Business Machines Corporation, American Telephone and Telegraph Company, and United States Steel Corporation would all be following the same capital budgeting policies merely because they draw their capital from the same capital markets. Nevertheless, the divisions of CONELP have many of the basic elements of contrast observable in these three companies. Therefore, why should each division follow the same capital budgeting policy? This argument concludes that using multiple return standards is a more satisfactory method of assuring the ability of each division to remain competitive within its industry.

B. *The Jurisdictional Question of Decisional Authority*

Prior to this inquiry, each division manager has had the authority to commit funds up to the limit of his division's depreciation charges. Typically, these decisions were not even reviewed informally by top management. Moreover, there were no restrictions (except that the authority was limited to projects requiring investments of less than $50,000) or even guides to limit the freedom of the division manager in making choices among projects.

Two issues have arisen with respect to this policy. First of all, the question has been raised: How much commitment authority should be delegated to the division level as against that preserved by the top-management level? Secondly, assuming some delegation of commitment authority is made, what restrictions (e.g., minimum-return criterion, type of projects, etc.) should be imposed to standardize or to narrow the scope of this authority?

A number of executives favor the continuance of the present liberal policy. However, the following alternative methods of limiting divisional commitment authority have been proposed:

1. *Dollar Expenditure Limitation:* Division managers should have unrestricted power to make commitments for new investments, provided the total dollar amount of each commitment does not exceed some set dollar limit (illustratively $10,000). With more time, top management can screen the most significant investment opportunities more carefully.

2. *Marginal Limitation:* Under this alternative, each division could commit funds to any project which clearly met company return standards by a wide margin. Top management, then, would only have to review expenditure proposals that were marginal (i.e., possibly questionable).

3. *Replacement Limitation:* Here, divisions would have the right to commit funds for replacement requirements only. Several individuals think this is the true intent of the present depreciation limitation.

4. *Intangible Limitation:* Several division managers believe strongly that projects, justified largely by such intangible considerations as competitive necessity, are difficult to present effectively to top management in a

written report. Moreover, these projects essentially involve complex value judgments. The division managers who are on the firing line believe that they are in the best position to make these judgments. Therefore, division managers should have final commitment authority over projects of this nature.

5. *Priority Limitation:* Division managers, under this alternative, would have no commitment authority. All projects would be submitted to top management for review. Division managers would, however, rank the projects submitted in accordance with their personal preferences (and perhaps code the projects by dollar size, etc.). Top management would then screen projects from all divisions on a truly competitive basis.

The alternatives outlined above inherently raise the question: Should standard procedures for evaluating projects at the divisional level be established to assure the desired degree of consistency among divisions? If so, what should these standards be, and in what ways should they differ from "top-level" criteria?

PERFORMANCE STANDARDS

One day while Mr. Holman was in the process of preparing a report which would set forth all recommended changes in the company's capital budgeting policies and practices, he was visited unexpectedly by Mr. Doyle, general manager of the industrial division. After a few friendly preliminary exchanges, Mr. Doyle commented:

All these new techniques for deciding whether a project is any good or not —frankly, I don't understand half of them. However, you know that when the system is all installed, we division managers are still going to be judged on how well we maintain our return percentages.[1] I came to ask you if, after you've finished writing up all the new procedures, you'd spell out how I should go about implementing these procedures and, at the same time, keep my performance standard up.

---

[1] Cf. CONELP (A), page 5 for a description of the performance standards by which division managers were evaluated.

ARGONAUT ELECTRONICS, INC.[1]

At the April, 1959, meeting of the board of directors of Argonaut Electronics, Inc., one director raised the question, "Has the company reached the point in time when it should sell common stock to the public for the first time?" This question had been raised several times before, but, in each instance, the directors had concluded that more could be gained by postponing the first public sale of stock. However, the directors recognized that one or more public issues of stock eventually would be necessary if they were to achieve their ambitious goal of building Argonaut Electronics rapidly into a large industrial enterprise.

In April, 1959, additional equity capital was not urgently needed, although funds could be used to strengthen the company's financial position, to institute operating economies, to accelerate the development of promising commercial products, and to provide greater flexibility for taking advantage of promising opportunities as they arose. The existence of what appeared to be an abnormally favorable opportunity for a public sale of stock motivated the directors to take a closer look at the relative advantages of such an issue in the immediate future. However, the directors did not feel under any pressure to sell stock unless the issue promised major advantages.

After considerable discussion, the six directors of Argonaut Electronics, all officers of the company, asked Mr. John A. Sutter, the treasurer, to determine whether it would be advantageous to raise $600,-000 through a public sale of common stock at a price of approximately $20 per share. His report would serve as the basis for more concrete discussion of the problem at the next board meeting one month hence.

Argonaut Electronics, Inc., a small company located in southern

---

[1] This case was made possible by the co-operation of a business firm which remains anonymous. It was prepared under the direction of Assistant Professor Robert F. Vandell as the basis for class discussion rather than to illustrate either effective or ineffective handling of an administrative situation.

California, was a developer and producer of electronic equipment for government and industry. The company had been formed with hopes of attracting outstanding engineers and scientists from nearby college faculties and student bodies to collaborate on research in an informal atmosphere. The caliber of the company's scientific staff was its principal asset, and Argonaut Electronics was recognized in the electronics industry for the quality of ideas that were being generated. The engineers were specialists in certain areas in the electronics industry, and Argonaut Electronics had made many significant contributions in research and development of electronic products. Almost one-third of all Argonaut's research and development bids to the government were accepted in contrast with an industry average of 10%.

HISTORICAL BACKGROUND

Argonaut had been formed in the fall of 1950 by John Sutter and James W. Marshall, engineers previously employed in a large West Coast electronics company. Messrs. Sutter and Marshall, together with Mr. Douglas Jason, a wealthy businessman from Los Angeles, entered into a three-way corporate "partnership" to which each man contributed equally. In addition to initial capital of $5,000, the company's primary assets were agreements with several outstanding engineers who had agreed to join the company as soon as volume could support their services. Since the company was located near California Institute of Technology, management believed it was in a favorable position to secure new engineering talent as needed.

Government contract work appeared to be the best way to support the engineering staff envisioned by the owners. The three men set out to promote the company to the point where it could become eligible to bid on government contracts for research and development work. Without a past performance record, progress was slow at first and sales in 1951 totaled only $675.

In April, 1952, Messrs. Sutter and Marshall secured the company's first prime contract—a government project that had to be completed by September, 1952.[2] Other companies had not bid on the contract because the time allotted was extremely short. However, Mr. Sutter and Mr. Marshall believed that they could fulfill the contract and submitted a bid that was accepted. Their engineers were gathered together, and on a

---

[2] A prime contract is awarded to one contractor who has the responsibility for the contract. The prime contractor may, in turn, award subcontracts to other companies for research and development or manufacturing of component parts.

"crash basis," this group developed, tested, and manufactured the electronic equipment ahead of the deadline. Largely due to this contract, sales in 1952 totaled $170,000, and the company incurred only a small loss for the year.

In the spring of 1953, Argonaut's reputation spread and research and development contracts came more easily. By June, 1953, the staff had increased to 70 people, and the company had accumulated a backlog of $500,000 in several cost-plus-fixed-fee research and development contracts (CPFF) and two fixed-price manufacturing contracts (FP). Mr. Sutter attributed this rapid success to the superior technical performance demonstrated by its first-rate engineering staff and to a lower overhead rate than competitors.

Although Mr. Jason had been elected president of the company and had handled the financing with the bank, he acted primarily as a silent partner. Mr. Sutter and Mr. Marshall were the operating heads of the company. After it became evident in the summer of 1953 that Argonaut Electronics was apparently destined to become a highly successful venture, Mr. Jason, through iniquitous means, issued additional stock to himself and acquired control of the company. When Mr. Sutter and Mr. Marshall objected to this move, Mr. Jason discharged them from their positions as officers of the company. Mr. Sutter and Mr. Marshall immediately undertook legal action to regain control of the company for themselves and for the engineers for whom it had been founded.

Meanwhile, the company was without technical leadership and began to deteriorate. Some of the key engineers expressed their dissatisfaction with the turn of events and left the company. Performance on contracts fell off sharply, and work was held up as more rigid inspection was instigated by the government. Only a handful of new contracts were received, and, in June, 1954, Mr. Jason was forced to purchase additional stock to help meet payrolls and to avoid a financial crisis. Throughout this period the company had lost money at a rapid rate primarily because of its inability to complete the two fixed-price contracts.

By midsummer of 1954, it appeared as if further losses would soon bankrupt the company, a situation Mr. Jason, as endorser of all loans, wished to avoid. By August of 1954, he capitulated and called for negotiations with Mr. Sutter and Mr. Marshall. The dispute was settled out of court. Mr. Jason surrendered his shares without reimbursement and relinquished all association with the company. Mr. Sutter and Mr. Marshall took over the sole voting stock and set about to rehire the former employees, to complete overdue contracts, to pay past-due bills, and to replenish the depleted backlog of orders. Mr. Marshall became president, and Mr. Sutter assumed the position of vice-president and treasurer.

Once Mr. Sutter and Mr. Marshall had regained control, the company grew steadily with sales increasing from $476,000 in 1955 to $1,850,000 in 1958, with a projected volume of $2,830,000 in 1959. Net income increased from $7,200 in 1955 to $38,000 in 1958 and was projected at $84,000 in 1959 (see Exhibits 1 and 2).

CURRENT OPERATIONS

CPFF Contracts

In 1958, approximately 75% of Argonaut's sales volume, or $1,370,000, came from prime government CPFF research and development contracts. Mr. Sutter believed that this phase of the business could continue to increase at a rate of about 50% per year for the next four or five years without straining the company's resources of men and facilities. Each year, the government had been spending an increasing portion of the growing national defense budget for electronics research and development contracts, and Argonaut Electronics concentrated its efforts in some of the most promising phases of this business. Argonaut's reputation and capabilities were growing steadily, and the company had developed a strong competitive position for recruiting needed engineering talent. Manpower did not appear to be a potential limiting factor.

Although Argonaut Electronics had the opportunity to grow at the rate of 50% per year in the government CPFF research and development phases of its business, management thought it might be preferable to refrain from further growth in this direction until the company had reached a more favorable balance between research and manufacturing revenues. Its long-term target was $1 of research revenues for every $5 to $10 of manufacturing. Consequently, revenues from CPFF contracts had been estimated for 1959 at the same dollar level as in 1958, or $1,370,000. Nevertheless, management thought that it might have to bid on new CPFF research and development contracts if it wished to preserve its reputation in basic research and maintain strong proprietary interests in certain research areas.[3] If these bids were accepted, the volume of research and development CPFF contracts could reach $1.6 million in

---

[3] A proprietary product was one for which the company had done the basic research and development work. In the instance of CPFF work the research was usually fully reimbursed by the government.

1959. This policy of restraining growth in CPFF lines might be re-evaluated if additional equity capital were raised.

One factor on the horizon did cause some concern to Mr. Sutter. The Armed Forces procurement agencies appeared to be shifting their purchasing policies toward putting entire weapons systems up for bid rather than just individual electronic components. Contracts for weapon systems were awarded to prime contractors who, in turn, awarded sub-contracts for individual equipment comprising the system. These systems contracts often amounted to $50 million or more, far beyond the bidding capacity of Argonaut Electronics. It appeared as if Argonaut would either have to bid on subcontracts or aim for some of the smaller systems contracts, perhaps on a joint basis with larger companies offering more diversified engineering staffs. However, a number of government agencies promised to continue awarding individual equipment contracts which could provide enough volume to support current CPFF volume.

Mr. Sutter was concerned that prime contractors might place greater weight than the government on financial strength in awarding their subcontracts, thereby placing Argonaut Electronics in a somewhat weakened competitive position. Moreover, the company would have to exert greater effort to develop contracts from a large group of prime contractors than it did when dealing with a small number of government agencies. Related promotion costs, nonreimburseable under government contracts, might increase total costs by as much as 2%. Mr. Sutter consequently wondered how the change in procurement policies would affect Argonaut's future ability to secure contracts.

Although Argonaut Electronics had never been in a strong financial position, it had always been able to finance CPFF research and development contracts. This was largely due to the relatively small investment required for these contracts. Inventory requirements equaled only one month's volume on the average. All facilities were rented, and the moderate investment required for equipment was financed largely by purchase mortgages or conditional sales contracts. Assets were written off as rapidly as possible, and cash flows generated from the projects were used to pay for the machinery.[4] Most expenses incurred on the contract were billed at the end of each month and usually were settled in about 75 days. In summary, total inventory and receivable funds requirements under CPFF contracts amounted to roughly 30% of the annual sales volume rate.

---

[4] Because of accelerated depreciation, the value of fixed assets tended to be understated on the balance sheet. For instance, a recent independent appraisal had placed a reproduction value after depreciation of $200,000 on fixed assets.

Additional working capital had been obtained by stretching accounts payable and by borrowing from a local bank with accounts receivable pledged as collateral (accepted at 90% of their face value). Mr. Sutter anticipated that future CPFF research and development contracts could be financed by similar means and that a portion of cash flows generated from these projects could be diverted to other corporate purposes without financial strain.

FP Contracts

Argonaut Electronics estimated that its profit margin before taxes and profit-sharing allocations on government CPFF contracts was running at only 4% of sales volume. As a consequence, management had looked forward to the day when it could bid on FP production contracts which could return profits equal to 12% of sales or greater before considering taxes and profit-sharing allocations.[5] However, FP contracts often involved greater risks. Bids were made on the basis of estimated costs, and the validity of these estimates depended in good part upon engineering ability to solve complex technical problems expeditiously. Management had moved cautiously in bidding on FP contracts—in part because it remembered the $60,000 lost on two FP contracts in 1953–1954, and because it did not believe that Argonaut Electronics was financially strong enough to support possible losses of this magnitude. Consequently, bids were submitted only on contracts where Argonaut Electronics had participated in the product development and was immediately familiar with the technical requirements and the probable production costs. Mr. Sutter believed that this tended to minimize but did not completely eliminate the risks associated with FP contracts.

From the beginning, Mr. Sutter and Mr. Marshall had set out to build proprietary know-how, research staff and facilities, and patents in areas where promising FP government contracts could be procured. In 1959, Argonaut's research staff was about as large as the staff of a progressive electronics company with sales of $50 million. Management hoped to be in a position to finance contracts when they arose so that it could protect the company's proprietary interests and capitalize upon them. At the moment, Argonaut was unlikely to win bids on contracts outside of its areas of specialization, and was in a very good position to win only those contracts resulting from its CPFF efforts.

Although the volume of FP contracts had grown steadily until it had reached a level of $350,000 in 1958, financing had not been a prob-

---

[5] Twenty-five per cent of income before taxes was set aside as a profit-sharing plan for employees.

lem. Working capital requirements for FP contracts had been financed through retained earnings, through loans with accounts receivable pledged as collateral, and by stretching payables. The capital investments necessary for FP contracts were somewhat larger than those required for CPFF contracts because of somewhat heavier investments in equipment and larger inventories as well as normal accounts receivable balances.[6] Early in 1959, Argonaut Electronics had bid to manufacture several pieces of equipment it had previously developed for the Navy and had received contracts totaling $1,700,000 by April, 1959, all except $500,000 to be completed in 1959. Moreover, the company expected to submit bids on contracts totaling perhaps as high as $4,500,000 on other Argonaut proprietary products. These contracts would be awarded during the 12-month period beginning in April, 1959, and Argonaut, through its proprietary interest, stood an excellent chance of getting the contracts. Sales from these contracts would be spread over an 18-month period beginning January 1, 1960. Mr. Sutter expected the volume of FP contracts would equal $2,800,000 in 1960 and mount steadily thereafter. For example, he anticipated that the volume of FP contracts might easily reach a level of $7,000,000, and perhaps significantly higher by 1962, provided financing appeared feasible.

With the contracts already received and the expectations of others, Argonaut management had been forced to seek new methods of financing for the new plant facilities and working capital required. Officers anticipated, for example, that fund requirements, excluding plant facilities, necessary to support a projected FP sales volume of $1,700,000 in 1959 would amount to $620,000, after considering progress payments.

Mr. Sutter did not wish to tie up funds in bricks and mortar and looked for other means of financing the estimated $250,000 required for a new plant. The company organized an independent realty corporation with only nominal capitalization. The realty company, in turn, leased a tract of land for 99 years from an Industrial Park Authority and negotiated a loan from an insurance company for 60% of the cost of a new, general-purpose plant. The balance of the funds was obtained by a second mortgage from the Industrial Park Authority and by a third mortgage granted by the company's administered profit-sharing trust. Rental payments amounting to $25,000 per year were scheduled to

---

[6] Inventories equal to approximately two months' FP sales volume were required. However, Argonaut had been able to secure progress payments, billed at 75% of monthly costs. Collections of receivables paralleled experience in CPFF lines. The balance of funds due were billed at the termination of the contract.

cover all outlays including taxes required by the realty company. Equipment purchases would be financed by means of a chattel mortgage from a finance company.

Historic sources, however, appeared inadequate to cover the sharp increases in requirements, particularly for inventories, caused by new FP contracts. A forecast of loan requirements through March, 1960, prepared in February, 1959, and unrevised to reflect higher sales expectations (see Exhibit 3), indicated needs of $770,000—$514,000 more than the bank loan balance on December 31, 1958. Although still less than accounts receivable balances, this projected loan compared with an equity base (at book value) of $241,000 on December 31, 1958, and with a projected equity base of $361,000 on March 31, 1960.

Argonaut Electronics had always maintained a very cordial relationship with its primary bank of account, Glendale Warranty Trust Company. The bank had continued to loan funds up to 90% of pledged accounts receivable despite a stated preference for limiting loans to the size of Argonaut's net worth. Although the bank had not expressed an unwillingness to continue lending under its existing arrangement, Mr. Sutter believed that it was unreasonable to request bank support of the amount envisioned, using accounts receivable as collateral.

Early in 1959, Argonaut Electronics had applied for a government V-loan to replace the accounts receivable financing. A V-loan was a line of credit with 90% of combined accounts receivable and inventories on specific government CPFF and FP contracts pledged as collateral. If the loan was granted, Argonaut could draw upon this line of credit up to a limit of $800,000. The Glendale bank would advance the funds at a 5% interest rate to the company under this V-loan, within limits defined by available collateral, and the government would guarantee the loan up to 80% of amounts borrowed. Although Mr. Sutter considered the chances of securing this loan were fair, a number of thorny problems remained to be ironed out. Also, Mr. Sutter wondered how large future borrowings could grow in relation to net worth before the government would no longer be willing to underwrite further debt. Preliminary investigations failed to produce any concrete guidelines on this matter.

Commercial Products

Perhaps the most promising avenue for future corporate development was the opportunity to exploit the creative ideas being generated by Argonaut engineers for commercial products. These opportunities had the dual advantage of promising higher profit margins and of reducing long-term dependence upon government defense expenditures, but were more risky. Argonaut Electronics already had developed two such commercial applications.

In late 1957, one company engineer convinced management that he could solve the complex technical problems involved in counting newspapers accurately. This technological advance, if accomplished, had applications to the newspaper industry since it enabled the paper to regulate output exactly, preventing costly overruns or premature press shutdowns. Moreover, the basic principle of this electronic device had potential applications in other phases of the publishing and printing industries. However, previous attempts to develop an accurate electronic counter for newspapers had all failed because of the high speed of the presses and of other technical considerations.

Argonaut management decided to invest $60,000 (most development expenses were written off as costs in 1957) in developing an automatic counter that could be installed on every newspaper press. The effort succeeded, and in 1958, the company was able to manufacture 22 counters selling for $6,000 per counter. Profit before taxes and profit sharing amounted to roughly 25% of sales. Shortly thereafter, at small additional expense, Argonaut developed a complete and improved counting system that could be used in lieu of individual counters on each press. It employed an electronic memory system and high-speed switching to count up to 120,000 units per minute, with the built-in capacity to total simultaneously the output of 40 different production, processing, or packaging operations. An exact quantity of product required could be dialed, and as soon as the counter recorded this total, it caused one or more alarm systems to flash a warning light, sound a buzzer, and automatically stop the presses. The complete counting system was to sell for a minimum of $50,000, or $10,000 per press if a newspaper had more than five presses. This model also promised a contribution to profits of 25%. Mr. Sutter recognized that these profits, unlike FP, probably were somewhat overestimated in view of a propensity for engineers to tinker with developed products in a manner likely to lead to raw material obsolescence. He believed this obsolescence, which was difficult to control, had probably cost the company $5,000 in 1958.

With firm orders in hand, management anticipated it would be possible to manufacture and sell 30 individual counters and two complete systems at the minimum price of $50,000. With about 1,750 daily newspapers in the country, larger sales were anticipated in the future. However, another company of Argonaut's size had recently introduced a comparable product at a similar price, and only technological know-how might keep competition from increasing. Working capital needs (accounts receivable and inventories) for the expected 1959 volume would approximate $70,000 on the average. No new machinery was needed in the counter and system manufacturing processes (mostly intricate assembly work).

In mid-1958 Argonaut engineers began to develop an artificial kidney for use in hospitals during kidney operations. Essentially, this system operated outside of the patient's body by electromechanical means and performed the normal kidney functions when the human kidney was inoperative. After a year of work and development expense costing approximately $60,000, the system had been perfected. It was enthusiastically received by the medical profession, and initial use attracted considerable interest among physicians.

Sales were solicited in the fall of 1958, and two artificial kidneys were sold in early 1959. By March of 1959, Argonaut Electronics had already accumulated sufficient orders for a sales volume of $240,000 in 1959, assuring a contribution to overhead of $60,000. At this volume, net working capital needs approximated $60,000, and no significant investments in new equipment were needed to produce the kidneys. Mr. Sutter hoped eventually that every one of the more than 5,000 hospitals in the country would require one or more units. Since each unit cost approximately $30,000, potential sales volume looked highly promising. However, other companies might well develop a similar product, which would reduce Argonaut's share of the market. Mr. Sutter knew that industry experience with similar products indicated competitive conditions would develop with a year or two of introduction, and that technical obsolescence was probable before five years had passed.

Despite the success of its two commercial ventures, Argonaut management was hesitant to launch research on more than one new industrial application per year. The chances of failure to develop the desired product seemed significantly less than under CPFF contracts, where Argonaut had an excellent record; however, even CPFF contracts occasionally required extensions when technological problems proved difficult to overcome. This meant that research expenditures on commercial developments could run substantially higher than initial estimates. Since Argonaut Electronics had to advance the funds for these commercial research projects from its own resources, these projects might tie up capital for longer periods than the company currently could afford. Moreover, in the event development problems proved unsurmountable, Argonaut Electronics would have to absorb the entire loss. Finally, even if the products were developed, there was no assurance that they could be marketed successfully, or manufactured at a reasonable cost.

In the final analysis, Mr. Sutter did not think Argonaut Electronics was currently strong enough to underwrite commercial research expenditures of more than $60,000 per year, regardless of how promising the development opportunities appeared. Mr. Sutter's cautious attitude was reinforced by knowledge of instances where other electronic firms had failed in commercial development work when they had seized upon the first few opportunities available.

Limiting commercial development work to one new product a year, nevertheless, required considerable restraint. In deciding upon the newspaper counter and artificial kidney, nearly 100 products, many equally as promising from a profit standpoint, had to be rejected. These alternatives appeared to require about the same amount of funds for development and for capital investment as the two products selected. In addition they seemed to have excellent chances (perhaps eight chances in ten) of both technological and marketing success. Prospects of possible future competition were more difficult to assess.

With additional financial resources, Mr. Sutter believed that Argonaut Electronics could increase the number of commercial ventures started each year severalfold and still choose from among projects promising to pay back estimated development costs (typically $60,000 before taxes) through profits in less than one year, and promising no significantly greater degree of risk.

DISCUSSION RELATED TO ISSUING OF EQUITY CAPITAL

The directors of Argonaut had first given serious consideration to the public sale of common stock in the spring of 1958. At that time one of Mr. Marshall's friends, Mr. George O. West, president of a firm specializing in the development and manufacture of component parts for analog computers, was forced to retire for reasons of health and wished to sell his ownership position (100% of outstanding stock) for $400,000. The company, Youngman Computer Company, had earned $67,000 after taxes in 1957 and appeared in the position to increase its profits to $100,000 in 1958 and to grow substantially thereafter. Argonaut Electronics was offered the first chance to purchase the stock, but the company could muster only $100,000 from various debt sources for the purchase. Even this sum promised to place the company in an extremely tight financial position thereafter.

Management believed that the offer was attractive, and it considered acquiring the stock by sponsoring a $300,000 public sale of part of the Youngman stock, purchasing the remainder for its own account. Upon investigation, Mr. Sutter learned that the Youngman stock could not be sold effectively during the slow summer months and September seemed the earliest feasible offering date. This date, however, was well beyond the period Mr. West was willing to wait. Moreover, underwriters were more interested in marketing Argonaut's stock than Youngman's. Various sources of venture capital were also investigated, but they were not interested in buying an interest in Youngman Computer Company per se. However, one venture capital firm offered to purchase 23,000 shares of Argonaut's stock for $300,000, which would have reduced the voting control position of Mr. Marshall and Mr. Sutter to less than 60%. In light of previous control difficulties and prospective capital requirements, this alternative appeared undesirable.

Argonaut Electronics subsequently "found" another buyer for Youngman Computer, a new company, Aurum Aeronautics, Inc., that had recently raised capital for other purposes. At the time of the acquisition, Aurum Aeronautics' common stock was selling for $1 per share; nine months later the market value had risen to trade in a range between $8 and $12 per share, due largely to the benefits of the acquisition.[7] While no such acquisition opportunity was in immediate prospect in 1959, Mr. Sutter anticipated that others of a similar nature would possibly come along in the future. Argonaut management did not wish to be caught in an inflexible financial position again should an equally attractive opportunity be presented.

At the April, 1959, meeting of the board of directors, one director suggested that the time may have come for Argonaut's first public sale of common stock. He noted that electronic stocks, in general, and the stocks of small research and development companies, in particular, had risen very sharply in price and were trading at extremely high price-earnings ratios. For example, Itek Corporation (over-the-counter) had risen from about $2 per share when trading began in July, 1958, to $63 per share (bid) in February, 1959—a price 140 times reported

---

[7] Argonaut received an option to buy 10,000 shares from Aurum Aeronautics at $1 per share in return for its part in the acquisition. These options could not be exercised until January, 1960.

earnings per share of $0.45 for the company's first year of operations ended September 30, 1958.[8] He wondered whether Argonaut Electronics would ever experience a climate for a public sale of stock that was as favorable as the present. The advantages and disadvantages of a public sale of stock either in late June or early September were discussed at length, and various considerations were raised.

The directors believed that the primary benefits gained from a stock sale would be the over-all improvement in the company's financial position which had several possible advantages. For example, it would substantially reduce the risk that an error in estimating for a FP contract might seriously undermine the company's financial resources and borrowing position. Also, it would tend to improve the company's chances of raising more debt capital in the future; enhance the possibilities of bidding on larger CPFF subcontracts; and increase flexibility thereby putting the company in a position to move swiftly when unexpected opportunities arose. Finally, it would enable the company to undertake the development of additional commercial products and thereby accelerate the company's growth.

A second advantage from a public sale of stock was the factor of timing which had precipitated the discussion in the April meeting of the directors. Conditions for raising equity capital were extremely favorable in the current market. Mr. Sutter thought it was quite possible that similar conditions might not exist again for several years. Mr. Sutter had grave doubts about the ability of some companies to live up to the market's current high expectations. Several times in the past the stocks for electronic companies had reached high levels (in relation to earnings) for temporary periods. However, several "glamour" issues failed to produce the promised growth, and some companies even went bankrupt. The resulting market disillusionment adversely affected market prices of all electronic stocks, and precipitous market declines were common. Mr. Sutter had serious doubts about the extremely high price-earnings ratios of many electronic stocks, and he questioned how the market would react to electronic stocks in the future if and when failures became more prevalent.

In this regard, an article in the April, 1959, issue of the *American Investor* published by the American Stock Exchange stated:

> More and more things are being done by electronics. This includes making —or losing—money in the stock market. It is not yet possible, however, for the

---

[8] All data adjusted for a five-for-one stock split in January, 1959.

investor simply to press the profit button and wait for the computer to calculate his new wealth. Prices of many electronic stocks advanced in 1958, and in general the group has performed conspicuously well in 1959. . . . Obviously when investors pay high prices for stocks of any company operating in a romantic industry, some can anticipate losses. . . . The (serious-minded) analyst warns: "All one can feel fairly sure of is that the aftermath of the boom in electronics will be the same as any other—more companies will fail, at least in a relative sense, than succeed."

Sale of common stock to the public would have a third advantage by giving more employees an opportunity to become owners of the company. Mr. Sutter and Mr. Marshall recognized that a company was no more than the people in it and that the success of Argonaut Electronics depended upon the ideas generated by the engineers. Early in 1955 management had inaugurated a stock purchase plan to permit employees to become a part of the company, but the number of participants had been limited to 25 key engineers, about 10% of the total personnel force. Mr. Sutter believed that the company's success to date had been a result of the spirit of joint entrepreneurship of the select group of key engineers and thought that this *esprit de corps* would permeate the entire organization if more employees could become owners of the company.

The strongest argument raised against the sale of stock was that Argonaut Electronics had no urgent need for $600,000—the minimum issue of equity funds considered economical by one prominent underwriter. The forecast (Exhibit 3) prepared by Mr. Sutter suggested no funds would be needed before 1960. With more capital, however, Argonaut management would consider increasing the number of planned commercial research projects each year from one to a maximum of three. This would require an additional commitment of $120,000 for development work in 1959. Production on FP contracts and on commercial products was currently scheduled in small lots in order to minimize inventory investments. With $50,000 more funds on hand, purchasing policies could be revised to derive economies of roughly $10,000 to $20,000 per year based on crude, preliminary estimates. The balance of the funds raised would be applied to reducing borrowings under the proposed V-loan, if secured, and to paying trade creditors more promptly, until further needs arose. The potential uses for funds, while desirable, were not urgent and might not compensate adequately for other disadvantages associated with public ownership.

Both Mr. Sutter and Mr. Marshall remembered the harrowing days of the previous ownership dispute and did not wish to expose themselves to such a risk again in the immediate future. However, they recognized they would eventually have to surrender absolute voting control (50% or more) if the company were going to grow into a sizable enterprise. Nevertheless, they hoped to preserve voting control until outside ownership could be distributed over a wide geographical area to thousands of small stockholders. Mr. Sutter believed it would be five or ten years before the company would be large enough to make it difficult for a large, private investor or a company to finance the purchase of a substantial number of shares of Argonaut Electronics. Moreover, both principals were in their middle 30's and could foresee no urgency for establishing a market value for their stock holdings for estate tax purposes.

Messrs. Sutter and Marshall were also apprehensive about selling common stock because they were no longer the sole stockholders in the company. Management had inaugurated a plan for the sale of stock to key employees and a deferred profit-sharing plan for all employees to encourage a feeling of ownership and a participation in the company's growth. The stock holdings of Messrs. Sutter and Marshall had declined to 73% of the total shares outstanding on December 31, 1958, and were expected to fall to 67% within a few months when all of the 100,000 authorized shares were issued.

The third factor weighing against sale of stock in the immediate future was the fact that Argonaut Electronics had not begun to realize its full earnings potential. Earnings after taxes in 1958 had amounted to $38,000, were running at the annual rate of $56,000 in the first half of 1959, and were estimated at an annual rate of $124,000 during the last quarter of 1959. Moreover, by 1961, Mr. Sutter believed these earnings could easily be $250,000. Sale of equity capital therefore might be premature. On the other hand, Mr. Sutter anticipated present sales growth rates could probably be sustained over the next five years at least, so that an equity sale might always look unattractive relative to future earning expectations.

Sale of stock might also be premature in mid-1959. The company wanted its first issue underwritten by a leading investment house to add market stature to the company and to enhance future chances of successful issues. Mr. Sutter had gained the impression from previous discussions with a reputable underwriter that the ideal time for a first issue of common stock generally occurred when a firm had reached the position where it could expect to issue 100,000 shares so that the shares could be distributed over a wide geographical area and a market developed for the stock. Moreover, the underwriter stated a preference for stocks priced between $10 and $20 to prevent the new issue from getting a reputation as a "dog." Finally he mentioned that his firm preferred companies with a net worth of at least $1 million and a stock issue where the minimum compensation to the underwriter would be $60,-000. Mr. Sutter did not believe that these goals probably would be reached for another two years. However, the underwriter appeared willing to consider a smaller issue—probably no less than $600,000—for a company with Argonaut's promise.

Mr. Sutter believed Argonaut's net proceeds per share issued—stated as a percentage of the stock's intrinsic market value—would be higher if the stock issue were postponed until the criteria mentioned by the underwriter were fulfilled because the offering price could be set closer to "the market" after a longer growth history. Moreover, the underwriting and related expenses for an issuance of $1 million would not be much higher than for an issuance of $600,000.

In reviewing the possible ramifications resulting from a public sale of stock, Mr. Sutter wondered whether public ownership of Argonaut Electronics' stock would necessitate a change in certain policies of the company. For instance, he questioned whether outside stockholders would be satisfied with retention of 100% of earnings and the profit-sharing plan.

From recent casual conversations with friends in the investment banking profession, Mr. Sutter held the impression that a new issue would be priced somewhat above 20 times the annualized rate of the most recent semiannual earnings per share. This meant that if the issue went public in the late fall of 1959, it might be priced at about $20 per share and require the issuance of 30,000 shares. Underwriting fees would approximate 10% of the planned issue of $600,000. Other costs associated with registration, etc., would probably amount to $20,000.

Mr. Sutter recognized that the nature of the company would be altered considerably if common stock were issued to the public. He thought that all of the expansion policies would have to be re-examined critically and perhaps new policies and goals established for operations after 1959. He did not think the directors were likely to change their limitation of a maximum of three new commercial ventures per year for the next few years. As a practical limit, management thought it would be difficult for total manufacturing sales to increase more than 60% per year after 1960 without placing too great a strain on management. However, excluding these rigid policies, management felt free to develop the most suitable set of expansion plans for using the funds that would be raised.

Exhibit 1

ARGONAUT ELECTRONICS, INC.

COMPARATIVE BALANCE SHEET, DECEMBER 31, 1951–1958

(Dollar figures in thousands)

	1951	1952	1953	1954*	1955	1956	1957	1958
ASSETS								
Current assets:								
Cash	$1.2	$ 0.2	$ 0.9	$ 8.4	$ 7.8	$ 4.6	$ 8.8	$ 7.9
Accounts receivable—net†	2.1	71.9	136.9	154.4	106.2	194.3	315.1	492.4
Inventory	0.9	6.2	7.3	4.7	4.7	5.9	52.2	234.9
Total current assets	$4.2	$78.3	$145.1	$167.5	$118.7	$204.8	$376.1	$735.2
Investment in subsidiary—at cost				7.3	29.7	29.8	29.8	29.8
Fixed assets—net	1.9	12.3	29.9	30.4	30.7	48.6	83.7	101.9
Other assets		0.7	36.4	10.3	9.2	9.6	7.8	15.4
Total assets	$6.1	$91.3	$211.4	$215.5	$188.3	$292.8	$497.4	$882.3
LIABILITIES AND NET WORTH								
Current liabilities:								
Bank loans		$63.8	$ 47.9	$ 42.0	$ 39.2	$ 77.7	$128.2	$256.4
Equipment notes				1.0	1.2	8.2	18.5	37.3
Accounts payable		2.8	38.8	43.2	18.9	59.2	97.1	218.0
Accruals		4.5	44.0	24.2	3.5	12.7	32.9	64.2
Total current liabilities		$71.1	$130.7	$110.4	$ 62.8	$157.8	$276.7	$575.9
Long-term debt:								
Subordinated note‡				$ 24.8	$ 24.7	$ 21.1	$ 10.1	$ 65.3
Equipment notes					5.6	9.1	9.0	
Loans from stockholders	$2.8	$ 2.8	$ 21.7					
Total long-term debt	$2.8	$ 2.8	$ 21.7	$ 24.8	$ 30.3	$ 30.2	$ 19.1	$ 65.3
Reserves			3.9	17.0	16.9			
Net worth:								
Common stock (authorized—100,000 shares; outstanding December 31, 1958—92,000 shares)	$5.0	$20.1	$ 90.2	$ 96.3	$104.4	$114.3	$163.3	$164.7
Earned surplus	(1.7)	(2.7)	(35.1)	(33.0)	(26.1)	(9.5)	38.3	76.4
Total net worth	$3.3	$17.4	$ 55.1	$ 63.3	$ 78.3	$104.8	$201.6	$241.1
Total liabilities and net worth	$6.1	$91.3	$211.4	$215.5	$188.3	$292.8	$497.4	$882.3

* Company reorganized in 1954.
† Accounts receivable assigned to secure bank loan.
‡ Subordinated notes are subordinated to creditors.

Exhibit 2

ARGONAUT ELECTRONICS, INC.

COMPARATIVE INCOME STATEMENT

FISCAL YEARS ENDING DECEMBER 31, 1951–1958

(Dollar figures in thousands)

	1951	1952	1953	1954	1955	1956	1957	1958
Net sales	$ 0.7	$170.1	$425.5	$391.4	$476.0	$631.8	$1,246.2	$1,850.4
Cost of goods sold		111.0	363.7	345.8	398.8	515.9	1,038.9	1,545.7
Gross profit	$ 0.7	$ 59.1	$ 61.8	$ 45.6	$ 77.2	$115.9	$ 207.3	$ 304.7
General and administrative expense	2.2	58.9	87.0	62.1	61.9	78.9	129.7	200.4
Profit-sharing contributions					2.4	5.5	17.4	21.4
Profit from operation	$(1.5)	$ 0.2	$(25.2)	$(16.5)	$ 12.9	$ 31.5	$ 60.2	$ 82.9
Interest and miscellaneous deductions		1.2	7.2	8.5	5.7	14.8	8.5	18.7
Income before taxes	$(1.5)	$ (1.0)	$(32.4)	$(25.0)	$ 7.2	$ 16.7	$ 51.7	$ 64.2
Income taxes							3.9	26.1
Net profit after taxes	$(1.5)	$ (1.0)	$(32.4)	$(25.0)	$ 7.2	$ 16.7	$ 47.8	$ 38.1

INCOME STATEMENT ANALYSIS—PERCENTAGES

	1951	1952	1953	1954	1955	1956	1957	1958
Net sales	100.0 %	100.0 %	100.0 %	100.0 %	100.0%	100.0%	100.0%	100.0%
Cost of goods sold		65.3	85.5	88.3	83.8	81.6	83.4	83.5
Gross profit	100.0 %	34.7 %	14.5 %	11.7 %	16.2%	18.4%	16.6%	16.5%
General and administrative expense	314.2	34.6	20.4	15.9	13.0	12.5	10.4	10.8
Profit-sharing contributions					0.5	0.9	1.4	1.2
Profit from operation	(214.2)%	0.1 %	(5.9)%	(4.2)%	2.7%	5.0%	4.8%	4.5%
Interest and miscellaneous deductions		0.7	1.7	2.2	1.2	2.3	0.7	1.0
Income before taxes	(214.2)%	(0.6)%	(7.6)%	(6.4)%	1.5%	2.7%	4.1%	3.5%
Income taxes							0.3	1.4
Net profit after taxes	(214.2)%	(0.6)%	(7.6)%	(6.4)%	1.5%	2.7%	3.8%	2.1%

Exhibit 3

ARGONAUT ELECTRONICS, INC.

PROJECTION OF FINANCIAL STATEMENTS BY QUARTERS

JANUARY 1, 1959—MARCH 31, 1960

(Dollar figures in thousands)

I. PRO FORMA INCOME STATEMENTS

	1st	2nd	3rd	4th	Total	1960 1st
Sales	$380	$620	$830	$1,000	$2,830	$1,060
Cost of goods sold	310	515	705	855	2,385	900
Gross profit	$ 70	$105	$125	$ 145	$ 445	$ 160
General and administrative expense*	45	47	55	55	202	57
Profit-sharing contributions	5	13	15	20	53	23
Operating profit	$ 20	$ 45	$ 55	$ 70	$ 190	$ 80
Other expenses†	6	7	8	9	30	10
Profit before taxes	$ 14	$ 38	$ 47	$ 61	$ 160	$ 70
Taxes	6	18	22	30	76	35
Net income	$ 8	$ 20	$ 25	$ 31	$ 84	$ 35

* Includes depreciation of $55,000 and development expenses on industrial products of $60,000.
† Largely interest expenses.
Note: This forecast was prepared in mid-February, 1959, using the following sales assumptions for the year 1959:

Government research and development contracts (CPFF)........$1,370,000
Government manufacturing contracts (FP).................... 1,120,000
Commercial products....................................... 340,000
$2,830,000

II. PRO FORMA BALANCE SHEET

	Mar. 31	June 30	Sept. 30	Dec. 31	1960 Mar. 31
ASSETS					
Cash	$ 10	$ 22	$ 34	$ 45	$ 45
Accounts receivable	495	535	700	860	885
Inventories	360	350	320	365	370
Other	30	30	30	30	30
Total current assets	$ 895	$ 937	$1,084	$1,300	$1,330
Fixed assets—net*	110	115	122	130	135
Other	46	46	46	46	46
Total assets	$1,051	$1,098	$1,252	$1,476	$1,511
LIABILITIES AND NET WORTH					
Notes payable—bank (or V-loan)	$ 388	$ 590	$ 630	$ 745	$ 770
Trade payable	193	42	116	158	156
Income tax payable†	19	24	46	76	73
Equipment loans	37	37	37	37	37
Progress payments billed	65	65	65	78	65
Accruals	41	18	18	18	18
Total current liabilities	$ 743	$ 776	$ 912	$1,112	$1,119
Equipment loans	58	52	45	38	31
Common stock and surplus‡	165	165	165	165	165
Earned surplus	85	105	130	161	196
Total liabilities and net worth	$1,051	$1,098	$1,252	$1,476	$1,511

* An investment of approximately $1,000 in new equipment was required for each $10,000 of incremental increase in government contract sales volume over estimates.
† Payable in equal installments by March 15 and June 15 following the close of the taxable year.
‡ Excluding consideration of 8,000 shares to be sold to employees during 1959 for approximately $25,000.

Appendix

TABLES FOR THE ANALYSIS OF CAPITAL EXPENDITURES

By Jerome Bracken and Charles J. Christenson

USE OF THE INVESTMENT TABLES

This appendix includes tables intended for use in the analysis of decisions to invest in captial assets such as plant and equipment. Acquisition of such assets normally involves an immediate outlay followed by a stream of earnings or costs over time. It may be desired as part of the analysis to compare the outlay with the earnings, or to compare the streams of costs of two methods of performing the same function.

The investment factors included in the booklet are tabulated for the following periods and rates:

Periods: Integral values from 1 through 50.
Rates: From 2% to 30% at 2% intervals, plus 15% table;
From 30% to 50% at 5% intervals;
From 50% to 100% at 25% intervals.

The tables are organized by rates, with the ten following factors tabulated on a single page for each rate:

1. Present value of $1.
2. Amount to which $1 will accumulate.
3. Present value of $1 per period received at the end of each period.
4. Present value of $1 per period received continuously during period.
5. Amount to which $1 paid at the end of each period will accumulate.
6. Amount to which $1 paid continuously during each period will accumulate.
7. Amount received at end of each period which will recover $1 of initial investment.
8. Amount received continuously during period which will recover $1 of initial investment.
9. Present value of sum-of-the-years'-digits depreciation on $1 of initial investment.
10. Present value of double-declining balance depreciation on $1 of initial investment.

It is assumed throughout these tables that interest is compounded on a "per period" basis, even when payments are made continuously.

397

It is essential to a valid comparison that all calculations in a given analysis be based upon the same period of compounding, although this requirement seems to be commonly ignored.[1]

IMPORTANT COMMENT ON NOTATION

In order to provide the same number of significant digits throughout the tables, the tables are presented in what is called "floating point" notation. Each entry in the tables consists of two parts:

1. A block of five digits which are the first five significant digits of the desired value.
2. A decimal-point indicator which locates the decimal point with respect to the five significant digits.

This notation can best be explained by means of several examples. Suppose that the following entry is found in the tables:

17917E 03.

The first five digits of the entry, "17917," are the first five significant digits of the quantity tabulated. The expression "E 03" gives the location of the decimal point, in this case after the *third* digit of the entry (or three digits to the right of the beginning of the entry). That is, the correct numerical value of the quantity tabulated is:

179.17.

If the decimal-point indicator is negative, as in the entry

73021E-03,

the decimal point is to be located by inserting the designated number of zeros ahead of the entry. The correct numerical value for the above entry is:

.00073021.

In short, the decimal-point indicator specifies the number of places the decimal point must be shifted away from the first digit of the entry. If the number following the letter "E" in the indicator is *positive,* the decimal point is shifted to the *right.* If the number is *negative* the decimal point is shifted to the *left.*

---

[1] For further discussion of this point, see Charles Christenson, "Construction of Present Value Tables for Use in Evaluating Investment Opportunities," *Accounting Review,* October, 1955, pp. 666–72.

EXAMPLES OF THE USE OF THE TABLES

1. *Present Value of $1*

This is the value today of the right to receive $1 at the end of *n* periods if money will earn *i* per period compounded periodically.

Example 1. What is the present value of $1 to be received at the end of the 17th period, calculated at a rate of 15% compounded periodically? In the table for 15% and on the line representing 17 periods we find the entry

$$92926E\text{-}01.$$

In accordance with the notation employed in this table, this represents a value of $0.092926.

Example 2. What is the present value of $13.45 to be received at the end of the 17th period, calculated at a rate of 15% compounded periodically? In Example 1 we obtained the present value of $1 under these conditions and need only multiply that value by 13.45 to obtain

$$\$(13.45) \times (0.092926) = \$1.2499 .$$

2. *Amount to Which $1 Will Accumulate*

This is the amount which will be returned in *n* years if $1 is invested today to earn *i* per period, compounded periodically, as in a savings account.

Example 3. To what amount will $1 accumulate in 17 periods if invested today to earn 15% per period, compounded periodically? In the table for 17 periods and 15%, we find the entry 10761E 02. This represents an amount of $10.761.

Example 4. How long will it take to double one's investment if it is invested to earn 15% per period? For five periods, we find the entry 20114E 01, or $2.0114, in the table. Thus, at 15%, an investment will double in value in just under five periods.

3. *Present Value of $1 per Period Received at End of Each Period*

Often an investment will return not a single payment but a series of payments. This column enables one to find the present value of such a series when the payments are all equal and received periodically at the end of each period.

Example 5. An investment returns $1 at the end of each of the next 17 periods. If money is worth 15% per period, compounded periodically, what is this investment worth? The entry in the table is 60472E 01, which gives a value of $6.0472.

Example 6. A building can be acquired for $60,472 and then leased out at annual payments of $10,000, to be paid at the end of each year for 17 years. At the end of 17 years the building will be worthless. What is the annual rate of return on the investment? According to Example 5, at 15% the annual payments would have a present value of $60,472. Since this is equal to the cost of the building, the rate of return is 15%.

Example 7. What is the present value of a series of payments of $1 made at the end of each period from the tenth through the seventeenth inclusive? This can be found as follows:

```
Present value for seventeen periods..........................$6.0472
Present value for nine periods...............................  4.7716
Present value tenth through seventeenth periods...............$1.2756
```

4. Present Value of $1 per Period Received Continuously during Period

Many nonfinancial investments are made in the expectation of receiving a return almost continuously rather than at the end of stated intervals. For such investments, Column 3 would understate the present value; receiving the return *during* the period rather than at its end increases its present value. The appropriate adjustment can, however, be determined by means of the calculus and is incorporated in this column.

Example 8. A machine can be acquired to produce a product which will be sold at a constant rate for five years, at which time the usefulness of the machine will be at an end. The contribution from the product (revenue less variable cost) is expected to be $1,000 per year. If money is worth 15% compounded anually, how much can be paid for the machine and still permit a contribution to be made to general overhead? From the table, we find that the present value of $1 per year received continuously is $3.5977, so that the machine has a value of $3,597.70.

5. Amount to Which $1 Received at the End of Each Period Will Accumulate

This column gives the amount which can be returned at some fixed future date if periodic payments of $1 are invested at compound interest, as in a periodic savings plan.

Example 9. If $1 is invested at the end of each of 17 periods to earn 15% compounded periodically, what will be the aggregate value of the investment at the end of the seventeenth period? The value obtained from the table is $65.075.

6. *Amount to Which $1 per Period Paid Continuously during Period Will Accumulate*

This column relates to Column 5 in the same way as Column 4 relates to Column 3. If payments are made during the year rather than at the end, they will earn interest over a longer period and hence will accumulate to a larger amount.

Example 10. If money is invested continuously at the rate of $1 per period to earn 15%, what will be the aggregate value of the investment at the end of the seventeenth period? In this case the value will be $69.842.

7. *Amount Received at End of Each Period Which Will Recover $1 of Initial Investment*

The tables for the present value of $1 per year, Columns 3 and 4, enable one to determine the present payment equivalent to a given stream. It is often useful to be able to invert this procedure: given an initial outlay, find the periodic stream of equivalent value. Columns 7 and 8 provide such results. Column 7 gives the equivalent stream in which payments are made at the end of each period. For brevity, we will refer to this function at the *capital recovery factor.*

Example 11. Consider the building described in Example 6. Suppose that its cost were $75,000 rather than the amount given in that example. What annual rent would have to be received to recover the investment if money is worth 15%? From Column 7, we find that the capital recovery factor is 0.16537. Multiplying this factor by the cost of the building, we determine that

$$(\$75{,}000)(0.16537) = \$12{,}402.75$$

is the required annual rent.

8. *Amount Received Continuously during Each Period Which Will Recover $1 of Initial Investment*

This table relates to Column 7 in the same way as Column 4 relates to Column 3. If payments are made during the year rather than at the end, a slightly smaller stream is required to recover a given investment.

Example 12. An operation is now being performed by hand at a cost of $5,000 per year. A machine is available which will reduce this cost to $1,000. The machine has an expected life of five years and costs $15,000. If money is worth 15%, and ignoring taxes, which alternative is cheaper? From Column 8, we find that the capital recovery factor is 0.27795. Hence, the initial cost of the machine is equivalent to an annual outlay of ($15,000) (0.27795) = $4,169.25 per year. When this amount is added to the operating costs of the machine, we see that the hand method is slightly less costly.

9. Present Value of Sum-of-the-Years'-Digits Depreciation on $1 of Initial Investment

While depreciation itself is not a cash item, it has tax consequences which do result in cash flow: as a tax-deductible expense, it reduces taxes paid, which is a cash outlay. Columns 9 and 10 enable the calculation of the tax writeoff under two accelerated write-off methods permitted by federal income tax laws.[2] Both tables assume that the tax credit will be taken in one lump sum at the end of each year of asset life. While other assumptions could be made, the exact circumstances are likely to vary from case to case, and it is believed that the assumption used will be reasonably appropriate in most of these.

Column 9 is to be used when sum-of-the-years'-digits depreciation is applicable.

Example 13. On the machine described in Example 12, what would be the present value at 15% of the tax credit on sum-of-the-years'-digits depreciation charges? According to Column 9, $1 of investment would produce depreciation charges, with a present value of $0.73238, so that the total present value is ($15,000) (0.73238) = $10,985.70. Taxes will be reduced by 52% of this amount, or $5,712.56.

10. Present Value of Double-Declining Balance Depreciation on $1 of Initial Investment

This table is used exactly as Column 9, except when double-declining balance depreciation is applicable. The federal income tax laws permit a change to be made from double-declining balance to straight-line depreciation. The tables assume that such a change will

---

[2] See, for example, R. N. Anthony, *Management Accounting* (rev. ed.; Homewood, Ill.: Richard D. Irwin, Inc., 1960), p. 144.

be made in the year in which the straight-line method begins to result in larger tax credits.

Example 14. If double-declining balance depreciation were applied to the machine described in Examples 12 and 13, the present value of depreciation charges on $1 of initial investment would be $0.73943. Hence the tax credits would have a present value of

$$(\$15,000)(0.73943)(0.52) = \$5,767.55 .$$

2% PER PERIOD

PERIOD	PRESENT VALUE OF $1	AMOUNT TO WHICH $1 WILL ACCUMULATE	PRESENT VALUE OF $1 PER PERIOD		AMOUNT TO WHICH $1 PER PERIOD WILL ACCUMULATE		AMOUNT PER PERIOD TO RECOVER $1 OF INVESTMENT		PRESENT VALUE OF DEPRECIATION	
			Received at End	Received Continuously	Received at End	Received Continuously	Received at End	Received Continuously	Sum-of-Years' Digits	Declining Balance
1	98039E 00	10200E 01	98039E 00	99016E 00	10000E 01	10100E 01	10200E 01	10099E 01		
2	96117E 00	10404E 01	19416E 01	19609E 01	20200E 01	20401E 01	51505E 00	50997E 00		
3	94232E 00	10612E 01	28839E 01	29126E 01	30604E 01	30909E 01	34675E-00	34333E-00	96764E 00	97189E 00
4	92385E 00	10824E 01	38077E 01	38457E 01	41216E 01	41627E 01	26262E-00	26003E-00	96136E 00	96376E 00
5	90573E 00	11041E 01	47135E 01	47604E 01	52040E 01	52559E 01	21216E-00	21006E-00	95513E 00	95613E 00
6	88797E 00	11262E 01	56014E 01	56573E 01	63081E 01	63710E 01	17853E-00	17676E-00	94897E 00	94839E 00
7	87056E 00	11487E 01	64720E 01	65365E 01	74343E 01	75084E 01	15451E-00	15299E-00	94287E 00	94100E 00
8	85349E 00	11717E 01	73253E 01	73985E 01	85830E 01	86685E 01	13651E-00	13516E-00	93683E 00	93353E 00
9	83676E 00	11951E 01	81622E 01	82436E 01	97546E 01	98519E 01	12252E-00	12131E-00	93085E 00	92633E 00
10	82035E 00	12190E 01	89826E 01	90721E 01	10950E 02	11059E 02	11133E-00	11023E-00	92492E 00	91906E 00
11	80426E 00	12434E 01	97868E 01	98844E 01	12169E 02	12290E 02	10218E-00	10117E-00	91905E 00	91203E 00
12	78849E 00	12682E 01	10575E 02	10681E 02	13412E 02	13546E 02	94560E-01	93626E-01	91324E 00	90496E 00
13	77303E 00	12936E 01	11348E 02	11461E 02	14680E 02	14827E 02	88118E-01	87249E-01	90749E 00	89810E 00
14	75788E 00	13195E 01	12106E 02	12227E 02	15974E 02	16133E 02	82602E-01	81787E-01	90179E 00	89121E 00
15	74301E 00	13459E 01	12849E 02	12977E 02	17293E 02	17466E 02	77825E-01	77057E-01	89614E 00	88451E 00
16	72845E 00	13728E 01	13578E 02	13713E 02	18639E 02	18825E 02	73650E-01	72923E-01	89055E 00	87779E 00
17	71416E 00	14002E 01	14292E 02	14434E 02	20012E 02	20212E 02	69970E-01	69279E-01	88501E 00	87124E 00
18	70016E 00	14282E 01	14992E 02	15141E 02	21412E 02	21626E 02	66702E-01	66044E-01	87952E 00	86469E 00
19	68643E 00	14568E 01	15678E 02	15835E 02	22841E 02	23068E 02	63782E-01	63152E-01	87409E 00	85830E 00
20	67297E 00	14859E 01	16351E 02	16514E 02	24297E 02	24540E 02	61157E-01	60553E-01	86871E 00	85190E 00

21	659778E 00	15157E 01	17011E 02	17181E 02	25783E 02	26040E 02	58785E-01	58205E-01	86337E 00	84565E 00
22	64684E 00	15460E 01	17658E 02	17834E 02	27299E 02	27571E 02	56631E-01	56073E-01	85809E 00	83942E 00
23	63416E 00	15769E 01	18292E 02	18475E 02	28445E 02	29132E 02	54668E-01	54129E-01	85286E 00	83331E 00
24	62172E 00	16084E 01	18914E 02	19102E 02	30422E 02	30725E 02	52871E-01	52349E-01	84768E 00	82722E 00
25	60953E 00	16406E 01	19523E 02	19718E 02	32030E 02	32350E 02	51220E-01	50715E-01	84255E 00	82125E 00
26	59758E 00	16734E 01	20121E 02	20322E 02	33671E 02	34007E 02	49699E-01	49209E-01	83746E 00	81531E 00
27	58586E 00	17069E 01	20707E 02	20913E 02	35344E 02	35697E 02	48293E-01	47816E-01	83242E 00	80948E 00
28	57437E 00	17410E 01	21281E 02	21493E 02	37051E 02	37421E 02	46990E-01	46526E-01	82743E 00	80367E 00
29	56311E 00	17758E 01	21844E 02	22062E 02	38792E 02	39179E 02	45778E-01	45327E-01	82248E 00	79797E 00
30	55207E 00	18114E 01	22396E 02	22620E 02	40568E 02	40972E 02	44650E-01	44209E-01	81759E 00	79230E 00
31	54125E 00	18476E 01	22938E 02	23166E 02	42379E 02	42802E 02	43596E-01	43166E-01	81273E 00	78673E 00
32	53063E 00	18845E 01	23468E 02	23702E 02	44227E 02	44668E 02	42611E-01	42190E-01	80792E 00	78119E 00
33	52023E 00	19222E 01	23989E 02	24228E 02	46112E 02	46571E 02	41687E-01	41275E-01	80316E 00	77574E 00
34	51003E 00	19607E 01	24499E 02	24743E 02	48034E 02	48513E 02	40416E-01	40416E-01	79844E 00	77033E 00
35	50003E 00	19999E 01	24999E 02	25248E 02	49994E 02	50493E 02	40002E-01	39607E-01	79376E 00	76501E 00
36	49022E-00	20399E 01	25489E 02	25743E 02	51994E 02	52513E 02	39233E-01	38846E-01	78913E 00	75972E 00
37	48061E-00	20807E 01	25969E 02	26228E 02	54034E 02	54573E 02	38507E-01	38127E-01	78453E 00	75452E 00
38	47119E-00	21223E 01	26441E 02	26704E 02	56115E 02	56674E 02	37821E-01	37447E-01	77998E 00	74934E 00
39	46195E-00	21647E 01	26903E 02	27171E 02	58237E 02	58818E 02	37171E-01	36804E-01	77547E 00	74426E 00
40	45289E-00	22080E 01	27355E 02	27628E 02	60402E 02	61004E 02	36556E-01	36195E-01	77101E 00	73920E 00
41	44401E-00	22522E 01	27799E 02	28077E 02	62610E 02	63234E 02	35972E-01	35617E-01	76658E 00	73423E 00
42	43530E-00	22972E 01	28235E 02	28516E 02	64862E 02	65509E 02	35417E-01	35068E-01	76219E 00	72929E 00
43	42677E-00	23432E 01	28662E 02	28947E 02	67159E 02	67829E 02	34890E-01	34546E-01	75785E 00	72443E 00
44	41840E-00	23901E 01	29080E 02	29370E 02	69503E 02	70195E 02	34388E-01	34049E-01	75354E 00	71999E 00
45	41020E-00	24379E 01	29490E 02	29784E 02	71893E 02	72609E 02	33910E-01	33575E-01	74927E 00	71484E 00
46	40215E-00	24866E 01	29892E 02	30190E 02	74331E 02	75071E 02	33453E-01	33123E-01	74504E 00	71011E 00
47	39427E-00	25363E 01	30287E 02	30588E 02	76817E 02	77583E 02	33018E-01	32692E-01	74084E 00	70546E 00
48	38654E-00	25871E 01	30673E 02	30979E 02	79353E 02	80144E 02	32280E-01	32280E-01	73669E 00	70084E 00
49	37896E-00	26388E 01	31052E 02	31362E 02	81941E 02	82757E 02	32204E-01	31886E-01	73257E 00	69629E 00
50	37153E-00	26916E 01	31424E 02	31737E 02	84579E 02	85422E 02	31823E-01	31509E-01	72849E 00	69177E 00

4% PER PERIOD

PERIOD	PRESENT VALUE OF $1	AMOUNT TO WHICH $1 WILL ACCUMULATE	PRESENT VALUE OF $1 PER PERIOD		AMOUNT TO WHICH $1 PER PERIOD WILL ACCUMULATE		AMOUNT PER PERIOD TO RECOVER $1 OF INVESTMENT		PRESENT VALUE OF DEPRECIATION	
			Received at End	Received Continuously	Received at End	Received Continuously	Received at End	Received Continuously	Sum-of-Years' Digits	Declining Balance
1	96154E 00	10400E 01	96154E 00	98064E 00	10000E 01	10199E 01	10400E 01	10197E 01		
2	92456E 00	10816E 01	18861E 01	19236E 01	20400E 01	20805E 01	53020E 00	51987E 00		
3	88900E 00	11249E 01	27751E 01	28302E 01	31216E 01	31836E 01	36035E-00	35333E-00	93712E 00	94526E 00
4	85480E 00	11699E 01	36299E 01	37020E 01	42465E 01	43308E 01	27549E-00	27012E-00	92526E 00	92988E 00
5	82193E 00	12167E 01	44518E 01	45403E 01	54163E 01	55239E 01	22463E-00	22025E-00	91363E 00	91561E 00
6	79031E 00	12653E 01	52421E 01	53463E 01	66330E 01	67648E 01	19076E-00	18705E-00	90222E 00	90133E 00
7	75992E 00	13159E 01	60021E 01	61213E 01	76783E 01	80552E 01	16661E-00	16336E-00	89102E 00	88784E 00
8	73069E 00	13686E 01	67327E 01	68665E 01	92142E 01	93973E 01	14853E-00	14553E-00	88004E 00	87435E 00
9	70259E 00	14233E 01	74353E 01	75831E 01	10583E 02	10793E 02	13449E-00	13187E-00	86926E 00	86150E 00
10	67556E 00	14802E 01	81109E 01	82721E 01	12006E 02	12245E 02	12329E-00	12089E-00	85868E 00	84869E 00
11	64958E 00	15395E 01	87605E 01	89345E 01	13486E 02	13754E 02	11415E-00	11193E-00	84830E 00	83643E 00
12	62460E 00	16010E 01	93851E 01	95716E 01	15026E 02	15324E 02	10655E-00	10448E-00	83812E 00	82425E 00
13	60057E 00	16651E 01	99856E 01	10184E 02	16627E 02	16957E 02	10014E-00	98193E-01	82812E 00	81254E 00
14	57748E 00	17317E 01	10565E 02	10773E 02	18292E 02	18655E 02	94669E-01	92825E-01	81830E 00	80093E 00
15	55526E 00	18009E 01	11118E 02	11339E 02	20024E 02	20421E 02	89941E-01	88189E-01	80667E 00	78974E 00
16	53391E 00	18730E 01	11652E 02	11884E 02	21825E 02	22258E 02	85820E-01	84148E-01	79921E 00	77867E 00
17	51337E 00	19479E 01	12166E 02	12407E 02	23698E 02	24168E 02	82199E-01	80597E-01	78992E 00	76798E 00
18	49363E-00	20258E 01	12659E 02	12911E 02	25645E 02	26155E 02	78993E-01	77454E-01	78080E 00	75741E 00
19	47464E-00	21068E 01	13134E 02	13395E 02	27671E 02	28221E 02	76139E-01	74655E-01	77185E 00	74719E 00
20	45639E-00	21911E 01	13590E 02	13860E 02	29778E 02	30370E 02	73582E-01	72148E-01	76306E 00	73709E 00

21	43883E-00	22788E 01	14029E 02	14308E 02	31969E 02	32604E 02	71280E-01	69891E-01	75442E 00	72731E 00
22	42196E-00	23699E 01	14451E 02	14738E 02	34248E 02	34928E 02	69199E-01	67851E-01	74594E 00	71766E 00
23	40573E-00	24647E 01	14857E 02	15152E 02	36618E 02	37345E 02	67309E-01	65998E-01	73761E 00	70830E 00
24	39012E-00	25633E 01	15247E 02	15550E 02	39083E 02	39859E 02	65587E-01	64309E-01	72942E 00	69907E 00
25	37512E-00	26658E 01	15622E 02	15932E 02	41646E 02	42473E 02	64012E-01	62765E-01	72138E 00	69011E 00
26	36069E-00	27725E 01	15983E 02	16300E 02	44312E 02	45192E 02	62567E-01	61348E-01	71348E 00	68128E 00
27	34682E-00	28834E 01	16330E 02	16654E 02	47084E 02	48020E 02	61239E-01	60045E-01	70572E 00	67270E 00
28	33348E-00	29987E 01	16663E 02	16994E 02	49968E 02	50960E 02	60013E-01	58844E-01	69809E 00	66425E 00
29	32065E-00	31186E 01	16984E 02	17321E 02	52966E 02	54019E 02	58880E-01	57733E-01	69059E 00	65603E 00
30	30832E-00	32434E 01	17292E 02	17636E 02	56085E 02	57199E 02	57830E-01	56703E-01	68322E 00	64793E 00
31	29646E-00	33731E 01	17588E 02	17938E 02	59328E 02	60507E 02	56855E-01	55748E-01	67598E 00	64005E 00
32	28506E-00	35081E 01	17874E 02	18229E 02	62701E 02	63947E 02	55949E-01	54859E-01	66887E 00	63229E 00
33	27409E-00	36484E 01	18148E 02	18508E 02	66209E 02	67525E 02	55104E-01	54030E-01	66187E 00	62473E 00
34	26355E-00	37943E 01	18411E 02	18777E 02	69858E 02	71246E 02	54315E-01	53257E-01	65499E 00	61729E 00
35	25342E-00	39461E 01	18665E 02	19035E 02	73652E 02	75116E 02	53577E-01	52533E-01	64823E 00	61004E 00
36	24367E-00	41039E 01	18908E 02	19284E 02	77598E 02	79140E 02	52887E-01	51856E-01	64158E 00	60290E 00
37	23430E-00	42681E 01	19143E 02	19523E 02	81702E 02	83326E 02	52240E-01	51222E-01	63504E 00	59595E 00
38	22529E-00	44388E 01	19368E 02	19753E 02	85970E 02	87678E 02	51632E-01	50626E-01	62861E 00	58909E 00
39	21662E-00	46164E 01	19584E 02	19974E 02	90409E 02	92206E 02	51061E-01	50066E-01	62229E 00	58241E 00
40	20829E-00	48010E 01	19793E 02	20186E 02	95025E 02	96914E 02	50523E-01	49539E-01	61607E 00	57584E 00
41	20028E-00	49931E 01	19993E 02	20390E 02	99826E 02	10181E 03	50017E-01	49043E-01	60996E 00	56942E 00
42	19258E-00	51928E 01	20186E 02	20587E 02	10482E 03	10690E 03	49540E-01	48575E-01	60394E 00	56310E 00
43	18517E-00	54005E 01	20371E 02	20776E 02	11001E 03	11220E 03	49090E-01	48133E-01	59802E 00	55693E 00
44	17805E-00	56165E 01	20549E 02	20957E 02	11541E 03	11771E 03	48665E-01	47716E-01	59220E 00	55086E 00
45	17120E-00	58412E 01	20720E 02	21132E 02	12103E 03	12343E 03	48262E-01	47322E-01	58647E 00	54493E 00
46	16461E-00	60748E 01	20885E 02	21300E 02	12687E 03	12939E 03	47882E-01	46949E-01	58084E 00	53909E 00
47	15828E-00	63178E 01	21043E 02	21461E 02	13295E 03	13559E 03	47522E-01	46596E-01	57529E 00	53339E 00
48	15219E-00	65705E 01	21195E 02	21616E 02	13926E 03	14203E 03	47181E-01	46261E-01	56983E 00	52778E 00
49	14634E-00	68333E 01	21341E 02	21766E 02	14583E 03	14873E 03	46857E-01	45944E-01	56446E 00	52229E 00
50	14071E-00	71067E 01	21482E 02	21909E 02	15267E 03	15570E 03	46550E-01	45643E-01	55917E 00	51688E 00

6% PER PERIOD

Period	Present Value of $1	Amount to Which $1 Will Accumulate	Present Value of $1 per Period		Amount to Which $1 per Period Will Accumulate		Amount per Period to Recover $1 of Investment		Present Value of Depreciation	
			Received at End	Received Continuously	Received at End	Received Continuously	Received at End	Received Continuously	Sum-of-Years' Digits	Declining Balance
1	94340E 00	10600E 01	94340E 00	97142E 00	10000E 01	10297E 01	10600E 01	10294E 01		
2	89000E 00	11236E 01	18334E 01	18879E 01	20600E 01	21212E 01	54544E 00	52970E 00	90830E 00	92000E 00
3	83962E 00	11910E 01	26730E 01	27524E 01	31836E 01	32782E 01	37411E-00	36332E-00	89149E 00	89816E 00
4	79209E 00	12625E 01	34651E 01	35681E 01	43746E 01	45046E 01	28859E-00	28027E-00	87515E 00	87811E 00
5	74726E 00	13382E 01	42124E 01	43375E 01	56371E 01	58046E 01	23740E-00	23055E-00		
6	70496E 00	14185E 01	49173E 01	50634E 01	69753E 01	71825E 01	20336E-00	19750E-00	85927E 00	85829E 00
7	66506E 00	15036E 01	55824E 01	57482E 01	83938E 01	86432E 01	17914E-00	17397E-00	84382E 00	83976E 00
8	62741E 00	15938E 01	62098E 01	63943E 01	98975E 01	10192E 02	16104E-00	15639E-00	82880E 00	82145E 00
9	59190E 00	16895E 01	68017E 01	70038E 01	11491E 02	11833E 02	14702E-00	14278E-00	81419E 00	80418E 00
10	55839E 00	17908E 01	73601E 01	75787E 01	13181E 02	13572E 02	13587E-00	13195E-00	79997E 00	78716E 00
11	52679E 00	18983E 01	78869E 01	81212E 01	14972E 02	15416E 02	12679E-00	12313E-00	78614E 00	77104E 00
12	49697E-00	20122E 01	83838E 01	86329E 01	16670E 02	17371E 02	11928E-00	11584E-00	77268E 00	75519E 00
13	46884E-00	21329E 01	88527E 01	91157E 01	18882E 02	19443E 02	11296E-00	10970E-00	75958E 00	74011E 00
14	44230E-00	22609E 01	92950E 01	95711E 01	21015E 02	21639E 02	10758E-00	10448E-00	74683E 00	72531E 00
15	41727E-00	23966E 01	97122E 01	10001E 02	23276E 02	23967E 02	10296E-00	99992E-01	73441E 00	71119E 00
16	39365E-00	25404E 01	10106E 02	10406E 02	25673E 02	26435E 02	98952E-01	96097E-01	72232E 00	69735E 00
17	37136E-00	26928E 01	10477E 02	10789E 02	28213E 02	29051E 02	95445E-01	92691E-01	71054E 00	68412E 00
18	35034E-00	28543E 01	10828E 02	11149E 02	30906E 02	31824E 02	92357E-01	89692E-01	69906E 00	67117E 00
19	33051E-00	30256E 01	11158E 02	11490E 02	33760E 02	34763E 02	89621E-01	87035E-01	68788E 00	65876E 00
20	31180E-00	32071E 01	11470E 02	11811E 02	36786E 02	37878E 02	87185E-01	84669E-01	67699E 00	64661E 00

21	29416E-00	33996E 01	11764E 02	12114E 02	39993E 02	41181E 02	85005E-01	82552E-01	66637E 00	63496E 00
22	27751E-00	36035E 01	12042E 02	12399E 02	43392E 02	44681E 02	83046E-01	80650E-01	65602E 00	62357E 00
23	26180E-00	38197E 01	12303E 02	12669E 02	46996E 02	48392E 02	81278E-01	78933E-01	64593E 00	61261E 00
24	24698E-00	40489E 01	12550E 02	12923E 02	50816E 02	52325E 02	79679E-01	77380E-01	63609E 00	60191E 00
25	23300E-00	42919E 01	12783E 02	13163E 02	54864E 02	56494E 02	78227E-01	75970E-01	62649E 00	59160E 00
26	21981E-00	45494E 01	13003E 02	13389E 02	59156E 02	60914E 02	76904E-01	74686E-01	61713E 00	58154E 00
27	20737E-00	48223E 01	13211E 02	13603E 02	63706E 02	65598E 02	75697E-01	73513E-01	60800E 00	57183E 00
28	19563E-00	51117E 01	13406E 02	13804E 02	68528E 02	70564E 02	74593E-01	72440E-01	59909E 00	56236E 00
29	18456E-00	54184E 01	13591E 02	13994E 02	73640E 02	75828E 02	73580E-01	71457E-01	59039E 00	55321E 00
30	17411E-00	57435E 01	13765E 02	14174E 02	79058E 02	81407E 02	72649E-01	70553E-01	58191E 00	54428E 00
31	16425E-00	60881E 01	13929E 02	14343E 02	84802E 02	87321E 02	71792E-01	69721E-01	57362E 00	53565E 00
32	15496E-00	64534E 01	14084E 02	14502E 02	90890E 02	93590E 02	71002E-01	68954E-01	56553E 00	52722E 00
33	14619E-00	68406E 01	14230E 02	14653E 02	97343E 02	10024E 03	70273E-01	68245E-01	55763E 00	51908E 00
34	13791E-00	72510E 01	14368E 02	14795E 02	10418E 03	10728E 03	69598E-01	67590E-01	54991E 00	51112E 00
35	13011E-00	76861E 01	14498E 02	14929E 02	11143E 03	11475E 03	68974E-01	66984E-01	54237E 00	50342E 00
36	12274E-00	81472E 01	14621E 02	15055E 02	11912E 03	12266E 03	68395E-01	66422E-01	53501E 00	49589E-00
37	11579E-00	86361E 01	14737E 02	15175E 02	12727E 03	13105E 03	67857E-01	65900E-01	52781E 00	48861E-00
38	10924E-00	91542E 01	14846E 02	15287E 02	13590E 03	13994E 03	57358E-01	65415E-01	52078E 00	48149E-00
39	10306E-00	97035E 01	14949E 02	15393E 02	14506E 03	14937E 03	66894E-01	64964E-01	51391E 00	47459E-00
40	97222E-01	10286E 02	15046E 02	15493E 02	15476E 03	15936E 03	66462E-01	64544E-01	50719E 00	46784E-00
41	91719E-01	10903E 02	15138E 02	15588E 02	16505E 03	16995E 03	66059E-01	64153E-01	50062E 00	46130E-00
42	86527E-01	11557E 02	15225E 02	15677E 02	17595E 03	18118E 03	65683E-01	63788E-01	49419E-00	45491E-00
43	81630E-01	12250E 02	15306E 02	15761E 02	18751E 03	19308E 03	65333E-01	63448E-01	48791E-00	44870E-00
44	77009E-01	12985E 02	15383E 02	15840E 02	19976E 03	20569E 03	65006E-01	63131E-01	48176E-00	44263E-00
45	72650E-01	13765E 02	15456E 02	15915E 02	21274E 03	21906E 03	64700E-01	62834E-01	47575E-00	43674E-00
46	68538E-01	14590E 02	15524E 02	15986E 02	22651E 03	23324E 03	64415E-01	62556E-01	46987E-00	43098E-00
47	64658E-01	15466E 02	15589E 02	16052E 02	24110E 03	24826E 03	64148E-01	62297E-01	46411E-00	42537E-00
48	60998E-01	16394E 02	15650E 02	16115E 02	25656E 03	26419E 03	63898E-01	62054E-01	45847E-00	41989E-00
49	57546E-01	17377E 02	15708E 02	16174E 02	27296E 03	28107E 03	63664E-01	61827E-01	45296E-00	41456E-00
50	54288E-01	18420E 02	15762E 02	16230E 02	29034E 03	29896E 03	63444E-01	61614E-01	44756E-00	40935E-00

(handwritten notes)

$[(1+i)^n - 1]/i$ — Amount of Annuity

Present Value of Annuity $[1-(1+i)^{-n}]/i$

PERIOD	PRESENT VALUE OF $1	AMOUNT TO WHICH $1 WILL ACCUMULATE	PRESENT VALUE OF $1 PER PERIOD — Received at End	— Received Continuously	AMOUNT TO WHICH $1 PER PERIOD WILL ACCUMULATE — Received at End	— Received Continuously	AMOUNT PER PERIOD TO RECOVER $1 OF INVESTMENT — Received at End	— Received Continuously	PRESENT VALUE OF DEPRECIATION — Sum-of-Years' Digits	— Declining Balance
1	92593E 00	10800E 01	92593E 00	96249E 00	10000E 01	10395E 01	10800E 01	10390E 01		
2	85734E 00	11664E 01	17833E 01	18537E 01	20800E 01	21621E 01	56077E 00	53947E 00		
3	79383E 00	12597E 01	25771E 01	26789E 01	32464E 01	33746E 01	38803E-00	37329E-00	88105E 00	89601E 00
4	73503E 00	13605E 01	33121E 01	34429E 01	45061E 01	46840E 01	30192E-00	29045E-00	85984E 00	86841E 00
5	68058E 00	14693E 01	39927E 01	41504E 01	58666E 01	60983E 01	25046E-00	24094E-00	83941E 00	84333E 00
6	63017E 00	15869E 01	46229E 01	48054E 01	73359E 01	76256E 01	21632E-00	20810E-00	81971E 00	81882E 00
7	58349E 00	17138E 01	52064E 01	54120E 01	89228E 01	92751E 01	19207E-00	18478E-00	80073E 00	79613E 00
8	54027E 00	18509E 01	57466E 01	59736E 01	10637E 02	11057E 02	17401E-00	16740E-00	78242E 00	77396E 00
9	50025E 00	19990E 01	62469E 01	64936E 01	12488E 02	12981E 02	16008E-00	15400E-00	76475E 00	75326E 00
10	46319E-00	21589E 01	67101E 01	69750E 01	14487E 02	15059E 02	14903E-00	14337E-00	74771E 00	73308E 00
11	42888E-00	23316E 01	71390E 01	74209E 01	16645E 02	17303E 02	14008E-00	13476E-00	73126E 00	71412E 00
12	39711E-00	25182E 01	75361E 01	78337E 01	18977E 02	19726E 02	13270E-00	12765E-00	71537E 00	69568E 00
13	36770E-00	27196E 01	79038E 01	82159E 01	21495E 02	22344E 02	12652E-00	12172E-00	70003E 00	67830E 00
14	34046E-00	29372E 01	82442E 01	85698E 01	24215E 02	25171E 02	12130E-00	11669E-00	68521E 00	66140E 00
15	31524E-00	31722E 01	85595E 01	88975E 01	27152E 02	28224E 02	11683E-00	11239E-00	67089E 00	64542E 00
16	29189E-00	34259E 01	88514E 01	92009E 01	30324E 02	31522E 02	11298E-00	10869E-00	65704E 00	62991E 00
17	27027E-00	37000E 01	91216E 01	94818E 01	33750E 02	35083E 02	10963E-00	10546E-00	64366E 00	61520E 00
18	25025E-00	39960E 01	93719E 01	97420E 01	37450E 02	38929E 02	10670E-00	10265E-00	63071E 00	60093E 00
19	23171E-00	43157E 01	96036E 01	99828E 01	41446E 02	43083E 02	10413E-00	10017E-00	61818E 00	58736E 00
20	21455E-00	46610E 01	98181E 01	10206E 02	45762E 02	47569E 02	10185E-00	97983E-01	60606E 00	57420E 00

21	19866E-00	50338E 01	10017E 02	10412E 02	50423E 02	52414E 02	99832E-01	96040E-01	59433E 00	56167E 00
22	18394E-00	54365E 01	10201E 02	10604E 02	55457E 02	57647E 02	98032E-01	94308E-01	58297E 00	54951E 00
23	17032E-00	58715E 01	10371E 02	10781E 02	60893E 02	63298E 02	96422E-01	92759E-01	57196E 00	53792E 00
24	15770E-00	63412E 01	10529E 02	10945E 02	66765E 02	69401E 02	94978E-01	91370E-01	56130E 00	52667E 00
25	14602E-00	68485E 01	10675E 02	11096E 02	73106E 02	75993E 02	93679E-01	90120E-01	55097E 00	51592E 00
26	13520E-00	73964E 01	10810E 02	11237E 02	79954E 02	83112E 02	92507E-01	88993E-01	54096E 00	50550E 00
27	12519E-00	79881E 01	10935E 02	11367E 02	87351E 02	90800E 02	91448E-01	87974E-01	53124E 00	49551E-00
28	11591E-00	86271E 01	11051E 02	11487E 02	95339E 02	99103E 02	90489E-01	87052E-01	52183E 00	48583E-00
29	10733E-01	93173E 01	11158E 02	11599E 02	10397E 03	10807E 03	89619E-01	86214E-01	51269E 00	47655E-00
30	99377E-01	10063E 02	11258E 02	11702E 02	11328E 03	11776E 03	88827E-01	85453E-01	50382E 00	46755E-00
31	92016E-01	10868E 02	11350E 02	11798E 02	12335E 03	12822E 03	88107E-01	84760E-01	49522E-00	45890E-00
32	85200E-01	11737E 02	11435E 02	11887E 02	13421E 03	13951E 03	87451E-01	84129E-01	48686E-00	45051E-00
33	78889E-01	12676E 02	11514E 02	11969E 02	14595E 03	15171E 03	86852E-01	83552E-01	47875E-00	44244E-00
34	73045E-01	13690E 02	11587E 02	12044E 02	15863E 03	16489E 03	86304E-01	83026E-01	47086E-00	43461E-00
35	67635E-01	14785E 02	11655E 02	12115E 02	17232E 03	17912E 03	85803E-01	82544E-01	46320E-00	42707E-00
36	62625E-01	15968E 02	11717E 02	12180E 02	18710E 03	19449E 03	85345E-01	82103E-01	45576E-00	41975E-00
37	57986E-01	17246E 02	11775E 02	12240E 02	20307E 03	21109E 03	84924E-01	81698E-01	44852E-00	41269E-00
38	53690E-01	18625E 02	11829E 02	12296E 02	22030E 03	22902E 03	84539E-01	81328E-01	44148E-00	40584E-00
39	49713E-01	20115E 02	11879E 02	12348E 02	23894E 03	24838E 03	84185E-01	80987E-01	43464E-00	39922E-00
40	46031E-01	21725E 02	11925E 02	12395E 02	25906E 03	26929E 03	83860E-01	80675E-01	42798E-00	39279E-00
41	42621E-01	23462E 02	11967E 02	12440E 02	28078E 03	29187E 03	83562E-01	80387E-01	42150E-00	38658E-00
42	39464E-01	25339E 02	12007E 02	12481E 02	30424E 03	31626E 03	83287E-01	80123E-01	41519E-00	38054E-00
43	36541E-01	27367E 02	12043E 02	12519E 02	32958E 03	34260E 03	83034E-01	79880E-01	40905E-00	37470E-00
44	33834E-01	29556E 02	12077E 02	12554E 02	35695E 03	37104E 03	82802E-01	79656E-01	40307E-00	36902E-00
45	31328E-01	31920E 02	12108E 02	12587E 02	38651E 03	40177E 03	82587E-01	79450E-01	39724E-00	36352E-0U
46	29007E-01	34474E 02	12137E 02	12617E 02	41843E 03	43495E 03	82390E-01	79260E-01	39157E-00	35817E-00
47	26659E-01	37232E 02	12164E 02	12645E 02	45290E 03	47078E 03	82208E-01	79085E-01	38603E-00	35298E-00
48	24869E-01	40211E 02	12189E 02	12670E 02	49013E 03	50949E 03	82040E-01	78924E-01	38064E-00	34793E-00
49	23027E-01	43427E 02	12212E 02	12694E 02	53034E 03	55128E 03	81886E-01	78775E-01	37539E-00	34303E-00
50	21321E-01	46902E 02	12233E 02	12717E 02	57377E 03	59643E 03	81743E-01	78638E-01	37026E-00	33826E-00

10% PER PERIOD

PERIOD	PRESENT VALUE OF $1	AMOUNT TO WHICH $1 WILL ACCUMULATE	PRESENT VALUE OF $1 PER PERIOD		AMOUNT TO WHICH $1 PER PERIOD WILL ACCUMULATE		AMOUNT PER PERIOD TO RECOVER $1 OF INVESTMENT		PRESENT VALUE OF DEPRECIATION	
			Received at End	Received Continuously	Received at End	Received Continuously	Received at End	Received Continuously	Sum-of-Years' Digits	Declining Balance
1	90909E 00	11000E 01	90909E 00	95382E 00	10000E 01	10492E 01	11000E 01	10484E 01		
2	82645E 00	12100E 01	17355E 01	18209E 01	21000E 01	22033E 01	57619E 00	54917E 00		
3	75131E 00	13310E 01	24869E 01	26092E 01	33100E 01	34729E 01	40211E-00	38326E-00	85525E 00	87319E 00
4	68301E 00	14641E 01	31699E 01	33258E 01	46410E 01	48694E 01	31547E-00	30068E-00	83013E 00	84045E 00
5	62092E 00	16105E 01	37908E 01	39773E 01	61051E 01	64055E 01	26380E-00	25143E-00	80614E 00	81100E 00
6	56447E 00	17716E 01	43553E 01	45696E 01	77156E 01	80953E 01	22961E-00	21884E-00	78321E 00	78253E 00
7	51316E 00	19487E 01	48684E 01	51080E 01	94872E 01	99540E 01	20541E-00	19577E-00	76128E 00	75642E 00
8	46651E-00	21436E 01	53349E 01	55974E 01	11436E 02	11999E 02	18744E-00	17865E-00	74030E 00	73118E 00
9	42410E-00	23579E 01	57590E 01	60424E 01	13579E 02	14248E 02	17364E-00	16550E-00	72022E 00	70783E 00
10	38554E-00	25937E 01	61446E 01	64469E 01	15937E 02	16722E 02	16275E-00	15511E-00	70099E 00	68528E 00
11	35049E-00	28531E 01	64951E 01	68147E 01	18531E 02	19443E 02	15396E-00	14674E-00	68257E 00	66430E 00
12	31863E-00	31384E 01	68137E 01	71490E 01	21384E 02	22437E 02	14676E-00	13988E-00	66491E 00	64407E 00
13	28966E-00	34523E 01	71034E 01	74529E 01	24523E 02	25729E 02	14078E-00	13418E-00	64798E 00	62516E 00
14	26333E-00	37975E 01	73667E 01	77292E 01	27975E 02	29352E 02	13575E-00	12938E-00	63174E 00	60694E 00
15	23939E-00	41772E 01	76061E 01	79803E 01	31772E 02	33336E 02	13147E-00	12531E-00	61616E 00	58985E 00
16	21763E-00	45950E 01	78237E 01	82087E 01	35950E 02	37719E 02	12782E-00	12182E-00	60120E 00	57340E 00
17	19784E-00	50545E 01	80216E 01	84163E 01	40545E 02	42540E 02	12466E-00	11882E-00	58683E 00	55791E 00
18	17986E-00	55599E 01	82014E 01	86050E 01	45599E 02	47843E 02	12193E-00	11621E-00	57302E 00	54300E 00
19	16351E-00	61159E 01	83649E 01	87765E 01	51159E 02	53676E 02	11955E-00	11394E-00	55974E 00	52893E 00
20	14864E-00	67275E 01	85136E 01	89325E 01	57275E 02	60093E 02	11746E-00	11195E-00	54697E 00	51539E 00

21	50257E 00	53469E 00	11020E-00	11562E-00	67152E 02	64002E 02	90743E 01	86487E 01	74003E 01	13513E-00
22	49023E-00	52286E 00	10866E-00	11401E-00	74916E 02	71403E 02	92032E 01	87715E 01	81403E 01	12285E-00
23	47852E-00	51148E 00	10729E-00	11257E-00	83457E 02	79543E 02	93203E 01	88832E 01	89543E 01	11168E-00
24	46725E-00	50051E 00	10608E-00	11130E-00	92852E 02	88497E 02	94268E 01	89847E 01	98497E 01	10153E-00
25	45653E-00	48994E-00	10500E-00	11017E-00	10319E 03	98347E 02	95237E 01	90770E 01	10835E 02	92296E-01
26	44621E-00	47975E-00	10404E-00	10916E-00	11455E 03	10918E 03	96117E 01	91609E 01	11918E 02	83905E-01
27	43637E-00	46991E-00	10318E-00	10826E-00	12706E 03	12110E 03	96917E 01	92372E 01	13110E 02	76278E-01
28	42689E-00	46043E-00	10241E-00	10745E-00	14081E 03	13421E 03	97645E 01	93066E 01	14421E 02	69343E-01
29	41784E-00	45127E-00	10172E-00	10673E-00	15594E 03	14863E 03	98306E 01	93696E 01	15863E 02	63039E-01
30	40911E-00	44243E-00	10110E-00	10608E-00	17259E 03	16449E 03	98908E 01	94269E 01	17449E 02	57309E-01
31	40076E-00	43389E-00	10055E-00	10550E-00	19090E 03	18194E 03	99454E 01	94790E 01	19194E 02	52099E-01
32	39270E-00	42564E-00	10005E-00	10497E-00	21103E 03	20114E 03	99951E 01	95264E 01	21114E 02	47362E-01
33	38499E-00	41766E-00	99599E-01	10450E-00	23319E 03	22225E 03	10040E 02	95694E 01	23225E 02	43057E-01
34	37753E-00	40994E-00	99193E-01	10407E-00	25756E 03	24548E 03	10081E 02	96086E 01	25548E 02	39143E-01
35	37039E-00	40247E-00	98827E-01	10369E-00	28436E 03	27102E 03	10119E 02	96442E 01	28102E 02	35584E-01
36	36347E-00	39525E-00	98496E-01	10334E-00	31385E 03	29913E 03	10153E 02	96765E 01	30913E 02	32349E-01
37	35684E-00	38825E-00	98198E-01	10303E-00	34628E 03	33004E 03	10184E 02	97059E 01	34004E 02	29408E-01
38	35041E-00	38148E-00	97928E-01	10275E-00	38196E 03	36404E 03	10212E 02	97326E 01	37404E 02	26735E-01
39	34424E-00	37491E-00	97684E-01	10249E-00	42120E 03	40145E 03	10237E 02	97570E 01	41145E 02	24304E-01
40	33825E-00	36855E-00	97464E-01	10226E-00	46437E 03	44259E 03	10260E 02	97790E 01	45259E 02	22095E-01
41	33249E-00	36238E-00	97264E-01	10205E-00	51186E 03	48785E 03	10281E 02	97991E 01	49785E 02	20086E-01
42	32691E-00	35640E-00	97083E-01	10186E-00	56409E 03	53764E 03	10300E 02	98174E 01	54764E 02	18260E-01
43	32153E-00	35059E-00	96919E-01	10169E-00	62155E 03	59240E 03	10318E 02	98340E 01	60240E 02	16600E-01
44	31631E-00	34496E-00	96771E-01	10153E-00	68475E 03	65264E 03	10334E 02	98491E 01	66264E 02	15091E-01
45	31126E-00	33949E-00	96636E-01	10139E-00	75428E 03	71890E 03	10348E 02	98628E 01	72890E 02	13719E-01
46	30637E-00	33418E-00	96514E-01	10126E-00	83076E 03	79180E 03	10361E 02	98753E 01	80180E 02	12472E-01
47	30164E-00	32902E-00	96403E-01	10115E-00	91488E 03	87197E 03	10373E 02	98866E 01	88197E 02	11338E-01
48	29705E-00	32401E-00	96303E-01	10104E-00	10074E 04	96017E 03	10384E 02	98969E 01	97017E 02	10307E-01
49	29261E-00	31913E-00	96212E-01	10095E-00	11092E 04	10572E 04	10394E 02	99063E 01	10672E 03	93704E-02
50	28829E-00	31439E-00	96129E-01	10086E-00	12212E 04	11639E 04	10403E 02	99148E 01	11739E 03	85186E-02

12% PER PERIOD

PERIOD	PRESENT VALUE OF $1	AMOUNT TO WHICH $1 WILL ACCUMULATE	PRESENT VALUE OF $1 PER PERIOD		AMOUNT TO WHICH $1 PER PERIOD WILL ACCUMULATE		AMOUNT PER PERIOD TO RECOVER $1 OF INVESTMENT		PRESENT VALUE OF DEPRECIATION	
			Received at End	Received Continuously	Received at End	Received Continuously	Received at End	Received Continuously	Sum-of-Years' Digits	Declining Balance
1	89286E 00	11200E 01	89286E 00	94542E 00	10000E 01	10589E 01	11200E 01	10577E 01		
2	79719E 00	12544E 01	16901E 01	17895E 01	21200E 01	22448E 01	59170E 00	55880E 00		
3	71178E 00	14049E 01	24018E 01	25432E 01	33744E 01	35730E 01	41635E-00	39320E-00	83079E 00	85148E 00
4	63552E 00	15735E 01	30373E 01	32161E 01	47793E 01	50607E 01	32923E-00	31093E-00	80221E 00	81414E 00
5	56743E 00	17623E 01	36048E 01	38170E 01	63528E 01	67268E 01	27741E-00	26199E-00	77512E 00	78088E 00
6	50663E 00	19738E 01	41114E 01	43534E 01	81152E 01	85929E 01	24323E-00	22970E-00	74944E 00	74907E 00
7	45235E-00	22107E 01	45638E 01	48324E 01	10089E 02	10683E 02	21912E-00	20694E-00	72507E 00	72017E 00
8	40388E-00	24760E 01	49676E 01	52601E 01	12300E 02	13024E 02	20130E-00	19011E-00	70194E 00	69250E 00
9	36061E-00	27731E 01	53282E 01	56419E 01	14776E 02	15645E 02	18768E-00	17725E-00	67995E 00	66711E 00
10	32197E-00	31058E 01	56502E 01	59828E 01	17549E 02	18582E 02	17698E-00	16714E-00	65906E 00	64284E 00
11	28748E-00	34786E 01	59377E 01	62872E 01	20655E 02	21870E 02	16842E-00	15905E-00	63918E 00	62043E 00
12	25668E-00	38960E 01	61944E 01	65590E 01	24133E 02	25554E 02	16144E-00	15246E-00	62026E 00	59901E 00
13	22917E-00	43635E 01	64235E 01	68017E 01	28029E 02	29679E 02	15568E-00	14702E-00	60224E 00	57914E 00
14	20462E-00	48871E 01	66282E 01	70183E 01	32393E 02	34299E 02	15087E-00	14248E-00	58507E 00	56016E 00
15	18270E-00	54736E 01	68109E 01	72118E 01	37280E 02	39474E 02	14682E-00	13866E-00	56869E 00	54247E 00
16	16312E-00	61304E 01	69740E 01	73845E 01	42753E 02	45270E 02	14339E-00	13542E-00	55306E 00	52557E 00
17	14564E-00	68660E 01	71196E 01	75387E 01	48884E 02	51761E 02	14046E-00	13265E-00	53815E 00	50977E 00
18	13004E-00	76900E 01	72497E 01	76764E 01	55750E 02	59032E 02	13794E-00	13027E-00	52390E 00	49467E-00
19	11611E-00	86128E 01	73658E 01	77994E 01	63440E 02	67174E 02	13576E-00	12822E-00	51027E 00	48050E-00
20	10367E-00	96463E 01	74694E 01	79091E 01	72052E 02	76294E 02	13388E-00	12644E-00	49724E-00	46695E-00

21	92560E-01	10804E 02	75620E 01	80072E 01	81699E 02	86508E 02	13224E-00	12489E-00	48478E-00	45419E-00
22	82642E-01	12100E 02	76446E 01	80947E 01	92503E 02	97948E 02	13081E-00	12354E-00	47284E-00	44199E-00
23	73788E-01	13552E 02	77184E 01	81728E 01	10460E 03	11076E 03	12956E-00	12236E-00	46140E-00	43047E-00
24	65882E-01	15179E 02	77843E 01	82426E 01	11816E 03	12511E 03	12846E-00	12132E-00	45044E-00	41945E-00
25	58823E-01	17000E 02	78431E 01	83048E 01	13333E 03	14118E 03	12750E-00	12041E-00	43992E-00	40901E-00
26	52521E-01	19040E 02	78957E 01	83604E 01	15033E 03	15918E 03	12665E-00	11961E-00	42983E-00	39900E-00
27	46894E-01	21325E 02	79426E 01	84101E 01	16937E 03	17934E 03	12590E-00	11890E-00	42014E-00	38951E-00
28	41869E-01	23884E 02	79844E 01	84544E 01	19070E 03	20192E 03	12524E-00	11828E-00	41083E-00	38041E-00
29	37383E-01	26750E 02	80218E 01	84940E 01	21458E 03	22721E 03	12466E-00	11773E-00	40188E-00	37175E-00
30	33378E-01	29960E 02	80552E 01	85294E 01	24133E 03	25554E 03	12414E-00	11724E-00	39328E-00	36343E-00
31	29802E-01	33555E 02	80850E 01	85609E 01	27129E 03	28726E 03	12369E-00	11681E-00	38500E-00	35551E-00
32	26609E-01	37582E 02	81116E 01	85891E 01	30485E 03	32279E 03	12328E-00	11643E-00	37703E-00	34789E-00
33	23758E-01	42092E 02	81353E 01	86143E 01	34243E 03	36259E 03	12292E-00	11609E-00	36935E-00	34062E-00
34	21212E-01	47143E 02	81566E 01	86367E 01	38452E 03	40716E 03	12260E-00	11578E-00	36195E-00	33362E-00
35	18940E-01	52800E 02	81755E 01	86568E 01	43166E 03	45707E 03	12232E-00	11552E-00	35482E-00	32692E-00
36	16910E-01	59136E 02	81924E 01	86747E 01	48446E 03	51298E 03	12206E-00	11528E-00	34794E-00	32047E-00
37	15098E-01	66232E 02	82075E 01	86907E 01	54360E 03	57560E 03	12184E-00	11507E-00	34130E-00	31428E-00
38	13481E-01	74180E 02	82210E 01	87049E 01	60983E 03	64573E 03	12164E-00	11488E-00	33490E-00	30832E-00
39	12036E-01	83081E 02	82330E 01	87177E 01	68401E 03	72428E 03	12146E-00	11471E-00	32871E-00	30259E-00
40	10747E-01	93051E 02	82438E 01	87291E 01	76709E 03	81225E 03	12130E-00	11456E-00	32273E-00	29707E-00
41	95953E-02	10422E 03	82534E 01	87392E 01	86014E 03	91078E 03	12116E-00	11443E-00	31694E-00	29175E-00
42	85673E-02	11672E 03	82619E 01	87483E 01	96436E 03	10211E 04	12104E-00	11431E-00	31135E-00	28662E-00
43	76494E-02	13073E 03	82696E 01	87564E 01	10811E 04	11447E 04	12093E-00	11420E-00	30594E-00	28167E-00
44	68298E-02	14642E 03	82764E 01	87636E 01	12118E 04	12831E 04	12083E-00	11411E-00	30070E-00	27689E-00
45	60980E-02	16399E 03	82825E 01	87701E 01	13582E 04	14382E 04	12074E-00	11402E-00	29563E-00	27227E-00
46	54447E-02	18367E 03	82880E 01	87758E 01	15222E 04	16118E 04	12066E-00	11395E-00	29072E-00	26781E-00
47	48615E-02	20571E 03	82928E 01	87810E 01	17059E 04	18063E 04	12059E-00	11388E-00	28596E-00	26349E-00
48	43404E-02	23039E 03	82972E 01	87856E 01	19116E 04	20201E 04	12052E-00	11382E-00	28134E-00	25931E-00
49	38754E-02	25804E 03	83010E 01	87897E 01	21420E 04	22681E 04	12047E-00	11377E-00	27686E-00	25527E-00
50	34602E-02	28900E 03	83045E 01	87934E 01	24000E 04	25413E 04	12042E-00	11372E-00	27252E-00	25135E-00

14% PER PERIOD

PERIOD	PRESENT VALUE OF $1	AMOUNT TO WHICH $1 WILL ACCUMULATE	PRESENT VALUE OF $1 PER PERIOD		AMOUNT TO WHICH $1 PER PERIOD WILL ACCUMULATE		AMOUNT PER PERIOD TO RECOVER $1 OF INVESTMENT		PRESENT VALUE OF DEPRECIATION	
			Received at End	Received Continuously	Received at End	Received Continuously	Received at End	Received Continuously	Sum-of-Years' Digits	Declining Balance
1	87719E 00	11400E 01	87719E 00	93726E 00	10000E 01	10685E 01	11400E 01	10669E 01		
2	76947E 00	12996E 01	16467E 01	17594E 01	21400E 01	22865E 01	60729E 00	56837E 00		
3	67497E 00	14815E 01	23216E 01	24806E 01	34396E 01	36751E 01	43073E-00	40313E-00	80758E 00	83078E 00
4	59208E 00	16890E 01	29137E 01	31132E 01	49211E 01	52581E 01	34320E-00	32121E-00	77592E 00	78934E 00
5	51937E 00	19254E 01	34331E 01	36681E 01	66101E 01	70627E 01	29218E-00	27262E-00	74615E 00	75278E 00
6	45559E-00	21950E 01	38887E 01	41549E 01	85355E 01	91200E 01	25716E-00	24068E-00	71814E 00	71816E 00
7	39964E-00	25023E 01	42883E 01	45819E 01	10730E 02	11465E 02	23319E-00	21825E-00	69176E 00	68697E 00
8	35056E-00	28526E 01	46389E 01	49565E 01	13233E 02	14139E 02	21557E-00	20176E-00	66689E 00	65740E 00
9	30751E-00	32519E 01	49464E 01	52851E 01	16085E 02	17187E 02	20217E-00	18921E-00	64343E 00	63049E 00
10	26974E-00	37072E 01	52161E 01	55733E 01	19337E 02	20661E 02	19171E-00	17943E-00	62128E 00	60498E 00
11	23662E-00	42262E 01	54527E 01	58261E 01	23045E 02	24622E 02	18339E-00	17164E-00	60035E 00	58160E 00
12	20756E-00	48179E 01	56603E 01	60479E 01	27271E 02	29138E 02	17667E-00	16535E-00	58056E 00	55944E 00
13	18207E-00	54924E 01	58424E 01	62424E 01	32089E 02	34286E 02	17116E-00	16019E-00	56182E 00	53902E 00
14	15971E-00	62613E 01	60021E 01	64130E 01	37581E 02	40154E 02	16661E-00	15593E-00	54408E 00	51966E 00
15	14010E-00	71379E 01	61422E 01	65627E 01	43842E 02	46844E 02	16281E-00	15238E-00	52725E 00	50173E 00
16	12289E-00	81372E 01	62651E 01	66940E 01	50980E 02	54471E 02	15962E-00	14939E-00	51129E 00	48473E 00
17	10780E-00	92765E 01	63729E 01	68092E 01	59118E 02	63165E 02	15692E-00	14686E-00	49613E-00	46891E-00
18	94561E-01	10575E 02	64674E 01	69103E 01	68394E 02	73077E 02	15462E-00	14471E-00	48173E-00	45389E-00
19	82948E-01	12056E 02	65504E 01	69989E 01	78969E 02	84376E 02	15266E-00	14288E-00	46603E-00	43986E-00
20	72762E-01	13743E 02	66231E 01	70766E 01	91025E 02	97258E 02	15099E-00	14131E-00	45500E-00	42654E-00

21	63826E-01	15668E 02	66870E 01	71448E 01	10477E 03	11194E 03	14954E-00	13996E-00	44258E-00	41405E-00
22	55988E-01	17861E 02	67429E 01	72046E 01	12044E 03	12868E 03	14830E-00	13880E-00	43075E-00	40216E-00
23	49112E-01	20362E 02	67921E 01	72571E 01	13830E 03	14777E 03	14723E-00	13780E-00	41946E-00	39098E-00
24	43081E-01	23212E 02	68351E 01	73032E 01	15866E 03	16952E 03	14630E-00	13693E-00	40869E-00	38033E-00
25	37790E-01	26462E 02	68729E 01	73435E 01	18187E 03	19432E 03	14550E-00	13617E-00	39840E-00	37029E-00
26	33149E-01	30167E 02	69061E 01	73789E 01	20833E 03	22260E 03	14480E-00	13552E-00	38856E-00	36071E-00
27	29078E-01	34390E 02	69352E 01	74100E 01	23850E 03	25483E 03	14419E-00	13495E-00	37915E-00	35164E-00
28	25507E-01	39204E 02	69607E 01	74373E 01	27289E 03	29157E 03	14366E-00	13446E-00	37015E-00	34298E-00
29	22375E-01	44693E 02	69830E 01	74612E 01	31209E 03	33346E 03	14320E-00	13403E-00	36153E-00	33477E-00
30	19627E-01	50950E 02	70027E 01	74821E 01	35679E 03	38122E 03	14280E-00	13365E-00	35326E-00	32691E-00
31	17217E-01	58083E 02	70199E 01	75005E 01	40774E 03	43566E 03	14245E-00	13332E-00	34534E-00	31943E-00
32	15102E-01	66215E 02	70350E 01	75167E 01	46582E 03	49772E 03	14215E-00	13304E-00	33773E-00	31227E-00
33	13248E-01	75485E 02	70482E 01	75308E 01	53204E 03	56846E 03	14188E-00	13279E-00	33043E-00	30545E-00
34	11621E-01	86053E 02	70599E 01	75433E 01	60752E 03	64912E 03	14165E-00	13257E-00	32341E-00	29890E-00
35	10194E-01	98100E 02	70700E 01	75541E 01	69357E 03	74106E 03	14144E-00	13238E-00	31667E-00	29264E-00
36	89418E-02	11183E 03	70790E 01	75637E 01	79167E 03	84588E 03	14126E-00	13221E-00	31018E-00	28663E-00
37	78437E-02	12749E 03	70868E 01	75721E 01	90351E 03	96537E 03	14111E-00	13206E-00	30393E-00	28088E-00
38	68804E-02	14534E 03	70937E 01	75794E 01	10310E 04	11016E 04	14097E-00	13194E-00	29792E-00	27535E-00
39	60355E-02	16569E 03	70997E 01	75859E 01	11763E 04	12569E 04	14085E-00	13182E-00	29213E-00	27004E-00
40	52943E-02	18888E 03	71050E 01	75915E 01	13420E 04	14339E 04	14075E-00	13173E-00	28654E-00	26493E-00
41	46441E-02	21533E 03	71097E 01	75965E 01	15309E 04	16357E 04	14065E-00	13164E-00	28115E-00	26002E-00
42	40738E-02	24547E 03	71138E 01	76008E 01	17462E 04	18658E 04	14057E-00	13156E-00	27596E-00	25529E-00
43	35735E-02	27984E 03	71173E 01	76047E 01	19917E 04	21281E 04	14050E-00	13150E-00	27094E-00	25075E-00
44	31346E-02	31902E 03	71205E 01	76080E 01	22715E 04	24271E 04	14044E-00	13144E-00	26609E-00	24633E-00
45	27497E-02	36368E 03	71232E 01	76110E 01	25906E 04	27679E 04	14039E-00	13139E-00	26140E-00	24210E-00
46	24120E-02	41459E 03	71256E 01	76135E 01	29542E 04	31565E 04	14034E-00	13135E-00	25687E-00	23800E-00
47	21158E-02	47264E 03	71277E 01	76158E 01	33688E 04	35995E 04	14030E-00	13131E-00	25248E-00	23404E-00
48	18560E-02	53881E 03	71296E 01	76178E 01	38415E 04	41045E 04	14026E-00	13127E-00	24824E-00	23022E-00
49	16280E-02	61424E 03	71312E 01	76195E 01	43803E 04	46802E 04	14023E-00	13124E-00	24413E-00	22652E-00
50	14281E-02	70023E 03	71327E 01	76210E 01	49945E 04	53365E 04	14020E-00	13122E-00	24015E-00	22294E-00

15% PER PERIOD

Period	Present Value of $1	Amount to Which $1 Will Accumulate	Present Value of $1 per Period		Amount to Which $1 per Period Will Accumulate		Amount per Period to Recover $1 of Investment		Present Value of Depreciation	
			Received at End	Received Continuously	Received at End	Received Continuously	Received at End	Received Continuously	Sum-of-Years' Digits	Declining Balance
1	86957E 00	11500E 01	86957E 00	93326E 00	10000E 01	10733E 01	11500E 01	10715E 01		
2	75614E 00	13225E 01	16257E 01	17448E 01	21500E 01	23075E 01	61512E 00	57313E 00		
3	65752E 00	15209E 01	22832E 01	24505E 01	34725E 01	37269E 01	43798E-00	40808E-00	79642E 00	82080E 00
4	57175E 00	17490E 01	28550E 01	30641E 01	49934E 01	53592E 01	35027E-00	32636E-00	76335E 00	77748E 00
5	49718E-00	20114E 01	33522E 01	35977E 01	67424E 01	72363E 01	29832E-00	27795E-00	73238E 00	73943E 00
6	43233E-00	23131E 01	37845E 01	40617E 01	87537E 01	93950E 01	26424E-00	24620E-00	70334E 00	70357E 00
7	37594E-00	26600E 01	41604E 01	44652E 01	11067E 02	11877E 02	24036E-00	22395E-00	67609E 00	67142E 00
8	32690E-00	30590E 01	44873E 01	48160E 01	13727E 02	14732E 02	22285E-00	20764E-00	65050E 00	64105E 00
9	28426E-00	35179E 01	47716E 01	51211E 01	16786E 02	18015E 02	20957E-00	19527E-00	62643E 00	61353E 00
10	24718E-00	40456E 01	50188E 01	53864E 01	20304E 02	21791E 02	19925E-00	18565E-00	60379E 00	58756E 00
11	21494E-00	46524E 01	52337E 01	56171E 01	24349E 02	26133E 02	19107E-00	17803E-00	58245E 00	56383E 00
12	18691E-00	53503E 01	54206E 01	58177E 01	29002E 02	31126E 02	18448E-00	17189E-00	56234E 00	54144E 00
13	16253E-00	61528E 01	55831E 01	59921E 01	34352E 02	36868E 02	17911E-00	16689E-00	54336E 00	52085E 00
14	14133E-00	70757E 01	57245E 01	61438E 01	40505E 02	43472E 02	17469E-00	16277E-00	52543E 00	50142E 00
15	12289E-00	81371E 01	58474E 01	62757E 01	47580E 02	51066E 02	17102E-00	15934E-00	50848E 00	48346E-00
16	10686E-00	93576E 01	59542E 01	63904E 01	55717E 02	59799E 02	16795E-00	15648E-00	49244E-00	46649E-00
17	92926E-01	10761E 02	60472E 01	64901E 01	65075E 02	69842E 02	16537E-00	15408E-00	47725E-00	45074E-00
18	80805E-01	12375E 02	61280E 01	65769E 01	75836E 02	81392E 02	16319E-00	15205E-00	46285E-00	43584E-00
19	70265E-01	14232E 02	61982E 01	66523E 01	88212E 02	94674E 02	16134E-00	15032E-00	44918E-00	42195E-00
20	61100E-01	16367E 02	62593E 01	67178E 01	10244E 03	10995E 03	15976E-00	14886E-00	43621E-00	40878E-00

No.										
21	53131E-01	18822E 02	63125E 01	67749E 01	11881E 01	12751E 03	15842E-00	14760E-00	42388E-00	39646E-00
22	46201E-01	21645E 02	63587E 01	68245E 01	13763E 01	14771E 03	15727E-00	14653E-00	41216E-00	38477E-00
23	40174E-01	24891E 02	63988E 01	68676E 01	15928E 01	17094E 03	15628E-00	14561E-00	40099E-00	37380E-00
24	34934E-01	28625E 02	64338E 01	69051E 01	18417E 01	19766E 03	15543E-00	14482E-00	39036E-00	36336E-00
25	30378E-01	32919E 02	64641E 01	69377E 01	21279E 01	22838E 03	15470E-00	14414E-00	38022E-00	35354E-00
26	26415E-01	37857E 02	64906E 01	69660E 01	24571E 01	26371E 03	15407E-00	14355E-00	37055E-00	34418E-00
27	22970E-01	43535E 02	65135E 01	69907E 01	28357E 01	30434E 03	15353E-00	14305E-00	36131E-00	33534E-00
28	19974E-01	50066E 02	65335E 01	70121E 01	32710E 01	35107E 03	15306E-00	14261E-00	35249E-00	32690E-00
29	17369E-01	57575E 02	65509E 01	70307E 01	37717E 01	40480E 03	15265E-00	14223E-00	34405E-00	31891E-00
30	15103E-01	66212E 02	65660E 01	70470E 01	43475E 01	46659E 03	15230E-00	14191E-00	33597E-00	31128E-00
31	13133E-01	76144E 02	65791E 01	70611E 01	50096E 01	53765E 03	15200E-00	14162E-00	32824E-00	30403E-00
32	11420E-01	87565E 02	65905E 01	70733E 01	57710E 01	61938E 03	15173E-00	14138E-00	32083E-00	29709E-00
33	99305E-02	10070E 03	66005E 01	70840E 01	66467E 01	71335E 03	15150E-00	14116E-00	31372E-00	29048E-00
34	86352E-02	11580E 03	66091E 01	70932E 01	76537E 01	82143E 03	15131E-00	14098E-00	30690E-00	28414E-00
35	75089E-02	13318E 03	66166E 01	71013E 01	88117E 01	94572E 03	15113E-00	14082E-00	30035E-00	27810E-00
36	65295E-02	15315E 03	66231E 01	71083E 01	10143E 01	10887E 04	15099E-00	14068E-00	29406E-00	27230E-00
37	56778E-02	17612E 03	66288E 01	71144E 01	11675E 01	12530E 04	15086E-00	14056E-00	28801E-00	26675E-00
38	49372E-02	20254E 03	66337E 01	71197E 01	13436E 01	14420E 04	15074E-00	14046E-00	28220E-00	26141E-00
39	42932E-02	23292E 03	66380E 01	71243E 01	15462E 01	16594E 04	15065E-00	14036E-00	27660E-00	25630E-00
40	37332E-02	26786E 03	66418E 01	71283E 01	17791E 01	19094E 04	15056E-00	14029E-00	27120E-00	25138E-00
41	32463E-02	30804E 03	66450E 01	71319E 01	20470E 01	21969E 04	15049E-00	14022E-00	26601E-00	24665E-00
42	28229E-02	35425E 03	66478E 01	71347E 01	23550E 01	25275E 04	15042E-00	14016E-00	26100E-00	24210E-00
43	24547E-02	40739E 03	66503E 01	71375E 01	27092E 01	29077E 04	15037E-00	14011E-00	25616E-00	23772E-00
44	21345E-02	46850E 03	66524E 01	71397E 01	31166E 01	33449E 04	15032E-00	14006E-00	25150E-00	23350E-00
45	18561E-02	53877E 03	66543E 01	71417E 01	35851E 01	38478E 04	15028E-00	14002E-00	24699E-00	22943E-00
46	16140E-02	61959E 03	66559E 01	71435E 01	41239E 01	44260E 04	15024E-00	13999E-00	24264E-00	22549E-00
47	14035E-02	71252E 03	66573E 01	71450E 01	47435E 01	50910E 04	15021E-00	13996E-00	23843E-00	22170E-00
48	12204E-02	81940E 03	66585E 01	71463E 01	54560E 01	58557E 04	15018E-00	13993E-00	23436E-00	21803E-00
49	10612E-02	94231E 03	66596E 01	71474E 01	62754E 01	67351E 04	15016E-00	13991E-00	23042E-00	21448E-00
50	92280E-03	10837E 04	66605E 01	71484E 01	72177E 01	77464E 04	15014E-00	13989E-00	22661E-00	21105E-00

16% PER PERIOD

PERIOD	PRESENT VALUE OF $1	AMOUNT TO WHICH $1 WILL ACCUMULATE	PRESENT VALUE OF $1 PER PERIOD		AMOUNT TO WHICH $1 PER PERIOD WILL ACCUMULATE		AMOUNT PER PERIOD TO RECOVER $1 OF INVESTMENT		PRESENT VALUE OF DEPRECIATION	
			Received at End	Received Continuously	Received at End	Received Continuously	Received at End	Received Continuously	Sum-of-Years' Digits	Declining Balance
1	86207E 00	11600E 01	86207E 00	92933E 00	10000E 01	10780E 01	11600E 01	10760E 01		
2	74316E 00	13456E 01	16052E 01	17305E 01	21600E 01	23285E 01	62296E 00	57788E 00		
3	64066E 00	15609E 01	22459E 01	24211E 01	35056E 01	37791E 01	44526E-00	41303E-00	78553E 00	81104E 00
4	55229E 00	18106E 01	27982E 01	30165E 01	50665E 01	54618E 01	35738E-00	33151E-00	75114E 00	76594E 00
5	47611E-00	21003E 01	32743E 01	35298E 01	68771E 01	74137E 01	30541E-00	28331E-00	71904E 00	72651E 00
6	41044E-00	24364E 01	36847E 01	39722E 01	89775E 01	96779E 01	27139E-00	25175E-00	68907E 00	68952E 00
7	35388E-00	28262E 01	40386E 01	43537E 01	11414E 02	12304E 02	24761E-00	22969E-00	66103E 00	65650E 00
8	30503E-00	32784E 01	43436E 01	46825E 01	14240E 02	15351E 02	23022E-00	21356E 02	63479E 00	62545E 00
9	26295E-00	38030E 01	46065E 01	49660E 01	17519E 02	18885E 02	21708E-00	20137E-00	61020E 00	59741E 00
10	22668E-00	44114E 01	48332E 01	52103E 01	21321E 02	22985E 02	20690E-00	19193E-00	58713E 00	57105E 00
11	19542E-00	51173E 01	50286E 01	54210E 01	25733E 02	27741E 02	19886E-00	18447E-00	56547E 00	54705E 00
12	16846E-00	59360E 01	51971E 01	56026E 01	30850E 02	33257E 02	19241E-00	17849E-00	54510E 00	52449E 00
13	14523E-00	68858E 01	53423E 01	57592E 01	36786E 02	39636E 02	18718E-00	17364E-00	52594E 00	50381E 00
14	12520E-00	79875E 01	54675E 01	58941E 01	43672E 02	47079E 02	18290E-00	16966E-00	50789E 00	48436E-00
15	10793E-00	92655E 01	55755E 01	60105E 01	51660E 02	55690E 02	17936E-00	16638E-00	49086E-00	46643E-00
16	93041E-01	10748E 02	56685E 01	61108E 01	60925E 02	65679E 02	17641E-00	16365E-00	47479E-00	44953E-00
17	80207E-01	12468E 02	57487E 01	61972E 01	71673E 02	77265E 02	17395E-00	16136E-00	45961E-00	43389E-00
18	69144E-01	14463E 02	58178E 01	62718E 01	84141E 02	90706E 02	17188E-00	15944E-00	44525E-00	41913E-00
19	59607E-01	16777E 02	58775E 01	63360E 01	98603E 02	10630E 03	17014E-00	15783E-00	43166E-00	40540E-00
20	51385E-01	19461E 02	59288E 01	63914E 01	11538E 03	12438E 03	16867E-00	15646E-00	41878E-00	39242E-00

21	44298E-01	22574E 02	59731E 01	64392E 01	13484E 03	14536E 03	16742E-00	15530E-00	40657E-00	38030E-00
22	38188E-01	26186E 02	60113E 01	64803E 01	15742E 03	16970E 03	16635E-00	15431E-00	39498E-00	36881E-00
23	32920E-01	30376E 02	60442E 01	65158E 01	18360E 03	19793E 03	16545E-00	15347E-00	38396E-00	35805E-00
24	28380E-01	35236E 02	60726E 01	65464E 01	21398E 03	23067E 03	16467E-00	15276E-00	37349E-00	34784E-00
25	24465E-01	40874E 02	60971E 01	65728E 01	24921E 03	26866E 03	16401E-00	15214E-00	36352E-00	33823E-00
26	21091E-01	47414E 02	61182E 01	65955E 01	29009E 03	31272E 03	16345E-00	15162E-00	35402E-00	32910E-00
27	18182E-01	55000E 02	61364E 01	66151E 01	33750E 03	36383E 03	16296E-00	15117E-00	34497E-00	32048E-00
28	15674E-01	63800E 02	61520E 01	66320E 01	39250E 03	42313E 03	16255E-00	15078E-00	33633E-00	31227E-00
29	13512E-01	74009E 02	61655E 01	66466E 01	45630E 03	49190E 03	16219E-00	15045E-00	32808E-00	30451E-00
30	11648E-01	85850E 02	61772E 01	66592E 01	53031E 03	57169E 03	16189E-00	15017E-00	32020E-00	29709E-00
31	10042E-01	99586E 02	61872E 01	66700E 01	61616E 03	66424E 03	16162E-00	14993E-00	31266E-00	29006E-00
32	86565E-02	11552E 03	61959E 01	66793E 01	71575E 03	77159E 03	16140E-00	14972E-00	30545E-00	28333E-00
33	74625E-02	13400E 03	62034E 01	66874E 01	83127E 03	89612E 03	16120E-00	14954E-00	29854E-00	27693E-00
34	64332E-02	15544E 03	62098E 01	66943E 01	96527E 03	10406E 04	16104E-00	14938E-00	29191E-00	27080E-00
35	55459E-02	18031E 03	62153E 01	67003E 01	11207E 04	12082E 04	16089E-00	14925E-00	28556E-00	26496E-00
36	47809E-02	20916E 03	62201E 01	67054E 01	13010E 04	14025E 04	16077E-00	14913E-00	27947E-00	25935E-00
37	41215E-02	24263E 03	62242E 01	67099E 01	15102E 04	16280E 04	16066E-00	14903E-00	27361E-00	25399E-00
38	35530E-02	28145E 03	62278E 01	67137E 01	17528E 04	18896E 04	16057E-00	14895E-00	26798E-00	24884E-00
39	30629E-02	32648E 03	62309E 01	67170E 01	20343E 04	21930E 04	16049E-00	14888E-00	26257E-00	24391E-00
40	26405E-02	37872E 03	62335E 01	67198E 01	23608E 04	25449E 04	16042E-00	14881E-00	25737E-00	23917E-00
41	22763E-02	43932E 03	62358E 01	67223E 01	27395E 04	29532E 04	16037E-00	14876E-00	25235E-00	23462E-00
42	19623E-02	50961E 03	62377E 01	67244E 01	31788E 04	34268E 04	16031E-00	14871E-00	24752E-00	23023E-00
43	16916E-02	59114E 03	62394E 01	67262E 01	36884E 04	39762E 04	16027E-00	14867E-00	24287E-00	22602E-00
44	14583E-02	68573E 03	62409E 01	67278E 01	42795E 04	46134E 04	16023E-00	14864E-00	23838E-00	22195E-00
45	12572E-02	79544E 03	62421E 01	67292E 01	49653E 04	53527E 04	16020E-00	14861E-00	23404E-00	21804E-00
46	10838E-02	92272E 03	62432E 01	67303E 01	57607E 04	62102E 04	16017E-00	14858E-00	22986E-00	21426E-00
47	93427E-03	10703E 04	62442E 01	67313E 01	66834E 04	72049E 04	16015E-00	14856E-00	22582E-00	21061E-00
48	80541E-03	12416E 04	62450E 01	67322E 01	77538E 04	83587E 04	16013E-00	14854E-00	22191E-00	20709E-00
49	69432E-03	14403E 04	62457E 01	67330E 01	89954E 04	96972E 04	16011E-00	14852E-00	21813E-00	20368E-00
50	59855E-03	16707E 04	62463E 01	67336E 01	10436E 05	11250E 05	16010E-00	14851E-00	21448E-00	20039E-00

18% PER PERIOD

Period	Present Value of $1	Amount to Which $1 Will Accumulate	Present Value of $1 per Period		Amount to Which $1 per Period Will Accumulate		Amount per Period to Recover $1 of Investment		Present Value of Depreciation	
			Received at End	Received Continuously	Received at End	Received Continuously	Received at End	Received Continuously	Sum-of-Years' Digits	Declining Balance
1	84746E 00	11800E 01	84746E 00	92163E 00	10000E 01	10875E 01	11800E 01	10850E 01		
2	71818E 00	13924E 01	15656E 01	17027E 01	21800E 01	23708E 01	63872E 00	58731E 00		
3	60863E 00	16430E 01	21743E 01	23646E 01	35724E 01	38851E 01	45992E-00	42291E-00	76456E 00	79219E 00
4	51579E 00	19388E 01	26901E 01	29255E 01	52154E 01	56719E 01	37174E-00	34182E-00	72774E 00	74383E 00
5	43711E-00	22878E 01	31272E 01	34009E 01	71542E 01	77803E 01	31978E-00	29404E-00	69364E 00	70190E 00
6	37043E-00	26996E 01	34976E 01	38037E 01	94420E 01	10268E 02	28591E-00	26290E-00	66201E 00	66295E 00
7	31392E-00	31855E 01	38115E 01	41451E 01	12142E 02	13204E 02	26236E-00	24125E-00	63263E 00	62844E 00
8	26604E-00	37589E 01	40776E 01	44344E 01	15327E 02	16668E 02	24524E-00	22551E-00	60531E 00	59627E 00
9	22546E-00	44355E 01	43030E 01	46796E 01	19086E 02	20756E 02	23239E-00	21369E-00	57987E 00	56742E 00
10	19106E-00	52338E 01	44941E 01	48874E 01	23521E 02	25580E 02	22251E-00	20461E-00	55615E 00	54051E 00
11	16192E-00	61759E 01	46560E 01	50635E 01	28755E 02	31272E 02	21478E-00	19749E-00	53401E 00	51617E 00
12	13722E-00	72876E 01	47932E 01	52127E 01	34931E 02	37988E 02	20863E-00	19184E-00	51330E 00	49344E-00
13	11629E-00	85994E 01	49095E 01	53392E 01	42219E 02	45914E 02	20369E-00	18729E-00	49392E-00	47273E-00
14	98549E-01	10147E 02	50081E 01	54464E 01	50818E 02	55266E 02	19968E-00	18361E-00	47576E-00	45336E-00
15	83516E-01	11974E 02	50916E 01	55372E 01	60965E 02	66301E 02	19640E-00	18060E-00	45872E-00	43561E-00
16	70776E-01	14129E 02	51624E 01	56142E 01	72939E 02	79323E 02	19371E-00	17812E-00	44271E-00	41896E-00
17	59980E-01	16672E 02	52223E 01	56794E 01	87068E 02	94688E 02	19149E-00	17608E-00	42766E-00	40362E-00
18	50830E-01	19673E 02	52732E 01	57347E 01	10374E 03	11282E 03	18964E-00	17438E-00	41348E-00	38921E-00
19	43077E-01	23214E 02	53162E 01	57815E 01	12341E 03	13421E 03	18810E-00	17297E-00	40011E-00	37586E-00
20	36506E-01	27393E 02	53527E 01	58212E 01	14663E 03	15946E 03	18682E-00	17179E-00	38749E-00	36329E-00

#										
21	35159E-00	37557E-00	17080E-00	18575E-00	18925E 03	17402E 03	58549E 01	53837E 01	32324E 02	30937E-01
22	34055E-00	36430E-00	16997E-00	18485E-00	22440E 03	20634E 03	58834E 01	54099E 01	38142E 02	26218E-01
23	33023E-00	35362E-00	16928E-00	18409E-00	26588E 03	24449E 03	59075E 01	54321E 01	45008E 02	22218E-01
24	32046E-00	34350E-00	16869E-00	18345E-00	31483E 03	28949E 03	59280E 01	54509E 01	53109E 02	18829E-01
25	31130E-00	33390E-00	16820E-00	18292E-00	37259E 03	34260E 03	59454E 01	54669E 01	62669E 02	15957E-01
26	30262E-00	32478E-00	16778E-00	18247E-00	44074E 03	40527E 03	59601E 01	54804E 01	73949E 02	13523E-01
27	29443E-00	31611E-00	16743E-00	18209E-00	52116E 03	47922E 03	59725E 01	54919E 01	87260E 02	11460E-01
28	28666E-00	30786E-00	16714E-00	18177E-00	61606E 03	56648E 03	59831E 01	55016E 01	10297E 03	97119E-02
29	27932E-00	30000E-00	16689E-00	18149E-00	72804E 03	66945E 03	59920E 01	55098E 01	12150E 03	82304E-02
30	27232E-00	29251E-00	16668E-00	18126E-00	86017E 03	79095E 03	59996E 01	55168E 01	14337E 03	69749E-02
31	26569E-00	28536E-00	16650E-00	18107E-00	10161E 04	93432E 03	60061E 01	55227E 01	16918E 03	59110E-02
32	25937E-00	27854E-00	16635E-00	18091E-00	12001E 04	11035E 04	60115E 01	55277E 01	19963E 03	50093E-02
33	25336E-00	27201E-00	16622E-00	18077E-00	14172E 04	13031E 04	60161E 01	55320E 01	23556E 03	42452E-02
34	24761E-00	26577E-00	16611E-00	18065E-00	16734E 04	15387E 04	60200E 01	55356E 01	27796E 03	35976E-02
35	24213E-00	25980E-00	16602E-00	18055E-00	19756E 04	18167E 04	60233E 01	55386E 01	32800E 03	30488E-02
36	23689E-00	25408E-00	16594E-00	18047E-00	23323E 04	21446E 04	60262E 01	55412E 01	38704E 03	25837E-02
37	23188E-00	24859E-00	16588E-00	18040E-00	27533E 04	25317E 04	60285E 01	55434E 01	45670E 03	21896E-02
38	22707E-00	24333E-00	16582E-00	18033E-00	32499E 04	29884E 04	60306E 01	55452E 01	53891E 03	18556E-02
39	22247E-00	23827E-00	16578E-00	18028E-00	38360E 04	35273E 04	60323E 01	55468E 01	63591E 03	15725E-02
40	21805E-00	23341E-00	16574E-00	18024E-00	45276E 04	41632E 04	60337E 01	55482E 01	75038E 03	13327E-02
41	21381E-00	22874E-00	16570E-00	18020E-00	53436E 04	49136E 04	60349E 01	55493E 01	88545E 03	11294E-02
42	20973E-00	22425E-00	16567E-00	18017E-00	63066E 04	57990E 04	60360E 01	55502E 01	10448E 04	95710E-03
43	20581E-00	21993E-00	16565E-00	18015E-00	74428E 04	68439E 04	60369E 01	55510E 01	12329E 04	81110E-03
44	20203E-00	21576E-00	16563E-00	18012E-00	87836E 04	80786E 04	60376E 01	55517E 01	14548E 04	68737E-03
45	19839E-00	21174E-00	16561E-00	18010E-00	10366E 05	95316E 04	60382E 01	55523E 01	17167E 04	58252E-03
46	19489E-00	20787E-00	16560E-00	18009E-00	12233E 05	11248E 05	60388E 01	55528E 01	20257E 04	49366E-03
47	19150E-00	20413E-00	16558E-00	18008E-00	14436E 05	13274E 05	60392E 01	55532E 01	23903E 04	41836E-03
48	18824E-00	20052E-00	16557E-00	18006E-00	17035E 05	15664E 05	60396E 01	55536E 01	28206E 04	35454E-03
49	18508E-00	19703E-00	16556E-00	18005E-00	20103E 05	18485E 05	60400E 01	55539E 01	33283E 04	30046E-03
50	18203E-00	19366E-00	16556E-00	18005E-00	23722E 05	21813E 05	60402E 01	55541E 01	39274E 04	25462E-03

20% PER PERIOD

Period	Present Value of $1	Amount to Which $1 Will Accumulate	Present Value of $1 per Period		Amount to Which $1 per Period Will Accumulate		Amount per Period to Recover $1 of Investment		Present Value of Depreciation	
			Received at End	Received Continuously	Received at End	Received Continuously	Received at End	Received Continuously	Sum-of-Years' Digits	Declining Balance
1	83333E 00	12000E 01	83333E 00	91414E 00	10000E 01	10970E 01	12000E 01	10939E 01		
2	69444E 00	14400E 01	15278E 01	16759E 01	22000E 01	24133E 01	65455E 00	59669E 00		
3	57870E 00	17280E 01	21065E 01	23107E 01	36400E 01	39929E 01	47473E-00	43276E-00	74460E 00	77418E 00
4	48225E-00	20736E 01	25887E 01	28397E 01	53680E 01	58885E 01	38629E-00	35214E-00	70563E 00	72290E 00
5	40188E-00	24883E 01	29906E 01	32806E 01	74416E 01	81632E 01	33438E-00	30482E-00	66980E 00	67882E 00
6	33490E-00	29860E 01	33255E 01	36480E 01	99299E 01	10893E 02	30071E-00	27413E-00	63678E 00	63823E 00
7	27908E-00	35832E 01	35046E 01	39541E 01	12916E 02	14168E 02	27742E-00	25290E-00	60632E 00	60254E 00
8	23257E-00	42998E 01	38372E 01	42092E 01	16499E 02	18099E 02	26061E-00	23757E-00	57817E 00	56954E 00
9	19381E-00	51598E 01	40310E 01	44218E 01	20799E 02	22816E 02	24808E-00	22615E-00	55211E 00	54014E 00
10	16151E-00	61917E 01	41925E 01	45990E 01	25959E 02	28476E 02	23852E-00	21744E-00	52796E 00	51292E 00
11	13459E-00	74301E 01	43271E 01	47466E 01	32150E 02	35268E 02	23110E-00	21068E-00	50553E 00	48844E-00
12	11216E-00	89161E 01	44392E 01	48697E 01	39580E 02	43418E 02	22526E-00	20535E-00	48467E-00	46573E-00
13	93464E-01	10699E 02	45327E 01	49722E 01	48497E 02	53199E 02	22062E-00	20112E-00	46524E-00	44514E-00
14	77887E-01	12839E 02	46106E 01	50576E 01	59196E 02	64936E 02	21689E-00	19772E-00	44712E-00	42599E-00
15	64905E-01	15407E 02	46755E 01	51288E 01	72035E 02	79020E 02	21388E-00	19498E-00	43019E-00	40851E-00
16	54088E-01	18488E 02	47296E 01	51882E 01	87442E 02	95921E 02	21144E-00	19275E-00	41435E-00	39221E-00
17	45073E-01	22186E 02	47745E 01	52376E 01	10593E 03	11620E 03	20944E-00	19093E-00	39952E-00	37724E-00
18	37561E-01	26623E 02	48122E 01	52788E 01	12812E 03	14054E 03	20781E-00	18944E-00	38561E-00	36324E-00
19	31301E-01	31948E 02	48435E 01	53131E 01	15474E 03	16974E 03	20646E-00	18821E-00	37254E-00	35030E-00
20	26084E-01	38338E 02	48696E 01	53417E 01	18669E 03	20479E 03	20536E-00	18720E-00	36025E-00	33817E-00

21	21737E-01	46005E 02	48913E 01	53656E 01	22503E 01	24684E 03	20444E-00	18637E-00	34867E-00	32691E-00
22	18114E-01	55206E 02	49094E 01	53855E 01	27103E 01	29731E 03	20369E-00	18569E-00	33776E-00	31631E-00
23	15095E-01	66247E 02	49245E 01	54020E 01	32624E 01	35787E 03	20307E-00	18512E-00	32745E-00	30643E-00
24	12579E-01	79497E 02	49371E 01	54158E 01	39248E 01	43054E 03	20255E-00	18464E-00	31771E-00	29711E-00
25	10483E-01	95396E 02	49476E 01	54273E 01	47198E 01	51775E 03	20212E-00	18425E-00	30850E-00	28838E-00
26	87355E-02	11448E 03	49563E 01	54369E 01	56738E 01	62239E 03	20176E-00	18393E-00	29977E-00	28012E-00
27	72796E-02	13737E 03	49636E 01	54449E 01	68185E 01	74797E 03	20147E-00	18366E-00	29149E-00	27235E-00
28	60663E-02	16484E 03	49697E 01	54515E 01	81922E 01	89866E 03	20122E-00	18343E-00	28362E-00	26498E-00
29	50553E-02	19781E 03	49747E 01	54571E 01	98407E 01	10795E 04	20102E-00	18325E-00	27615E-00	25803E-00
30	42127E-02	23738E 03	49789E 01	54617E 01	11819E 02	12965E 04	20085E-00	18309E-00	26904E-00	25142E-00
31	35106E-02	28485E 03	49824E 01	54656E 01	14193E 02	15569E 04	20070E-00	18296E-00	26227E-00	24516E-00
32	29255E-02	34182E 03	49854E 01	54688E 01	17041E 02	18693E 04	20059E-00	18286E-00	25582E-00	23920E-00
33	24379E-02	41019E 03	49878E 01	54714E 01	20459E 02	22443E 04	20049E-00	18277E-00	24966E-00	23354E-00
34	20316E-02	49222E 03	49898E 01	54737E 01	24561E 02	26943E 04	20041E-00	18269E-00	24378E-00	22813E-00
35	16930E-02	59067E 03	49915E 01	54755E 01	29483E 02	32342E 04	20034E-00	18263E-00	23816E-00	22299E-00
36	14108E-02	70880E 03	49929E 01	54771E 01	35390E 02	38822E 04	20028E-00	18258E-00	23279E-00	21806E-00
37	11757E-02	85056E 03	49941E 01	54784E 01	42478E 02	46597E 04	20024E-00	18254E-00	22764E-00	21336E-00
38	97974E-03	10207E 04	49951E 01	54794E 01	50984E 02	55927E 04	20020E-00	18250E-00	22271E-00	20886E-00
39	81645E-03	12248E 04	49959E 01	54803E 01	61190E 02	67124E 04	20016E-00	18247E-00	21797E-00	20454E-00
40	68038E-03	14698E 04	49966E 01	54811E 01	73439E 02	80559E 04	20014E-00	18245E-00	21344E-00	20041E-00
41	56698E-03	17637E 04	49972E 01	54817E 01	88136E 02	96682E 04	20011E-00	18243E-00	20908E-00	19644E-00
42	47248E-03	21165E 04	49976E 01	54822E 01	10577E 03	11603E 05	20009E-00	18241E-00	20489E-00	19262E-00
43	39374E-03	25398E 04	49980E 01	54827E 01	12694E 03	13925E 05	20008E-00	18239E-00	20086E-00	18896E-00
44	32811E-03	30477E 04	49984E 01	54830E 01	15234E 03	16711E 05	20007E-00	18238E-00	19698E-00	18543E-00
45	27343E-03	36573E 04	49986E 01	54833E 01	18281E 03	20054E 05	20005E-00	18237E-00	19324E-00	18204E-00
46	22786E-03	43887E 04	49989E 01	54836E 01	21939E 03	24066E 05	20005E-00	18236E-00	18964E-00	17876E-00
47	18988E-03	52665E 04	49990E 01	54838E 01	26327E 03	28880E 05	20004E-00	18236E-00	18617E-00	17561E-00
48	15823E-03	63197E 04	49992E 01	54839E 01	31594E 03	34657E 05	20003E-00	18235E-00	18283E-00	17256E-00
49	13186E-03	75837E 04	49993E 01	54841E 01	37913E 03	41590E 05	20003E-00	18235E-00	17959E-00	16963E-00
50	10988E-03	91004E 04	49994E 01	54842E 01	45497E 03	49909E 05	20002E-00	18234E-00	17647E-00	16678E-00

22% PER PERIOD

PERIOD	PRESENT VALUE OF $1	AMOUNT TO WHICH $1 WILL ACCUMULATE	PRESENT VALUE OF $1 PER PERIOD		AMOUNT TO WHICH $1 PER PERIOD WILL ACCUMULATE		AMOUNT PER PERIOD TO RECOVER $1 OF INVESTMENT		PRESENT VALUE OF DEPRECIATION	
			Received at End	Received Continuously	Received at End	Received Continuously	Received at End	Received Continuously	Sum-of-Years' Digits	Declining Balance
1	81967E 00	12200E 01	81967E 00	90685E 00	10000E 01	11064E 01	12200E 01	11027E 01		
2	67186E 00	14884E 01	14915E 01	16502E 01	22200E 01	24561E 01	67045E 00	60600E 00		
3	55071E 00	18158E 01	20422E 01	22594E 01	37084E 01	41028E 01	48966E-00	44259E-00	72557E 00	75694E 00
4	45140E-00	22153E 01	24936E 01	27589E 01	55242E 01	61118E 01	40102E-00	36247E-00	68471E 00	70306E 00
5	37000E-00	27027E 01	28636E 01	31682E 01	77396E 01	85627E 01	34921E-00	31564E-00	64738E 00	65713E 00
6	30328E-00	32973E 01	31669E 01	35037E 01	10442E 02	11553E 02	31576E-00	28541E-00	61322E 00	61519E 00
7	24859E-00	40227E 01	34155E 01	37788E 01	13740E 02	15201E 02	29278E-00	26464E-00	58190E 00	57858E 00
8	20376E-00	49077E 01	36193E 01	40042E 01	17762E 02	19651E 02	27630E-00	24974E-00	55312E 00	54498E 00
9	16702E-00	59874E 01	37863E 01	41890E 01	22670E 02	25081E 02	26411E-00	23872E-00	52664E 00	51524E 00
10	13690E-00	73046E 01	39232E 01	43404E 01	28657E 02	31705E 02	25489E-00	23039E-00	50222E 00	48789E-00
11	11221E-00	89116E 01	40354E 01	44646E 01	35962E 02	39787E 02	24781E-00	22398E-00	47966E-00	46343E-00
12	91978E-01	10872E 02	41274E 01	45663E 01	44874E 02	49646E 02	24228E-00	21899E-00	45878E-00	44086E-00
13	75391E-01	13264E 02	42028E 01	46498E 01	55746E 02	61675E 02	23794E-00	21506E-00	43942E-00	42050E-00
14	61796E-01	16182E 02	42646E 01	47181E 01	69010E 02	76350E 02	23449E-00	21195E-00	42145E-00	40166E-00
15	50653E-01	19742E 02	43152E 01	47742E 01	85192E 02	94253E 02	23174E-00	20946E-00	40473E-00	38453E-00
16	41519E-01	24086E 02	43567E 01	48201E 01	10493E 03	11609E 03	22953E-00	20746E-00	38915E-00	36863E-00
17	34032E-01	29384E 02	43908E 01	48578E 01	12902E 03	14274E 03	22775E-00	20586E-00	37461E-00	35406E-00
18	27895E-01	35849E 02	44187E 01	48886E 01	15840E 03	17525E 03	22631E-00	20456E-00	36101E-00	34050E-00
19	22865E-01	43736E 02	44415E 01	49139E 01	19425E 03	21491E 03	22515E-00	20350E-00	34829E-00	32799E-00
20	18741E-01	53358E 02	44603E 01	49346E 01	23799E 03	26330E 03	22420E-00	20265E-00	33636E-00	31631E-00

21	15362E-01	65096E 02	44756E 02	49516E 01	29135E 03	32233E 03	22343E-00	20195E-00	32515E-00	30548E-00
22	12592E-01	79418E 02	44882E 02	49656E 01	36644E 03	39435E 03	22281E-00	20139E-00	31462E-00	29535E-00
23	10321E-01	96889E 02	44985E 02	49770E 01	43586E 03	48222E 03	22229E-00	20092E-00	30470E-00	28587E-00
24	84599E-02	11821E 03	45070E 03	49864E 01	53275E 03	58941E 03	22188E-00	20055E-00	29535E-00	27697E-00
25	69343E-02	14421E 03	45139E 03	49940E 01	65096E 03	72019E 03	22154E-00	20024E-00	28652E-00	26864E-00
26	56839E-02	17594E 03	45196E 03	50003E 01	79517E 03	87974E 03	22126E-00	19999E-00	27817E-00	26078E-00
27	46589E-02	21464E 03	45243E 03	50055E 01	97110E 03	10744E 04	22103E-00	19978E-00	27027E-00	25339E-00
28	38188E-02	26186E 03	45281E 03	50097E 01	11857E 04	13119E 04	22084E-00	19961E-00	26278E-00	24640E-00
29	31301E-02	31947E 03	45312E 03	50132E 01	14476E 04	16016E 04	22069E-00	19948E-00	25568E-00	23981E-00
30	25657E-02	38976E 03	45338E 03	50160E 01	17671E 04	19550E 04	22057E-00	19936E-00	24894E-00	23355E-00
31	21030E-02	47550E 03	45359E 03	50183E 01	21568E 04	23862E 04	22046E-00	19927E-00	24252E-00	22763E-00
32	17238E-02	58012E 03	45376E 03	50202E 01	26323E 04	29123E 04	22038E-00	19919E-00	23642E-00	22199E-00
33	14129E-02	70774E 03	45390E 03	50218E 01	32125E 04	35541E 04	22031E-00	19913E-00	23060E-00	21664E-00
34	11582E-02	86344E 03	45402E 03	50231E 01	39202E 04	43371E 04	22026E-00	19908E-00	22506E-00	21154E-00
35	94931E-03	10534E 04	45411E 04	50241E 01	47836E 04	52924E 04	22021E-00	19904E-00	21976E-00	20669E-00
36	77812E-03	12852E 04	45419E 04	50250E 01	58370E 04	64579E 04	22017E-00	19901E-00	21470E-00	20205E-00
37	63780E-03	15679E 04	45426E 04	50257E 01	71222E 04	78797E 04	22014E-00	19898E-00	20986E-00	19762E-00
38	52279E-03	19128E 04	45431E 04	50263E 01	86901E 04	96143E 04	22012E-00	19895E-00	20523E-00	19338E-00
39	42852E-03	23336E 04	45435E 04	50267E 01	10603E 05	11731E 05	22009E-00	19894E-00	20080E-00	18933E-00
40	35124E-03	28470E 04	45439E 04	50271E 01	12937E 05	14312E 05	22008E-00	19892E-00	19654E-00	18544E-00
41	28790E-03	34734E 04	45441E 04	50274E 01	15784E 05	17462E 05	22006E-00	19891E-00	19246E-00	18171E-00
42	23599E-03	42375E 04	45444E 04	50277E 01	19257E 05	21305E 05	22005E-00	19890E-00	18854E-00	17813E-00
43	19343E-03	51698E 04	45446E 04	50279E 01	23494E 05	25993E 05	22004E-00	19889E-00	18478E-00	17469E-00
44	15855E-03	63071E 04	45447E 04	50281E 01	28664E 05	31713E 05	22003E-00	19888E-00	18115E-00	17138E-00
45	12996E-03	76947E 04	45449E 04	50282E 01	34971E 05	38691E 05	22003E-00	19888E-00	17767E-00	16820E-00
46	10652E-03	93875E 04	45450E 04	50284E 01	42666E 05	47204E 05	22002E-00	19887E-00	17431E-00	16513E-00
47	87315E-04	11453E 05	45451E 05	50285E 01	52054E 05	57590E 05	22002E-00	19887E-00	17108E-00	16217E-00
48	71570E-04	13972E 05	45451E 05	50285E 01	63506E 05	70261E 05	22002E-00	19887E-00	16796E-00	15932E-00
49	58664E-04	17046E 05	45452E 05	50286E 01	77479E 05	85719E 05	22001E-00	19886E-00	16495E-00	15657E-00
50	48085E-04	20797E 05	45452E 05	50287E 01	94525E 05	10458E 06	22001E-00	19886E-00	16205E-00	15391E-00

24% PER PERIOD

Period	Present Value of $1	Amount to Which $1 Will Accumulate	Present Value of $1 per Period		Amount to Which $1 per Period Will Accumulate		Amount per Period to Recover $1 of Investment		Present Value of Depreciation	
			Received at End	Received Continuously	Received at End	Received Continuously	Received at End	Received Continuously	Sum-of-Years' Digits	Declining Balance
1	80645E 00	12400E 01	80645E 00	89976E 00	10000E 01	11157E 01	12400E 01	11114E 01		
2	65036E 00	15376E 01	14568E 01	16254E 01	22400E 01	24992E 01	68643E 00	61524E 00	70743E 00	74044E 00
3	52449E 00	19066E 01	19813E 01	22105E 01	37776E 01	42147E 01	50472E 00	45238E-00	66488E 00	68425E 00
4	42297E-00	23642E 01	24043E 01	26825E 01	56842E 01	63419E 01	41593E-00	37279E-00	62628E 00	63672E 00
5	34111E-00	29316E 01	27454E 01	30630E 01	80484E 01	89797E 01	36425E-00	32647E-00		
6	27509E-00	36352E 01	30205E 01	33699E 01	10980E 02	12250E 02	33107E-00	29674E-00	59118E 00	59368E 00
7	22184E-00	45077E 01	32423E 01	36175E 01	14615E 02	16306E 02	30842E-00	27644E-00	55918E 00	56636E 00
8	17891E-00	55895E 01	34212E 01	38171E 01	19123E 02	21335E 02	29229E-00	26198E-00	52995E 00	52236E 00
9	14428E-00	69310E 01	35655E 01	39780E 01	24712E 02	27572E 02	28047E-00	25138E-00	50319E 00	49245E-00
10	11635E-00	85944E 01	36819E 01	41079E 01	31643E 02	35305E 02	27160E-00	24344E-00	47865E-00	46511E-00
11	93834E-01	10657E 02	37757E 01	42125E 01	40238E 02	44893E 02	26485E-00	23739E-00	45608E-00	44078E-00
12	75673E-01	13215E 02	38514E 01	42970E 01	50895E 02	56784E 02	25965E-00	23272E-00	43529E-00	41846E-00
13	61026E-01	16386E 02	39124E 01	43651E 01	64110E 02	71527E 02	25560E-00	22909E-00	41610E-00	39840E-00
14	49215E-01	20319E 02	39616E 01	44200E 01	80496E 02	89810E 02	25242E-00	22625E-00	39835E-00	37993E-00
15	39689E-01	25196E 02	40013E 01	44642E 01	10082E 03	11248E 03	24992E-00	22400E-00	38190E-00	36318E-00
16	32008E-01	31243E 02	40333E 01	45000E 01	12601E 03	14059E 03	24794E-00	22222E-00	36663E-00	34770E-00
17	25813E-01	38741E 02	40591E 01	45288E 01	15725E 03	17545E 03	24636E-00	22081E-00	35242E-00	33356E-00
18	20817E-01	48039E 02	40799E 01	45520E 01	19599E 03	21867E 03	24510E-00	21968E-00	33918E-00	32044E-00
19	16788E-01	59568E 02	40967E 01	45707E 01	24403E 03	27227E 03	24410E-00	21878E-00	32683E-00	30837E-00
20	13538E-01	73864E 02	41103E 01	45858E 01	30300E 03	33873E 03	24329E-00	21806E-00	31527E-00	29712E-00

21	10918E-01	91592E 02	41212E 01	45980E 01	37746E 03	42114E 03	24265E-00	21749E-00	30445E-00	28672E-00
22	88049E-02	11357E 03	41300E 01	46078E 01	46906E 03	52333E 03	24213E-00	21702E-00	29430E-00	27698E-00
23	71007E-02	14083E 03	41371E 01	46157E 01	58263E 03	65004E 03	24172E-00	21665E-00	28477E-00	26792E-00
24	57264E-02	17463E 03	41428E 01	46221E 01	72346E 03	80717E 03	24138E-00	21635E-00	27579E-00	25942E-00
25	46180E-02	21654E 03	41474E 01	46273E 01	89809E 03	10020E 04	24111E-00	21611E-00	26734E-00	25146E-00
26	37242E-02	26851E 03	41511E 01	46314E 01	11146E 04	12436E 04	24090E-00	21592E-00	25936E-00	24397E-00
27	30034E-02	33295E 03	41542E 01	46348E 01	13831E 04	15432E 04	24072E-00	21576E-00	25183E-00	23694E-00
28	24221E-02	41286E 03	41566E 01	46375E 01	17161E 04	19147E 04	24058E-00	21563E-00	24470E-00	23029E-00
29	19533E-02	51195E 03	41585E 01	46397E 01	21290E 04	23753E 04	24047E-00	21553E-00	23795E-00	22403E-00
30	15753E-02	63482E 03	41601E 01	46414E 01	26409E 04	29465E 04	24038E-00	21545E-00	23154E-00	21809E-00
31	12704E-02	78718E 03	41614E 01	46428E 01	32757E 04	36547E 04	24031E-00	21539E-00	22546E-00	21247E-00
32	10245E-02	97610E 03	41624E 01	46440E 01	40629E 04	45330E 04	24025E-00	21533E-00	21968E-00	20713E-00
33	82620E-03	12104E 04	41632E 01	46449E 01	50390E 04	56220E 04	24020E-00	21529E-00	21418E-00	20206E-00
34	66629E-03	15008E 04	41639E 01	46457E 01	62494E 04	69724E 04	24016E-00	21525E-00	20894E-00	19724E-00
35	53733E-03	18611E 04	41644E 01	46463E 01	77502E 04	86469E 04	24013E-00	21523E-00	20394E-00	19264E-00
36	43333E-03	23077E 04	41649E 01	46467E 01	96113E 04	10723E 05	24010E-00	21520E-00	19917E-00	18826E-00
37	34946E-03	28616E 04	41652E 01	46471E 01	11919E 05	13298E 05	24008E-00	21519E-00	19461E-00	18407E-00
38	28182E-03	35483E 04	41655E 01	46474E 01	14781E 05	16491E 05	24007E-00	21517E-00	19025E-00	18007E-00
39	22728E-03	43999E 04	41657E 01	46477E 01	18329E 05	20450E 05	24005E-00	21516E-00	18608E-00	17624E-00
40	18329E-03	54559E 04	41659E 01	46479E 01	22729E 05	25359E 05	24004E-00	21515E-00	18208E-00	17257E-00
41	14781E-03	67653E 04	41661E 01	46481E 01	28185E 05	31446E 05	24004E-00	21514E-00	17825E-00	16906E-00
42	11920E-03	83890E 04	41662E 01	46482E 01	34950E 05	38994E 05	24003E-00	21514E-00	17457E-00	16568E-00
43	96132E-04	10402E 05	41663E 01	46483E 01	43339E 05	48353E 05	24002E-00	21513E-00	17104E-00	16244E-00
44	77526E-04	12899E 05	41663E 01	46484E 01	53741E 05	59959E 05	24002E-00	21513E-00	16765E-00	15933E-00
45	62521E-04	15995E 05	41664E 01	46485E 01	66640E 05	74351E 05	24002E-00	21512E-00	16439E-00	15633E-00
46	50420E-04	19833E 05	41665E 01	46485E 01	82635E 05	92196E 05	24001E-00	21512E-00	16125E-00	15344E-00
47	40661E-04	24593E 05	41665E 01	46486E 01	10247E 06	11432E 06	24001E-00	21512E-00	15822E-00	15066E-00
48	32791E-04	30496E 05	41666E 01	46486E 01	12706E 06	14176E 06	24001E-00	21512E-00	15531E-00	14798E-00
49	26445E-04	37815E 05	41666E 01	46486E 01	15756E 06	17579E 06	24001E-00	21512E-00	15249E-00	14539E-00
50	21326E-04	46890E 05	41666E 01	46487E 01	19537E 06	21798E 06	24001E-00	21512E-00	14978E-00	14290E-00

26% PER PERIOD

PERIOD	PRESENT VALUE OF $1	AMOUNT TO WHICH $1 WILL ACCUMULATE	PRESENT VALUE OF $1 PER PERIOD		AMOUNT TO WHICH $1 PER PERIOD WILL ACCUMULATE		AMOUNT PER PERIOD TO RECOVER $1 OF INVESTMENT		PRESENT VALUE OF DEPRECIATION	
			Received at End	Received Continuously	Received at End	Received Continuously	Received at End	Received Continuously	Sum-of-Years' Digits	Declining Balance
1	79365E 00	12600E 01	79365E 00	89285E 00	10000E 01	11250E 01	12600E 01	11200E 01		
2	62988E 00	15876E 01	14235E 01	16015E 01	22600E 01	25425E 01	70248E 00	62443E 00		
3	49991E-00	20004E 01	19234E 01	21639E 01	38476E 01	43285E 01	51990E 00	46214E-00	69010E 00	72462E 00
4	39675E-00	25205E 01	23202E 01	26102E 01	58480E 01	65790E 01	43100E-00	38311E-00	64608E 00	66638E 00
5	31488E-00	31758E 01	26351E 01	29644E 01	83480E 01	94145E 01	37950E-00	33733E-00	60639E 00	61747E 00
6	24991E-00	40015E 01	28850E 01	32456E 01	11544E 02	12987E 02	34462E-00	30811E-00	57052E 00	57355E 00
7	19834E-00	50419E 01	30833E 01	34687E 01	15546E 02	17489E 02	32433E-00	28829E-00	53801E 00	53570E 00
8	15741E-00	63528E 01	32407E 01	36458E 01	20588E 02	23161E 02	30857E-00	27429E-00	50847E 00	50148E 00
9	12493E-00	80045E 01	33657E 01	37864E 01	26940E 02	30308E 02	29712E-00	26411E-00	48157E-00	47151E-00
10	99150E-01	10086E 02	34648E 01	38979E 01	34945E 02	39313E 02	28862E-00	25655E-00	45701E-00	44430E-00
11	78691E-01	12708E 02	35435E 01	39864E 01	45031E 02	50659E 02	28221E-00	25085E-00	43453E-00	42018E-00
12	62453E-01	16012E 02	36060E 01	40567E 01	57739E 02	64956E 02	27732E-00	24651E-00	41391E-00	39817E-00
13	49566E-01	20175E 02	36555E 01	41124E 01	73751E 02	82969E 02	27356E-00	24316E-00	39495E-00	37847E-00
14	39338E-01	25421E 02	36949E 01	41567E 01	93926E 02	10567E 03	27065E-00	24058E-00	37748E-00	36040E-00
15	31221E-01	32030E 02	37261E 01	41918E 01	11935E 03	13426E 03	26838E-00	23856E-00	36134E-00	34407E-00
16	24778E-01	40358E 02	37509E 01	42197E 01	15138E 03	17030E 03	26661E-00	23698E-00	34641E-00	32902E-00
17	19665E-01	50851E 02	37705E 01	42418E 01	19173E 03	21570E 03	26522E-00	23575E-00	33257E-00	31532E-00
18	15607E-01	64072E 02	37861E 01	42594E 01	24259E 03	27291E 03	26411E-00	23478E-00	31970E-00	30263E-00
19	12387E-01	80731E 02	37985E 01	42733E 01	30666E 03	34499E 03	26326E-00	23401E-00	30772E-00	29098E-00
20	98308E-02	10172E 03	38083E 01	42844E 01	38739E 03	43581E 03	26258E-00	23341E-00	29655E-00	28015E-00

21	78022E-02	12817E 03	38161E 01	42932E 01	48911E 03	55025E 03	26204E-00	23293E-00	28611E-00	27015E-00
22	61922E-02	16149E 03	38223E 01	43001E 01	61728E 03	69444E 03	26162E-00	23255E-00	27634E-00	26081E-00
23	49145E-02	20348E 03	38273E 01	43056E 01	77877E 03	87611E 03	26128E-00	23225E-00	26718E-00	25213E-00
24	39004E-02	25639E 03	38312E 01	43100E 01	98225E 03	11050E 04	26102E-00	23202E-00	25857E-00	24399E-00
25	30955E-02	32305E 03	38342E 01	43135E 01	12386E 04	13935E 04	26081E-00	23183E-00	25048E-00	23639E-00
26	24568E-02	40704E 03	38367E 01	43163E 01	15617E 04	17569E 04	26064E-00	23168E-00	24286E-00	22924E-00
27	19498E-02	51287E 03	38387E 01	43185E 01	19687E 04	22148E 04	26051E-00	23156E-00	23567E-00	22253E-00
28	15475E-02	64621E 03	38402E 01	43202E 01	24816E 04	27918E 04	26040E-00	23147E-00	22887E-00	21619E-00
29	12282E-02	81423E 03	38414E 01	43216E 01	31278E 04	35188E 04	26032E-00	23140E-00	22245E-00	21022E-00
30	97473E-03	10259E 04	38424E 01	43227E 01	39420E 04	44348E 04	26025E-00	23134E-00	21636E-00	20457E-00
31	77359E-03	12927E 04	38432E 01	43236E 01	49679E 04	55889E 04	26020E-00	23129E-00	21058E-00	19923E-00
32	61396E-03	16288E 04	38438E 01	43243E 01	62606E 04	70432E 04	26016E-00	23125E-00	20510E-00	19416E-00
33	48727E-03	20522E 04	38443E 01	43248E 01	78894E 04	88755E 04	26013E-00	23122E-00	19989E-00	18934E-00
34	38672E-03	25858E 04	38447E 01	43252E 01	99416E 04	11184E 05	26010E-00	23120E-00	19493E-00	18476E-00
35	30692E-03	32581E 04	38450E 01	43256E 01	12527E 05	14093E 05	26008E-00	23118E-00	19020E-00	18041E-00
36	24359E-03	41052E 04	38452E 01	43259E 01	15786E 05	17759E 05	26006E-00	23117E-00	18569E-00	17625E-00
37	19333E-03	51726E 04	38454E 01	43261E 01	19891E 05	22377E 05	26005E-00	23116E-00	18139E-00	17228E-00
38	15343E-03	65175E 04	38456E 01	43262E 01	25063E 05	28196E 05	26004E-00	23115E-00	17728E-00	16849E-00
39	12177E-03	82120E 04	38457E 01	43264E 01	31581E 05	35528E 05	26003E-00	23114E-00	17334E-00	16487E-00
40	96645E-04	10347E 05	38458E 01	43265E 01	39793E 05	44767E 05	26003E-00	23113E-00	16958E-00	16139E-00
41	76702E-04	13037E 05	38459E 01	43266E 01	50140E 05	56407E 05	26002E-00	23113E-00	16597E-00	15807E-00
42	60075E-04	16427E 05	38459E 01	43266E 01	63178E 05	71075E 05	26002E-00	23113E-00	16251E-00	15487E-00
43	48313E-04	20698E 05	38460E 01	43267E 01	79605E 05	89555E 05	26001E-00	23112E-00	15919E-00	15181E-00
44	38344E-04	26080E 05	38460E 01	43267E 01	10030E 06	11284E 06	26001E-00	23112E-00	15600E-00	14886E-00
45	30432E-04	32860E 05	38460E 01	43268E 01	12638E 06	14218E 06	26001E-00	23112E-00	15293E-00	14603E-00
46	24152E-04	41404E 05	38461E 01	43268E 01	15924E 06	17915E 06	26001E-00	23112E-00	14998E-00	14331E-00
47	19168E-04	52169E 05	38461E 01	43268E 01	20065E 06	22573E 06	26000E-00	23112E-00	14714E-00	14068E-00
48	15213E-04	65733E 05	38461E 01	43268E 01	25282E 06	28442E 06	26000E-00	23111E-00	14441E-00	13815E-00
49	12074E-04	82824E 05	38461E 01	43269E 01	31855E 06	35837E 06	26000E-00	23111E-00	14177E-00	13571E-00
50	95824E-05	10436E 06	38461E 01	43269E 01	40137E 06	45154E 06	26000E-00	23111E-00	13923E-00	13336E-00

28% PER PERIOD

PERIOD	PRESENT VALUE OF $1	AMOUNT TO WHICH $1 WILL ACCUMULATE	PRESENT VALUE OF $1 PER PERIOD		AMOUNT TO WHICH $1 PER PERIOD WILL ACCUMULATE		AMOUNT PER PERIOD TO RECOVER $1 OF INVESTMENT		PRESENT VALUE OF DEPRECIATION	
			Received at End	Received Continuously	Received at End	Received Continuously	Received at End	Received Continuously	Sum-of-Years' Digits	Declining Balance
1	78125E 00	12800E 01	78125E 00	88613E 00	10000E 01	11342E 01	12800E 01	11285E 01		
2	61035E 00	16384E 01	13916E 01	15784E 01	22800E 01	25861E 01	71860E 00	63355E 00	67355E 00	70945E 00
3	47684E-00	20972E 01	18684E 01	21193E 01	39184E 01	44444E 01	53521E 00	47186E-00	62823E 00	64938E 00
4	37253E-00	26844E 01	22410E 01	25418E 01	60156E 01	68231E 01	44624E-00	39342E-00	58762E 00	59931E 00
5	29104E-00	34360E 01	25320E 01	28719E 01	86999E 01	98678E 01	39494E-00	34820E-00		
6	22737E-00	43980E 01	27594E 01	31298E 01	12136E 02	13765E 02	36240E-00	31951E-00	55113E 00	55469E 00
7	17764E-00	56295E 01	29370E 01	33313E 01	16534E 02	18754E 02	34048E-00	30018E-00	51824E 00	51647E 00
8	13878E-00	72058E 01	30758E 01	34887E 01	22163E 02	25139E 02	32512E-00	28664E-00	48851E-00	48213E-00
9	10842E-00	92234E 01	31842E 01	36117E 01	29369E 02	33312E 02	31405E-00	27688E-00	46157E-00	45223E-00
10	84703E-01	11806E 02	32689E 01	37078E 01	38593E 02	43773E 02	30591E-00	26970E-00	43708E-00	42522E-00
11	66174E-01	15112E 02	33351E 01	37828E 01	50398E 02	57164E 02	29984E-00	26435E-00	41477E-00	40139E-00
12	51699E-01	19343E 02	33868E 01	38415E 01	65510E 02	74304E 02	29526E-00	26032E-00	39438E-00	37974E-00
13	40390E-01	24759E 02	34272E 01	38873E 01	84853E 02	96244E 02	29179E-00	25725E-00	37570E-00	36042E-00
14	31554E-01	31691E 02	34587E 01	39231E 01	10961E 03	12433E 03	28912E-00	25490E-00	35855E-00	34277E-00
15	24652E-01	40565E 02	34834E 01	39510E 01	14130E 03	16027E 03	28708E-00	25310E-00	34276E-00	32686E-00
16	19259E-01	51923E 02	35026E 01	39729E 01	18187E 03	20628E 03	28550E-00	25171E-00	32819E-00	31226E-00
17	15046E-01	66461E 02	35177E 01	39899E 01	23379E 03	26518E 03	28428E-00	25063E-00	31471E-00	29897E-00
18	11755E-01	85071E 02	35294E 01	40033E 01	30025E 03	34056E 03	28333E-00	24980E-00	30223E-00	28671E-00
19	91836E-02	10889E 03	35386E 01	40137E 01	38532E 03	43705E 03	28260E-00	24915E-00	29063E-00	27547E-00
20	71747E-02	13938E 03	35458E 01	40218E 01	49421E 03	56056E 03	28202E-00	24864E-00	27983E-00	26504E-00

```
   9                    17.4
 60.0                   4.66
 43.2                   ────
   26.8                 1044
                        1044
                        696
                        ──────
                        81.084      124.6
                                     70.7
                                    ─────
                                     53.9
                        $81.08     +10.8
                          .06      ─────
                        ───────     43.2
                        4.86.48
                                     82.6
First                                103.6
Issue          ≈ 81.00             ──────
               − 4.90               196.2
              ─────────             82.6
              $ 76.10               43.2
                                   ──────
                                    125.8


                    ≈ 6 5 7 0 0 0.
  76.10 / 50,000,000.00
          45 6 6 0
          ─────────
           4 3 4 00
           3 8 0 5 0
          ──────────
            5 3 5 00
            5 3 2 70
           ──────────
              2 3 0 00
```

875-5434

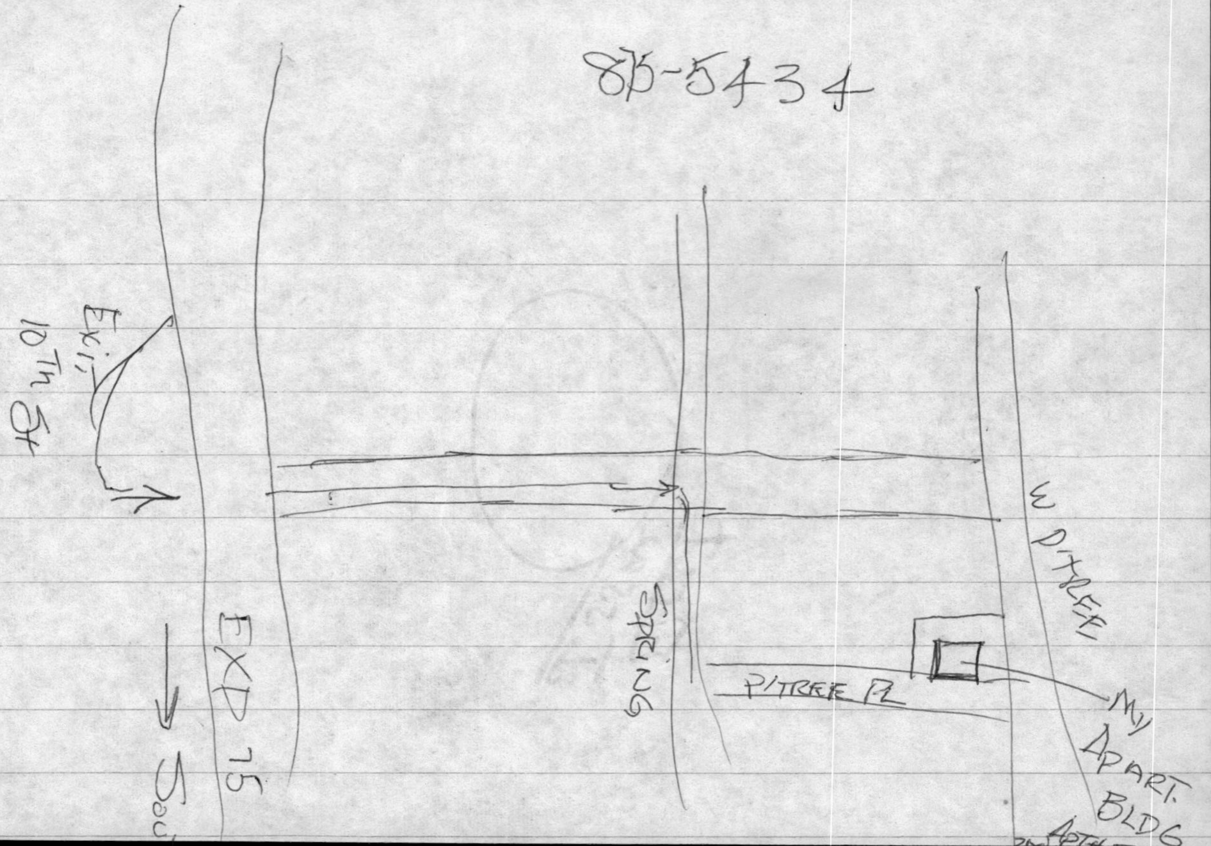

	(1)	(2)	(3)	(4)	(5)	(6)	(7)	(8)	(9)	(10)
21	25542E-00	26977E-00	24825E-00	28158E-00	71865E 03	63359E 03	40282E 01	35514E 01	17841E 03	56052E-02
22	24645E-00	26036E-00	24795E-00	28123E-00	92101E 03	81200E 03	40331E 01	35558E 01	22836E 03	43791E-02
23	23812E-00	25156E-00	24771E-00	28096E-00	11800E 04	10404E 04	40370E 01	35592E 01	29230E 03	34211E-02
24	23032E-00	24331E-00	24752E-00	28075E-00	15116E 04	13327E 04	40401E 01	35619E 01	37414E 03	26728E-02
25	22304E-00	23556E-00	24738E-00	28059E-00	19359E 04	17068E 04	40424E 01	35640E 01	47890E 03	20881E-02
26	21620E-00	22827E-00	24726E-00	28046E-00	24791E 04	21857E 04	40443E 01	35656E 01	61300E 03	16313E-02
27	20979E-00	22140E-00	24718E-00	28036E-00	31744E 04	27987E 04	40457E 01	35669E 01	78464E 03	12745E-02
28	20374E-00	21492E-00	24711E-00	28028E-00	40644E 04	35833E 04	40468E 01	35679E 01	10043E 04	99568E-03
29	19805E-00	20880E-00	24705E-00	28022E-00	52036E 04	45877E 04	40477E 01	35687E 01	12855E 04	77788E-03
30	19266E-00	20300E-00	24701E-00	28017E-00	66617E 04	58732E 04	40484E 01	35693E 01	16455E 04	60772E-03
31	18756E-00	19751E-00	24698E-00	28013E-00	85281E 04	75187E 04	40490E 01	35697E 01	21062E 04	47478E-03
32	18273E-00	19230E-00	24695E-00	28010E-00	10917E 05	96250E 04	40494E 01	35701E 01	26960E 04	37092E-03
33	17815E-00	18735E-00	24693E-00	28008E-00	13975E 05	12321E 05	40497E 01	35704E 01	34509E 04	28978E-03
34	17379E-00	18265E-00	24692E-00	28006E-00	17889E 05	15772E 05	40500E 01	35706E 01	44171E 04	22639E-03
35	16964E-00	17817E-00	24690E-00	28005E-00	22899E 05	20189E 05	40502E 01	35708E 01	56539E 04	17687E-03
36	16569E-00	17390E-00	24689E-00	28004E-00	29312E 05	25843E 05	40503E 01	35709E 01	72370E 04	13818E-03
37	16192E-00	16983E-00	24689E-00	28003E-00	37521E 05	33080E 05	40504E 01	35711E 01	92634E 04	10795E-03
38	15832E-00	16594E-00	24688E-00	28002E-00	48028E 05	42343E 05	40505E 01	35711E 01	11857E 05	84338E-04
39	15488E-00	16222E-00	24688E-00	28002E-00	61476E 05	54200E 05	40506E 01	35712E 01	15177E 05	65889E-04
40	15158E-00	15866E-00	24687E-00	28001E-00	78691E 05	69377E 05	40507E 01	35712E 01	19427E 05	51476E-04
41	14842E-00	15525E-00	24687E-00	28001E-00	10073E 06	88804E 05	40507E 01	35713E 01	24866E 05	40215E-04
42	14540E-00	15199E-00	24687E-00	28001E-00	12893E 06	11367E 06	40508E 01	35713E 01	31829E 05	31418E-04
43	14249E-00	14885E-00	24687E-00	28001E-00	16503E 06	14550E 06	40508E 01	35713E 01	40741E 05	24545E-04
44	13970E-00	14585E-00	24686E-00	28000E-00	21124E 06	18624E 06	40508E 01	35714E 01	52148E 05	19176E-04
45	13702E-00	14296E-00	24686E-00	28000E-00	27039E 06	23839E 06	40508E 01	35714E 01	66750E 05	14981E-04
46	13443E-00	14018E-00	24686E-00	28000E-00	34610E 06	30514E 06	40508E 01	35714E 01	85439E 05	11704E-04
47	13195E-00	13750E-00	24686E-00	28000E-00	44301E 06	39058E 06	40508E 01	35714E 01	10936E 06	91439E-05
48	12955E-00	13493E-00	24686E-00	28000E-00	57705E 06	49994E 06	40508E 01	35714E 01	13998E 06	71437E-05
49	12724E-00	13244E-00	24686E-00	28000E-00	72583E 06	63992E 06	40509E 01	35714E 01	17918E 06	55810E-05
50	12501E-00	13005E-00	24686E-00	28000E-00	92906E 06	81910E 06	40509E 01	35714E 01	22935E 06	43602E-05

30% PER PERIOD

Period	Present Value of $1	Amount to Which $1 Will Accumulate	Present Value of $1 per Period		Amount to Which $1 per Period Will Accumulate		Amount per Period to Recover $1 of Investment		Present Value of Depreciation	
			Received at End	Received Continuously	Received at End	Received Continuously	Received at End	Received Continuously	Sum-of-Years' Digits	Declining Balance
1	76923E 00	13000E 01	76923E 00	87958E 00	10000E 01	11434E 01	13000E 01	11369E 01		
2	59172E 00	16900E 01	13609E 01	15562E 01	23000E 01	26299E 01	73478E 00	64260E 00		
3	45517E-00	21970E 01	18161E 01	20766E 01	39900E 01	45624E 01	55063E 00	48155E-00	65772E 00	69489E 00
4	35013E-00	28561E 01	21662E 01	24770E 01	61870E 01	70745E 01	46163E-00	40372E-00	61125E 00	63321E 00
5	26933E-00	37129E 01	24356E 01	27849E 01	90431E 01	10340E 02	41058E-00	35907E-00	56987E 00	58215E 00
6	20718E-00	48268E 01	26427E 01	30218E 01	12756E 02	14586E 02	37839E-00	33092E-00	53290E 00	53698E 00
7	15937E-00	62749E 01	28021E 01	32041E 01	17583E 02	20105E 02	35687E-00	31210E-00	49975E-00	49852E-00
8	12259E-00	81573E 01	29247E 01	33442E 01	23858E 02	27280E 02	34192E-00	29902E-00	46994E-00	46419E-00
9	94300E-01	10604E 02	30190E 01	34521E 01	32015E 02	36607E 02	33124E-00	28968E-00	44304E-00	43443E-00
10	72538E-01	13786E 02	30915E 01	35350E 01	42619E 02	48733E 02	32346E-00	28288E-00	41869E-00	40769E-00
11	55799E-01	17922E 02	31473E 01	35988E 01	56405E 02	64497E 02	31773E-00	27787E-00	39660E-00	38418E-00
12	42922E-01	23298E 02	31903E 01	36479E 01	74327E 02	84989E 02	31345E-00	27413E-00	37648E-00	36292E-00
13	33017E-01	30288E 02	32233E 01	36857E 01	97625E 02	11163E 03	31024E-00	27132E-00	35812E-00	34401E-00
14	25398E-01	39374E 02	32487E 01	37147E 01	12791E 03	14626E 03	30782E-00	26920E-00	34131E-00	32679E-00
15	19537E-01	51186E 02	32682E 01	37370E 01	16729E 03	19128E 03	30598E-00	26759E-00	32588E-00	31131E-00
16	15028E-01	66542E 02	32832E 01	37542E 01	21847E 03	24981E 03	30458E-00	26637E-00	31169E-00	29713E-00
17	11560E-01	86504E 02	32948E 01	37674E 01	28501E 03	32590E 03	30351E-00	26543E-00	29859E-00	28425E-00
18	88924E-02	11246E 03	33037E 01	37776E 01	37152E 03	42481E 03	30269E-00	26472E-00	28648E-00	27240E-00
19	68403E-02	14619E 03	33105E 01	37854E 01	48397E 03	55340E 03	30207E-00	26417E-00	27525E-00	26155E-00
20	52618E-02	19005E 03	33158E 01	37914E 01	63017E 03	72056E 03	30159E-00	26375E-00	26483E-00	25150E-00

21	40475E-02	24706E 03	33193E 01	37961E 01	82021E 03	93787E 03	30122E-00	26343E-00	25512E-00	24223E-00
22	31135E-02	32118E 03	33230E 01	37996E 01	10673E 04	12204E 04	30094E-00	26318E-00	24607E-00	23361E-00
23	23950E-02	41754E 03	33253E 01	38024E 01	13885E 04	15876E 04	30072E-00	26299E-00	23762E-00	22560E-00
24	18423E-02	54280E 03	33272E 01	38045E 01	18060E 04	20651E 04	30055E-00	26285E-00	22970E-00	21812E-00
25	14172E-02	70564E 03	33286E 01	38061E 01	23488E 04	26857E 04	30043E-00	26274E-00	22227E-00	21114E-00
26	10901E-02	91733E 03	33297E 01	38073E 01	30544E 04	34926E 04	30033E-00	26265E-00	21529E-00	20459E-00
27	83855E-03	11925E 04	33305E 01	38083E 01	39718E 04	45415E 04	30025E-00	26258E-00	20873E-00	19845E-00
28	64504E-03	15503E 04	33312E 01	38090E 01	51643E 04	59051E 04	30019E-00	26253E-00	20254E-00	19267E-00
29	49618E-03	20154E 04	33317E 01	38096E 01	67146E 04	76778E 04	30015E-00	26249E-00	19669E-00	18722E-00
30	38168E-03	26200E 04	33321E 01	38100E 01	87300E 04	99823E 04	30011E-00	26246E-00	19117E-00	18207E-00
31	29360E-03	34060E 04	33324E 01	38104E 01	11350E 05	12978E 05	30009E-00	26244E-00	18594E-00	17720E-00
32	22585E-03	44278E 04	33326E 01	38106E 01	14756E 05	16873E 05	30007E-00	26242E-00	18098E-00	17259E-00
33	17373E-03	57561E 04	33328E 01	38108E 01	19184E 05	21936E 05	30005E-00	26241E-00	17628E-00	16822E-00
34	13364E-03	74830E 04	33329E 01	38110E 01	24940E 05	28517E 05	30004E-00	26240E-00	17180E-00	16406E-00
35	10280E-03	97279E 04	33330E 01	38111E 01	32423E 05	37074E 05	30003E-00	26239E-00	16755E-00	16010E-00
36	79075E-04	12646E 05	33331E 01	38112E 01	42151E 05	48197E 05	30002E-00	26239E-00	16350E-00	15634E-00
37	60827E-04	16440E 05	33331E 01	38113E 01	54797E 05	62657E 05	30002E-00	26238E-00	15963E-00	15275E-00
38	46790E-04	21372E 05	33332E 01	38113E 01	71237E 05	81456E 05	30001E-00	26238E-00	15595E-00	14931E-00
39	35992E-04	27784E 05	33332E 01	38114E 01	92609E 05	10589E 06	30001E-00	26237E-00	15242E-00	14604E-00
40	27686E-04	36119E 05	33332E 01	38114E 01	12039E 06	13766E 06	30001E-00	26237E-00	14905E-00	14290E-00
41	21297E-04	46954E 05	33333E 01	38114E 01	15651E 06	17896E 06	30001E-00	26237E-00	14583E-00	13990E-00
42	16382E-04	61041E 05	33333E 01	38114E 01	20347E 06	23265E 06	30000E-00	26237E-00	14273E-00	13702E-00
43	12602E-04	79353E 05	33333E 01	38114E 01	26451E 06	30245E 06	30000E-00	26237E-00	13977E-00	13425E-00
44	96938E-05	10316E 06	33333E 01	38115E 01	34386E 06	39219E 06	30000E-00	26237E-00	13692E-00	13160E-00
45	74567E-05	13411E 06	33333E 01	38115E 01	44702E 06	51114E 06	30000E-00	26237E-00	13419E-00	12905E-00
46	57360E-05	17434E 06	33333E 01	38115E 01	58113E 06	66449E 06	30000E-00	26237E-00	13157E-00	12660E-00
47	44123E-05	22664E 06	33333E 01	38115E 01	75546E 06	86383E 06	30000E-00	26237E-00	12904E-00	12424E-00
48	33941E-05	29463E 06	33333E 01	38115E 01	98210E 06	11230E 07	30000E-00	26237E-00	12661E-00	12196E-00
49	26108E-05	38302E 06	33333E 01	38115E 01	12767E 07	14599E 07	30000E-00	26236E-00	12426E-00	11977E-00
50	20083E-05	49793E 06	33333E 01	38115E 01	16598E 07	18978E 07	30000E-00	26236E-00	12200E-00	11765E-00

35% PER PERIOD

Period	Present Value of $1	Amount to Which $1 Will Accumulate	Present Value of $1 per Period		Amount to Which $1 per Period Will Accumulate		Amount per Period to Recover $1 of Investment		Present Value of Depreciation	
			Received at End	Received Continuously	Received at End	Received Continuously	Received at End	Received Continuously	Sum-of-Years' Digits	Declining Balance
1	74074E 00	13500E 01	74074E 00	86390E 00	10000E 01	11663E 01	13500E 01	11575E 01		
2	54870E 00	18225E 01	12894E 01	15038E 01	23500E 01	27407E 01	77553E 00	66497E 00		
3	40644E-00	24604E 01	16959E 01	19778E 01	41725E 01	48662E 01	58966E 00	50560E 00	62101E 00	66092E 00
4	30107E-00	33215E 01	19969E 01	23290E 01	66329E 01	77357E 01	50076E 00	42938E-00	57230E 00	59598E 00
5	22301E-00	44840E 01	22200E 01	25891E 01	99544E 01	11609E 02	45046E-00	38624E-00	52953E 00	54311E 00
6	16520E-00	60534E 01	23852E 01	27817E 01	14438E 02	16839E 02	41926E-00	35949E-00	49182E-00	49714E-00
7	12237E-00	81721E 01	25075E 01	29244E 01	20492E 02	23899E 02	39880E-00	34195E-00	45842E-00	45852E-00
8	90642E-01	11032E 02	25982E 01	30301E 01	28664E 02	33430E 02	38489E-00	33002E-00	42872E-00	42453E-00
9	67142E-01	14894E 02	26653E 01	31084E 01	39696E 02	46296E 02	37519E-00	32170E-00	40220E-00	39539E-00
10	49735E-01	20107E 02	27150E 01	31664E 01	54590E 02	63666E 02	36832E-00	31581E-00	37844E-00	36951E-00
11	36841E-01	27144E 02	27519E 01	32094E 01	74697E 02	87116E 02	36339E-00	31158E-00	35706E-00	34694E-00
12	27289E-01	36644E 02	27792E 01	32412E 01	10184E 03	11877E 03	35982E-00	30852E-00	33776E-00	32673E-00
13	20214E-01	49470E 02	27994E 01	32648E 01	13848E 03	16151E 03	35722E-00	30630E-00	32027E-00	30885E-00
14	14974E-01	66784E 02	28144E 01	32823E 01	18795E 03	21920E 03	35532E-00	30467E-00	30437E-00	29270E-00
15	11092E-01	90158E 02	28255E 01	32952E 01	25474E 03	29709E 03	35393E-00	30347E-00	28987E-00	27824E-00
16	82160E-02	12171E 03	28337E 01	33048E 01	34490E 03	40224E 03	35290E-00	30259E-00	27660E-00	26508E-00
17	60859E-02	16431E 03	28398E 01	33119E 01	46661E 03	54419E 03	35214E-00	30194E-00	26443E-00	25317E-00
18	45081E-02	22182E 03	28443E 01	33172E 01	63092E 03	73582E 03	35158E-00	30146E-00	25323E-00	24225E-00
19	33393E-02	29946E 03	28476E 01	33210E 01	85275E 03	99453E 03	35117E-00	30111E-00	24289E-00	23228E-00
20	24736E-02	40427E 03	28501E 01	33239E 01	11522E 04	13438E 04	35087E-00	30085E-00	23333E-00	22308E-00

21	18323E-02	54577E 03	28519E 01	33261E 01	15565E 04	18153E 04	35064E-00	30066E-00	22447E-00	21461E-00
22	13572E-02	73679E 03	28533E 01	33276E 01	21023E 04	24518E 04	35048E-00	30051E-00	21623E-00	20675E-00
23	10054E-02	99466E 03	28543E 01	33288E 01	28390E 04	33111E 04	35035E-00	30041E-00	20855E-00	19947E-00
24	74471E-03	13428E 04	28550E 01	33297E 01	38337E 04	44711E 04	35026E-00	30033E-00	20138E-00	19269E-00
25	55164E-03	18128E 04	28556E 01	33303E 01	51765E 04	60371E 04	35019E-00	30027E-00	19468E-00	18636E-00
26	40862E-03	24472E 04	28560E 01	33308E 01	69893E 04	81513E 04	35014E-00	30023E-00	18839E-00	18043E-00
27	30268E-03	33038E 04	28563E 01	33312E 01	94365E 04	11005E 05	35011E-00	30020E-00	18249E-00	17488E-00
28	22421E-03	44601E 04	28565E 01	33314E 01	12740E 05	14859E 05	35008E-00	30017E-00	17694E-00	16966E-00
29	16608E-03	60211E 04	28567E 01	33316E 01	17200E 05	20060E 05	35006E-00	30015E-00	17171E-00	16475E-00
30	12302E-03	81285E 04	28568E 01	33318E 01	23222E 05	27082E 05	35004E-00	30014E-00	16678E-00	16011E-00
31	91128E-04	10974E 05	23569E 01	33319E 01	31350E 05	36562E 05	35003E-00	30013E-00	16211E-00	15573E-00
32	67502E-04	14814E 05	28569E 01	33319E 01	42324E 05	49300E 05	35002E-00	30012E-00	15770E-00	15159E-00
33	50002E-04	19999E 05	28570E 01	33320E 01	57138E 05	66638E 05	35002E-00	30012E-00	15352E-00	14766E-00
34	37038E-04	26999E 05	28570E 01	33320E 01	77137E 05	89962E 05	35001E-00	30012E-00	14955E-00	14394E-00
35	27436E-04	36449E 05	28571E 01	33321E 01	10414E 06	12145E 06	35001E-00	30011E-00	14577E-00	14039E-00
36	20323E-04	49206E 05	28571E 01	33321E 01	14058E 06	16396E 06	35001E-00	30011E-00	14218E-00	13702E-00
37	15054E-04	66428E 05	28571E 01	33321E 01	18979E 06	22135E 06	35001E-00	30011E-00	13876E-00	13381E-00
38	11151E-04	89677E 05	28571E 01	33321E 01	25622E 06	29882E 06	35000E-00	30011E-00	13550E-00	13074E-00
39	82601E-05	12106E 06	28571E 01	33321E 01	34590E 06	40340E 06	35000E-00	30011E-00	13239E-00	12781E-00
40	61186E-05	16344E 06	28571E 01	33322E 01	46696E 06	54460E 06	35000E-00	30011E-00	12942E-00	12502E-00
41	45323E-05	22064E 06	28571E 01	33322E 01	63040E 06	73521E 06	35000E-00	30011E-00	12657E-00	12234E-00
42	33572E-05	29786E 06	28571E 01	33322E 01	85104E 06	99253E 06	35000E-00	30011E-00	12385E-00	11977E-00
43	24868E-05	40212E 06	28571E 01	33322E 01	11489E 07	13399E 07	35000E-00	30011E-00	12124E-00	11731E-00
44	18421E-05	54286E 06	28571E 01	33322E 01	15510E 07	18089E 07	35000E-00	30011E-00	11874E-00	11495E-00
45	13645E-05	73286E 06	28571E 01	33322E 01	20939E 07	24420E 07	35000E-00	30011E-00	11634E-00	11268E-00
46	10108E-05	98936E 06	28571E 01	33322E 01	28267E 07	32967E 07	35000E-00	30010E-00	11403E-00	11050E-00
47	74871E-06	13356E 07	28571E 01	33322E 01	38161E 07	44505E 07	35000E-00	30010E-00	11181E-00	10841E-00
48	55460E-06	18031E 07	28571E 01	33322E 01	51517E 07	60082E 07	35000E-00	30010E-00	10968E-00	10639E-00
49	41081E-06	24342E 07	28571E 01	33322E 01	69548E 07	81111E 07	35000E-00	30010E-00	10762E-00	10444E-00
50	30431E-06	32862E 07	28571E 01	33322E 01	93890E 07	10950E 08	35000E-00	30010E-00	10564E-00	10257E-00

40% PER PERIOD

PERIOD	PRESENT VALUE OF $1	AMOUNT TO WHICH $1 WILL ACCUMULATE	PRESENT VALUE OF $1 PER PERIOD		AMOUNT TO WHICH $1 PER PERIOD WILL ACCUMULATE		AMOUNT PER PERIOD TO RECOVER $1 OF INVESTMENT		PRESENT VALUE OF DEPRECIATION	
			Received at End	Received Continuously	Received at End	Received Continuously	Received at End	Received Continuously	Sum-of-Years' Digits	Declining Balance
1	71429E 00	14000E 01	71429E 00	84915E 00	10000E 01	11888E 01	14000E 01	11777E 01		
2	51020E 00	19600E 01	12245E 01	14557E 01	24000E 01	28531E 01	81667E 00	68696E 00	58795E 00	63006E 00
3	36443E-00	27440E 01	15889E 01	18889E 01	43600E 01	51832E 01	62936E 00	52940E 00	53769E 00	56279E 00
4	26031E-00	38416E 01	18492E 01	21984E 01	71040E 01	84453E 01	54077E 00	45488E-00	49414E-00	50884E 00
5	18593E-00	53782E 01	20352E 01	24194E 01	10946E 02	13012E 02	49136E-00	41332E-00		
6	13281E-00	75295E 01	21680E 01	25773E 01	16324E 02	19406E 02	46126E-00	38800E-00	45619E-00	46265E-00
7	94865E-01	10541E 02	22628E 01	26901E 01	23853E 02	28357E 02	44192E-00	37174E-00	42296E-00	42432E-00
8	67760E-01	14758E 02	23306E 01	27706E 01	34395E 02	40889E 02	42907E-00	36093E-00	39371E-00	39101E-00
9	48400E-01	20661E 02	23790E 01	28282E 01	49153E 02	58433E 02	42034E-00	35359E-00	36783E-00	36271E-00
10	34572E-01	28925E 02	24136E 01	28692E 01	69814E 02	82995E 02	41432E-00	34852E-00	34484E-00	33782E-00
11	24694E-01	40496E 02	24383E 01	28986E 01	98739E 02	11738E 03	41013E-00	34499E-00	32431E-00	31627E-00
12	17639E-01	56694E 02	24559E 01	29196E 01	13923E 03	16552E 03	40718E-00	34251E-00	30590E-00	29711E-00
13	12599E-01	79371E 02	24685E 01	29346E 01	19593E 03	23292E 03	40510E-00	34077E-00	28933E-00	28024E-00
14	89993E-02	11112E 03	24775E 01	29453E 01	27530E 03	32728E 03	40363E-00	33953E-00	27435E-00	26510E-00
15	64281E-02	15557E 03	24839E 01	29529E 01	38642E 03	45938E 03	40259E-00	33865E-00	26075E-00	25158E-00
16	45915E-02	21780E 03	24885E 01	29584E 01	54199E 03	64432E 03	40185E-00	33802E-00	24837E-00	23933E-00
17	32796E-02	30491E 03	24918E 01	29623E 01	75978E 03	90323E 03	40132E-00	33758E-00	23706E-00	22828E-00
18	23426E-02	42688E 03	24941E 01	29651E 01	10647E 04	12657E 04	40094E-00	33726E-00	22669E-00	21818E-00
19	16733E-02	59763E 03	24958E 01	29670E 01	14916E 04	17732E 04	40067E-00	33704E-00	21716E-00	20897E-00
20	11952E-02	83668E 03	24970E 01	29685E 01	20892E 04	24837E 04	40048E-00	33687E-00	20837E-00	20050E-00

21	85371E-03	11714E 04	24979E 01	29695E 01	29259E 04	34783E 04	40034E-00	33676E-00	20024E-00	19271E-00
22	60979E-03	16399E 04	24985E 01	29702E 01	40972E 04	48708E 04	40024E-00	33668E-00	19270E-00	18550E-00
23	43557E-03	22959E 04	24989E 01	29707E 01	57371E 04	68203E 04	40017E-00	33662E-00	18570E-00	17883E-00
24	31112E-03	32142E 04	24992E 01	29711E 01	80330E 04	95497E 04	40012E-00	33658E-00	17917E-00	17261E-00
25	22223E-03	44999E 04	24994E 01	29714E 01	11247E 05	13371E 05	40009E-00	33655E-00	17308E-00	16683E-00
26	15873E-03	62998E 04	24996E 01	29715E 01	15747E 05	18720E 05	40006E-00	33653E-00	16738E-00	16142E-00
27	11338E-03	88198E 04	24997E 01	29717E 01	22047E 05	26209E 05	40005E-00	33651E-00	16204E-00	15635E-00
28	80987E-04	12348E 05	24998E 01	29718E 01	30867E 05	36694E 05	40003E-00	33650E-00	15702E-00	15160E-00
29	57848E-04	17287E 05	24999E 01	29718E 01	43214E 05	51373E 05	40002E-00	33649E-00	15230E-00	14712E-00
30	41320E-04	24201E 05	24999E 01	29719E 01	60501E 05	71924E 05	40002E-00	33649E-00	14785E-00	14291E-00
31	29514E-04	33882E 05	24999E 01	29719E 01	84702E 05	10069E 06	40001E-00	33648E-00	14365E-00	13893E-00
32	21082E-04	47435E 05	24999E 01	29720E 01	11858E 06	14097E 06	40001E-00	33648E-00	13968E-00	13517E-00
33	15058E-04	66409E 05	25000E 01	29720E 01	16602E 06	19736E 06	40001E-00	33648E-00	13592E-00	13161E-00
34	10756E-04	92972E 05	25000E 01	29720E 01	23243E 06	27631E 06	40000E-00	33648E-00	13235E-00	12823E-00
35	76828E-05	13016E 06	25000E 01	29720E 01	32540E 06	38684E 06	40000E-00	33647E-00	12897E-00	12502E-00
36	54877E-05	18223E 06	25000E 01	29720E 01	45556E 06	54157E 06	40000E-00	33647E-00	12575E-00	12197E-00
37	39198E-05	25512E 06	25000E 01	29720E 01	63779E 06	75820E 06	40000E-00	33647E-00	12269E-00	11906E-00
38	27998E-05	35716E 06	25000E 01	29720E 01	89290E 06	10615E 07	40000E-00	33647E-00	11977E-00	11629E-00
39	19999E-05	50003E 06	25000E 01	29720E 01	12501E 07	14861E 07	40000E-00	33647E-00	11699E-00	11364E-00
40	14285E-05	70004E 06	25000E 01	29720E 01	17501E 07	20805E 07	40000E-00	33647E-00	11433E-00	11112E-00
41	10204E-05	98005E 06	25000E 01	29720E 01	24501E 07	29127E 07	40000E-00	33647E-00	11179E-00	10870E-00
42	72882E-06	13721E 07	25000E 01	29720E 01	34302E 07	40778E 07	40000E-00	33647E-00	10936E-00	10633E-00
43	52059E-06	19209E 07	25000E 01	29720E 01	48023E 07	57089E 07	40000E-00	33647E-00	10703E-00	10417E-00
44	37185E-06	26893E 07	25000E 01	29720E 01	67232E 07	79925E 07	40000E-00	33647E-00	10480E-00	10204E-00
45	26561E-06	37650E 07	25000E 01	29720E 01	94124E 07	11190E 08	40000E-00	33647E-00	10266E-00	10000E-00
46	18972E-06	52710E 07	25000E 01	29720E 01	13177E 08	15665E 08	40000E-00	33647E-00	10060E-00	98041E-01
47	13551E-06	73793E 07	25000E 01	29720E 01	18448E 08	21931E 08	40000E-00	33647E-00	98626E-01	96155E-01
48	96795E-07	10331E 08	25000E 01	29720E 01	25828E 08	30704E 08	40000E-00	33647E-00	96726E-01	94341E-01
49	69140E-07	14464E 08	25000E 01	29720E 01	36159E 08	42986E 08	40000E-00	33647E-00	94898E-01	92593E-01
50	49385E-07	20249E 08	25000E 01	29720E 01	50622E 08	60180E 08	40000E-00	33647E-00	93137E-01	90910E-01

45% PER PERIOD

PERIOD	PRESENT VALUE OF $1	AMOUNT TO WHICH $1 WILL ACCUMULATE	PRESENT VALUE OF $1 PER PERIOD — Received at End	PRESENT VALUE OF $1 PER PERIOD — Received Continuously	AMOUNT TO WHICH $1 PER PERIOD WILL ACCUMULATE — Received at End	AMOUNT TO WHICH $1 PER PERIOD WILL ACCUMULATE — Received Continuously	AMOUNT PER PERIOD TO RECOVER $1 OF INVESTMENT — Received at End	AMOUNT PER PERIOD TO RECOVER $1 OF INVESTMENT — Received Continuously	PRESENT VALUE OF DEPRECIATION — Sum-of-Years' Digits	PRESENT VALUE OF DEPRECIATION — Declining Balance
1	68966E 00	14500E 01	68966E 00	83524E 00	10000E 01	12111E 01	14500E 01	11973E 01		
2	47562E-00	21025E 01	11653E 01	14113E 01	24500E 01	29672E 01	85816E 00	70858E 00		
3	32802E-00	30486E 01	14933E 01	18085E 01	45525E 01	55135E 01	66966E 00	55294E 00	55804E 00	60191E 00
4	22622E-00	44205E 01	17195E 01	20825E 01	76011E 01	92057E 01	58156E 00	48019E-00	50677E 00	53301E 00
5	15601E-00	64097E 01	18755E 01	22714E 01	12022E 02	14559E 02	53318E 00	44025E-00	46288E-00	47853E-00
6	10759E-00	92941E 01	19831E 01	24018E 01	18431E 02	22322E 02	50426E 00	41636E-00	42507E-00	43255E-00
7	74203E-01	13476E 02	20573E 01	24916E 01	27725E 02	33578E 02	48607E-00	40134E-00	39228E-00	39479E-00
8	51175E-01	19541E 02	21085E 01	25536E 01	41202E 02	49900E 02	47427E-00	39160E-00	36367E-00	36235E-00
9	35293E-01	28334E 02	21438E 01	25963E 01	60743E 02	73566E 02	46646E-00	38516E-00	33858E-00	33499E-00
10	24340E-01	41085E 02	21681E 01	26258E 01	89077E 02	10788E 03	46123E-00	38083E-00	31644E-00	31114E-00
11	16786E-01	59573E 02	21849E 01	26462E 01	13016E 03	15764E 03	45768E-00	37791E-00	29680E-00	29059E-00
12	11577E-01	86381E 02	21965E 01	26602E 01	18973E 03	22979E 03	45527E-00	37592E-00	27930E-00	27244E-00
13	79839E-02	12525E 03	22045E 01	26698E 01	27612E 03	33440E 03	45362E-00	37455E-00	26363E-00	25652E-00
14	55061E-02	18162E 03	22100E 01	26765E 01	40137E 03	48609E 03	45249E-00	37362E-00	24952E-00	24230E-00
15	37973E-02	26334E 03	22136E 01	26811E 01	58298E 03	70605E 03	45172E-00	37298E-00	23678E-00	22964E-00
16	26189E-02	38185E 03	22164E 01	26843E 01	84632E 03	10250E 04	45118E-00	37254E-00	22522E-00	21820E-00
17	18061E-02	55368E 03	22182E 01	26865E 01	12282E 04	14874E 04	45081E-00	37224E-00	21470E-00	20790E-00
18	12456E-02	80283E 03	22195E 01	26880E 01	17818E 04	21580E 04	45056E-00	37203E-00	20508E-00	19851E-00
19	85903E-03	11641E 04	22203E 01	26890E 01	25847E 04	31303E 04	45039E-00	37188E-00	19625E-00	18996E-00
20	59243E-03	16880E 04	22209E 01	26897E 01	37488E 04	45401E 04	45027E-00	37178E-00	18814E-00	18212E-00

#										
21	40858E-03	24475E 04	22213E 01	26902E 01	54367E 04	65844E 04	45018E-00	37172E-00	18065E-00	17491E-00
22	28178E-03	35489E 04	22216E 01	26906E 01	78843E 04	95486E 04	45013E-00	37167E-00	17372E-00	16825E-00
23	19433E-03	51459E 04	22218E 01	26908E 01	11433E 05	13847E 05	45009E-00	37164E-00	16730E-00	16209E-00
24	13402E-03	74616E 04	22219E 01	26910E 01	16579E 05	20079E 05	45006E-00	37161E-00	16132E-00	15636E-00
25	92427E-04	10819E 05	22220E 01	26911E 01	24041E 05	29116E 05	45004E-00	37160E-00	15575E-00	15103E-00
26	63743E-04	15688E 05	22221E 01	26912E 01	34860E 05	42219E 05	45003E-00	37159E-00	15054E-00	14605E-00
27	43961E-04	22748E 05	22221E 01	26912E 01	50548E 05	61219E 05	45002E-00	37158E-00	14567E-00	14140E-00
28	30318E-04	32984E 05	22222E 01	26912E 01	73296E 05	88768E 05	45001E-00	37157E-00	14109E-00	13703E-00
29	20909E-04	47827E 05	22222E 01	26913E 01	10628E 06	12872E 06	45001E-00	37157E-00	13680E-00	13292E-00
30	14420E-04	69349E 05	22222E 01	26913E 01	15411E 06	18664E 06	45001E-00	37157E-00	13275E-00	12906E-00
31	99447E-05	10056E 06	22222E 01	26913E 01	22346E 06	27063E 06	45000E-00	37157E-00	12893E-00	12541E-00
32	68584E-05	14581E 06	22222E 01	26913E 01	32401E 06	39241E 06	45000E-00	37157E-00	12533E-00	12197E-00
33	47299E-05	21142E 06	22222E 01	26913E 01	46982E 06	56900E 06	45000E-00	37157E-00	12192E-00	11871E-00
34	32620E-05	30656E 06	22222E 01	26913E 01	68124E 06	82504E 06	45000E-00	37156E-00	11868E-00	11562E-00
35	22497E-05	44451E 06	22222E 01	26913E 01	98779E 06	11963E 07	45000E-00	37156E-00	11562E-00	11268E-00
36	15515E-05	64454E 06	22222E 01	26913E 01	14323E 07	17347E 07	45000E-00	37156E-00	11271E-00	10990E-00
37	10700E-05	93458E 06	22222E 01	26913E 01	20768E 07	25153E 07	45000E-00	37156E-00	10993E-00	10724E-00
38	73793E-06	13551E 07	22222E 01	26913E 01	30114E 07	36471E 07	45000E-00	37156E-00	10730E-00	10472E-00
39	50892E-06	19650E 07	22222E 01	26913E 01	43666E 07	52883E 07	45000E-00	37156E-00	10478E-00	10230E-00
40	35098E-06	28492E 07	22222E 01	26913E 01	63315E 07	76681E 07	45000E-00	37156E-00	10238E-00	10000E-00
41	24205E-06	41313E 07	22222E 01	26913E 01	91807E 07	11119E 08	45000E-00	37156E-00	10008E-00	97801E-01
42	16693E-06	59904E 07	22222E 01	26913E 01	13312E 08	16122E 08	45000E-00	37156E-00	97890E-01	95695E-01
43	11513E-06	86861E 07	22222E 01	26913E 01	19302E 08	23377E 08	45000E-00	37156E-00	95790E-01	93678E-01
44	79398E-07	12595E 08	22222E 01	26913E 01	27988E 08	33897E 08	45000E-00	37156E-00	93777E-01	91744E-01
45	54757E-07	18262E 08	22222E 01	26913E 01	40583E 08	49150E 08	45000E-00	37156E-00	91847E-01	89888E-01
46	37763E-07	26481E 08	22222E 01	26913E 01	58846E 08	71268E 08	45000E-00	37156E-00	89994E-01	88106E-01
47	26044E-07	38397E 08	22222E 01	26913E 01	85326E 08	10334E 09	45000E-00	37156E-00	88215E-01	86394E-01
48	17961E-07	55675E 08	22222E 01	26913E 01	12372E 09	14984E 09	45000E-00	37156E-00	86504E-01	84746E-01
49	12387E-07	80729E 08	22222E 01	26913E 01	17940E 09	21727E 09	45000E-00	37156E-00	84858E-01	83160E-01
50	85428E-08	11706E 09	22222E 01	26913E 01	26013E 09	31504E 09	45000E-00	37156E-00	83273E-01	81633E-01

50% PER PERIOD

PERIOD	PRESENT VALUE OF $1	AMOUNT TO WHICH $1 WILL ACCUMULATE	PRESENT VALUE OF $1 PER PERIOD		AMOUNT TO WHICH $1 PER PERIOD WILL ACCUMULATE		AMOUNT PER PERIOD TO RECOVER $1 OF INVESTMENT		PRESENT VALUE OF DEPRECIATION	
			Received at End	Received Continuously	Received at End	Received Continuously	Received at End	Received Continuously	Sum-of-Years' Digits	Declining Balance
1	66667E 00	15000E 01	66667E 00	82210E 00	10000E 01	12332E 01	15000E 01	12164E 01		
2	44444E-00	22500E 01	11111E 01	13702E 01	25000E 01	30829E 01	90000E 00	72984E 00		
3	29630E-00	33750E 01	14074E 01	17355E 01	47500E 01	58575E 01	71053E 00	57619E 00	53086E 00	57613E 00
4	19753E-00	50625E 01	16049E 01	19791E 01	81250E 01	10019E 02	62308E 00	50527E 00	47901E-00	50617E 00
5	13169E-00	75938E 01	17366E 01	21415E 01	13187E 02	16262E 02	57583E 00	46696E-00	43512E-00	45156E-00
6	87791E-01	11391E 02	18244E 01	22498E 01	20781E 02	25626E 02	54812E 00	44449E-00	39767E-00	40607E-00
7	58528E-01	17086E 02	18829E 01	23220E 01	32172E 02	39673E 02	53108E 00	43067E-00	36550E-00	36906E-00
8	39018E-01	25629E 02	19220E 01	23701E 01	49258E 02	60742E 02	52030E 00	42193E-00	33767E-00	33758E-00
9	26012E-01	38443E 02	19480E 01	24021E 01	74887E 02	92347E 02	51335E 00	41629E-00	31342E-00	31120E-00
10	17342E-01	57665E 02	19653E 01	24235E 01	11333E 03	13975E 03	50882E 00	41262E-00	29217E-00	28837E-00
11	11561E-01	86498E 02	19769E 01	24378E 01	17100E 03	21086E 03	50585E 00	41021E-00	27343E-00	26879E-00
12	77073E-02	12975E 03	19846E 01	24473E 01	25749E 03	31753E 03	50388E 00	40861E-00	25681E-00	25159E-00
13	51382E-02	19462E 03	19897E 01	24536E 01	38724E 03	47752E 03	50258E 00	40756E-00	24198E-00	23654E-00
14	34255E-02	29193E 03	19931E 01	24579E 01	58186E 03	71752E 03	50172E 00	40686E-00	22870E-00	22315E-00
15	22837E-02	43789E 03	19954E 01	24607E 01	87379E 03	10775E 04	50114E 00	40639E-00	21674E-00	21125E-00
16	15224E-02	65684E 03	19970E 01	24625E 01	13117E 04	16175E 04	50076E 00	40608E-00	20593E-00	20054E-00
17	10150E-02	98526E 03	19980E 01	24638E 01	19685E 04	24275E 04	50051E 00	40588E-00	19610E-00	19090E-00
18	67664E-03	14779E 04	19986E 01	24646E 01	29538E 04	36425E 04	50034E 00	40574E-00	18715E-00	18213E-00
19	45109E-03	22168E 04	19991E 01	24652E 01	44317E 04	54649E 04	50023E 00	40565E-00	17896E-00	17416E-00
20	30073E-03	33253E 04	19994E 01	24656E 01	66485E 04	81986E 04	50015E 00	40559E-00	17143E-00	16685E-00

21	20049E-03	49879E 04	19996E 01	24658E 01	97738E 04	12299E 05	50010E 00	40555E-00	16451E-00	16014E-00
22	13366E-03	74818E 04	19997E 01	24660E 01	14962E 05	18450E 05	50007E 00	40552E-00	15810E-00	15395E-00
23	89105E-04	11223E 05	19998E 01	24661E 01	22443E 05	27676E 05	50004E 00	40550E-00	15218E-00	14823E-00
24	59403E-04	16834E 05	19999E 01	24662E 01	33666E 05	41516E 05	50003E 00	40549E-00	14667E-00	14292E-00
25	39602E-04	25251E 05	19999E 01	24662E 01	50500E 05	62275E 05	50002E 00	40548E-00	14154E-00	13798E-00
26	26401E-04	37877E 05	19999E 01	24662E 01	75752E 05	93413E 05	50001E 00	40548E-00	13675E-00	13337E-00
27	17601E-04	56815E 05	20000E 01	24663E 01	11363E 06	14012E 06	50001E 00	40547E-00	13228E-00	12906E-00
28	11734E-04	85223E 05	20000E 01	24663E 01	17044E 06	21018E 06	50001E 00	40547E-00	12808E-00	12502E-00
29	78226E-05	12783E 06	20000E 01	24663E 01	25567E 06	31528E 06	50000E 00	40547E-00	12414E-00	12123E-00
30	52151E-05	19175E 06	20000E 01	24663E 01	38350E 06	47291E 06	50000E 00	40547E-00	12043E-00	11766E-00
31	34767E-05	28763E 06	20000E 01	24663E 01	57525E 06	70937E 06	50000E 00	40547E-00	11694E-00	11430E-00
32	23178E-05	43144E 06	20000E 01	24663E 01	86288E 06	10641E 07	50000E 00	40547E-00	11364E-00	11112E-00
33	15452E-05	64716E 06	20000E 01	24663E 01	12943E 07	15961E 07	50000E 00	40547E-00	11052E-00	10811E-00
34	10301E-05	97074E 06	20000E 01	24663E 01	19415E 07	23941E 07	50000E 00	40547E-00	10756E-00	10527E-00
35	68676E-06	14561E 07	20000E 01	24663E 01	29122E 07	35912E 07	50000E 00	40547E-00	10476E-00	10257E-00
36	45784E-06	21842E 07	20000E 01	24663E 01	43683E 07	53868E 07	50000E 00	40547E-00	10210E-00	10000E-00
37	30525E-06	32762E 07	20000E 01	24663E 01	65525E 07	80802E 07	50000E 00	40547E-00	99573E-01	97563E-01
38	20348E-06	49144E 07	20000E 01	24663E 01	98287E 07	12120E 08	50000E 00	40547E-00	97166E-01	95240E-01
39	13566E-06	73716E 07	20000E 01	24663E 01	14743E 08	18180E 08	50000E 00	40547E-00	94872E-01	93025E-01
40	90438E-07	11057E 08	20000E 01	24663E 01	22115E 08	27271E 08	50000E 00	40547E-00	92683E-01	90910E-01
41	60292E-07	16586E 08	20000E 01	24663E 01	33172E 08	40906E 08	50000E 00	40547E-00	90592E-01	88890E-01
42	40195E-07	24879E 08	20000E 01	24663E 01	49758E 08	61359E 08	50000E 00	40547E-00	88594E-01	86957E-01
43	26796E-07	37318E 08	20000E 01	24663E 01	74637E 08	92039E 08	50000E 00	40547E-00	86681E-01	85107E-01
44	17864E-07	55978E 08	20000E 01	24663E 01	11196E 09	13806E 09	50000E 00	40547E-00	84848E-01	83334E-01
45	11909E-07	83967E 08	20000E 01	24663E 01	16793E 09	20709E 09	50000E 00	40547E-00	83092E-01	81633E-01
46	79397E-08	12595E 09	20000E 01	24663E 01	25190E 09	31063E 09	50000E 00	40547E-00	81406E-01	80000E-01

75% PER PERIOD

Period	Present Value of $1	Amount to Which $1 Will Accumulate	Present Value of $1 per Period — Received at End	Present Value of $1 per Period — Received Continuously	Amount to Which $1 per Period Will Accumulate — Received at End	Amount to Which $1 per Period Will Accumulate — Received Continuously	Amount per Period to Recover $1 of Investment — Received at End	Amount per Period to Recover $1 of Investment — Received Continuously	Present Value of Depreciation — Sum-of-Years' Digits	Present Value of Depreciation — Declining Balance
1	57143E 00	17500E 01	57143E 00	76583E 00	10000E 01	13402E 01	17500E 01	13058E 01		
2	32653E-00	30625E 01	89796E 00	12034E 01	27500E 01	36856E 01	11136E 01	83094E 00		
3	18659E-00	53594E 01	10845E 01	14535E 01	58125E 01	77899E 01	92204E 00	68799E 00	42566E-00	47425E-00
4	10662E-00	93789E 01	11912E 01	15964E 01	11172E 02	14973E 02	83951E 00	62640E 00	37451E-00	40400E-00
5	60927E-01	16413E 02	12921E 01	16781E 01	20551E 02	27542E 02	79866E 00	59592E 00	33315E-00	35190E-00
6	34815E-01	28723E 02	12869E 01	17247E 01	36964E 02	49539E 02	77705E 00	57980E 00	29924E-00	31067E-00
7	19895E-01	50265E 02	13068E 01	17514E 01	65687E 02	88034E 02	76522E 00	57098E 00	27110E-00	27824E-00
8	11368E-01	87964E 02	13182E 01	17666E 01	11595E 03	15540E 03	75862E 00	56605E 00	24747E-00	25161E-00
9	64962E-02	15394E 03	13247E 01	17753E 01	20392E 03	27329E 03	75490E 00	56327E 00	22742E-00	22977E-00
10	37121E-02	26939E 03	13284E 01	17803E 01	35785E 03	47960E 03	75279E 00	56170E 00	21022E-00	21132E-00
11	21212E-02	47143E 03	13305E 01	17831E 01	62724E 03	84063E 03	75159E 00	56081E 00	19534E-00	19570E-00
12	12121E-02	82500E 03	13317E 01	17848E 01	10987E 04	14724E 04	75091E 00	56029E 00	18236E-00	18220E-00
13	69264E-03	14438E 04	13324E 01	17857E 01	19237E 04	25781E 04	75052E 00	56000E 00	17095E-00	17049E-00
14	39579E-03	25266E 04	13328E 01	17862E 01	33674E 04	45131E 04	75030E 00	55984E 00	16085E-00	16018E-00
15	22617E-03	44215E 04	13330E 01	17865E 01	58940E 04	78992E 04	75017E 00	55974E 00	15186E-00	15107E-00
16	12924E-03	77376E 04	13332E 01	17867E 01	10316E 05	13825E 05	75010E 00	55969E 00	14379E-00	14294E-00
17	73850E-04	13541E 05	13332E 01	17868E 01	18053E 05	24195E 05	75006E 00	55966E 00	13653E-00	13565E-00
18	42200E-04	23697E 05	13333E 01	17869E 01	31594E 05	42342E 05	75003E 00	55964E 00	12995E-00	12907E-00
19	24114E-04	41469E 05	13333E 01	17869E 01	55291E 05	74101E 05	75002E 00	55963E 00	12398E-00	12311E-00
20	13780E-04	72571E 05	13333E 01	17869E 01	96759E 05	12968E 06	75001E 00	55962E 00	11852E-00	11767E-00
21	78741E-05	12700E 06	13333E 01	17869E 01	16933E 06	22694E 06	75001E 00	55962E 00	11352E-00	11269E-00
22	44995E-05	22225E 06	13333E 01	17869E 01	29633E 06	39714E 06	75000E 00	55962E 00	10892E-00	10812E-00
23	25711E-05	38893E 06	13333E 01	17869E 01	51858E 06	69500E 06	75000E 00	55962E 00	10467E-00	10390E-00
24	14692E-05	68063E 06	13333E 01	17869E 01	90751E 06	12162E 07	75000E 00	55962E 00	10074E-00	10000E-00
25	83956E-06	11911E 07	13333E 01	17869E 01	15881E 07	21284E 07	75000E 00	55962E 00	97094E-01	96389E-01
26	47975E-06	20844E 07	13333E 01	17869E 01	27792E 07	37248E 07	75000E 00	55962E 00	93701E-01	93026E-01
27	27414E-06	36478E 07	13333E 01	17869E 01	48637E 07	65183E 07	75000E 00	55962E 00	90535E-01	89889E-01
28	15665E-06	63836E 07	13333E 01	17869E 01	85115E 07	11407E 08	75000E 00	55962E 00	87575E-01	86958E-01
29	89515E-07	11171E 08	13333E 01	17869E 01	14895E 08	19962E 08	75000E 00	55962E 00	84802E-01	84211E-01
30	51152E-07	19550E 08	13333E 01	17869E 01	26066E 08	34934E 08	75000E 00	55962E 00	82198E-01	81633E-01
31	29229E-07	34212E 08	13333E 01	17869E 01	45616E 08	61135E 08	75000E 00	55962E 00	79749E-01	79208E-01
32	16703E-07	59871E 08	13333E 01	17869E 01	79828E 08	10699E 09	75000E 00	55962E 00	77441E-01	76923E-01
			13333E 01	17869E 01	13262E 09	18723E 09	75000E 00	55962E 00	75262E-01	74767E-01

100% PER PERIOD

PERIOD	PRESENT VALUE OF $1	AMOUNT TO WHICH $1 WILL ACCUMULATE	PRESENT VALUE OF $1 PER PERIOD		AMOUNT TO WHICH $1 PER PERIOD WILL ACCUMULATE		AMOUNT PER PERIOD TO RECOVER $1 OF INVESTMENT		PRESENT VALUE OF DEPRECIATION	
			Received at End	Received Continuously	Received at End	Received Continuously	Received at End	Received Continuously	Sum-of-Years' Digits	Declining Balance
1	50000E 00	20000E 01	50000E 00	72135E 00	10000E 01	14427E 01	20000E 01	13863E 01		
2	25000E-00	40000E 01	75000E 00	10820E 01	30000E 01	43281E 01	13333E 01	92420E 00		
3	12500E-00	80000E 01	87500E 00	12624E 01	70000E 01	10099E 02	11429E 01	79217E 00	35417E-00	40278E-00
4	62500E-01	16000E 02	93750E 00	13525E 01	15000E 02	21640E 02	10667E 01	73936E 00	30625E-00	33594E-00
5	31250E-01	32000E 02	96875E 00	13976E 01	31000E 02	44724E 02	10323E 01	71551E 00	26875E-00	28812E-00
6	15625E-01	64000E 02	98437E 00	14202E 01	63000E 02	90890E 02	10159E 01	70415E 00	23884E-00	25154E-00
7	78125E-02	12800E 03	99219E 00	14314E 01	12700E 03	18322E 03	10079E 01	69861E 00	21456E-00	22335E-00
8	39062E-02	25600E 03	99609E 00	14371E 01	25500E 03	36789E 03	10039E 01	69587E 00	19455E-00	20068E-00
9	19531E-02	51200E 03	99805E 00	14399E 01	51100E 03	73722E 03	10020E 01	69450E 00	17782E-00	18229E-00
10	97656E-03	10240E 04	99902E 00	14413E 01	10230E 04	14759E 04	10010E 01	69382E 00	16365E-00	16694E-00
11	48828E-03	20480E 04	99951E 00	14420E 01	20470E 04	29532E 04	10005E 01	69349E 00	15152E-00	15403E-00
12	24414E-03	40960E 04	99976E 00	14423E 01	40950E 04	59078E 04	10002E 01	69332E 00	14103E-00	14297E-00
13	12207E-03	81920E 04	99988E 00	14425E 01	81910E 04	11817E 05	10001E 01	69323E 00	13187E-00	13341E-00
14	61035E-04	16384E 05	99994E 00	14426E 01	16333E 05	23636E 05	10001E 01	69319E 00	12381E-00	12504E-00
15	30518E-04	32768E 05	99997E 00	14427E 01	32767E 05	47273E 05	10000E 01	69317E 00	11667E-00	11768E-00
16	15259E-04	65536E 05	99998E 00	14427E 01	65535E 05	94547E 05	10000E 01	69316E 00	11029E-00	11113E-00
17	76294E-05	13107E 06	99999E 00	14427E 01	13107E 06	18910E 06	10000E 01	69315E 00	10458E-00	10528E-00
18	38147E-05	26214E 06	00000E 00	14427E 01	26214E 06	37819E 06	10000E 01	69315E 00	99415E-01	10001E-00
19	19073E-05	52429E 06	00000E 00	14427E 01	52429E 06	75639E 06	10000E 01	69315E 00	94737E-01	95243E-01
20	95367E-06	10486E 07	00000E 00	14427E 01	10486E 07	15128E 07	10000E 01	69315E 00	90476E-01	90912E-01
21	47684E-06	20972E 07	00000E 00	14427E 01	20972E 07	30255E 07	10000E 01	69315E 00	86580E-01	86959E-01
22	23842E-06	41943E 07	00000E 00	14427E 01	41943E 07	60511E 07	10000E 01	69315E 00	83004E-01	83335E-01
23	11921E-06	83886E 07	00000E 00	14427E 01	83886E 07	12102E 08	10000E 01	69315E 00	79710E-01	80001E-01
24	59605E-07	16777E 08	00000E 00	14427E 01	16777E 08	24204E 08	10000E 01	69315E 00	76667E-01	76924E-01
25	29802E-07	33554E 08	00000E 00	14427E 01	33554E 08	48409E 08	10000E 01	69315E 00	73846E-01	74074E-01
26	14901E-07	67109E 08	00000E 00	14427E 01	67109E 08	96818E 08	10000E 01	69315E 00	71225E-01	71429E-01
27	74506E-08	13422E 09	00000E 00	14427E 01	13422E 09	19364E 09	10000E 01	69315E 00	68783E-01	68966E-01

INDEX OF CASES

INDEX OF CASES

This book has been set on the Linotype in 10, 11, and 12 point Garamond #3, leaded 1 point. Case and section titles are in 18 point Garamond Bold; section numbers are in 18 point Garamond. The size of the type page is 27 by 45 picas.